Violence against Prisoners of War
in the First World War

In this groundbreaking new study, Heather Jones provides the first in-depth and comparative examination of violence against First World War prisoners. She shows how the war radicalised captivity treatment in Britain, France and Germany, dramatically undermined international law protecting prisoners of war and led to new forms of forced prisoner labour and reprisals, which fuelled wartime propaganda that was often based on accurate prisoner testimony. This book reveals how, during the conflict, increasing numbers of captives were not sent to home front camps but retained in western front working units to labour directly for the British, French and German armies – in the German case, by 1918, prisoners working for the German army endured widespread malnutrition and constant beatings. Dr Jones examines the significance of these new, violent trends and their later legacy, arguing that the Great War marked a key turning-point in the twentieth-century evolution of the prison camp.

HEATHER JONES is Lecturer in International History at the London School of Economics and Political Science. Her previous publications include *Untold War. New Perspectives in First World War Studies* (co-edited with Christoph Schmidt-Supprian and Jennifer O'Brien, 2008).

Studies in the Social and Cultural History of Modern Warfare

General Editor
Jay Winter, *Yale University*

Advisory Editors
Omer Bartov, *Brown University*
Carol Gluck, *Columbia University*
David M. Kennedy, *Stanford University*
Paul Kennedy, *Yale University*
Antoine Prost, *Université de Paris-Sorbonne*
Emmanuel Sivan, *Hebrew University of Jerusalem*
Robert Wohl, *University of California, Los Angeles*

In recent years the field of modern history has been enriched by the exploration of two parallel histories. These are the social and cultural history of armed conflict, and the impact of military events on social and cultural history.

Studies in the Social and Cultural History of Modern Warfare presents the fruits of this growing area of research, reflecting both the colonization of military history by cultural historians and the reciprocal interest of military historians in social and cultural history, to the benefit of both. The series offers the latest scholarship in European and non-European events from the 1850s to the present day.

A full list of titles in the series can be found at:

www.cambridge.org/modernwarfare

Violence against Prisoners of War in the First World War

Britain, France and Germany, 1914–1920

Heather Jones

To Andrea,

with every best wish,

Heather Jones

CAMBRIDGE
UNIVERSITY PRESS

CAMBRIDGE UNIVERSITY PRESS
Cambridge, New York, Melbourne, Madrid, Cape Town,
Singapore, São Paulo, Delhi, Mexico City

Cambridge University Press
The Edinburgh Building, Cambridge CB2 8RU, UK

Published in the United States of America by Cambridge University Press, New York

www.cambridge.org
Information on this title: www.cambridge.org/9781107638266

First published 2011
Reprinted 2012
First paperback edition 2013

A catalogue record for this publication is available from the British Library

Library of Congress Cataloguing in Publication Data
Jones, Heather, 1978–
Violence against prisoners of war in the First World War : Britain, France, and
Germany, 1914–1920 / Heather Jones.
    p.   cm. – (Studies in the social and cultural history of modern warfare; 34)
Includes bibliographical references and index.
ISBN 978-0-521-11758-6 (hardback)
1. World War, 1914–1918 – Prisoners and prisons, British.   2. World War,
1914–1918 – Prisoners and prisons, French.   3. World War, 1914–1918 –
Prisoners and prisons, German.   4. Prisoners of war – Violence against – Great
Britain – History – 20th century.   5. Prisoners of war – Violence against – France –
History – 20th century.   6. Prisoners of war – Violence against – Germany –
History – 20th century.   7. World War, 1914–1918 – Conscript labor.
8. Repatriation – Europe – History – 20th century.   I. Title.
D805.A2J66   2011
940.4′72–dc22
                                                                        2011000395

ISBN 978-1-107-63826-6 Paperback

Contents

    violence against prisoners of war, 1922–39   315

    Epilogue: the legacy of First World War captivity in
    1939–45   356

    Conclusion   371

    Glossary of foreign terms   377
    Bibliography   378
    Index   440

Illustrations

Tables

Acknowledgements

This book originated as a doctoral dissertation, submitted to Trinity College, University of Dublin, in 2006, where I benefited from the generous assistance of many friends and scholars. I am particularly indebted to my former thesis supervisor, Alan Kramer, for his constant support, encouragement and advice. I am also extremely grateful to John Horne for his many thoughtful comments regarding this project; his assistance has been absolutely invaluable. It has been a privilege to work with two such remarkable historians. This study would also have been much the poorer were it not for the wonderful collegiality of my former postgraduate colleagues at the Department of Modern History, Trinity College, Dublin, Edward Madigan, Jennifer O'Brien, Catriona Pennell, Christoph Schmidt-Supprian, Claudia Siebrecht and Vanessa Ther.

A large number of scholars from outside Trinity also helped me to write this history. Jay Winter, as external thesis examiner, provided crucial insights that have greatly benefited the whole book; I would like to thank him here for all his kind assistance. I also owe a considerable debt of thanks to the following people who provided comments on parts of different chapters or help with sources: Odon Abbal, Andrew Barros, Rainer Benedick, Tom Burke, Santanu Das, Richard van Emden, Leen Engelen, Richard Evans, Heinz-Gerhard Haupt, Uta Hinz, Gerhard Hirschfeld, Arne Hofmann, Isabel V. Hull, Victoria Kingston, Gerd Krumeich, Paul Lerner, Reinhard Nachtigal, Eunan O'Halpin, Pierre Purseigle, Alon Rachamimov, Sophie de Schaepdrijver, Gary Sheffield, Dennis Showalter, Matthew Stibbe, Fabien Théofilakis, Riccarda Torriani, Alexander Watson, Thomas Weber, Oliver Wilkinson and Neville Wylie. In Berlin and Paris, Annette Becker, Christoph Jahr, Christoph Prochasson, and Jens Thiel were particularly generous with their time and their advice. Nicolas Beaupré, Mathilde von Bülow, Yaël Dagan, Dorota Dakowska, Anne Duménil, Caroline Moine, Daniel Steinbach and Astrid Swenson constantly provided support and historical discussion during my archive stints. A special note of thanks also goes to Catherine Fahy, Paris

O'Donnell, Jérôme and Sylvie Blondet, and Susie and Richard Elliott, who hosted me on many different occasions.

I am grateful to the Irish Research Council for the Humanities and Social Sciences for funding this study. For a crucial research grant and for providing the opportunity for constant intellectual discussion, I would like to thank the Board of the Historial de la Grande Guerre, Péronne. Trinity College, Dublin provided important scholarship support and also travel grants from the Grace Lawless Lee Fund and the Trinity Association and Trust. The European University Institute funded a valuable postdoctoral year which allowed me to work further on the question of prisoners. It has been a privilege to complete this study while teaching at the London School of Economics and Political Science; I would particularly like to thank my LSE colleagues David Stevenson, Dominic Lieven, Kristina Spohr-Readman, Paul Preston and MacGregor Knox. I would also like to thank Michael Watson at Cambridge University Press for his guidance and help, as well as the outstanding book production team: Daniel Dunlavey, Chloe Howell and David Watson.

In different archives and libraries, I have been assisted by many people, unfortunately too numerous to list here: I would like to note my debt of gratitude to all of those who helped at the many institutions where this research was carried out. Particular thanks are due, however, to a number of people who went above and beyond the call of duty in their assistance. The research for this book was made much easier by the wonderful staff of Trinity College Library, in particular the late Anne Walsh. I also owe a debt of thanks to Irina Renz at the Institut für Zeitgeschichte, Stuttgart; Jürgen-K. Mahrenholz from the Lautarchiv, at the Music Department of the Humboldt University, Berlin; Franz Moegle-Hofacker at the Hauptstaatsarchiv, Stuttgart; Karl-Heinz Leven, at the Freiburg Institut für Geschichte der Medizin; and Achim Fuchs at the Bavarian Kriegsarchiv, Munich. The staff at the Service Historique de l'Armée de Terre, Vincennes were continually resourceful in answering my queries about obscure collections. The ever helpful Fabrizio Bensi at the International Red Cross Archives, Geneva, and Bernhardine Pejovic at the United Nations Library, Geneva, made research much easier. Rémy Guillot, Geoffrey Geraud and the staff of the Bibliothèque de Documentation Internationale Contemporaine at Nanterre and the Musée d'Histoire Contemporaine at Les Invalides went out of their way on many occasions.

The Imperial War Museum and the National Archives at Kew were a pleasure to work with. I would also particularly like to thank the National Library of Scotland for their assistance with sourcing the cover image. Every effort has been made to trace copyright holders and to obtain their permission for the use of copyright material. The author apologises for any errors or omissions and would be grateful if notified of any corrections that should be incorporated in future reprints or editions of this book. Chapters 1, 2, 3 and 4 incorporate some material which appeared previously in the following articles or book chapters: Heather Jones, 'Encountering the "Enemy": Prisoner of War Transport and the Development of War Cultures in 1914', in Pierre Purseigle, ed., *Warfare and Belligerence. Perspectives in First World War Studies* (Boston and Leiden: Brill Academic Publishers, 2005), pp. 133–62; Heather Jones, 'Un tournant dans la guerre: le typhus dans les camps de prisonniers de guerre allemands en 1915', in John Horne ed., *Vers la guerre totale. Le tournant de 1914–15* (Paris, Tallandier, 2010); Heather Jones, 'The German Spring Reprisals of 1917. Prisoners of War and the Violence of the Western Front', *German History*, 26 (2008), pp. 335–56; Heather Jones, 'The Final Logic of Sacrifice? Violence in German Prisoner of War Labor Companies in 1918', *The Historian*, 68, 4 (2006), pp. 770–91. I thank the editors for their permission to use this material.

Finally, I am especially grateful to my family. My brother, Mark Jones, has debated history with me for many years. His comments have greatly improved this study. My parents, Stuart and Valerie Jones, have always enthusiastically supported my work; this book is dedicated to them, for their love, their encouragement and their example.

Abbreviations

AA	Auswärtiges Amt
ACICR	Archives du Comité international de la Croix-Rouge, Geneva
AN	Archives Nationales, Paris
ASV	Achivio Segreto Vaticano (Vatican Archives)
BA	Bundesarchiv, Berlin-Lichterfelde
BA-MA	Bundesarchiv-Militärarchiv, Freiburg
BDIC-MHC Les Invalides	Bibliothèque de Documentation Internationale Contemporaine-Musée d'Histoire Contemporaine, Les Invalides
BDIC-MHC Nanterre	Bibliothèque de Documentation Internationale Contemporaine-Musée d'Histoire Contemporaine, Nanterre
BHStA IV	Bayerisches Hauptstaatsarchiv, Abteilung IV Kriegsarchiv, Munich
DA	Direction de l'Arrière
GQG	Grand Quartier Général (French Military Headquarters)
GstA PK	Geheimes Staatsarchiv Preußischer Kulturbesitz, Berlin-Dahlem
HLRO	House of Lords Record Office
HStA STUTT	Württembergisches Hauptstaatsarchiv, Stuttgart
IbAK	First Bavarian Army Corps
IWM	Imperial War Museum, Department of Documents, London
MAE	Archives du Ministère des Affaires Étrangères (French Foreign Ministry Archives)
NCO	Non-Commissioned Officer

OHL	Oberste Heeresleitung (German Army Supreme High Command)
PG	Prisonnier de Guerre
RAMC	Royal Army Medical Corps (British)
SHAT	Service Historique de l'Armée de Terre, Vincennes
TCD	Trinity College, University of Dublin
TNA	The National Archives, London (formerly the Public Record Office)

Introduction

The First World War unleashed a paroxysm of violence, both within Europe and overseas. Marking a major radicalisation of warfare, the extent of this violence and its effect on societies has long attracted the attention of scholars. In the interwar period, accounting for how violence was collectively represented and sanctioned through cultural practices was an underlying theme of the work of Marc Bloch, Sigmund Freud and Jean Norton Cru, among others.[1] Later military historians analysed the brutal nature of trench combat on the western front in enormous detail.[2] More recently, there has been a new wave of historical analysis, exploring the cultural context of combatant violence, both on the battlefield and against civilian populations; this has been accompanied by an ongoing debate as to how the war contributed to a violent European post-war political climate.[3] Yet despite this wealth of scholarship, one

[1] See, for example, Marc Bloch, 'Réflexions d'un historien sur les fausses nouvelles de la Guerre, 1921', in Annette Becker and Étienne Bloch, eds., L'Histoire, la Guerre, la Résistance (Paris, 2006), pp. 293–316. Sigmund Freud, Civilization and Its Discontents (New York, 1930); Jean Norton Cru, Témoins. Essai d'analyse et de critique des souvenirs de combattants édités en français de 1915 à 1928 (Paris, 1929).

[2] See, for example, the work of Tony Ashworth, Trench Warfare 1914–1918. The Live and Let Live System (London, 2000); John Keegan, The Face of Battle. A Study of Agincourt, Waterloo and the Somme (London, 1976); Wolfram Wette, ed., Der Krieg des kleinen Mannes. Eine Militärgeschichte von unten (Munich and Zurich, 1995). See also the related cultural history on the war experience or 'Kriegserlebnis' in Germany: Gerhard Hirschfeld, Keiner fühlt sich hier mehr als Mensch. Erlebnis und Wirkung des Ersten Weltkriegs (Frankfurt am Main, 1996).

[3] The surge in recent interest in First World War combatant violence has produced a wealth of new studies. Among the most groundbreaking, see Alan Kramer, Dynamic of Destruction. Culture and Mass Killing in the First World War (Oxford, 2007); John Horne and Alan Kramer, German Atrocities, 1914. A History of Denial (New Haven and London, 2001); Stéphane Audoin-Rouzeau and Annette Becker, 14–18. Retrouver la Guerre (Paris, 2000); Stéphane Audoin-Rouzeau and Annette Becker, 'Violence et consentement. La "culture de guerre" du premier conflit mondial', in Jean-Pierre Rioux and Jean-François Sirinelli, eds., Pour une histoire culturelle (Paris, 1997), pp. 251–71; Stéphane Audoin-Rouzeau, Les Armes et la chair. Trois objets de mort en 14–18 (Paris, 2009); Isabel V. Hull, Absolute Destruction. Military Culture and the Practices of War in Imperial Germany (Ithaca and London, 2005); Joanna Bourke, Dismembering the Male. Men's Bodies, Britain and the

1

crucial aspect of wartime violence has been largely overlooked. Violence against the estimated 7 to 9 million prisoners of war taken in the conflict has not been addressed in the existing historiography, with the exception of the battlefield practice of prisoner killing; however, even this subject has largely only been briefly discussed as part of broader debates on the nature of trench warfare. The scale of violence against captives remains unknown.[4]

This book sets out to investigate this forgotten issue – violence against combatant prisoners of war – through an analysis of the captivity experiences of British, French and German military prisoners captured on the western front. More specifically, it aims to explore the wide range of different kinds of enemy violence that prisoners endured on the battlefield, in transit, in labour companies and in the prison camp, as well as the ways that governments and the public at large influenced the use of violence against captives; a particular focus here is the public's role in

---

Great War (London, 1996); Joanna Bourke, *An Intimate History of Killing. Face-to-Face Killing in Twentieth-Century Warfare* (London, 1999); Niall Ferguson, *The Pity of War. Explaining World War I* (London, 1998), pp. 339–66; Antoine Prost, 'Les Limites de la brutalisation. Tuer sur le front occidental, 1914–1918', *Vingtième Siècle. Revue d'Histoire*, 81 (2004), pp. 5–20. On the broader impact of First World War combatant violence on societies and also on the general relationship between violence and the state, see George L. Mosse, *Fallen Soldiers. Reshaping the Memory of the World Wars* (Oxford, 1990); Bernd Hüppauf, ed., *War, Violence and the Modern Condition* (Berlin, 1997); Alf Lüdtke and Bernd Weisbrod, eds., *No Man's Land. Extreme Wars in the 20th Century* (Göttingen, 2006); Mark Mazower, 'Violence and the State in the Twentieth Century', *The American Historical Review*, 107, 4 (2002), pp. 1158–78; Michael Geyer, 'War and Terror. Some Timely Observations on the German Way of Waging War', *AICGS Humanities*, 14 (2003), pp. 47–69; Omer Bartov, *Murder in Our Midst. The Holocaust, Industrial Killing and Representation* (Oxford, 1996); Stéphane Audoin-Rouzeau, Annette Becker, Christian Ingrao and Henry Rousso, eds., *La Violence de guerre, 1914–1945. Approches comparées des deux conflits mondiaux* (Brussels, 2002); John Horne, 'War and Conflict in Contemporary European History, 1914–2004', *Zeithistorische Forschungen/Studies in Contemporary History*, Online-Ausgabe, 1 (2004), H3, www.zeithistorische-forschungen.de/site/40208266/default.aspx, accessed 18 March 2010; Dirk Schumann, 'Europa, der Erste Weltkrieg und die Nachkriegszeit. Eine Kontinuität der Gewalt?' *Journal of Modern European History*, 1, 1 (2003), pp. 24–43; Benjamin Ziemann, 'Germany after the First World War – a Violent Society? Results and Implications of Recent Research on Weimar Germany', *Journal of Modern European History*, 1, 1 (2003), pp. 80–95; Adam Seipp, *The Ordeal of Peace. Demobilization and the Urban Experience in Britain and Germany, 1917–1921* (Farnham and Burlington, 2010).

4 For the total estimated number of prisoners of war taken in the conflict, see Jochen Oltmer, 'Einführung. Funktionen und Erfahrungen von Kriegsgefangenschaft im Europa des Ersten Weltkriegs', in Jochen Oltmer, ed., *Kriegsgefangene im Europa des Ersten Weltkriegs* (Paderborn, 2006), p. 11. For detailed discussion on battlefield prisoner-killing see Ferguson, *The Pity of War*, pp. 367–94, and Niall Ferguson, 'Prisoner Taking and Prisoner Killing in the Age of Total War. Towards a Political Economy of Military Defeat', *War in History*, 11, 2 (2004), pp. 148–92; Bourke, *An Intimate History of Killing*; Tim Cook, 'The Politics of Surrender. Canadian Soldiers and the Killing of Prisoners in the Great War', *The Journal of Military History*, 70, 3 (2006), pp. 637–65; Prost, 'Les Limites de la brutalisation'.

defining acceptable violent practices through shifting social, political and legal understandings of what constituted transgressive 'atrocities' or acceptable 'reprisals'. The violent act is thus not considered in isolation: while relating the reality of brutal treatment, with its painful, often traumatic, impact upon individual captives, this book also seeks to contextualise how forms of collective violent practices against prisoners developed in three countries and how these reflected changing societal values, as the idea of what constituted violence against prisoners evolved throughout the conflict.

Enemy violence against captives merits being singled out for this kind of study because it was a very distinct wartime phenomenon: unlike violence between combatants, the prisoner was unable to defend himself, nor could he flee. He was thus part of a very particular, unequal captivity power dynamic, which was inherently coercive: the prison camp system was based upon the long-term submission of the prisoner to his captor's superior ability to use violent force, a submission which began at the moment of capture. In this regard, all Great War captivity, even the most comfortable, to some extent functioned through the threat of violence; indeed, in accordance with international law, all combatant prisoners of war were subject to the military law of their captor army during captivity, which meant they lived with the threat of corporal punishment for certain misdemeanours and often lost certain rights, for example, the right to refuse to work.[5] To become a prisoner was therefore to come under the exclusive control of omnipresent systems of power, ultimately based on violent physical force.

The kind of violence which forms the subject of this book can thus be defined as the use or threat of physical force, both discriminate and indiscriminate, against a prisoner of war, by an enemy subject. It is a deliberately broad definition, as the aim here is to investigate the full range of those acts which contemporaries at the time considered constituted enemy violence against prisoners of war, which was described in public debate using multiple different terms, the euphemisms 'mistreatment' or 'reprisal' being particularly popular. Such public interpretations mattered during the conflict: violations of a prisoner's right to bodily and mental integrity became part of a broader symbolic framework of violence that defined captivity. Shooting prisoners out of hand was one of the most dramatic types of violence, but it was far from the only one, nor was it always the most notorious: making captives work under shellfire, beatings, corporal punishment, mistreating the sick, starvation rations and even

---

[5] On military law and prisoners in Germany, see Uta Hinz, *Gefangen im Großen Krieg. Kriegsgefangenschaft in Deutschland, 1914–1921* (Essen, 2006), pp. 141–68.

threats of violence were all equally prominent in the debates on violent treatment during the war and thus feature in this study. The one kind of violence not covered here is sexual violence; due to the complete absence of any mention of this topic in the source material, it was not possible to include it.

There are three key reasons for focusing upon violence against prisoners. First, the kinds of violence against captives that emerged during the First World War offer a fundamental insight into the radicalisation processes at the heart of the conflict: as Stéphane Audoin-Rouzeau and Annette Becker have argued, 'the specific violence of war is a prism, which refracts many things that are otherwise invisible'.[6] Violence against prisoners, both on and off the battlefield, was not a set of static practices; it evolved as the conflict continued. It can thus show us how wartime extremisms developed. What constituted legitimate forms of violence against captives was a key question that preoccupied European wartime elites and the general public alike throughout the war; it was one which was constantly renegotiated within societies and also at a transnational level in close reciprocal relationship to what allied or enemy states were doing to their captives. This legitimacy debate operated at several different levels: what was actually practised as prisoner treatment; what was known about those practices by the population at large; and finally what was publicly endorsed. By encouraging hostility towards the enemy, violence against prisoners of war thus played a highly significant role in mobilising home front populations. In sum, studying violence against prisoners of war provides valuable insights into the escalation of wartime brutalisation, as well as the cultural limits placed upon this process, through changing understandings of acceptable 'norms', what was considered permissible, and 'extremes', the outer limits of what could be publicly condoned. The assumption here, building upon Walter Benjamin's differentiation in his 'Critique of Violence', is that wartime violence is not a natural constant – rather it is a 'product of history' that is socially and culturally conditioned, emerging in different ways at certain historical junctures; in part, this study also reflects Wolfgang Sofsky's work, with its suggestion that we need to explore the relationship between violence and culture in more detail, although it rejects his idea that because violence is innate in human nature, cultural structures ultimately always serve to facilitate it.[7]

---

[6] Audoin-Rouzeau and Becker, *14–18. Retrouver la Guerre*, p. 25.
[7] Walter Benjamin, 'Critique of Violence', in Marcus Bullock and Michael W. Jennings, eds., *Walter Benjamin. Selected Writings*, vol. I: *1913–1926* (Cambridge, Mass., and London, 1996), p. 237. Wolfgang Sofsky, *Traktat über die Gewalt* (Frankfurt, 1996),

In this way, this book provides a new perspective on some of the existing interpretations of the war. Isabel Hull has argued that there was a cultural predilection for extremes of violence in the German army, a 'dynamic of destruction' which caused it to always opt by default for the most ruthless method to achieve its aims; building on Hull's analysis, Alan Kramer's recent work has suggested that this dynamic existed in other armies too and that 'for all sides in the war, enemy civilians and other non-combatants came to be regarded to a greater or lesser degree as targets of war policy, even as legitimate objects of violence'.[8] By following the evolution of violence against prisoners of war, in three countries, this book is able to show that there was a drive towards extremes in the German army, as Hull has argued; however, this German ruthlessness was only the farthest and most extreme end of a developmental spectrum, whereby mass captivity, as well as new forms of forced labour, unleashed a dynamic of radicalisation of violence against prisoners which affected all three states and their armies. The idea of brutalisation, first posited by George Mosse, is thus presented here as a process which was already occurring within polities during the conflict.[9] The key conclusion that emerges, however, is that in the British and French cases this radicalisation dynamic was ultimately impeded due to political structures and cultural norms in these two countries that differed from the German case; these acted as impediments that offset the drive towards radicalisation.

Second, through studying violence against prisoners this book aims to show the real extent of prisoner mistreatment during the conflict and the policies that facilitated this development. Violence against prisoners is taken here as a crucial indicator for broader mistreatment patterns. In particular, this book argues that the key overlooked innovation of the First World War was the forced labour company. As the war continued, a significant percentage of non-officer prisoners of war were retained at the western front to work for their captor army in labour companies – an innovation adopted by all three national armies studied here. This was a breach of international law: while the 1907 Hague Convention allowed other-rank prisoners to work for the captor state, it stipulated that they should not be put to work directly for their captor's war effort.[10] These

---

pp. 219–26. See also Sofsky's discussion of societies during war: Wolfgang Sofsky, *Violence. Terrorism, Genocide, War* (London, 2003), p. 118. For a critique of Sofsky's view, see Alan Kramer, 'The War of Atrocities. Murderous Scares and Extreme Combat', in Lüdtke and Weisbrod, eds., *No Man's Land*, pp. 11–34, where Kramer argues that violence is largely determined by historical context.

[8] Hull, *Absolute Destruction*; Kramer, *Dynamic of Destruction*, p. 3.

[9] Mosse, *Fallen Soldiers*.

[10] James Scott Brown, ed., *The Hague Conventions and Declarations of 1899 and 1907* (Washington, D.C., and Oxford, 1915), p. 109; Hinz, *Gefangen im Großen Krieg*, p. 53.

men endured a much harsher captivity which contrasted greatly to that of their peers who were evacuated to home front camps, effectively creating two contrasting captivity systems. The advent of this 'dual' system, of home front camps and labour companies at the front, radicalised prisoner of war treatment; prisoners in labour companies were often exposed to frequent violence, particularly in the German army. This book reveals the extent of the labour company system for the first time and emphasises the importance of reintegrating this early, significant development into the longer-term historical trajectory of the evolution of forced labour and the prison camp in the first half of the twentieth century, which would go on to be marked by the widespread use of mass imprisonment and forced labour, from the gulags of Russia to Franco's Spain and the horrors of the Nazi concentration camp system.

Thus this book provides a new perspective upon an ongoing debate in the existing historiography on First World War prisoners of war as to whether captives were generally humanely or badly treated. Until fifteen years ago, the overall history of captivity during the Great War was largely forgotten, under-researched due to the popular and historical focus upon the horrors of the camps of the Second World War, as well as the severe destruction of archive sources in Germany and Britain in aerial bombardments in 1939–45.[11] However, recently there has been a series of new publications on Great War captivity, most of which focus on prisoner living conditions. These can be broadly divided into two interpretations. The first, presented in the work of Odon Abbal, Richard Speed, Rémy Cazals, Kai Rawe, Rainer Pöppinghege and Alon Rachamimov, broadly views the war as the last phase of a nineteenth-century humanitarian culture, which protected prisoners from the extremes of mistreatment seen in later twentieth-century conflicts; Rachamimov concludes in his study of prisoners of war in Russia that 'when we want World War I to be the worst cautionary example of war' then captivity at best 'has a marginal place'.[12] More nuanced, Uta Hinz's impressive recent study of prisoners of war in Germany accepts that significant deterioration in prisoner living

---

[11] Second World War bombing destroyed the archives of the German army at Potsdam and damaged First World War British Red Cross prisoner of war records.

[12] Alon Rachamimov, *PoWs and the Great War. Captivity on the Eastern Front* (Oxford and New York, 2002), p. 228; Richard B. Speed III, *Prisoners, Diplomats and the Great War. A Study in the Diplomacy of Captivity* (New York and London, 1990), pp. 2–12; Rawe, '... *wir werden sie schon zur Arbeit bringen'. Ausländerbeschäftigung und Zwangsarbeit im Ruhrkohlenbergbau während des Ersten Weltkrieges* (Essen, 2005); Odon Abbal, *Soldats oubliés. Les prisonniers de guerre français* (Esparon, 2001), pp. 9–11; Eckart Birnstiel and Rémy Cazals, eds., *Ennemis fraternels 1914–1915. Hans Rodewald, Antoine Biesse, Fernand Tailhades, Carnets de guerre et de captivité* (Toulouse, 2002); Sylvie Caucanas, Rémy Cazals and Pascal Payen, eds., *Les Prisonniers de guerre dans l'histoire. Contacts entre peuples et*

conditions occurred but argues that this was due to 'the structural economic changes caused by the war', rather than any violent radicalisation of wartime attitudes to prisoners; for Hinz, the boundaries set in international law to protect prisoners were largely kept: 'in this regard the First World War was not a total war'.[13] The second interpretation, presented in the work of Annette Becker, Giovanna Procacci and Mark Spoerer, emphasises poor Great War captivity conditions; Procacci and Spoerer point to the high death rates among Italian and British prisoners respectively, with Procacci citing the deaths of 100,000 of the 600,000 Italian captives held by Germany and Austria-Hungary.[14] For these historians, the war was marked by particularly ruthless prisoner treatment; indeed, Becker goes on to argue that it established patterns which later resurfaced in the 1939–45 conflict.[15] At issue in these two diverging historiographical interpretations, which are both represented in the contributions to Jochen Oltmer's recent edited book of essays on Great War captivity, is whether the First World War marked the key watershed moment in Europe's twentieth century treatment of prisoners of war: indeed, one historian, a proponent of the benevolent captivity interpretation of the Great War, François Cochet, contended that it was only after the Second World War that a process of deregularisation set in, as international law protecting prisoner rights in war was sidelined.[16]

These two contrasting interpretations are fully contextualised for the first time through the analysis of violence against prisoners presented here, which reveals the existence of what were, in practice, effectively

---

cultures (Carcassonne, 2003); Rainer Pöppinghege, *Im Lager unbesiegt. Deutsche, englische und französische Kriegsgefangenen-Zeitungen im Ersten Weltkrieg* (Essen, 2006). See also the work of Katja Mitze, 'Das Kriegsgefangenenlager Ingolstadt während des Ersten Weltkriegs', Doctoral Thesis, University of Münster, 1999, which also largely adopts the benevolent captivity theme.

[13] Hinz, *Gefangen im Großen Krieg*, p. 362.

[14] Annette Becker, *Oubliés de la Grande Guerre, humanitaire et culture de guerre 1914–1918. Populations occupées, déportés civils, prisonniers de guerre* (Paris, 1998); Giovanna Procacci, *Soldati e prigionieri italiani nella Grande Guerra, con una raccolta di lettere inedite* (Turin, 2000); Mark Spoerer, 'The Mortality of Allied Prisoners of War and Belgian Civilian Deportees in German Custody during the First World War. A Reappraisal of the Effects of Forced Labour', *Population Studies*, 60, 2, (2006), pp. 121–36; Giovanna Procacci, '"Fahnenflüchtige jenseits der Alpen". Die italienischen Kriegsgefangenen in Österreich-Ungarn und Deutschland', in Oltmer, ed., *Kriegsgefangene im Europa des Ersten Weltkriegs*, p. 196. See also the negative view of captivity in Jean-Claude Auriol, *Les Barbelés des bannis. La Tragédie des prisonniers de guerre français en Allemagne durant la Grande Guerre* (Paris, 2002).

[15] Becker, *Oubliés de la Grande Guerre*. See also Annette Becker, 'Suppressed Memory of Atrocity in World War I and Its Impact on World War II', in Doris L. Bergen, ed., *Lessons and Legacies VIII. From Generation to Generation* (Illinois, 2008), p. 66.

[16] François Cochet, *Soldats sans armes. La captivité de guerre. Une approche culturelle* (Brussels, 1998), p. 3, p. 4. Oltmer, ed., *Kriegsgefangene im Europa des Ersten Weltkriegs*.

'dual' captivity systems in Britain, France and Germany; although there was some bureaucratic overlap in their administration, the prisoner of war labour system in each country functioned largely autonomously from the home front camps. What emerges is that the benevolent captivity interpretation is one which is overly dependent upon sources from home front camps; the darker interpretation of widespread mistreatment stems mainly from the prisoner of war labour company system. This is not to claim that home front camps were always benign sites of incarceration – far from it. However, it is to argue that by tracing levels of violence in both home front camps and front labour companies from 1914 until 1920, when the last German prisoners were repatriated from France, the different patterns of mistreatment in the two systems emerge more clearly; the divergent forms and levels of violence to be found in different parts of these incarceratory systems, and the fluctuating scale of violence during different phases of the war, help to explain the contrasting historical impressions of Great War captivity and to present a more accurate picture of the scale and location of prisoner abuses. Indebted to the work of Hinz and Becker in particular, this book ultimately contends that the prisoner labour company system marked a watershed in western European ideas regarding forced labour.

Third, this book is intended as a contribution to the development of the comparative history of the First World War, a burgeoning scholarly field, albeit one which has until now largely focused upon two-way national comparisons.[17] By deliberately studying three countries, the different patterns of violence against prisoners across three European states become visible for the first time; moreover, a central premise of this study is that comparing states on both sides of the conflict reduces the risk of partisan interpretations or of drawing overly simplistic national oppositions between victims and perpetrators of violence. Methodologically, this book draws upon two key approaches to historical comparison set out by Marc Bloch and Michel Espagne. As a clearly

---

[17] Recent comparative studies include: Alexander Watson, *Enduring the Great War. Combat, Morale and Collapse in the German and British Armies, 1914–1918* (Cambridge, 2008); Thomas Weber, *'Our Friend "the Enemy"'. Elite Education in Britain and Germany before World War I* (Stanford, 2008). There have also been a number of edited volumes which present the history of the war in a comparative way: see, in particular, Jenny Macleod and Pierre Purseigle, eds., *Uncovered Fields. Perspectives in First World War Studies* (Boston and Leiden, 2004); Jay Winter and Jean-Louis Robert, eds., *Capital Cities at War, Paris, London, Berlin, 1914–1919*, vol. I (Cambridge, 1997), and vol. II: *A Cultural History* (Cambridge, 2007). See also Pierre Purseigle's thoughtful discussion of the value of local and regional comparative studies in 'Warfare and Belligerence. Approaches to the First World War', in Pierre Purseigle, ed., *Warfare and Belligerence. Perspectives in First World War Studies* (Boston and Leiden, 2005), pp. 1–37.

legally defined category found within all three states, where they generated
very similar source materials, such as interviews with escapers and memoirs, prisoners of war represent an ideal subject for a synchronic comparative study of the kind advocated by Marc Bloch.[18] However, this book
additionally goes beyond the straightforward synchronic juxtaposition of
the three countries as three separate units of comparison, to also look at
these units as wholly interactive with each other; this is the transnational
dimension to this history.[19] The transnational sphere includes multiple
levels of interaction such as bilateral and multilateral relations between the
three states, as well as with other countries, national responses to enemy
policies and constructed popular rumours about enemy practices; it also
encompasses engagement with the international public sphere, with its
discourses and debates about prisoner treatment. All affected how ideas
about violence against prisoners of war were formed and practices condoned or rejected. This book attempts to deal with the complexity of this
transnational sphere by building upon the work of Michel Espagne, which
calls for historians to consider historical 'transfer', how ideas travel from
one society to another and are changed into hybrid forms through the very
process of exchange; thus this book treats violence as both a physical
behaviour pattern within each country and a concept partly constructed
through transnational interactions.[20] Both Bloch's and Espagne's different approaches to historical comparison are constantly used throughout
this book, although at certain points it has proved appropriate that the
narrative focus in detail upon a particular national experience.

The work of Bénédicte Zimmermann and Michael Werner has recently
highlighted the pitfalls of comparison, contending that selecting one
historical theme to compare across multiple linguistic zones is an arbi-
trary, artificial process whereby the historian creates a framework out of
linguistic categories which do not always directly conceptually translate

---

[18] Marc Bloch, 'A Contribution towards a Comparative History of European Societies', in
   Land and Work in Medieval Europe (London, 1967), p. 47.
[19] On theories on comparison in history see Hans-Gerhard Haupt and Jürgen Kocka,
   'Comparative History. Methods, Aims, Problems', in Deborah Cohen and Maura
   O'Connor, eds., *Comparison and History. Europe in Cross-National Perspective* (New York
   and London, 2004); Philipp Ther, 'Beyond the Nation. The Relational Basis of a
   Comparative History of Germany and Europe', *Central European History*, 36, 1 (2003),
   pp. 45–73; John Breuilly, 'Introduction. Making Comparisons in History', in John
   Breuilly, ed., *Labour and Liberalism in Nineteenth-Century Europe. Essays in Comparative
   History* (Manchester and New York, 1992), pp. 1–25; Michael Werner and Bénédicte
   Zimmermann, 'Beyond Comparison. Histoire Croisée and the Challenge of Reflexivity',
   History and Theory, 45, 1 (2006), pp. 30–50; Michel Espagne, 'Sur les limites du com-
   paratisme en histoire culturelle', *Genèses*, 17, 1 (1994), pp. 112–21.
[20] Deborah Cohen, 'Comparative History. Buyer Beware', *Bulletin of the German Historical
   Institute, Washington*, 29 (2001), p. 24.

between different cultures; indeed, particular concepts may exist in one culture that are not even present in another.[21] As far as is possible, this problem is circumvented here by comparing a subject which enjoyed a common legal definition in international law at the outset of the war in all three countries studied: what constituted unacceptable prisoner treatment was set out in the 1864 and 1906 Geneva Conventions, which provided protection for enemy wounded, and the 1907 Hague Convention on Land Warfare, with its stipulation that prisoners of war be treated 'humanely'.[22] Thus while acknowledging that, to some extent, the term violence in English does not mean exactly the same thing as its counterparts *violence* in French or *Gewalt* in German, this study takes as its comparative starting point the argument that there was considerable overlap in how contemporaries in all three countries conceptualised violence against captives in 1914; this facilitates historical comparison, even if, as the war continued, these shared understandings began to break down along national lines.

Ultimately, comparison is also a highly suitable approach given that prisoners of war experienced the war in a conceptually hybrid, transnational way, located in a liminal cultural space between home state and captor nation. The aid effort which developed to assist them clearly illustrates this: British, French and German prisoners provoked similar humanitarian mobilisations in their home countries as charitable organisations used the European postal system, which continued to function during the war, to send prisoners aid parcels; regimental care associations, *départemental* care committees, religious charities, national Red Cross organisations, and individual families, sustained a mammoth humanitarian aid effort which helped to alleviate prisoner hardship.[23] And from 1916, the French government organised the delivery of bread and biscuits to French prisoners in German camps.[24] All these efforts involved transnational exchanges and a reciprocal learning curve between cultures.

[21] Werner and Zimmermann, 'Beyond Comparison'.

[22] Brown, ed., *The Hague Conventions and Declarations of 1899 and 1907*, p. 108; Cochet, *Soldats sans armes*, p. 11; Georges Cahen-Salvador, *Les Prisonniers de guerre (1914–1919)* (Paris, 1929), p. 17.

[23] On aid to prisoners, see Heather Jones, 'International or Transnational? Humanitarian Action during the First World War', *European Review of History*, 16, 5 (2009), pp. 697–713. See also Parliamentary Paper, Cd. 8615, *Report of the Joint Committee Appointed by the Chairmen of Committees of the House of Lords and the House of Commons to Enquire into the Organisation and Methods of the Central Prisoners of War Committee* (London, 1917). See also *Reports by the Joint War Committee and the Joint War Finance Committee of the British Red Cross Society and the Order of St John of Jerusalem in England on Voluntary Aid Rendered to the Sick and Wounded at Home and Abroad and to British Prisoners of War, 1914–1919* (London, 1921), pp. 544–87.

[24] Abbal, *Soldats oubliés*, pp. 88–9.

Comparison is all the more vital as the existing recent historiography on prisoners has been heavily weighted towards single-nation studies, reflecting the fact that the national framework still dominates First World War historiography, as noted by Jay Winter and Antoine Prost; moreover, the focus has been almost entirely upon prisoners of war in either German or Russian captivity.[25] British and French prisoner treatment has been largely ignored. Thus until now the attitudes and motivations governing Germany's behaviour towards prisoners have remained largely hidden, as the transnational reciprocity dimension which drove prisoner policy was overlooked; indeed, at present there is still no monograph on German prisoners of war in France or German prisoners in Britain, although the latter are the focus of a forthcoming doctoral study.[26] For most historians, the First World War still remains fundamentally the war of the trench, not the prison camp.

It is important to note one other significant issue which facilitates comparison. The key structures which acted as limitations upon violence against prisoners were transnational and functioned relatively similarly in all three countries. The first of these structural checks upon violence, international humanitarian law, has already been mentioned: Britain, France and Germany had all ratified the Hague and Geneva Conventions, although the German army had been far more reluctant to accept them than the British or French, with one senior figure, Colmar von der Goltz, governor-general of Belgium in 1914, describing the Hague Convention as 'silly negotiations and agreements'.[27] This shared international law provided a common framework of standards for all three countries, even if, as the war radicalised, it was rapidly undermined and frequently ignored, a process significantly aggravated by the fact that it was never clear whether a captor state's internal military law took precedence over international law when the two clashed; this often led to international law being breached.[28] Pre-war international law had envisaged that prisoners would be disciplined according to a

[25] Antoine Prost and Jay Winter, *The Great War in History. Debates and Controversies, 1914 to the Present* (Cambridge, 2005), p. 195. On British prisoners in Germany see Robert Jackson, *The Prisoners 1914–1918* (London, 1989), which is based only on Imperial War Museum sources; on Canadian prisoners in Germany see Jonathan Vance, *Objects of Concern. Canadian Prisoners of War through the Twentieth Century* (Vancouver, 1994); Desmond Morton, *Silent Battle. Canadian Prisoners of War in Germany, 1914–1919* (Toronto, 1992).

[26] Brian K. Feltman, 'The Culture of Captivity: German Prisoners, British Captors and Manhood in the Great War, 1914–1920', Ph.D. thesis, Ohio State University, 2010.

[27] Horne and Kramer, *German Atrocities*, pp. 151, 215–16.

[28] See the discussion in Herbert Belfield, 'The Treatment of Prisoners of War', *Transactions of the Grotius Society. Problems of Peace and War*, 9 (1923), pp. 140–1. See also the discussion in Hinz, *Gefangen im Großen Krieg*, pp. 43–70.

state's own internal military law. However, during the conflict this gave rise to disputes, due to the contrasting levels of harsh disciplinary measures allowable against captives according to the different military law codes in operation in each state and the radicalised wartime implementation of certain permitted forms of corporal punishment at the local level, particularly in Germany and France; this increasingly clashed with the general stipulation in the Hague Convention of 1907 that prisoners be treated 'humanely'.[29] Another problem was that internal military law was often very complex, allowing local commandants great leeway at the start of the war in how they implemented it: for example, in Germany, prisoners were subject to the German Military Law Codebook (*Militärstrafgesetzbuch*) of 1872, as well as the Military Courts Code and the Order on Discipline (*Disziplinarstrafordnung*).[30] To resolve these very real problems, in 1916, Germany and France agreed to suspend the implementation of all official military sentences passed in accordance with each state's internal military law against individual prisoners of war for misdemeanours to after the end of the war; in 1917, a similar agreement was made between Germany and Britain.[31] Both these agreements were also applied retrospectively to all sentences issued since the outbreak of the conflict, offering prisoners who had been found guilty a certain amount of protection; they also meant that, on the rare occasions that a prisoner of war was sentenced to death by military tribunal, the sentence was suspended. In fact, during the war, there was a great reluctance on the part of official military trials on the home front to issue death sentences against prisoners, often for reasons of reciprocity, as such sentences affected the enemy's treatment of its captives; when a prisoner was tried under military law in the German, French or British home front systems, the most usual sentence was solitary confinement or, in extreme cases, penal servitude. Indeed, according to one source, only two French prisoners and no British prisoners were sentenced to death in Germany during the whole war, and suspended sentences were never carried out.[32] In the British case, there were 3,842 military trials of prisoners of war during the conflict; in total, however, only twenty-two death sentences were issued to both prisoners of war

---

[29] Brown, ed., *The Hague Conventions and Declarations of 1899 and 1907*, p. 108; on the French adoption, on the basis of reciprocity, of harsher disciplinary measures against German prisoners who were sentenced to solitary confinement during the war, see Cahen-Salvador, *Les Prisonniers de guerre*, p. 98. On Germany, see Hinz, *Gefangen im Großen Krieg*, pp. 156–69.

[30] Hinz, *Gefangen im Großen Krieg*, p. 141.   [31] *Ibid.*, p. 143.

[32] Wilhelm Doegen, *Kriegsgefangene Völker*, vol. I: *Der Kriegsgefangenen Haltung und Schicksal in Deutschland* (Berlin, 1919 [1921]), pp. 138–9.

and civilians by military courts between 4 August 1914 and 31 March 1920.[33] The desire to avoid enemy retribution was a major factor in the limited official use of the death penalty in military law against captives; this helps to explain why the worst, most violent punishments of prisoners discussed in this book are largely to be found at the grassroots level, where official military trials were not involved. Most violence was informal, ordered directly by local commanders according to their own interpretation of military law or acting on their own autonomy, or was randomly carried out by guards.[34] In this regard, the camps of the First World War do not form the kind of comprehensive juridico-political state of complete 'exception', where all civic and military legal norms are suspended, all forms of transgressive violence permissible and 'everything is possible', which the philosopher Giorgio Agamben identifies occurring in Second World War concentration camps in his discussion of the camp as the '"Nomos" of the modern'.[35] In the Great War, a coherent, externally codified, military juridical system continued to theoretically apply to internal prison camp life in each country. The fact that this military law framework continued to exist – even if it was not always fully implemented or rigorously observed by guards or local commanders, as during the 1918 mistreatment of prisoners in German army labour companies – is important, as it demonstrates that First World War captivity never became a space beyond all legal jurisdiction.

The second key check on violence against prisoners was the development of a system of transnational neutral inspections of prisoner of war camps which applied in all three countries. Carried out by neutral governments, who were each assigned a particular set of prisoner nationalities for whom they acted as a 'protector power', as well as by the International Committee of the Red Cross, these inspections allowed for prisoner treatment to be monitored; they also established parameters for what constituted unacceptable violence.[36] As neutral powers, the Spanish monitored German treatment of French prisoners, while the Swiss checked upon German prisoners in France. The Americans were responsible for inspecting the treatment of German prisoners in Britain and British prisoners in Germany; after American entry into the war, these tasks fell to the Swiss and Dutch

---

[33] War Office, *Statistics of the Military Effort of the British Empire during the Great War 1914–1920* (London, 1922), p. 672.

[34] Hinz, *Gefangen im Großen Krieg*, p. 156.

[35] Giorgio Agamben, *Homo Sacer. Sovereign Power and Bare Life* (Stanford, 1998), pp. 166–76.

[36] Frédéric Yerly, 'Grande Guerre et diplomatie humanitaire. La mission Catholique Suisse en faveur des prisonniers de guerre (1914–1918)', *Vingtième Siècle*, 58 (1998), pp. 13–28.

respectively.[37] However, it was the International Red Cross which played the greatest role; as well as forwarding parcels and post to prisoners and liaising between national Red Cross organisations, its *Agence International des Prisonniers de Guerre*, established in 1914, investigated and publicly condemned incidents of prisoner mistreatment.[38] The Vatican was also involved, pressuring states into improving prisoner treatment.

As the war continued, neutral inspections also led to the development of a system of prisoner exchanges, whereby badly injured or ill prisoners were repatriated home. These began tentatively in March 1915, when seriously wounded prisoners, who were incapable of ever fighting again, were exchanged between France and Germany via Switzerland; later they were extended to captured medical personnel.[39] Further categories qualifying for exchange were codified in two wartime agreements between Britain and Germany at The Hague in June 1917 and July 1918. Two Franco-German prisoner agreements, known as the Berne Accords, were also signed during the war; the first, negotiated in 1917, entered into force in March 1918; the second was agreed in April 1918.[40] A system for transferring ill or wounded prisoners from their captor state to more comfortable internment conditions in neutral countries also developed; initially prisoners were moved to Switzerland; later the Netherlands also took part in a similar internment scheme. The existence of international inspections and exchanges provided some protection to prisoners, although the overall number of captives exchanged was very small relative to the total number of wartime captives, and inspectors were sometimes deliberately deceived by captor state administrations or refused entry to certain camps; indeed, neutral inspectors were never granted access to prisoners held by Germany in the occupied territories of France and Belgium.[41] Moreover, prisoners were often threatened with punishment if they complained to inspectors; their

---

[37] On the protecting powers see Speed, *Prisoners, Diplomats and the Great War*, pp. 19–20; Pöppinghege, *Im Lager unbesiegt*, p. 61; Howard S. Levie, 'Prisoners of War and the Protecting Power', *The American Journal of International Law*, 55, 2 (1961), pp. 374–97.

[38] Gradimir Djurović, *L'Agence centrale de recherches du Comité International de la Croix-Rouge. Activité du CICR en vue du soulagement des souffrances morales des victimes de guerre* (Geneva, 1981), p. 42.

[39] On exchanges see *Le Régime des prisonniers de guerre en France et en Allemagne au regard des conventions internationales, 1914–1916* (Paris, 1916).

[40] Neville Wylie, 'The 1929 Prisoner of War Convention and the Building of the Inter-war Prisoner of War Regime', in Sibylle Scheipers, ed., *Prisoners in War* (Oxford, 2010), p. 94.

[41] In camps in Austria-Hungary, in 1918, instructions were given that Spanish inspectors should only be shown 'healthy' prisoners; those in poor condition were to be hidden. Hannes Leidinger and Verena Moritz, 'Kriegsgefangene in der Donaumonarchie 1914–1918', in Oltmer, ed., *Kriegsgefangene im Europa des Ersten Weltkriegs*, p. 62. See also Hinz, *Gefangen im Großen Krieg*, pp. 79–80.

complaints could jeopardise a country's international reputation and so were often suppressed by captors.[42]

In practice, therefore, the power of transnational structures, such as international law and neutral inspections, to limit violence against prisoners, greatly depended upon the attitudes of national administrative systems, in particular, the bureaucratic institutions established to control enemy prisoners and to provide aid to a country's own men, held prisoner in enemy territory. Nationally distinctive, these administrative systems dealt differently with the issue of violence against prisoners – and their attitudes also changed as the war went on. The interaction between national administrative institutions and the transnational cultural and bureaucratic structures intended to limit violence evolved differently in each state; in general, Britain and France were more receptive to neutral intervention or international law than Germany.

The structure of the national bureaucracies responsible for managing prisoner of war issues was thus key to levels of violence against captives within a given country. Where there was strict centralisation and civilian government control, such as in France, where the treatment of enemy prisoners was initially based upon a relatively enlightened Ministerial Instruction of 21 March 1893 and carefully coordinated by the *Service Général des Prisonniers de Guerre*, a department established within the French Ministry of War in autumn 1914, the use of violence against prisoners largely evolved in accordance with national policies.[43] Indiscriminate violence by guards was thus generally curtailed for most of the war. Although the French system became more militarised as the war went on, particularly when in 1916 the *Inspection Générale des Prisonniers de Guerre* (IGPG) took over running many functions which had been under the *Service Général*, civilian input remained significant. The whole system remained under the overall civilian control of the Ministry of War, controlled by France's democratically elected civilian government. Georges Cahen-Salvador, a civil servant, who directed the *Service Général*, was responsible for prisoner policy decisions for most of the conflict. This did not prevent France from largely abandoning the 1893 Ministerial Instruction as too liberal in late 1915, in favour of basing prisoner treatment upon reciprocity with Germany; however, it did ensure that prisoner treatment was subject to largely effective government monitoring.

The power of civilian input and centralisation to limit violence against enemy prisoners was also clear in the British case, where from August

---

[42] See the accounts in The National Archives, London (TNA) WO 161/99, no. 1060, Private Edward Page and no. 862, Private William Beeby.
[43] Cahen-Salvador, *Les Prisonniers de guerre*, pp. 21, 44–6, 117.

1914, the treatment of German prisoners in Britain was directly controlled by the Department of Prisoners of War at the War Office, headed by Lieutenant-General Sir Herbert Belfield; it strictly regulated the use of violence against captives, which in the British system was generally only permitted in very specific, stringently controlled disciplinary contexts, as a punishment for misdemeanours set out in British military law. The main contrast with the French system, where the *Service Général* was responsible for both French prisoner treatment and monitoring German treatment of French captives, was that, in Britain, the Foreign Office controlled British policy regarding British prisoners of war held by Germany; indeed, in 1916, the Foreign Office founded its own Prisoner of War Department under Lord Thomas Newton to handle the increasing work involved. This made the British system slightly less centralised than the French and did lead to tensions between the War Office and the Foreign Office as the war went on, as both vied to influence government responses to German prisoner mistreatment. An additional civilian committee, the Government Committee on the Treatment by the Enemy of British Prisoners of War, established under the auspices of the Foreign Office in 1915, but with considerable autonomy, interviewed repatriated and exchanged British prisoners to collect evidence of any German prisoner mistreatment.[44] Headed by Sir Robert Younger, a judge of the Chancery Division and effectively run by the committee secretary, Adelaide Livingstone, an American woman married to a British officer, its interviews and reports were impressively rigorous; the interviews, often carried out by civilian lawyers, have been used extensively as source material on German violence against prisoners for this book.[45]

The German administration of enemy prisoners of war was the least centralised and the farthest removed from civilian government control, factors which led to widespread local variations in the levels of violence permitted against captives, to an inability to rein in indiscriminate random violence by guards and also to very haphazard adherence to national policies at the local level. Indeed, it is fair to suggest that due to Germany's unique regional framework, any 'national' policy on prisoner treatment remained an aspiration for much of the war. Two systems of control operated simultaneously: at the outbreak of war, Germany was divided into wartime military regions, administered by regional district

---

[44] J. F. Willis, *Prologue to Nuremberg. The Politics and Diplomacy of Punishing War Criminals of the First World War* (Westport, Conn., and London, 1982), p. 22.

[45] See the series TNA WO 161/95; WO 161/96; WO 161/97; WO 161/98; WO 161/99; WO 161/100; WO 161/101. However, the full series represents the testimony of only approximately 1.7 per cent of British prisoners captured by Germany.

commanders answerable to the Kaiser alone. These men had direct responsibility for all prisoners within their military region; they frequently delegated considerable powers to individual camp commandants, who thus had considerable autonomy regarding all aspects of prisoner life, including the extent to which the use of violence remained within the boundaries of existing military law. At the same time, the Prussian Ministry for War (the Prussian *Kriegsministerium*) was responsible for issuing prisoner guidelines, intended to harmonise similar standards of prisoner treatment across the Wilhelmine Reich.[46] These policy guidelines were sent to the district military commanders, who in the first two years of the war frequently ignored them; they were also sent to regional war ministries and to the German armies on the western front. In theory, these Prussian instructions on prisoner treatment were meant to take precedent over those from regional war ministries; Bavaria, Saxony and Württemberg retained their own Ministries for War in the German federal system. In reality, the Prussian Ministry for War found it difficult to implement its orders. Its lack of control over the regional district commanders who had charge of the prison camps was a major problem, as was its inability to effectively influence army behaviour towards prisoners on the western front. Its own internal administrative disorder, with different overlapping internal sections responsible for deciding prisoner policy, was also a factor.[47] Coordination of prisoner policy across Germany did improve as the war went on, with General Emil von Friedrich, head of the *Unterkunftsabteilung* at the Prussian Ministry for War, which was the main section responsible for prisoner issues, increasingly demanding that its instructions be respected. Policy towards prisoners was also increasingly linked to the treatment of German prisoners in enemy hands, which was monitored by the *Abteilung für Kriegsgefangenenschutz im Ausland und Völkerrechtsverletzungen* in the Prussian Ministry for War. However, the overall German administrative system remained labyrinthine and inefficient: widespread and often unregulated violence against prisoners thus continued to be a problem. Its decentralised nature, as well as the fact that civilian government had barely any input into prisoner policy, helps to explain the higher levels of violence which emerged in the German case.

Yet poor coordination is only part of the story: the German administration also differed from the British and the French in its acceptance of

---

[46] See also Hinz, *Gefangen im Großen Krieg*, pp. 71–4.
[47] *Handbuch über den Königlich Preussischen Hof und Staat für das Jahr 1914* (Berlin, 1913), p. 145; *Handbuch über den Königlich Preussischen Hof und Staat für das Jahr 1918* (Berlin, 1918), p. 142.

the use of extreme violence against prisoners of war during reprisal phases. On occasion, as this book will show, it adopted reprisal policies that deliberately led to prisoner deaths. Thus we are faced with a paradox. In comparison with previous conflicts, the bureaucratic management of prisoners of war was far more developed during the First World War: this often ensured a greater measure of protection for prisoners, as state bureaucracies took over or assisted the military with the organisation of food distribution systems, supervised disciplinary practices by guards or enforced the hygiene standards necessary to avoid epidemics, all factors which had cost prisoner lives in previous wars; even in the German case, where these bureaucratic advances were slowest and worst coordinated, particularly in 1914–15, when epidemics of typhus broke out because of inadequate supervision of camp hygiene, there was still overall a net modernisation of administrative procedures in comparison with the nineteenth century. However, these very same administrative improvements could also facilitate and coordinate more effective uses of radical violence against prisoners, where cultural norms permitted. This becomes clearly visible during reprisal sequences. The cultural rationale behind modernisation thus mattered: where it was driven by humanitarian agendas, modernisation offered prisoners greater protection than when it was motivated simply by the wartime state's desire to avoid the destabilising effects of mass chaos in the prison camps or the need to exploit prisoner of war labour.

In particular, the need for prisoner labour, in the context of the massive manpower demands of trench warfare, changed the nature of violence against other-rank prisoners; in contrast, officer prisoners, segregated into specially privileged officer prisoner of war camps on the home front, were, in all three countries, rarely exposed to any physical mistreatment. In the Great War, violence was now as likely to be used to force a captive from the ranks to work as to kill him; indeed, from the point of view of the wartime state, his value as a labourer meant that it was important to keep him alive, once he had entered into captivity. Hence, during the war, a whole host of forms of violent practices were adopted that usually stopped just short of killing other-rank captives; generally the purpose was to intimidate, humiliate, force obedience, punish or coerce, but not to kill outright, with the obvious exception of violence at the moment of capture itself, where fatalities occurred when quarter was refused or revoked on the spot. Violence against prisoners in captivity thus operated within certain thresholds during the conflict – limitations which stemmed from the specific modernisation processes unleashed by the new industrialised warfare, with its simultaneous creation of both mass captivity and the need for mass labour.

For this reason, this book, while it discusses prisoner killing at the battlefront, contends that it is also crucially important to study the other kinds of non-fatal violence practised in captivity throughout the war, if we wish to assess the full extent to which radicalisation processes were at work. In fact, prisoner death rates can offer only the roughest indication of general levels of violence within the British, French and German captivity systems: first, because not all deaths were directly attributable to violence, and second, because they can tell us nothing about non-fatal violent practices. Death rates do, however, provide an imperfect barometer for gauging how far the drive towards absolute extremes of violence went during the war, although their value is circumscribed by the fact that so much of the available data is incomplete. In fact, in the German case, we do not even have reliable statistics on how many prisoners Germany captured, let alone exactly how many died in German captivity, a problem illustrated by Table 1. In 1918, the German army, disintegrating under pressure, stopped registering newly captured prisoners; records for the rest of the war were largely destroyed in Second World War bombing and interwar publications do not concur on overall figures.[48] The most realistic figures for the number of British and French prisoners of war held in camps in Germany remain those of the French Deputy Gratien Candace of 520,579 French prisoners, and the *Statistics of the Military Effort of the British Empire during the Great War, 1914–1920*, which estimated 175,624 British prisoners; however, even these are based on incomplete records of numbers of captives repatriated.[49] Figures for Germans held in Britain and France, given in Table 2, diverge less but there are still discrepancies between different sources on total deaths or captures. And for all three countries, the available figures do not distinguish between deaths which occurred in prisoner of war labour companies working on the western front and deaths in home front areas.

Taking the most reliable sources results in a very rough maximum estimate of some 811,203 British and French prisoners captured by Germany. This is the sum of Candace's figure and the *Statistics of the Military Effort* total, plus an additional estimate of some 115,000 unregistered British and French prisoners in the German occupied territories of France and Belgium, which is based on the only available, incomplete,

---

[48] Hans Weiland and Leopold Kern, eds., *In Feindeshand. Die Gefangenschaft im Weltkriege in Einzeldarstellungen*, 2 vols. (Vienna, 1931), statistical appendix; Doegen, *Kriegsgefangene Völker*, pp. 12–29.

[49] Gratien Candace, *Rapport fait au nom de la Commission des affaires extérieures* no. 5676, Chambre des Députés, onzième législature, session de 1919, annexe au procès-verbal de la 2e séance du 11 février 1919 (Paris, 1919); War Office, *Statistics of the Military Effort*, pp. 632–5.

Table 1. *The different estimates of the total number of British and French prisoners captured by Germany, and French and British prisoner deaths in German captivity during the First World War.*[a]

	British prisoners captured by Germany[b]	French prisoners captured by Germany[c]	British prisoner deaths in German captivity	French prisoner deaths in German captivity
Interwar publications				
W. Doegen	182,009	535,411	5,525	17,069
G. Cahen-Salvador		520,579		38,963
H. Weiland and L. Kern	360,400	535,400	11,000	17,000
G. Candace		520,579		
L. Marin		506,000		
Stat. of the Milit. Effort	175,624	446,300	12,425	
Bulletin		844,000		
TNA WO 161/82	175,624		12,425	
SHAT 12 N 3	171,000	486,000		
Völkerrecht	185,329	535,411	5,547	17,308
M. Huber		549,000		19,000
Post-1945 publications				
A. Becker		600,000		20,000
O. Abbal		520,579		Min: 18,822 Max: 38,963
N. Ferguson	191,652	Min: 446,300 Max: 500,000		
U. Hinz III		500,000		
A. Rachamimov	360,400	535,400	11,000	17,000
R. Speed	185,329	535,411		

[a] The following works were used to compile Tables 1 and 2: Interwar period: Doegen, *Kriegsgefangene Völker*, p. 28, Prisoners captured by Germany on 10 October 1918; Candace, *Rapport fait au nom de la Commission des affaires extérieures*; Cahen-Salvador, *Les Prisonniers de guerre*, pp. 281, 284, 291; Reichstag, *Das Werk des Untersuchungsausschusses der Verfassunggebenden Deutschen Nationalversammlung und des Deutschen Reichstages, 1919–1928*, ed. E. Fischer et al., 3rd series, *Völkerrecht im Weltkrieg*, vol. III, part I (Berlin, 1927), p. 715; Michel Huber, *La Population de la France pendant la Guerre* (Paris, 1931). pp. 131–8; War Office, *Statistics of the Military Effort*, pp. 329, 352, 632–5; Jakob Reinhardt, 'Die Zurückführung der deutschen Kriegsgefangenen aus Frankreich', *Süddeutsche Monatshefte*, 11, 22 (August 1925), p. 29; *Bulletin de l'Office d'Information – Office d'Information des Oeuvres de secours aux prisonniers de guerre rattaché à l'Agence des Prisonniers de Guerre de la Croix-Rouge française, 1918*, p. 3002, cited in Bernard Delpal, 'Prisonniers de guerre en France (1914–1920)', in André Gueslin and Dominique Kalifa, eds., *Les Exclus en Europe, 1830–1930* (Paris, 1999), p. 149; Service Historique de l'Armée de Terre (SHAT), 16 N 525, GQG Bureau de Personnel – Pertes, Dossier no. 2, Prisonniers de Guerre, États numériques; SHAT, 12 N 3, no. 31. Nombre de prisonniers de chaque nationalité faits par les divers belligerents – (demandé de M. Louis Marin, Rapporteur général de la Commission du Budget de la Chambre des Deputés) 1919, 27 sept.–14 novembre, no. 13056. Chambre des Deputés, Commission du Budget – 27.9.1919, M. Louis Marin to Mr le Président du Conseil, Ministre de la Guerre; Weiland and Kern, *In Feindeshand*, vol. II, Statistical Appendix; TNA, WO 161/82, War Office, *Statistical Abstract of Information Regarding the Armies at Home and Abroad, 1914–1920*, June 1920, pp. 332, 628, 633–6; Louis Marin, *Journal Officiel*, Annexe no. 633, 1920, p. 44. Post-1945: Becker, *Oubliés de la Grande Guerre*, pp. 15, 361; Uta Hinz 'Kriegsgefangene', in Gerhard Hirschfeld, Gerd Krumeich and Irina Renz, eds., *Enzyklopädie Erster Weltkrieg* (Paderborn, Munich, Vienna, Zurich, 2003), p. 641; Ferguson, *The Pity of War*, pp. 295, 369; Speed, *Prisoners, Diplomats and the Great War*, pp. 195, 76; Abbal, *Soldats oubliés*, p. 23; Rachamimov, *POWs and the Great War*, pp. 39–42.

[b] Unless otherwise stated prisoners from the British Empire are included in these estimates. Civilian prisoners are excluded.

[c] French colonial prisoners are also included. Civilian prisoners are excluded.

Table 2. *The different estimates of the total number of German prisoners captured by France and Britain, and of German prisoner deaths in French or British captivity during the First World War.*

	German prisoners of war captured by Britain[a]	German prisoners of war captured by France	German prisoner deaths in British captivity	German prisoner deaths in French captivity
Interwar publications				
H. Weiland and L. Kern	328,900	429,200	10,000	25,200 dead, 43,250 missing
Stat. of the Mil. Effort	306,593[b]	392,425	9,349	
TNA,WO 161/82	308,864	392,425	9,467	
Süddeutsche Monatsh.		421,000		22,105
German prisoner graves			2,662[c]	
SHAT 16 N 525		392,425		
SHAT 12 N 3	311,000	359,000		
Völkerrecht	328,020	424,157[d]	9,939	25,229[e]
G. Cahen-Salvador		327,373		
Post-1945 Publications				
U. Hinz	328,000	350,000		
R. Speed III	328,000	350,000		

[a] Unless otherwise stated, these figures are for the total number of German prisoners of war captured on all fronts and include naval prisoners. Civilian internees are excluded.

[b] Number of German prisoners of war held by the UK on 20 January 1919. War Office, *Statistics of the Military Effort*, pp. 630–1. This figure does not include German naval prisoners.

[c] This figure is for German First World War burials located as follows: across the UK (263); at Cannock Chase War Cemetery (256); and Cannock Chase German Military Cemetery (2,143), where Germans who died in the UK in 1914–19 were collectively reinterred between 1964 and 1966. These burials are mainly of prisoners of war but also include Zeppelin crews who were shot down. www.cannockchasedc.gov.uk/cannockchase/wargraves.htm, accessed 10 August 2005, and home.arcor.de/kriegsgefangene/cemetery/cannockchase.html, accessed 10 August 2005. This figure does not include German prisoners who died in British captivity buried in France.

[d] This figure is for German prisoners captured by France and Belgium.

[e] This figure is for German prisoners who died in French and Belgian captivity.

statistic for the number of British and French captives liberated there at the end of the war; this figure of 115,000 is highly problematic, as it is in all likelihood an underestimate due to the chaos of the Armistice phase and as it is not clear to what extent Candace or the *Statistics of the Military Effort* included prisoners in the German-occupied territories in their totals.[50]

Indeed, as interwar estimates for British and French prisoner deaths in Germany, which suggest a maximum of 51,388 and a minimum of 22,525 fatalities for the two nationalities, do not state whether the occupied territories are included or not, it is necessary to exclude the occupied territory statistic of 115,000 prisoners altogether when calculating overall death rates, in order to avoid any potential danger of counting the occupied territory prisoners twice. Thus estimated *maximum* death statistics for each of the two Allied prisoner nationalities emerge as 7.48% for French prisoners held in Germany proper, based on 38,963 deaths out of 520,579 French captives, and a British death rate of 7.07% based upon 12,425 deaths out of 175,624 British captives. These rates are for the whole war. In comparison, Mark Spoerer calculated annual rates of 52 per thousand for British and Commonwealth prisoners against 12 per thousand for French captives in Germany, showing a bigger differential between these nationalities; however, Spoerer's findings are annual figures which have been weighted to take into account the much longer average length of time of 2.6 years spent in German captivity by the majority of French prisoners, as against 1.2 years for the average British prisoner. His figures also do not include deaths of prisoners from wounds received in action prior to captivity.[51]

In the case of Germans held by France, if we take approximately 392,425 as a relatively reliable estimate, based upon the weekly tallies in the SHAT archive file 16 N 525 and the highest death figure of approximately 25,229, we arrive at a maximum estimated death rate of 6.42%. Given that there is very little divergence in the different figures on German deaths in French captivity, this appears a relatively realistic figure, one, it should be noted, that is far below the 16% cited in some interwar German propaganda, which misleadingly counted battlefield missing as dead prisoners of war.[52] Again, in the British case, taking 10,000 as the highest figure for German deaths in British captivity and

---

[50] Bundesarchiv, Berlin-Lichterfelde (BA), R 904/77, f. 3, Kriegsministerium, Unterkunfts-Kriegsabteilung, Nr. 2068.11.18 U.K. to Staatsekretär Erzberger.

[51] Spoerer, 'The Mortality of Allied Prisoners of War', p. 129.

[52] The figure of 16 per cent is cited uncritically in Rüdiger Overmans, '"In der Hand des Feindes". Geschichtsschreibung zur Kriegsgefangenschaft von der Antike bis zum Zweiten Weltkrieg', in Overmans, ed., *In der Hand des Feindes, Kriegsgefangenschaft von der Antike bis zum Zweiten Weltkrieg* (Cologne, Weimar, Vienna, 1999), p. 9.

328,900 as the highest estimate for captures, gives us a maximum death rate of approximately 3.04%, far lower than the mortality rate estimates for prisoners held in French or German captivity.

All of the above calculations, apart from Spoerer's figures, are overall rates for the whole of the war. Given that these are maximum estimates, which include deaths from all causes, not just violence, this indicates that levels of *fatal* violence against British, French and German prisoners were relatively low, although again it has to be remembered that the occupied territories, where the evidence indicates that violence against captives was most widespread, cannot be effectively analysed from the available data. To place these figures in context, in the First World War, Romanian prisoners had an overall mortality rate of almost 29% in German captivity, based on German figures, which may well be an underestimate, while Italians in Austro-Hungarian captivity had a death rate of just under 20%.[53] Clearly some Great War prisoner nationalities benefited from more safeguards than others; British, French and German western front captives did not fare worst.

The figures also indicate that captivity was overall less violent than frontline infantry life; cumulatively, for the whole war, 12.9% of all those who served in the British army died or were killed, according to Jay Winter, which is greater than the above estimates for death rates for British and French prisoners in Germany.[54] In comparison, 16.8% of those mobilised in the French army and 15.4% of those mobilised in the German army died or were killed.[55] This helps explain why in some quarters, in interwar France in particular, there was resentment at prisoners who were seen as having escaped the risks of the trenches; it also shows the real protection which British captivity, where the total death rate was just 3.04%, offered German soldiers, although it should be noted that this was not dramatically lower than the *annual* death rate in the German army, which averaged out at 34 per thousand across 1914–18.[56] One must also factor in that prisoners of war in home front camps (but not in the prisoner labour company system) were also spared the risk of being wounded on the battlefield, a substantial danger for infantry at the front: 31.5% of all those who served in the British army were wounded in the war; in the French army, the figure was 40%; although contextualising the risk of non-fatal battlefield wounds against the dangers of prisoner of war life is a problematic measure of assessment, as we

---

[53] Kramer, *Dynamic of Destruction*, p. 65.
[54] Jay Winter, *The Great War and the British People* (London and Basingstoke, 1985), Table 3.3, p. 73.
[55] *Ibid.*, Table 3.4, p. 75. See also Kramer, *Dynamic of Destruction*, p. 2.
[56] Kramer, *Dynamic of Destruction*, p. 2.

lack comparable figures for how many prisoners were wounded from violence by captors during captivity.[57]

However, if we break the statistics down further, a slightly more nuanced image of captivity emerges; during some periods of the war, it was actually more dangerous to be a British prisoner in Germany than an ordinary British soldier. Between 1 October 1917 and 30 September 1918, other ranks in the British army had a death rate of 4.0%; Mark Spoerer has calculated an annual death rate among British prisoners of 5.2% for this same phase, which was the period of the conflict when Germany took the vast majority of its British prisoners.[58] Thus, for this short final phase of the conflict, the intensity of deaths among British prisoners was comparable to the mortality risks of non-captured British soldiers. Moreover, the maximum death rate estimates calculated above, of around 6–7% for British and French prisoners in Germany, are actually higher than those for their Second World War counterparts: Rüdiger Overmans puts death rates during the 1939–45 conflict at around 2–3% for German prisoners in Britain, and British and French prisoners in Germany; S. P. Mackenzie estimates deaths among British prisoners in Germany at 5.1% by spring 1945.[59] Without any data for prisoner deaths in the German-occupied territories of Belgium and northern France in 1914–18, comparisons with the Great War must remain provisional. However, clearly First World War captivity did involve real mortality risks – assumptions that it was always 'safer' to be a prisoner than an ordinary soldier in the conflict do not hold up. What mattered was *when* a man was captured: for example, a French infantry soldier, taken prisoner in August 1914, and thereby spared the terrible bloodletting of the subsequent war years, faced a reduced risk of dying than a man who remained in a French infantry unit for the remainder of the conflict. However, given that the highest French battlefield casualties were in 1914 and 1915, a French soldier captured later, in 1917 or 1918, benefited much less from captivity proportionally in terms of a reduced time-span exposure to the trenches in an infantry unit; he was also far more likely to end up in the prisoner of war labour company system which effectively kept him at the western front.[60] The fact that 50% of French prisoners taken by Germany were captured by August 1915 is thus highly relevant to any

---

[57] Winter, *The Great War and the British People*, p. 73. Audoin-Rouzeau and Becker, *14–18. Retrouver la Guerre*, p. 34.

[58] Winter, *The Great War and the British People*, Table 3.8, p. 87; Spoerer, 'The Mortality of Allied Prisoners of War', p. 129.

[59] Overmans, '"In der Hand des Feindes"', p. 14. S. P. Mackenzie, 'The Treatment of Prisoners of War in World War II', *The Journal of Modern History*, 66, 3 (1994), p. 510.

[60] On the high death rates in armies in 1914 and 1915 see Kramer, *Dynamic of Destruction*, p. 34.

comparison of front-line and captivity mortality risk: for these early French prisoners, long-term German captivity did offer a measure of relative safety by reducing their trench exposure, especially if considered in conjunction with the weighted annual death rate of just 1.2% (12 per thousand) for French prisoners in Germany in Spoerer's findings; for their comrades, captured later, the relative safety of captivity was less pronounced. In sum, the extent to which captivity protected a man from the trenches was subject to considerable chronological variation across the conflict.[61]

Finally, one has also to consider that focusing upon how captivity compared to the dangers of the trenches occludes the fact that prisoners faced greater risk relative to civilians in peacetime, as indicated by a comparison with pre-war civilian death rates. This is shown by a comparison with statistics for pre-war urban mortality for women aged between twenty and forty in 1913 in London, Berlin and Paris, a roughly equivalent age cohort to the dominant age profile of prisoners, men of military service age. For London, the death rate for women in the 20–40 age bracket in 1913 was between 2.5 and 5.8 per thousand; for Berlin, the rate was between 4.7 and 6 per thousand; while for Paris, it was between 5.39 and 7.75 per thousand; this is far below the 52 per thousand rate which Spoerer estimates for British and Commonwealth prisoner deaths in Germany in the last year of the war.[62] Obviously, there are problems with this comparison – urban dwellers' death rates do not correlate to national averages, nor do pre-war female rates correspond to their male equivalents and class differences are not taken into account – but these figures do provide evidence that wartime captivity compared negatively to peacetime urban living conditions.

Thus captivity did entail a certain level of increased risk of death. Yet, overall, what the figures for captivity mortality indicate is that any radicalisation of *fatal* violence against German, French and British prisoners during the war clearly remained beneath a certain threshold – given that the estimated maximum total death rates here, which include deaths from *all* causes, fall between 3.04% and 7.48%. The exposure of British, French and German captives in the three countries to fatal violence was thus always a minority phenomenon during the war. Yet, although only a minority died in captivity, those who witnessed prisoner deaths were often traumatised, particularly if the death was caused by violence.

---

[61] Spoerer, 'The Mortality of Allied Prisoners of War', pp. 127, 129.

[62] These figures are taken from appendices A.10, A.11 and A.12 in Winter and Robert, eds., *Capital Cities at War*, vol. I., pp. 572–4. Spoerer, 'The Mortality of Allied Prisoners of War', p. 125, p. 129.

The impact of any one fatal incident thus spread far beyond the individual; in particular, it contributed to widespread fears and myths among captives regarding the prevalence of fatal violence.

Statistics can only bring us so far, however: fatal violence offers insight into just one aspect of radicalisation, albeit an important one. Non-fatal violence was as relevant to brutalisation processes. Thus it is necessary to investigate the full range of violent practices against captives and their impact upon the public image of captivity. For this reason, this book is divided into three parts, each of which closely explores how violent practices and representations interacted during a different phase of the war and its aftermath, an approach which reveals the mechanisms or mediating structures which facilitated the social translation of violent practices into cultural discourses, and vice versa. The first part explores the radicalising impact of the representation of violence against prisoners during the opening two years of the conflict, looking in chapter 1 at violent civilian reactions to prisoners in 1914 and, in chapter 2, at how ideas of what constituted an atrocity against prisoners changed up to 1916. The second part of this book investigates radicalising military attitudes in 1916–18, looking at the role of violence in reprisals in chapter 3 and at how violence operated within the prisoner of war labour company system in chapters 4 and 5. The third part considers the legacy of wartime violence against prisoners, examining, in chapter 6, how the issue radicalised public attitudes during the repatriation phase. The ways in which remembrance practices later evolved between 1921 and 1939 to marginalise the history of violence against captives is the subject of chapter 7, with a brief epilogue on how this book relates to our understanding of Second World War prisoner treatment.

The order of the three parts here is deliberate. This study contends that the way certain kinds of violence against prisoners was represented in the first two years of the war culturally legitimised an escalation in violent military practices against captives, which in turn polarised memories of prisoner treatment in the immediate post-war period. Representations are understood here as the different ways in which socially determined narratives are constructed, orally, textually and visually, to convey particular cultural messages about violence; their interaction with military practices, the collective understanding and organisation of violence within armies was fundamental to escalation, as part I will now show.

Part I

Propaganda representations of violence against prisoners

Introduction to part I

Violence poses a challenge for historical analysis, as it encompasses both the reality of the human experience of physical force and the discursive web of perceptions, rumour and narrated meanings which regulates and interprets that reality. To understand a particular wartime violent action, it is thus necessary to consider it in the context of the different meanings which make up its discursive web. For this reason, the first section of this study will closely examine how, early in the war, popular meaning was attributed to particular accounts of violence against captives. The purpose here is to find out more about the crucial initial relationship between the violent incident and the cycle of wartime significations it provoked – in other words, how particular propaganda 'cycles' about prisoners developed out of real incidents of brutality against captives. Only by looking at how wartime societies perceived violence against prisoners is it possible to understand how such violence happened.

This will be done here by first examining in detail in chapter 1 how widespread civilian violence against prisoners of war in 1914 was represented in contemporary wartime media. Second, chapter 2 will explore how three early wartime propaganda 'cycles' concerning violence against prisoners led to the further radicalisation of prisoner mistreatment, through an examination of 1914–15 media debates surrounding the battlefield shootings of prisoners; accounts of prisoner beatings; and finally, the mistreatment of sick captives.

This part presents two key arguments. First, that propaganda often reflected prisoner of war experience relatively accurately – in this respect, the findings here correlate with the latest research on Great War propaganda by John Horne, Alan Kramer, Adrian Gregory and others, which has found that the wartime media contained far fewer atrocity exaggerations or myths than interwar commentators, such as Sir Arthur Ponsonby, later claimed.[1] This is not to contend that all propaganda in the First World War

---

[1] Horne and Kramer, *German Atrocities*; Adrian Gregory, *The Last Great War. British Society and the First World War* (Cambridge, 2008), pp. 40–70.

was true – far from it. But it is to assert that propaganda relating to violence against prisoners of war in 1914 and 1915 largely drew upon real events. Second, this section contends that the *representation* of violence against prisoners became more extreme between August 1914 and early 1916, provoking a radicalisation of attitudes against prisoners and thereby laying the foundation for later deteriorations in prisoner treatment. These years marked an important opening stage out of which more radicalised violent practices against prisoners developed and came to be socially legitimised; the military use of forced prisoner labour which happened in 1916–18 cannot be understood without exploring these origins. As Hannah Arendt observed, 'violence – as distinct from power, force, or strength – always needs *implements*'.[2] Cycles of violent representations in the media in 1914 and 1915 became reproductive tools for the violent actions they reported. These cycles were not state-fabrications, although state reports and investigations often provided the eyewitness account material which drove them.

To continue it is necessary to break down the term violence into two parts: action and discursive phenomenon. In the case studies here, violence as action is explored using different witness testimonies and administrative sources. From this examination it is then possible to move on to explore how violence against prisoners was socially understood. This opening section will seek to answer how the radicalisation of public and private discourses about prisoners in the early years of the war both reflected and exacerbated a radicalisation of violent action towards them.

[2] Hannah Arendt, *On Violence* (London, 1970), p. 4.

1 Encountering the 'enemy': civilian violence towards prisoners of war in 1914

Introduction: pre-war civilian expectations of wartime captivity

In 1886, the German artist Anton von Werner depicted a French soldier being taken prisoner during the Franco-Prussian war.[1] The image is one of chivalry, order and calm; the prisoner kisses his wife goodbye, while one of his captors gently cradles the couple's baby.[2] The reality of capture in the 1870–1 conflict, in which the majority of French prisoners captured at Sedan endured catastrophic living conditions at Inges before their transport to Germany, is excluded here.[3] Clearly, this imaginative artistic interpretation, by one of Wilhelmine Germany's leading court painters, provided a sanitised version of the historical realities of the state's foundational conflict. However, it also offers an important late nineteenth-century interpretation of wartime capture. Two key characteristics of the painting stand out: it presents a highly romantic vision of the prisoner of war and it makes no reference to wartime violence.

In fact, a romantic view of the prisoner of war, and the dissociation of violence from wartime capture, marked pre-1914 attitudes across Europe. Werner's image reflected a widespread cultural tendency to deny the concomitant historical relationship between wartime capture, violence and power. Believing that uncontrolled violence was a feature of man in his primitive state, Europeans thought their own cultural progress towards ever more civilised societies had eradicated violent behaviour towards

---

[1] The painting was recently acquired by the German Historical Museum, Berlin. Angelika Wachs, Deutsches Historisches Museum, Presseinformation, Berlin, 7. Februar 2001, www.dhm.de/presseinfos/2001020701.html. Accessed 14.9.2005. I am grateful to Claudia Siebrecht for bringing this picture to my attention.

[2] An earlier version of this chapter appeared in Purseigle, ed., *Warfare and Belligerence*, pp. 133–62.

[3] Katja Mitze, '"Seit der babylonischen Gefangenschaft hat die Welt nichts derart erlebt." Französische Kriegsgefangene und Franctireurs im Deutsch-Französischen Krieg 1870/71', in Overmans, ed., *In der Hand des Feindes*, p. 242.

Figure 1. Anton von Werner (1843–1915), 'Kriegsgefangen' (1886), depicting a scene from the Franco-Prussian War, 1870–1 at Jouy-aux-Arches, near Metz.

prisoners of war by western European armies.[4] As a French doctoral thesis on prisoners of war, written by Eugène Vassaux in 1890, stated:

The fate of prisoners of war has followed the different epochs of reason: the most civilised countries ransom them, exchange them and return them; the semi-barbaric peoples appropriate them and reduce them to slaves; simple savages massacre them without torturing them; and the most savage peoples torment them, cut their throats and eat them.[5]

Examined by Louis Renault, Professor of International Law at the University of Paris, who would later lead French accusations about German mistreatment of prisoners in 1914 and 1915, Vassaux's thesis illustrated the optimism of late nineteenth-century attitudes towards war:

[4] 'By the early part of the twentieth century the concept of civilisation was used by people in Western societies to refer to a completed process', Jonathan Fletcher, *Violence and Civilization. An Introduction to the Work of Norbert Elias* (Cambridge, 1997), p. 9. Even Georges Sorel, the proponent of revolutionary violence, admitted in 1908 that violence was generally perceived as uncivilised: 'there are so many legal precautions against violence, and our upbringing is directed towards so weakening our tendencies towards violence that we are instinctively inclined to think that any act of violence is a manifestation of a return to barbarism', Georges Sorel, *Reflections on Violence* (New York, 1941 [1908]), p. 205.

[5] Eugène Vassaux, 'Des prisonniers de guerre et des otages en droit romain et en droit français', doctoral thesis, Faculté de Droit de Paris (Paris, 1890), p. 1.

Today there is a new idea of war. Until recently, war set the whole population of each country against each other; it was war between the citizens of each nation. Nowadays, war is nothing more than a relationship between states. A state combats another state, but it is no longer the case that a whole people fight another people. The aim of war is no longer to annihilate the adversary but to impose such and such a view upon him and in order to do this it is only necessary to deprive a state of its forces temporarily. In war, one seeks only to prevent the largest number of adversaries from taking active part in the hostilities and one offers them [prisoners of war] complete liberty without any ransom or the signature of a peace treaty. Immense progress has taken place in the relationship between victors and vanquished. The soldier who defends his country is not punished like a criminal; he should not suffer any penalty or humiliation. He is to be considered as a free man acting within his rights. He should not suffer any ill-treatment.[6]

Such assumptions marked pre-1914 moral attitudes about the treatment of prisoners of war during any future war in Europe. The development of international laws of war in the fifty years preceding the 1914–18 conflict further illustrates this. The Geneva Conventions of 1864 and 1906 attributed neutral status to the enemy captured wounded on the battlefield. He was now to receive the same medical care as his captor's own casualties.[7] Once physically incapable of fighting, the soldier regained the status of a non-combatant – as in Vassaux's thesis, the category of 'enemy' was a temporary one which only applied to the armed, fighting soldier.

The Hague Convention of 1907 also reflected this attitude that, once captured, a soldier reverted to quasi-civilian status. A prisoner of war was to be allowed to retain all his personal belongings; he was not to be confined within a camp or fort unless this was absolutely necessary; he was to be paid a wage or salary depending on his rank; and was not to be employed on work directly related to the captor state's war effort.[8] The Hague Convention was designed for a war where prisoners would be granted their freedom on parole after capture. Having given their word of honour that they would not rejoin the fight, they would be exchanged or allowed to live as free civilians within their captor's country. This view was predicated upon the kind of conflict Vassaux described, where local populations were not caught up in war hatreds, allowing the prisoner to live freely in their midst.

Although atrocities against prisoners of war were reported during colonial conflicts and the Balkan wars, these were interpreted as symptomatic of the less civilised status of certain Turkish, Slav or indigenous colonial peoples. Europeans were optimistic that they could eradicate violence

---

[6] *Ibid.*, p. 9.   [7] William Edward Hall, *International Law* (Oxford, 1880), Appendix 6, pp. 696–7.
[8] Brown, ed., *The Hague Conventions and Declarations of 1899 and 1907*, pp. 108–10.

from the experience of military capture within the borders of western Europe. By codifying universal laws of war, they could impose order through legal regulation upon the wartime world, in the same way that increased legal intervention and codification had successfully ordered the civic peacetime sphere of the pre-1914 European state. Thus, by 1914, the prisoner of war had gradually gained a protected cultural and legal status very similar to that of a non-combatant. This drew upon existing moral attitudes of the period: in particular, in pre-war Edwardian England a key determinant of correct masculine behaviour, embedded in the public school ethos, was that violence should not be used against an opponent who was unable to defend himself. This sentiment lingered after the outbreak of war: one of the first British books published on the prisoner of war, following the declaration of hostilities, still viewed the prisoner in pre-war terms, which recall the work of Anton von Werner:

Romance clings to the prisoner of war and in every age (at least in every modern age) and every country ladies have ogled him, petted him when they could and helped or tried to help him to escape ... We have heard also of Bavarian damsels winking at our kilted Highlanders and surreptitiously conveying little gifts to them. It was thus of old and always.[9]

The development of this pre-war romantic understanding of the prisoner of war as a defenceless non-combatant explains why accounts of the mistreatment of prisoners provoked such outrage and surprise in 1914 and 1915, proving a key means of mobilising public anger at the enemy. Although certain pre-war romantic attitudes to prisoners lingered on in aspects of the wartime portrayal by belligerents of their *own* captured soldiers as romanticised helpless victims of the enemy, the overall pre-war romantic vision of captivity swiftly radicalised in September 1914, to be replaced by much harsher, violent representations of prisoner treatment.

For, when war broke out in 1914, the issue of violence against prisoners of war instantly became a popular topic. Far from Vassaux's predictions, the mass mobilisation of conscript armies and widespread literacy meant that local hatreds and popular involvement in national conflict in 1914 were greater than ever before; the corollary of this was that the public *image* of who constituted a legitimate enemy figure expanded, and the distinction between the enemy combatant and the enemy prisoner of war

[9]   Tighe Hopkins, *The Prisoner of War* (London, 1914), pp. 9–11. In a similar vein, *The Times* published a poem in Latin entitled 'Prisoners of War' on 18 September 1914, which extolled a romantic vision of mercy in battle: 'Whose valour in this strife, war's chance in mercy preserveth. I to preserve their freedom alike in mercy resolved am. Deem it a gift, giv'n gladly, the great gods thereto.'

broke down, with immediate effect in some areas: faced with prisoners of war being transported through their towns and cities for the first time in August and September 1914, many civilians reacted violently.[10]

Rapid radicalisation of civilians against prisoners did not occur everywhere; a micro-history of its development reveals significant local and national differences. To illustrate this, this chapter will investigate two case studies in turn: the arrival of German prisoners of war in France and the arrival of French and British prisoners of war in Germany; where relevant to these case studies, reference will also be made to the reaction of British civilians to their first German prisoners. However, the fact that civilian violence occurred at all is highly revealing, precisely because it emerged so suddenly and broke with the cultural beliefs of the pre-war period. Civilians, as culturally designated non-combatants, were the last grouping the pre-war world had expected to mistreat defenceless, and often wounded, prisoner soldiers – indeed, they are very rarely seen as physical perpetrators of First World War violence more generally in the existing historiography. This chapter will highlight that civilians were actually a key group that perpetrated violence against captives in 1914.

Such civilian violence against prisoners in 1914 and the media response to it thus provide key insights into the origins of the larger-scale patterns of violence against captives that would later emerge during the war; it set a significant precedent, whereby an image of transgressive violence against prisoners by the enemy was established, in what was a relatively transnational public domain, in a way that legitimised further violent radicalised civilian responses in retaliation. What becomes rapidly clear from this focus on 1914 is that reports of civilian violence against prisoners were more than just state-fabricated propaganda – the relationship between representation and reality emerges as far more complex here than the traditional understanding of First World War propaganda allows for: the media both reflected and distorted the reality of prisoners' experiences.[11]

In 1914, initial *representations* of real acts of violence by civilians against prisoners fuelled further violent behaviour against captives, creating

---

[10] A breakdown of combatant and non-combatant categories can also be observed in the German army treatment of Belgian civilians during the invasion in 1914. Women, children, clerics and medical personnel were often considered as enemy agents. See Horne and Kramer, *German Atrocities*.

[11] The following works outline the *étatiste* view of First World War propaganda: Arthur Ponsonby, *Falsehood in Wartime. Containing an Assortment of Lies Circulated throughout the Nations during the Great War* (London, 1928); James Morgan Read, *Atrocity Propaganda, 1914–1919* (New Haven, 1941); M. L. Sanders and Philip M. Taylor, *British Propaganda during the First World War, 1914–18* (London and Basingstoke, 1982). For a detailed critique of this approach see Horne and Kramer, *German Atrocities*, and Prost and Winter, *The Great War in History*, pp. 155–6.

nascent 'cycles of violence'; later in the war, these representation-based cycles would spiral into full-scale cycles of violent military reprisals against prisoners. 1914, as the next section will show, marked a new era in the complex relationship between prisoners of war, violence and the media.

Civilian violence against prisoners: establishing the 'enemy'

All across Europe there was great curiosity and excitement about the first prisoners of war. In the Vatican, Pope Benedict XV received reports from French clerics who described how in 1914 German crowds insulted wounded French military prisoners and the French religious travelling with them as medical carers.[12] At Schneidemühl, close to the German border with Russia, excited, curious crowds gathered to stare at the arrival of the first Russian prisoners.[13] In the small Irish town of Templemore in Co. Tipperary, the local nationalist newspaper, *The Tipperary Star*, announced its delight that the local barracks would house German prisoners, potential allies in a national struggle against Britain, depicting the captured German troops as 'men of splendid physique ... marched from the railway to the barracks ... they sang all the way. Fine singers.'[14] This singing motif was particularly apt. To paraphrase the famous song, it was indeed a long way from Tipperary to Schneidemühl in 1914. However, the phenomenon of excitement and curiosity at the arrival of prisoners was common to both.

Civilian interest in prisoners of war was to be expected. However, in some parts of France and Germany, civilian curiosity and excitement rapidly disintegrated into violence – crowds shouted insults, spat at or hurled objects at prisoners, on occasion even attacking captives who were wounded. Why did such strong civilian reactions occur, only weeks into the war? And why did they occur in some areas, but not in others?

The first key factor was the context of national mobilisation. This played a major role in the outbreak of civilian violence against prisoners in 1914. Although historiographical discussions continue regarding how quickly wartime mobilisation, with its concomitant labelling and dehumanisation of the 'enemy', appeared at local levels, it appears clear that

---

[12] Archivio Segreto Vaticana (ASV), Segretaria di Stato, Guerra, anno 1914–1918, rubrica 244, fasc. 137, f. 104, Letter from Bishop of Versailles to Vatican, 20.9.1915, enclosing written statements from two priests deported with French military prisoners in September 1914.

[13] Jo Mihaly, *'Da gibt's ein Wiedersehn!' Kriegstagebuch eines Mädchens 1914–1918* (Freiburg and Heidelberg, 1982), p. 48.

[14] *The Tipperary Star*, 3.10.1914, p. 5, and 29.8.1914, p. 5.

hostility to prisoners was, in part, provoked by how rapidly, and how strongly, civilians felt emotionally involved in the conflict.[15] Traditionally, the army was the sole legal repository of violence in war. However, mass conscription, the popular press and the growth of nationalism meant that in 1914 many civilians felt personally called to act against the perceived threat to their nation – every citizen was called upon to stop spies and saboteurs.[16] Mobilisation thus triggered a powerful individual response, be it fear or euphoria; violent reaction by a population to arriving prisoners of war in 1914 appears to have been closely linked to the overall investment of a locality in the war effort.

An integral part of this mobilisation was the establishment of fear and hatred of the enemy figure and widespread xenophobia: this marked the first stage in the development of a war culture – the system of cultural supports that allowed populations to adapt to and perpetuate conflict. In 1914, this process was a key motivation for civilian violence against prisoners.[17] Aggressive behaviour towards prisoners represented a form of bonding on the home front against the external enemy – a type of socially 'constructive' aggression.[18] In many cases, violence towards prisoners, verbal or physical, was used to popularise and culturally teach the new mark of 'otherness' of the enemy, a means of defining the new wartime boundaries that divided belligerent groupings – a key blooding in the wartime culture of friend and foe for civilians.[19] Other factors such as public feelings of impotence, desire for vengeance and a displaced sense of frustration at the disruption of daily life by war also played a role.[20]

None of this had been predicted in international law. In 1914, it contained little regarding the treatment of prisoners during transport to prison camps. Although the pre-war Geneva Conventions established the principle that wounded prisoners should be treated in the same manner as the wounded of one's own side, and the Hague Convention on Land Warfare of 1907 established that prisoners should be treated

---

[15] On this subject see Jeffrey Verhey, *The Spirit of 1914. Militarism, Myth and Mobilisation in Germany* (Cambridge, 2000); Jean-Jacques Becker, *1914. Comment les français sont entrés dans la guerre. Contribution à l'étude de l'opinion publique printemps-été 1914* (Paris, 1977).

[16] Becker, *1914*, pp. 497–514.

[17] On cultural mobilisation see John Horne, ed., *State, Society and Mobilization in Europe during the First World War* (Cambridge, 1997), pp. 1–17.

[18] On 'constructive' aggression see Gerda Siann, *Accounting for Aggression. Perspectives on Aggression and Violence* (London, Sydney and Boston, 1985), p. 4.

[19] On German and French images of the 'enemy' see Michael Jeismann, *Das Vaterland der Feinde. Studien zum nationalen Feindbegriff und Selbstverständnis in Deutschland und Frankreich 1792–1918* (Stuttgart, 1992).

[20] On xenophobia at the outbreak of war, see Hew Strachan, *The First World War*, vol. I: *To Arms* (Oxford, 2001), pp. 105–8, and Becker, *1914*, pp. 497–514.

humanely, the specifics of prisoner transport, including the feeding of prisoners, their sleeping conditions, their exposure to enemy populations and medical treatment on the journey, were not dealt with in any detail.[21] This meant that in each country the treatment of prisoners in 1914 – and, in particular, their exposure to civilian violence – depended upon the military resources and, most importantly, the wartime mobilisation culture of the captor nation. These, in turn, were greatly influenced by how many prisoners a country captured. This was the second key factor which influenced how and why violence by civilians occurred.

The vast disparity in the numbers of prisoners captured by Germany, compared to France and Britain, in 1914 is crucial to this analysis. 1914 was a period of mobile warfare, which resulted in a higher number of prisoners than trench combat allowed for and Germany took by far the lion's share. In August alone, 8,190 British prisoners were taken – a remarkably high figure, given the total British casualties for the entire month of 14,409, and the relatively small size of the British Expeditionary Force, which numbered about 90,000 men on 22 August 1914.[22] German prisoner-taking was helped by the fall of French defensive centres: the fall of Maubeuge alone saw 40,000 French soldiers captured; the British retreat from Mons resulted in another high prisoner tally.[23] Germany claimed by December 1914 to have captured 3,459 French officers and 215,905 French other ranks, together with 492 British officers and 18,824 British other ranks – 15,313 of these British prisoners were captured between August and October 1914.[24] In addition, by March 1915, Germany had captured over 359,277 Russians.[25] After the shift to trench-fighting, the numbers of prisoners captured by Germany dropped off considerably, with only 369 British captured in December 1914, out of total British casualties of 11,079 that month.[26] Ironically, despite Germany's impressive prisoner figures, Helmut von Moltke, the German Chief of

---

[21] Brown, ed., *The Hague Conventions and Declarations of 1899 and 1907*.

[22] Of the British soldiers reported missing in August 1914 almost all would be found to be prisoners of war, unlike the missing of later battles. The National Archives, London (TNA), WO 161/82, Statistical Abstract of Information regarding the Armies at Home and Abroad, 1914–1920, June 1920, p. 253. J. M. Bourne, *Britain and the Great War* (New York and London, 1989), p. 18. See also Martin Gilbert, *First World War* (London, 1995), p. 43.

[23] A. Armin, ed., *Die Welt in Flammen. Illustrierte Kriegschronik, 1914* (Leipzig, 1915), p. 235.

[24] *Ibid.*, p. 459. TNA, WO 161/82, Statistical Abstract, 1914–1920, p. 253. By 10 March 1915 the Germans had captured 3,748 French officers and 230,503 French other ranks, and 506 British officers and 20,031 British other ranks. Doegen, *Kriegsgefangene Völker*, pp. 28–9.

[25] Doegen, *Kriegsgefangene Völker*, pp. 28–29.

[26] TNA, WO 161/82, Statistical Abstract, 1914–1920, p. 253.

Staff, was disappointed as the numbers did not indicate the imminent collapse of the opposing armies:

We have had successes, but we have not yet gained victory. Victory means the annihilation of the enemy's power of resistance. When million-strong armies confront each other, the victor takes prisoners. Where are our prisoners?[27]

Von Moltke's expectation of high capture rates in 1914 contradicts subsequent German propaganda arguments that failings in the German care of prisoners in 1914 were due to the fact that very large numbers of captives were not anticipated. As an American observer, Daniel McCarthy, pointed out, the Germans always claimed they had been 'taken by surprise at the number of prisoners taken during the fall of 1914'.[28] In reality, prisoners were expected, but the necessary detailed planning for their arrival and accommodation had not been put in place.[29] For Germany, under pressure to keep to the rigorous Schlieffen plan, the dispatch and delivery of enemy prisoners presented difficulties for a rail network already heavily burdened by the demands of transporting troops and supplies to the front.[30]

In comparison with Germany, the French and British took far fewer men prisoner at the start of the war. By September 1914, the French had captured 250 German officers and 13,500 men.[31] The battle of the Marne added 25,000 German prisoners to their number.[32] By 1 January 1915, the French held 45,700 German prisoners in total.[33] If the number of German prisoners held by France was relatively low, the number held by Britain was even smaller. Military and naval prisoners held in the UK in January 1915 amounted to 10,000.[34]

This disparity in the numbers of prisoners captured had considerable effect. The sheer numbers of prisoners arriving in or passing through German cities meant that it was difficult to keep them segregated from the local inhabitants; the likelihood of hostile interactions was thus far greater. The prisoner also became a highly visible symbol of Germany's military successes to a much greater extent than in France or Britain. The

---

[27] Holger Afflerbach, *Falkenhayn. Politisches Denken und Handeln im Kaiserreich* (Munich, 1994), p. 182.

[28] Daniel J. McCarthy, *The Prisoner of War in Germany. The Care and Treatment of the Prisoner of War with a History of the Development of the Principle of Neutral Inspection and Control* (London, 1918), p. 177.

[29] Hinz, *Gefangen im Großen Krieg*, p. 69.

[30] John Keegan, *The First World War* (London, 1998), pp. 31–7.

[31] Cahen-Salvador, *Les Prisonniers de guerre*, p. 29.

[32] *Ibid.*, p. 30.   [33] *Ibid.*, p. 45.

[34] Comité International de la Croix-Rouge, *Documents publiés à l'occasion de la Guerre de 1914–1915. Rapports de MM. Ed. Naville, V. Van Berchem, Dr C. de Marval et A. Eugster sur leurs visites aux camps de prisonniers en Angleterre, France et Allemagne* (Paris and Geneva, 1915), p. 8.

number of prisoners arriving in a country was a key factor in their reception and one which differentiated Germany from the Entente in 1914.

Finally, it is important to note that civilian violence towards prisoners in 1914 generally occurred in train stations, at a point when new prisoners were at their most exhausted, after a long journey.[35] In France, as in Germany and Britain, officer prisoners largely travelled in passenger carriages, although some British officers arriving in Germany travelled in wagons; other-rank prisoners were transported by rail from the front in third-class carriages and in livestock wagons. The train journey to the prison camp took a considerable length of time in 1914: some German prisoners travelled for forty-nine hours across France from the front to Pau; British prisoners captured by the Germans at Cambrai and sent to Torgau took four days to get there. The journey to the prison camp was often long and difficult, leaving prisoners tired and unkempt, enhancing their defeated appearance. The poor transport conditions meant prisoners arrived dishevelled, which encouraged civilians to view the enemy as inferior and as different. It also sent the message to onlookers that their own military did not expect prisoners to be comfortably treated. Prisoners also arrived still wearing their battlefield uniform – marking them as the 'enemy'. These factors made violence more likely.

Case study 1: the arrival of German prisoners of war in France, August–October 1914

Having examined the mobilisation context for the arrival of prisoners of war in 1914, it is now necessary to look at civilian violence against prisoners in more detail, starting with France. The arrival of the first German prisoners of war in France revealed diverse wartime cultures in existence within the same country. In government and administration circles any civilian violence towards prisoners was regarded as unchivalrous, uncivilised and a threat to public order. Despite this, in some areas, French crowds reacted violently. In northern areas close to the fighting zone, the hatred expressed towards prisoners by civilians was often particularly marked.[36] In other parts of France, passing prisoners were jeered, spat at and verbally insulted. In France, civilian violence towards prisoners emerged from below within local populations, rather than being orchestrated from above by the authorities.

[35] On railway stations and their wartime cultural role see Adrian Gregory, 'Railway Stations. Gateways and Termini', in Winter and Robert, eds., *Capital Cities at War*, pp. 23–56.

[36] See, for example, Bundesarchiv-Militärarchiv, Freiburg (BA-MA), PH2 / 588, Schwarze Liste derjenigen Engländer, die sich während des Krieges gegenüber deutschen Heeresangehörigen völkerrechtswidrigen Verhaltens schuldig gemacht haben, f. 115, Interview with Otto Schlagk, captured on 11.9.1914, who reports crowds throwing stones at wounded prisoners at Chery and at Fismes, and prisoners being insulted at Fère-en-Tardenois.

German prisoners captured by France in 1914 were dispersed to eighty-three different prisoner of war camps all across the country.[37] One German prisoner, Gustav Schubert, recalled how the wagon he travelled in across France had been used to transport horses, and the stench of horse urine hurt the prisoners' eyes.

No one who has not himself experienced it can imagine how awful the five days we spent in the train were. A great number of the prisoners were ill. Some had diarrhoea, others vomited, however, no one could leave the wagon and all such waste remained in it. Even answering the call of nature had to take place in the corner of the wagon ... In some wagons there were wounded prisoners whose wounds began to produce pus and were infested by maggots ... we were treated worse than livestock.[38]

Schubert's account was published in 1915 after his repatriation. The initial repatriations of prisoners in 1915 provided the first accurate information in France, Germany and Britain regarding the treatment of prisoners by the enemy, and, given the wartime context, they often focused on the worst elements of a prisoner's experience during the journey from the front: for example, ex-prisoners on each side accused the enemy of transporting wounded prisoners in cattle trucks.

In fact, in both Germany and France other-rank prisoners, including wounded prisoners, frequently travelled in cattle trucks, due to a shortage of hospital trains.[39] Both countries underestimated the number of wounded prisoners which industrial warfare would cause, and the severity of their injuries. Hence the use of dirty cattle trucks to transport wounded men, presenting a real danger of infection and gangrene in the era before antibiotics. Scarcity of proper trains was a major problem: France had only seven hospital trains operating during the first week of the war and was forced to improvise additional transport for the wounded.[40] The German rail network used the same wagons that had brought German soldiers to the front to transport both prisoners and German 'walking wounded' back to Germany; the large number of Russian prisoners taken

---

[37] Service Historique de l'Armée de Terre, Vincennes (SHAT), 7 N 1993, Dépôts de Prisonniers. Carte Cantonale de la France par régions et subdivisions de région de corps d'armée, 1914.

[38] Gustav Schubert, *In Frankreich kriegsgefangen. Meine Erlebnisse auf dem Vormarsch der 1. Armee durch Belgien und Frankreich sowie in der französischen Kriegsgefangenschaft*, 2nd edn (Magdeburg, 1915), pp. 110–12.

[39] Marcel Peschaud, *La Guerre et les transports. Politique et fonctionnement des transports par chemin de fer pendant la guerre* (Paris and New Haven, 1926), p. 79; Reichsarchiv, *Der Weltkrieg 1914 bis 1918. Die militärischen Operationen zu Lande*, 14 vols., *Das deutsche Feldeisenbahnwesen*, vol. I: *Die Eisenbahnen zu Kriegsbeginn* (Berlin, 1928), p. 98.

[40] Peschaud, *La Guerre et les transports*, p. 79.

at the battle of Tannenberg at the end of August 1914 placed this German system under real pressure.[41]

In contrast to the negative symbolic message about prisoners' status, which the poor transport conditions projected, instructions from the French civilian authorities focused upon respecting prisoners. At a government and administration level, there was strong disapproval of any civilian violence against prisoners of war. The principal government desire was to avoid public disorder. The French government was kept informed of public reaction to the war in 1914 through Prefects' Reports sent in from each *Département*: the reports for seventy-eight *Départements*, returned to the *Ministère de l'Intérieur* in August and September 1914, were surveyed as a sample for this study. Of these, the vast majority did not describe the arrival of military prisoners of war at all: only six reported a hostile crowd gathering to harass prisoners and thirteen *Départements* recorded the arrival of prisoners of war without incident. Most officials, such as the *Commissaire Spécial* at Saint-Étienne station, cited the measures that had been taken to avoid any disorder as the reason for the calm.[42] In several *Départements*, such as the Gironde, Allier, Bouches-du-Rhône and Meurthe-et-Moselle, Prefects even reported that German civilians were attacked while prisoner of war convoys arrived without incident.

The Prefects played down any mob behaviour towards prisoners. Their reports reveal that the French administration disapproved of jeering at prisoners of war. Moreover, the French government was against crowds gathering at stations for any reason during the mobilisation period as it tried to preserve a sense of calm and to dispel rumour. Attempts were made to keep the public away from trains carrying wounded, for example: the general commanding the 10th region declared that 'stations must be evacuated during the passage of trains carrying wounded'.[43] Level crossings along the railways were to be closed.[44] In some areas the time of arrival of trains, including those transporting prisoners, was kept secret.[45]

Furthermore, in the opening months of the war, the French administration still held onto certain older chivalrous ideas regarding prisoners, allowing German officers a relative freedom on parole, for example.[46] This is illustrated by the actions of the Prefect of Belfort, who responded to 'several hostile cries these past few days when German prisoners

---

[41] Gilbert, *First World War*, p. 49.
[42] Archives Nationales, Paris (AN), F7.12936, Dossier Loire. Report by the Commissariat Spécial for Saint-Étienne station to the Ministre de l'Intérieur, 23.9.1914.
[43] AN, F7.12936, Prefect of Bouches-du-Rhône to the Ministre de l'Intérieur, 7.9.1914.
[44] AN, F7.12937, Prefect of la Manche to the Ministre de l'Intérieur, 8.8.1914.
[45] *Ibid.*, Prefect of the Rhône to the Ministre de l'Intérieur, 11.8.1914.
[46] Cahen-Salvador, *Les Prisonniers de guerre*, pp. 31–2.

passed' with a poster campaign calling on locals to 'respect adversaries taken with arms in hand for the defence of their country'.[47] This campaign was effective and the transport through the town of a German officer took place the following day 'in total calm'.[48] Similarly, the Prefect of Meurthe-et-Moselle on 8 August 1914 visited the hospitals where he 'saluted the German wounded and embraced the French'.[49]

However, in many areas the viewpoint of the local French population differed from that of the civilian authorities. The recommendations of the French government were not always adhered to at the local level; civilian crowds interacted with prisoners relatively frequently and hostile reactions did occur. One Prefect reported that when a convoy of German prisoners arrived at Clermont-Ferrand, 'although precautions had been taken to keep their arrival secret, several hundred people awaited their train and accompanied them from the station ... the crowd shouted angrily at the prisoners and sang the Marseillaise'.[50] According to Gustav Schubert, when he arrived at his destination on 18 September 1914, 'the population at first acted very hostilely' but, after a little while, accepted the prisoners and came to beg souvenirs from them.[51] Schubert stated that 'Germans ... for an apple or a piece of chocolate or cigarette would offer a button, so a real barter business developed'.[52] Hans Rodewald, a wounded German prisoner transported across France on 11–13 September 1914, recalled similar treatment:

We stopped at all the important stations, where we were given water, and a thin soup with some bread. Everywhere civilians, mostly women, ran to our wagons to beg us for a *souvenir*. If one did not give them a uniform button loop or a button they became impertinent and rude ... the public became more and more aggressive and harassing, especially the old: they waved sticks and canes, cursed us and insulted us.[53]

In some places these hostile crowds became violent, throwing stones. At Carcassonne, a French guard, Louis Barthas, recalled civilians' outright anger towards arriving prisoners in 1914: 'Gentlemen brandished their canes, ladies threatened with their sun umbrellas, urchins threw stones, and the over-excited pulled out knives and jumped onto the track only to be held back by the sentries.'[54]

---

[47] AN, F7.12937, Prefect of Belfort to the Ministre de l'Intérieur, 6.8.1914.
[48] *Ibid.*   [49] *Ibid.*, Prefect of Meurthe-et-Moselle to the Ministre de l'Intérieur, 11.8.1914.
[50] AN, F7.12937, Prefect of Puy-de-Dôme to the Ministre de l'Intérieur, 19.8.1914.
[51] Schubert, *In Frankreich kriegsgefangen*, p. 114.   [52] *Ibid.*
[53] Birnstiel and Cazals, eds., *Ennemis fraternels*, pp. 84–5.
[54] Louis Barthas, *Les Carnets de guerre de Louis Barthas, tonnelier 1914–1918* (Paris, 1997), pp. 20–1.

The extent of such local civilian violence becomes clear from an examination of statements collected between 1915 and 1918 by the Prussian *Kriegsministerium* from German captives repatriated from France, as part of an investigation into French prisoner mistreatment.[55] These provide detailed accounts of a prisoner's background, capture and entire captivity experience.[56] A survey of thirty of these statements, made by prisoners captured in 1914, reveals that seventeen record French civilian crowds behaving violently to prisoners during the period between capture and arrival at their prison camp. Of the seventeen, sixteen reported a violent civilian reaction during the German prisoner's train journey through France and ten also reported civilian hostility prior to entraining in the north of France. Only six recorded crowd violence occurring at their final destination.

This sample is a limited one. However, it allows for some useful analysis. Twenty-five of the prisoners were wounded when captured and transported. Importantly, most violence towards prisoners in France occurred at stations away from major urban centres in smaller towns such as Le Puy, Tarbes and Vitre. The only exceptions to this were Rouen, Orléans and Limoges. September 1914 had the highest number of prisoners transported (24) and all seventeen incidents of civilian hostility occurred during this month. Only ten prisoners referred to the behaviour of the French guards: in five cases the guards sought to protect prisoners from crowd violence, in five they did not intervene or acquiesced. However, significantly, the guards did not perpetrate acts of violence against the prisoners themselves. The principal incidents which prisoners recalled were having buttons stolen (9 cases), being spat at (11 cases), verbal abuse (13 incidents) and stone throwing (11 incidents).

French civilian violence stemmed from popular anger at the German invasion, blamed on Germany's leaders. One prisoner recalled how the crowd's anger 'was not only directed at us but also in a very horrid way against our German royal family'.[57] Incidents were worst in the northern areas of France, near to the fighting, where civilians reacted furiously to passing prisoners. A prisoner, Adolf Michael, recounted that, on the way to Châlons after capture, 'we came through a town where the inhabitants were so enraged that the guards had to raise their revolvers and threaten to hit them'.[58]

---

[55] BA-MA, PH2 / 33, Kriegsministerium. Militär-Untersuchungsstelle für Verletzungen des Kriegsrechts. Anlagenband II zu der Liste derjenigen Franzosen, die sich besonders roh und grausam gegen deutsche Gefangene gezeigt haben.
[56] *Ibid.*   [57] BA-MA, PH2 / 33, f. 158, Statement by Walter Schicht, 18.10.1917.
[58] *Ibid.*, f. 173, Statement by Adolf Michael, 27.10.1917.

Crowd incidents that did occur were a spontaneous reaction by the French population and not organised; however, the violence involved was notably vicious. One prisoner outlined how, travelling through France, 'we were so threatened and jeered at by civilians that the guards had difficulty keeping the doors of the wagon closed. Stones were thrown at us. I saw a Bavarian soldier with a head injury caused by this.'[59] Another prisoner, Otto Möhle, recalled that

At one station a man in civilian clothing climbed into a wagon containing badly wounded Germans. He asked one of them if he wanted something to drink, whereupon he emptied a can of water over the wounded man's head and spat at him in the face saying 'the Germans are all barbarians'.[60]

Möhle, captured while sick in hospital in Reims, on 13 September 1914, described being led 'with three comrades through the finest streets of Reims to the town hall for interrogation. Along the way we were shouted at by the civilian population and had stones thrown at us.'[61]

As in many of the German accounts, Möhle reveals that the hostility of the civilian population towards prisoners reflected the attitude of some military personnel. During interrogation, Möhle's group was refused food for twenty-four hours as the French officer told them they had to learn to go hungry as they 'had had it too good in Belgium'.[62] Violent reactions towards prisoners by civilians did not occur in a vacuum – such attitudes were also to be found within the army, which explains why guards did not always make much of an effort to protect prisoners from the civilian crowds. However, there is a very important distinction to be made here. Civilian violence was extremely physical. Throwing objects at prisoners was intended to injure them – on some occasions the targets were prisoners already bearing battlefield injuries. In contrast, there are virtually no reports of French guards physically abusing their charges. French guards transporting prisoners to their camps in 1914 did not hit, kick or beat them, although off-duty soldiers on occasion joined in with hostile civilian crowds.

British observers noted the vehemence of the French reaction. Field Marshal Sir John French informed the War Office on 19 September 1914 that in some cases 'the populace have assumed a menacing attitude towards the prisoners'.[63] At this point the British government was tentatively debating whether to hand over German prisoners taken by

[59] Ibid., f. 272, Statement by Paul Michaelis, 30.10.1917.
[60] Ibid., f. 6, Statement by Otto Möhle, 13.8.1917.   [61] Ibid.   [62] Ibid.
[63] TNA, WO 32/5365, 1 A, Field Marshal Sir John French to the Secretary of the War Office, 19.9.1914.

Britain to the French but fear of German reprisals led to the idea being dropped.[64] The British attitude towards German prisoners was generally more moderate in August and September 1914, as the following account by British bishop Llewelleyn H. Gwynne indicates. Gwynne saw 'about sixty German prisoners at the docks' in St Nazaire on 8 September as they embarked on a ship for England:

> They were marched out of a docks' shed between British soldiers – the French crowd booed and booed and were very threatening. I saw some of the younger prisoners look rather terrified at first at the sight of the crowds while other older ones seemed amused. The British soldiers were more of a guard against the French mob than against the prisoners escaping. When they had boarded the ship which had to pass through a narrow dock way, the French soldiers and others threw stones at the port holes with great vehemence. If all that is told of the cruelty of the German soldiers be true, they richly deserve the hatred of the mob, but it was an exhibition of great indignity to see a crowd give vent to their feeling against prisoners, which is like hitting a man when he is down to an Englishman. One Frenchman tied a knife to a stick and tried to prod the prisoners between the guards.[65]

Gwynne's sympathetic attitude towards German prisoners mirrors other British sources from the opening months of the war. Surgeon-Lieutenant Commander A. J. Gilbertson recorded his experience tending to wounded German prisoners on board a ship transport from Dunkirk to Cherbourg, in October 1914. For Gilbertson, the German prisoners were 'boys, clean, poor physique, not eager'.[66] Once on board the British, French and German wounded got on well together: 'all men very plucky, and those able to walk just staggered up the gangway, but after an hour's rest and bits of soup they were full of beans and chatter, playing cards, chaffing the Germans in a very friendly manner exchanging buttons etc.'[67] German prisoners also reported a difference between French and British attitudes towards them. One prisoner, Paul Niegel, noted that in his hospital in Le Havre in September 1914:

[64] *Ibid.*

[65] University of Birmingham, Special Collections, Diaries of Llewelleyn H. Gwynne, Bishop of Khartoum, Army Chaplain (4th Class) 1914–1915, Deputy Chaplain-General 1915–1919. Acc. 18 F/1/52. I am grateful to Edward Madigan for bringing this source to my attention. A week later, Gwynne observed, the French hostility towards German prisoners had somewhat abated: 'Though some shout and curse it is only fair to say there are others, as for instance the ladies at the station, who meet every train and give tea and food to their German enemies.' *Ibid.*

[66] The Imperial War Museum (IWM), 92/46/1, Surgeon Lieutenant Commander A. J. Gilbertson, RNVR, Diary for 1914, Thursday, 30.10.1914.

[67] Gilbertson described how during his night watch he saw 'one curious sight a German and a Frenchy cuddled up close together like brothers sleeping soundly'. *Ibid.*

While we were in Le Havre we were frequently insulted and threatened by the French sentries. If we did not get into bed fast enough they threatened us with their rifles. When British soldiers replaced the French guards this changed. The English soldiers behaved much more honourably to us and did not hassle us.[68]

Another prisoner, Otto Schlagk, captured in 1914, related that the British soldiers behaved more honourably than the French to their German captives, and would secretly give their prisoners some of the food they received from French women at train stations.[69]

The British public also reacted more moderately than the French towards the first prisoners of war. German prisoners recorded little public hostility to them on their arrival in the UK.[70] Curiosity was the dominant public reaction in 1914, as recounted by the author Vera Brittain, who motored out to Frimley Common to see the first German prisoners of war.

And though one feels almost mean going to look at them as if one were going to the Zoo, yet since it is a sight that has never been seen in England before and probably never will be again after this war, it was of too great interest to be missed. Although there is a board standing by the entrance to the camp saying that this thoroughfare is forbidden to the public the day we were there the public were so numerous that one could hardly see the thoroughfare. Cora and I got quite close to the imprisoned Germans.[71]

An officer regulating traffic at Frith Hill described it as worse than Ascot Races.[72] A British journalist, Michael McDonagh, present at the arrival in Frimley of the first German prisoners from the Aisne on 23 September 1914, recorded:

The people of the place crowded the station to see them ... There was no hostile demonstration. A few spectators kept their distance, scowling at the Germans and muttering curses. Most of the people crowded round the prisoners and their curiosity quickly warmed into friendliness to the point of giving them cigarettes, apples, cakes and bottles of ginger beer, which the prisoners accepted very thankfully. Only the officers stood apart and refused, rather curtly, offers of refreshments.[73]

---

[68] BA-MA, PH2 / 33. f. 133, Interview with Paul Niegel.
[69] BA-MA, PH2 / 588, Schwarze Liste derjenigen Engländer, die sich während des Krieges gegenüber deutschen Heeresangehörigen völkerrechtswidrigen Verhaltens schuldig gemacht haben, f. 115, Interview with Otto Schlagk.
[70] Ibid.
[71] Vera Brittain, Chronicle of Youth. Great War Diary 1913–1917, ed. Alan Bishop (London, 2000), p. 111.
[72] Ken Clarke, Clarke's Camberley at War (1914–1918) (Camberley, 1986), p. 15.
[73] Michael McDonagh, In London during the Great War. The Story of a Journalist (London, 1935), pp. 26–7.

Indeed, *The War Illustrated* on 24 October 1914 complained that the British were 'too kind to our German prisoners'.[74] It attempted to dissuade British civilians from giving gifts to arriving German prisoners, describing the 'flabby sentimentality' of those local residents at Frimley who 'presented them with chocolates and cigarettes and filled their water-bottles with beer'.[75] It published a picture of 'a little English girl' presenting chocolate to 'men whose comrades – nay, perhaps these very men – have been criminally assaulting and cutting off the hands of little girls like herself in Belgium and France'.[76] The British public generally was slower to react with hostility to prisoners than the French or Germans. With few German prisoners in British captivity in August and September 1914, they appeared a novelty rather than a threat. It was spring 1915 when the first accounts from German ex-prisoners appeared describing hostile English crowds jeering German prisoners at railway stations, particularly after the sinking of the *Lusitania*.[77]

Ultimately, analysing French civilian violence towards prisoners in detail reveals several key conclusions. First, the violence was not orchestrated by the civilian authorities. Second, the French military did not provoke it, although when it broke out they often only did the bare minimum to protect the captives from the crowds. Third, the comparison with Britain shows that such violence was not inevitable. It is also important to note that when civilian violence against prisoners did break out, it was often remarkably extreme – throwing stones at wounded prisoners required a considerable level of anger. It appears that French civilians were interpreting the demeaning condition of prisoners during transport as an invitation to perpetrate further humiliation upon the enemy. There was also an important element of crowd psychology involved as people were caught up in the behaviour of a group.[78] Who made up these crowds and whether they represented the feelings of the whole French population is difficult to assess. However, the fact that violence by civilians occurred indicates that within weeks of the outbreak of war a proportion of the French population viewed prisoners as legitimate targets for popular anger.

---

[74] *The War Illustrated*, 24 October 1914, p. 236.   [75] *Ibid.*   [76] *Ibid.*

[77] BA-MA, PH2 / 588, f. 96, Report by Dr Hesper, Stabsarzt, relating how the train of prisoners he travelled on from Southend to Frith Hill was attacked near London on 15 April 1915 by a crowd who broke the windows, wounding a British officer. The camp at Frith Hill was also attacked in April 1915 by stone-throwing British soldiers. See also f. 121, Interview with Paul Boek Fritz, who reported being hit in a British station in May 1915.

[78] Jeffrey Verhey masterfully outlines the difficulty of defining 1914 crowds in his work: *The Spirit of 1914*, pp. 75–87.

Case study 2: the arrival of British and French prisoners of war in Germany, August–October, 1914

The German situation evolved slightly differently from the French. In contrast to France or Britain in 1914, there was a recent historical precedent in Germany for the arrival of large numbers of prisoners of war. Germany took 380,000 French prisoners of war in the Franco-Prussian war of 1870, who were welcomed by the local German population in 'an atmosphere of popular celebration and festivity ... The inhabitants of Munich brought beer, tobacco and sausages for the prisoners ... Berliners gave cigars.'[79] In 1914, the very first prisoners of war were initially welcomed in Germany, like their predecessors of 1870.[80] This alarmed the German authorities, both military and civilian, who immediately cracked down on such behaviour. Their orders in 1914 were indicative of a harsher attitude towards prisoners than the French civilian authorities. The director of the military railway service (*Chef des Feldeisenbahnwesens*) was instructed on 13 August by the Prussian *Kriegsministerium* that unwounded prisoners were to receive nothing at stations:

> Unwounded prisoners – regardless of whether they are officers or other ranks – are under no circumstances to be given voluntary food gifts ... This is only permitted for wounded prisoners. The stations where prisoner transports are stopped for a long period are to be sealed off to prevent interaction between the public and the prisoners of war.[81]

The Prussian *Kriegsministerium* issued further instructions on 20 August, ordering that public displays of kindness to prisoners be stopped:

> Already during the transport of French prisoners of war improper behaviour has occurred. Not only have the prisoners of war been given as many presents as departing German troops, women have also asked them for signed postcards and mementoes ... The *Kriegsministerium* asks for the necessary steps to be taken so that these events, which in the light of the treatment of German citizens by the enemy populations, are shameful, will be immediately stopped ... All available means are to be used to carry this out.[82]

The phrase 'all available means' allowed for wide-ranging interpretations.[83]

[79] Rainer Bendick, 'Les Prisonniers de guerre français en Allemagne durant la guerre de 1870–71', in Caucanas, Cazals and Payen, eds., *Les Prisonniers de guerre dans l'histoire*, p. 190.

[80] Verhey, *The Spirit of 1914*, pp. 80–2.

[81] Bayerisches Hauptstaatsarchiv, Abteilung IV Kriegsarchiv, Munich (BHStA IV), M Kr 1630, K. M. Berlin, Nr. 371/8.14, U3, enclosed letter from Groener, KM Berlin to Chef des Feldeisenbahnwesens I.Sekt. III b 217 g. geheim, Betrifft abtransport von Gefangenen, 13.8.1914.

[82] BHStA IV, M Kr 1630, K. M. Berlin, Nr. 371/8.14, U3, Wild v. Hohenborn to M. des Innern, Fernhalten des Publikums von Kriegsgefangenen, 20.8.1914.

[83] *Ibid.*

As in France, despite the official orders that prisoners were to be segregated from civilians, on the ground in many stations this did not occur. Once the element of euphoria, present in early August, wore off, a corresponding hostility developed towards those seen as responsible for obstructing German victory. Violent mob reaction against Allied prisoners became relatively common in Germany by late August 1914. It is likely that German civilians were also influenced by the official attitudes that kindness towards prisoners was unpatriotic.

Prisoners were genuinely shocked by the violent behaviour of German civilians. This impression emerges from both memoir and archive sources. Following his exchange back to France, a French prisoner, Gaston Riou, recalled 'what a welcome the citizens of Sarrebrück gave us. My ears still ring from their howls.'[84] Lieutenant-Colonel Reginald Bond recalled the hostile reaction of the German civilian population towards British prisoners arriving at Torgau in early September 1914 in his memoirs: 'the whole mass of people seemed to be trying to get at the prisoners ... There was one old woman who distinguished herself by the violence of her denunciations and the directness of her aim ... with three well-delivered spits! Old German women can spit!'[85] A French prisoner, Captain Pasqual, who was also transported to Torgau on 11 September 1914, reported in a confidential statement to the French authorities:

An indescribable journey, crammed into third class carriages and cattle wagons which had not been cleaned, surrounded by a population that was over-excited and hostile. The women of the German Red Cross refused us bread and water ... In all the stations we passed the crowd sang; at all the level crossings children, accompanied by their teachers, insulted our old officers, many of whom wore the 1870 medal; the towns were decorated with flags; the bells rang.[86]

A French prisoner, Léon Blanchin, captured on 27 August 1914, wrote in his memoir: 'What to say of that journey? It was monotonous ... it was sad: we travelled into exile. It was very uncomfortable ... In certain stations we were shouted at, and people waved fists at us. In general, however, the

---

[84] On 2 September 1914, Riou was transported 'across the Rhineland, the Palatinate, Baden, Wurttemberg and Bavaria during three days and three nights. In all the stations and even in the countryside, groups of peasants and masses of citizens shouted and booed ... threatened us with their fists, gestured cutting our necks, poking out our eyes ... Running children waving flags were lined along the track ... The sight of a red cross brassard seemed to send them into a sort of epileptic fury: "kill them, kill them, the ambulance men! These are the men who kill our wounded."' Gaston Riou, *The Diary of a French Private. War Imprisonment 1914–15* (Paris, 1916), pp. 1–2, 31.

[85] Reginald Coppleston Bond, *Prisoners Grave and Gay* (Edinburgh and London, 1935), pp. 35–41.

[86] SHAT, 6 N 47, October 1915, Report by Capitaine de Réserve Pasqual, Service de l'État-Major, on his captivity at Torgau-sur-Elbe (Silesia).

population was calm, even sad.'[87] Testimony sent to the German Foreign Ministry from a Belgian Dominican monk, transported to Germany from Louvain alongside British and Belgian prisoners of war, described German soldiers jeering at prisoners.[88] The Vatican also received similar reports of the experiences of priests deported from Belgium and France alongside civilians and prisoners of war.[89] German witnesses also noted the civilian hostility to prisoners. The schoolboy Heinrich Himmler wrote on 30 August 1914 in his diary describing the station at Landshut: 'full of curious Landshuters who were crude and almost violent as the *severely* wounded Frenchmen (who are surely worse off than our wounded in that they are prisoners) were given bread, water'.[90]

These civilian reactions indicate that there was considerable public anger towards prisoners, particularly in German urban centres, and little attempt was made on the ground to keep prisoners and civilians apart. In fact, in some areas, the local military authorities encouraged German civilians to come and view the new captives. The Commandant of Lechfeld camp in Bavaria even made a tidy business from charging civilian visitors for entry, donating the entrance fee, of 20 Pfennigs per person, to the German Red Cross.[91] On one Sunday in August 1914 thousands of civilians visited the camp.[92] There are also references in prisoners' accounts to groups of schoolchildren at German stations, singing or being shown prisoners, which did not occur in German prisoners' accounts of their reception in France.[93]

---

[87] Léon Blanchin, *Chez eux. Souvenirs de guerre et de captivité* (Paris, 1916), p. 57. The French prisoner, Edmond Rénault Désiré, captured on 22.8.14, recalled a similar journey: Jean-Pierre Guéno and Yves Laplume, *Paroles de Poilus. Lettres et Carnets du front (1914–1918)* (Paris, 1998), p. 31.

[88] Politisches Archiv des Auswärtigen Amtes, Berlin (AA), R 20882, Akten betreffend den Krieg 1914, Grausamkeiten in der Kriegsführung und Verletzungen des Völkerrechts, f. 75, Report from P. Vincent M. (Laurent) Dillen, geborener Belgier und Bürger der Stadt Löwen, Prior der Dominikaner aus Löwen, Schilderung der Bestrafung Löwens, 9.9.1914.

[89] ASV, Segretaria di Stato, Guerra, anno 1914–1918, rubrica 244, fasc. 137, ff. 32, 104, deportation account by Truffant, priest of the Diocese of Lille, Paroisse du Sacre Coeur, and f. 111, account by Abbé Aubry.

[90] Gilbert, *The First World War*, p. 63.

[91] BHStA IV, M Kr 1630, Extract from *Münchner Neueste Nachrichten*, 5.9.1914 and M Kr 1631, Bavarian KM, Graf von Hertling to Auswärtiges Amt, 12.10.1914.

[92] *Ibid.*

[93] A French prisoner, the ironically named Sergeant Allemand, related in a confidential account of his captivity to the French authorities that during his journey the German crowd 'cried at us "Paris capout" accompanying these words with gestures of cutting off our heads'. Allemand also recalled that civilian crowds, including schoolchildren brought by their teachers, came to jeer at his prison camp in September–October 1914. SHAT, 6 N 22, Rapport du Sergent Allemand, fait prisonnier à Maubeuge et rentré en France après évasion. Ministère de la Guerre, Direction de l'Aéronautique Militaire, Cabinet du Directeur.

The key difference with France, however, was that in 1914, Germany had captured prisoners from many countries. This led to a differentiated reaction in Germany to prisoners of different nationalities. For example, Russian prisoners were not highly regarded. An order in the German 8th Army on 31 August 1914, on the transport of Russian prisoners from the eastern front, stated that 'feeding the prisoners is not possible as due to the uncertainty of the Eastern army's supply lines, all food to hand must be reserved for the German troops ... Prisoners must be treated strictly ... They are not to be given water at first; while they are in the vicinity of the battlefield it is good for them to be in a broken physical condition.'[94] Captured Russian officers were to 'march on foot and must feel the humiliation of captivity. The prisoners are to carry the packs of their guards as they march and are to pull the captured field guns and machine guns.'[95] This military attitude of disrespect towards Russian prisoners was mirrored by that of German civilians. A children's book described Hindenburg's prisoners in derogatory rhyme: 'What is that for an army? The devil only knows! Flat caps, raised caps, broad braiding, silver braiding, shabby coats without buttons, bony Kalmykian heads.'[96] Some civilians took an even harsher line, fearing food shortages because of the number of Russians captured. Schoolgirl Piete Kuhr noted the following conversation about Russian prisoners in Schneidemühl in her diary, in October 1914:

What will we do with all these prisoners! We now see so many prisoner of war transports through our station that the long brown coats and the tattered trousers no longer arouse any curiosity. Fräulein Gumprecht, who came to coffee today, said the prisoners will only bring famine and disease into the country. 'Why don't they just shoot the fellows dead?' she asked.[97]

Kuhr thought it terrible that 'people now must even shoot prisoners dead'.[98] In fact, by 8 January 1915, the Prussian *Kriegsministerium*, 'for security reasons', ordered guards to open fire on any escaping prisoner following only one warning call.[99]

---

[94] BA-MA, PH5 / 185, 8. Armee, I.AOK.1141g, Erfahrungen des I. Reservekorps auf dem Gebiete des Gefangenenwesens, der Trophän usw. Kortau, 31.8.1914.

[95] *Ibid.*

[96] 'Hindenburgs Gefangene', in Kriegskinderspende deutscher Frauen, ed., *Vater ist im Kriege. Ein Bilderbuch für Kinder* (Berlin and Leipzig, n.d.), cited in Gerd Hankel, *Die Leipziger Prozesse. Deutsche Kriegsverbrechen und ihre strafrechtliche Verfolgung nach dem Ersten Weltkrieg* (Hamburg, 2003), p. 321.

[97] Mihaly, *'Da gibt's ein Wiedersehn!'* p. 85.   [98] *Ibid.*

[99] Geheimes Staatsarchiv Preußischer Kulturbesitz, Berlin-Dahlem (GstA PK), I. Abt. Rep. 77, tit. 1713, Korps der Landgendarmerie, Spez. I, Nr. 73 b I, Band I, Korps der Land-Gendarmerie. Special-Akten betreffend Mobilmachung 1914. Kriegsministerium. Nr. 1482/12.14.C.3, 11. Ang. Berlin, 8.1.1915.

However, while there was contempt for Russian prisoners, and some hostility towards the French, popular hatred and anger in Germany was greatest towards British prisoners in 1914. British and French accounts specifically point out that where French and British captives travelled together, German civilians directed more anger at the British.[100] One British prisoner described how 'the French and Belgians got what they wanted at the stations. There were four unwounded Frenchmen in our horse-box who got food and drink but the guards would not let them give us any.'[101] On one occasion, British officers were made to travel in unclean cattle wagons with their men, while French officers in the train travelled first class.[102] Former British prisoners were quick to accuse the German army of mistreatment because it transported wounded British prisoners in dirty cattle wagons, risking infection of open wounds, and because prisoners often did not have their dressings changed during the journey.[103] As the orders on Russian prisoners show, the German army *was* capable of behaving harshly towards captives in 1914. However, the chaos of distributing military resources in the initial months of the war also played a part. No army had adequate systems in place for the massive casualties which occurred. The British accusations hid the fact that even their own army was finding it difficult to dress all its German prisoners' wounds: Surgeon-Lieutenant Commander A. J. Gilbertson found that the seriously wounded German prisoners he was transporting on 30 October 1914 had not had their wounds dressed for ten days, including a German boy shot through both lungs and both legs.[104]

The extent of hostility to British prisoners arriving in Germany was considerable. In 1915, the British government, recognising the potential propaganda value of accounts of prisoner mistreatment and seeking evidence for post-war war crimes trials, established the British Government Committee on the Treatment by the Enemy of British Prisoners of War. It interviewed all repatriated, escaped or Swiss-interned British prisoners of war about their experiences. In spring 1918, this committee produced a

[100] TNA, MF 124.233, Parliamentary Paper, Cd. 8084, Miscellaneous no. 3, *Report on the Transport of British Prisoners of War to Germany, August–December 1914* (London, 1918) (hereafter *RTBP*), Sergeant Crockett, Maubeuge–Friedrichsfeld, September 1914, p. 38.
[101] *RTBP*, Private C. H. Fussell, Cambrai–Sennelager, September 1914, p. 41. *RTBP*, Lieutenant H. G. Henderson, Tourcoing–Osnabrück, 12–14 November 1914, p. 25. Exact dates of journeys are cited when stated in the report.
[102] *RTBP*, Lieutenant C. E. Wallis, Laon–Mainz, 30 October–2 November 1914, p. 23; *RTBP*, Lieutenant R. D. Middleditch, Courtrai–Munster, 12–15 December 1914, p. 29; *RTBP*, Captain A. S. Fraser, Douai–Paderborn, 30 October–3 November 1914, p. 24.
[103] *RTBP*, introduction.
[104] IWM, 92/46/1, Diary of Surgeon Lieutenant A. J. Gilbertson, RNVR, 30.10.1914.

parliamentary report on the German transport of British prisoners in 1914: *Report on the Transport of British Prisoners of War to Germany, August–December 1914*. The report contains seventy-six extracts from interviews with NCOs and other ranks and forty-eight extracts from interviews with British officers; it was later publicised as a pamphlet, *The Quality of Mercy. How British Prisoners of War Were Taken to Germany in 1914*, with an introduction by John Keble Bell.[105] By matching the extracts published in the report with the original committee interviews they were taken from and reading other unpublished interviews which the committee carried out, it becomes clear that the material cited in the published Parliamentary Report is reliable.[106] The Parliamentary Report describes hostility to British prisoners during their journeys to thirty-eight German cities and towns, including Wittenberg, Brunswick, Frankfurt, Cologne, Mainz, Friedrichsfeld and Hanover. In contrast to civilian reaction to prisoners in France, public hostility to prisoners in Germany occurred in large urban centres. The vast majority of the incidents cited occurred in September and October 1914.

The violence towards British prisoners, described in the report, was quite marked. A British sergeant stated that at Cologne 'the crowd of soldiers, civilians, women and children amused themselves by throwing buckets of water over us. Any utensil which would hold water was eagerly seized; clean water, dirty water and even urine was used.'[107] Private Dodd reported how 'we went on by train ... The Germans wrote *"Engländer"* outside in chalk and at every station we were jeered at, especially some Scots in kilts, who were dragged out and insulted, called *"Fräulein"* and kicked.'[108] Another private reported that 'at every station the guard kicked a lot of us out for the populace to see. The people spat in our faces and threw stones and 6-inch nails, &c. at us.'[109] In Aachen, on 2 September 1914, British officer prisoners believed their lives in danger when drunken Uhlans and railway employees attacked their carriage.[110] One prisoner,

---

[105] Bell used the pseudonym Keble Howard.

[106] The report quotes faithfully from the original interviews and provides a substantial selection of extracts. It also matches evidence from other sources. For example, an Irish prisoner, P. Aylward, exchanged to Holland in 1918, described in a private letter how he was transported in 1914: 'We left Louvain packed in trucks with just standing room, wounded and all ... jolting along we had occasional stops when the doors were opened and a crowd of civilians gathered round jeering the *"Engländer"*.' National Archives of Ireland, M 6808, shelf 2/478/9, Letter from P. Aylward, v. Boetzerlaerlaan 187, The Hague, Holland, to the Rev. Jackson, 3.3.1918.

[107] *RTBP*, Sergeant R. Gilling, Mons–Osnabrück, September 1914, p. 42.

[108] *Ibid.*, Private J. Dodd, Mons–Sennelager, August 1914, p. 32.

[109] *Ibid.*, Private C. Brash, Cambrai–Sennelager, August–September 1914, p. 33.

[110] *Ibid.*, Captain Beaman, Mons–Torgau, 1–4 September 1914, p. 8.

Trooper Grassick, who was wounded, described how en route for Bielefeld hospital, the guard opened the doors 'at the stations ... to show us to civilians, who threw stones at us and hit us with sticks'.[111]

This civilian violence was fuelled by German anger at British involvement in the war and the feeling that British troops were mercenaries (*Geldsoldaten*). This was exacerbated by anti-British propaganda, such as that described by Matthew Stibbe in his book on German anglophobia.[112] The rumours that the British used dumdum bullets further provoked mob passions against British prisoners. In addition, the belief in mutilation by the enemy had an enormous impact in Germany: the German press depicted German wounded or prisoners being killed and mutilated by Belgian and French civilians or by colonial troops serving in the British and French armies. One post-war German pamphlet published a November 1914 account that German prisoners were decapitated by French colonial troops at a French station.[113] British RAMC officers stated that their clasp-knives were shown to German crowds and described as tools used to mutilate German wounded.[114] Stories of dumdum bullets and of German wounded being mutilated probably resulted from the unfamiliar effect of high explosives and shrapnel, stripping and mutilating bodies.[115] Their widespread dissemination in 1914 helps explain the negative reaction to Allied prisoners. Tales of violence against German prisoners in Allied hands also sparked anger. The German Red Cross authorities at Cologne were convinced that German prisoners were attacked by angry mobs in France while 'we have seen many, many thousands of French prisoners transported through Cologne and they have not experienced the slightest mistreatment'.[116]

Other factors also led to popular hostility towards prisoners arriving in Germany. Prisoners arrived in German stations which were crowded with tense soldiers on their way to the front and German civilians. As a British prisoner, Major Peebles, reported, 'our guards were loaded with food,

---

[111] *Ibid.*, Trooper T. Grassick, Mons–Bielefeld, September 1914, p. 36.

[112] Matthew Stibbe, *German Anglophobia and the Great War 1914–1918* (Cambridge, 2001), pp. 10–32.

[113] Auswärtiges Amt, *Liste über Fälle, die sich auf planmäßige Ermordung und Misshandlung einer größeren Zahl von deutschen Kriegsgefangenen durch farbige Truppen beziehen* (Berlin, 1919), p. 1.

[114] *RTBP*, Major H. B. Kelly, Cambrai–Aachen, 5–7 September 1914, p. 15.

[115] Horne and Kramer, *German Atrocities*, p. 119; Robert Weldon Whalen, *Bitter Wounds. German Victims of the Great War, 1914–1939* (London and Ithaca, 1984), p. 50.

[116] ASV, Segretaria di Stato, Guerra 1914–1918, rubrica 244, fasc.132, f. 37, Report of a meeting of the Kriegshilfe der Vereinigten Vereine vom Roten Kreuz, Cologne, 19.12.1915. British sources differ however. See L. J. Austin, *My Experiences as a German Prisoner* (London, 1915), pp. 42–3, describing mob violence at Cologne.

cigars, &c, at every stop, everywhere there were enormous crowds of people singing, shouting, spitting, cursing, children drawn up with flags singing *"Deutschland über Alles"* and *"Die Wacht am Rhein"*.[117] Such crowds were not necessarily representative of the entire German population. They were often at the station to see their loved ones off to war and were, therefore, more likely to be hostile towards enemy prisoners. In addition, prisoners were often transported in trains alongside German wounded.[118] The first sight of large numbers of seriously wounded German troops aroused public emotion, which was then vented on nearby prisoners.[119] The prisoners' trains were also often delayed in sidings at stations in order that German troop trains on the way to the front might pass unobstructed. This led to greater exposure of prisoners to local populations.[120] Moreover, as one British prisoner recalled, 1 September 1914 was Sedan day, a celebration of victory in 1870: 'stations were thronged with seething masses of holiday citizens'.[121] The hostile German crowds encountered must be understood in this context.

Furthermore, the prisoners' feelings of suppressed fear, vulnerability and disorientation rendered them particularly sensitive to any show of German hostility and exacerbated the highly vivid nature of their memories of crowd anger. The effects of sleep deprivation, wounds, hunger and cold took their toll. Journeying in a closed train to an unknown destination through a foreign enemy country enhanced their confusion. Prisoners rarely understood the language of their captors or the French and Belgian civilian prisoners, with whom they often travelled, and found the shouts of German crowds all the more frightening because incomprehensible. This language barrier led to frustration on all sides. One British prisoner described how he saw a German officer 'strike some of the wounded ... because they did not understand him and get out of his way'.[122] Prisoners easily misinterpreted German actions, such as the opening of the wagon doors at railway stations, which they believed was in order that they could be stared at, but which was probably also to allow them fresh air, since their accounts describe ventilation in the wagons as very poor.[123]

[117] *RTBP*, Major Arthur Peebles, Cambrai–Torgau, 31 August 1914, p. 7.
[118] Major R. F. Meiklejohn, for example, describes German wounded and 150 British prisoners travelling together. *RTBP*, Major R. F. Meiklejohn, Cambrai–Brunswick, 3–6 September 1914, p. 13.
[119] Whalen, *Bitter Wounds*, p. 24.
[120] *RTBP*, Major Arthur Peebles, Cambrai–Torgau, 31 August–3 September 1914, p. 8, and Major R. F. Meiklejohn, Cambrai–Brunswick, 3–6 September 1914, p. 14.
[121] Bond, *Prisoners Grave and Gay*, p. 35. For a similar account of German crowd hostility see Austin, *My Experiences as a German Prisoner*, pp. 42–3, describing mob violence at Cologne.
[122] *RTBP*, Major Furness, Mons–Torgau, 1–4 September 1914, p. 9.
[123] *Ibid.*, Major Vandaleur, Douai–Krefeld, 17–20 October 1914, p. 21.

For many class-conscious British officers, often products of a particular English 'gentlemanly' culture of masculinity, the fact that they travelled to Germany in third- or fourth-class carriages added to their disorientation.[124] They were insulted by having to travel alongside ordinary soldiers, having to pay for their own meals and not being allowed to call a cab to take them to or from railway stations. Officers were shocked at having their coats, buttons or personal belongings stolen.[125] What the British prisoners found traumatic in 1914 demonstrates the extent to which the war that unfolded was at odds with the imagined war that troops had expected to fight. These 1914 prisoners believed in the observation of a gentlemanly war culture, corresponding with the pre-war conventions of Geneva and The Hague. The prisoners' train journey also effectively marked their indefinite separation from their own home front. It was the inverse of the collective gaze of the cheering crowds that had sent them off so recently, reinforcing the traumatic absence of the home culture, which the prisoners both remembered and desired.

Part of this disorientation was gendered: prisoners found the violent behaviour of German women when encountering prisoners at stations a particularly shocking transgression of gender norms in 1914. Wounded British prisoners claimed that they were treated worse than German casualties, as they were specifically refused all attention and food by the German Red Cross, particularly by its female members.[126] One witness, Private Harvey, saw a fellow prisoner 'wounded in the mouth, go to the German Red Cross at the station to get his wound dressed and the Red Cross woman spat in his face'.[127] The German Red Cross was not always hostile to British prisoners: one prisoner said they 'behaved very decently all the time I had anything to do with them. They did their best.'[128] However, in some cases, it appears they did behave hostilely to prisoners in late August–early September 1914. Of the seventy-six NCOs and other ranks whose interviews are cited in the British Parliamentary Report,

---

[124] On British 'gentlemanly' culture, see John Tosh, 'What Should Historians Do with Masculinity? Reflections on Nineteenth Century Britain', *History Workshop Journal*, 38, 1 (1994), pp. 179–202. See also Peter Parker, *The Old Lie. The Great War and the Public School Ethos* (London, 1987).

[125] *RTBP*, Captain Beresford, Cambrai–Mainz, 16–20 October 1914, p. 20.

[126] As one prisoner wrote 'At all the large stations [there] were German Red Cross Aid Posts. The German wounded were taken out, their wounds dressed and they were given food and drink in abundance. When I asked the Red Cross authorities for food and drink for the British and French wounded, it was refused ... At Hanover the Red Cross official I addressed spat on the platform and walked away.' *RTBP*, Captain G.H. Rees, Cambrai–Döberitz, 3–8 September 1914, p. 12.

[127] *Ibid.*, Private A. Harvey, Journey to Friedrichsfeld, October 1914, p. 49.

[128] *Ibid.*, Private P. Connolly, Journey to Kassel, November 1914, p. 50.

forty-eight describe being spat at, hit, insulted or refused aid by the German Red Cross, almost always by a Red Cross woman.[129]

On some occasions, the German Red Cross incidents were due to British prisoners confusing who was actually in the Red Cross and who was in patriotic volunteer organisations, such as the *Vaterländische Frauenvereine*, who were extremely active in providing refreshments at stations. Other incidents, however, probably resulted from the cultural constraints that controlled how German women could behave towards the 'enemy'. According to Ute Daniel, in August 1914, the first transports of French prisoners arriving in Germany were given a warm reception in many places by women,

the friendly tone of which raised a cry of indignation heard in newspaper articles, letters to the editor and petitions ... In the eyes of the critics the regaling of prisoners with wine and chocolate constituted an unpatriotic act. The orders of the Elberfeld rail commander to the train stations under his jurisdiction provide a good example of this sentiment. As he wrote: '"during the transport of prisoners of war German women and girls have sometimes behaved in an undignified manner. I request that station masters intervene in the strongest manner as soon as our national honour is offended by such elements."' Other military officers issued similar announcements and, in some cities, also reintroduced the stocks for such women.[130]

The cultural penalties for German women who were seen as being too friendly to the enemy were clearly very significant, and this may have led to them acting hostilely towards prisoners in order to avoid social disapproval. However, such constraints not only applied to German women. In 1914, female behaviour became closely associated with ideals of national pride and purity in both France and Germany, and was scrutinised accordingly. In the Corrèze *Département* in France, the Prefect reported to the *Ministre de l'Intérieur* that he had alerted the military authorities to 'certain totally inappropriate acts by the ladies of the Red Cross under the surveillance of a guarding officer in Brive station, who offered chocolate and beer to prisoners passing through'.[131] Similarly, Simone de Beauvoir recalled her experience as a child distributing food to French troops at the local station in September 1914:

---

[129] Robert Vansittart of the British Foreign Office was a key proponent of this view of German women, even reiterating it in his 1958 memoirs. Robert Vansittart, *The Mist Procession. The Autobiography of Lord Vansittart* (London, 1958), p. 157.

[130] Ute Daniel, *The War from Within. German Working-Class Women in the First World War* (Oxford and New York, 1997), pp. 23–4. This debate continued into the post-war period in Germany. See Rosa Kempf, 'Die deutschen Kriegsgefangenen und die deutschen Frauen', *Die Frau*, 28 (1920/21), pp. 330–4.

[131] AN, F7.12937, Prefect of Corrèze Département to the Ministre de l'Intérieur, 24.8.1914.

One day a woman offered a German prisoner a glass of wine. There were murmurs of disapproval from the other women. 'Well!' she said. 'They're men, too, like the others.' The sounds of disapproval grew stronger ... I stared with studied horror at the woman who was known from then on as the 'Frau'. In her I beheld at last Evil incarnate.[132]

The importance of the ritualised acts of giving food and other gifts to parting troops, and refusing prisoners, must be read in terms of a contested mobilisation space, with home troops leaving and prisoners arriving simultaneously, in the same stations. The giving of chocolate or cigarettes became an act of national affirmation in the wartime moral economy of sacrifice, binding the home front and fighting troops, civilians and combatants, particularly when carried out by women. The captured diary of a German soldier reveals how widespread this ritualised giving was in Germany in August 1914:

9 August 1914. 1h 30 The battalion left Berlin to scenes of public enthusiasm. At Rathenau ... soup and beef ... At Stendal coffee. At Gardelegen *Tartines* and sausage ... At Lehrte water and postcards. At Linden-les-Hanovre [sic] *Tartines fourrées*, raspberries, cake, chocolate. The world of youth is truly a chic one for us ... 10 August ... coffee, and filled bread. At Hamm coffee, bread rolls and postcards. At Scharnhorst near Dortmund rice and beef ... I was given cigarettes and a box of matches. Around me pressed all the best young girls of the town, each more beautiful and attractive than the previous one ... pity we can't take them all with us.[133]

Departing soldiers received similar gifts in France.[134] The act of giving these items, known as 'love gifts' (*Liebesgaben*) in Germany, thus became a mobilising act of national appropriation of 'our' soldiers leaving for the front, and its corollary was to deny the same gifts to the enemy, embodied by the prisoner of war or even to act violently towards him. Such female violence also occurred away from stations. Indeed, in one case in France, in 1915, a nun, Sister Saint-Pierre, repeatedly mistreated wounded German prisoners she was nursing, hitting them in the face or on the buttocks, causing one prisoner to weep with humiliation that a nun could hit him, 'a married man', in this way.[135] The shunning of prisoners had become a form of national and social bonding for patriotic women

---

[132] Simone de Beauvoir, *Memoirs of a Dutiful Daughter* (London, 1959), pp. 26–7.

[133] SHAT, 5 N 556, Prisonniers de guerre allemands. Diaries taken from captured prisoners, Carnet de campagne de Fusilier M. de la 12e Cie du II Régiment de la Garde à Pied.

[134] AN, F7.12935, Dossier Haute-Savoie, Prefect of Châlon-sur-Seine to Ministre de l'Intérieur, 19.8.1914.

[135] Archives du Comité International de la Croix Rouge, Geneva (ACICR), FAW 140/3, [140/1], 1.5.18, Red Cross, Berlin to CICR, Otto Westerkamp aus Recklinghausen (1/3 Garde Regt z.f.); also BA-MA, PH2 / 33, f. 138, Heinrich Nutzhorn.

volunteers in both Germany and France. This new bonding process created new taboos; showing overt kindness to a prisoner was one of them.

The media coverage of 1914 civilian violence against prisoners – the cycle of representations

Civilian violence against arriving prisoners soon received coverage in the European media. It gave rise to a particular cycle of representations which was as influential as the events themselves in constructing public opinion during the first years of the war. In 1914, the arrival of the first prisoners was a heavily publicised event: prisoners were photographed and sketched. For example, in France the artist Marcel Eugène Louveau-Rouveyre produced a series of sketches of German prisoners at railway stations.[136] Photographs of prisoners arriving were frequently printed on postcards and in newspapers – violence against captives in 1914 rapidly caught public attention.

This process of publicising the arrival of prisoners soon merged real eyewitness accounts, government propaganda and popular myth to create a powerful media discourse about civilian violence against captives – a discourse which was institutionalised within national war histories and publicised in the contemporary press. This process homogenised the different complex factors at play in the early public reactions to prisoners of war into a crudely simplified stereotypical version in which enemy civilians were cruel to helpless prisoners while the home nation's civilians were disciplined and kind to them.

The initial official accusations of mistreatment of prisoners during transport in 1914 were made by the British: Germany, whose propaganda had focused on allegations of mistreatment of German civilians in France and Britain, found itself forced to respond to accusations that British military prisoners had been mistreated by German civilians. While Germany and France focused upon questions of prisoners being shot or mutilated on the battlefield, the story of the wounded British prisoner mistreated by German civilians achieved notoriety in Britain in December 1914 when an escaped British officer, Major Vandaleur from Krefeld camp, reported his poor treatment during the journey into Germany after capture.[137]

During 1915–16, however, the 1914 transport issue became more widely publicised in all three countries as more repatriated prisoners'

---

[136] Bibliothèque de Documentation Internationale Contemporaine-Musée d'Histoire Contemporaine, Les Invalides (BDIC-MHC Les Invalides) Or F3 1311–20.

[137] *The Times*, 10.4.1915, p. 10.

accounts became available. On 12 March 1915, *The Times* published a prisoner's report describing German crowds jeering in railway stations in 1914. *The Times History of the War* in 1916 reported that for British prisoners in 1914 'the journey to captivity was ever terrible'.[138] These British accusations had such influence that in June 1915 the German government made an official response:

If the English pretend that they were attended to during the journey only after the French, the reason is to be found in the quite comprehensible bitterness of feeling among the German troops who respected the French on the whole as honourable and decent opponents, whereas the English mercenaries had in their eyes adopted a cunning method of warfare from the very beginning and when taken prisoners bore themselves in an insolent and provocative mien.[139]

A 1915 German publication on the treatment of Allied prisoners of war, *Les Prisonniers de guerre en Allemagne*, attempted to justify the hostile treatment of British prisoners of war during the initial prisoner transports of 1914:

One is not surprised by the hostile manifestations of the first days [of war] towards the English who without any reason had allied themselves with the adversaries of Germany and whose policies had for years been directed towards isolating and weakening our country.[140]

The real events which some prisoners had experienced soon elided into crude propaganda as shown in Figures 2 and 3.

Such pictures popularised the original stories of 1914 prisoners, and homogenised them into a standard mythic image which may have influenced prisoners' own later understanding of events. The two examples here provide an interesting comparison of how the French and the British interpreted the same phenomenon. It was all a long way from the work of Anton von Werner. In both pictures, the fact that the prisoners are wounded is emphasised. In the British case, it is the treatment of wounded prisoners by German Red Cross women during the transport that matters – for the French artist and prisoner of war, André Warnod, the whole German population, including children, take part in attacking wounded French captives. Both pictures, however, endorse the extension of the concept of the 'enemy' beyond the German soldier

---

[138] *The Times History of the War* (London, 1916), vol. VI, p. 253.   [139] *Ibid.*, pp. 254–6.

[140] Prof. Dr A. Backhaus, *Die Kriegsgefangenen in Deutschland. Gegen 250 Wirklichkeitsaufnahmen aus deutschen Gefangenenlagern, mit einer Erläuterung von Professor Dr. Backhaus* (Siegen, 1915), p. 6. 30,000 copies of this book were produced in German, English, French, Spanish and Russian.

RED CROSS OR IRON CROSS?

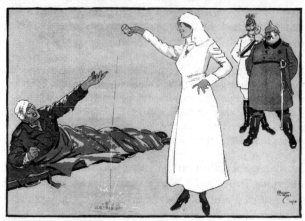

WOUNDED AND A PRISONER
OUR SOLDIER CRIES FOR WATER.

THE GERMAN "SISTER"
POURS IT ON THE GROUND BEFORE HIS EYES.

THERE IS NO WOMAN IN BRITAIN
WHO WOULD DO IT.

THERE IS NO WOMAN IN BRITAIN
WHO WILL FORGET IT.

Figure 2. Poster by David Wilson, 'Red Cross or Iron Cross?' Imperial War Museum, IWM PST 2762.

to encompass the wider German population. The French picture further enhances this effect by its use of colour for the French prisoner victims and black and white for the German perpetrators. The artist, André Warnod, was a prisoner of the Germans during the war and may have based his drawing upon personal experience. Yet at the same time both pictures depict the prisoner as a helpless demilitarised victim and non-combatant.

The discourse on German civilian violence that emerges in these images also appeared in textual form. The French government publication

Figure 3. André Warnod, 'Les Prisonniers de guerre!' Drawing of French prisoners arriving in Germany. Bibliothèque de Documentation Internationale Contemporaine et Musée d'Histoire Contemporaine (BDIC-MHC Les Invalides), Est FL 1837.

Le Régime des prisonniers de guerre, published in Paris in 1916, outlined comparatively the treatment of German and French prisoners in 1914.[141] For German prisoners taken in France, it claimed:

The transport of prisoners from the place of capture to that of their internment takes place as far as possible in third-class carriages ... It is only in the case of necessity and in the absence of any possible damage to a prisoner's health that goods wagons, specially adapted for this use, are employed ... Precautions are taken to protect the prisoners from any crowd demonstrations during stops in stations: lowering the windows or opening the curtains is prohibited; the general public are not allowed to stand on the platforms, and the train is halted on a special track at a distance from the station ... Almost always, the calm and the dignity of the French crowd have rendered these precautions unnecessary. The popular indignation, vividly expressed on other occasions, is always contained before unarmed enemies, and there is no case where a German prisoner has suffered brutal treatment during the transport.[142]

In contrast, the book outlined how French prisoners in Germany endured

The inexpressible suffering of a journey of many days in livestock wagons, where in the enormous majority of cases, the prisoners, including sick and wounded, were

---

[141] See also Dr de Christmas, *Le Traitement des prisonniers français en Allemagne d'après l'interrogatoire des prisonniers ramenés d'Allemagne en Suisse* (Paris, 1917), p. 101.

[142] *Le Régime des prisonniers de guerre en France et en Allemagne au regard des conventions internationales 1914–1916*, p. 11.

crammed without food or medicine ... Expressions of hatred ... howling, stone-throwing, bottle-throwing, theft in all the stations of buttons from uniforms and of *Képis* – were usual in the first months of the war when the majority of prisoners arrived.[143]

Clearly, the behaviour of civilians towards arriving prisoners of war had become one of the propaganda war's signifiers of a country's position on the wartime civilisation–barbarism axis.[144]

Germany responded to this Entente discourse in a variety of ways. German prisoners' memoirs recounting poor treatment during their transport in France were published in 1915–16. Albums of photographs showing Allied prisoners arriving in peaceful German towns were widely distributed. Accusations of French mobs mistreating German prisoners were published in German propaganda booklets.[145] Yet, in reality, both the Franco-British and the German material published on the 1914 transport of prisoners manipulated actual events into a wartime cultural framework of simplistic homogeneous moral representations. A useful comparison can be made here with the absence of complaints regarding prisoners' post-war repatriation journeys. After the Armistice, many French prisoners of war travelled to Switzerland in overcrowded, badly heated trains which, according to the International Committee of the Red Cross, were unsuitable, particularly for sick prisoners.[146] This uncomfortable journey, however, did not correspond to any topography of wartime hatred and prejudice in the way that the 1914 prisoners' journeys had; thus, its exigencies were fast forgotten. Moreover, as this

---

[143] *Ibid.*, p. 15.

[144] This discourse was not restricted to social elites. In Britain, a journalist writing in the local newspaper the *Camberley News* described German prisoners arriving at Frith Hall camp in England: 'my mind reverted to the stories told by wounded British soldiers who had fallen into the Germans' hands, and contrasted the treatment meted out to them with what was accorded to the German prisoners as they passed the silent spectators in that village street. I thought of the brutal ill-treatment by the German guards on the train. Wretched British prisoners crowded into the cattle trucks, starving and begging for water; of the stones and filth flung at them and of the misery of long journeys by rail and road in the depths of winter without overcoats, and in many cases without boots ... and then I thanked God that I had seen the British reception of German prisoners and the lessons it contained and hoped that among the prisoners in that column were some with first hand knowledge of the savage way in which British prisoners had been treated under similar circumstances, so that they could compare it with the experience of that day.' Article from the *Camberley News*, cited in Clarke, *Clarke's Camberley at War*, p. 15.

[145] Auswärtiges Amt, *Die Gefangenen-Misshandlungen in Entente-Ländern. Noten der deutschen Regierung an die Neutralen Staaten* (Berlin, 1918), translated as *German Government. Maltreatment of Prisoners in Allied Countries. Notes by the German Government to Neutral States* (Berlin, 1919).

[146] Bruno Cabanes, 'Finir la guerre. L'expérience des soldats français (été 1918–printemps 1920)', doctoral thesis, University of Paris I – Panthéon Sorbonne UFR d'histoire, 2 vols. (2002), vol. II, p. 435.

example shows, both public and prisoners' attitudes towards what constituted hardship had altered by the end of 1918. Nevertheless, even after the war ended, Germany still felt the need to rebut the Allies' claims that in 1914 German civilians had mistreated prisoners in the Reichstag's inquiry into German conduct during the war. The results of this German inquiry, published in the series *Völkerrecht im Weltkrieg*, counter-accused the Allies of mistreating German prisoners during transport and generally refuted the French claims in *Le Régime des prisonniers de guerre*; significantly, the allegations made in the British Parliamentary Paper were not referred to.[147] Ultimately, the most important result of this media discourse on violence against prisoners of war by civilians in 1914 was the section stating that prisoners should be protected from the public, which was included in the 1929 Geneva Convention that still applies today.[148]

Conclusion

On the basis of the available sources, it is difficult to make any direct comparison about the scale of civilian violence towards prisoners in Germany and France in 1914. However, it is evident that in both countries civilians were actively involved in aggression towards arriving enemy captives at the outset of the war. The patterns of violence also reveal similarities between the German and French situations: the forms of civilian group behaviour which emerged were almost identical – spitting, shouting, throwing stones, refusing food or water. The means used to transport prisoners were also very similar in both countries and prisoners in both cases were often traumatised witnesses, suffering from wounds, disorientation and culture shock. Civilian social concerns regarding women's interaction with prisoners were almost identical, although they received more media attention in Germany. In both France and Germany, civilians showed their anger at the enemy by displaying hostility towards those of its men who had been captured. They also expressed their anxiety and fear at the dramatic outbreak of war; prisoners served as a metonym for

---

[147] Prof. Dr Meurer, 'Verletzungen des Kriegsgefangenenrechts', in Reichstag, *Völkerrecht im Weltkrieg*, vol. III, part I, pp. 165–77.

[148] The 1929 Geneva Convention states (Part 1, Art. 2): 'Prisoners of war ... must be treated at all times with humanity and must be protected, particularly against acts of violence, insults and public curiosity.' Part 8, Art. 25, states: 'unless military events render it necessary, sick or wounded prisoners of war shall not be transported if their recovery might be compromised by the journey'. Gustav Rasmussen, *Code des prisonniers de guerre. Commentaire de la Convention du 27 juillet 1929, relative au traitement des prisonniers de guerre* (Copenhagen, 1931), pp. 108 and 115–16.

the war onto which they could project their frustrations, their anguish and show solidarity.

However, although the overall trends were in some ways alike, there were differences between France and Germany at a local level. More of the German population encountered prisoners given that Germany had considerably more prisoners to transport in 1914. German crowds showed more hostility to particular prisoner nationalities, differentiating between them. French and German crowds were hostile to prisoners for different reasons: in the first instance French civilians were largely reacting against the invasion; in the German case, stories of mutilation of the wounded were a major cause. Government reaction also differed. Whereas the French government wanted to keep its population calm and feared crowds gathering, German authorities appear to have been less concerned, regarding crowds as positive signs of patriotism and a means of mobilising civilian support for the war. There is more evidence of prisoners being deliberately displayed as booty in Germany than in France. German authorities were also prepared to acknowledge that there had been popular anger towards British prisoners during the ensuing propaganda battle on the prisoner transport issue. The French authorities ignored all evidence that any German prisoners had been mistreated by civilians in 1914.

Overall, the pattern that emerges from the arrival of prisoners is one of remarkably rapid mobilisation of spontaneous collective public anger in both Germany and France, which adopted similar mechanisms of expression. There were regional variations and motivations, but the spontaneity of the civilian reaction is telling. It reveals the powerful impact the outbreak of war had upon regionally disparate areas and the rapidity with which civilians entered into a culture of hatred, accepting the stereotype of the 'enemy' as a basis for abandoning peacetime moral norms. Hostile civilian behaviour towards captives sent out a powerful message to the military in each country that violence against prisoners was popularly sanctioned and had public approval.

This early wartime violence by civilians reveals a significant shift away from the pre-war tendency to view prisoners of war as a specially protected group. The strength of this is illustrated by the fact that in many cases German and French civilians were prepared to throw stones at wounded prisoners. However, in the media discourse which ensued from the crowd hostility in 1914, Germany was on the defensive. It is noteworthy that Britain and France proved to be much better at exploiting the accounts of mistreatment of their prisoners, both textually and visually, than Germany was. This pattern would continue through 1915 as the next chapter will show.

The transport of prisoners of war in 1914 also illustrates that the relationship between propaganda and event during the First World War was never a stable one. Real prisoners' eyewitness evidence became part of a fluid media discourse that continued to evolve into the post-war era. However, this case study of civilian violence can only provide insights into one early aspect of this process. The type of violence which civilians practised against prisoners in 1914 was shocking, but it was not initially perceived as an *atrocity*. How the representation of violence against prisoners radicalised between late 1914 and 1916 into multiple atrocity depictions will be examined in the following chapter.

2 Legitimate and illegitimate violence against prisoners: representations of atrocity, 1914–16

> Great part of the information obtained in war is contradictory, a still greater part is false, and by far the greatest part is of a doubtful character ... As a general rule, ... everyone is inclined to magnify the bad in some measure.   Carl von Clausewitz, *On War*.[1]

Introduction

In a recent essay on war literature, Bernd Hüppauf described how 'since the First World War propaganda has stood for the absolute opposite of truth'.[2] Yet, as the previous chapter has shown, the real relationship between representations of violence and wartime experience was much more complex. As the events of 1914 illustrated, violence by civilians against prisoners of war, reported in the media, served to exacerbate the polarisation of European populations and to undermine the legally protected status of the prisoner in wartime. However, this pattern did not stop with civilian violence against prisoners arriving on the home front. Rather it was repeated throughout the first sixteen months of the war, as other incidents of prisoner mistreatment emerged in public discourse in a similar fashion to form cycles of violent representations, which ultimately undermined prisoners' rights, by encouraging lower social and military expectations of how prisoners were to be treated. These early wartime discourses on prisoner mistreatment were closely interrelated and over time they led to widespread cognitive assumptions: by 1915, it had become the norm to depict *any* prisoner mistreatment by the enemy as an atrocity, regardless of cause, scale or extremity.

This escalation in atrocity depictions in 1914–16 did not occur by default. It is necessary to interrogate it in more detail and to ask why representations of prisoners of war became so violent. How did this radicalisation occur? It is important also to consider whether this process

---

[1] Carl von Clausewitz, *On War* (Ware, 1997 [1832]), pp. 64–5.
[2] Bernd Hüppauf, 'Kriegsliteratur', in Hirschfeld *et al.*, eds., *Enzyklopädie Erster Weltkrieg*, p. 181.

developed in different ways within the military, in comparison to the home front. This chapter will explore these questions by examining three case studies. First, the depiction of battlefield capture in 1914 and 1915 will be assessed, to see how the theme of shooting prisoners upon surrender became widespread and how this in turn led to a depiction of the enemy prisoner as a perpetrator of war crimes. Second, the portrayal of beatings of prisoners within prisoner of war camps will be considered, to highlight how propaganda, based on real reports, exacerbated radicalisation. Third, the depiction of sickness among prisoners of war will be analysed to show how in 1915 and 1916 prisoner illness was represented as an enemy atrocity, rather than a traditional wartime phenomenon, and came to be situated within a wider, all-encompassing portrayal of the prisoner of war experience as violent. Together these case studies reveal the rapid erosion of pre-war norms – what Jay Winter and Antoine Prost recently called 'the degeneration of the limits on extreme violence in wartime in the first phase of the war'.[3] A degeneration of limits can be clearly traced here in the relationship between these violent representations and violent acts towards prisoners – a relationship which undermined the status of prisoners of war, as countries reciprocated the behaviour of which their enemy stood accused.

Governments were central to this process of violent escalation due to their role in publicising incidents of real prisoner mistreatment by the enemy. During the opening phase of the war, governments constantly redefined what constituted a wartime atrocity against prisoners in the light of the ongoing information they received about how the enemy was treating its captives; real accounts of abuses thus helped governments reformulate their views of what constituted legitimate or illegitimate prisoner treatment, leading them to issue public protests against enemy behaviour and to demand that neutral states and international groups, such as the Vatican and the International Committee of the Red Cross, who were in a position to investigate prisoner abuses, should intervene.[4] Passed between enemy belligerents via neutral states, such diplomatic protests highlighted the clash between pre-war normative expectations

---

[3] Prost and Winter, *The Great War in History*, p. 171.

[4] Surprisingly robust channels kept governments and armies informed about how the enemy was treating its prisoners, including reports by the representatives of the neutral 'protector' powers and by the International Red Cross who inspected camps; information from escaped and exchanged prisoners; interviews with captured enemy combatants; information from prisoners' letters sent home, or from letters sent to prisoners of war, where families often mentioned prisoner treatment in their own country; and information from journalists from neutral countries who had been allowed to visit prison camps. For example, as early as September 1914, German prisoners of war in France were able to write home and their letters provided a source of information for both captor and home governments.

and wartime realities, by constantly referring back to pre-war customs and international law which governments believed were being transgressed. These public protests by governments, coupled with information from repatriated prisoners, in turn fuelled popular press discourses that increasingly associated captivity with radical forms of violence. Although some of these press discourses were exaggerated, it was simply not the case that governments deliberately fabricated accusations of prisoner mistreatment in the media; rather, in 1914 and 1915, cultural representations of prisoner mistreatment were both the expression of belligerents' belief that violence was actually occurring, as well as reportage – merging the evidence of real prisoner mistreatment with an almost eschatological expectation of enemy cruelty towards captives. In this way, the process of converting real events into symbolic denigration of the enemy accelerated to create atrocity discourses in which violence against prisoners of war was perceived in an oppositional manner to the glorified violence of the *champ d'honneur*.[5] While the combatant experience of violence was enshrined in a litany of positive value meanings as sacrifice, courage, heroism, honour and stoicism, violence against prisoners of war was depicted in utterly contrasting terms as barbaric, atrocious, cruel and cowardly. This chapter will now explore how the public image of surrender on the battlefield which was established in 1914 and 1915 led to capture being associated with violent atrocity.

Case study 1: battlefield violence against prisoners at the moment of surrender, 1914–15

The seminal initial representations of violence against prisoners emerged from the battlefields of 1914 and, in particular, the extreme violence of the German invasion of France and Belgium. Capture was linked with atrocity from the very outset of the war, with both sides believing that the enemy was killing prisoners on the battlefield. The killing of prisoners of war at or immediately after the moment of surrender was obviously not a new development in warfare; it had frequently occurred in previous conflicts. Indeed existing studies by Niall Ferguson and Joanna Bourke, among others, have argued that it was a relatively common form of violence against prisoners during the First World War.[6] However, what was new in 1914–15 was the very rapid translation of such killings into radicalised propaganda discourses which encouraged further

SHAT, 6 N 23, Croix-Rouge française – états des envois [commission des PG] 30.9.1914, état des envois faits du 11 au 29 sept. 1914. Lettres de prisonniers allemands à leurs parents – 1376, Lettres des parents au prisonniers allemands – 1248.

[5] On the spread of atrocity rumours see Bloch, 'Réflexions d'un historien', pp. 293–316.

[6] On the scale of prisoner killing during the war see Ferguson, *The Pity of War*, pp. 367–94, and 'Prisoner Taking', pp. 148–92; Bourke, *An Intimate History of Killing*; Cook, 'The Politics of Surrender'.

violent escalation. For this reason, this study will not seek to assess the scale of battlefield prisoner killing during the whole 1914–18 conflict which, as other historians have already acknowledged, is practically impossible to gauge and which is beyond the scope of this book. Instead it will explore battlefield prisoner killings in terms of how the *depiction* of such violence against prisoners in the first phase of the war redefined popular attitudes towards captives and atrocity.

The first accounts of the killing of prisoners of war, which appeared during the invasion, fuelled a strong belief among British, French and German soldiers that exceptional violence towards prisoners was occurring. On the German side, a remarkably powerful belief developed that wounded German troops captured by enemy soldiers and civilians were being killed and their bodies mutilated.[7] Tales of mutilation abounded: one German civilian, repatriated from London to Germany on 26 August 1914, related that at Dijon train station French soldiers showed him twelve ears and sixteen noses carried in their bags.[8] Such tales fed the belief in mutilation in the German army. Wounded German soldiers tended by nuns in Blégny were terrified: 'they had been told that in Belgium the wounded had their eyes gouged out, were poisoned, were finished off'.[9] In Warsage in Belgium on 5–6 August 1914, German soldiers bound an old man accused of cutting off the ears and gouging out the eyes of wounded Germans to the wheel of a wagon.[10] At Noményy, German soldiers told a French civilian: 'There can be no mercy because the French are no longer taking prisoners; they are gouging out the eyes of our wounded and cutting off their members ...'[11] The mutilation belief led to a crucial cognitive association: the enemy prisoner was not associated merely with combat, but was perceived as the *perpetrator* of war crimes. This belief negatively influenced German attitudes to both civilian and combatant prisoners of war. The German army was the first to make this cognitive shift but the Allies soon followed.

The belief that taboo forms of violence towards prisoners were being perpetrated by the enemy radicalised German soldiers' behaviour. Tales of the mutilation of the dead and wounded stood as cultural shorthand for desecration. Despite the fact that there was no evidence for mutilation,

---

[7] See, for example, AA, R 20880, Bd. 1, f. 55, Extract from a private letter by Prince Heinrich XXXIII relating the cruelty of Belgian Franktireurs against the German troops, 20.8.1914.
[8] AA, R 20882, f. 2, Robert Müller, 1.9.1914.
[9] Horne and Kramer, *German Atrocities*, p. 14.   [10] *Ibid.*   [11] *Ibid.*, p. 64.

soldiers continued to believe in it, largely because it imbued the violence
of the opening weeks of the war with eschatological meaning. The Mutilation
allowed German soldiers to view the enemy in Manichaean terms – not
simply as a military adversary to be defeated, but as part of a belief system
based upon a battle between good and evil. The mutilation belief was
probably inherited by troops in 1914 from the German army's earlier
experience in colonial wars; in particular, the mutilation of soldiers'
corpses by the Herero in 1904–6.[12] The belief system that had developed
around what constituted enemy barbarism in Africa was transferred
almost entirely intact to the European battlefield. It was no coincidence
that in 1914, when Germany accused Entente soldiers and civilians generally of killing and mutilating German wounded, it particularly singled
out Entente colonial troops, who, it alleged, murdered the wounded and
dismembered corpses. In 1915, the German Foreign Office published a
report cataloguing accusations of such war crimes by Entente colonial
troops, largely based on hearsay; a second followed in 1919 after the
German revolution.[13] This belief that German prisoners were being killed
and mutilated on the battlefield had serious long-term implications. It led
Germany to claim that the use of colonial troops in Europe was a war
crime. In some cases, it also led German troops to give no quarter to black
soldiers. Lieutenant-Colonel Gerold von Gleich reported a popular joke
in the army in 1914 that related how a Bavarian NCO killed a large
number of black prisoners.[14] In July 1915 and July 1917, German soldiers
told the writer Gregor Huch that army commanders had told them they
did not wish to see any black prisoners of war taken.[15]

Moreover, the mutilation belief appears to have radicalised a particularly ruthless initial German reaction to prisoners during the invasion of

[12] On mutilation of corpses during the African wars see Hull, *Absolute Destruction*, pp. 136,
210. This German fear of the wounded being murdered and mutilated was in many ways a
mirror image of the Allied belief that the Germans were cutting off Belgian and French
children's hands – a belief system which also drew upon colonial references to Belgian
practices in the Congo. Mutilation of enemy corpses remained an important motif
throughout the First World War – in his 1933 memoir, one British soldier described
finding a corpse whose eyes had been deliberately gouged out at Ghissignies. Guy
Chapman, *A Passionate Prodigality. Fragments of an Autobiography* (London, 1965
[1933]), p. 272.
[13] Auswärtiges Amt, *Völkerrechtswidrige Verwendung farbiger Truppen auf dem europäischen
Kriegsschauplatz durch England und Frankreich* (Berlin, 1915); Auswärtiges Amt, *Liste über
Fälle, die sich auf planmäßige Ermordung und Misshandlung einer größeren Zahl von deutschen
Kriegsgefangenen durch farbige Truppen beziehen* (Berlin, 1919).
[14] Württembergisches Hauptstaatsarchiv, Stuttgart (HStA STUTT), M 660, Nachlass
Gleich, Meine Erlebnisse im Feldzug 1914, III. Teil. Die Verlängerung des rechten
Heeresflügels, Diary 22 September 1914, p. 27.
[15] Gregor Huch, 'Die belgische Schande. Ein Briefwechsel', *Der Deutsche*, Heft 1, JG 1
(1919), pp. 69–70.

France and Belgium. An escaped French prisoner related how, during the march after his capture on 7 September 1914: 'one of our comrades ... pushed by a German soldier, thinking it was a comrade who wanted to pass him out, pushed back automatically. He was shot immediately – the execution taking place before us.'[16] In Herstal, on 5–6 August 1914, ninety Belgian prisoners of war and civilians were shot.[17] At Aarschot, on 19 August over twenty captured Belgian soldiers were shot and their bodies thrown into a river.[18] At Ethe an unknown number of prisoners of war were killed on 23 August.[19] The most dramatic incident occurred at nearby Goméry the same day, when troops from the German Infantry Regiment 47, massacred approximately 150 wounded French soldiers at a large improvised dressing station, marked with the Red Cross.[20] The surrender of the improvised dressing station and all the wounded French soldiers in its vicinity had been accepted by a German lieutenant at 11 a.m. According to the French doctor, Sedillot, who carried out the surrender, the German lieutenant found all in order and left some soldiers to attend to the wounded and to destroy the French arms which had been handed over.[21] Shortly afterwards, however, a German NCO arrived who ordered all the medical staff shot and who set fire to the dressing station with the French wounded inside, believing that a shot had been fired from the building. Any wounded who tried to flee were brutally killed. Sedillot described the scene in his report:

The men tried to flee through the windows and the rear doors but they were forced back or fell as they were shot at. Others must have got further away because I heard cries of 'they are going to kill us'. These were futile attempts to escape ... The Germans cried 'here's another, here's another'.[22]

Badly injured, Dr Sedillot survived, hiding in a cellar surrounded by the corpses of the wounded soldiers he had tended. Finally, the following afternoon a German captain arrived and accepted Sedillot's surrender, although he insisted on executing several other wounded French soldiers and a French doctor as *franc-tireurs*. When Sedillot protested the German captain replied 'It is war (*Es ist Krieg*).'[23] Sedillot asked the French authorities that his report not be published for fear that the Germans might enact reprisals against prisoners of war still in their hands.[24]

[16] SHAT, 7 N 1187, Déclarations de prisonniers de guerre français évadés à la légation de France à la Haye, 1915–1916. Rapports d'évadés ou rapatriés transmis par Gouv. de Boulogne, Charles Dausque and Louis Vauchel statements.
[17] Horne and Kramer, *German Atrocities*, p. 14.   [18] *Ibid.*, p. 26.
[19] *Ibid.*, p. 59.   [20] *Ibid.*
[21] SHAT, 6 N 22, Rapport du Docteur Sedillot, aide-major de 1ère classe au 26me régiment d'artillerie, blessé le 23 août 1914, fait prisonnier le 24 et rapatrié par Pontarlier le 23 mars 1915.
[22] *Ibid.*   [23] *Ibid.*   [24] *Ibid.*

Similar incidents of prisoner killing were reported by British troops. In October 1914, Lieutenant R. D. Middleditch was captured wounded, as he was escorted on a stretcher by members of the Royal Army Medical Corps. The stretcher party walked into a large group of German soldiers. As medical personnel, the British stretcher bearers should have been treated as non-combatants. Following his return to Britain, Middleditch recounted in interview:

As everyone was unarmed Captain Winter [RAMC] surrendered. As far as I remember, an officer or an under-officer put a revolver at Captain Winter's head and the four stretcher-bearers were put up against a wall and shot stone dead. I myself was left lying in a field of cabbages and though I was in a semi-unconscious state I distinctly remember one of the stretcher-bearers saying 'My God! They're going to shoot us,' and I remember the sound of the shots. The reason given for this action was I believe that the English were using 'dum-dum' bullets. After this there was a lot of talking and an officer came up who could talk English and prevented the Germans from shooting Captain Winter.[25]

Prisoner killing thus clearly predated the onset of trench warfare – it was an initial German army response to the demands and fears of the invasion phase. Interviews with British officers captured in 1914, and repatriated later in the war, provide evidence that international law was not being kept by all German army units. One British officer prisoner was well treated when captured on 26 August 1914 but warned that, should any prisoner in his party escape, all the others would be shot.[26] Another officer prisoner reminded a German military doctor of the Geneva Convention, only to be told that 'he was not complying with the conventions'.[27] Captain R. W. Thomas of the Munster Fusiliers described his capture on 27 August 1914:

A number of German soldiers came through a gap in the hedge close to where I was lying; they were very angry and excited and I distinctly saw them bayoneting several wounded men. There was an angry crowd of them around Captain Rawlinson (also wounded) and myself and I believe they would also have bayoneted us but that an officer came up just in time to stop them.[28]

Significant variations in attitudes towards prisoner-taking clearly existed in 1914 in the German army. On occasion this extended to different units on the same battlefield, where one group of German soldiers administered the *coup de grâce* to wounded enemy, only for another group to follow and give

[25] TNA, WO 161/95, Interview no. 28, Lieutenant R. D. Middleditch.
[26] TNA, WO 161/95, Interview no. 25, Major E. H. Jones.
[27] TNA, WO 161/95, Interview no. 22, Captain H. O. Sutherland.
[28] TNA, WO 161/95, Interview no. 27, Captain R. W. Thomas.

medical assistance to any survivors they found.[29] The German army also reacted particularly harshly to any enemy soldiers found in hiding in forests or villages, having been cut off from the retreat of their armies prior to the battle of the Marne.[30] It ordered that those who did not give themselves up were to be shot as *franc-tireurs*. This order was carried out – one German lieutenant-colonel noted that at Cuy, on 19 September 1914, he had ordered the execution of several French cavalrymen found wearing civilian clothing.[31] Civilians who hid Allied soldiers or helped them escape faced the death penalty.[32] Some prisoners managed to escape back into unoccupied France, bringing with them information about these measures, again fuelling the association of capture with killing.[33] This association became widespread in 1914: the German Foreign Office learned from French prisoners that 'the absurd rumour has been deliberately spread through the French army that the Germans kill all their prisoners'.[34] German military leaders became concerned that this belief made the French reluctant to surrender and asked the Foreign Office to publish information in the Swiss papers that 'French prisoners of war are so well treated that many of them have openly stated that they are better cared for in German captivity than in their French garrison'.[35]

German sources support Allied accounts that a negative attitude towards prisoners was relatively common in the German army in 1914. Major Koebke serving in Artillerie-Regiment 3, noted in his diary on 20 November 1914:

The anger at the British was . . . enormous. Very few prisoners were taken according to statements from the front and where there was the occasional one he had nothing to smile about during his trip to the rear. It was the purest gauntlet run. Today I saw another three prisoners on the street . . . and heard the indignant calls to their guard: 'shame on you for taking prisoners!'[36]

[29] See, for example, the account of capture on 16.10.1914 at St Mihiel given by a repatriated French prisoner, Charles Hennebois: C. Hennebois, *Journal d'un Grand Blessé. Aux mains de l'Allemagne* (Paris, 1916), pp. 20–32.

[30] One particularly interesting case study on this subject is Ben Macintyre's, *A Foreign Field. A True Story of Love and Betrayal during the Great War* (London, 2001).

[31] HStA STUTT, M 660, Nachlass Gleich, Oberstleutnant Gerold von. Meine Erlebnisse im Feldzug 1914. III Teil: Die Verlängerung des rechten Heeresflügels, 19.9.1914, p. 8.

[32] Helen McPhail, *The Long Silence. Civilian Life under the German Occupation of Northern France, 1914–1918* (London and New York, 1999), p. 126.

[33] AN, F7.12936, Nord, Lille, Prefect to Minister of the Interior, 28.8.1914.

[34] AA, R 20880, Bd. 1, f. 43–54, Abschrift ZU.A.17845.14.

[35] AA, R 20880, Bd. 1, f. 43, Grosser Generalstab, Section IIIB, no. 5834, Geheim to AA, 18.8.1914.

[36] BA-MA, Militärgeschichtliche Sammlung 2/2361: Artillerie-Regiment 3. Kriegstagebuch des Majors a.D. Koebke. Bd. 1, Einleitung und Mobilmachung, Westl. Kriegsschauplatz, 1914.

A German medical officer noted: 'Again and again one hears that our people are not giving quarter any more and ruthlessly beat down everything which comes before their guns … Prisoners of war cost too much money and men as guards to be of advantage to Germany at the moment.'[37] These ambiguous attitudes among German officers towards prisoners were also shared by the Kaiser.[38] Wilhelm II, in his infamous 'Hun' speech, had told German soldiers sent to put down the Boxer rebellion in China 'to give no quarter to the Chinese'; in 1914, he made a similar statement to 'take no prisoners' to at least one assembly of troops going to France.[39]

Perhaps the best-documented incident of German prisoner killing was that of Major-General Stenger, who was eventually tried at the post-war war crimes trials held at Leipzig in 1921 for ordering in August 1914 that all French wounded found on the battlefield should be shot and no prisoners taken, in order to ensure that his advancing soldiers were not attacked from behind.[40] Stenger was acquitted at Leipzig, despite the fact that the French government had compiled overwhelming evidence that he had ordered his troops to give no quarter in Lorraine on 21 and 26 August 1914.[41] The French began collecting evidence against Stenger in 1914 – significantly they interviewed German prisoners of war from his regiment who had received his order.[42] The prisoners' evidence backed up the accusations of French witnesses. However, through their testimony, these German prisoners were effectively admitting that their units had been ordered to commit war crimes; for the French too the distinction between the prisoner of war and the war criminal was now blurring. Indicative of this shift was the fact that the first court martial of prisoners of war for crimes committed prior to capture took place in France on 2 October 1914, when three German prisoners were sentenced to imprisonment for pillage.[43]

It is important to state that the German army was not automatically shooting all military prisoners in 1914. Tens of thousands of British and French prisoners were sent to camps in Germany, and British interview evidence attests to many cases of wounded men being taken prisoner and treated humanely for their injuries.[44] The French High Command was

[37] HStA STUTT, M 660, Nachlass Generaloberarzt Dr. Max Erwin Wilhelm Flammer, Diary entry, 28.9.1914, p. 19.
[38] Hull, *Absolute Destruction*, pp. 119–26. See also the discussion in Horne and Kramer, *German Atrocities*, pp. 148–9.
[39] Willis, *Prologue to Nuremberg*, pp. 9, 13. See also Hull, *Absolute Destruction*, p. 29.
[40] SHAT, 6 N 23, Buat, copie, Mr le Président du Conseil, 1.5.1915, p. 6.
[41] Horne and Kramer, *German Atrocities*, p. 194.   [42] *Ibid.*
[43] Willis, *Prologue to Nuremberg*, p. 13.
[44] See TNA, WO 161/95 interviews and WO 161/96.

even beginning to panic that its troops were surrendering too easily, issuing an order on 28 November 1914 that 'any military individual taken prisoner <u>unwounded</u> will be the subject of an inquiry upon his return from captivity to establish if there is a case for him to be court-martialled, for either desertion or for abandoning his post in the face of the enemy or if any other disciplinary sanctions should be taken.'[45] Clearly, despite the widespread discourse on German prisoner killing, many French soldiers on the ground still believed it safe to surrender – evidence that it remained a minority of German units, albeit a significant one, that gave no quarter. However, the available evidence does suggest that there were more cases of deliberate prisoner killing in the German army than in the British or French armies in 1914.

Overall, what this analysis shows is that from the very outset of the war, capture in all three armies became intimately associated with atrocity. The prisoner killing that occurred in 1914 radicalised popular representations of battlefield violence against prisoners of war and lowered expectations of good prisoner treatment. The real shootings of prisoners which occurred on the battlefield in 1914 rapidly mutated into exaggerated representations of violence and death. One illustration of this is the widespread rumour that the Germans had tortured and crucified a captured Canadian soldier, which swept through the trenches in April 1915.[46] Despite an investigation by the Canadian Judge Advocate General's Office, no substantive evidence for the crucifixion account ever emerged.[47] However, the rumour illustrates the extent to which, in all armies, by 1915, capture and violent atrocity had become inextricably associated with each other.

A key corollary of this process was that the enemy captive increasingly became negatively associated with atrocity. In Britain and France, a widespread belief in enemy cruelties meant that the German prisoner of war was increasingly depicted as a perpetrator of war crimes, as illustrated in Figures 4, 5 and 6. In Figure 4 a German prisoner muses upon how a visiting Frenchwoman reminds him of her compatriot who, the caption strongly implies, was raped and executed by him and his comrades. The message from the picture is clear – kindness to prisoners is unacceptable because of the crimes they may have committed prior to capture.

---

[45] SHAT, 7 N 143, Dossier 1, Le Ministre de la Guerre, Circular no. 5437 to M. M. les Gouverneurs Militaires de Paris et de Lyon; Les Généraux Commandant les régions; le Général Commandant les forces de terre et de mer de l'Afrique du nord; le Général, Commissaire Résident Général de France au Maroc, Commandant en Chef, 16.12.1914. Underlining in original.

[46] Ponsonby, *Falsehood in Wartime*, pp. 91–3; James Hayward, *Myths and Legends of the First World War* (Stroud, 2002), pp. 101–11.

[47] *Ibid.*

Figure 4. D. Widhopff, 'Remorse. How pretty she is, this little Frenchwoman and how she resembles the woman that we shot in the trenches ... after.' Bibliothèque de Documentation Internationale Contemporaine et Musée d'Histoire Contemporaine (BDIC-MHC, Les Invalides), Or 2059.

Such public attitudes became widespread; after the war, the British writer Vera Brittain recalled her concern when she was sent to nurse German prisoners at Étaples in 1917:

Before the war I had never been in Germany and had hardly met any Germans ... So it was somewhat disconcerting to be pitch-forked, all alone ... into the midst of thirty representatives of the nation, which, as I had repeatedly been told, had crucified Canadians, cut off the hands of babies and subjected pure and stainless females to unmentionable 'atrocities'. I didn't think I had really believed all those

Figure 5. Jean-Louis Forain (1852–1931), 'Childhood Memories (the Prisoners Passing), "Tell me Mummy! ... Is it those men there who killed Daddy?"' *Le Figaro*, 23.11.1916.

Figure 6. Adolphe Willette, '... You're not afraid Tropmann?' Caricature from October 1914.

stories but I wasn't quite sure. I half expected that one or two of the patients would get out of bed and try to rape me, but I soon discovered that none of them was in a position to rape anybody ... at least a third of the men were dying.[48]

[48] Vera Brittain, *Testament of Youth. An Autobiographical Study of the Years 1900–1925* (London, 1978 [1933]), p. 374.

The message that German prisoners of war were perpetrators of violence was reinforced in images such as that in Figure 5.

Another example is provided in Figure 6, a 1914 cartoon, where the German prisoner is revealed to have cut the hands off civilian victims before finally being captured by the Allies. Significantly, this image depicts the Allied soldiers about to execute their captive who is being provided with a blindfold. The prisoner is asked if he is afraid to die and replies 'no! But before dying I would have liked to have seen Carcassonne!' The inference is that Germany intends to conquer all of France. The severed hands are used in the image to designate the German prisoner as barbarian.[49] In this illustration it is the protectors of 'civilisation' and not the Germans who are preparing to shoot a prisoner. The implication was that German prisoners were perpetrators of war crimes and, as such, their execution was lawful.

Such representations of the prisoner as perpetrator clearly marked a significant degeneration in the status of the captive. The cognitive association of the prisoner with enemy war crimes also encouraged real retaliation by Allied troops against German prisoners: Sir John French, Commander-in-Chief of the British Expeditionary Force, wrote shortly after the Bryce Report was published that the 'outrages' committed by the Germans had angered his troops to the extent that they were taking very few prisoners.[50] Indeed in the whole of 1915, the British army took only 6,372 Germans prisoner, while the French, on their much longer stretch of front, took 49,588.[51] In the French army too, atrocity stories were used to legitimise prisoner killing in 1915, as illustrated in a French soldier's letter:

In this sector we do not take prisoners, neither does the other side. We shoot in the trenches all those found with pared down bullets on them, that is to say all, and they shoot all our men who have velvet trousers, even those covered in blue overalls, on the pretext that they are *franc-tireurs*. So prisoners are rare; they do not dare to come over to surrender.[52]

---

[49] This image is reproduced in Horne and Kramer, *German Atrocities*, p. 209. Carcassonne was the location of a French prisoner of war camp for German officers. On Adolphe Willette see Jean-Pierre Auclert, *La Grande Guerre des crayons. Les noirs dessins de la propagande en 1914–1918* (Paris, 1981), p. 58. Another example of the German prisoner of war as perpetrator of war crimes is given in *ibid.*, p. 56, where a wounded German prisoner is shown about to knife the French military doctor caring for him.

[50] Read, *Atrocity Propaganda, 1914–1919*, p. 7.

[51] War Office, *Statistics of the Military Effort*, p. 632. SHAT, 16 N 525, Dossier no. 2, Prisonniers de Guerre, États numériques 1915, mars–1917, novembre.

[52] SHAT, 6 N 23, Fonds Buat, Correspondance août 1914–octobre 1915, Mai 1915, note, author's name not given.

The association of capture with atrocity had become widespread; the real scale of prisoner killing impossible to ascertain.[53] As the war went on, the French established 'mopping-up' units known as *nettoyeurs des tranchées*, whose task was to kill German wounded left lying on the battlefield during French advances, an aspect of combatant violence that Annette Becker and Stéphane Audoin-Rouzeau describe as one of the most taboo subjects of the conflict.[54] By 1916, some units of the British army received orders not to take prisoners during the battle of the Somme.[55] Such Allied prisoner killing remained a highly ambiguous action; although it occurred in the heat of battle throughout the war, it never gained official military approval and public opinion remained deeply ambivalent towards those who committed such acts, as Figure 7, by a French artist entitled 'Thoughtless murderer. A French soldier who has just killed a German prisoner', reveals.

While the association of the prisoner of war with the perpetration of war crimes may have helped legitimise prisoner killing on the battlefield, it also led to an escalation in prisoner reprisals. The actions of the British Admiralty offer perhaps the best example of the powerful impact which the image of the German prisoner of war as perpetrator had on prisoner treatment in 1914 and 1915. Within a year of the beginning of the war, the British Admiralty was in favour of abandoning the existing regulations which protected enemy prisoners from violence. First Sea Lord John Fisher threatened to resign if the government did not agree to shoot German prisoners of war in reprisal for zeppelin attacks on Britain.[56] An official Admiralty reprisal policy against prisoners soon followed, when, angered by German U-boat attacks on British shipping, Winston Churchill, the First Lord of the Admiralty, decided to treat all captured U-boat crews as war criminals. The Board of Admiralty announced on 8 March 1915 that thirty-nine German submarine crew captured on the U-8 and U-12 would be specially confined in naval detention barracks rather than in prisoner of war camps.[57] Their trial, however, would await the end of the war. Although symbolically segregated as war criminals, the submarine prisoners were not treated particularly badly. An American inspection which interviewed the most senior German officer among these prisoners out of earshot of the guards, was told

---

[53] See the discussion on prisoner killing in Prost, 'Les limites de la brutalisation', pp. 5–20.
[54] Audoin-Rouzeau and Becker, *14–18. Retrouver la Guerre*, pp. 54–6. On the role of *nettoyeurs* see Prost, 'Les limites de la brutalisation', p. 13.
[55] Ferguson, *The Pity of War*, p. 384.
[56] Martin Gilbert, *Churchill. A Life* (London, 2000), p. 296.
[57] Willis, *Prologue to Nuremberg*, pp. 17–22.

Figure 7. Pierre Gérbaud, 'Thoughtless murderer. A French soldier who has just killed a German prisoner.' Bibliothèque de Documentation Internationale Contemporaine et Musée d'Histoire Contemporaine (BDIC-MHC, Les Invalides), Or 1233.

that he had absolutely no complaints to make as to their actual treatment. He did, however, protest that their internment in the Detention Barracks was not worthy of prisoners of war. Apart from this he had no further complaint to make.[58]

---

[58] The House of Lords Record Office (HLRO), Bonar Law Papers, BL/50/3/45, Report of an inspection by Grafton Minot from the American Embassy in Berlin, 1.5.1915.

Conditions at Chatham, where these men were held, were far from spartan. Facilities for the twenty-nine U-boat crew held there included a gymnasium, a covered recreation room, an officers' smoking room, an officers' mess room, a schoolroom, a chapel, and indoor and outdoor recreation areas.[59]

On the German side, the British segregation of U-boat crews provoked an escalatory reaction which was also more symbolic than violent. On 20 March 1915, Germany announced reprisals: thirty-nine British prisoners of war from distinguished British families, including a close relative of Grey, the son of a former British Ambassador to Germany, and a variety of other young scions of aristocratic families, were sent to military and ordinary German prisons.[60] They were then encouraged to write home to describe their harsh treatment. However, these reprisals were relatively mild. An American inspector wrote: 'They are not in solitary confinement but are allowed several hours a day together. The rooms seem clean and the food far from bad. Of course it is severe discipline but not half as bad as even I feared.'[61]

The German reprisal worked. Pressure mounted for the Admiralty to change policy – on 27 April and 5 May 1915, there were major debates in the House of Commons on the German treatment of British prisoners of war. When the Conservatives joined the new British coalition government of National Unity, Churchill's was one of the first scalps they demanded. He was replaced at the Admiralty by the Conservative Sir Arthur Balfour, who immediately announced that all U-boat crews would receive treatment 'absolutely identical' to other prisoners of war.[62] However, behind the scenes, the Admiralty and the War Office agreed in June 1915 that submarine prisoners would be kept undisclosed in naval custody for an initial period after capture before being sent to official War Office prisoner of war camps once the Admiralty felt it had got all possible information from them. Moreover, they would be sent to camps 'where there are no

---

[59] The American inspector noted 'I was interested to observe that for the sake of courtesy, steps had been taken to the end that the British non-commissioned officers should come into as little communication as possible under the circumstances with either the crews or the officers. I noticed that in one detail this was accomplished by the fact that the recreation places were so arranged that it was not necessary for a guard to watch the men.' *Ibid*.

[60] *Ibid*. In July 1915, Germany attempted a similar reprisal action against France, segregating fifty French officers in a fortress. France threatened identical reprisals and the German action was called off. Cahen-Salvador, *Les Prisonniers de guerre*, pp. 49–50.

[61] HLRO, Bonar Law Papers, BL/50/3/45, Letter from Grafton Minot, American Embassy Berlin to Mrs Graham Watson, 14.5.1915.

[62] Willis, *Prologue to Nuremberg*, p. 21.

prisoners likely to be repatriated'.[63] However, among the general public and most Liberal Party politicians, Churchill's prisoner policy was generally seen as a debacle. It had totally destroyed any public confidence in prisoner reprisals, making British politicians highly reluctant to use them later in the war; indeed, Britain almost completely avoided using reprisals after 1915 and those sanctions it did later consider imposing on German prisoners were extremely mild.[64] For British public opinion, in 1915, the association of the German prisoner of war with enemy war crimes was not enough to justify reprisals that risked British prisoners' well-being; indeed for some commentators in the reprisals debate the submarine prisoners could not even be considered as the perpetrators of war crimes. As one former naval commander wrote in 1915: 'the action of the German submarine officers cannot be classified as espionage or as a war crime'; reprisals were likely to be 'denounced as methods of barbarism' and prove counterproductive.[65] The Director of the Department of Prisoners of War at the War Office viewed reprisals as un-British: 'our national characteristics are opposed to the ill-treatment of a man who has no power to resist and this especially in the case of one who is not personally responsible for the acts complained of'.[66]

Yet although the Admiralty reprisals were short-lived, feelings towards German submarine crew prisoners ran high in the British navy in 1915 and some British naval officers even refused to take German submarine crews prisoner. The most famous example occurred when the Captain of HMS *Baralong* ordered the shooting of the surviving crew of a German U-boat who were awaiting rescue after the *Baralong* sank their submarine, seventy miles south of Queenstown (Cobh) in August 1915.[67] One American witness on a nearby cargo ship, twenty-two-year-old J. M. Garrett, stated upon his return to America:

I hope never to see or hear of again a scene like I witnessed when the naked Germans in the water and hanging to ropes on the side of the Nicosian and the officer were

---

[63] TNA, ADM 1/8446/15, Procedure to be adopted regarding prisoners of war captured from enemy submarines, NID, 8395.

[64] TNA, CAB 24/63, 'Summary of reprisals taken by the British and German governments since the start of the war', 12/9/1918. See also TNA, FO 369/1450, Maj. Gen. Sir Herbert Belfield, 'Report on Directorate of Prisoners of War', September 1920, pp. 57–8.

[65] Graham Bower, 'The Laws of War. Prisoners of War and Reprisals', in *Problems of the War*, vol. I: *British Institute of International and Comparative Law. Papers Read before the Society in the Year 1915* (Oxford, 1915), pp. 24, 31.

[66] TNA, FO 369/1450, Maj. Gen. Sir Herbert Belfield, 'Report on Directorate of Prisoners of War', September 1920, pp. 57–8.

[67] BHStA IV, M Kr 14127, Mob 9. Verletzungen d. Kriegsrechts, Auswärtiges Amt, Der Baralong Fall, Copy sent to bayer. Militär. Bevollm. Empf. 20.8.16, Copy of legal statement, J. M. Garrett, 5.10.1915.

murdered. We were instructed by British members of the crew not to say anything about how the Germans were killed who escaped from the submarine.[68]

Germany immediately publicised the *Baralong* incident, embarrassing the British government, which, alarmed by the adverse propaganda fall-out, denied any shootings had occurred, even publishing a pamphlet, entitled *Does the British Navy Take Prisoners?* to reassure the British public and remind them of German war crimes.[69] Ultimately, the overall analysis of naval reprisals policy in 1915 shows that the British public rejected any violent mistreatment of prisoners, seeing it as damaging to Britain's reputation, thereby halting any further radicalisation. However, the Admiralty's actions clearly highlight how the elision of the categories of German prisoner of war and war crimes perpetrator had occurred amongst some key groups within the British establishment, encouraging a more negative view of the captive.

Case study 2: violent representations and the German prison camp in 1915

The increasing association of the prisoner of war with extreme violence, evident in the radicalised portrayal of battlefield capture that emerged at the outset of the war, was also reinforced in Britain and France by the depiction of the German prisoner of war camp, which, in 1914–15, became identified with the transgression of violent norms. As with the battlefield, mistreatment of the prisoner of war in the prison camp came to be framed in the language of extreme atrocity, illustrating the ongoing redefinition in wartime of what constituted an atrocity against captives. This occurred even when the prison camp mistreatment concerned, such as beatings or corporal punishment, did not actually mark a major break with traditional forms of violence against captives that had occurred in previous wars – or even necessarily differ much from corporal punishments permitted in the captive's own home army. Again these depictions linking the prisoner of war and violence developed because of incidents of real abuses which became widely publicised. Reports of beatings in German camps were common in 1915, as the historian Uta Hinz has shown.[70] This reflected the fact that prisoners were subject to the military law of the captor nation and German military law permitted a wide range of corporal punishments. The head of the

---

[68] *Ibid.*

[69] Anonymous, *Does the British Navy Take Prisoners?* (London, n.d. [1916]). Even the post-war British film *The Battles of the Coronel and Falkland Islands* (made in 1927, directed by Walter Summers, produced with Admiralty assistance) implicitly referred to this question of naval treatment of prisoners, emphasising British ships rescuing all surviving Germans from the water after battle, and even saving the German mascot – a dachshund – from a watery grave. The film was made in conjunction with the British Admiralty, the Navy League and an Advisory Committee. The specific depiction of the British navy's treatment of prisoners of war should not be seen as coincidental.

[70] See Hinz, *Gefangen im Großen Krieg*, pp. 84, 158–9.

British Prisoner of War Department at the War Office, Lieutenant-General Sir Herbert Belfield, felt that the German military code was to blame for the infliction of heavy punishments for 'seemingly trivial offences' on prisoners.[71] For example, the punishment of tying a prisoner to a post for hours was permitted in German military law in 1915; it was only removed as a punishment in May 1917.[72] Depictions of this punishment were frequently reproduced in Allied propaganda and became an iconic symbol of British and French prisoners' suffering.

For Uta Hinz, prisoner beating was particularly prevalent in Germany in 1914–15 because guards needed to control large numbers of enemy prisoners in improvised camps without adequate clear instructions as to what disciplinary punishments were permitted.[73] However, the mobilisation of prisoner labour in 1915 also played a role: as Germany mobilised its prisoner labour force for the wartime economy in 1915, prisoners were sent to live in improvised camps near factories and mines; by August 1916, 86 per cent of prisoners held in the XIIIth Armeekorps area were working outside their camps.[74] For both civilian and military overseers, violence served as a means of making captives work. As Paul Reusch, the Director of the *Gutehoffnungshütte Aktiengesellschaft* in Oberhausen, wrote, the employment of prisoners of war would be impossible if one stuck to the instructions given by the Ministry for War:

We are in the position that we do what we consider necessary. Therefore, if a prisoner will not comply, we let him go hungry for two to three days without seeking any further instructions. This occurs with the silent approval of the military administration. It is naturally a breach of the Hague Agreement. The military administration is, however, delighted when we can enforce a little order onto the men in this way.[75]

Another commentator, Ernst von Borsig, reported on the treatment of British prisoners of war in Berlin:

There seems to have been quite violent scenes here. The *Landsturm* men who deal with these people [prisoners], amused themselves with the British in silent little rooms. What happened in there I do not officially know; I only know of it privately and cannot give any further information about it.[76]

---

[71] Belfield, 'The Treatment of Prisoners of War', p. 140.
[72] Hinz, *Gefangen im Großen Krieg*, pp. 163–4.   [73] *Ibid.*, p. 160.   [74] *Ibid.*, p. 128.
[75] Jens Thiel, *'Menschenbassin Belgien'. Anwerbung, Deportation und Zwangsarbeit im Ersten Weltkrieg* (Essen, 2007), p. 68, fn 60.
[76] *Ibid.*

During the early phase of the war, British NCOs were key in instigating collective prisoner refusals to perform particular tasks, out of a desire not to help the German war effort. Such strikes were violently crushed. Private Frank Byrne from Dublin reported how 'about 500 men were sent at various times from Limburg to work in a foundry at Husten. Men returning from Husten reported that any prisoner refusing to work (filling blast furnaces) was locked up for three days without food and severely flogged.'[77] The use of violence to force prisoners to work was widespread, ruthless and involved cooperation between civilian managers and prison guards.

Former prisoners, who had escaped or been exchanged, described frequent beatings in German captivity. The accounts of escaped French prisoners who arrived in the Netherlands in 1915 were almost unanimous that prisoners were very badly fed in Germany and frequently hit by their guards. One escaped prisoner, Gendarme Grangeot, described the frequent beating of Russian captives.[78] Louis Lennaitre, captured at Maubeuge, reported being treated 'with brutality and very badly fed' at Sennelager camp.[79] Jean-Celestin Rabasteus reported 'like all my comrades I was badly fed and mistreated every time I refused to work'.[80] Arthur Guillot, captured on 22 August 1914, reported being 'very badly fed at Meschede camp and very badly treated everywhere'.[81] The prisoners received only barley soup in the mornings, soup in the evenings with a small portion of fish, and lunch was a very weak carrot stew along with 250 grams of bread which contained potato. When the prisoners refused to work in a mine they were forced to comply by sentinels with bayonets.[82] Lucien Roussel stated that at Quedlinburg camp there was 'insufficient food and bad, bad treatment [beatings, tied to posts, being hit with rifle butts etc.]'.[83]

These accounts are revealing. Escapers from different locations in Germany were reporting the same pattern of experiences: hunger and

---

[77] TNA, WO 161/99, no. 871, Private Frank Byrne.

[78] SHAT, 7 N 1187, Déclarations de prisonniers de guerre français évadés à la légation de France à la Haye, 1915–1916, Rapports d'évadés ou rapatriés transmis par Gouv. de Boulogne, Boulogne, 1.11.1915. Région du nord, Gendarmerie, Détachement de Boulogne sur mer, Reseignements recueillis à l'interrogatoire du Gendarme Grangeot évadé d'allemagne [sic] où il était prisonnier de guerre. Grangeot was captured wounded on 25.9.1914 and escaped 17.10.1915. There are a considerable number of interviews in this box which outline the same pattern of hunger and beatings.

[79] *Ibid.*, Louis Lennaitre.   [80] *Ibid.*, Jean-Celestin Rabasteus.

[81] *Ibid.*, Arthur Guillot. Another prisoner, Ernest Nicaulaud described how at Meschede in 1915 he suffered 'terrible hunger ... The food was bad to the extent that many comrades died of hunger. Things dreadful.' *Ibid.*, Ernest Nicaulaud.

[82] *Ibid.*   [83] *Ibid.*, Lucien Roussel.

beatings. One 1915 censor report noted that French prisoners had taken to signing their letters with synonyms for hunger: '*Créban de Fan, San Car ni Pan, Lasaoutan*'.[84] These were all slang among French soldiers for '*nous crèvons de faim*' (we are dying of hunger).[85] Hunger, in 1915, occurred because the system of supplying prisoners with parcels from home had not yet properly developed because of the time it took Germany to provide lists and camp addresses of all those captured in 1914. However, the prisoners' hunger also crucially reveals, as Uta Hinz has argued, that Germany had already decided in early 1915 to provide prisoners with an inadequate ration in order to husband food for its own army and population in the light of the British blockade.[86]

The beatings reported by the French escapers matched those reported by British prisoners, who were also physically abused. Private William Beeby reported how at Gießen camp: 'The discipline was so strict that it caused the guards to be rather rough at times. Some of the prisoners were slightly bayoneted on occasion.'[87] Ex-prisoner Private Frank Byrne reported: 'Men were frequently tied up for two hours to posts and deprived of their dinner. The English were treated worse than the French, but the Russians even worse than the English. The Russians were flogged for instance in a way in which no others were.'[88] Another British prisoner, Private William Woodward, reported that as a punishment for not washing their hands after going to the latrine prisoners were tied to a post for two hours a day and that 'several men fainted after being cut down from the post as they were tied up so that just the tips of the toes touched the ground'.[89] Figure 8, by an ex-prisoner, provides a visual depiction of the brutality of beatings in Germany, highlighting the deliberate humiliation of the captive, who is stripped naked from the waist down.[90]

Such testimony by former prisoners fuelled a highly negative impression of German captivity as violent in Britain and France; it also provided the Allies with a major propaganda advantage, as Germany was unable to effectively deny ex-prisoners' accounts of frequent beatings. German

---

[84] SHAT, 5 N 556, Cabinet du Ministre, Bureau des Informations Militaires, 1915–1919, Le Lieutenant Baron du dépôt des prisonniers de guerre de Montauban à Monsieur le Chef d'escadron Marguier, Commandant le dit dépôt, 2.3.1915. p. 19.
[85] *Ibid.*   [86] Hinz, *Gefangen im Großen Krieg*, pp. 214, 246–7.
[87] TNA, WO 161/99, Interview no. 862, Private William Charles Beeby.
[88] *Ibid.*, no. 871, Private Frank Byrne.   [89] *Ibid.*, no. 866, Private William John Woodward.
[90] See for example Parliamentary Paper, Cd. 8480, *Correspondence Respecting the Use of Police Dogs in Prisoners' Camps in Germany*, misc. no. 9, 1917 (London, 1917). See also the discussion on the British and French protests regarding harsh German prisoner discipline, in Hinz, *Gefangen im Großen Krieg*, p. 156. Figures 8 and 9 are reproduced by kind permission of Odon Abbal.

Figure 8. Jean-Pierre Laurens, 'La Schlague [The Beating]' from *Prisonniers de guerre. Cahier à la mémoire des compagnons de captivité du camp de Wittenberg* (Paris, 1918).

propaganda was also at a disadvantage on this issue of prisoner mistreatment because similar reports of beatings did not emerge on this scale regarding home front camps in Britain and France in 1915. This contrast may possibly be explained by different military cultures, as well as the fact that, in 1915, the British and French had barely begun to use prisoner labour; in contast, prisoners in Germany were already being substantially integrated into the war economy, a process which increased violence, as a means of making captives work.

The surviving sources indicate that complaints by German prisoners held by Britain in the early phase of the war largely related to minor issues. One German prisoner complained that 'the treatment was generally orderly but here and there, there would be the odd officer who would hassle us, for example, leaving us to stand for a long time in the rain while waiting for our pay'.[91] Another ex-prisoner complained about the inadequate accommodation at Horsham in 1914:

Here, I was disgracefully accommodated upon a damp field fenced off with barbed wire ... We had to sleep four men to a tent upon the damp floorboards without anything under us. For a cover we had only a thin woollen blanket. After a few days

[91] BA-MA, PH2 / 588, f. 18, Nr. 600.16.ZVI, Kommandantur-Gericht, account by Kaufmann Albert Fruchtnicht.

we were brought to Dyffryn Aled in North Wales and put up in an old country house. The sanitary facilities were very bad at the start. There were only two faulty toilets for 70 people. The floor was not thick so that urine would leak down into the room below where the meals were taken.[92]

However an accusation of physical violence by guards did occur at Leigh camp, where an ex-prisoner, Otto Schlagk, stated that the guards had shot a prisoner around April–May 1915. The different parts of the camp in a former factory were closed at 9 p.m. and prisoners had to be in their own section by this time. One night, a German prisoner named Schmidt lingered too long in a neighbouring section and found the doors closed. In order to return to his own section he tried to climb the barbed wire. The British guards shot him and he died of his wounds.[93] The guards believed Schmidt was trying to escape. His comrades believed he had been illegally killed. Schlagk alleged that at Leigh camp on Fridays and Saturdays the guards were often drunk, as they were paid on Fridays and this made them annoy the prisoners. However, 'it never came to any physical abuse. The commandant was very concerned with discipline and was supported by the German N.C.O.s'.[94]

Similarly, for camps in the interior of France in 1915, there are relatively few accounts of prisoner beatings. Indeed, some of the evidence, albeit from an internal French source, points to a relaxed regime in certain camps. A postal censor's report on letters from German prisoners at Montauban camp on 2 March 1915 outlined that the captives were writing favourably of their captivity. He reported:

the prisoners are unanimous in declaring that the French guards are good to them. They had expected to be physically mistreated, in accordance with the norms established in the German army. They are very happy to find a milder, if firm, discipline, replace that which was based on being hit ... The expression '*sehr nett*' (very nice) occurs quite frequently in their correspondence.[95]

The prisoners were particularly content that they received coffee, tea and hot chocolate.[96] The one complaint was that the guards would not help the prisoners practise their French: 'they told us,' one prisoner wrote, 'that the people of the south of France were chatty. Well, they must have sent us soldiers from the north here because it is difficult to make them talk.'[97]

---

[92] *Ibid.*, f. 31, Nr. 367.4.18.Z.V.I. Friedrichsort 2.4.18 Ausgetauschte [sic] Marine-Assistenarzt der Reserve, Dr. Arno Kirsche von SMS 'Mainz'.
[93] *Ibid.*, f. 115, 12.12.1917, Nr. 1071.1.18.Z.V.I., Interview with Otto Schlagk.   [94] *Ibid.*
[95] SHAT, 5 N 556, Cabinet du Ministre, Bureau des Informations Militaires, 1915–1919, Le Lieutenant Baron du dépôt des prisonniers de guerre de Montauban à Monsieur le Chef d'escadron Marguier, Commandant le dit dépôt, 2.3.1915.
[96] *Ibid.*   [97] *Ibid.*

Another difficulty for the prisoners was that they were not accustomed to French food – eating white bread without butter was foreign to them. They wanted black bread and butter or fat to spread on it.[98]

Thus it appears that the relatively higher levels of violence in German camps in the early phase of the war reinforced the association of German captivity with mistreatment and atrocity in Allied countries.[99] Representations of violence against prisoners in German prison camps in 1914–15 were used by the Allies to provide moral justification for the conflict and to keep populations mobilised. Overall, the key trend which emerges from the examination of both the depiction of battlefield mistreatment of prisoners and prison camp beatings in 1914–15 is that during this key first year a belief that prisoner mistreatment was occurring developed into an *expectation* of atrocity in all three countries studied here.

Case study 3: the depiction of illness among prisoners of war

This expectation of atrocity becomes very clear if we analyse how belligerents reacted to reports of epidemics in prisoner of war camps. By 1915, violence against prisoners was expected of the enemy; even illness among prisoners of war came to be portrayed as a form of enemy atrocity, illustrating how the definitions of what constituted violent practice against prisoners of war were changing. How this occurred will be examined here, first in relation to a major typhus epidemic in German camps in spring 1915 and, second, in relation to sickness among German prisoners of war sent by France to North African camps in 1914 and 1915. These two incidents were pivotal in bringing about a further radicalisation of atrocity representations, as prisoner sickness came to be seen as an integral part of an overall wartime discourse on prisoner atrocities in Germany, France and Britain. Violence was increasingly broadly interpreted, to include extremes of negligence or the violation of a prisoner's right to bodily integrity – his right to special consideration once ill.

Typhus in German camps in 1915

The outbreak of a widespread typhus epidemic in German prisoner of war camps in 1915 has been largely overlooked by historians, with the

---

[98] *Ibid.*

[99] See the post-war discussion at the Grotius Society in 1919 describing the beating of British prisoners in German camps as widespread. Geo. G. Phillimore and Hugh H. L. Bellot, 'Treatment of Prisoners of War', *Transactions of the Grotius Society*, vol. V: *Problems of Peace and War* (1919), pp. 58, 47–64.

exception of two recent studies: Uta Hinz in her book *Gefangen im Großen Krieg. Kriegsgefangenschaft in Deutschland, 1914–1921* briefly discusses the epidemic in order to illustrate the poor hygiene conditions in the early prisoner of war camps.[100] Paul Weindling's study *Epidemics and Genocide in Eastern Europe, 1890–1945* mentions the 1915 typhus wave only cursorily; his main focus is upon how, following the discovery in 1909 that lice carried the illness, pre-war and interwar German public and military health campaigns against parasites came to define typhus as a 'threat from the East' and as a disease of 'racially inferior peoples'.[101] Weindling convincingly shows how this earlier association later contributed to the depiction of Jews, Slavs and Roma in Nazi propaganda as racially inferior 'lice carriers' who were to be eradicated. However, his book does not explore how the 1915 epidemic impacted upon the image of the prisoner of war in Germany, associating the prisoner with contagion. Thus how the 1915 epidemic was perceived in Germany, as well as its impact in France and Britain, remains largely unexplored.

In fact, the British and French governments rapidly defined the 1915 typhus outbreak within well-established paradigms of violent German war crimes against prisoners, rather than as an epidemiological threat from the east. This process was predicated upon broadening the definition of violence against prisoners in two key ways: first, the Allies portrayed extremes of negligence, such as poor sanitation, bad food, absence of clothing and overcrowding in German camps in 1915, as forms of contextual violence against the individual captive. Second, the Allied argument adopted the logic that violence could be understood in terms of the violation of a prisoner's right to health and entitlement to special care once ill. Within a prison camp system, where guards had the power of ultimate recourse to violence over their charges, a sick prisoner was particularly vulnerable, having no access to any assistance other than that provided or allowed by his captors. Typhus was thus depicted as another German atrocity. This is particularly clear if we examine the British response.

On 17 March 1915, Major W. B. Fry of the Royal Army Medical Corps (RAMC) died of typhus in a German prisoner of war camp at Wittenberg, one of three medics to succumb to the disease at Wittenberg camp that spring, out of a group of six RAMC doctors.[102] His death was well documented: the three surviving RAMC officers, Major Priestley, Captain Vidal

---

[100] Hinz, *Gefangen im Großen Krieg*, pp. 102–6.
[101] Paul Weindling, *Epidemics and Genocide in Eastern Europe, 1890–1945* (Oxford, 2000), pp. 15, 73–107.
[102] Commonwealth War Graves Commission, Details of graves registered at Berlin Southwestern Cemetery, Berlin, Brandenburg. Provided by Ms Erna Rodelez, Commonwealth War Graves Commission, Ieper.

and Captain Lauder, who had been at Wittenberg camp, were repatriated after the epidemic and provided accounts to the British authorities of how Fry died while treating British prisoners suffering from typhus; in addition, the location of his body and date of death were recorded by the Imperial War Graves Commission.[103] Fry's three colleagues' accounts of his death provided a graphic insight into the scale of the typhus epidemic in Wittenberg camp in 1915, and the British authorities lost no time in publishing this information in a parliamentary paper for propaganda purposes in April 1916. Citing from interviews with the repatriated men, the paper outlined appalling hygiene conditions during the epidemic, describing: 'delirious men waving arms brown to the elbow with faecal matter. The patients were alive with vermin.'[104] One doctor attempted 'to brush what he took to be an accumulation of dust from the folds of a patient's clothes and he discovered it to be a moving mass of lice'.[105] Yet beyond emotive descriptions of horrific sanitary conditions, the parliamentary paper specifically portrayed the Wittenberg epidemic as a German war crime.

This parliamentary paper revealed how seriously the British viewed the Wittenberg case. There were two central British accusations: first, that the German authorities, German medical staff and the chief German doctor, Dr Aschenbach, had abandoned the prisoners to their fate, deserting the camp once the typhus outbreak was confirmed, as the paper reported:

No communication was held between the prisoners and their guards except by means of directions shouted from the guards or officers remaining outside the wire entanglements of the camp. All supplies for the men were pushed into the camp over chutes ... No medical attention the whole time was provided by the German staff.[106]

The Germans were also accused of failing to provide appropriate medical care for the prisoners: bedpans, paper, dressings, mattresses and beds were not supplied for the sick. Second, the parliamentary paper claimed that the German authorities had been negligent in failing to prevent an epidemic, by not combating lice in the camp, where Russian, French and British prisoners mixed freely. For the British there was no debate: lice caused typhus and the German authorities had deliberately ignored the

---

[103] It should be noted that all the German references to the 1915 epidemic refer to *Fleckfieber*, which translates into English as typhus, an illness spread by lice. This should not be confused with '*Typhus*' in German, which refers to *Unterleibtyphus* or *Paratyphus*, which translates into English as typhoid.

[104] Parliamentary Paper, Cd. 8224, *Report by the Government Committee on the Treatment by the Enemy of British Prisoners of War Regarding the Conditions Obtaining at Wittenberg camp during the Typhus Epidemic of 1915* (London, 1916) (hereafter *RGCT*), Enclosure in no. 1, p. 5.

[105] *Ibid.*   [106] *Ibid.*

risk posed to prisoners' lives. The British RAMC survivors described between 250 and 300 cases of typhus among the British prisoners of whom sixty died, and alluded to a much higher death rate among the French and Russians.[107]

The evidence regarding Wittenberg was compelling. Although it was a camp for ordinary soldiers, the German authorities had moved a number of medical officer prisoners there, including the British RAMC officers, to combat the epidemic: under the 1906 Geneva Convention, Germany was entitled to retain captured enemy medical personnel as long as they were required to care for their own men who were sick or wounded prisoners of war.[108] This meant that there were medical witnesses present who could provide very accurate testimony regarding conditions: one French doctor, Georges Monvoisin, even wrote his post-war doctoral thesis on the epidemic, based on his notes, one of several French medical theses which were produced during the war on typhus in German prisoner of war camps.[109] Monvoisin substantiated the British accusations, stating that typhus was first diagnosed on 18 January 1915 and that the camp was quarantined. 'No German could come near. There was only a cordon of sentries located 50 to 100 metres from the perimeter. Orders were conveyed to us by telephone or shouted from a distance ... We were abandoned to our sad fate ...'[110] Monvoisin claimed that in total there were 3,500 cases of typhus among prisoners at Wittenberg camp during the epidemic and that of these 400 died.[111] He described 'an average death rate of 11%' which broke down to '4% for Russians' and '17 to 18%' for

---

[107] *RGCT*, p. 7. For an unofficial account of the epidemic at Wittenberg see the memoir by Arthur Green, *The Story of a Prisoner of War by No. 6646, 1st Somerset Light Infantry* (London, 1916).

[108] *RGCT*, p. 1, Enclosure in no. 1. The claim that prisoners were left to compatriot prisoner doctors tallies with other sources: Paul Weindling found that Russian prisoners with typhus were also left to be tended by Russian doctors in spring 1915. Weindling, *Epidemics and Genocide*, p. 80. On the Geneva Convention see *Le Régime des prisonniers de guerre en France et en Allemagne au regard des conventions internationales, 1914–1916*, p. 54.

[109] See Georges Monvoisin, *Le Typhus exanthématique, son traitement par les injections intraveineuses de sérum de convalescents, à propos de l'épidémie de typhus du camp de prisonniers de Wittemberg (1914–1915)* (Paris, 1919); Monvoisin's was not the only French medical study on the 1915 epidemic: Marie-Joseph Dautrey, 'Deux epidémies de typhus exanthématique dans les camps de prisonniers d'Allemagne, Langensalza et Cassel, 1915', doctoral thesis (Nancy, 1919). See also Gaston Timsit, *Contribution à l'étude de typhus exanthématique par la relation de cas observés au camp de prisonniers de guerre de Cassel* (Algiers, 1915); Georges Cazal-Gamelsy, *Une épidémie dans un camp de prisonniers, contribution à l'étude clinique du typhus exanthématique* (Toulouse, 1920).

[110] Monvoisin, *Le Typhus exanthématique*, p. 26. Note that the date that Monvoisin gives for the start of the epidemic differs from that given by German sources.

[111] *Ibid.*, p. 147.

French prisoners, but which reached 25–30% during March and April 1915.[112] Of the thirty-two doctors of all nationalities working in Wittenberg camp, Monvoisin states that twenty-one caught typhus and eight died.[113] Like the RAMC officers, Monvoisin stated that the lack of medical supplies, washing facilities and clean clothing was to blame for the epidemic, observing that it 'began in January at the point when the prisoners were covered in lice' and 'disappeared in June when the disinfection vats, finally obtained, began to function'.[114]

American embassy sources also support the British case. Refused access during the epidemic, the American inspector Lithgow Osborne finally visited the camp after the typhus outbreak had ended; his report was so critical that the American Ambassador, James W. Gerard, delayed its delivery to London and Berlin until he had had an opportunity to inspect Wittenberg himself.[115] In his memoirs, Gerard described Wittenberg as the worst camp he ever visited, believing that 'the prisoners there had been knocked about and beaten in a terrible manner by their guards'.[116] This claim also appeared in a second British parliamentary paper on Wittenberg, which published accusations by ex-prisoners that the German guards had beaten captives and used guard dogs against them; one prisoner claimed the sentries had set dogs upon sick prisoners seeking to use the latrines until the date when the guards fled the camp due to fear of typhus.[117] Physical violence by guards and the typhus epidemic were conflated in these accounts, the two German 'crimes' being presented as interchangeable.

These British accusations against Wittenberg proved a propaganda victory, leading them to issue an additional white book on typhus in the camp, as well as a separate parliamentary paper, published in October 1916, which accused the German authorities of negligence during a typhus epidemic at Gardelegen camp in spring 1915; again this was based on extracts from interviews with repatriated prisoners which described how the camp was placed in quarantine and the prisoners abandoned to their fate.[118] The parliamentary papers on Wittenberg and Gardelegen were subsequently translated into French, Spanish, Dutch and Swedish for readers in neutral countries, thus illustrating

---

[112] *Ibid.*, p. 101.   [113] *Ibid.*, p. 102.   [114] *Ibid.*, p. 56.

[115] James W. Gerard, *My Four Years in Germany* (London, 1918), pp. 117–20.   [116] *Ibid.*

[117] *Correspondence Respecting the Use of Police Dogs in Prisoners' Camps in Germany*, Cmd. 8480, p. 5.

[118] Parliamentary Paper, Cd. 8351, *Report on the Typhus Epidemic at Gardelegen by the Government Committee on the Treatment by the Enemy of British Prisoners of War during the Spring and Summer of 1915* (London, 1916); Speed, *Prisoners, Diplomats and the Great War*, p. 67.

once again the complex relationship between truth and propaganda during the First World War and the increasing association of captivity with atrocity in the first two years of the war.

A similar process occurred in France, where news of a typhus epidemic at Kassel-Niederzwehren camp in spring 1915 was used to stoke popular indignation against Germany; again the central accusation was that typhus was a German war crime:

The German doctors cannot have been ignorant of the French discoveries concerning the transmission of this illness by parasites and the ease with which an epidemic can be stopped by the simple disinfection of men and their belongings. Yet they let an epidemic develop which took on such proportions that thousands of men died in the above named camps ... One has to demand if from the outset they really desired to prevent the epidemic.[119]

An official French publication in 1916, described 'French soldiers with typhus, in agony' in overcrowded barracks, where 'the crowding was so great that ... the dying had to be disentangled, often soiled with their own faeces'.[120]

The imagery used to describe the typhus epidemic portrayed Germany as failing to fulfil one of the basic tenets of civilisation – nursing the sick. The British and French thus made a direct link with the imagery that had dominated in 1914, which had depicted the Germans as barbarians who shot dead French and British wounded on the battlefield.[121] In turn, extreme violence on the battlefield in 1915 was legitimised by this dehumanisation of Germans, which the repetitive depiction of prisoners abandoned to typhus reinforced. Significantly, there was no comparable outbreak of typhus in British or French camps during the 1914–18 war: typhus in prisoner of war camps was firmly established as a *German* war atrocity.

The notoriety of the Wittenberg, Gardelegen and Kassel cases was such that it tended to mask the extent of the typhus epidemic throughout the German camp system in 1915. Typhus broke out in thirty major German prisoner of war camps between January and July 1915, mostly located in north Germany.[122] In March 1915, when the epidemic peaked, some 11,862 British, French, Russian and Belgian prisoners had the disease according to post-war German estimates; in total, in the whole epidemic,

---

[119] Christmas, *Le Traitement des prisonniers français en Allemagne*, p. 11.
[120] *Le Régime des prisonniers de guerre en France et en Allemagne au regard des conventions internationales, 1914–1916*, p. 61.
[121] Horne and Kramer, *German Atrocities*, p. 14.
[122] August Gärtner, 'Einrichtung und Hygiene der Kriegsgefangenenlager', in Otto von Schjerning, ed., *Handbuch der ärztlichen Erfahrungen im Weltkriege 1914/18*, vol. VII: *Hygiene*, ed. Wilhelm Hofmann (Leipzig, 1922), p. 261.

Figure 9. Jean-Pierre Laurens, 'Typhus, Wittenberg, January–May 1915'. From *Prisonniers de guerre. Cahier a la mémoire des compagnons de captivité du camp de Wittenberg* (Paris, 1918).

some 44,732 prisoners of war in Germany caught typhus.[123] To place this in perspective, by June 1915, Germany had captured an estimated 848,556 prisoners.[124] At the very least, therefore, the overall infection rate among prisoners can be estimated at 5.27 per cent. In some camps the situation was clearly overwhelming: at Kottbus camp between January and May 1915, 6,509 prisoners out of 9,400 fell ill.[125]

The scale of the epidemic and the fact that it occurred at roughly the same time as a major typhus outbreak in Serbia between January and April 1915, which cost over 200,000 civilian lives in six months, led the German authorities to opt for strict quarantine measures to prevent typhus spreading from prisoner of war camps to German civilians.[126] Typhus was a real problem in prisoner of war camps in eastern Europe in 1915: the German epidemic paralleled one in Austria-Hungary, where mortality rates were often very high: for example, in Mauthausen camp in January 1915, up to 186 prisoners a day died of typhus.[127] Serious epidemics also broke out in

---

[123] *Ibid.*, p. 260.   [124] Doegen, *Kriegsgefangene Völker*, pp. 28–9.
[125] Gärtner, 'Einrichtung', p. 261.
[126] Weindling, *Epidemics and Genocide*, pp. 76–80; Monvoisin, *Le Typhus exanthématique*, p. 37.
[127] Hannes Leidinger and Verena Moritz, 'Verwaltete Massen. Kriegsgefangene in der Donaumonarchie 1914–1918', in Oltmer, ed., *Kriegsgefangene im Europa des Ersten Weltkriegs*, pp. 35–6.

Table 3. *Location and dates of typhus epidemics in German prisoner of war camps in 1915.*

NAME OF CAMP	START OF EPIDEMIC	END OF EPIDEMIC
Altdamm	1.6	17.7
Bergerdamm	30.1	9.2
Brandenburg a.H.	8.1	9.6
Bütow	4.4	7.6
Czersk	8.3	1.8
Danzig-Troyl	30.3	21.8
Erfurt	9.3	21.4
Frankfurt a. O.	9.1	11.6
Gardelegen	26.2	21.7
Görlitz	6.5	6.8
Guben	8.2	11.3
Halbe	24.2	23.8
Hammerstein	7.4	8.7
Heilsberg	30.6	–
Heuberg	5.3	14.5
Kassel	20.2	3.10
Kottbus	15.1	24.5
Lamsdorf	1.3	13.8
Langensalza	16.2	15.7
Lügumkloster	20.5	30.8
Ohrdruf	9.2	29.7
Rastatt	1.6	18.9
Sagan	8.2	10.6
Schneidemühl	4.1	13.9
Soltau	1.7.	12.8
Stargard i.P.	12.1	25.4
Stralkowo	12.4	24.9
Witttenberg	16.1	23.7
Zerbst	5.3	16.4
Zossen	4.3	20.5

Note: Taken from August Gärtner, 'Einrichtung und Hygiene der Kriegsgefangenenlager', in Wilhelm Hoffmann, ed., *Handbuch der ärztlichen Erfahrungen im Weltkriege 1914/18*, vol. VII (Leipzig, 1922), p. 261.

Russian camps in 1915; there was a particularly high death rate from typhus at Tockoe camp in winter 1915–16.[128] The absolute segregation

[128] Reinhard Nachtigal, 'Seuchen unter militärischer Aufsicht in Rußland. Das Lager Tockoe als Beispiel für die Behandlung der Kriegsgefangenen 1915/16', *Jahrbücher für Geschichte Osteuropas*, 48 (2000), pp. 363–87; Reinhard Nachtigal, 'Seuchenbekämpfung als Probleme der russischen Staatsverwaltung. Prinz Alexander von Oldenburg und die

of the prisoners – and in some cases such as Wittenberg, the German abandonment of the camp inmates to total seclusion – was seen as logical in this context.

The association of the foreign captive with disease thus became the norm in Germany in 1915. In February 1915, a German girl, Piete Kuhr, who tried to approach Schneidemühl prisoner of war camp, was chased away by a guard who told her no one could go near the camp because of illness there.[129] A British ex-prisoner from Schneidemühl camp described how:

About February 1915 typhus swept over the camp; nearly all the camp was down with it. There were 2,000 deaths in a couple of months but the English only lost about 22 of their number. The men died so fast that they could not bury them properly; they were laid in trenches in deal boxes blackened with tar. On the average there would be about 20 deaths in the morning and the same number in the afternoon. There was no identification or notification of the deaths to the men's friends. You could die and your own comrade would not know you were dead. When the men fell sick they were carried, bed and blankets and all and put down on the floor in some huts which were wired off and left to die or recover … No German doctors came.[130]

An exchanged British prisoner related similar mass typhus deaths at Langensalza camp 'due to the verminous state of the camp' in 1915, while a German army doctor described being given the command of medical personnel in a prisoner of war camp in 1915 as a 'death sentence'.[131]

As a result of the typhus epidemic, in Germany prisoner of war camps became associated with contagion and death. In the pre-antibiotic era the mortality rate for typhus was usually around 20 per cent.[132] This matches that given in the German post-war medical history of the war for French prisoners (21.55 per cent). The Russian prisoner death rate was lower (7.46 per cent) as Russians apparently had a level of immunity from childhood to the disease.[133] However, the total number of deaths remains unclear. If we consider the case of Kassel-Niederzwehren camp the difficulty in ascertaining exact death rates becomes evident. August Gärtner writing in the German medical history of the war cited only 803 prisoner

Kriegsgefangenen der Mittelmächte', *Medizinhistorisches Journal*, 39 (2004), pp. 135–63; Reinhard Nachtigal, *Kriegsgefangenschaft an der Ostfront, 1914–1918* (Frankfurt am Main, 2005), p. 72.

[129] Mihaly, *'Da gibt's ein Wiedersehn'*, pp. 142–3.

[130] TNA, WO 161/99, no. 1092, Interview with Private J. McGinlay.

[131] TNA, WO 161/98, no. 288, on Langensalza; Karl-Heinz Leven, *Die Geschichte der Infektionskrankheiten. Von der Antike bis ins 20. Jahrhundert* (Landsberg/Lech, 1997), p. 133.

[132] *Ibid.*   [133] Gärtner, 'Einrichtung', p. 262.

deaths of all nationalities at Kassel-Niederzwehren during the epidemic.[134] Gärtner was in a position to know the correct figures – he was called in from Jena specifically to deal with the epidemic in Kassel in 1915.[135] Yet other witnesses disagreed: a French doctor repatriated from Kassel-Niederzwehren claimed that 2,300 prisoners had died during the epidemic there: 1,600 French and 700 Russians.[136] The headstone on the mass grave at the camp records 2,000 Russian dead without specifying in what year they died.[137] Finally, the post-war German investigation into the Kassel-Niederzwehren case found that 1,280 prisoners of war had succumbed to typhus.[138]

The discrepancy between the available figures in the case of Kassel reveals the unreliability of the death statistics in post-war official publications: the official post-war account of prisoner treatment published by Wilhelm Doegen in conjunction with the Ministry of the Reichswehr stated that in total during the whole war only 2,895 Russian prisoners died of typhus.[139] August Gärtner reported that throughout Germany 4,248 prisoners of war (of whom 1,226 were French) died of typhus in 1915. However, Gärtner admitted that this figure was probably too low as it did not include those whose cause of death had been misdiagnosed at the outbreak of the epidemic or those who died in hospitals outside prisoner of war camps.[140] Wilhelm Doegen's figures for the overall number of British prisoners in Germany also show that, between 10 August and 10 September 1915, the overall number of British prisoners in Germany dropped by 417, possibly indicating that British prisoner deaths from typhus may have cancelled out any net German gains in British prisoners of war from new captures.[141]

---

[134] *Ibid.*, p. 261.
[135] *Ibid.*, p. 262. Christmas, *Le Traitment des prisonniers français en Allemagne*, p. 28.
[136] *Ibid.*, pp. 27–37. Rapport adressé au ministère de la guerre le 12.8.15 par le Docteur David [Alphonse], médécin-major de 1er classe, sur l'epidémie de typhus exanthématique, qui a sévi au camp de Cassel, de janvier à juillet 1915. At the Leipzig trials the French claimed 3,000 prisoners died at Kassel-Niederzwehren in the epidemic. See Hankel, *Die Leipziger Prozesse*, p. 341.
[137] As noted during a visit to the graveyard in August 2003.
[138] Hinz, *Gefangen im Großen Krieg*, pp. 103–4.
[139] Doegen, *Kriegsgefangene Völker*, pp. 56–7.
[140] Gärtner, 'Einrichtung', p. 260, p. 262. Uta Hinz has also noted that Gärtner's figures are unreliable, Hinz, *Gefangen im Großen Krieg*, p. 103.
[141] This figure of 417 was calculated from the figures in Doegen's work given for the overall monthly tally of British prisoners reported in prisoner of war camps in Germany throughout 1915: new captures and prisoner deaths are reflected in the net increase or decrease in these prisoner figures. Doegen, *Kriegsgefangene Völker*, pp. 28–9, Zahlentafel sämtlicher eingebrachten [sic] Kriegsgefangenen während der Kriegsdauer bis zum 10. Oktober 1918. As a post-war right-wing publication Doegen's statistics should not be considered absolutely reliable.

Germany responded to the Allied propaganda that the epidemic was a German war crime with a defensive discourse that incorporated epidemiological paradigms, depicting typhus as a foreign contamination. Gärtner asserted in the post-war German medical history that, in 1914, German doctors knew nothing of typhus, which was 'unknown in the country apart from a few rare cases in the eastern border regions among vagabonds and the lowest class of society'.[142] Moreover, he misleadingly claimed it was not initially known that lice spread the disease.[143] The German discourse also argued that lice-infested Russian prisoners caused the typhus. Therefore, it was simply an unfortunate consequence of war.[144] Moreover, the German authorities correctly pointed out that German guards and medical staff had died from typhus caught in the camps. In particular, they emphasised Kassel-Niederzwehren camp where forty German guards and medical staff died, including Professor Hermann Knackfuss from the Kasseler Kunstakademie, a personal friend of the Kaiser.[145]

Although it was true that German medical staff had contracted typhus, the overall German version of events was disingenuous. There was detailed knowledge in Germany in 1915 about the link between poor hygiene and typhus. The fact that typhus was carried by lice had been generally accepted by German scientists by 1914, although there was still debate as to whether human-to-human transmission of the disease was also possible.[146] The Austrians had also recognised the link: military regulations in 1911 and civil legislation of 1913 identified lice as the likely cause of typhus.[147]

German researchers, such as Bernhard Nocht, were among the foremost European experts on typhus, which had been the focus of research by scientists during the Balkan wars of 1912 and 1913.[148] When the first case of typhus was identified in the Russian prisoner of war camp in Kottbus in 1914, Nocht alerted the military authorities that the louse was in all probability the main carrier of the illness.[149] Several German researchers, such as the zoologist Stanislaus von Prowazek, even carried out experiments in the prison camps at the height of the epidemic.[150] Prowazek caught the illness at Kottbus camp and died as a result, later to be

---

[142] Gärtner, 'Einrichtung', p. 259.   [143] *Ibid.*
[144] Hinz, *Gefangen im Großen Krieg*, p. 104.
[145] 'Eine Trutzburg für die Toten. Briten und Engländer ruhen auf dem Keilsberg – Friedhöfe mit höchst unterschiedlichem Charakter', *Extra Tip*, Kassel, 11.6.2003, p. 13.
[146] Weindling, *Epidemics and Genocide*, p. 15.   [147] *Ibid.*
[148] Leven, *Die Geschichte der Infektionskrankheiten*, p. 133. Weindling, *Epidemics and Genocide*, p. 15, pp. 73–4.
[149] Weindling, *Epidemics and Genocide*, p. 77.   [150] *Ibid.*, p. 76.

venerated as a martyr by the Nazi researchers Ernst Rodenwaldt and Heinz Zeiss; in Schneidemühl camp, medical professors Ludolf Brauer and Wilhelm His researched the disease.[151]

Yet despite this knowledge, the German response to the epidemic in 1915 was initially remarkably slow when compared with the emphasis upon delousing within the German army from the outbreak of the war in 1914. The German army had already been faced with typhus in 1914 when it had broken out among German soldiers in the 2nd Army.[152] However, it was only in March 1915 that the President of the Reich Health Office convened a conference in Berlin on how to combat the disease in prison camps. The slow reaction to the prisoner epidemic appears to have been due to a refusal on the part of some of the military to initially accept that lice alone were responsible. According to Weindling:

Scientists felt that the military should have operationalized delousing far more rapidly than was in fact the case. While military authorities imposed draconian measures fearing another unknown means of contagion, medical scientists tried to stabilize the situation by providing unassailable proof that the louse was sole vector. By spring 1915, the Posen professor of hygiene Wernicke instructed Field Marshal von Hindenburg on how the body louse spread typhus.[153]

There was also a significant racial aspect that determined the slow initial reaction of the German authorities. Karl-Heinz Leven outlines that during the war 'for German hygienists, typhus had a racial component; it was seen as affecting the Russians and Polish who were seen as indolent, and in particular, as affecting the Jewish population'.[154] This motif of typhus as a threat from the 'East', which had existed in Germany before the war, was profoundly reinforced by the 1915 epidemic.[155] Typhus was perceived as endemic among eastern populations and as a normal, inevitable part of life for Russian prisoners, whose culture and hygienic attitudes were considered primitive.[156] During the war, the German authorities even tried to use the typhus epidemic to try to divide the Allies – denying

---

[151] www15.bni-hamburg.de/bni/bni2/neu2/getfile.acgi?area=geschichte&pid=131, accessed 27.10.2005; Weindling, *Epidemics and Genocide*, pp. 78–9.

[152] Reichswehrministerium, *Sanitätsbericht über das deutsche Heer (Deutsches Feld- und Besatzungsheer) im Weltkriege 1914/18*, 3 vols. (Berlin, 1934–8), vol. I, p. 126. See also Wolfgang Eckart, 'Epidemien', in Hirschfeld *et al.*, eds., *Enzyklopädie Erster Weltkrieg*, p. 459.

[153] Weindling, *Epidemics and Genocide*, pp. 76–7.

[154] Leven, *Die Geschichte der Infektionskrankheiten*, p. 133.

[155] Weindling, *Epidemics and Genocide*, pp. 73–80.

[156] See, for example, the German cartoons of Russian prisoners reproduced in Uta Hinz, '"Die deutschen 'Barbaren' sind doch die besseren Menschen". Kriegsgefangenschaft und Gefangene "Feinde" in der Darstellung der deutschen Publizistik 1914–1918', in Overmans, ed., *In der Hand des Feindes*, pp. 339–62.

all German responsibility and blaming the Russian prisoners entirely as the carriers of typhus lice, brought from their homeland to 'contaminate' a hygienic, typhus-free Reich; this trope even became a source of wartime humour in several cartoons that poked fun at Russian prisoners as primitive, one of which, in 1916, depicted Russian captives fighting over a pet louse named 'Cherminchen'.[157] Even in late 1915, the year of the epidemic, *Simplicissimus* published a cartoon showing the 'barbarian' Russian benefiting from being washed, disinfected and educated in German captivity.[158] As Uta Hinz has pointed out, by blaming the epidemic on Russian prisoners, the German authorities effectively insinuated that through their alliance with Russia the British and French governments were themselves to blame for the death of their soldiers.[159]

The British and French response was to emphasise that it was a German decision to mix British, French and Russian prisoners; in their propaganda depicting typhus as a war crime, they blamed this move, along with poor camp hygiene facilities, for the epidemic, rather than presenting the Russians as contaminated typhus-carriers.[160] The French and British believed that the order by the German Chief of the General Staff on 1 October 1914 to mix the different nationalities of Allied prisoners together was intended to humiliate British and French prisoners by making them share quarters with Russians and colonial prisoners whom the German military regarded as less civilised. They may have been correct: when the post-war head of the prisoners of war department at the German Ministry for War, General Fransecky, was queried in 1919 about this decision he refused to answer, stating that investigators could 'draw their own conclusions as to the motive of this order'.[161]

Ultimately, however, the German army's failure to delouse prisoners and to provide adequate sanitation in prison camps was the major contributory factor that explains why the typhus epidemic raged on such a disastrous scale.[162] There was no provision for disinfection in many of the provisional prisoner of war camps in 1914–spring 1915 and no quarantining of newly arrived prisoners from other captives. Conditions for other-rank prisoners of war in Germany in the winter of 1914 were exceptionally poor, as recalled by repatriated men: Döberitz camp consisted of 'four

---

[157] *Ibid.*   [158] *Ibid.* See Figure 18 in this book.
[159] Hinz, *Gefangen im Großen Krieg*, p. 104.
[160] TNA, WO 32/5608, no. 64, Wittenberg Case. The Director of the French *Service des Prisonniers de Guerre*, Georges Cahen-Salvador, blamed the mixing of French and Russian prisoners for the epidemic: Cahen-Salvador, *Les Prisonniers de guerre*, p. 37.
[161] TNA, WO 32/5608, no. 64, Wittenberg Case.
[162] TNA, WO 161/98, no. 288, on Langensalza camp in 1914–15; Speed, *Prisoners, Diplomats and the Great War*, pp. 66–7.

large tents, each holding some hundreds; we had no beds, only straw and a blanket. No sanitary arrangements; no water or nothing.'[163] Sennelager camp in September 1914 was 'an open field enclosed with wire ... there were no tents or covering of any kind. There were about 2,000 prisoners in it – all British. We lay on the ground with only one blanket for every three men.'[164] At Hameln camp, in October–November 1914, prisoners were lodged 'for the first six weeks in trenches covered with canvas awnings. The bedding consisted of shavings and each man had one blanket ... The dirt and vermin etc. were frightful. Washing facilities consisted of one tap for some 7,000 men.'[165] Minden camp in September 1914 was described in similar terms by an escaped French prisoner, Adjutant Lucien Debond, who recalled 13,000 prisoners sleeping on wet soil in the rain without shelter or blankets.[166] Only on 24 September were the prisoners transferred into wooden buildings; Debond claimed that by then some prisoners had died of the cold.[167] Bavarian War Ministry documents reveal that during the opening six months of the war prison camp organisation was chaotic, with a major shortage of prisoner accommodation and no coordinated policy for sanitation, clothing or delousing; by December 1915, 926 French other-rank prisoners and 349 French civilian prisoners had died in Bavarian camps.[168] This was also the case in north Germany: the Foreign Office in Berlin was informed as late as September 1915 that journalists were still not to be allowed to visit Zossen or Döberitz prisoner of war camps because they were not yet in a fit state to be seen:

The camps are in no way finished; only the most basic of shelters is standing so that the accommodation at the present time appears scarcely presentable ... Our military successes will be the best propaganda abroad.[169]

Similar chaotic conditions prevailed at Wittenberg during the winter of 1914 and spring 1915. The French doctor Georges Monvoisin described an overcrowded, unsanitary camp where 14,000 men were held without access to soap, hot water or a change of clothes. They lacked an individual

[163] TNA, WO 161/98, no. 462, Private A. Crossley.
[164] TNA, WO 161/98, no. 536, Private Charles Brash.
[165] TNA, WO 161/99, no. 871, Private Frank Byrne.
[166] SHAT, 7 N 1187, Rapports d'évadés ou rapatriés transmis par Gouv. de Boulogne, Adjutant Lucien Debond.
[167] Ibid.
[168] BHStA IV, M Kr 1630. For death statistics see BHStA IV, M Kr 13785, Übersicht der im Bereich der bayerischen Armee seit Kriegsausbruch bis einschliesslich 10.12.15 verstorbenen Kriegsgefangenen Belgier, Engländer, Franzosen und Russen.
[169] AA, R 20883, f. 148, Gardekorps, Stellvertr. Generalkommando. Berlin, Ia Nr. 9671 to AA, 16.9.1915.

straw mattress, sharing three apiece.[170] Moreover, Monvoisin revealed that there was a cholera epidemic in Wittenberg camp in December 1914 which resulted in sixty prisoners becoming ill, thirty of whom died.[171] The response to the cholera epidemic *was* effective – the German authorities began a vaccination programme for the prisoners. However, this epidemic does not appear to have served as a warning regarding the urgent need to improve hygiene and to introduce appropriate quarantine measures in all camps: the need to delouse prisoners was given practically no consideration in the winter of 1914–15.

The priority, above all in 1915, once typhus broke out, was to protect the German population from an epidemic. This explains why the German authorities were so successful in organising quarantine protection for German civilians living near camps, whereas they failed to protect prisoners from the spread of the disease. In the whole war, there were only 1,279 cases of typhus among the entire German population, most spread by soldiers on leave from Russia or the Balkans.[172] This contrasts dramatically with the spread of the disease unchecked in spring 1915 throughout thirty different prisoner of war camps.

During the immediate post-war period, the Allies continued to view the typhus epidemics as war crimes. The view persisted particularly among the French that the Germans had deliberately tried to encourage the typhus epidemic in order to kill prisoners. Both the British and the French pushed for judicial enquiries and they succeeded in bringing about two post-war German investigations into the two particular camps where the 1915 typhus epidemic had been particularly notorious: Wittenberg and Kassel-Niederzwehren. The British accusations regarding Wittenberg camp were examined by a post-war German Commission of Enquiry into prisoner treatment established by Matthias Erzberger after the collapse of the *Kaiserreich* and led by Professor Walter Schücking, a world-renowned expert in international law. It found against the British case:

A violation of international law in the matter of treatment of prisoners at Wittenberg camp during the epidemic in the year 1915, did not take place. The Commission were of the opinion that greater precautions might have been taken, and greater preparations made in advance, to meet an outbreak of contagious diseases in camps.[173]

Yet the evidence of the chief German doctor at Wittenberg during the epidemic, Dr Aschenbach, largely concurred with the British accusations.

---

[170] Monvoisin, *Le Typhus exanthématique*, pp. 16–18, pp. 24–5.   [171] *Ibid.*, p. 25.
[172] Leven, *Die Geschichte der Infektionskrankheiten*, p. 133.
[173] TNA, WO 32/5608, no. 64, Memorandum to Major-General Sir Richard Ewart.

He admitted the camp was overcrowded, German personnel were with-drawn and British doctors and personnel substituted and that food was supplied to the camp by a special mechanical contrivance to avoid the spread of the epidemic to the town.[174] Moreover, Dr Aschenbach admit-ted that he was 'seldom in the hospital himself; the same was true of his assistant'.[175] A British observer caustically remarked on the Commission hearing: 'the evidence of prisoners-of-war themselves is not heard, so that the value of an investigation into the Wittenberg case ... was questionable'.[176]

The French government took a case against the commandant of Kassel-Niederzwehren camp, Generalmajor Benno Kruska, and the chief of the camp guard, Generalleutnant Hans von Schack, at the post-war Leipzig war crimes trials, which were held in Germany in 1921, following the failure of the Allies to force Germany to extradite suspects the Allies wished to try for breaches of the laws of war.[177] For the Allies, the Leipzig case reinforced their definition of typhus in prison camps as a German war crime. However, the trial was a fiasco for the French. Kruska had the support of the courtroom; his defence accused a key French witness, an Alsatian who had been serving in the German army, of being a traitor.[178] For the French, the typhus was interpreted as a deliberate wartime violence against their soldiers: one French witness who took the stand accused Kruska of saying that he would fight the war 'in his own way' and claimed that Kruska deliberately allowed the typhus to spread.[179] Another claimed Kruska had said the French and Russian prisoners should be mixed together so the French could get to know their Allies better, adding: 'what does it matter if the French have a few lice more or less'.[180] The case against Kruska failed, as his intent to cause harm to the prisoners could not be proven. The court concluded that the French had not 'a shadow of evidence'.[181] However, key information which surfaced during the trial was ignored. A report by the Prison Camp Inspectorate of the XI Army Corps from 4 May 1915 stated that the camp commandant had failed to recognise the 'great danger of a typhus epidemic and implemented the necessary measures far too late.

[174] Ibid.   [175] Ibid.   [176] TNA, WO 32/5608, Memorandum to Sir Richard Ewart.
[177] Archives du Ministère des Affaires Étrangères (MAE), Correspondance politique et commerciale, Série Y, Internationale, 589, Archives de la mission de l'Avocat Général, Paul Matter, au procès de Leipzig 1921, ff. 98–124, 12.7.1921.
[178] Ibid.   [179] Ibid.
[180] MAE, Correspondance politique et commerçiale, Série Y, Internationale, 589, Archives de la mission de l'Avocat Général, Paul Matter, au procès de Leipzig 1921, ff. 98–124. 12.7.1921, f. 119.
[181] Hankel, Die Leipziger Prozesse, p. 342.

There was also a failure to adequately instruct doctors and officers, and to energetically and efficiently use the available personnel.'[182] Another memo from 9 August 1919 gave the opinion of another general from the XI Army Corps who stated: 'General Kruska was a very imprudent and not very active camp commandant and was little loved by the prisoners ... The conditions outlined in the French report – apart from the overestimate of the numbers who died and fell sick – are in general accurate.'[183] Indifference was clearly a factor in the failure to respond to the typhus outbreak at Kassel.[184]

The 1915 typhus epidemic reveals a pattern of negligence at the heart of the German prisoner of war camp system during the first year of the war. Its significance was enormous; as Uta Hinz has pointed out, the epidemic marked a major turning point within the German camp system as the authorities were

forced for the first time to construct camp buildings or to improve them as a result of the experience of the typhus epidemics. Within a few months the structure of the German prison camp fundamentally changed. From improvised camps, the equivalent of small towns developed, with their own administration and infrastructure.[185]

A proper system of delousing prisoners, involving mass bathing, shaving body hair and putting clothing in disinfection ovens or fumigation chambers, was established in the wake of the epidemic, which meant that typhus did not reappear in prison camps in Germany after 1915, although in 1918, prison camps saw another epidemic in the form of the Spanish influenza. However, a significant cognitive association, linking typhus with the eastern front prisoner of war, developed during 1915, as did an obsession with prison camp hygiene after the epidemic; the *Münchener Medizinische Wochenschrift* even published an article on how to organise prison camp hygiene to avoid infectious disease which suggested inoculating prisoners against smallpox and cholera.[186] There were longer-term consequences, too: as Paul Weindling has pointed out, a key legacy of the First World War was that 'delousing became routine ... By the time of the Second World War migrants and deportees had become conditioned to expect the ordeal of delousing at border crossings, ports, railway junctions and on entry to camps.'[187] This 'routine', which developed further in the interwar period, was ultimately used to disguise the gas chambers at Auschwitz.

---

[182] *Ibid.*, p. 346.   [183] *Ibid.*
[184] Hinz, *Gefangen im Großen Krieg*, p. 105.   [185] *Ibid.*, p. 106.
[186] See Dr. G. Seiffert, Lager Lechfeld, 'Hygienische Erfahrungen bei Kriegsgefangenen'. Special edition of the *Münchener Medizinische Wochenschrift*, 1915, no. 1, pp. 35–6, and no. 2, pp. 68–70, BHStA IV, no. 2950.
[187] Weindling, *Epidemics and Genocide*, p. xv.

Yet overall the 1915 epidemic highlights another important shift in attitude: the revelation that for British and French contemporaries, prisoner mistreatment of any kind, including the outbreak of typhus in a camp, had come to be perceived as a form of violent atrocity – rather than as an historical inevitability of war. The Allies' response was to depict typhus in prison camps within their existing 'German war crime' paradigm. Paradoxically, this reaction reveals the high Allied expectations of how prisoners should be treated – any gap between their expectations and reality was a 'crime'. In this way, the typhus epidemic was used to stoke popular hatred of Germany and to legitimise the Allied war effort. Ultimately, the prisoner with typhus represented a victim in Allied propaganda; for the German authorities in 1915, he came to embody their worst wartime fears of 'eastern' contamination and epidemic among the Reich population.

Sickness among German prisoners in French camps in North Africa

The shift in attitude in 1915 towards viewing prisoner sickness as a form of *violence* perpetrated upon captives by the enemy was not limited to the British and French, however. In Germany, too, a similar atrocity discourse emerged, regarding illness among German captives, sent by the French government to prisoner of war camps in Morocco, Tunisia and Algeria. Here too, an expectation of atrocity clearly determined how prisoner sickness was interpreted and, once again, real incidents of prisoner mistreatment fuelled a broader cycle of atrocity beliefs, as Germany collected evidence from repatriated prisoners of harsh living conditions in the North African camps.[188]

In the first year of the war, France sent significant numbers of German captives to its North African territories. By 1 April 1915, there were 4,834 German prisoners in Algeria and Tunisia; by January 1916 there were 12,000.[189] Most were working on engineering or public works projects.[190] German prisoners were also sent to Morocco, where, in April 1915, 5,356 captives were working on railway building at Casablanca, Rabat, Meknès and Fez.[191] Wounded prisoners were also sent to hospitals

[188] BA-MA, Msg 200 / 327, 29-page report of evidence of prisoner abuse in North Africa.
[189] SHAT, 6 N 23, Commission Interministérielle des Prisonniers de Guerre, État du travail des prisonniers de guerre, 1.4.1915; Odon Abbal, 'Le Maghreb et la Grande Guerre. Les camps d'internement en Afrique du Nord', in *Les Armes et la Toge. Mélanges offerts à André Martel* (Montpellier, 1997), p. 631.
[190] Abbal, *Les Armes et la Toge*, p. 631.
[191] SHAT, 6 N 23, Commission Interministérielle, Etat, 1.4.1915.

in North Africa. Once again class was a determinant of treatment: German officer prisoners remained in metropolitan France.

In Tunisia and Algeria, the prisoners were under the control of the *Général Commandant les armées de terre et de mer de l'Afrique du Nord*, General Moynier.[192] In Morocco, the administration of the Governor-General, Louis Hubert Gonzalve Lyautey, controlled the prison camps. Lyautey intended that the presence of German prisoners in Morocco would symbolically humiliate Germany, in revenge for its pre-war attempts to win political influence in the country, where: 'Before the European war, the Germans enjoyed considerable prestige in the eyes of the natives'.[193] For this reason, Lyautey believed it was important to take energetic measures to 'affirm in the eyes of the natives our power and our superiority over the enemy'.[194] In 1916, he stated 'it was necessary to convince the Moroccan people that we were and remain the stronger power. We have sought to do this through a series of measures', including, 'bringing 8,000 German prisoners to Morocco, who are employed on public works'.[195]

Germany quickly protested at German prisoners being sent to Africa, as a belief that prisoners were subject to mistreatment by non-white guards in North African camps rapidly spread. Such fears were fuelled by the fact that prisoners in North Africa had practically no postal link with Germany; their relatives had little information about their fate.[196] A meeting of the Cologne Red Cross War Help Group on 19 December 1915 was informed that 'our prisoners in Algeria and Morocco must endure the worst humiliation and mistreatment. They are handed over to the vengeful animal lusts of the blacks.'[197] This fear of French colonial soldiers was largely provoked by racist prejudice, exacerbated by only a handful of real incidents: in North Africa, five German prisoners were killed by Arab guards during escape attempts.[198] However, prisoners were subject to the same harsh military discipline as French Zouaves, enduring the '*tambour*' punishment in many camps, where a man was disciplined by being forced to lie still for long periods in a tiny tent

---

[192] Abbal, *Les Armes et la Toge*, p. 623.
[193] United Nations Archives, Geneva, Archives of the League of Nations, P.153, Archives Lyautey, Chapitre VI, Maroc 1914, Doc. 7.
[194] *Ibid.*   [195] *Ibid.*, Chapitre VII, Maroc 1915–1920, Doc. 1.
[196] Baron d'Anthouard, *Les Prisonniers allemands au Maroc. La campagne de diffamation allemande. Le jugement porté par les neutres. Le témoignage des prisonniers allemands* (Paris, 1917), p. 37.
[197] ASV, Segretaria di Stato, Guerra anno 1914–18, rubrica 244, fasc. 132, f. 41, Kriegshilfe der Vereinigten Vereine vom Roten Kreuz Cöln [sic] Abt. IV: Ausschuss für Angehörigen-Abende to Msgr. Pacelli, 10.3.1916.
[198] Abbal, 'Le Maghreb et la Grande Guerre', p. 628.

exposed to the sun.[199] They were also subject to random acts of coercion: prisoner Oskar Wachler recounted that at Ferryville camp in Tunisia:

The commandant of the camp, Captain Grand was a very unpleasant man who made our lives very hard and hassled the prisoners a lot. He often hit them with his whip, even in the face. However, I never saw this personally.[200]

Prisoner Alfred Scheler described how at Tizi Ouzou:

a Bavarian NCO called Kiestein from a railway regiment was put on the floor and his hands and feet tied to posts. He had to lie like that on his stomach for half an hour because when the commandant ordered us to leave our tents, he [Kiestein] had said 'they deserve a bloody good hiding'. A man from Alsace reported what he had said to the sentry.[201]

Scheler also recounted how German prisoners were stoned by 'well-dressed' French women at Marseille and Algiers when embarking and disembarking on their fourteen-day transport by sea to North Africa.[202] Oskar Wachler also described his journey, travelling wounded from Marseille to Tunis in November 1914, as very difficult: 'We were loaded onto a ponton – a type of cattle ship – where we spent ten days without blankets lying on lousy straw. It was impossible to sleep because of the cold.'[203]

The association of North African captivity with harsh, violent treatment rapidly became interwoven with representations of sickness: Germany claimed the climate was making the captives ill, thereby fuelling a widespread popular German belief that the French were deliberately risking the health of their German charges; the pro-French American writer Edith Wharton, who travelled extensively in Morocco during the war, described these German protests about the African climate as 'absurd'.[204] Yet the reality was that many German prisoners in North Africa did fall sick, finding it hard to cope with local food, and the heat. One prisoner, Oskar Wachler, described how, in April 1915:

---

[199] Comité International de la Croix-Rouge, *Documents publiés à l'occasion de la Guerre Européenne 1914–1916. Rapports de M. le Dr A. Vernet et M. Richard de Muralt sur leurs visites aux depôts de prisonniers en Tunisie et de MM. P. Schazmann et Dr O.-L. Cramer sur leurs visites aux depôts de prisonniers en Algérie en décembre 1915 et janvier 1916* (Geneva, 1916), pp. 83–9. (Hereafter CICR, *Rapports Vernet, Muralt, Schazmann et Cramer.*)

[200] BA-MA, PH2 / 33, f. 16–21, Interview with Oskar Wachler.

[201] *Ibid.*, f. 191, Interview with Alfred Scheler.   [202] *Ibid.*

[203] *Ibid.*, f. 16, Interview with Oskar Wachler; see also a similar account in f. 76, Interview with Erl. Arnold.

[204] Edith Wharton, *In Morocco* (New York and London, 1920), p. 81. See the Project Gutenberg Literary Archive Foundation: www.gutenberg.org/catalog/world/readfile? pageno=80&fk_files=48137, accessed 15.12.2005. On German protests, see d'Anthouard, *Les Prisonniers allemands au Maroc.*

I and sixty comrades were sent to Ferryville camp on the north coast of Tunisia. The diet here was unbalanced. For eight weeks we had only rice at midday and in the evenings. Then for many weeks only horse beans etc. which are hard on the stomach and made many of us sick.[205]

Another ex-prisoner reported a dysentery epidemic at his camp at Khanga-Sidi-Nadgi, and gruelling desert marches.[206] He recalled the French guards stating that 'they did not understand why the government had sent us to build pointless roads in these God-forsaken areas where the climate was so bad that no European would ever wish to settle there'.[207] The prisoner concluded that the French government was deliberately trying to kill its captives.[208] A German letter to the Vatican requested that the church intercede on behalf of 120 German prisoners sick with fever at Miliana camp in Algeria.[209]

French records of the ailments affecting German prisoners repatriated from North Africa to France in 1916 reveal that many were suffering from anaemia, due to malaria and the almost total lack of red meat in their diet.[210] Some were repatriated due to eye damage from the sun.[211] The International Committee of the Red Cross was allowed to inspect the North African camps, which it did several times at the behest of the German government; the first inspections took place in February 1915.[212] These International Red Cross inspections found that almost all of the German prisoners sent to North Africa caught malaria.[213] Initially, this unfamiliar sickness had given rise in Germany to the rumour that their prisoners in North Africa all had tuberculosis. However, International Red Cross inspections found very few cases of TB: 'when we encountered a pale or thin man in the camps we questioned him thinking to find a tuberculosis sufferer, but it was always the same reply: malaria'.[214] Prisoner Alfred Scheler recalled how at Sikh-ou-Meddour [sic], in August 1915, 'malaria broke out. The sick remained lying where

[205] BA-MA, PH2 / 33, ff. 16–21, Interview with Oskar Wachler.
[206] BA-MA, Msg 200 / 427, 'Aus den Erfahrungen einer vierjährigen Gefangenschaft in Algerien und Frankreich', *Deutsche Medizinische Wochenschrift*, 28, pp. 771–3, 10.7.1919.
[207] *Ibid.*   [208] *Ibid.*
[209] ASV, Segretaria di Stato, Guerra anno 1914–18, rubrica 244, fasc. 132, f. 37, Geheimrat Greve to Cardinal Amette, Archbishop of Paris, 1.3.1916.
[210] SHAT, 3 H 260, Rapatriement grands blessés, prisonniers allemands du Maroc 1915–1916.
[211] *Ibid.*
[212] BA, R 901/84525. See also Comité International de la Croix-Rouge, *Documents publiés à l'occasion de la Guerre de 1914–1915, Rapports de MM. Dr C. de Marval (3ème et 4ème voyages) et A. Eugster (2ème voyage) sur leurs visites aux camps de prisonniers en France et en Allemagne*, 2nd series (Geneva, 1915). (Hereafter CICR, *Rapports Marval*.)
[213] ACICR, 432/II/10/c.37, CICR, *Rapports Vernet, Muralt, Schazmann et Cramer*, p. 57.
[214] *Ibid.*, p. 24.

they were until they lost consciousness. Only then were they sent to hospital in Tizi Ouzou. I also ended up there.'[215] Red Cross inspectors found that 'it was malarial fever that the prisoners feared the most'.[216]

In Tunisia, International Red Cross inspectors also found that almost all the prisoners had suffered badly from diarrhoea after their arrival from France and that typhoid had also occurred.[217] Prisoners were inoculated against typhoid on arrival.[218] Despite this, there was a major typhoid outbreak at Monastir in 1915. 'Quite a large number of prisoners caught the illness and many died,' Red Cross inspectors noted during inspections in December 1915 and January 1916.[219] According to the French, the cases of typhoid only occurred among those German prisoners who had refused inoculation by claiming that they had already been vaccinated. The Red Cross inspectors decided that the prisoners were, therefore, themselves to blame for the epidemic.[220] However, the inspectors reported that they were unable to interrogate a key witness, the German prisoner interpreter Borgstoff. They nevertheless concluded that 'after asking many questions we have become convinced that the prisoners generalised too hastily' from the typhoid fever.[221] The epidemic had

broken out suddenly in a widespread manner with a particular malignancy; the hospitals saw a sudden influx of sick. It does not seem that there were mistakes or negligence to blame but simply large material difficulties to overcome and a particularly strong strain of illness which led to the men dying in two or three days and sometimes sooner … As for the bad reputation of the hospital at Monastir, it is surely undeserved as this establishment does not exist. See how one writes history![222]

Questions have to be asked regarding the reliability of the Red Cross reports. Their simplistic approach to investigating the typhoid epidemic in Monastir was astounding – it did not occur to them that the original hospital could have been closed, renamed or moved following the epidemic. The Red Cross also provided no overall death statistics for prisoners in North Africa in its reports.[223] It even admitted that death rates for Algerian camps were not available when its inspectors enquired.[224]

Despite the absence of death rates, the Red Cross inspector Dr de Marval concluded from his inspections of camps in Tunisia and Algeria in February 1915 that the overall situation in North African camps was good:

---

[215] BA-MA, PH2 / 33, f. 191, Interview with Alfred Scheler.
[216] ACICR, 432/II/10/c.37, CICR, *Rapports Vernet, Muralt, Schazmann et Cramer*, p. 59.
[217] CICR, *Rapports Marval*, p. 8.   [218] *Ibid.*
[219] ACICR, 432/II/10/c.37, CICR, *Rapports Vernet, Muralt, Schazmann et Cramer*, p. 24.
[220] *Ibid.*   [221] *Ibid.*, pp. 44–8, p. 49.   [222] *Ibid.*   [223] *Ibid.*   [224] *Ibid.*, p. 59.

Prisoners in Algeria and Tunisia have no reason to complain, and they do not complain. Generally very well treated they have an easy life in a marvellous land with a healthy climate. Several of the more philosophical even told me that in the midst of the material and mental misery of being prisoners of war they had at least the consolation of seeing 'an interesting land'.[225]

Subsequent inspectors who visited Tunisia and Algeria in December 1915 and January 1916 came to similar conclusions, despite encountering widespread malaria among the prisoners and reporting that in several camps the prisoners looked exhausted and unwell.[226]

The Red Cross inspections caused controversy in Germany, where their favourable claims about North Africa were not believed. Suspicions grew that the French were duping neutral inspectors. One German prisoner reported that when the Swiss Medical Commission came to inspect his camp in North Africa in March 1916,

the rooms were crowded with sick. About an hour before the commission arrived the sick who could walk were taken into the wood to create the impression that the conditions were healthy in the camp. Once the commission were gone the sick were brought back out of the wood.[227]

The German government asked for further International Red Cross inspections to be carried out by Swiss Germans and organised that the inspectors report to the *Kriegsministerium* representative, Major Pabst von Ohain, about their trip, before they presented their findings to their superiors in Geneva.[228] This breach of protocol angered the International Committee of the Red Cross, as it implied that it was pressuring its inspectors to make their reports favourable to France.[229] The International Committee of the Red Cross was further alienated by the German decision to launch reprisals against French prisoners of war. In order to force France to remove its German prisoners from North Africa, in 1916 Germany sent 30,000 French prisoners to work in harsh conditions in reprisal camps in German-occupied Russia; in response to the reprisal, the French government quickly agreed to evacuate their North African camps and all German prisoners were transferred to camps in France by the end of the year.[230] Once again, the belief that violence against captives was occurring had led to an escalation in prisoner

[225] CICR, *Rapports Marval*, p. 11.
[226] ACICR, 432/II/10/c.37, CICR, *Rapports Vernet, Muralt, Schazmann et Cramer*, p. 8.
[227] BA-MA, PH2 / 33, f. 191, Interview with Alfred Scheler.
[228] ACICR, 432/II/8,10, 11 B and C, carton 41.   [229] *Ibid.*
[230] SHAT, 6 N 110, Journal hebdomadaire de l'Inspection générale des prisonniers de guerre [semaine du 30 avril au 6 mai 1916]. See chapter 3 for a detailed discussion of these reprisals.

reprisals as Germany initiated deliberate prisoner mistreatment to protect its own men in French captivity.

Important comparisons can be made between the typhus epidemics in German camps in 1915 and the typhoid and malaria outbreaks among German prisoners in North Africa the same year. In both cases, there was a desire on the part of the military administration to humiliate prisoners. In the German case, the aim was to humiliate British and French captives by putting them into barracks alongside Russian peasant soldiers; in the French case, the intention was to demean German prisoners by placing them under colonial guards. Thus in the first year of the war, the desire of the military to humiliate took precedence over prisoners' welfare. This was the prerequisite for the subsequent negligent attitude towards safeguarding prisoners' health. In both cases, the general public concluded that the enemy had deliberately caused prisoners to fall sick and sickness in captivity was perceived as a form of wartime atrocity.

The comparative context is important here, as it shows the key role that negligence played in the outbreak of epidemic illness. Widespread fatal illness only emerged in two western cases in 1914–15: the typhus epidemics of spring 1915 in Germany, and malaria and typhoid in North Africa. Thus sickness among prisoners was not a universal phenomenon in 1914–15 and was not an automatic or an inevitable result of improvised accommodation. Despite significant problems in organising camps and distributing resources, there were no epidemics among German prisoners of war held in Britain or in metropolitan France in 1914–15, which illustrates that it was possible to protect prisoners' health, even when states were forced to use improvised and inadequate accommodation.

A brief outline of camps in Britain and France in 1914 and 1915 reveals the extent of the initial disorder and improvisation. In Britain, German prisoners of war were initially lodged in empty barracks, disused factories, in tents and on board ships anchored off the coast while suitable camps were prepared for them. The British were unprepared for prisoners of war – one Admiralty minute looked to 'the French war at the commencement of the last century' for its precedent for how to organise the exchange of prisoner information.[231] Conditions on the ships were far from ideal and German prisoners of war complained of cramped living conditions. Lieutenant-General Sir Herbert Belfield, who headed the War Office Department of Prisoners of War, admitted after the war that 'the ships though modern and well equipped were most unsatisfactory. It was extremely difficult to exercise proper supervision, sanitation was a constant cause of anxiety and

[231] TNA, ADM 1/8393/304, N. F. Oliver, D.I.D., Minute, 3.9.1914.

they were very expensive.'[232] Crucially, however the prisoners were well fed: Belfield admitted that 'the scale of rations issued by us to prisoners of war, other than officers, was at first liberal, and this was especially so in view of the enforced idleness to which those in this country were condemned for the first eighteen months of the war'.[233] The British did not send German other-rank prisoners to work outside prisoner of war camps until 1916.[234] Even then there were only 5,332 prisoners working outside camps in Britain by September 1916.[235] These factors protected captives' health.

Inspectors from the International Red Cross viewed the British camps favourably in 1915, despite their improvised nature, finding that 'the power of the commandant is much more limited than in other countries'.[236] They observed that the Kaiser's birthday had been celebrated in all the prisoner of war camps they visited in Britain.[237] German prisoners, however, were less satisfied. Stabsarzt Dr Hesper recalled that in 1914:

In Frith Hill camp in England the worst possible hygienic conditions existed and it was only after repeated demands that I was able to obtain an improvement. Similarly in Southend on board the ships the Ivernia and the Saxonia the conditions were very unhealthy and it took a long time before they improved.[238]

In France, the situation was similar – camps were improvised at the outbreak of war in military barracks, old fortresses and tents; often this accommodation proved unsuitable. One German officer held in the Hôpital de l'Arsenal, at Brest in September 1914, described the rooms as damp and cold.[239] The food was insufficient until November. He was moved to a fifteenth-century fortress, Château d'Anne, which was also damp and cold: after a month all the prisoners had rheumatism.[240] At Lourdes, German prisoners initially slept on straw on the bare floor of a fortress.[241] France was also short of medical dressings in September and

[232] Belfield added that 'prisoners were moved into huts or buildings as soon as these could be provided, thus freeing the ships and factories which were urgently required for other purposes. Tents were used at all times, they being boarded and warmed in winter; but tent-life seems to have been very novel to all and was at first the cause of many complaints from the prisoners, their governments and the representatives of neutral governments charged with watching their interests.' Belfield, 'The Treatment of Prisoners of War', pp. 139–40.

[233] Ibid., p. 139.   [234] Jackson, The Prisoners, p. 140.

[235] TNA, CAB 42/20/7, Memorandum on the employment of prisoners of war for the Adjutant-General, 23.9.1916.

[236] Comité International de la Croix-Rouge, Rapports de MM. Ed. Naville, V. van Berchem, Dr C. de Marval et A. Eugster, p. 10.

[237] Ibid., p. 26.   [238] BA-MA, PH2 / 588, f. 96, Dr. Hesper, Stabsarzt.

[239] BA-MA, Msg 200 / 590, Bericht über Gefangenschaft in Brest.   [240] Ibid.

[241] Willy Frerk, Kriegsgefangen in Nordafrika. Aus dem Tagebuche des deutschen Gardegrenadiers Eduard von Rohden (Siegen, 1917), p. 39.

October – wounded prisoners complained that the French medical system did not provide adequate medical resources for them.[242]

Yet despite this level of organisational improvisation, sickness did not emerge on any significant scale in camps in metropolitan France or in the United Kingdom. For sickness to emerge a level of negligence was necessary which went beyond the general improvisation of camps, which occurred in these geographic locations. Widespread malaria, typhus or typhoid required a level of administrative indifference to the welfare of prisoners of war to be present. These conditions existed in certain parts of the German camp system in 1915 where typhus was able to break out because safeguards had been ignored. Similarly, they existed in French North Africa. The desire to humiliate enemy prisoners and the lack of accountability within the military in Germany and French North Africa made it less likely that camp administrators and their superiors would react appropriately and with the necessary speed when sickness first broke out to ensure that epidemics were avoided.

Conclusion

Between the outbreak of war in 1914 and Christmas 1915, significant change had occurred in how the prisoner of war was represented. The prisoner was almost exclusively associated with violence, either as perpetrator or victim. Moreover, this violence was now defined as atrocity – as the most extreme and outrageous type of radical moral transgression. Much of the prisoner mistreatment that occurred during this first phase of the war actually reflected abuses which had happened in previous conflicts: shoddy accommodation, battlefield shooting of the wounded, epidemics in prison camps and harsh prison camp discipline. The difference was that now, because they clashed so fundamentally with European pre-war expectations, such incidents were defined in propaganda representations as atrocity, the most extreme, taboo and shocking form of social understanding of violence. This occurred regardless of whether or not the term atrocity was actually appropriate for a particular incident. This radicalised representation of the prisoner of war laid the foundation for subsequent significant deteriorations in prisoner treatment, which occurred between 1916 and 1918.

There are two key points at issue here. First, the real and surprising amount of violence against prisoners in 1914 and 1915, particularly by the German army, reveals that the opening phase of the war saw a relatively

---

[242] BA-MA, Msg 200 / 427, 'Feuilleton aus den Erfahrungen einer vierjährigen Gefangenschaft in Algerien und Frankreich', 10.7.1919.

sustained disintegration of the pre-war legal and cultural limitations that had been placed upon violence against captives, affecting both military and home front cultural attitudes. This disintegration occurred more rapidly and more extensively in Germany than in Britain and France. In Britain, in particular, while some radicalisation occurred within the military, society at large was slow to follow: the general public, in contrast to the navy, proved most reluctant in 1915 to sanction reprisals against captives. Second, the way that violence against prisoners was represented was crucial. Depicting the prisoner as either a perpetrator or a victim of war crimes undermined the former pre-war representation of the prisoner as a neutral, universalised figure defined by international law. The voyeuristic, compelling shock value of violence also meant that recounting prisoner atrocities interested the general public far more than the description of more mundane aspects of prison camp life: the image of the passive prisoner, subjected to the extremes of mistreatment and violence, became a fetish of wartime society.

Far from being a marginal group, prisoners were thus central to the radicalisation of the conflict in Germany, France and Britain and a fundamental part of each country's wartime self-image. Prisoners were not immune from the totalisation processes which the war unleashed or a neutral bloc removed from the conflict. Their accounts of mistreatment, conveyed through cycles of representations, fuelled the sense of outrage that mobilised populations to fight. Such accounts also legitimised increasingly violent practices towards prisoners, in the guise of reciprocity, as the next section will show.

Part II

Violence and prisoner of war forced labour

Introduction to part II

By 1916, important precedents had been set. As part I has shown, the image of the prisoner of war had become firmly associated with atrocity in cultural representations in Britain, France and Germany. This set in place an escalatory dynamic: representations of violence actually discursively popularised and legitimised the very violent practices against prisoners which they were intended to condemn, as they sparked calls for retaliation and also created cultural expectations of further atrocity among both civilians and military. The complex, symbiotic relationship which emerged between violent practices and the violent image, both textual and iconographic, during the early years of the war, thus fed cycles of violence against prisoners of varying intensity. This process, in turn, fuelled new violent propaganda images – and further mistreatment. Violence against prisoners was therefore not a stable constant. It was an ever-changing trajectory, influenced by frequently revised expectations regarding permitted and prohibited practices as well as by military necessity.

Prisoners themselves were complicit in this escalation dynamic, as exchanged and repatriated former captives were the main source of the information which fuelled their own representation. In this sense, prisoners were not the passive subjects of their own historicisation, as the media portrayed them. Statements from ex-prisoners largely determined the accusations made by the belligerent governments about prisoner atrocities; prisoner testimony was assessed by armies and governments, who tried to ascertain the extent of both positive and negative captivity experiences and draw overall conclusions about the accuracy of any mistreatment claims. This explains why propaganda on war crimes against prisoners generally remained relatively close to real prisoner experiences: underlying all these representations, to a greater or lesser extent, were actual incidents of violence against prisoners of war which ex-prisoners had reported.

However, although representations largely interpreted real acts of violence against prisoners relatively accurately, there was constantly a problem of gauging the extent of mistreatment: popular representations magnified the impact of particular incidents – in wartime the scale of enemy prisoner abuse was very difficult to assess, and populations rapidly failed to distinguish between the particular and the general. The discourse on prisoner abuse by the enemy thus often merged different real incidents, reported by traumatised witnesses, into a confection of confused dates, locations and generalised assumptions. Prisoner beatings in one or two camps soon morphed into the indictment of prison camps across an entire country, fuelling the further escalation of retaliatory measures and obscuring the fact that, while much of the violence reported by prisoner witnesses in 1914 and 1915 was real, it was also sporadic. This process also operated around an unconscious rule of *selection*: representations of violence against prisoners always showed the enemy as the perpetrator. There was no transparency whatsoever within societies regarding their own internal failings in prisoner treatment.

By producing lower public and military *expectations* of how prisoners could be treated, and by encouraging the belief that enemy violence against captives was widespread and in breach of international law, popular representations in 1914 and 1915 also had a negative impact on actual military practices, encouraging armies to relax pre-war regulations protecting prisoners. By 1916, this process was also exacerbated by arguments that prisoner welfare should be secondary to military necessity. Thus popular representations and military needs were increasingly operating in tandem to legitimise significant deteriorations in prisoner welfare – a trend which grew stronger in the second half of the war. This is illustrated by one issue in particular, which impacted above all others – the military demand for prisoner labour. It unleashed a powerful escalatory dynamic, which culminated in increasing violence against prisoners of war.

The next section of this book will examine this process more closely by looking at prisoner labour in detail. It will investigate how changing cultural expectations in 1916, regarding how prisoners could be used as workers, radicalised military practices, increasing violence against captives, and consider how the interaction between popular representations and military needs drove this escalation. In order to explore this, part II will focus upon one previously unstudied case study – the development of the prisoner of war labour company.[1]

---

[1] No study has yet been published on the belligerent armies' direct use of forced prisoner labour. Both Isabel Hull and Uta Hinz have highlighted the absence of research on the German army's treatment of western front prisoner labourers in occupied France and Belgium: Hull, *Absolute Destruction*, p. 321; Hinz, *Gefangen im Großen Krieg*, p. 357.

Prisoner labour companies were units of prisoners which worked exclusively for their captor army at or near the western front and rear zone areas, often on supply and communication lines. The establishment of prisoner labour companies effectively created a war zone forced labour system, with its own separate administration, largely cut off from the home front prison camps; although directives issued for home front camps were passed on to the labour company commanders, they had enormous latitude to ignore them, and, in the German and French case, frequently did. In prisoner of war labour companies, we see the most extreme forms of violence against prisoners of war emerging – for this reason the whole of part II of this book is devoted to discussing them.

Part II consists of three chapters. Chapter 3 will explore how the initial decisions were taken in the British, German and French armies to form prisoners of war into army labour units and how the formation and development of these prisoner of war labour companies resulted in a direct increase in the amount of violence to which prisoners were subjected, particularly through reprisal sequences. Chapter 4 examines how the demand for forced labour led to a particular dynamic of increasing violence against captives in German army prisoner of war labour companies in 1917 and 1918. Chapter 5 investigates whether an increase in violence against prisoners also occurred in British and French prisoner of war labour companies in 1918.

3 The development of prisoner of war labour companies on the western front: the spring reprisals of 1917

I see these pitiful creatures working every day; their faces haggard, numbed. They advance harassed by fatigue, their insides ravaged with hunger. Five men receive one loaf a day. They sleep in a barracks on the bare ground without a blanket, having only their clothes as covering. And it is every day, every day the same suffering. If you could see them! A spectacle of misery, of horror. I am not yet hardened enough by war to look on indifferently. I am seized with rage at seeing such things.

Letter found on a captured German soldier, written to his parents, describing French prisoners of war held in reprisal camps behind the German lines, 28 February 1917.[1]

Introduction: cycles of violence

One of the most significant and overlooked uses of forced labour in the First World War was the development of a mass prisoner of war workforce by armies on the western front. In 1915, the German army began using Russian prisoners of war, on a trial basis, in western front labour companies. In 1916, the British and French armies followed suit, deciding to permanently retain increasing numbers of prisoners of war in new labour companies for army needs.[2] The same year, the German system, using Russian prisoners, rapidly developed. This military use of forced prisoner labour subsequently dramatically expanded on the western front, leading to major redefinitions of what constituted the legitimate limits of violence against prisoners of war. It also reveals just how far removed prisoners of war were by 1916–17 from their pre-war protected legal status – they were now incorporated into military labour units *within* their captor's army. Lower military expectations regarding how prisoners could be treated facilitated this development.

---

[1] SHAT, 16 N 2469, D.9, f. 82, DA/7445, translation of a letter found on a German prisoner, sent to Direction de l'Arrière by 4th Army, État-Major, 2e Bureau, 5.5.1917.

[2] I am grateful to Matthew Brown and Daniel Siemens, who commented upon an earlier draft of this chapter, presented to the Transatlantic Doctoral Seminar at the German Historical Institute, Washington, 13–16 April 2005. An earlier version of this chapter was also published in *German History*: Heather Jones, 'The German Spring Reprisals of 1917. Prisoners of War and the Violence of the Western Front', *German History*, 26 (2008), pp. 335–56.

The purpose of this chapter is to show how the military need for prisoner labour directly resulted in a new ruthlessness within armies towards exposing prisoners to violence. Placing prisoners in army labour companies within the battle zone resulted in types of violence against French, British and German prisoners in 1916 and 1917 which differed in form and scale to those of 1914 and 1915. This was particularly the case in the German army, which initiated new forms of severe collective reprisals during this period in reaction to the Allies' use of German captives in prisoner of war labour companies. These reprisals saw prisoners forced to work in hazardous conditions for the German army at or near the front line. The development of these new, very violent reprisals and the widespread foundation of prisoner of war labour companies were thus closely interlinked and will be explored simultaneously here, in order to obtain broader insights into the nature of wartime violence.

The existing historiography, by Stéphane Audoin-Rouzeau, Annette Becker, Isabel Hull, John Horne and Alan Kramer among others, has almost exclusively focused upon inter-combatant battlefield violence and violence against civilians; however, it raises many interesting theoretical questions which can also be applied to prisoner reprisals.[3] In particular, new historical work on violence has debated the extent to which battlefield 'brutalisation' occurred in 1914–18: what Annette Becker and Stéphane Audoin-Rouzeau define as a process of totalisation at the heart of the war that was 'profoundly linked to a successive breach of thresholds or degrees of violence'.[4] Indeed, the existing analysis of First World War violence has largely been dominated by these two paradigms: brutalisation and totalisation.[5] The first attributes the dramatic levels of violence during the war to a process occurring 'from below' – the widespread brutalisation of

---

[3] See Audoin-Rouzeau and Becker, *14–18. Retrouver la Guerre*; Horne and Kramer, *German Atrocities*; Kramer, *Dynamic of Destruction*. The relationship between violence and irrational decision-making in the German army has recently been explored by Isabel Hull in her book *Absolute Destruction*. Michael Geyer has also examined the question of rationality and attitudes to violence in the German army at the end of the war in 'Insurrectionary Warfare. The German Debate about a *Levée en masse* in October 1918', *Journal of Modern History*, 73 (2001), pp. 459–527.

[4] I am indebted to the work of Annette Becker and Stéphane Audoin-Rouzeau, which developed the concept of brutalisation, first outlined by George Mosse in his book *Fallen Soldiers. Reshaping the Memory of the Two World Wars*. See Audoin-Rouzeau and Becker, 'Violence et consentement', p. 256. The idea that the war brutalised a generation has recently been challenged by Benjamin Ziemann in his book *War Experiences in Rural Germany, 1914–1923* (Oxford and New York, 2007).

[5] For a definition of 'total' war, see Stig Förster's introduction in Roger Chickering and Stig Förster, eds., *Great War, Total War. Combat and Mobilization on the Western Front, 1914–1918* (Cambridge, 2000), pp. 1–15. On the concept of 'totalisation', see John Horne's discussion in Horne, ed., *State, Society and Mobilization*, pp. 1–17.

combatants, due to the nature of the war experience in the trenches; the second posits that increased 'totalised' violence was an inevitable corollary of the shift at state and military levels towards waging 'total' industrialised war. Both these paradigms represent valuable theoretical tools. Indeed, the only existing, brief, historiographical references to collective reprisals against prisoners, by Marc Michel and Annette Becker, refer to them in these terms, with Michel concluding that the 1917 reprisals were due to a mixture of 'brutalisation' and 'intoxication' with violence on the part of populations, and Becker contending that prisoners were 'the first victims of the vicious circle of totalisation', because of a spiralling reprisal dynamic throughout the war.[6] Yet how the processes of brutalisation and totalisation actually operated remains relatively unclear: the more detailed case study investigation here, of how collective reprisals against prisoners interacted with new military labour needs to propel an escalation in violence, sheds new light on brutalisation processes at work – suggesting that they were highly contingent, depending upon individual 'cycles of violence'.

The reprisal 'cycles' against labour company prisoners in 1916–17 are thus highly significant. Collective reprisals against prisoners illustrate the development of new forms of violence and the expansion of wartime violent practices beyond established combat patterns – and thus, to some extent, a process of escalation or totalisation. They provide us with an insight into how violence actually evolved and escalated through reciprocal reactions to enemy behaviour which made increased violence appear logical. This created a 'cycle of violence' which drove wartime totalisation. These reprisals also highlight how the increasing demand for prisoners' forced labour – often justified using the argument of military necessity – greatly exacerbated this process. However, an examination of this 1916–17 reprisals violence also challenges some of the assumptions regarding totalisation during the war. First, collective reprisals reveal that there was no constant, linear increase in violence. Rather violence occurred in cycles which emerged and disappeared according to different factors; the evolution of a particular cycle also varied between national armies. War violence was thus extremely heterogeneous. Second, totalisation was not inevitable or unlimited: reprisals could escalate violent practice but de-escalation was also possible if a cycle of violence faltered. Moreover, reprisals violence was always a process of negotiation: if it redefined new violent practices as acceptable it was also subject to cultural

---

[6] Marc Michel, 'Intoxication ou "brutalisation"? Les représailles de la Grande Guerre', in Nicholas Beaupré and Christian Ingrao, eds., *14–18. Aujourd'hui, Today, Heute*, vol. IV: *Marginaux, marginalité, marginalisation* (2001); Becker, *Oubliés de la Grande Guerre*, p. 121.

constraints which created boundaries that limited violent behaviour – and it was also limited by the continuing need for prisoner labour. In sum, reprisals against prisoners illustrate the processes which developed to justify transgression of the norms of violence by framing it as an act of self-defence, and highlight a continual evolutionary tension between perceptions of what constituted legitimate or illegitimate violence. Finally prisoner reprisals show us that wartime violence was not necessarily irrational or indiscriminate; nor, for that matter, was the totalisation process it engendered. Rather, both were controlled and often highly rational and measured – with increases in violence deliberately directed towards obtaining a particular goal. By looking at collective prisoner reprisals it becomes possible to examine closely how the cycle of violence interacted with the totalisation process; concomitantly the limits of totalisation also become clear.

This chapter will now explore how the practice of violence against prisoners evolved, looking at the establishment of prisoner labour companies and collective reprisals during the period 1915–17. First, it will examine how the foundation of prisoner of war labour companies led to increased violence against prisoners of war in the German and French armies; second, it will investigate the new German collective reprisals which developed in tandem with the new labour companies; and finally it will consider what conclusions can be drawn from a study of reprisals regarding how the cultural limits of acceptable violence against prisoners changed, and what the implications of this are for our understanding of wartime violence.

The foundation of prisoner of war labour companies in the German army

The collective reprisals of spring 1917 represented planned, systemic violence against British and French prisoners working for the German army on the western front; however, they occurred against a backdrop of incidents of non-reprisal violence against prisoner workers that long predated 1917 – in particular, physical violence against Russian prisoner workers. Prisoner of war labour companies were first established in the German army in 1915, using Russian prisoners captured in the East.[7] This was the first such use of prisoners of war by any army on the western front;

---

[7] BA-MA, PH5 / II / 455, f. 130. Circular telegram from Chef des Generalstabes des Feldheeres to Armeeoberkommandos 2, 3, 4, 5, 6, 7, 9, Oberbefehlshaber Ost [zugl. für die unterstellten Armeen] A. A. v. Strantz, v. Falkenhausen, Gaede, v. Woyrsch, Bugarmee, Gouv. Metz, Strassburg, Lille, 22.9.1915.

the British and French prisoner of war labour companies were only established in 1916.[8] On 22 September 1915, the German Chief of Staff announced that prisoner of war labour companies were to be used in the army zone:

> Over the coming period several prisoner of war labour battalions (each made up of 4 companies of 500 men with 1 *Landsturm* Company as guards) will be established on a trial basis. These battalions are to be set to work on non-military work (building camps and roads, agricultural work etc.). Prisoners already being used on this work ... are to be organised and their number and location is to be reported.[9]

These first German prisoner labour companies only contained Russian prisoners. French, British and Belgian prisoners continued to be evacuated to camps in Germany: 'Where French, English and Belgian prisoners of war have been put to work, they should be replaced by Russian prisoners of war ... Their transfer to German prisoner of war camps is to take place once the replacements have arrived.'[10] Uniform rations for the Russian prisoners in prisoner labour companies were not established until 30 December 1916. Until that date

> rations for feeding prisoners of war in the zone of operations (*Operationsgebiet*) and behind the lines (*Etappengebiet*) were not fixed, in order to allow the army commands (*Armeeoberkommandos*), observing the greatest economy, to provide adequate food (*auskömmliche Verpflegung*) according to the different real needs of the working prisoners and the available food supplies. It is the duty of all involved in setting these rations to continually remember that the home population, including those employed as heavy labourers, have to endure the greatest of food restrictions and, therefore, it is not permissible to feed prisoners better than our hard working population at home.[11]

---

[8] TNA, WO 32/5098, 1B, Formation of Prisoner of War Companies, No. A.G. b 2006/4, 27.7.1916; SHAT 16 N 2467, D.1, f. 34, 520/DA, no. 2046/DA, 9.6.1916.

[9] BA-MA, PH5 / II / 455, f. 130. Circular telegram from Chef des Generalstabes des Feldheeres to the following: Armeeoberkommandos 2, 3, 4, 5, 6, 7, 9, Oberbefehlshaber Ost [zugl. für die unterstellten Armeen]. A. A. v. Strantz, v. Falkenhausen, Gaede, v. Woyrsch, Bugarmee, Gouv. Metz, Strassburg, Lille.

[10] 'Soweit französische, englische und belgische Kriegsgefangene zu Arbeitsleistungen herangezogen sind, wird ihr Ersatz durch russische Kriegsgefangene erfolgen ... Die Überführung in deutsche Kriegsgefangenenlager ist mit Eintreffen des Ersatzes zu bewirken.' BA-MA, PH5 / II / 455, f. 127. 24.9.1915. Generalquartiermeister, IIa Nr. 26306. Circular to all Armee-Oberkommandos and Etappeninspektionen des Westens, the Generalgouvernant in Belgium, the Befehlshaber der Tr. I. Luxemburg, den Herrn 2. Kommandanten des Gr.H.Qu. A copy of the order was also sent 'Zur Kenntnis' to the Oberbefehlshaber Ost, the Königliches Kriegsministerium Berlin, the Stab des Herrn Kriegsministers and the Auswärtiges Amt.

[11] BA-MA, PH5 / II / 455, f. 39, G.H.Q., Generalintendant des Feldheeres III.d. Nr. 3025/12.16 to sämtliche Armeeintendanturen and Feldintendanturen selbständiger Truppenverbände, 30.12.1916.

Within the moral economy of wartime a hierarchy of prisoners of war had been established. Initially, only Russians were to be sent to work permanently in the more demanding, spartan world of the labour company work camps being established in the militarised area, to the rear of the front in occupied Belgium and France. This differential treatment of captives based upon nationality broke with the idea of the same standard, universal treatment for all prisoners of war which pre-war international law had sought to establish. It sent out a dangerous symbolic message about the value of a Russian prisoner in 1915 compared to that of a British, French or Belgian captive, fuelling an existing problem of Russian prisoners being abused, which had already emerged in German home front camps: a Prussian *Kriegsministerium* order on 29 July 1915 revealed that, despite orders that prisoners were not to be mistreated, 'Russian prisoners continue to be subjected to beatings by German personnel – often in the most violent manner.'[12]

The result of the symbolic demotion of Russian prisoners of war to battle zone forced labourers was soon clear. Although the initial German army orders stated that these prisoners were only to be used for non-military work, on the ground these prisoner workers were treated harshly and often sent to work near the front. Their exposure to violence took three broad forms: corporal punishment, random beatings and working under shellfire. Violence was a common form of punishment: in June 1916, Nestor Hersent, a civilian living in St Leger, noted in his diary that 'two Russian prisoners of war who had escaped were tortured when recaptured ... They have their hands tied behind their backs and then are hung up by a belt.'[13] Violence was an important tool for discipline from the very outset of the prisoner labour company system. Random beatings were also common, illustrating that, while it was the initial decision by higher command levels to authorise prisoner labour near the front that facilitated their mistreatment, it was the actions of individual guards that escalated the situation; beatings of Russian prisoners emerged from below in the German army.

Alongside such experiences of individualised violent punishments, prisoners also endured violence as a collective group: orders that Russian prisoners should not work under shellfire were frequently not obeyed in 1915 and 1916. On 6 November 1916, an order in the Sixth Bavarian Army stated, 'recently there has been an increase in the cases where different Russian

---

[12] BHStA IV, Gen.Kdos IbAK, Bund 183, Folder 8, Akten des GeneralKommandos I. Armee Korps, Kriegsgefangene Mannschaften 1914–1916, KM Berlin, Nr. 546/15g. U3, Geheim, 29.7.1915. The beating of Russian prisoners was widespread in home front German camps: see Hinz, *Gefangen im Großen Krieg*, pp. 82–3, 158.

[13] IWM, London, 93/21/1, The Diary of Nestor Hersent, 27.6.1916.

prisoner camps and workplaces have been shelled by enemy artillery'.[14] In one case alone, six Russian prisoners were killed, and twenty-three wounded.[15] On 24 December 1915, the Fourth Army Command (*Armeeoberkommando* 4) found it necessary 'because of different incidents' to impose 'restrictions on the employment of Russian prisoners', outlining that they should not be made to work under enemy shellfire.[16] This cyclical pattern, where prisoners were exposed to violence because of decisions made at a local level, prompting higher command levels to issue orders to protect captive labour, which in turn were frequently disregarded on the ground, leading to new orders, was a feature of the German labour company system in 1915 and 1916. Labouring in a militarised zone where neutral inspections were prohibited, these Russian prisoners experienced a particularly violent captivity.[17]

The German prisoner of war labour company system rapidly expanded. In February 1916, an appendix to the new Reichstag Memorandum on the Economic Measures taken by the *Bundesrat* stated that 'some 250,000' prisoners were employed along lines of communication.[18] By August 1916, of the 1,625,000 prisoners of war in German hands, 253,000 were working in areas behind the lines.[19] This represented 16 per cent of the total number of prisoners held by Germany.[20] These prisoners were particularly vulnerable to mistreatment, as the exposure of Russian prisoners working in labour companies to direct violence from their guards and indirect violence from shellfire clearly illustrates.

This ongoing violence against Russian prisoner workers to some extent set a precedent for later prisoner mistreatment by establishing a culture of brutality within prisoner of war labour companies. However, debilitating as these initial violent practices against Russian prisoners were, they must be distinguished from collective prisoner reprisals, as violence against Russian captives was not a deliberate, coordinated policy adopted by the army to obtain a specific goal from an enemy government. Moreover, in a number of cases, the disciplinary violence meted out to individual Russian prisoners actually mirrored the corporal punishments doled out to ordinary German soldiers under German military law.

---

[14] BHStA IV, Gen.Kdos IbAK, Bund 183, Oberkommando der Armee-Abtg, von Strantz, Ic Nr. 22340/16.

[15] *Ibid.*

[16] BA-MA, PH5 / II / 454, f. 288, AOK 4, Ic Nr. 3223, 24.12.1915.

[17] ACICR, 444/IV/c.59, Rapport sur la situation des prisonniers de la guerre dans les territoires du nord de la France occupée par les armées allemandes.

[18] TNA, MUN 4/6527, Employment of prisoners of war in Germany 18.2.16.

[19] Rawe, '. . . *wir werden sie schon zur Arbeit bringen!*', p. 79.

[20] Ulrich Herbert, *A History of Foreign Labor in Germany, 1880–1980. Seasonal Workers/ Forced Laborers/Guest Workers* (Michigan, 1990), p. 91.

In contrast, reprisals violence was orchestrated by official orders and used against enemy prisoners only. It was also more extreme, deliberately risking prisoners' lives. The events of 1916 illustrate this difference clearly – the worst violence against captives that year was not against Russian prisoner workers on the western front. It occurred on the eastern front, when the German army initiated a sequence of particularly severe reprisals, sending British and French captives to the Baltic zone to work in spartan conditions with little food or shelter, in retaliation for the French treatment of German prisoners in North Africa and the British use of German prisoners in labour companies in France.

It is worth examining these eastern front reprisals in some detail because they marked a significant radicalisation point: although collective reprisals against prisoners were relatively common throughout the war, prior to 1916, they had taken predominantly mild forms. Not expressly prohibited in international law, reprisals had first emerged amid the accusations and counter-accusations of atrocity which marked the opening months of the conflict, when France and Germany had quickly resorted to a reciprocal system of prisoner treatment, whereby the Germans would allow or refuse French prisoners in Germany exactly the same privileges or rights as German prisoners were allowed in France and vice versa. This system of reciprocity was policed by the use of relatively limited reprisals; it rapidly superseded the pre-war corpus of international law on prisoners of war: the Hague Convention on Land Warfare of 1907 and the Geneva Convention of 1864, revised in 1906.[21] In this way, each belligerent used the prisoners of war it held as surety, retaliating against them for any bad treatment against its own men held captive by the enemy.

This was not a new phenomenon: reprisals against prisoners had been common in earlier European conflicts.[22] In the early years of the First World War reprisals were often petty: refusing prisoners access to their post, or confiscating Christmas parcels, for example; other reprisals were more punitive, such as the German decision to place prisoners from intellectual backgrounds in special reprisal work camps in 1915.[23] The form of reprisal that emerged in 1916 which involved forcing prisoners to

---

[21] Brown, ed., *The Hague Conventions and Declarations of 1899 and 1907*, p. 110.

[22] On prisoner treatment in earlier conflicts see Caucanas *et al.*, eds., *Les Prisonniers de guerre dans l'histoire*, and Overmans, ed., *In der Hand des Feindes*.

[23] SHAT, 16 N 2468, D.4, f. 60, Ministère de la Guerre, Service Général des Prisonniers de Guerre, No. 66.689, 27.11.1916. In 1916, a British cabinet circular noted 'a growing tendency on the part of the Germans – avowedly by way of reprisal for any real or imagined harshness in the treatment of their own men in other countries – to punish the prisoners of those countries by withholding their parcels altogether'. TNA, CAB 37/151/1. File circulated by Robert Cecil, July 1/16. On the so-called 'intellectual' reprisals in 1915, see Michel, 'Intoxication ou "brutalisation"?', pp. 180–4.

carry out certain types of very hard manual labour on subsistence rations under shellfire was of a very different nature, however, and marked a major escalation in prisoner mistreatment.

It is important to note that a further shift in popular representations of violence against prisoners was fundamental to this radicalisation. By 1916, armies and populations were prepared to openly admit their role as perpetrators of violence against captives, where it was represented as a reprisal, as illustrated by comments made by the French expert in international law Louis Renault:

> From the point of view of absolute justice, it is easy to say that the violation of international law by one belligerent does not justify the other to also violate it on his side ... that this risks legitimising grave abuses ... This is evident but it is no less evident that with regard to certain belligerents there is no other way of obtaining redress for distressing practices.[24]

This attitude was also reflected in Germany, where severe reprisals were believed to be 'required'.[25]

This new radicalisation of reprisals in 1916 also represented a power struggle over policy in Germany; there was disagreement about reprisals between the Foreign Office, which opposed harsher collective retaliation against captives, and the Prussian Ministry for War, which was pushing for more severe measures on behalf of the German Army Supreme High Command, the *Oberste Heeresleitung* (OHL).[26] Agreement was finally reached between the two ministries on 31 March 1916, on the following basis: reprisals were only legitimately to be used where a misdemeanour against German subjects had been committed by the enemy and 'where it

---

[24] Preface by Louis Renault to *Le Régime des prisonniers de guerre en France et en Allemagne au regard des conventions internationales, 1914–1916*, p. vii.

[25] As stated in a 1916 propaganda publication with an introduction in English, French and German which contextualised reprisals as follows: 'From the instant that an enemy soldier, overcome by force of arms, falls within the power of the Germans he is no longer regarded as a foeman but as a human being for whose welfare they are responsible to humanity. Whenever Germany has been compelled to resort to harsher measures against prisoners of war it inevitably followed as a consequence of bad treatment accorded Germans imprisoned in hostile countries. These severe reprisals were implacably required in order to mitigate the lot of the mistreated Germans and compel the enemy to observe the laws of humanity. That innocent persons were injured by these repressive measures was inevitable but it is the hard duty of the German government to provide by every conceivable means for the welfare of their own brave warriors who have fallen into the hands of the enemy and this obligation is paramount to any one which they may owe to hostile prisoners.' ACICR, 431/III/j/c.31, Commission allemande d'enquête, English-language introduction to *Kriegsgefangene in Deutschland/Prisonniers de guerre en Allemagne/Prisoners of War in Germany* (Fribourg, c.1916).

[26] Alfred Gautier, Vice-President of the International Committee of the Red Cross, 'Traitement des Prisonniers de Guerre en Allemagne', *Revue Internationale de la Croix-Rouge*, 2e année, no. 1, in *Bulletin International de la Croix-Rouge*, 31e année, nos. 209–14 (1920), p. 694.

could be proved that the blame for this lay with the enemy government and not with a subordinate authority'.[27] The reprisal measure ordered was to be analogous to the action taken by the foreign state against German subjects and the enemy belligerent had to be notified in advance.[28]

The way was now clear for an escalation in the military practice of violent reprisals; within a month, the German army launched its harsh new eastern front reprisal measure. In April 1916, it sent an estimated 30,000 French prisoners of war from camps in Germany to German-occupied Russian territory to work in deliberately poor conditions on reduced rations. This was in response to growing concerns that German prisoners of war sent by the French to labour in difficult conditions in Morocco, Algeria and Tunisia were being mistreated.[29] The German army sent many of these French reprisals prisoners to Courland, located in modern-day Latvia; in 1916, this area was part of a military zone under the exclusive control of the German Eastern Supreme Command (*Ober-Ost*), to the rear of the eastern front.[30] The French prisoners were encouraged to write home about their predicament. This, the German army hoped, would pressurise the French government into improving conditions for German prisoners in North Africa: the collective humilia-tion of prisoners of war through mistreatment was to be used as a way of gaining leverage over their home state. Over sixty postcards from these prisoners even reached the International Committee of the Red Cross in Geneva, prompting its first denunciation of reprisals, which it described as a 'barbarity'.[31]

The scrawled postcards to the International Red Cross were revealing. One prisoner wrote that 'we are reduced to eating grass to sustain ourselves ... we all hope that this torture will soon end'.[32] Another wrote how 'we must not laugh or sing or smoke or read or even have a group conversation. All gaiety is prohibited and the food does not change. I ask myself what will become of us leading this existence as our forces diminish.'[33] Another prisoner, Pierre Lecomte, wrote to his wife: 'we are the only ones to be treated as slaves and not as soldiers'.[34]

The fate of these French captives was soon shared by a smaller group of 2,000 British prisoners, drawn mainly from Döberitz camp, who, in May

---

[27] *Ibid.*   [28] *Ibid.*   [29] D'Anthouard, *Les Prisonniers allemands au Maroc*, pp. 1–8.

[30] On this region, see Vejas Gabriel Liulevicius, *War Land on the Eastern Front. Culture, National Identity and German Occupation in World War I* (Cambridge, 2000).

[31] ACICR, 445/I/c.59, 12.7.1916.

[32] ACICR, 445/III/c.60, Postcard from Russia from a prisoner named only as Charles to his sister, 24.6.1916.

[33] *Ibid.*, Prisoner's postcard to his mother from Ostolsti-Schaulen, 10.6.1916.

[34] Michel, 'Intoxication ou "brutalisation"?', pp. 188–9.

1916, were also sent east to Courland. They were sent to camps at Angersee (Engures Ezers), Mitau (Jelgava), Wainoden (Vainode) and Libau (Liepāja) in German-occupied Russia in retaliation for the British diverting some 1,500 German prisoners of war from the UK to work in Rouen and Le Havre in April 1916.[35]

These German prisoners working at Rouen and Le Havre formed the first permanent British prisoner of war work units in France. They were created in April 1916 as part of a Franco-British deal brokered by Albert Thomas, French Undersecretary of State for Munitions, to ease congestion in French ports.[36] The British would provide a small number of prisoner working units to load and unload French ships. In exchange the French gave the British army direct access to forests and quarries which helped it to overcome a tonnage crisis in spring 1916, caused by German submarine warfare and the difficulties of bringing wood and stone to the British army from the UK.[37] The British government then decided to expand the initial experiment with German labour in France a step further and to form several more German prisoner of war units to exploit these forests and quarries.

In contrast to the German and French situations, the impetus for organising permanent prisoner labour units to work for the British army came from the War Office, rather than the military commanders: Lord Kitchener, the British Minister for War, was the chief proponent of this new use of prisoners of war on a permanent basis in France. The British army's Commander-in-Chief, Sir Douglas Haig, was initially strongly opposed to using any prisoner workers in France, believing that they would provide indifferent labour and could escape.[38] The French found it difficult to understand this reluctance, believing the British were unwilling to make their German prisoners work hard; Thomas informed Lloyd George that he would happily 'find them intensive work'.[39]

Haig was eventually forced to relent; the first transport of 750 German prisoners from Britain to work at Rouen port occurred on 5 April 1916.[40] Yet unlike the German situation, the British use of German prisoner workers in France was initially carefully monitored by the War Office, which set out strict preconditions for the prisoners' employment:

---

[35] TNA, MUN 4/6527, 121/works/219, Department of Prisoners of War, WO to Sir Douglas Haig, 31.3.1916. The areas cited are in present-day Poland and the Baltic States.

[36] HLRO, LG /D/17/6/31, U. F. Wintour to David Lloyd George, 12.2.1916; TNA, MUN 4/6527, Albert Thomas to David Lloyd George, 1.3.1916.

[37] Ferguson, *The Pity of War*, p. 283; TNA, MUN 4/6527, Walter Runciman to Sir Douglas Haig, 23.3.1916.

[38] TNA, MUN, 4/6527, Sir Douglas Haig to War Office, 18.3.1916.

[39] TNA, MUN 4/6527, Albert Thomas to David Lloyd George, 1.3.1916.

[40] TNA, MUN 4/6527, 121/works/219, War Office to Sir Douglas Haig, 31.3.1916.

They must be guarded by English troops; they must be adequately accommodated and fed; they should be housed near their work which should not be near the front; the work should be so supervised that the technical and possibly dangerous part of it should be in the hands of skilled French or Englishmen and the heavy unskilled labour done by the Germans.[41]

Furthermore Lieutenant-Colonel Sir Herbert Belfield, head of the Department of Prisoners of War at the War Office, proposed that '"camps" in France shall be treated exactly the same as those in the United Kingdom'.[42]

Yet the German prisoners sent to Rouen noticed a difference in comparison to their camps in the UK. 'In Dorchester we had it good,' ex-prisoner Max Scheuer stated.[43] Work was voluntary there and prisoners were paid 8 shillings a week. In Rouen, in contrast, he had to 'work partly in the harbour, partly on building roads and waterworks for 16 Pfennig a day'.[44] He received less food, although it was 'tastily prepared'.[45] Other ex-prisoners were highly critical of conditions in Rouen. Eugen Hofmeister described the accommodation as 'utterly inadequate', with primitive toilet facilities and water from jerry cans that tasted of oil.[46] The camp commandant was 'brutal' to the prisoners.[47] Karl Folger described how prisoners were given too little food and were often forced to work in wet clothes in the rain.[48] Several of the prisoners complained that the French civilian population spat at them or hit them. According to ex-prisoner Peter Kickert, this frequently resulted in the British guards and French civilians shouting at each other.[49] Changed expectations of how prisoners could be treated had paved the way for a deterioration in British military practice towards captives. Similarly, the German army expectation of enemy prisoner mistreatment meant that it automatically assumed that the British action constituted an atrocity which called for the most severe response – reprisals.

It was in retaliation for this British move to employ German prisoners at Rouen and Le Havre that the German army leadership sent British prisoners in May 1916 to join the French in reprisal camps at the eastern front. Despite this, however, the British army decided to further expand their use of German prisoner labour in France in summer 1916, developing a fully organised system of prisoner of war labour companies. On 15 July 1916, GHQ requested that the War Office allow it to 'employ German prisoners

---

[41] TNA, MUN 4/6527, 11 a, 121/works, B. B. Cubitt to Sir Douglas Haig, 5.2.1916.
[42] TNA, MUN 4/6527, 121/works/219, War Office to Sir Douglas Haig, 31.3.1916.
[43] BA-MA, PH2 / 26, f. 38, Interview with Max Scheuer.
[44] Ibid.   [45] Ibid.   [46] BA-MA, PH2 / 588, f. 33, Interview with Eugen Hofmeister.
[47] Ibid.   [48] BA-MA, PH2 / 26. f. 51, Interview with Karl Folger.
[49] Ibid., f. 43, Interview with Peter Kickert.

of war on roads in army areas and in quarries on lines of communication as necessity for this work is urgent'.[50] Belfield replied that he had no objection but that 'they must not be employed within range of enemy artillery'.[51] It was Belfield, as Director of the Department of Prisoners of War at the War Office, who provided the 'provisional orders and instructions' for the size, equipment, discipline and accommodation of these prisoner of war labour companies on 27 July 1916.[52] Each company was to contain 425 prisoners.[53] Belfield personally inspected the prisoner of war labour companies in France on 30 August 1916 and found that

they are entirely employed in advanced positions, in front of railheads, on the maintenance of roads which are used by motor and horse transport. Whereas army commanders were at first very half-hearted in the employment of these companies they now find that their services are so valuable that applications for the formation of new companies are frequent and no limit has so far been set out on the numbers ... German prisoners in our prisoner of war company 'camps' in France ... are reasonably well-housed, well-fed and clothed and the conditions are generally good; but this cannot be brought home to the German government for I understand that our military authorities in France deprecate the idea of any visits being paid to these 'camps' by members of the American Embassy in Paris. This attitude seems to me to be entirely reasonable as the 'camps' are, as I have said, almost in the zone of immediate hostilities and the means of transport are scanty.[54]

Belfield was fully cognisant of the danger of further German reprisals. 'It is a matter for serious consideration,' he wrote in August,

as to what acts of reprisal may be taken by the German authorities for this work. It seems probable that they will do something of this kind ... It is a matter for consideration whether the formation of such companies should be continued indefinitely or whether their place should not be taken by the Kaffir and Chinese labour which it is intended to send to France.[55]

Belfield realised, however, that the decision to use prisoner labour companies would be difficult to reverse: 'we shall find it very difficult to abandon with dignity a policy which has been deliberately adopted'.[56] By 5 October 1916, there were twenty-eight prisoner of war labour companies and a depot company in France employing 12,300 prisoners.[57] Significantly, in September 1916, Belfield decided to divest

[50] TNA, WO 32/5098, 68 A, GHQ to DPW, WO, 15.7.1916.
[51] Ibid., 69 A, DPW to GHQ, 17.7.1916.
[52] Ibid., 1 B, Formation of Prisoner of War Labour Companies, AG b 20006/4, 27.7.1916.
[53] Ibid.   [54] TNA, WO 32/5098, DPW, WO Register no. 0103/8472, minutes no. 9, 30.8.1916.
[55] Ibid., Register no. 0103/8472, Minutes no. 9, 30.8.1916.
[56] Ibid., 9 A, WO to GHQ, draft letter, Sept. 1916.
[57] Peter T. Scott, 'Captive Labour. The German Companies of the B.E.F., 1916–1920', The Army Quarterly and Defence Journal, 110, 3 (1980), pp. 319–31.

control of managing the prisoner labour companies to GHQ: 'whereas the camps at Havre and Rouen will be treated in all respects as English camps, all instructions regarding prisoner of war labour companies ... will be addressed to G.H.Q'.[58] Henceforth, British prisoner of war labour companies, like their German army counterparts, would be controlled almost exclusively by the Army High Command.

This British decision to expand their use of German prisoner labour in France occurred in full knowledge of the German reprisals being inflicted on British prisoners at the eastern front. Military necessity, however, triumphed over humanitarian concerns. The War Office learned that British captives on the eastern front were 'employed ... under conditions of great hardship, parcels of supplies, if received at all, arriving only after long delays and no representative of the American Embassy in Berlin having been permitted to visit them'.[59] The War Office's description belied the severity of what was actually happening. One British prisoner sent on these reprisals, Able Seaman James Farrant, described how guards beat prisoners who refused to work, with the butt ends of their rifles. Those men who still resisted working 'were taken by the Uhlans to some trees outside the Lager and tied up, the Uhlans banging them in their faces with their fists'.[60] The punishment of *Anbinden* (also known by its French name *poteau*) – tying a prisoner to a pole and leaving him hanging by his arms – was widely practised. The accommodation consisted of cow sheds or shelters built from turf. The reprisal prisoners worked for eleven hours a day felling trees. Their rations were two cups of coffee, three slices of bread and a bowl of soup per day.[61] Hardly surprisingly, the prisoners began eating nettles and raw ears of corn found growing wild.

It is worthwhile comparing the different reaction to these eastern front reprisals in France and Britain. The French government, alarmed at the arrival of letters from French reprisals prisoners pleading for assistance and in need of extra prisoner labour to deal with a shortage of agricultural workers in France, soon made the decision to compromise.[62] Negotiations between Germany and France began in August 1916 with Spanish mediation, and in September a deal was reached: France evacuated all German prisoners from North Africa, in exchange for the return of all French reprisals prisoners in German-occupied Russia to prisoner of war camps in Germany.[63] The totalisation process – the escalation of

---

[58] TNA, WO 32/5098, 8A, DPW, WO to GHQ, 7.9.1916.

[59] TNA, WO 32/5098, 9A, WO to GHQ, September 1916.

[60] Extract from the diary of Able Seaman James Farrant in Michael Moynihan, ed., *Black Bread and Barbed Wire. Prisoners in the First World War* (London, 1978), p. 18.

[61] *Ibid.*   [62] SHAT, 16 N 2468, D.4, f. 69 bis, 5.12.1916.

[63] D'Anthouard, *Les Prisonniers allemands au Maroc*, pp. 1–8.

violent practices against prisoners – in this case was halted. In contrast, the British prisoners in Courland experienced an ongoing increase in violence. Unlike the French, the British government refused to negotiate and the British prisoners remained in German-occupied Russia throughout the winter of 1916–17.

The eastern front reprisals thus revealed just how unwilling the Allies were to coordinate their prisoner treatment. In August 1916, the Russians, British and French discussed whether to adopt a collective reprisals policy in response to Germany's actions against its Allied captives. The question of implementing a common regime for German prisoners in Allied countries was even suggested in the French national assembly by deputy Géo Gerald as a means of combating Germany's 'barbarism' towards French prisoners.[64] By late autumn, however, the British and French governments had rejected the idea, as both wished to retain the freedom to respond independently to German prisoner treatment.[65] The French Ministry for Foreign Affairs observed that 'the enemy does not apply the same measures to the prisoners of each allied nation. It can be the Russians, the French or the English who are the victims of a particular reprisal and the means to bring it to an end are not and cannot be the same.'[66] The French noted that they had already brought about the return of their prisoners from the eastern front reprisal camps to Germany, whereas the British had not.[67] London and Paris also diverged in their attitudes towards imposing reprisals; following the disaster of the Admiralty action against German submarine prisoners in 1915, Britain was very reluctant to inflict any prisoner reprisals. Sir Edward Grey, the Secretary of State for Foreign Affairs, wrote to Paul Cambon, the French Ambassador in London:

His Majesty's Government have abstained almost entirely from, and are opposed in principle to reprisals as a means of securing the better treatment of prisoners of war. It is to be feared that reprisals would only provoke the German government to still worse treatment and thus fail in their object while entailing on British and French authorities increasingly harsh treatment of prisoners in their hands which it would become repugnant to inflict.[68]

A French memo on the subject considered the British position rather incongruous given that they 'were the first to use reprisals against German prisoners' in 1915.[69]

---

[64] MAE, Série A, Paix, 64, f. 39, question écrite remise par Géo Gerald, 9.11.1916.
[65] *Ibid.*, f. 29, Projet de reponse à la question écrite remise le 9 novembre à la présidence de la Chambre des Députés par M. Géo Gerald, 19.11.1916.
[66] *Ibid.*   [67] *Ibid.*   [68] *Ibid.*, f. 40, Sir Edward Grey to Paul Cambon, 2.10.1916.
[69] *Ibid.*, f. 29.

While the British refused to implement reprisals or to negotiate, the German army continued to maintain British prisoners of war at the eastern front. Conditions for these British reprisals prisoners in spring 1917 were far worse than in 1916. One former prisoner described how,

Owing to the thermometer showing 29 degrees centigrade below zero ... many of the men were brought in with frost bite ... On 6 April we were amazed to hear that 11 men were dead and nearly 200 in hospital, most of them serious cases. Everyone became very depressed ... It would be beyond the powers of any man no matter how able or fluent to describe in writing the impression it left as you gazed upon these human wrecks, starved, frozen and unwashed. Simply a frame of bones covered with skin, breathing and looking at you with eyes sunk deep into their sockets.[70]

Able Seaman James Farrant described men collapsing at work from hunger. On 1 March 1917, he wrote that he had worked '50 yards from the first line, 150 yards from the Russian line, pulling sleighs loaded with timbers, frequently had to take shelter from machine-gun fire. German soldiers in trenches bore us no malice and were surprised that we should be working here.'[71] On 11 March he noted in his diary that he was made to work for 'nearly 20 hours' shovelling snow in the trenches: 'one man collapsed. It was the coldest night yet, 10 degrees Fahrenheit below zero.'[72] He was shocked to discover, during disinfection in spring 1917, how ill his companions looked: 'we were like skeletons; shoulder bones, hip bones, knees and elbows were horribly prominent'.[73] Another ex-prisoner reported:

Many men were unable to finish the day's work and collapsed at the time of the midday halt which lasted 20 minutes. They were left lying in the snow till night, when we others carried them home. There were usually 50 or 60 who had to be carried on the shoulders or helped home, too weak to walk. Those of us who were working in the forest were able to make a kind of stretcher which made it easier to carry the men. Some were dead without our knowing it before they arrived at the camp and quite a number died in the night and were found dead the next morning, the sentries bayoneting them to convince themselves that they were not shamming.[74]

Even Sir Reginald Acland, a member of the 1918 British Committee of Enquiry into Breaches of the Laws of War investigating war crimes against prisoners, who dissented from the general committee view that British prisoners had been mistreated by Germany on any large scale during the war, acknowledged in 1922 that the severe treatment of British prisoners

---

[70] TNA, WO 161/100, Interview no. 2803, Sergeant J. Morrison, RMLI.
[71] Moynihan, ed., *Black Bread and Barbed Wire*, p. 23.   [72] *Ibid.*, p. 24.   [73] *Ibid.*, p. 27.
[74] TNA, WO 161/100, no. 3006, Private C. Brown.

who were 'marched up to the frozen river Aar [sic] on the eastern front' was an atrocity 'unparalleled in the course of the war', and had not the slightest 'doubt that it was ordered almost in its details by superior authorities in Germany'.[75] An internal British report based on interviews with exchanged, escaped or repatriated prisoners stated that, of 500 prisoners who arrived at one eastern front reprisal camp in February 1917, 'at the end of April 1917 there were only 77 men left ... 23 having died and 400 having been sent to hospital'.[76] The report was not published until 1945; some of the interviews on which it was based are still to be found at the National Archives at Kew.[77] What began in 1916 as a limited German reprisal measure clearly deteriorated in the winter of 1916–17 into something much more ruthless. Ultimately, it was only in autumn 1917 that these British reprisals prisoners were finally sent back to camps in Germany, when Britain ceased using German prisoner labour units in French ports; although the British army continued to expand its use of German prisoner labour companies elsewhere in France, the eastern front reprisals were now officially ended.[78]

Thus 1916 set important precedents. First, the widespread abuse of Russian prisoners of war labouring on the western front established a culture of physical brutality in prisoner labour companies. Second, the fact that the eastern front reprisals by Germany appeared to have successfully influenced French policy encouraged the use of such methods to protect German prisoners in French hands. Third, 1916 also illustrates the very particular limits set to reprisal violence. Social class hierarchies were strictly observed. No officer prisoners were ever considered for such treatment.[79] Certain humane boundaries were also set. While wounded prisoners had been sent to reprisal camps within Germany in 1915, only fit prisoners were sent on the 1916 eastern front reprisals, and prisoners who were wounded or fell sick were evacuated from the reprisal camps in Courland for treatment.[80] In some cases, in 1917, British prisoners,

---

[75] Sir Reginald Acland in a comment during a debate at the Grotius Society, *Transactions of the Grotius Society*, 8 (1922), p. 36. It appears Acland means either the Kurländische Aa (Lielupe) or the Livländische Aa (Gauja) in Latvia.

[76] The report was included as an appendix to J. H. Morgan's book, *Assize of Arms. Being the Story of the Disarmament of Germany and Her Rearmament*, vol. I (London, 1945), Appendix IV, p. 261. For the interviews on which it was partly based see TNA, WO 161/100 series.

[77] *Ibid.*

[78] SHAT, 16 N 2469, D.8, f. 12, M. de la G. to C. en C., 9.4.1917. TNA, CAB 24/63, f.220, 'Summary of reprisals taken by the British and German governments since the beginning of the war', 12.9.1918.

[79] Although reprisals against officers did occur, they never involved manual labour camps in the army zone.

[80] Michel, 'Intoxication ou "brutalisation"?', p. 184.

desperate for evacuation, even 'deliberately chopped off their fingers in the hope that they would be sent to hospital'.[81] Hunger and long working hours were the principal punishments inflicted during the eastern reprisals in 1916. 'Our bodies had dwindled until our legs were no larger than an ordinary man's wrist and everybody was completely emaciated. We were all like a lot of children almost imbecile in our conversation and unable to think consecutively. The only conversation of any interest was food, food, food,' one former prisoner recalled in interview.[82] The psychological strain on prisoners was clearly severe. Finally, the numbers of prisoners involved in the harshest phase of the eastern front reprisals in the winter of 1916–17 were quite small – some 2,000 British prisoners. The deterioration in their condition and treatment largely occurred in early 1917, as the western front too was witnessing real prisoner mistreatment by both France and Germany.

Nevertheless, reprisal cycles within the German army in 1916 were clearly increasingly ruthless. Certain types of mistreatment had become legitimate when inflicted as a means to an end – a military equivalent of Bethmann Hollweg's doctrine that 'Not kennt kein Gebot (necessity knows no law).'[83] The term 'reprisal' officially justified behaviour which would otherwise have been seen as morally questionable; established customs restricting violence against British and French prisoners captured by Germany were being renegotiated. This development will now be compared with new patterns of violence against prisoners emerging in the French army in 1916.

Violence against prisoners of war before the 1917 spring reprisals: the French army

Philippe Pétain once remarked that Verdun was not only a great eastern fortress destined to block an invasion, but that it was also the moral boulevard of France.[84] The phrase reveals the enormous symbolic importance the French invested in their Verdun defences. However, Verdun was also important for another reason. For it was at this moral boulevard that the French army significantly remodelled its policy towards German prisoners of war and it was this shift in French policy that provoked Germany into further reprisals.

---

[81] TNA, WO 161/100, no. 3006.   [82] Ibid.
[83] Imperial Chancellor Bethmann Hollweg's speech to the German Reichstag, 4.8.1914. Collected Diplomatic Documents Relating to the Outbreak of the European War (London, 1915), p. 438.
[84] Annette Becker, Les Monuments aux morts. Patrimoine et mémoire de la Grande Guerre (Paris, 1988), p. 13.

In May 1916, the French Ministry of War made two key decisions that considerably altered prisoner treatment. The first, based on the argument that the Germans were already doing the same, rescinded the restriction that prisoners of war could not be employed on work directly connected to the war effort, a stipulation enshrined in the Hague Convention of 1907.[85] The second created an entirely new category of prisoner labourer. The French Ministry of War approved French army requests that a certain proportion of the prisoners it captured should be directly employed by the army in the army zone. Following this decision, on 9 June 1916, an initial 10,600 German prisoners were formed into prisoner of war labour companies, each made up of 425 prisoners.[86] By 1 September 1916, French army headquarters wrote to the Ministry of War in Paris that the 10,600 prisoners were not enough. It proposed that a proportion of all new prisoners captured be allocated to the army to form new prisoner of war labour companies as

The work required to the rear of the front of military operations and for the development of offensives has become increasingly urgent ... There is no other means to remedy the enormous deficit between the labour requirements and the resources available other than organising and employing in the armies numerous units of prisoner workers.[87]

The numbers of Germans thus employed rapidly increased. By 26 January 1917, 22,915 German prisoners were working in the French prisoner of war labour companies, 5,978 of whom worked for the 2nd Army.[88]

Control of the kinds of work these prisoner labour companies were assigned and where they were housed was very lax. There were considerable variations in prisoner living conditions between companies. Conditions were especially bad at the Verdun battlefield and its environs, the area controlled by the 2nd Army Command. In August 1916, many of its prisoner workers were sleeping in tents with 'no means of protecting themselves from bad weather as they have no blanket or canvas. Some have only a coat.'[89] Most of the prisoners working in this area never received any allocation of bedding straw.[90] Such supply problems existed in other French armies too. In the 3rd Army one general noted on 25 August 1916 that the prisoners of war 'do not have any blankets; very few of them

---

[85] Cahen-Salvador, *Les Prisonniers de guerre*, p. 126.
[86] SHAT, 16 N 2467, D.1, f. 34, 520/DA, order no. 2046/DA, 9.6.1916.
[87] SHAT, 16 N 2467, D.1, f. 134, 2846/DA to M. de la Guerre, 1.9.1916.
[88] SHAT, 16 N 525, État des Prisonniers se trouvant dans la Zone des Armées le 26 Janvier 1917.
[89] SHAT, 19 N 512, Cie de P.G., Cahier de Correspondance, avril 1916–novembre 1917, no. 352, 28.8.1916.
[90] *Ibid.*, no. 102, 17.6.1916.

have a coat. In order to obtain the best level of production and to avoid pulmonary and abdominal infections, I think it necessary . . . to provide each of them with a second-hand blanket and later with a coat for the winter.'[91]

In addition to these poor living conditions, prisoner labourers in the 2nd Army Zone also had to work under shellfire. One of the most dangerous locations for these German prisoner labourers was Baleycourt, where, on 29 July 1916, a German prisoner died and another was injured.[92] The French report named them as Georg Sigl and Arthur Hock. In all likelihood the French had spelled the German names incorrectly as the incident was confirmed to German military intelligence by a German prisoner from the same working party who identified them as Georg Siegl and another man named Koch.[93] Between 15 and 25 October alone, seven prisoners died from shellfire incidents at Baleycourt.[94] The worldly possessions of prisoner Wedebrock, one of those killed, amounted to a wallet, 3 Pfennig, his photograph and identity tags.[95]

This exposure of prisoners to indirect violence was known to higher levels of the French Command. An internal report stated that:

It is certain that in the 2nd Army the prisoners are employed under fire . . . the following losses have occurred in Prisoner Labour company number 53: 30 November 1916: 12 killed and 5 wounded at Faubourg Pavé at Verdun. 12 December 1916: 5 wounded at Tavannes. 24 December 1916: 1 killed and 1 wounded at Douaumont.[96]

Lieutenant-Colonel Maquard, who inspected French prisoner labour companies in the army zone, provides further insights into prisoner of war labour company number 53. Based at Cabaret Ferme, these prisoners were lodged in dug-outs.[97] Hygiene conditions there were 'bad. There are numerous cases of dysentery and enteritis.'[98] Working at the heart of the Verdun battlefield, 100 of these prisoners were building a track at Fort Douaumont and 1,200 were bringing material to Douaumont, and also to

---

[91] SHAT, 16 N 2467, D.1, f. 132, 3e armée État-Major, DES, General Legrand, to DA, 25.8.1916.

[92] SHAT 19 N 512, no. 247, 30.7.1916.

[93] *Ibid*; also BA-MA, PH2 / 33, f. 362, 2.8.1918, Interview with Anton Lauber.

[94] SHAT, 19 N 512, Cie de P. G. Cahier de Correspondance, avril 1916–nov 1917, no. 609, 23.10.1916; BA-MA, PH2 / 33, f. 362, 2.8.1918, Interview with Anton Lauber.

[95] SHAT, 19 N 512, Cie de P. G. Cahier de Correspondance, avril 1916–nov 1917, no. 601, 21.10.16.

[96] SHAT, 16 N 2468, D.5, f. 47, 8.1.1917, GQG, Note relative à l'emploi des prisonniers de guerre dans la Zone des Armées.

[97] SHAT, 16 N 2732, GQG, DA, Inspection des Troupes d'étapes, unités indigènes, 25.12.1916, Rapport du Lt.-Col. Maquard . . . a.s. de l'inspection passée à la Cie. PG 53 à Verdun.

[98] *Ibid*.

Fort Vaux, labouring 'under the fire of the enemy'.[99] As the location was so dangerous, Maquard even requested that French guards who were fathers of large families be replaced by men upon whose lives fewer children depended.[100] The fate of the German prisoner workers aroused no such concern. One prisoner, Hermann Herigsohn, who escaped from a Verdun labour company in January 1917, recalled how the prisoners lived in accommodation '1,40m high and 1,40m wide. A man could not stand upright in it; you could also not stretch out fully when lying down. The ground was very damp. In places there was water on it.'[101] Herigsohn stated that during his time with the company, working behind Fort Douaumont, forty-five prisoners were killed or wounded and two or three men were sent to hospital daily wounded or sick. He complained to a French major that 'I had not expected this of a great nation.'[102] The major replied that Germany was doing the same.[103] The prisoners received no gas masks although gas grenades were being used in the area.[104] Herigsohn recounted how, when working,

We received a direct hit and had 8 badly wounded. While we were waiting there for the work to be assigned to us, we received a second direct hit which wounded four among us. With this, the prisoners ran back to the camp. There a French officer ordered us back to work. One of us, an NCO explained that we refused to go. He was then threatened with being shot ... Then the French officer got another more senior officer and he said to us that it was army orders that we must work here; he would gladly spare us this work but it had to be. Upon this, we went back to work. We had to bring planks and boards to the second French line behind Fort Douaumont through the Souilly gorge ... The following night we were suddenly awoken and an order was read out to us that we were duty bound to obey our commanders. In the case of refusal to obey the leader of the German group concerned would be shot. His successor would also be shot if another refusal to obey occurred.[105]

Such harsh working conditions took their toll. A German prisoner, Georg Oeder, who worked in a French 2nd Army field hospital in December 1916, recalled that 'the prisoners from the working companies at the front only came to us in the field hospital when, because of severe sickness, they were no longer able to work. Many came with fully frost-bitten feet that were already completely black. In addition, they were eaten all over their body by vermin and as most were suffering from diarrhoea, they soiled themselves over and over with their own faeces.'[106]

---

[99] *Ibid.*   [100] *Ibid.*
[101] BA-MA, PH2 / 33, f. 109, Interview 26.4.1917 with Hermann Herigsohn.   [102] *Ibid.*
[103] *Ibid.*   [104] *Ibid.*   [105] *Ibid.*
[106] BA-MA, PH2 / 33, f. 357, Interview with Sanitäts-Sergeant Georg Oeder, exchanged to Switzerland, 20.10.1917.

In part, this poor treatment was due to supply problems which dogged
the newly established prisoner of war companies. However, cultural attitudes also played an important role; the indifference to these captives'
welfare indicates a certain attitude that prisoners were expendable –
revealing an ongoing process of brutalisation. Although never justified
as an official reprisal, this treatment was also certainly perceived in terms
of retaliation by the French personnel involved. In October 1916, the
commandant of the 21st company of prisoners of war at Vraincourt-
Auzeville passed on a complaint from a French military doctor that 'the
numerous sick prisoners at Vraincourt camp' were ill because they did not
have boots and were receiving 'insufficient' rations of fats.[107] The doctor
requested more boots and better rations. The reply from his superior, the
commandant at Souilly camp, a major military zone holding camp for
German prisoners taken at Verdun, was that a doctor was

Only supposed to report on the prisoners' health, not demand supplies which
according to military regulations he is not qualified to make judgments about . . . In
this instance, it would be salutary to let him know that the treatment inflicted upon
our compatriots who are prisoners in the Army Zone and in the interior of
Germany, does not allow us to treat our enemies with the indulgence which he
seems to desire for them.[108]

Such attitudes help explain why, in contravention of orders, prisoners
held at Souilly camp were working an eleven-hour day and why a dysentery epidemic broke out there in late December 1916.[109] Conditions at
Souilly camp were extremely bad during this period with overcrowding
and inadequate shelter. The camp was knee-deep in slime.[110] As dysentery had 'appeared in almost all the prisoners' by 17 January 1917, the
camp doctor ordered the camp quarantined.[111] He complained that he
had not enough fuel to maintain the temperature necessary for the recovery of the sick.[112] The German medical orderly, Georg Oeder, described
how during the epidemic 'half the sick were in wooden barracks and half in
a tent on tiny amounts of stinking straw . . . The men were left without care
lying in their own faeces. By 19 December to my knowledge three men
died.'[113] On 19 January 1917, there were 376 prisoners with dysentery in
Souilly camp.[114]

---

[107] SHAT, 19 N 512, Cie de P.G., Cahier de Correspondance, avril 1916–novembre 1917,
no. 561, 9.10.1916.
[108] Ibid.   [109] Ibid., no. 681, 20.11.1916; Ibid., no. 860–2, no. 890.
[110] BA-MA, PH2 / 33, f. 109, Interview with Hermann Herigsohn.
[111] SHAT, 19 N 512, Cahier de correspondance avril 1916–nov. 1917, no. 860–2, no. 890.
[112] Ibid.   [113] BA-MA, PH2 / 33, f. 357, Interview with Georg Oeder.
[114] SHAT, 19 N 512, cahier de correspondance avril 1916–novembre 1917, dossier PG
1070.

French military attitudes towards German prisoners evolved in relation to German treatment of French captives. An order from the French 2nd Army Command on disciplining prisoners stated that

Treatment ... must be conceived of in reprisal for the sufferings which our own have experienced in camps in Courland and Lithuania. Any act of indulgence, any regard whatsoever for a Boche prisoner is a punishable act of weakness and will be the object of severe sanctions by the higher command. Any misdemeanour by a prisoner must be punished with the greatest severity and the punishment must be immediate and without mercy.[115]

The attitude of the French rear command (*Direction de l'Arrière*) which oversaw the prisoner labour companies was that the orders from the French army leadership and the instructions from the Ministry of War in Paris regarding how German labour company prisoners were to be treated, housed and fed were too liberal. When the *Général Directeur des Étapes et des Services* of the 10th Army wrote in December 1916 that it was 'very regrettable' that these instructions existed, the *Direction de l'Arrière* responded that the commander of the 10th Army should feel free to

take the necessary measures without recourse to your intervention or mine to obtain from prisoners a serious output, rigorous discipline and to ensure that they are kept in conditions of comfort and alimentation which are not superior to those of French soldiers stationed near them. I would invite you to follow this principle to regulate the regime of the prisoners employed in your army zone in future.[116]

This was an effective pledge to turn a blind eye to lower command levels who did not fully adhere to the official instructions on prisoners of war. Given such attitudes, there was little effort made to monitor prisoner of war labour companies to ensure that regulations from French Army Headquarters or ministerial directives were being kept. Commandant Gay, the overall commander of prisoner labour companies in the 2nd Army, even openly admitted that, although the order from French Army Headquarters regulating prisoner of war companies had stated that prisoners' work should be carried out under the same conditions as that of French *troupes d'étapes*,

because of the urgency of the work to be carried out and the orders to obtain the greatest possible productivity from prisoners in the 2nd Army ... it has not been

---

[115] SHAT, 16 N 2468, D.4, f.140, Copie de la Note 2515, SP46, 15.9.16, Ordre donné par Groupement ABC de la IIe Armée, transmis à titre de compte-rendu, aux armées le 22.10.1916.
[116] SHAT, 16 N 2468, D.4, f. 94, 9581/DA, 13.12.1916; SHAT, 16 N 2468, D.4, f. 94, 9581/DA, 13.12.1916.

possible to stick to these prescriptions. Therefore during the summer months, daylight hours permitting, prisoners at Souilly laboured for 11 hours a day.[117]

It is difficult to assess how the prisoners reacted to these conditions. The French censor's reports on prisoners in labour companies working for the 10th Army remarked that prisoners' letters were 'extremely empty'.[118] Prisoners working for the 6th Army complained in their letters of sleeping in tents, of being bombed by German planes and of insufficient and monotonous food.[119] The letters of prisoners working in the 5th Army simply revealed 'a unanimous desire for peace'.[120]

As the above evidence illustrates, the establishment of French prisoner of war labour companies, which were poorly supplied and, in their first six months of existence, rarely inspected, resulted in a major deterioration in prisoner treatment, exposing German prisoners to the violence of bombardment from their own compatriots. The situation was particularly bad in the French 2nd Army at Verdun. Information from escapers about the harsh living conditions of these German prisoners led the German army to opt once again for collective reprisals in January 1917, in an attempt to force the French army to rectify its prisoner treatment. The commander of the French 2nd Army when these prisoner abuses occurred at France's moral boulevard was Georges Robert Nivelle and his superior, commanding the *Groupe d'armées du Centre*, Philippe Pétain. The location of Pétain's headquarters was at Souilly; the deterioration in prisoner treatment that provoked German reprisals against French captives was occurring at the very heart of the French war effort.[121]

The German spring reprisals, 1917

Michel Foucault once described the use of violence in the penal system of the early nineteenth century as 'the great spectacle of physical punishment ... the theatrical representation of pain'.[122] Foucault's intention was to illustrate how these elements disappeared from the prison landscape as the nineteenth century progressed. Yet, in some ways, these

[117] SHAT, 19 N 512, Cie de P. G. Cahier de Correspondance, avril 1916–nov. 1917, no. 681, 20.11.1916.
[118] SHAT, 16 N 2468, D.4, f. 27, Rapport Mensuel sur la correspondance des prisonniers de guerre de la 10e Armée, 1.12.1916.
[119] *Ibid.*, f. 52, Rapport Mensuel sur la correspondance des prisonniers de guerre de la 6e Armée, 5.12.1916
[120] *Ibid.*, f. 134, Rapport Mensuel sur la correspondance des PG de la 5e Armée, 24.12.1916. Information on the 5th Army was included in this report.
[121] Antoine Prost, 'Verdun', in Pierre Nora, ed., *Realms of Memory. The Construction of the French Past*, vol. III: *Symbols* (Chichester and New York, 1998), p. 381.
[122] Michel Foucault, *Discipline and Punish. The Birth of the Prison* (London, 1979), p. 14.

Figure 10. Jules Adler, 'A Bavarian Prisoner,' Souilly camp, February 1917. Bibliothèque de Documentation Internationale Contemporaine et Musée d'Histoire Contemporaine (BDIC-MHC, Les Invalides), Or PE 107.

themes re-emerged in a different captivity context in 1917. Similar phenomena – the endorsement of punishment as spectacle and a media representation of prisoners' physical pain – lay behind the German army's collective reprisals in spring 1917. The reprisals were to punish France for her perceived mistreatment of German prisoners working in French army labour companies, as outlined in the previous section, and this punishment was to be highly visible, carried out symbolically upon French prisoners whose real suffering would chastise the metaphorical body of the French nation for its misdeeds. In a very real way, therefore, the German spring reprisals of 1917 used violence as spectacle and theatre.

This was evident from the very outset. On 5 January 1917, the French received a German ultimatum that, if France did not withdraw all German prisoner of war labourers to a distance of thirty kilometres behind the front, Germany would retaliate.[123] This retaliation consisted of keeping all newly captured French prisoners at the front and sending between 10,000 and 20,000 French prisoners from camps in Germany to join them.[124] A propaganda campaign was launched by the German army leadership, the OHL, to inform German troops of Allied mistreatment of German prisoners so that they would be supportive of reprisals against their French captives.[125] On 16 January 1917, the German government announced that the French had not replied to its request within the stipulated time and a reprisal order was issued by the OHL on 21 January.[126]

The order read that prisoners were to have 'no provision of protection from the weather; no hygienic care; only meagre food; long and exhausting work without any restrictions, including transport of munitions and fortification work under enemy fire'.[127] French prisoners in working companies were to be housed in any kind of accommodation available, regardless of its quality. With this reprisal move, Hindenburg and Ludendorff's new *Oberste Heeresleitung* (OHL) effectively brought the pattern of forced labour reprisals, carried out the previous year on the eastern front, to the west; as in the 1916 eastern front reprisals, publicity was also of paramount importance. Outgoing post from prisoners was to be forwarded with speed 'so that the treatment will become known about in France'.[128] Again, as in 1916, the totalisation process operated within certain limits: while the punishment of *Anbinden* – tying prisoners to a pole or tree – was to be allowed, significantly the order also stated that beatings were not permitted. Prisoners captured wounded and officer prisoners were also once more exempt from reprisals. However, these restrictions notwithstanding, the reprisals still encompassed a variety of forms of violence against captives: prisoners were deliberately subjected to enemy shellfire, exposure, forced labour and malnutrition.

---

[123] *The Times*, 22.1.1917.   [124] Becker, *Oubliés de la Grande Guerre*, p. 121.

[125] BA-MA, Nachlass von Trotta gen. Treyden, N 233 / 32. Copy of AOK 3 order from 19.1.1917. Also SHAT, 16 N 2468, D.6, no. 113, Annexe 1, section d'information. Extraits des radiotélégrammes allemands concernant le traitement des prisonniers allemands en France.

[126] *The Times*, 22.1.1917.

[127] BA-MA, PH5 / II / 455, f. 00031, Telegramm vom 21.1.1917, Ic28302 to Armee Oberkommando 4. The same order was issued by Armee Oberkommando 3 on 24.1.1917.

[128] *Ibid.*

The French could see the reprisal camps from their own lines.[129] French reports noted that 'on 28 January, the Germans installed reprisals camps at 120 locations along the front and very near the firing line, each containing 80 to 100 prisoners, putting them especially in the villages which are most often bombarded'.[130] The spectacle of their comrades trapped under French shellfire was very unsettling for French troops. One French observer reported seeing 'the Germans pushing French prisoners under the fire of our artillery near Côte 304'.[131]

The prisoner reprisals came at a very tense phase of the war for both Germany and France. Following the massive losses in the Somme and Verdun battles of 1916, the German military leadership decided to retreat to a stronger defensive position on the western front and to focus upon the outcome of the unrestricted submarine warfare campaign, which began on 1 February 1917.[132] In the German army, the reprisals thus began just weeks before the retreat to the new defensive Hindenburg/Siegfried line took place on 16–19 March 1917 and the whole issue provided an important propaganda diversion on the home front; the reprisals may also possibly have been intended to distract the Allied armies on the ground from noticing the German military preparations for retreating. Most importantly, the reprisals provided valuable extra labour at a time when the German army badly required additional forced workers: the final phase of building the Hindenburg/Siegfried line, as well as the five-week implementation of a massive scorched earth policy, codenamed Operation Alberich, between 9 February and 15 March, which preceded the German withdrawal to the Hindenburg/Siegfried line's new defences, were highly labour-intensive actions, which, as the historian Michael Geyer has convincingly argued, could not have occurred without the massive use of forced civilian and prisoner labour.[133] From late 1916 on, prisoner labour had been used to construct the new Hindenburg/ Siegfried line defences – some 26,000 prisoner of war workers were involved – and it is not implausible that the need for extra workers in spring 1917, to replenish manpower resources, may well have been a factor in the initial decision to launch the reprisals in January 1917,

---

[129] SHAT, 16 N 2468, D.6, f. 113, Annexe 3, Information from 4th Army based on plane and troop observations.

[130] SHAT, 16 N 2469, D.7, f. 110, GQG, 4044/DA, 30.3.1917.

[131] SHAT, 16 N 2469, D.7, f. 110, DA/4044, C. en C. to M. de la Guerre, 30.3.1917.

[132] David Stevenson, *1914–1918. The History of the First World War* (London, 2004), p. 312.

[133] On the construction of the Hindenburg/Siegfried line defences, see Michael Geyer, 'Rückzug und Zerstörung 1917', in Gerhard Hirschfeld, Gerd Krumeich and Irina Renz, eds., *Die Deutschen an der Somme, 1914–1918. Krieg, Besatzung, Verbrannte Erde* (Essen, 2006), pp. 163–78.

significantly the same month that the military leadership finally decided upon the date for their strategic withdrawal to the new defensive line. The two decisions thus may well have interacted: indeed, under the auspices of the reprisals policy, not only were newly captured prisoners retained as labour for the German army at the front but thousands of prisoners were also moved from German home front camps to the army working companies.[134] Hence the reprisals coincided with a moment when the German army was in great need of additional workers, a turning-point which was instrumental in convincing Ludendorff that in future the army needed to vastly increase its use of forced labour.[135] The spring 1917 reprisals must also be seen in the context of Germany's wider efforts to deal with wartime manpower shortages which gave rise to increasingly radical attitudes towards civilian labour on the German home front, with the passing of the Auxiliary Service Law in December 1916, which instigated mandatory labour service for all German males during the war and restricted the freedom of workers to change jobs. In sum, the reprisals occurred in the context of a widespread shift within Germany towards the totalisation of wartime labour.

In France, where the Nivelle Offensive was being prepared, the question of removing all German prisoner labour to a distance of thirty kilometres was rejected out of hand by the French military. The French Commander-in-Chief, Georges Robert Nivelle, was adamant that the French should establish their own reprisal camps for German prisoners in retaliation and even selected potential reprisal camp sites at locations under fire in the French front line.[136] Nivelle also publicised the reprisals to his troops to deter French surrenders, believing this would 'at least serve as a warning to French soldiers of the end that awaits them should they fall into enemy hands and increase their hatred for an implacable enemy, making them prefer anything to the horrors of captivity'.[137] The irony was that, although ordinary soldiers endured hard labour under shellfire, this was seen as culturally acceptable. When demanded of prisoners, on very poor rations, by the enemy, however, it was perceived as violently abhorrent. It was not the exposure of men to violence, but rather the cultural legitimacy of the context of that exposure that mattered.

---

[134] *Ibid.* Annette Becker estimates that 10,000 French prisoners were moved to the front from camps in Germany. Becker, *Oubliés de la Grande Guerre*, p. 121.

[135] Geyer, 'Rückzug und Zerstörung', pp. 168, 172.

[136] SHAT, 16 N 2468, D.6, no. 113, 5875/DA, Nivelle to Ministère de la Guerre, 25.2.1917.

[137] SHAT, 16 N 2469, D.7, f. 47, GQG, État-Major, C. en C. to M. de la Guerre, Cabinet, 17.3.1917.

The French government, unaware of the fact that the French 2nd Army had been employing German prisoners under shellfire at Verdun, became increasingly concerned about how the French army was treating its prisoner labour companies. It refused Nivelle's request to set up reprisal camps behind French lines and demanded to know where German prisoners were working.[138] In fact, the British too had begun to demand similar information from the French army: Adelaide Livingstone, the American secretary of the British Committee on the Treatment by the Enemy of British Prisoners of War, requested to be allowed to inspect the French prisoner of war labour companies in January 1917. Her request was refused.[139]

Nivelle denied that any German prisoners had been employed under shellfire. He fed the French government misinformation throughout spring 1917, claiming that the Germans had launched reprisals because 'certain German military authorities are angry about the ease with which many of their units were taken prisoner during the December engagements before Verdun. It is, therefore, probably the case that the German leaders are seeking every means to inspire in their soldiers a horror of captivity.'[140] The French Commander-in-Chief avoided informing his government that German prisoners had frequently worked under shellfire in the autumn of 1916. Instead he wrote on 17 March 1917 requesting that the Minister for War instruct the press to 'focus particularly at the moment ... upon the bad treatment inflicted upon French prisoners by the Germans'.[141] Nivelle helpfully enclosed documents on the theme which could be used to write suitable articles.

On 11 March 1917, following a British refusal to limit their employment of German prisoners to thirty kilometres behind the front, the reprisals were extended by the OHL to include all newly captured British prisoners. In total, across the whole of the spring reprisals period, as many as 33,000 French and British other-rank prisoners may have been affected.[142] With its own new military push looming, the battle of Arras (April–May 1917), an increasingly concerned British government looked

---

[138] SHAT, 16 N 2468, D.6, no. 143, 6411/DA, C. en C. to M. de la Guerre, 1.3.1917.
[139] SHAT, 16 N 2468, D. 5, no. 75, sous-secrétaire d'état, service de santé militaire to Mr le Général, C. en C., 10.1.1917.
[140] SHAT, 16 N 2469, D.7, f. 34, 290/DA, Nivelle to M. de la Guerre, Cabinet, 15.3.1917.
[141] SHAT, 16 N 2469, D.7, no. 47, C. en C. to M. de la Guerre, 17.3.1917.
[142] Wilhelm Doegen states that 23,184 British and French other ranks were captured during the spring reprisals period, although a portion of these would have been captured wounded and thus been exempt from reprisals. Doegen, *Kriegsgefangene Völker*, pp. 28–9. Annette Becker estimates that 10,000 French prisoners were moved to the front from camps in Germany. Becker, *Oubliés de la Grande Guerre*, p. 121.

to the French to coordinate a common Allied policy: at the Anglo-French conference in London on 12 March 1917, the reprisals question was discussed in detail. Some civilian politicians present suggested that the Allies should consider withdrawing their German prisoner labourers to a twenty-kilometre distance, but military figures attending rejected this. General Nivelle said that he could not alter the twenty kilometre rule as it was important for the French Army to have this labour. Sir Douglas Haig said that he did not even agree to 20 kilometres. He said that Britain had actually employed prisoners of war on work within 5 miles of the fighting line, though they were not exposed to shellfire. He attached great importance to the employment of these prisoners of war.[143] It was decided that no change in where the Allies employed prisoners would occur. The conference concluded that 'we were at liberty to utilise German prisoners of war as we thought fit'.[144]

However, the debate at the Anglo-French conference had miscalculated on one point. The German reprisals policy was based on the fact that the French and British governments were very vulnerable to public opinion. The spring reprisals were played out before the general public in France, Britain and Germany in a way that previous reprisals had not been. Newspapers such as *The Times* reported the prisoners' predicament.[145] Thousands of letters from the reprisals prisoners began to arrive at family homes, at the International Committee of the Red Cross, the Vatican, the Australian High Commission in London and the Canadian High Commission.[146] Shocked relatives forwarded the letters they received to prefects, mayors, local councils and the War Office in London. The Prefect of Meurthe et Moselle wrote to Nivelle on 1 April 1917 that 'many families in Nancy have received letters from their sons who are prisoners in Germany, informing them that they are on reprisals. They were brought to the front some time ago and forced to work on fortifications under the fire of the French guns.'[147] Such letters fed into the existing well-developed public expectation of atrocity by the enemy against prisoners of war, leading to a rapid public outcry that governments do something to stop the German reprisals.

The prisoners had been carefully informed of what to write home. Their letters all insisted that they were being held in reprisal because German prisoners of war were working behind the British and French firing lines.

---

[143] TNA, WO 32/5098, 90a, Minutes of the Anglo-French Conference, 12.3.1917.
[144] *Ibid.*   [145] *The Times*, 22.1.1917.
[146] TNA, WO 32/5381, 46a and 47a. Also ASV, Affari Ecclesiastici Straordinari, Stati Ecclesiastici, anno 1916–1918, pos. 1412, fasc. 550, 15.2.1917.
[147] SHAT, 16 N 2469, D.8, f. 9, GQG, 1 Bureau, 7.4.1917.

Private Jack Smart wrote to his family that 'we are absolutely starving ...
we have nothing else but a wet floor to sleep on and nothing to cover us ...
it is all through the British government having German prisoners working
just behind the firing line. The sooner the government remove [sic] the
German prisoners further back the sooner we will be better treated.'[148]
Rifleman T. M. Kenna wrote: 'They are keeping us working in their
trenches, they say their prisoners is [sic] working in ours ... There is
eight of your boys here and I hope that no more comes [sic] for it is
cruelty.'[149] Another prisoner letter stated: 'They [sic] nearly working us
to death, and don't give us much grub and they make us work up in their
trenches from daylight till dark and our shells come very close to us.'[150]
Lance-Corporal M. Birmingham wrote to his former unit:

Just a few lines which no doubt will surprise you and the rest of the Boys to say I
was taken prisoner ... and I am working behind the line through our government
keeping the German prisoners behind our lines. We are getting bad treatment until
justice is done to their men, they say, so the sooner our officials takes it into
consideration [sic] the better it will be for us, so no more. From Brum. Write
soon old boy.[151]

The French prisoners, who had been in the reprisal camps since
January, wrote more graphically: 'We are forced to work for the
German army under the fire of the French artillery and yesterday 9
of my comrades were hit by a shell ... 19 grams of meat per man for 4
days and every 4 days a loaf of KK bread that weighs 1200 grams and
that is all.'[152] Prisoner Sergeant Paul Barthelémy wrote: 'do they
know of our dangerous situation in France? Are they trying to improve
it?'[153] Gilbert Lasausse informed his cousin: 'We are in a lamentable
state and work under artillery fire. We have suffered casualties – dead
and wounded. Try to speak with those of influence to make these
reprisals end.'[154] 'Tens of men fall each day on the road, victims of
cold and hunger. It is our seventh week of martyrdom,' another
prisoner stated, writing to his uncle that 'this work consists of working
on improving trenches before the German positions under the fire of
the French batteries ... Please hide the truth of this at all costs from

[148] TNA, WO 32/5381, 28a, Letter from Private Jack Smart, 28.3.1917.
[149] *Ibid.*, Postcard from no. 1021, Rifleman T. M. Kenna, 7th Royal Irish Rifles, n.d.
    forwarded to D.M.I. for information from G.H.Q., 7 May 1917.
[150] *Ibid.*, no. 29, S. Kerry to Mr H. Morris, Manager, Jersey Gas Works, 18.3.1917.
[151] *Ibid.*, 31 a, Lance-Corporal M. Birmingham to Pte T. Chapman, 17.3.1917.
[152] SHAT, 16 N 2469, D.9, f. 36, Extract of letter from a French prisoner passed on to
    GQG, 20.4.1917.
[153] SHAT, 16 N 2469, D.8, f. 123, Sgt P. Barthelémy to Mlle J. Nicey, 13.4.1917.
[154] SHAT, 16 N 2469, D.9, f. 77, DA/7456, Gilbert Lasausse to Célestin Thiron, 1.4.1917.

Maman.'[155] Some German soldiers observing these French reprisals prisoners were moved to pity. 'I am not yet hardened enough by war to look on indifferently,' one wrote home to his parents, 'I am seized with rage at seeing such things … They search in the rubbish to appease their hunger … the sufferings of these men are terrible. Every day many of them fall during work either because of hunger or because of exhaustion.'[156]

The German reprisals rapidly became public knowledge in Britain, France, and also in Germany. On 4 March 1917, the Prussian Minister for War, Hermann von Stein, announced these new collective reprisals against prisoners on the western front to the Reichstag; his speech was received with warm applause and widely reported in the German press, which referred to thousands of German prisoners 'discovered working close behind the French front in the range of the fire of our own guns'.[157] Von Stein's comments caused consternation for the families of German prisoners, who flooded the German Red Cross at Frankfurt with demands for information.[158] 'To our great surprise we learned that the prisoners who have an address like yours are all behind the French front and even in the firing zone,' one anxious letter written from Cologne to a German prisoner in France stated. 'I am very worried; yet you wrote to us that you were working in a locomotive depot.'[159]

Von Stein's speech illustrates how the ruthlessness of the reprisal move was justified. He emphasised that 'it was not easy' to enact reprisal treatment of prisoners that mirrored the enemy treatment of German captives; he also insisted that German soldiers did not directly physically harm prisoners.[160] His position was supported by Gustav Stresemann, who endorsed the reprisals, stating that 'we take such measures in the expectation and belief that only immediate retaliation in the form of such reprisals' could protect German prisoners from French mistreatment – a French action that Stresemann described as a 'return to the age of barbarism' which would make one 'doubt in human progress'.[161] In contrast, the Social Democrats, while condemning French mistreatment, protested that Germany should not enter into a 'competition in barbarism' with

---

[155] SHAT, 16 N 2469, D.8, f. 127, DA 2730, 13.2.1917.
[156] *Ibid.*, D.9, f. 82, DA/7445. Letter found on a captured German soldier, 5.5.1917.
[157] *The Times,* 24.3.1917, p. 7. *The Times,* 5.3.17, p. 7.
[158] SHAT, 16 N 2469, D. 7, f. 94, rapport sur la correspondance des prisonniers de guerre dans la IIe Armée, 3137/DA, 27.3.1917.
[159] SHAT, 16 N 2469, D.7, f. 72, GAN, DE, État Major, no. 1473, Rapport mensuel sur la correspondance des PG stationnés dans la zone de la DE, 20.3.1917.
[160] *Verhandlungen des Reichstages,* XIII. Legislaturperiode, II. Session, vol. 309, Stenographische Berichte (Berlin, 1870–1939; 1917), 85. Sitzung, 1 March 1917, 2446.
[161] *Ibid.* 2468.

other nations; SPD Deputy Keil also suggested that if reprisals were necessary, they should target the upper-class enemy officer prisoner, 'not the simple soldier' who had 'no responsibility' for the wrongdoing of the French government.[162]

The emotional charge of the reprisals prisoners' letters ultimately proved too much for the French government and, 'owing to pressure of French public opinion', on 27 March 1917, Nivelle was informed that the government had ordered that all German prisoners were to be withdrawn to thirty kilometres behind the French lines.[163] This move must be seen in context: France was experiencing a significant wave of domestic protest actions, beginning with a major strike by Parisian female textile workers on 8 January 1917; in the wake of the overthrow of the Tsarist regime in Russia through strike actions in February 1917, the French government greatly feared the domestic rise in popular discontent with the war.[164] It could not afford to be seen to do nothing to aid its prisoners in German hands. Nivelle initially attempted to resist the French government's request, asking them to defer the decision. The withdrawal of the German prisoners would 'result in the army being unable to use an important section of prisoner labour on work necessary for the preparation of active operations, resulting in serious delays,' he wrote.[165] It would create an unacceptable 'scandalous contrast if we withdraw the German prisoners from Toul and Belfort, when the Germans are making our own work at 1,100 metres from the front'.[166]

Nivelle's protests were to no avail. The French government was powerful enough to refuse its Commander-in-Chief, even as he prepared for a massive offensive. The withdrawal of German prisoner labourers to thirty kilometres was to be carried out 'as swiftly as possible' and completed by 5 May 1917 at the latest; significantly, this decision meant that German prisoner labourer units were removed from the thirty-kilometre front area just as discontent within the French army, following the failure of the Chemin des Dames offensive, escalated into widespread mutinous protest in May 1917; thus any security threat that prisoner workers might potentially have posed during the mutinies was avoided.[167] Moreover, the French government also appointed a new inspector to provide it with direct information on conditions for German prisoners of war labouring

[162] *Ibid.*, 2454.   [163] TNA, WO 32/5098, W.O. to General Wilson, G.H.Q., 14.4.1917.
[164] Jean-Baptiste Duroselle, *La Grande Guerre des Français, 1914–1918. L'incompréhensible* (Paris, 2002), p. 201.
[165] SHAT, 16 N 2469, D.7, f. 111, 4041/DA to M. de la G., 30.3.1917.   [166] *Ibid.*
[167] SHAT, 16 N 2469, D.7, f. 152, M. de la G. to G.Q.G., 3.4.1917. On the mutinies, see Duroselle, *La Grande Guerre des Français*, pp. 202–5.

for the French army and ensure that government orders on prisoner treatment were obeyed.[168] The British, initially angered that the French did not consult them before agreeing to the German demand, soon followed suit.[169] On 27 April, the British cabinet ordered that all German prisoner workers were to be withdrawn to thirty kilometres distance from the front.[170] The order was carried out by 27 May 1917.[171] Having reluctantly given in to the German thirty-kilometre demand, the Allies proceeded to abide by this new limitation remarkably tenaciously: for the remainder of the conflict, Britain and France did not employ German prisoner labour companies within thirty kilometres of the front. Indeed, when British and German delegates met in The Hague in June 1917, to negotiate directly on prisoner of war treatment, they even included an article emphasising the thirty-kilometre limit in the agreement they signed.[172]

Once the news that all German prisoners had been withdrawn to thirty kilometres reached Germany, the collective reprisals effectively ended and the British and French prisoners were removed from the German front line by mid-June 1917 to a distance of thirty kilometres, where they remained working for the German army.[173] Yet although they were no longer working at the front, these prisoner workers continued to experience mistreatment: reprisals prisoners who were still fit were retained in the occupied territories where conditions remained harsh. One post-war account from a British prisoner, Leonard Thompson, captured in April 1917 and retained to work in France until the following Christmas, recalled how

we lived on pearl barley boiled in coppers and bread or cake made of weed-seed. Then we were put into a forest to make charcoal and sometimes the Germans shot into our legs as we marched. We never knew what they would do next. They chose boys to thrash. I don't know why I was chosen but I was a favourite for this thrashing and was always being taken off for a beating. George Holmes ... was one of the people who died from the ill-treatment.[174]

---

[168] *Ibid.*, D.9, f. 139, M. de la G., IGPG, 11.4.1917.
[169] TNA, CAB 24/63, War Cabinet, Prisoners of War, 'Summary of reprisals taken by the British and German governments since the beginning of the war', 12.9.1918.
[170] TNA, WO 32/5098, no. 113a, W.O. to G.H.Q., 27.4.1917.
[171] *Ibid.*, no. 120 a, AG, G.H.Q. to W.O., 17.5.1917.
[172] BA-MA, PH5 / II / 449 f. 76, Heeresgruppe Kronprinz Rupprecht to AOK 4, 19.6.1918; IWM, 91/44/1 HEB 1/1 Papers of Lieutenant-General Sir Herbert Belfield, Director of Prisoners of War 1914–1920, Diary of the conference at The Hague, 23 June–7 July 1917.
[173] TNA, WO 32/5098, no. 126a, Sir W. Townley, to FO, 16.6.1917. BA-MA, PH5 / II / 456, f. 168, Kriegsministerium Nr. 21103.17.U.5/1 to all AOKs, 5.6.1917. See also f. 159, G. Qu. M. to all AOKs, tgm, n.d.
[174] Ronald Blyth, *Akenfield. Portrait of an English Village* (London, 1969), p. 42.

Prisoners categorised as sick or unfit when the reprisals ended were evacuated to camps in Germany.[175] The German army could ill afford to spare them – its ever-increasing labour needs were driving a deterioration in prisoner conditions, as it forced men to work on rations which even the army leadership acknowledged were inadequate. As Ludendorff noted in July 1917,

because of overwork and underfeeding, the productivity of labourers working for the army and in the occupied territories [prisoners of war etc.] is continually decreasing. A general increase in food is out of the question, although in particular cases better food may be tried and those employed on heavy manual labour may be given extra. The exchange of exhausted and sick prisoners for fully fit ones from Germany is not possible because of the damage it would cause to the home front economy. For this reason, all means must be used to preserve the available valuable and irreplacable labour strength for the long-term. Careful consideration of accommodation, clothing, appropriate preparation and division of food is, therefore, invaluable. Above all the work demanded ... must be proportionate to the small amount of food provided.[176]

Those reprisals prisoners who were sent to Germany were searched for any documentary evidence of their experience. All diaries or letters were taken from them. Moreover, those prisoners who had been held in the reprisal camps were deliberately excluded from consideration for exchange to Switzerland or repatriation to their home country to prevent them providing information about German front-line installations.[177] Having experienced the worst of the German prisoner of war system they were now condemned to remain within it for the rest of the war.[178]

Conclusion

Writing about another very different war, Hannah Arendt remarked that one definition of a war crime was the 'factor of gratuitous brutality'.[179] From the German army's point of view the spring reprisals of 1917 did not fall into this category. The exposure of British and French prisoners to shellfire was anything but gratuitous. It was a calculated policy, designed

---

[175] BA-MA, PH5 / II / 456, f. 159, G.Qu. M. to all AOKs, tgm, n.d.
[176] BA-MA, PH5 / II / 456, f. 131, Abschrift, Chef des Generalstabes des Feldheeres to all AOKs, II Nr. 59071 op., gez. Ludendorff, 4.7.1917.
[177] BA-MA, PH5 / II / 456, Kriegsministerium UK dept, Nr. 54.17.UK to AOK, 22.4.1917.
[178] BA-MA, PH5 / II / 454, ff. 208–25, Kriegsministerium, Unterkunftsdepartement, Nr. 54.17.UK, 22.4.1917.
[179] Hannah Arendt, *Eichmann in Jerusalem. A Report on the Banality of Evil* (London, 1994), p. 256.

to protect German prisoners held by the French in appalling conditions. And it had worked.

Yet the kind of violence, both physical and psychological, which the OHL was prepared to sanction during the spring reprisals took a heavy toll on the prisoners involved. The destruction of the German army archive at Potsdam during the Second World War means that statistics detailing the exact cost of the reprisals in prisoner lives may never be found; in their absence, however, there is considerable anecdotal evidence of malnutrition and death. British prisoners who witnessed some of those who had been on reprisals arriving in Germany were shocked by their condition. 'They looked very bad and were all so weak that we had to carry them on stretchers from the station to the camp,' a private at Hameln camp recalled.[180] 'They could not walk from sheer exhaustion ... they were absolutely exhausted from starvation and some were frost-bitten,' another remembered.[181] Pte H. J. Clarke, a British prisoner at Giessen (sic) camp, wrote in his diary on 13 May 1917, upon seeing 260 French prisoners arriving back after the spring reprisals:

May I never behold again such specimens of humanity. With hollow eyes and sunken cheeks, their clothes hanging on them like sacks, torn and filthy, starved into semi-insanity, they rushed the guards, broke through the barbed wires and ran to us for food. That which we gave them although hard as iron, disappeared rapidly. It was of course impossible to feed all, the last comers ran to the waste tubs and scrambled for the refuse.[182]

Clarke stated that '580 men left Giessen on January 14th 1917 for work behind the German lines, 260 returned, of the remainder 192 died of starvation and brutality or were shot in cold blood. 128 were admitted to hospital on their return to camp since when many have died.'[183] Clarke's account matches other evidence. One German order on 1 June 1917 stated that complaints had been received from camps in Germany that prisoners of war sent to them because they were sick or no longer capable of working (*arbeitsunfähig*) in labour companies in the army zone 'are frequently in such poor condition that they die soon after delivery. With a view to the present shortage of labour it is absolutely imperative to avoid further such cases.'[184] In future such prisoners were only to be

---

[180] TNA, FO, 383/268, no. 118077, Statement by Frederick Thorne, 14.6.1917.
[181] *Ibid.*, no. 118079, Statement by Thomas Lever, 14.6.1917.
[182] Malcolm Hall, *In Enemy Hands. A British Territorial Soldier in Germany, 1915–1919* (Stroud, 2002) p. 87. Diary entry by H. J. Clarke, Giessen (sic) camp 13.5.1917.
[183] *Ibid.* Punctuation in quotations is H. J. Clarke's own.
[184] BA-MA, PH5 / II / 456, Generalquartiermeister to Oberbefehlshaber Ost, Alle Heeresgruppen, Alle AOKs u. Et.Insp., Mil. Verw. Rümanien, B.d.G. West, Ost, E.S., 1.6.1917.

Figure 11. 'The return from reprisals'. From: *Derrière les barbelés Scènes de la vie des prisonniers de guerre. Camps de Lechfeld, Landshut, Puchheim, Ingolstadt, Mannheim*. Sketches made during captivity by an anonymous French Prisoner 'Marix'. Bibliothèque de Documentation Internationale Contemporaine et Musée d'Histoire Contemporaine (BDIC-MHC, Les Invalides), F Piéce 114 (F).

transported to camps in Germany if the medical view was that they were capable of surviving the journey.[185]

To end with the question posed at the outset: what, ultimately, do these collective reprisals tell us about the changing nature of violence during the First World War? There are three main conclusions to be drawn here. First, the reprisals show us how the totalisation process was often determined by internal national decisions: in the French case, civilian government sought to regain control of prisoner treatment from a high command which had gained considerable autonomy of action due to French desperation to defend Verdun at any cost. In the German case, a calculated gamble was made to exploit the French and British public's sense of outrage at prisoner atrocities, at the deliberate cost of prisoners' health and, in some cases, lives. This gamble, first made in the eastern reprisals of 1916, was further developed in 1917. In the short term it worked – the Allies were forced to change policy and treat their prisoner workers better. However, although the reprisals did represent a victory of sorts for Germany, they were also to some extent counterproductive. They risked alienating neutrals, damaging Germany's international reputation, and they may have dissuaded British and French troops from surrendering in

[185] *Ibid.*

1917.[186] In this regard, it is important to note that the reprisals reveal different patterns of managing violence and of legitimising certain violent behaviour towards prisoners within the French and German armies: prisoner mistreatment, largely the result of poor battlefield conditions or the brutalisation of individual officers in the French case, was institutionalised and publicly justified, in the German army reprisal response.

Second, the reprisals illustrate a process of brutalisation occurring at the level of attitudes – a key factor driving totalisation. The reprisals changed the culturally constructed perceptions of what constituted acceptable violence against prisoners in the German army, encouraging the belief that prisoners were expendable when needs dictated. These attitudes would have a profound influence, as conditions for prisoners working for the German army deteriorated in late 1917 and 1918, as the next chapter will show – indeed this change in attitudes facilitated the later mistreatment. Ultimately, it was in terms of such cultural attitudes that the spring reprisals mattered.

Third the reprisals reveal the heterogeneous nature of First World War violence. The spring reprisals sequence shows that the war gave rise to a plurality of forms of violence, not all of which fit the thesis of mass, indeterminate industrial slaughter; German reprisals violence was skilfully targeted, utilising a vulnerable group to obtain geo-political leverage over the enemy.[187] Violence was not a linear process of continual escalation – rather fluctuating cycles of violence dictated the process of totalisation in the French and German armies and governments. Studying such a 'cycle of violence' illustrates that the totalisation of warfare was not a homogeneous or irreversible process: in the French case, it was possible for civilian government to intervene and exert control over the army, reversing a deterioration in prisoner treatment. Nor was totalisation always irrational: the spread of violence to new categories of target such as prisoners of war in the German army was a calculated retaliatory response; it was neither uncontrolled nor ineffective, as it achieved an improvement in French behaviour. It was also not based on irrational propaganda – the reality of French prisoner mistreatment shows that German propaganda was not always fabricated or inaccurate. Moreover,

---

[186] This argument cannot be taken too far – despite the 1917 reprisals, enormous numbers of British troops surrendered in spring 1918. For the argument that successfully encouraging surrender was a factor in Allied victory in 1918 see Ferguson, 'Prisoner Taking', pp. 148–92.

[187] The idea of the war as an irrational mass indiscriminate slaughter was part of the post-war *Zeitgeist* and has greatly influenced our image of the conflict ever since. See Bartov, *Murder in Our Midst*, for an interpretation of how societies responded to the idea of indiscriminate battlefield violence.

totalisation *could* co-exist alongside certain limitations: reprisal violence was carefully mitigated – once they fell sick prisoners were removed from reprisals and wounded prisoners were never selected for them. The spread of violent practices to targeting prisoners did mark a significant new degree of totalisation. However, this totalisation was largely a rational process which went hand in hand with both political and military decision-making. The civilian sphere was actively engaged with the question of totalisation and, at times, endorsed it: indeed, given the reality of French prisoner mistreatment, many centrist and right-wing German politicians, as well as civilians, accepted reprisal violence as necessary. It was public knowledge following von Stein's Reichstag speech. This throws into question post-war claims that the home front was ignorant of battlefield violence; the reprisals of 1917 show the close interaction between the home front and the battle front, regarding escalating violence – an interaction which many civilians later attempted to distance themselves from during the post-war period.

In fact, it was this civilian reaction that fundamentally mattered. The subsequent longevity or future development of a reprisal sequence depended largely upon public reactions in 1914–18. The war thus gave rise to a developing power dynamic between modernity and the reception of violent practice. Reprisal violence was not historically random. With mass media and mass citizen armies, violence had a new symbolic impact which potentially exceeded its immediate strategic battlefield value – it could be used to manipulate enemy public opinion; by provoking outrage it could also provoke changes in policy. The representation of violence against prisoners of war as atrocity in 1914–15 had grown into the *deliberate* use and manipulation of atrocities against prisoners – in the form of reprisals – for strategic ends. The German army was the most receptive to this new reality.

Ultimately, however, it was the decision by armies to use prisoners in military labour companies *permanently* near and, at times, on the battle-field that marked *the* major wartime shift in the existing paradigms of captivity. Prisoners' welfare was now subordinated to military labour needs – army commands knew that locating them in and around the war zone dramatically reduced their standard of living and placed them at risk of shelling. It also forced them to work directly upon their captor's war effort, both a breach of pre-war international law and a source of mental suffering for captives. This subordination of prisoners' welfare to the military demands of the captor army occurred in all three armies studied here, by the end of 1916. Although the German army was the most ruthless towards its prisoner workers, the French and British had also accepted that prisoner welfare was subordinate to military labour needs.

However, the process of breaching successive thresholds of violence against prisoners which began in 1914, and escalated dramatically with the establishment of prisoner labour companies, was suddenly halted in the French and British armies when they accepted the thirty-kilometre agreement with Germany in 1917. The British and French strictly enforced this limit, never again employing prisoner labour companies near the front; they used colonial and British infantry labourers in front-line areas instead. In contrast, in the German case escalation continued, as the next chapter will show.

4   From discipline to retribution: violence in German prisoner of war labour companies in 1918

Into sheds capable of accommodating at the utmost 450 men, over 1,000 men were crowded. The sanitary and washing arrangements were so primitive as to be practically non-existent. The provision of food and medical attention was wholly insufficient and no parcels or letters reached the camp. In a very short time the men were starving, verminous and in a filthy condition with the inevitable consequence that dysentery appeared almost at once and men began to die with appalling rapidity. In spite of the terrible condition of the men they were forced to engage in heavy work behind the lines at long distances from the camp and practically no excuse of weakness or sickness was accepted as relieving them from work. Men in the last stages of dysentery were driven out to work and fell and died by the road.

Report on conditions at Flavy-le-Martel camp in occupied France, from the British summary of the case against Emil Müller at the Leipzig War Crimes Trials, 1921, based on testimony from twenty-seven former British prisoners.[1]

Introduction

By 1918, a mass forced labour system had developed on the western front, as the British, French and German armies retained captured prisoners to work indefinitely in their prisoner of war labour companies. This was a military incarceratory system that was now almost entirely separate to that which existed on the home front, with its much better-resourced camps. Conditions were worst, however, for those prisoners who were working in labour companies for the German army. In numerous interviews carried out in summer 1918 with escaped British prisoners who had been taken in the German spring offensive in March, the same motifs of starvation, beatings and sickness occur; former prisoners even referred to captives picking nettles to boil as food or as medicine.[2] Escaped prisoners told of cold and of men fainting from malnutrition: 'We slept on cement floors,

---

[1] Parliamentary Paper, Cd. 1450, vol. 12, *German War Trials. Report* (London, 1921), p. 10.
[2] Parliamentary Paper, Cd. 9106, *Report on the Treatment by the Germans of Prisoners of War taken during the Spring Offensives of 1918* (London, 1918). The interviews cited in the

no blankets, no straw, and fires were not allowed. Our bread ration sometimes failed for thirty-six hours. Lots of men fell sick and fainted from exhaustion. There was a lot of dysentery, and the only medicine we got was nettle leaves boiled in water.'[3] One escaped prisoner described life at Villers camp in April 1918:

The work was very hard and continuous. We dared not rest a moment. If we did, the sentries would strike us with the butt end of their rifles ... The prisoners were very weak and exhausted. During the spell between 12 and 1 they used to wander round collecting nettles, which they brought to the camp at night to eat. We were given no opportunity for washing. There was a pump at the cookhouse but the pump handle was removed to prevent us using it. The guards would give us no water. There was no heating or warming apparatus given us and there was no means of drying our clothes. If we got wet we had to remain wet.[4]

Several of these interviews with ex-prisoners were used to compile a British parliamentary paper on German prisoner abuses in 1918; they were also used to gather evidence of war crimes for post-war trials.[5] In 1921, the German Supreme Court (*Reichsgericht*), hearing the Allies' war crimes allegations at trials at Leipzig, was presented with a case brought by the British government, detailing allegations that British prisoners of war in a labour company at Flavy-le-Martel in 1918 had died from beatings, exhaustion and starvation.

In sum, the individual stories of ex-prisoners, who worked in German army prisoner of war labour companies, correspond with a broader picture of real progression towards extreme prisoner mistreatment in the German army in late-1917 and 1918. This was a site of major escalation of violence against captives; the radicalisation visible here marked a watershed in wartime prisoner mistreatment. This chapter will now examine why violence against prisoners became so widespread within the German army prisoner of war labour company system in 1918, looking at how, in the German case, the drive towards extreme mistreatment of prisoner labour that emerged during reprisals in 1916 and 1917 developed unchecked. The aim here is to explore several key questions. First, what was the overall context for violence and how prevalent was it: how exactly were British and French prisoners of war treated in 1918 while working for the German army in occupied France and Belgium? Second, was the use of violence against prisoner workers in the occupied zone deliberate army policy – an active decision to disregard alternative measures for managing

Parliamentary Paper have been traced back to the original full text of their interview in the WO 161 files at the National Archives, Kew, and it is clear that the published citations repeat exactly what the prisoner witness stated to the interviewer.
[3] *Ibid.*, p. 6.   [4] *Ibid.*, p. 4.   [5] *Ibid.*

prisoner labour – or the random result of individual initiatives by guards on the ground? Finally, was the violence practised against prisoner of war workers considered exceptional in the eyes of contemporaries? The next part of this book, chapter 5, will then consider Entente treatment of prisoner labour in 1918 by way of comparison, to see whether German army practices were evolving similarly to or diverging from those of the British and French military.

To begin, this chapter will examine the situation on the ground for prisoners working directly for the German army in autumn 1917. By September 1917, the German army had a well-established system of prisoner of war labour companies containing British and French prisoners working in areas to the rear of the front (*Etappengebiete*). This prisoner labour system operated against the backdrop of an occupation situation where the German military controlled all aspects of civilian life and exploited the occupied territories ruthlessly.[6] Occupied Belgium was divided into three zones: a northern area controlled by the German military governor; the *Etappengebiete* rear areas behind the front controlled by the rear echelon inspectors (*Etappen-Inspektion*) of each of the seven German armies; and the front areas of military operations (*Operationsgebiete*) administered by the Field Administrations (*Feldintendanturen*) of the various German armies at the front.[7] Occupied France was divided into two militarised zones only: *Etappengebiete* and *Operationsgebiete*. The focus here will be upon prisoner labour companies working in the *Etappengebiete* and *Operationsgebiete* in both France and Belgium; these prisoner workers experienced harsh living conditions throughout the winter of 1917.

Prisoner living conditions in the occupied territories before the German spring offensive

Mortagne, St Saulve, Denain and Marchiennes are not especially well known placenames from the First World War. However, they represent an appropriate point to begin an examination of the living conditions of British and French prisoners of war working for the German army in autumn 1917: the *Etappen-Inspektion* records of the German Sixth (Bavarian) Army reveal that its prisoner companies were accommodated in improvised camps at these locations, situated in former schools or large houses which had survived the ravages of combat. Into these buildings several hundred prisoners were often crammed with the minimum

---

[6] Hull, *Absolute Destruction*, pp. 227–62.   [7] *Ibid.*, p. 227.

provision for sanitation. In October 1917, 100 British prisoners from the *Engländer Kommando 3* were located at Mortagne. They lived, ate and slept in one room in what had been a civilian home before the war. Two-storey wooden plank bunks had been erected to serve as beds. There were no sacks to serve as mattresses: the prisoners had two blankets and slept on dirty wood shavings. They received 'some 350 grams of bread' as their daily bread ration and few parcels reached them.[8] The prisoners were working on road building for eight hours a day. Local civilians passed them extra food from time to time. The prisoners had no coats and each man had only one shirt and one pair of underwear. Their footwear was fully worn out; some men had no proper footwear at all. The latrine was a pit in the ground. There was no running water. Instead, the men were bathed every fourteen days in a nearby factory. Hardly surprisingly, the men's health was described as poor and there were high sickness rates.[9] In addition to the sick in the camp *Lazarett* (hospital quarters), fifteen prisoners were *revierkrank* (in the sickbay) in October 1917. In August 1917, two prisoners in the camp died.[10]

At St Saulve, in October 1917, 193 other British prisoners from the *Engländer Kommando 3* were accommodated in an improvised camp in a former schoolroom. Here the prisoners had no opportunity to bathe at all, although in contrast to Mortagne they did have access to running water in the yard for washing. Again the prisoners had no coats and only some had a change of underwear. Their clothing was described by the inspector as 'very worn', needing to be supplemented.[11] There was such a shortage of blankets that some prisoners had no bed covering at all. They worked for eight hours a day unloading and loading cargo, with an hour-long march to and from their workplace. This work was carried out on a daily ration of 600 grams of bread and 100 grams of meat. However, prisoners here also received food parcels.

---

[8] BHStA IV, Etappen-Inspektion 6, Gefangenen Kommando, Bd. 199, Tagebuch 3, Abschrift des Kriegstagebuches der Gefangenen-Inspektion 106 für die Zeit vom 1.10.17 bis 31.12.1917, Akt 3. Etappen-Inspektion 6. Armee 30.10.17, Anlage 15, Zusammenfassendes Endurteil des Kommandeurs der Gefangenen-Inspektion 6 über die Besichtigungsreisen am 4.6 und 23.10.17, Inspektion of Engländer Kommando 3, Mortagne, Major Gross und Hauptmann Georg.

[9] *Ibid.*

[10] BHStA IV, Et.Inspektion 6, Bund 203, Engländer Kommando 3, 1917, September, October, November.

[11] BHStA IV, Et.Inspektion, Gefangenen Kommando, Bd. 199, Tagebuch 3, Abschrift des Kriegstagebuches der Gefangenen-Inspektion 106 für die Zeit vom 1.10.17 bis 31.12.1917, Akt 3, Et.Inspektion 6 Armee 30.10.17, Anlage 15, Zusammenfassendes Endurteil des Kommandeurs der Gefangenen-Inspektion 6 über die Besichtigungsreisen am 4.6 und 23.10.17, Major Gross und Hauptmann Georg.

At Denain, where 209 British prisoners from the *Engländer Kommando 3* were working, the accommodation was in a former hospital building. The prisoners had access to water for washing in the yard and were brought each week for a bath in the town. They received rations of 330 grams of bread and 110 grams of meat daily. They worked a six-hour day. Seventeen prisoners were sick in the camp *Lazarett* and ten others were *revierkrank*.

Conditions for French prisoners working for the German army in October 1917 varied. At Marchiennes, French prisoners from the *Franzosen Kommando 14* were accommodated in a former civilian house.[12] All rooms were heated and had windows and doors which closed properly. Water was available in the yard and the clothing of the prisoners was in order, although they had last been deloused in May 1917. The prisoners' health was good. Only two were sick. The prisoners received a ration per day of 330 grams of bread and 70 grams of meat. Local civilians gave them extra food. The prisoners were employed on work at the station.

In October 1917, the German *Etappen* Inspectors passed all of the above camps as suitable for prisoners to stay in during the cold winter months. Their reports give an insight into the types of camps which by late 1917 had sprung up across the *Etappengebiete* and *Operationsgebiete* of the German army. Several key points emerge. First, although all the prisoners were paid the same amount, 30 Pfennig, the rations they were receiving differed substantially from camp to camp even though all were engaged upon heavy manual labour. Moreover, the 'wages' the prisoners earned were not to be paid until after the end of the war, which, in effect, meant they worked without any financial reward. Second, the prisoners in these camps received or bartered for crucial food supplements from local civilians without which their condition would be jeopardised, particularly as the bread ration they were receiving was made up of substitute ingredients and the work camps they lived in had no official canteen from which to buy extra food.[13] Extra food from parcels was also not guaranteed in the occupied territories. At a meeting to discuss the administration of prisoner labour in October 1917 it was acknowledged by the German

---

[12] *Ibid.*

[13] The flour content of prisoners' bread was open to question. An order from the *Generalintendant des Feldheeres* stated that any addition of bran or husks to the flour for prisoners' bread rations must maintain a minimum nutritional value equal to that of 400 grams of bread made from 94 per cent of rye flour, illustrating that some dilution of the flour content was standard practice. BA-MA, PH5/II/456, f. 55, General Intendant des Feldheeres IIId Nr. 254.11.17, Gr.H.Qu. to alle Armee-Oberkommandos usw. 13.11.1917.

officers present that prisoners were so frequently moved from camp to camp and, indeed, often from the administration of one German army to another, that the delivery of parcels and post to them was very irregular.[14]

Third, these inspection reports show that the accommodation and clothing of the prisoners was generally substandard by late 1917. Finally, rations were defined according to whether a prisoner was sick, doing ordinary manual labour or considered as a 'heavy labourer' (*Schwerarbeiter*). Ordinary workers received 400 grams of bread per head per day. For men doing especially heavy work as *Schwerarbeiter*, this could be raised to 600 grams of bread. Sick prisoners received 400 grams or less. An order from the Intendant General of the Field Army (*Generalintendant des Feldheeres*) on 13 November 1917 specified that 'sick or convalescent prisoners in convalescent companies, convalescent homes etc. are to receive the ordinary worker's ration if according to medical advice this will return them to full working strength within the foreseeable future'.[15] What ration was to be given if medical advice maintained that they were unlikely to return to work is not clear.

How many prisoners did fall sick from these conditions? Paybooks from several of the *Engländer Kommando 3* working camps in the 6th (Bavarian) Army provide an insight into the extent of illness and the amount of time off which prisoners received.[16] The following sickness rates are drawn from the paybooks of *Kommandos* based at Le Hamage, Nomain-Delmez and Néchin, during the period September to November 1917.[17] For the purposes of this analysis men counted as 'sick' were those who were in hospital, marked as *Lazarett* (L), or marked as sick, *krank* (K), on five days or more in one month. This excludes minor illnesses and thus represents the *minimum* sickness rates. It also excludes those men who may have succeeded in pretending to be sick for a day to avoid working. German army medical staff were under considerable pressure to pass prisoners as fit for work: if a man remained off work for five days or more he was clearly

---

[14] BHStA IV, Et.Inspektion, Gefangenen Kommando, Bd. 199, Tagebuch 3, Abschrift des Kriegstagebuches der Gefangenen-Inspektion 106 für die Zeit vom 1.10.17 bis 31.12.1917, Abschrift, Entwurf, Niederschrift zur Besprechung über Gefangenen- und Arbeiterangelegenheiten, abgehalten in Valenciennes am 4 Oktober 1917.

[15] BA-MA, PH/5/II/456, f. 55, General Intendant des Feldheeres IIId Nr. 254.11.17, Gr.H. Qu. to alle Armee-Oberkommandos usw. 13.11.1917.

[16] It should be noted that prisoners never received cash for their work. If they were paid at all, it was in camp tokens, which could only be exchanged for goods or food in prison camp canteens – and there were generally no prison camp canteens in working camps in the occupied territories.

[17] BHStA IV, Et.Inspektion 6, Bund 203, Engländer Kommando 3, September, Oktober, November 1917.

very ill. It should also be noted that the prisoners in each *Kommando* remained largely the same across the three months. Some men marked sick for one month would be marked *Lazarett* the next.

Table 4. *Sickness rates in the* Engländer Kommando 3 *working camp at Le Hamage, September–November 1917.*

Month	Total number of prisoners in Kommando	Number of days worked	Number of prisoners marked sick for five days or more	Number of prisoners marked Lazarett	Total number of prisoners sick	Percentage sick
Company begins work at Hamage mid-September	49	16	1	5	6	12%
October	49	27	6	3	9	18%
November (company moves from Le Hamage camp on 14.11.1917 and is replaced by a Russian Kommando)	49	11	6	2	8	16%

Table 5. *Sickness rates in the* Engländer Kommando 3 *working camp at Nomain-Delmez, September–November 1917.*

Month	Total number of prisoners in Kommando	Number of days worked	Number of prisoners marked sick for five days or more	Number of prisoners marked Lazarett	Total number of prisoners sick	Percentage of prisoners sick
September	84	26	1	11	12	14%
October	83	27	4	12	16	19%
November (the prisoners are moved to work elsewhere on 14.11.1917)	83	12	7	1	8	10%

Table 6. *Sickness rates in the* Engländer Kommando 3 *working camp at Néchin, September–November 1917*

Month	Total number of prisoners in *Kommando*	Number of days worked	Number of prisoners sick for five days or more	Number of prisoners in *Lazarett*	Total number of prisoners sick	Percentage of prisoners sick
September	201	25	28	39	67	33%
October	202	27	38	35	73	36%
November (the company left Néchin on 14.11.1917)	202	12	27	34	61	30%

Evidently, sickness rates varied from place to place. However, those at Néchin would clearly give an army short of labour resources cause for concern. The high sick rates were probably aggravated by the poor living conditions and short amount of time off. According to the paybooks, prisoners usually received one day off a week, which was normally Sunday. However, on occasion they worked for nine or ten days without a break or worked in different weekly shifts. If the prisoners' work was substandard their wage was cut from 30 to 20 Pfennig as a punishment. For what was classed as 'excellent' work prisoners were occasionally allocated 40 Pfennig as an inducement.[18] This was also the usual pay for NCO prisoners. The paybooks effectively served as a record of the money due to a prisoner when the war ended.

On occasion prisoners missed work because they were undergoing punishment in the camp lock-up (*Arrestlokal*), which was usually an improvised cell. In Nomain-Delmez, no prisoner was marked in *Arrest* during this entire period. In Néchin, the rate was much higher; five prisoners were in *Arrest* in September; four different men in October; and two in November, with one man placed in the *Arrestlokal* for over fourteen days. Moreover, at Néchin, the paybook shows that the letter K for sick (*krank*) often followed upon the letter A (*Arrest*). Several men who had been in arrest were listed as sick for days afterwards, indicative of severe punishment conditions. However, no prisoners were listed in the paybooks as having died at Le Hamage, Nomain-Delmez or Néchin during these three months.

[18] BHStA IV, Et.Inspektion 6, Bund 203, Engländer Kommando 3, September, Oktober, November 1917.

The paybooks, like the *Etappen-Inspektion* records, do not provide any description of the prisoners themselves. However, an interview with an ex-prisoner, a Durham fruiterer, named Arthur Leggett, reveals that the condition of these captives was poor by early 1918. Leggett, captured at Ypres in April 1915, saw those prisoners from the *Engländer Kommando 3* who had been sent back to Germany. An escaper, he was interviewed by the British Government Committee on the Treatment by the Enemy of British Prisoners of War on 6 May 1918 and described how

At the end of January or early in February 1918 1,400 men came into Friedrichsfeld from working behind the German lines. I think they were E.K.3 men. Some had been there 14 or 15 months and had never had a parcel or a letter. They were in a terrible state. The German doctor himself admitted he had never seen men in such a condition. You could not recognise some of them as human beings. As soon as they arrived some of them had to be carried into the hospital and some had collapsed before they reached the camp. There were a lot of parcels waiting for these men in our camp and the camp officials, the English N.C.O.s distributed them. Some men were drawing from 10 to 12 parcels, and, being in such a weak state, many of them collapsed from having too much to eat at once. A lot of them had dysentery when they came in, and a few died. These men were like skeletons and were very depressed. They said many of them had died.[19]

While Leggett was watching the arrival of prisoners who had escaped the rigours of *Engländer Kommando 3* for a German home front camp, the Sixth Army *Etappen-Inspektion* was submitting its monthly report. On 1 February 1918, it reported that inspections had been carried out in January on camps in the *Engländer Kommando 4* at Camphin, Wez-Welvain and Hollain; the *Franzosen Kommando 14* at St Amand, Orchies, La Tombe, Pecq and Deuze; the *Engländer Kommando 5* at Marquin, Orcq, Tournai and Quevaucamps; and the *Engländer Kommando 3* at Quartes, Condé and Néchin. It described the accommo-dation in general as 'good'. The clothing of the prisoners was 'adequate, in some cases good'.[20] Most significantly it reported that the prisoners' food was 'tastily prepared and the increased bread ration of 500 grams had contributed greatly to an improvement in work performance'.[21]

The obsession with work performance revealed by the 6th Army *Etappen-Inspektion* was no accident. By 1918, the German army was dependent upon a prisoner labour system which had greatly expanded from its earlier origins in 1916, described in chapter 3. The German Sixth Army alone commanded multiple Prisoner of War Labour Battalions

[19] TNA, WO 161/100, no. 1804, Interview with Arthur Leggett, Private 1620, 8th Durham Light Infantry.
[20] BHStA IV, Et.Inspektion 6, Bd. 199, Abschrift, Etappen-Inspektion 6. Armee, 1.2.1918.
[21] *Ibid.*

(*Kriegsgefangenen-Arbeiter-Bataillone*), Prisoner of War Working Commandos (*Kriegsgefangenen Kommandos*) and Civilian Worker Battalions (*Zivilgefangenen-Arbeiter-Bataillone*). By 1918, it also had two Military Prisoner Companies (*Militär-Gefangenen-Kompagnien*) made up of German troops who had committed disciplinary offences, which earlier in the war would have been punished with a prison term but now resulted in the offender being sent into a punishment labour company to work at the front. This *Militär-Gefangenen-Kompagnien* system in the German army was established on 3 October 1917.[22]

The interwar German commentator, Hermann Cron, revealed the scale of the prisoner labour system which had developed in occupied France and Belgium, stating that by the Armistice there were 151 Prisoner of War Labour Battalions (*Kriegsgefangenen-Arbeiter-Bataillone*), 57 French Prisoner of War Commandos (*Franzosen Kommandos*), 26 British Prisoner of War Commandos (*Engländer Kommandos*), 38 Romanian Commandos (*Rumänien Kommandos*), 22 Italian Commandos (*Italiener Kommandos*) and 2 Portuguese Commandos (*Portugiesen Kommandos*), as well as 34 Civilian Worker Battalions (*Zivil-Arbeiter-Bataillone*), 10 Civilian Worker Columns (*Zivil-Arbeiter-Kolonnen*) and 78 Military Prisoner Companies, made up of German military prisoners (*Militär-Gefangenen-Kompagnien*).[23] Given that a prisoner of war battalion consisted of 2,000 prisoners, and a company of 500, Cron here attests to a substantial labour resource of approximately 400,000 prisoners of war, many of whom were Russians, and an unknown number of civilians, which the German army drew upon to resolve its manpower shortage. In addition, British and French prisoners of war were also working in German army Field Railway (*Rekodeis*) units, building and maintaining the occupied territories' rail network; according to Hermann Cron there were 8 civilian labour companies and 80 prisoner of war labour companies working for the Field Railway, among them 6 companies composed of miners, together with 7 Russian detachments for the railway workshops in the lines of communication.[24] These units were under the separate control of the German army Field Railway command.

Any overall estimate of how many captive labourers were working for the German army, however, is difficult to calculate: some prisoner labour battalions were under strength by the end of the war. An escaped Russian declared in January 1918 that a prisoner of war 'labour battalion on the

---

[22] Hermann Cron, *Geschichte des deutschen Heeres im Weltkriege, 1914–1918* (Berlin, 1990 [1937]), p. 263; translated as *Imperial German Army, 1914–1918. Organisation, Structure, Orders of Battle* (West Midlands, 2001).
[23] Cron, *Geschichte des deutschen Heeres*, p. 263.   [24] Cron, *Imperial German Army*, p. 213.

western front originally consisted of 2,000 men but the processes of starvation, accidents, exposure, unmerciful beatings and death, have reduced it to about 500 men and sometimes to much less. The same process of disintegration was going on in all the battalions.'[25]

One reason for the German army's worsening wartime labour resources was, ironically, a declaration of peace. Although the Treaty of Brest-Litovsk freed troops for the western front, it also imposed the withdrawal of the German army's most important labour resource – Russian prisoners of war – from work in the occupied territories as a prelude to their repatriation.[26] On 10 January 1918, the Quartermaster-General's office ordered that in the interests of Germany's negotiations with Russia, all Russian prisoners working at the front were to be exchanged to camps in Germany and replaced by prisoners of other nationalities.[27] This order was not fully implemented and many Russian prisoners remained in the occupied territories. However, by 20 January 1918, the German 6th Army had brought in 4,000 British prisoners to take over from 4,000 Russians who had been labouring in the *Operationsgebiete*.[28] The *Operationsgebiet* was the zone between the front-line trenches and the rear *Etappengebiet* area. This January exchange effectively sent these British prisoners to work in the front operations area.

This decision illustrates the increasing ruthlessness regarding prisoners of war emerging in the German army. The realisation that the forthcoming major German offensive would be the last before the arrival of American troops made a real impact on the battlefield, led to an intense reappraisal of resources and a determination to use all available manpower to the utmost. It also resulted in the German army breaching many of the agreements reached with the Allies about prisoner labour in 1917, such as the prohibition on the employment of British and French prisoners within thirty kilometres of the front. The impact of this increased ruthlessness

---

[25] 'Forced Labour for Germany', *Morning Post*, 3.1.1918.
[26] BA-MA, PH5 / II / 454, f. 19, f. 32, f. 40. An instruction from the Kriegsministerium Nr. 1544/5.18.U1 on 27 May 1918, emphasised that 'In all events, it must be ensured that Russian prisoners really see an overall improvement in their situation.' As part of this process of improving the conditions of Russian prisoners, the Generalquartiermeister ordered that, from 25 March 1918 on, all Orthodox Russian and Jewish religious holidays were to be kept. *Ibid.*, f. 101 Ic Nr. 11779. The shift in attitude towards Russian prisoners began in December 1917. A new order issued stated that 'Russian prisoners are to be well treated. All unnecessary hard measures against them are to be avoided and use of arms against them should only occur in the case of an absolute emergency.' See *ibid.*, f. 155, Heeresgruppe Kronprinz Rupprecht to AOK 4, 18.12.1917.
[27] BA-MA, PH5 / II / 454, f. 153. Generalquartiermeister order to all AOKs.
[28] BHStA IV, Et.Inspektion, Gefangenen Kommando Bd. 199, Tagebuch 4, Abschrift des Kriegstagebuches der Gefangenen-Inspektion 106 für die Zeit vom 1.1.1918 bis 31.3.1918, AOK 6 VI, 20.1.1918.

was most clearly to be seen in the treatment of prisoners of war taken by the German army during the 1918 spring offensives, which resulted in tens of thousands of British and French prisoners flooding the established western front German army prisoner of war work camp system of 1917. This was the context for the widespread use of violence against prisoner labours working for the German army in the last year of the war.

Prisoner living conditions in the occupied territories during the German spring offensive

The offensive launched on 21 March 1918, known as the *Kaiserschlacht* or the Ludendorff Offensive, involved one of the largest concentrations of troops and munitions of the entire war.[29] It also involved some of the most detailed planning; the allocation of troop strengths, munitions and guns was carefully assessed and reassessed in the weeks prior to the battle.[30] Yet despite these meticulous preparations, little provision was made for the prisoners which the offensive was likely to produce. This lack of attention to prisoners continued once the offensive began. In fact, prisoners were considered so peripheral that many British troops who surrendered were given no escort to the rear of the German lines but simply left to make their own way back. Others were ordered to carry back the German wounded.[31]

The lack of planning was not the only problem. The sheer number of men captured in such a remarkably short space of time initially overwhelmed the German army. Martin Middlebrook estimates that some 21,000 British prisoners were taken on the first day of the offensive alone.[32] Some 75,000 British prisoners were taken between 21 March and 5 April, along with 15,000 French.[33] For the majority of these men the war was most definitely not over. Unwounded, non-officer prisoners taken during the spring offensive were kept in occupied France and Belgium in newly improvised work camps. After capture, prisoners were

---

[29] Martin Kitchen, *The German Offensives of 1918* (Stroud, 2001), p. 62.

[30] Malcolm Brown, *The Imperial War Museum Book of 1918. Year of Victory* (London, 1998), pp. 38–9.

[31] TNA, WO 161/100, no. 1781, Interview with Private Tulloch. Also no. 1783, Interview with Private Chilton, and nos. 1782, 1785, 1787, 1788, 1789, 1790, 1791. French prisoners were similarly used. See BA-MA, PH5 / II / 470, f. 00018, letter from the Spanish Embassy, conveying a French protest at this practice and the result of the German investigation, Abschrift K.H.Qu, 26.9.1918, admitting that it had occurred in April 1918, 'without the knowledge of the *Generalkommandos*' at the time.

[32] Martin Middlebrook, *The Kaiser's Battle, 21 March 1918. The First Day of the German Spring Offensive* (London, 1978), p. 322.

[33] Martin Kitchen, 'Michael-Offensive', in Hirschfeld, Renz and Krumeich, eds., *Enzyklopädie Erster Weltkrieg*, p. 714.

This survey has its limitations. Sixteen represents a very small sample. Another important point to stress is that of these men, eleven had escaped before the end of May 1918, and the remaining five had left the work camps by the end of September, so the experience of prisoners who remained in work camps in summer 1918 is underrepresented and the situation in October is not covered here. Moreover, the prisoners' accounts of their time in captivity were determined by the issues they chose to mention to the interviewer. It should be noted that the interviewer only recorded what the prisoner recounted. If the prisoner did not explicitly mention in interview that he did not have a blanket, it cannot be assumed that he did have one. However, the survey provides a good general outline of the average prisoner experience at many different German army work camp locations: poor accommodation and random acts of violence.

These former prisoners' accounts reveal two key points. First, although work camp accommodation quality varied, in the majority of cases it was seriously deficient. In thirteen out of the sixteen cases surveyed, it lacked any heating, roof or running water; prisoners arriving at this rudimentary accommodation were already filthy and tired, following upon several days' stay in a holding pen out in the open, where conditions were very inadequate, a fact mentioned in interview by twelve of the prisoners in the above sample. Given the lack of blankets reported in the work camps, lack of heating was a serious issue. The lack of running water also led to unsanitary conditions, as did overcrowding, and the fact that prisoners were very rarely afforded the chance to wash or provided with a change of clothing – nine of the sample said their camp had no washing facilities.

The following examples typify the types of accommodation prisoners experienced. Courchelettes camp in April 1918 was described as

Two huts and a shed ... Wire beds were given us but there were no blankets. There was water and we used our steel helmets for basins but it was difficult to wash and impossible for the prisoners to keep clean; also we were troubled with vermin ... We worked at unloading barges of coal, wood and stone. The prisoners got very weak from hunger and many fell sick whilst at work; on an average about three were taken back to the cage each day ... The condition of the prisoners towards the 1st of May became deplorable owing to the dirt, the want of food and the vermin and many of them were covered with boils and sores.[41]

At Marchiennes, 3,000 British prisoners were 'lodged in a building which had been a glass factory, and our quarters were very much overcrowded ... No beds or blankets were provided, only a little straw. We had to sleep on the floor and the cold was very severe. The place was very dirty and we were troubled a

---

[41] TNA, WO 161/100, no. 1781, Interview with Private Tulloch.

good deal with vermin.'[42] As at Courchelettes, prisoners used their helmets to carry water for washing. At Douai, prisoners were 'lodged in a brick kiln. We had to lie on the floor; there were no beds or blankets or even straw. The place was very dirty and the vermin were very troublesome ... We were able to make fires in the kilns. There were no facilities for washing.'[43] The prisoners worked on a railroad where 'shells frequently fell within 200 or 300 yards of us'.[44] At Buissey,

the prisoners' accommodation was in a large house. But there was not nearly sufficient room for so large a number and there was much overcrowding ... Many prisoners there were ill but the German doctor, who came every morning to see the prisoners, very seldom passed a man sick and during the six days I was there many men had to go to work who were unfit and really ill.[45]

Similar conditions were reported at Bazancourt.[46] Even allowing for the poor conditions front-line troops endured in the trenches, this accommodation was inadequate. It was permanently overcrowded and, unlike front-line troops, prisoners were not regularly rotated to better billets.

Second, what emerges from this interview sample is that these prisoners were often sent to work near the front, in breach of the thirty-kilometre limit agreed in 1917 – exposing them on occasion to shellfire. These prisoners' accounts of working in the firing zone are corroborated by other evidence which reveals that this work was officially sanctioned by the German Army Supreme High Command (OHL). Early during the March offensive the decision was made to temporarily suspend the thirty-kilometre agreement made in 1917 with Britain and France that no British, French or German prisoners were to work within thirty kilometres of the firing zone. An order was issued on 23 March 1918 by the OHL that 'newly captured prisoners of war taken by the armies can provisionally be put into prisoner formations according to need and used on the operation front (*Operationsfront*) for road and railway building tasks'.[47]

Significantly, this order relaxing the thirty-kilometre restriction was the first major decision the OHL issued on prisoners with regard to the spring

---

[42] *Ibid.*, no. 1783, Interview with Private Chilton   [43] *Ibid.*   [44] *Ibid.*   [45] *Ibid.*

[46] A prisoner described this camp as follows: 'wooden huts were built, 120 men to each hut. The beds were of wire netting in three tiers, head to head in the middle of the hut with narrow passages round them and no lighting or heating apparatus. After a short time we were supplied with palliasses of paper and wooden shavings for blankets. Later on we received a thin blanket and a ground sheet. This was in July. The 120 men in each hut was [sic] great overcrowding and the smell caused was very bad.' TNA, WO 161/100, no. 2537, Interview with Sergeant William Rhodes.

[47] This order was OHL II 81455 op.vom 23.3.18, related in BA-MA, PH5 / II / 453, f. 96, Abschrift, AOK 4, IcA 6939. See same order at PH5 / II / 449, f. 13, AOK 4, Abt.Ic A, nr.7301, 23.5.1918. The inspection of these hastily formed camps was entrusted to

offensive – a full two days after it began. No attempt was even made to cloak this shift in policy by claiming that the British and French had breached the thirty-kilometre agreement first. The German action was also a clear breach of Article 25 and Article 32 of the first Berne Accord, which entered into force on 15 March 1918, between the French and German governments, which stated that French and German prisoners of war should not be housed or employed within thirty kilometres of the front.[48] For the OHL, prisoners could be exposed to shellfire if necessary – their safety was completely subordinated to the demands of military necessity. The cultural demarcation between the forms of violence considered appropriate for use against the enemy in the field and those permitted against prisoners of war was breaking down.

The German case was unique. Following the 1917 agreement that prisoners should not work within thirty kilometres of the front, the British and French armies maintained a total prohibition on prisoner of war labour companies working within the thirty-kilometre line. Although British and French units often used newly captured German prisoners at the front to carry in the wounded during battles, this work was temporary, lasting several days at most and did not involve the established prisoner of war labour companies. Moreover, no orders have emerged to indicate that prisoner of war front-line work was sanctioned by French or British higher command levels in 1918.

The British were keenly attentive to any German breach of the thirty-kilometre agreement. In February 1918, they sent a note to the German government to ask whether, since the agreement's inception in 1917, any British prisoners had been made to work within the thirty-kilometre zone.[49] Lord Newton, head of the Department of Prisoners of War at the Foreign Office, even mooted reprisals against German prisoners working for the British in France, although Sir Herbert Belfield at the War Office resisted, feeling that: 'I am certain that if we again adopt a policy of employing the Germans within the 30 kilometre limit, we should have a recurrence of the brutalities which existed before we and they reached an agreement on the subject.'[50]

Captain Feuchter, who was the head of the *Kriegsgefangenen-Arbeiter-Bataillon* 29. He was, therefore, hardly an independent inspector – some of the provisionally formed companies were attached to his KAB 29 or took over work camp sites its units had previously occupied. On Feuchter's appointment, see BA-MA, PH 5 / II/ 453, f. 96.

[48] BA-MA, PH5 / II / 453, f. 92, Verfügungen über Kriegsgefangenenangelegenheiten, Band 2, Abschrift from Generalquartiermeister to all AOKs.

[49] BA-MA, PH5 / II / 453, f. 222, Abschrift, Heeresgruppe Kronprinz Rupprecht, Oberkommando Ia/NO. Nr. 40206, 8.2.1918.

[50] TNA, WO 32/5381, 98 B, Sir Herbert Belfield to Lord Newton, 13.2.1918.

Evidence from the records of the 29th German prisoner of war labour battalion, KAB 29, which was guarded by a Bavarian unit, while working in the 4th Army zone, reveals how near the front prisoners were working.[51] One report on 14 May 1918 stated that all prisoners in the Prisoner of War Batallions 29 and 144, working in the German 4th Army for the *Gruppe Ieperen*, were employed

forwards of the thirty kilometre line. If all prisoners of war have to be removed to a distance of thirty kilometres then the *Gruppe* can no longer find work for them. The *Gruppe* requests 4,800 men to replace the prisoners of war. Without replacement workers most of the rear zone work activities will cease.[52]

Prisoners were aware that working inside of thirty kilometres was illegal.[53] Eleven French soldiers from the French 13th Infantry Regiment wrote on 17 May 1918 to the German officer commanding their work camp at Halluin, stating that they were working at a distance of less than thirty kilometres from the front and that shells had fallen close to where they worked:

Yet the conventions ratified between the governments stipulate that concentration camps should not be located under thirty kilometres from the front; and that the tasks carried out by prisoners should not have anything to do with those of national defence. However, every day work groups are asked for at the camp to work at the stations, such as those at Comines and Wervicq, unloading shells. These stations are a very short distance from the firing lines.[54]

An internal German army memo, from 3 September 1918, confirmed that prisoners taken in April and May by the 4th Army had been working within the thirty-kilometre zone, and that until June over a thousand French prisoners had been working at Halluin.[55] On 17 May 1918, there were 1,166 French prisoners in total there.[56] The German inter-rogation officer at Halluin Prisoner of War Holding Camp (*Gefangenensammelstelle*) remarked acerbically that 'it is indicative of the difference between the two nationalities that so far not one of the British

---

[51] BHStA IV, Kr. Gef. Arb. Batl. 29. Bund 3.

[52] BA-MA, PH5 / II / 457, f. 10, Gruppe Ieperen to AOK 4, 14.5.1918.

[53] According to Ernie Stevens, a former prisoner interviewed in 1999, soldiers in the British army had been given lectures on war conventions 'before we even left for France'. Richard van Emden, *Prisoners of the Kaiser. The Last POWs of the Great War* (Barnsley, 2000), p. 60.

[54] BA-MA, PH5 / II / 457, f. 4, Gefangenensammelstelle Halluin, Vernehmungsoffizier 17.5.1918. Another letter was 'a collective protest by French prisoners of the 88th Infantry Regiment located at Halluin'. BA-MA, PH5 / II / 457, f. 5.

[55] BA-MA, PH5 / II / 449, f. 59, Arb. 8982, AOK 4 to die Beauftragten des General-quartiermeisters West, 3.9.1918.

[56] BA-MA, PH5 / II / 457, f. 8, Gruppe Flandern, Gen.Kdo XRK betr. Kriegsgefangene, to AOK 4, 17.5.1918.

(*Engländer*), who carry out the same work at the same location, has complained. This is all the more surprising as the British have recently borne the brunt of the most regrettable gas shell accident.'[57]

Three prisoners from the 88th Infantry Regiment who escaped from Halluin on 21 May 1918 brought news of the prisoners' plight to the attention of the French government.[58] One escaped prisoner told of being forced to dig trenches for the Germans under shellfire. The French reaction contrasted strongly with the British reluctance to resort to reprisals. The French government issued a very strongly worded protest note in July 1918, threatening reprisals upon German prisoners within a month should French prisoners not be immediately removed from the thirty-kilometre zone. The French note stated that accounts of French prisoners working in the firing zone 'are too numerous and too grave in nature ... for the blame to be laid upon subordinates (*Untergebenen*). The responsibility for this treatment lies with the German Army Supreme Command and the Kaiser's government.'[59]

Ultimately, French reprisals were not necessary as the German army had already decided to reinstate the thirty-kilometre rule by the time the French protest note was received. On 17 May, the OHL began to issue orders that the thirty-kilometre rule should once again be kept.[60] From this point on, frequent reminder orders were issued that French and British prisoners should not be used within thirty kilometres of the firing line. Where possible, they were to be replaced by Italian or Portuguese prisoners or Belgian or French civilian workers, categories for whom no thirty-kilometre agreement existed. Orders to this effect were issued on 19 May, 4 June, 11 June, 19 June, 25 June, 13, 21 and 24 October 1918 – the frequent reminders an indication that the thirty-kilometre rule was continuing to be breached right up to the end of the war.[61] In June, British and French prisoners were still working in the thirty-kilometre zone. On 12 June 1918, General Sixt von Armin wrote to the *Heeresgruppe Kronprinz Rupprecht* that there were 13,962 prisoners working for the 4th Army in total, including 2,858 British and 5,661 French prisoners; 2,519 of these prisoners were due to be transferred

[57] *Ibid.*, f. 3.
[58] BA-MA, PH5 / II / 449, f. 70, Abschrift zu kr.2.IX.5.2364, Schweizerisches politisches Departement, French Note Verbale enclosed.
[59] *Ibid.*
[60] BA-MA, PH5 / II / 449, f. 52, Abt.Ic.A.7225, A.H., 19.5.1918. Also f. 00051, Generalquartiermeister, Ic Nr. 24332, 17.5.1918.
[61] BA-MA, PH5 / II / 449, f. 79, f. 78; BA-MA, PH5 / II / 449, f. 00011, AOK 4 Abt. Arb. Nr. 7910, 25.6.1918; BA-MA, PH5 / II / 449, f. 3, AOK 4, Abt.Ic.A.7225, 19.5.1918; BHStA IV, Gen.Kdos IbAK, Bund 38, AOK 18 rm Ic, 24.10.1918 and 13.10.1918; BA-MA, PH5 / II / 457, f. 0063, AOK 4, Arb. Nr. 9802, Circular to all Generalkommandos, Et. Inspektion 4, Gouvernement Antwerpen etc., A.H.Qu., 21.10.1918.

elsewhere and Armin argued that if the remaining French and British captives were removed to a distance of 30 kilometres, 'the working strength of 6,000 men would be lost. As a result the timely completion of the *Hagen* preparations would be put at risk, if no replacement workers are provided.'[62] On 9 August, an inspection of prisoner of war labour companies referred to French prisoners who had only been moved out of the thirty-kilometre zone three weeks earlier.[63] There was a clear conflict of interest between the German army's labour needs and the thirty-kilometre restriction – and this may have reflected a deeper clash between the Prussian *Kriegsministerium*, which still stood by the thirty-kilometre agreement in 1918, and the OHL. Indeed, the *Kriegsministerium* only learned of the extent of the German army's breaches of the 1917 agreement during the preliminary negotiations preceding the Anglo-German Hague Conference on prisoners of war in July 1918, when the British sent the *Kriegsministerium* delegates some of the evidence they had gathered.[64] Up to the very end of the war, breaches of the thirty-kilometre rule by the German army continued to occur. Interviewed after their liberation by the Allied armies in October 1918, French civilians confirmed that British prisoners had been labouring near the front. Twenty-one-year-old Jean Deparis, from Clary, described how he was employed at Roisel, twelve kilometres from the front, where he saw between 300 and 400 British prisoners working. He stated that prisoners had been killed during air raids by Allied planes and that 'the soldiers who guarded them frequently hit them with their rifle butts because they were not working fast enough, or slapped them'.[65] His comments were supported by two other French civilians, Adolphe Toilliez and Gustave Dedon, who had worked in the same civilian labour company as Deparis at Roisel. Dedon described prisoners being killed by aerial bombardment.[66]

All the evidence concurs that prisoners were not only exposed to violence in the form of shellfire. Labour company prisoners working for the German army in 1918 were threatened, kicked, cuffed or beaten at

---

[62] BA-MA, PH5 / II / 449, f. 78, Abschrift, AOK 4 Arb. Nr. 7667, to Heeresgruppe Kronprinz Rupprecht, 12.6.1918.

[63] BHStA IV, Kriegsgefangenen-Arbeiter-Bataillon, Nr. 29, Abschrift, Bericht über Besichtigung der Gefangenenlager im Bereich des AOK 4, Rekodeis 1 und der BdKM 3 und 5, 9.8.1918.

[64] BHStA IV, Kriegsgefangenen-Arbeiter-Bataillon, Nr. 29, Abschrift Kriegsministerium, message from Generalquartiermeister Ic 28051 to AOK 4, 4.6.1918.

[65] TNA, WO 32/5188, 37 A, Copy of French Procès-Verbal with Jean Deparis, Adolphe Toilliez and Gustave Dedon on 26.10.1918.

[66] *Ibid.* Dedon described how '15 days before the Allied advance, British soldiers, prisoners, were still working with us 12 kilometres from the front; the Allied shells fell 4 kilometres from where we were at Thincourt. I saw the guards being brutal with the prisoners, several of whom were killed by the aerial bombardments.'

will. With few exceptions, violence towards prisoners working in the occupied zones was widespread; physical coercion to make prisoners work was the norm. One task commonly assigned to prisoners was loading and unloading German shells. Drummer Leslie Rudd described the violence used to force prisoners to do this work at a camp at Sailly, five miles from the firing line:

We were under the direction of guards; some had W's on their shoulder straps and others O's with a crown underneath. They treated us very badly and beat us with sticks and rifles all times of the day. Many of us were in a bad state and incapable to work from dirt and lack of food. It was a regular thing for us to lose our bread ration and we had a very small quantity of bread and coffee and soup given us. One day we refused to load shells and one of our men complained to a German staff officer who spoke English, telling him it was wrong to expect us to load shells for them and that we wanted to make a general complaint. His only reply was to line us up in a squad and to order that the first man who refused to work should be instantly shot.[67]

'If we talked to the Belgians we got a beating,' Drummer Rudd also recalled.[68] Another prisoner recounted: 'We were shown a lot of cruelty, men being hit with rifles in the small of the back often without cause. Two men (I do not know their names) were carried in from work after being hit and died in camp.'[69] Private Thomas Martleton described a three-day march after capture where wounded and unwounded prisoners alike journeyed on foot to Denain. The prisoners were not fed on the journey and the guard was 'rough ... the wounded suffered very much and we did our best to help them along'.[70] At Douai, the guards kicked and used the butt ends of their rifles to hit prisoners who did not get up quickly enough.[71] Another prisoner working behind the lines recorded in his diary how, on 22 April 1918, the 'interpreter asked if anyone wanted to go sick and one man unwisely said he did. The officer came and looked at him and then gave him a punch in the face which knocked him down.'[72] Another unpublished prisoner diary, kept by Private William Wilkinson, recorded how he was seriously injured when a guard hit him.[73] One British prisoner recaptured by German soldiers after a failed escape attempt in July 1918 told his German interrogators that he had escaped because of his fear of being beaten and described how he had witnessed a German sergeant flog

---

[67] TNA, WO 161/100, no. 1785, Interview with Drummer Leslie Rudd.
[68] Ibid., no. 1785, Interview with Drummer Leslie Rudd
[69] Ibid., no. 2816, Interview with Private John Stewart Dixon.
[70] Ibid., no. 1789, Interview with Private Thomas Martleton.
[71] Ibid., no. 1791, Interview with Corporal Joseph Page.   [72] Jackson, The Prisoners, p. 20.
[73] Diary of Private William Wilkinson, 2/8/1918, cited in Oliver Wilkinson, 'Captured! What Was the Experience of a British Prisoner of War during the First World War?' (undergraduate dissertation, University of Lancaster, 2007), p. 23.

British prisoners.[74] Violence against prisoners was so common that his claims were accepted without further question. The German interrogator noted that 'the Briton has a strongly developed sense of honour. For this reason physical mistreatment should absolutely not happen.'[75]

There are several explanations for this violence against prisoners. First, it was a security measure. Prisoner labour was never ideal at the best of times: captives were reluctant to assist their enemy's war effort; and so many of them working to the rear of the German army raised security issues. Any coordinated action by prisoners could seriously threaten the German advance – indeed, unsubstantiated rumours of such a mass rebellion occasionally circulated. Security fears were so great that in 1917 sabotage by prisoners was punishable by death.[76] In part, this fear of prisoners resulted from real acts of sabotage. A Russian prisoner, working for the Bavarian army, reported on 18 October 1918 that British prisoners were deliberately damaging the shells they were loading.[77] However, much of this fear was due to the large-scale paranoia about prisoner sabotage which had developed in Germany before 1918.[78] Keeping prisoners working close to the fighting lines also meant that escapers did not have far to go to regain their liberty and escapes would provide crucial reconnaissance information to the Allies. Camp sentries thus had permission to shoot any man in the act of escaping. Fugitives risked their lives: prisoners trying to cross no man's land were shot at by the Germans and, on occasion, by the Allies who mistook them for the enemy.[79] The concern about the number of escapes was so great that in September 1918 the German army instituted a reward of 20 Marks for German troops who caught escaped prisoners.[80]

---

[74] BHStA IV, Kriegsgefangenen-Arbeiter Bataillon, Nr.29, Schriftstücke für Engländer-Kommando XI, Nr. 13678, Italiener Kommando 1, Kriegsgefangenen Inspektion 4 an das Engländer Kommando XI, Interrogation of George Robert Hall, 6.7.1918.

[75] Ibid.

[76] BHStA IV, Gen.Kdos IbAK, Bund 183, Abschrift, Generalquartiermeister, III 1142 geh/741, 5.5.1917.

[77] BHStA IV, Kriegsgefangenen-Arbeiter Bataillon Nr. 29, Abschrift, Oberkommando der H.Gr. Herzog Albrecht, Abt.Ib.no.15809, 18.10.1918.

[78] See, in particular, the orders on escape materials being sent to French officers in officer camps in Germany. BHStA IV, Gen.Kdos IbAK, Bund 183, Kriegsministerium Berlin, Unterkunft, 1047/5.18, 25.6.1918. See also Doegen, Kriegsgefangene Völker, pp. 140–72. See also Hinz, Gefangen im Großen Krieg, pp. 144–7 on sabotage hysteria.

[79] In one case, four British prisoners who had almost reached the British lines killed a German soldier who stumbled upon their hiding place. All four prisoners were recaptured and executed by firing squad. The incident only came to light when a German padre who had attended the execution wrote to the family of one of the prisoners. TNA, WO 141/41 British Military Mission, Berlin to the Secretary, War Office, 4.6.1919.

[80] BHStA IV, Gen.Kdos IbAK, Bund 183, Armee Oberkommando 18, IIa Nr. 25120. 21.9.1918.

The treatment of escapers also illustrates the second explanation for violence against prisoners – its disciplinary function. Escapers who were recaptured were physically punished. At Flavy-le-Martel camp, 'two men tried to escape but were recaptured and made to stand to attention for three hours facing the sun on a hot day. Both collapsed, and they were put into a small hut three yards square for 10 days on bread and coffee.'[81] Some failed escapers were sent to Fort Flines or Fort Macdonald, punishment prisons with hard labour regimes. At Fort Flines, where recalcitrant French and British prisoners were punished, the regime was tough. One prisoner, Sapper George Waymark, who secretly kept a diary during his time in the fort, wrote on 27 June 1918 describing how a guard used to set his Alsatian dog upon the prisoners who were not working fast enough: 'I've seen a number of men suddenly bowled over by the dog with it standing over them with bared teeth at their throat. Beyond a scratch I don't think the dog bit them, but the effect on the men so treated can be imagined. The Prussian thought it a huge joke.'[82] The work the men were set to was exhausting. Waymark wrote on 3 July that he had been unloading wood from trucks 'stripped to the waist, blinded with perspiration and swines of guards. I couldn't stand up when we had finished. How long will this last?'[83] The prisoners were starving – to the extent that they fought over potato peelings found on the road. On 13 July 1918, Waymark wrote of the first signs of dropsy among the prisoners: 'We are all suffering more or less with swelling in some part of the body. One or two men have faces so large that their eyes are hardly visible. It affects me in the legs and I can only think it is due to the watery food we are getting.'[84] His legs remained swollen throughout August although he was made to continue working. In September, Waymark was in the sick bay as a result.[85]

Fort Flines and Fort Macdonald had served as disciplinary prisons for recalcitrant prisoners of war since 1915. They had well-established harsh regimes of violence, long working days and little food. Perhaps the most revealing point of all regarding prisoner work camps in 1918 is that such special punishment camps were considered by the German army to no longer be of much use. Conditions in normal work camps throughout the occupied territories were so bad by summer 1918 that

a period in a disciplinary punishment camp (*Disziplinarstraflager*) is not perceived as a punishment by prisoners, as life in a disciplinary camp is scarcely distinguishable from life in the other prisoner of war camps.[86]

---

[81] TNA, WO 161/100, no. 2816, Interview with Private John Dixon.
[82] Moynihan, ed., *Black Bread and Barbed Wire*, p. 149.
[83] *Ibid.*, p. 150.   [84] *Ibid.*, p. 152.   [85] *Ibid.*, p. 152.
[86] BA-MA, PH5 / II / 452, f. 24, der Beauftragte des Generalquartiermeisters West, III.d. Nr. 70607.

Violence was no longer reserved for the function of punishing prisoner misdeeds. By 1918, it was spontaneous and commonplace throughout the labour company system to an extent not adequately explained by its security or disciplinary functions.

This highlights a third explanation: violence against prisoners emerged from below, within the lower ranks of the German army in 1918, because of labour needs; to meet the massive work targets required necessitated the use of force. Within a forced labour system, violence thus had an inherent function of labour compulsion. This was aggravated by the fact that guards, whose task was not only to guard but also to enforce work output, were outnumbered. By 1918, the German army did not have enough men to serve as prison camp guards: the guards for prisoner of war labour companies were all from the *Landsturm* infantry, often old, wounded or unfit.[87] Guards thus resorted to violence to enforce control. This helps explain the increasingly brutal treatment meted out to prisoner workers in labour companies from March 1918 on. Beatings became so common that frequent orders had to be issued reminding guards that such treatment threatened the German army's labour resources and that beating prisoners was officially prohibited – these orders appear to have had little effect in stopping violence by guards on the ground.[88] Higher command levels were clearly concerned that violence against prisoners by guards was irrational and indiscriminate. It had also become disproportionate to the result it was intended to achieve, as prisoners stopped associating being beaten with having committed a misdemeanour. The paradox was that the whole labour system, suffering badly from food shortages, was unable to function without the widespread use of physical force against captives, yet the OHL and the Quartermaster-General's office could no longer limit or control the application of this force, which resulted in damage to the labourers the German army so badly needed. Thus violence within this forced labour system escalated in a similar way to political violence which, as Hannah Arendt has argued, spreads throughout the whole 'body politic' if it fails to achieve its initial goals rapidly.[89] As discipline within the German army began to collapse during late summer 1918 and the German retreat in the autumn, guards became increasingly adept at taking out their frustrations physically upon prisoner workers, spreading this violence throughout the army; a sign of

---

[87] Cron, *Imperial German Army, 1914–1918*, p. 234.
[88] BA-MA, PH5 / II / 452, f. 00076, Dem Herrn Oberbefehlshaber durch Herrn Oberquartiermeister. 10.10.1918. See also the 1917 order issued to stop the 'many' cases where Russian prisoners are being 'hit by their guards': BHStA IV, Gen.Kdos IbAK, Bund 183, Armee Abtg C, Armeeoberkommando, Nr. 40684/17, 31.12.17.
[89] Arendt, *On Violence*, p. 80.

an overall shift from a military culture of control to one of violent retribution, as anger at the Allies' advance was taken out on enemy captives.[90] The *Kriegsministerium* even intervened on 23 September 1918, stating that it had learned of heavy-handed mistreatment of prisoners 'from cases where prisoners had died violent deaths and from other evidence'.[91] It warned that such cases 'will be used by our enemies to rouse hatred against Germans' and that 'such mistreatment leads to suffering for German prisoners in enemy hands'.[92] It pointed out that much of prisoners' incorrect behaviour was due to misunderstandings arising from the language difference.

There is also a fourth explanation: violence against prisoners was legitimised by the example which the OHL had set in its disregard for prisoners' welfare, creating precedents which, it failed to recognise, had directly led to this situation of ever-increasing violence against captive labourers in 1918. As shown in chapter 3, the prisoner of war labour company system had used violence as a disciplinary tool from its inception; violence against Russian prisoners had initially emerged from below within the army. However, by 1918, violence against prisoners had received official encouragement: the reprisals of 1916 and 1917 had sent out a message from the OHL that such violence could be used as a means to an end and the OHL had further endorsed violence against captive workers during the Ludendorff Offensive when it sanctioned prisoner labour in the operations area to achieve military aims. In 1918, guards were imitating their leaders – random violence against prisoners was practised to achieve short-term output goals, even though beating hungry prisoner workers was counterproductive in the long term. It was a response by German lower ranks to the OHL's own doctrine of military necessity.

Finally, to some extent the problem also resulted from the German army's own structure. Although general orders were issued that prisoners were not to be mishandled, no action was ever taken to punish mistreatment and great latitude was given to lower command levels. This was a classic example of what Isabel V. Hull has described as the 'mission tactics' which operated in the German army: 'Under mission tactics,

---

[90] As Charles Tilly has pointed out, 'rising uncertainty spurs wielders of violent means on either side of an us-them boundary to direct their means of destruction at those on the boundary's other side'. Charles Tilly, *The Politics of Collective Violence* (Cambridge, 2003), p. 229.

[91] BHStA IV, Kriegsgefangenen-Arbeiter Bataillon, Nr. 29, Abschrift, Kriegsministerium, Nr. 63/7.18, U3, 23.9.1918. For another copy of this order see BA-MA, PH5 / II / 452, f. 70.

[92] BHStA IV, Kriegsgefangenen-Arbeiter Bataillon, Nr. 29, Abschrift, Kriegsministerium, Nr. 63/7.18, U3, 23.9.1918.

commanders issued general orders outlining the task at hand and left the details of accomplishment to their subordinates.'[93] Thus the higher army echelons ordered that guards should be careful to maintain prisoners' physical strength, while at the same time leaving it completely up to subordinates how to get the desired amount of work from their charges. The only punishment guards received was if a prisoner escaped.[94]

However, ultimately, one key factor provides the crucial additional rationale behind the beatings – the fact that prisoners were starving. Hunger dominated the lives of prisoners working for the German army in 1918; guards, faced with the problem of how to force malnourished men to continue to work, often found violence the easiest option. Feeding the huge numbers of new captives taken in the spring offensive was a logistical nightmare in an army which, by late 1917, was already feeding its prisoner workers in the occupied territories the bare minimum. The British Government Committee interviews reveal the effect of inadequate rations: 'Many of the men were fading shadows'; 'the prisoners were literally starving, and many of them had become weak and ill already for want of nourishment'; 'all the men were very weak from lack of nourishment and it was a common sight to see them fall over when waiting for the issue of food'; 'the effect of this feeding was that everyone lost weight and rapidly became very low in condition. I personally lost over two stone and I would have gone on losing weight.'[95] The German army was aware of the problem – an order from the Intendant General of the Field Army (*Generalintendant des Feldheeres*) on 8 May 1918 stated that 'the food designated for prisoners of war has recently become increasingly sparse (*immer knapper*) so that the fulfilment of all requests is no longer possible'.[96] One prisoner summed up the rations in April 1918 as 'coffee substitute with no sugar or milk at 4 am. At 2.30 pm after coming in from work, barley boiled in water, very thin. At 6 pm coffee and bread ration of a quarter of a loaf of black bread.'[97]

Parcels did not reach these captives for two reasons. First, as outlined above, a great many of these prisoners had not been able to send a postcard to notify the British authorities of their existence or had not

[93] Hull, *Absolute Destruction*, p. 116.

[94] BA-MA PH5 / II / 452, f. 00082. Extract from Nachtrag zu den Dienst- und Wachtvorschriften für die Kommandos der bayerischen Bewachungskompagnie in den Arbeitslagern des [sic] Kriegsgefangenen A. Battalion, no. 29.

[95] TNA, WO 161/100, no. 1785, Interview with Drummer Leslie Rudd; no. 1787, Interview with Private C. Street; no. 1791, Interview with Cpl Joseph Page; no. 2537, Interview with Sergeant William Rhodes.

[96] BA-MA, PH5 / II / 453, f. 95, Generalintendant des Feldheeres, III d Nr. 889.5.18, 8.5.1918.

[97] TNA, WO 161/100, Interview no. 1789, Thos. Martleton.

been registered by Germany with the International Red Cross. Second, those prisoners who had been registered had to give a *Stammlager* (main camp) in Germany as their postal address because their frequent movements between work camps in the occupied zone meant they had no fixed camp address there; it was to the *Stammlager* in Germany that prisoners' parcels were sent for forwarding. This policy reduced the number of personnel, both German and prisoner, required for work camp administrative tasks in the *Etappen* area, freeing up manpower. In reality, in 1918, many parcels were never forwarded on from *Stammlager* to the occupied territories, and those that were were often stolen en route or stockpiled at depots. As a rule only camps with over 5,000 prisoners in Germany could act as a *Stammlager*.[98]

This postal system for work camps in the occupied territories had been in operation since 1915.[99] It had never worked well. By 1918, the whole German parcel system for prisoners was in such chaos that neutral powers had protested and the German army recognised the validity of these complaints regarding parcels in June 1918.[100] In September 1918, the Quartermaster-General's office (*Generalquartiermeister*) wrote that 'numerous complaints from enemy governments about irregularities in prisoners' post reveal that in numerous units the importance of supplying prisoners with post from home in the interest of maintaining their working strength is not properly recognised'.[101] Indeed, by October 1918, the Intelligence Section of the German army complained that camp commandants and postal censors were also blocking prisoners' letters, resulting in the loss of a useful intelligence source.[102] In the absence of parcels, prisoners turned to bartering for food: in one typical example, Corporal Joseph Page described exchanging a silver wristwatch for a loaf and a half of bread at Marchiennes.[103] Some German troops saw the prisoners' hunger as an opportunity for profit, selling them bread and cigarettes at inflated prices, to the annoyance of their commanders.[104]

---

[98] BHStA IV, Gen.Kdos IbAK, Bund 183, KM Berlin, Nr. 891/3.15.UK, 10.4.1915.
[99] *Ibid.*
[100] BHStA IV, Gen.Kdos IbAK, Bund 183, Abschrift, Ic Nr. 28500, 14.6.1918; See also BHStA IV, Gen.Kdos IbAK, Bund 183, Generalquartiermeister, Ic Nr. 33106, 1.7.1918.
[101] BA-MA, PH5 / II / 452, f. 125, Abschrift, Generalquartiermeister Ic Nr. 46811 to all AOKs des Westens, 8.9.1918.
[102] BA-MA, PH5 / II / 457, f. 39, Generalquartiermeister, Ic Nr. 52828, Gr.H.Qu., 11.10.1918.
[103] TNA, WO 161/100, no. 1791, Interview with Corporal Joseph Page.
[104] BHStA IV, Gen.Kdos IbAK, Bund 183, Generalkommando bayer. IAK Korpstagesbefehl, K.H.Qu., 28.7.1918. One German army inspector saw the problem in a different

Several prisoners were traumatised by the difficult conditions they endured in German army labour companies in 1918. Private Henry Emerson from Miletown, Co. Tyrone, was captured on 28 March 1918 and escaped on 15 September 1918. When interviewed in October 1918, the interviewer found him 'a difficult witness; willing, seemingly, but one who found it difficult to express himself. He gave me an impression of having received worse treatment than he was able to express clearly.'[105] Given Emerson's account of life in captivity, this comment is disturbing. Emerson described to the interviewer how, from 21 April to 30 June, at Esmery-Hallon, he was forced to work eight hours a day without a break, seven days a week. The prisoners lived in an old building with 'no roofs, no beds, no blankets, no protection from the weather'.[106] Emerson remained in the clothes he was captured in throughout his captivity – some five and a half months. He and his fellow prisoners were continually beaten and kicked by the guard: 'this was the usual thing; the guards constantly ill-treated us like this. There was no one to complain to; if we complained to an officer he would give us the same.'[107] For most of his captivity, Emerson was effectively sleeping rough, with no blanket, in shelled-out buildings which served as temporary camps. He was carrying out heavy manual labour on a single meal a day, consisting of a quarter of a loaf of bread, turnip soup and coffee made from barley – a situation which illustrates the extreme deprivation forced labourers endured on the western front by 1918.

Emerson's case was not exceptional. Another prisoner, Corporal Arthur Speight, who worked on the rail network in the *Etappengebiet* described how

we began our day's work by being walked on and walloped with sticks while it was still dark. Then we were shoved into lines of four men and issued with a drink of coffee made from burnt barley. A piece of bread was the day's ration but as most of the fellows were nearly mad for food the first one got the most – if he was strong enough to keep it![108]

One German guard allowed the prisoners to collect and cook snails.[109] Such conditions took their toll. Speight described how in summer 1918 the prisoners began to die:

light: in a 4th Army report in August, he stated that it was his belief that British prisoners captured in the March offensive were 'far inferior in build and working strength to the French'. BHStA IV, Kriegsgefangenen-Arbeiter Bataillon, Nr. 29. Abschrift, 9.8.18, Bericht über Besichtigung der Gefangenenlager im Bereich des AOK 4, Rekodeis 1 und der BdKM 3 und 5.

[105] TNA, WO 161/100, no. 2536, Interview with Private Henry Emerson, 1.10.1918.
[106] *Ibid.*   [107] *Ibid.*   [108] Arthur Speight, cited in Jackson, *The Prisoners*, pp. 25–6.
[109] *Ibid.*, p. 24.

It was a common sight to see about six men pulling a cart through the village with about twenty dead men piled on it ready for burial ... One incident stands out in my mind which should give some idea as to the state some of these men had come to. The ration of bread had evidently been issued from old stock and was quite unfit to eat being bright green in colour. Corporal Costello ... to make sure of none of the bad bread finding its way to the sick men ... threw it into the open latrine. Two wrecks of humanity crawled into the latrine on hands and knees and plunged their arms into the filth to recover the bread. Costello yelled at them that the stuff would kill them, but still they were intent upon getting it, whereupon Costello ran forward and flung them bodily from the hole. He then turned away and said: 'Well, I don't know, the poor —s [sic] will die anyway.'[110]

Two early post-war memoirs by French ex-prisoners describe similarly poor living conditions. Fernand Relange was taken prisoner in April 1918; Georges Caubet was captured in June of the same year. After capture, Relange had to bury the German and British dead for fifteen days. The prisoners were not provided with water to wash their hands after handling the bodies, which he described as 'decomposed – many were crawling with maggots'.[111] Of the twenty-two parcels sent to Relange while he worked behind the German lines, only two arrived, both of which had been plundered. Relange's account echoes many of the complaints in the British interviews: he had to work carrying German shells; his prison camp at Ham was bombed by French planes on 28 May, resulting in eighteen prisoners killed and forty-five wounded; he was fed a watered-down 'beet and barley soup' and suffered badly from hunger; and the prisoners were all covered in lice.[112] Relange and his companions took to stealing potatoes from the German stores to survive. At Buronfosse camp, Relange described appalling conditions: 1,500 prisoners were lodged in tents in a field; severe rain led to problems with mud; the guards were 'ferocious' to their charges.[113] When the seat to the latrine broke, five prisoners fell into the waste below. It was impossible to get water to wash them. When some parcels containing tins did arrive for one prisoner, a German NCO poured the contents of all the tins together in a bucket in the middle of the camp, mixing meat, condensed milk, chocolate, tinned vegetable, sugar and soap. This impossible mix was then given to the prisoner. The man wept. His food supply for six weeks had been spoiled. Relange described how

After 25 days we were nothing more than skeletons which dragged themselves in the mud of the camp. 50 men died of misery. When we demanded a medical

---

[110] Ibid., pp. 25–6.
[111] Fernand Relange, *Huit mois dans les lignes allemands. Souvenirs d'un prisonnier de Belleherbe* (Besançon, 1919), pp. 1–6.
[112] Ibid., p. 9.   [113] Ibid.

inspection we paraded before a major seated in an armchair in a corner of the camp. We paraded in Indian file 3 metres from him and heard him call '*Weg, los, raus*'.[114]

During the retreat, Relange claimed that one day the prisoners marched thirty-five kilometres on 500 grams of bread, a spoonful of marmalade and a tiny piece of cheese; the following day they marched eighteen kilometres. Georges Caubet's account of his four-week captivity in occupied France, written in October 1918, detailed similar events: poor conditions in the open air in the holding cage after capture; work loading and unloading shells; guards hitting prisoners; no postal service.[115] In a work camp at Saint Quentin the prisoners exchanged 'our great coats, our boots … shoes' for bread.[116]

Elderly British veterans who were held in the occupied territories in 1918 recalled similar experiences when interviewed for a documentary in the late 1990s. Ernie Stevens remembered being made to work at carrying boxes of ammunition from a railhead to the German line. Thomas Spriggs described how at Tournai he saw four British prisoners fighting over a bucket of pig-swill due to their hunger.[117] Walter Humprys recalled how

We were always hungry. We used to pick a few mushrooms and mangolds as we cleared the old battlefields. It was repugnant eating mangolds, potato peelings, nettles and dandelions but hunger finally overcame discretion. We became so weak that our legs shook under us and a march of a mile and a half fatigued us.[118]

The reason for the repeated references to nettles and dandelions in many of the former prisoners' accounts is simple. From late 1917 on, the German army instructions for prisoner working companies encouraged the use of wild flowers and plants 'such as nettles, sorrel and dandelion' as a supplement for the prisoners' inadequate rations.[119]

The fact that by 1918 many prisoners were too malnourished to perform effectively as a workforce thus helps to explain the widespread use of violence by guards. However, this situation was exacerbated by decisions

---

[114] *Ibid.*

[115] Georges Caubet, *Instituteur et Sergent. Mémoires de guerre et de captivité* (Carcassonne, 1991), pp. 47–61.

[116] *Ibid.*, p. 58.

[117] Thomas Spriggs (b.1897), cited in Emden, *Prisoners of the Kaiser*, p. 119; Ernie Stevens (b.1899), *ibid.*, p. 60.

[118] Walter Humprys (b.1897) cited in Emden, *Prisoners of the Kaiser*, p. 118.

[119] BHStA IV, Gen.Kdos IbAK, Bund 183, Generalquartiermeister, Ia Nr. 37 996, 29.9.1917. See also TNA, WO 161/100, Interview no. 1783, Private Chilton, who recalls prisoners gathering dandelion roots to eat at Buissey camp; BHStA IV, Gen.Kdos IbAK, Bund 38, Abschrift, Der Beauftragte des Generalquartiermeisters West, III d no.99707, 7.10.1918.

taken by higher command levels in the German army which knew that prisoners were totally inadequately fed, yet continued to force them to work and failed to effectively enforce measures to protect their health – indeed, on occasion higher command levels undermined such measures. Some of these measures will now be assessed here in turn: the orders issued to protect prisoners' working strength which were not carried out; the decision to keep sick or weakened prisoners in the occupied zone rather than transferring them to main camps (*Stammlager*) in Germany where living conditions were better; and the decision to strictly prohibit all civilian attempts to give prisoners food.

The first key factor which undermined prisoners' health in 1918 was the failure to enforce or coordinate the orders issued by various command levels to try to protect prisoner health. German sources reveal that the weakened condition of prisoner labourers was known at command level. Indeed, in work camps controlled by the 4th Army, some French, British and Italian prisoners were weighed monthly from April 1918 on to assess their condition.[120] From orders issued in the Bavarian 6th and the Prussian 4th Armies it is clear that it was an open secret within the command structure that the workers were not adequately fed. The *Armeeoberkommando 18* admitted in July 1918 that 'correct behaviour towards prisoners and feeding of prisoners in the camps would greatly reduce the number of prisoner escapes. In many cases inadequate food is the reason for the escape.'[121] Attempts were made to add food supplements to prisoners' diets – they were provided with extra mushrooms, weak prisoners were to be given *Nährhefe* (nutrient yeast), and the ban on prisoners using money to order foodstuffs to be sent to them from abroad was lifted.[122] However, prisoners' rations were still the target of drastic measures to spare resources. On 18 June 1918 an order from the *Generalkommando I. bayer. Armee Korps* revealed that

In recent times, multiple requests have been sent to the *Armeeoberkommando* for heavy worker rations and the higher bread ration of up to 600 grams to be issued to prisoners in cases where it does not seem that there exists a compelling need for the better food. For the most part, the doctors' certificates accompanying such requests only state that the prisoners should be considered as heavy labourers, and because of this, should receive the heavy worker (*Schwerarbeiter*) rations and the higher bread rations. The fact that prisoners of war are working at heavy

[120] BA-MA, PH5 / II / 447.

[121] BHStA IV, Gen.Kdos IbAK, Bund 38, Landsturm und Gefangenen Inspektion, Ic/Iq Nr. 19827, 30.7.1918.

[122] BHStA IV, Kriegsgefangenen-Arbeiter Bataillon, Nr. 29, Generalintendant d.Feldg. IIId. Nr. 987.6.18. 13.6.1918. Also BHStA IV, Kriegsgefangenen-Arbeiter Bataillon, Nr. 29, Kriegsministerium, Nr. 2303/2.18.U.5/4.19.4.1918.

manual labour tasks does not on its own justify, without additional reasons, extra food. Due to the difficult food supply situation such rations can only be approved when they are absolutely necessary to maintain prisoners in strength and in working condition. To avoid the exhaustion of prisoners only the strong should be put to work at heavy labour tasks, the weak or sick should be set to lighter work. It is also recommended that prisoners who have been working on heavy labour tasks for a long period should be set to work on lighter tasks, such as in agriculture or in repair workshops. If these methods still do not prevent the prisoners' weakening, then requests for the heavy labourer rations should be sent in. The doctors' certificates enclosed in these requests must provide irrefutable proof of the need for the increased rations.[123]

In other words, by summer 1918, employment on heavy labour tasks no longer automatically qualified a prisoner for heavy worker rations.

As prisoners became increasingly malnourished, several measures were taken to try to preserve their labour strength. From June 1918 on, repeated orders outlined the special attention that was to be paid to prisoners' welfare. Prisoners were only to work for a maximum of eight hours a day and orders were issued that they should not be beaten by their guards. The eight-hour day was 'to ensure that the working strength of prisoners is used to the maximum (*voll ausgenutzt*) but not weakened by overstrain'.[124] Beatings by the guards were 'strictly prohibited. All guards are relied upon to do all that seems necessary to maintain the working strength and work motivation (*Arbeitsfreudigkeit*) of the prisoners and to do all that is ordered by the army.'[125] Sick prisoners were not to be sent to work. Prison camps were also to be camouflaged to protect them from aerial bombardment.[126] An order issued on 7 October 1918 in the 6th Army

asked once again for all units which have charge of prisoners of war, civilian prisoner battalions etc. to pay attention to ensuring the good treatment of the prisoners, correct feeding (*sachgemässe Ernährung*), observation of the health instructions, and consideration for the prisoners' working strength (*Schonung der Arbeitskräfte*).[127]

---

[123] BHStA IV, Gen.Kdos IbAK, Bund 183, Gen.Kdo I. bayer. AK, Ausschnitt aus Verordnungsblatt der Armee Abteilung C, 1918, Seite 319, Nr. 835, Schwerarbeiterportionen und erhöhte Brotportion für Kriegsgefangene 18.6.1918.

[124] BHStA IV, Kriegsgefangenen-Arbeiter Bataillon, Nr. 29, AOK 4, Arb. Nr. 7675, 18.6.1918.

[125] BA-MA, PH5 / II / 452, f. 00076, Dem Herrn Oberbefehlshaber durch Herrn Ober-quartiermeister 10.10.1918.

[126] BHStA IV, Gen.Kdos IbAK, Bund 38, Landsturm und Gefangenen Inspektion 118, Deutsche Feldpost 158, B.B. Nr. G. 6600.

[127] BHStA IV, Gen.Kdos IbAK, Bund 38, Abschrift, Der Beauftragte des Generalquartier-meisters West, III d no.99707, 7.10.1918 (underlining in original). See also BA-MA, PH5 / II / 457, f. 38 for another copy of this order.

The order emphasised that 'all means should be used, to preserve this valuable and irreplaceable labour resource – the amount of work demanded should not be set too high and should be adapted to the condition of the prisoners. All over-exhaustion (*Überanstrengung*) should be avoided.'[128] It stated that to protect prisoners 'accommodation should be as near to the workplace as possible so that the prisoners do not arrive at work tired by a long march and footwear is not worn out, unnecessarily'.[129] Where possible

the men must find a warm room when they return from work thoroughly frozen and wet through and be able to dry their things. Each prisoner is to receive two blankets in winter and as protection from bad weather should bring blankets or a coat to their workplace with them ... As morning and evening food soup is better than a thin coffee. The food should be varied. Wild plants should be used.[130]

The order also emphasised that the postal service in most camps was not yet organised: 'the blame lies mainly with the *Stammlager*'.[131] It called for this to be remedied as 'parcels from home provide a valuable supplement of food'.[132]

Such orders to protect prisoners were issued because the German army needed its captive labour to remain fit enough to work; they rarely mentioned the Hague Convention or other international law. However, the fear that the Allies might punish *their* German prisoner labourers in reprisal also played a role. On 1 July 1918, for example, an order was issued, reminding troops of the impact on German prisoners of war abroad of prisoner mistreatment by German soldiers.[133] By October 1918, there was also a concern that the state of the prisoner labourers might result in Allied punishment after the war. A telegram from General Headquarters to the 4th Army Command on 30 October stated that

during the present necessary transfers of prisoner of war camps it is of the utmost importance that particular attention is paid to the feeding, clothing and accommodation of prisoners so that damage to their health will be completely avoided. Otherwise it cannot be ruled out that poor prisoner treatment will be used against us politically by the Entente and will also result in bad treatment for German prisoners.[134]

Yet although there were clearly considerable pragmatic motivations for ensuring a minimum of prisoner care, the orders issued to protect

---

[128] *Ibid.* [129] *Ibid.* [130] *Ibid.* [131] *Ibid.* [132] *Ibid.*

[133] BHStA IV, Gen.Kdos IbAK, Bund 183, Generalquartiermeister, Ic Nr. 33106, 1.7.1918. See also a copy of this order: BA-MA, PH5 / II / 452, f. 249, Abschrift, Generalquartiermeister, Ic Nr. 33106, 1.7.1918.

[134] BHStA IV, Kriegsgefangenen-Arbeiter Bataillon, Nr. 29, Abschrift, Tgm Gr.H.Qu. to AOK 4, 30.10.1918. See also a copy of this order in BA-MA, PH5 / II / 452, f. 16, Tgm from G.H.Qu., Generalquartiermeister Ic Nr. 56905.

prisoners were not properly enforced on the ground and they were often undermined by subsequent orders. For example, although frequent orders reiterated that British and French prisoners should not be used within thirty kilometres of the front, in September 1918, a separate order allowed for French prisoners to be employed within the thirty-kilometre zone as a reprisal.[135] Where one order stated that guards should not hit prisoners, others demanded that guards 'handle prisoners strictly (*strenge Handhabung*)' to prevent escapes.[136] In addition, lower-level command groups often adopted differing policies. One inspection report on prisoner labour company camps in the 4th Army written on 13 September 1918 related that:

1. In one *Generalkommando*, despite the best personal efforts of the camp commandant at the Corps Provision Office (*Korps-Proviantamt*) the special foodstuffs for prisoners had not been delivered. The Economic Affairs Offices (*Intendanturen*) and Provision Offices must absolutely ensure that the special foodstuffs for prisoners are supplied, where there are enough stocks available.
2. In one *Generalkommando* the prisoners were only given a rest day every 14 days. Working prisoners must be given a day off each week – where possible, a Sunday.
3. At one *Generalkommando* the working day including the march there and back was from 12 to 16 hours a day ... At one camp the latrine pit was not walled although it was near the newly installed pumps. Great care should be taken with the installation of pumps and supply of water in prisoner camps to avoid sickness and to give the prisoners the opportunity to thoroughly clean their person and their clothing.[137]

The inspector reiterated in the report that prisoners should not work for more than eight hours a day. If their place of work was further than four kilometres away, the march there and back was to be counted as working time. Yet a memo written *in response* to this report stated that the 4th Army Command (*Oberkommando*) had ordered that prisoners should work for ten hours a day.[138]

There were similar contradictions between the German army's policies towards its labour companies and the Prussian *Kriegsministerium*. At the same time that army orders were being issued not to make sick prisoners work, other instructions from the *Kriegsministerium* in Berlin were being circulated to prisoner labour companies informing commanders that

---

[135] BHStA IV, Gen.Kdos IbAK, Bund 38, A.H.Qu, 14.9.18, Armeeoberkommando 18, Ic/ Iq Nr. 20797.
[136] BHStA IV, Gen.Kdos IbAK, Bund 38, Armeeoberkommando 18, Ic/Iq Nr. 17809, 17.5.1918.
[137] BA-MA, PH5 / II/ 452, f. 00112, Armeeoberkommando 4, Arb. Nr. 9174, 13.9.1918.
[138] BA-MA, PH5 / II / 452, f. 00113, Arb. Nr. 9180, 13.9.1918.

prisoners were faking illnesses to win time off, by using a nail to infect themselves with petroleum to create swellings, fever and headaches; by rubbing salt into slight wounds to cause inflammation and by swallowing salt and soap to cause stomach and intestinal cramps.[139] This *Kriegsministerium* alert largely related to prisoners in Germany – there was an almost total absence of soap in the work camps in the western occupied territories, although petroleum was used there on occasion for delousing. However, such instructions illustrate the continuing suspicion of prisoners' illnesses, which constantly undermined orders to protect weak or sick captives in prisoner labour companies from hard manual labour.

The disparity between the orders issued to protect prisoners' health and the reality on the ground should not come as any surprise for several reasons. First, there was never any sanction implied or enforced by the orders issued on prisoner treatment against those guards or camp commandants who breached their stipulations. Second, the need to continue to maintain an adequate output of work from the key labour resource available to the German army in a demanding wartime situation undermined the orders issued to protect that labour resource: any measures to cut prisoners' working time or allow them extra rest days reduced the intense short-term output which commandants were under pressure to deliver. Finally, the only serious measure that would truly have protected prisoners' health would have been to increase their rations to a par with German troops. This option, however, was never taken. Moreover, prisoners were not allowed to buy any extra food from the local population, unlike German troops.[140]

The second key factor which undermined prisoners' welfare was a change of policy by the German army, which in 1918 removed an important protection that had existed for sick captive workers. In 1917, prisoners who became severely ill and unfit to work were often sent to a *Stammlager* in Germany. This transfer to a *Stammlager* offered sick or weak prisoners certain benefits. There was immediate access to better nutrition in large camps in Germany, usually through the prisoners' camp committee, which organised donations of food from other prisoners for those who had not received parcels. There was often access to the collective bread and biscuit deliveries sent from Berne and Copenhagen and paid for by the British and French governments. Arrival in a *Stammlager* also provided a prisoner with a morale boost at leaving the devastated

---

[139] BA-MA, PH5 / II / 453, f. 64, Kriegsministerium, Sanitätsdepartement, Nr. 4365/4.18.S 2 geh. 10.6.1918.
[140] BA-MA, PH5 / II / 452, f. 113, Arb. Nr. 9180, 13.9.1918.

Etappen area. There was much better accommodation than in the occupied territories, with proper beds and blankets and sometimes recreational facilities – *Stammlager* were frequently purpose-built, with large barrack rooms. Finally, almost all *Stammlager* had a hospital section. It was to this that men who arrived from working in the occupied zone were invariably sent. German doctors working in *Stammlager* were also far less likely to pass a very sick man as fit for work than those in the occupied territories. They were under less pressure to do so and some were civilians who had not adopted hardline military attitudes towards sick prisoner workers. They appear to have generally done their utmost to assist very ill prisoners who arrived from the occupied zone.

By spring 1918, however, the transfer system had changed. The problem was that prisoners transported to Germany owing to sickness were never returned to the labour company work camps in the occupied territories if they recovered. The OHL had no power over prisoners once they arrived in Germany, as camps there were directly under the District Military Commanders, who answered to the Kaiser. Therefore, new prisoner convalescent systems were established within the occupied territories in order to stop this continual labour seepage to Germany. On 17 March 1918, an order from the Quartermaster-General stated that sick prisoners of war would be sent to hospitals in Belgium at Liège and Antwerp and returned to their work companies once passed as fit.[141] The 6th Army had already established its own convalescent homes in September 1917 at convents in Warchin and Wez-Welvain for British or Russian prisoner workers who after a short rest period could be returned to their working companies without being sent to Germany.[142] The 6th Army *Etappen-Inspektion* also started a convalescence section for weak prisoners at Conflans.[143] By October 1918, it also had a convalescence section at La Capelle for prisoners working for the army *Generalkommandos*.

The effect of this policy was to create an enclosed system of prisoner labour within the occupied territories, largely outside public knowledge in Germany. Sick prisoners kept in the occupied territories had practically no access to parcels and had to deal pyschologically with the likelihood

---

[141] BHStA IV, Et.Inspektion, Gefangenen Kommando, Bd. 199, Tagebuch 4, Abschrift des Kriegstagebuches der Gefangenen-Inspektion 106 für die Zeit vom 1.1.1918 bis 31.3.1918. Der Beauftragte des Generalquartiermeisters West III d Nr. 26094, no.14, 17.3.1918.

[142] BHStA IV, Et.Inspektion, Gefangenen Kommando, Bd. 199, Kriegstagebuch 1.7.1917–30.9.1917, Anlage 1 Tagb. Nr. 2155/17.

[143] BHStA IV, Gen.Kdos IbAK, Bund 183, Armee Abtg C, Armee Oberkommando, Arbo Nr. 34301/17, 12.11.1917.

that they would be sent back to the same work camp and its spartan conditions if they recovered their fitness. Prisoners *were* still sent to Germany if it became clear that they would not be able to physically work again, but the new convalescent system was intended to reduce the numbers of prisoners transferred.

Some prisoners believed this army policy was to hide the situation in the occupied territories from the German public. In March 1918, the *Morning Post* quoted an escaped Russian prisoner who had been working behind the lines and who claimed that

The sick, the injured and those utterly worn out and unfit are never sent back to Germany to their original camps but are kept behind the front, there to die. The officials are afraid of the effect on their own people of the horrible sight these men present. They are like men who stalk out of their graves, animated skeletons, bones covered with skin, cheeks without flesh, deeply sunken eyes.[144]

As prisoners became increasingly malnourished in the occupied territories in September and October 1918, the situation deteriorated. An order from *Etappen-Inspektion 18* on 4 October 1918 stated that prisoners who had been working for the army *Generalkommandos* in the Operations area and who were no longer able to work due to physical weakness could not be exchanged for less-exhausted prisoners working to the rear in the *Etappen* zone as this would 'quickly wear out all the *Etappen-Inspektion* reserves'.[145] Effectively, by October, sick prisoners could no longer be moved after convalescence to less demanding work zones.

In fact, the general policy was now to delay prisoner evacuation from the work camps to proper hospitals whenever possible. On 14 October 1918, a telegram from the *Feldsanitätschef* at German General Headquarters outlined this:

1. Sick prisoners of war who are sick for up to three weeks are to be treated at their existing location.
2. Sick prisoners of war with a predicted treatment period of 3 to 6 weeks are only to be sent to the prisoner of war hospital (*Lazarett*) at Liège after consultation with the army doctor at Brussels.
3. In cases with a predicted sickness period of over 6 weeks, as well as permanent inability to work, the prisoner is to be sent to Germany.[146]

Thus unless a prisoner was clearly permanently incapacitated by sickness or injury, his evacuation from a work camp to an army hospital was

---

[144] BA, AA R 901/54412, *Morning Post* cutting, 'Forced labour for Germany', 3.1.1918.
[145] BHStA IV, Gen.Kdos IbAK, Bund 38, Etappen-Inspektion 18, Abt Ib, Nr. 50759, Arbeitsunfähige Kriegsgefangene, 4.10.1918.
[146] BA-MA, PH5 / II / 452, f. 34, Abschrift, Tgm H.Qu. Mezières to AOK 4, B.d.G. (Beauftragte des Generalquartiermeisters) West, III.d.112045, 14.10.1918.

unlikely; the policy was that as many sick prisoners as possible were to be treated at their work location. Where prisoners did get access to hospitals the treatment was often good, but access was often delayed until the last phase of illness: for example, Private John Dixon, a British prisoner worker who was suffering from dysentery and starvation, was sent to the German hospital at Cugny with ten other prisoners, three of whom died on admittance, despite what Dixon describes as excellent care from the German doctors and nurses, who even managed to procure 'eggs, white bread, rice, milk, meat, cocoa, vegetables and wine for their very ill prisoner charges'.[147]

Dixon's experience was not an isolated incident – British prisoners had been dying at Cugny field hospital from dysentery since April 1918. For their relatives obtaining information about what had happened to these men was extremely difficult, making the process of grieving protracted. Most were never reported as prisoners. The mother of Rifleman Joe Clarke, who died at Cugny of dysentery on 22 April, wrote letters to the King's Royal Rifle Corps, to the Red Cross, to the War Office and to a family friend at Le Havre, desperate to find out what had happened to her teenage son, reported only as missing.[148] On 15 July 1918, the International Committee of the Red Cross informed her that Joe, captured in March, had died of dysentery as a prisoner of war at Cugny and was buried there.[149] His mother initially refused to accept the news and wrote to repatriated prisoners from the same battalion as Joe in December 1918. One of them, Rifleman E. Powell, replied:

We had a rather rough time and fellows as I no [sic] for a fact were dying from this dysentery but I hope sincerely that you hear very shortly of him being alive. I am sure you are putting me to no trouble whatever I would only be glad to help you as I no [sic] what a Mother feels towards her son and also how my own mother was.[150]

After advertising in the *Daily Sketch* for news of her son, without success, Mrs Clarke finally accepted that he was dead; in 1920 his body was exhumed and moved to a British cemetery. How many of those who were posted as missing actually died as prisoners of war in the occupied territories in 1918 may never be known.

The third key decision which undermined prisoners' well-being in 1918 was the German army prohibition on all interaction between the civilians of the occupied territories and prisoners of war. Civilians were

---

[147] TNA, WO 161/100, Interview no. 2816, Private John Dixon.
[148] Helen Cleary, 'The Human Face of War' www.bbc.co.uk/history/worldwars/wwone/humanfaceofwar_gallery_07.shtml, accessed 30.11.09.
[149] *Ibid.*   [150] *Ibid.*

believed to be abetting prisoners in their attempts to escape by secretly providing them with maps or compasses, or worse, plotting rebellion or sabotage with them. Undoubtedly this did on occasion occur. The *Generalkommando* of the *XVIII Reservekorps* wrote to *Armeeoberkommando 4* on 25 May in one typical letter that

In spite of the strictest measures, it is very difficult to prevent prisoners from establishing contact with the civilian population and exchanging letters and parcels ... Already individual prisoners have escaped, most while at work, and of these few have been recaptured, which leads to the conclusion that the civilian population supported the escapers in every way, and in particular, supplied them with civilian clothing.[151]

At Halluin, the problem was compounded by the fact that a number of the French prisoners working there came from the area. This had caused 'understandable upset among the population and led them to continually try to make contact with the prisoners', giving them parcels, letters, news and notes 'on their way to and from work, despite threatened punishments and other reprisal measures'.[152] However, in most incidents, it appears that civilians, in particular, women, simply desired to give prisoners food. German guards' violent enforcement of the prohibition on civilian–prisoner interaction greatly reduced prisoners' access to a source of additional food – a remarkably short-sighted policy when the German army was struggling with the problem of malnourishment among its prisoner labourers.

All interaction between prisoners and civilians was totally prohibited in 1918 and considerable violence was used to enforce this measure.[153] Guards frequently beat any prisoners or civilians who tried to contravene it. One British prisoner witnessed how

French civilians offered us food but if anyone left the ranks to get it they were struck by the guards with the butts of their rifles and an order was given that the sentries had instructions to fire on anyone who left the ranks ... In a village ... just outside Montigny a French peasant woman threw mangold wurzels to the prisoners. She had only thrown two when three Germans from the garrison in the village rushed at her and threw her down and kicked her.[154]

---

[151] BA-MA, PH5 / II / 459, f. 26, Generalkommando XVIII Reservekorps to Armeeoberkommando 4, 25.5.1918.

[152] BA-MA, PH5 / II / 457, f. 9, Gefangenen Sammelstelle, Halluin, Vernehmungsoffizier to N.O.4, 14.5.1918.

[153] BHStA IV, Gen.Kdos IbAK, Bund 38, Landsturm und Gefangenen Inspektion 118, Deutsche Feldpost 158, B.B. Nr. G.6600, Betr. Bestimmungen über den Wachdienst bei Gefangenen-Formationen. See also Parliamentary Paper, Cd. 9106, *Report on the Treatment by the Germans of Prisoners of War taken during the Spring Offensives of 1918*, p. 3.

[154] TNA, WO 161/100, Interview no. 1791, Interview with Corporal Joseph Page.

He also recalled how, at Hordain, civilians who had initially been allowed to assist the prisoners with food and clothes were prevented from doing so after three days: 'There was an order that anyone disobeying would be fined and I saw a woman brought before the commandant for this reason.'[155] On occasion the actions by guards seem to have been vindictive: a former prisoner wrote in his memoirs how 'as we approached Caudry, the civilians tried hard to give us a little bread but the Germans charged them from time to time with their lances ... One brave woman threw us half a loaf of bread from her bedroom window and the sentry put his lance through every pane.'[156] The elderly William Easton, interviewed in 1999, recounted a similar incident near Mons.[157] The civilians' persistent efforts showed considerable generosity – the bread ration for Belgian civilians dropped as low as 190 grams between March and October 1918.[158]

In at least one case, a civilian was shot for trying to give prisoners food. On 12 October 1918, in a famous incident, a German guard shot and fatally wounded Yvonne Vieslet, a Belgian child of ten, who was attempting to give her school lunch to some French prisoners held at Marchienne-au-Pont.[159] Rumours of other such shootings abounded: a repatriated French civilian from Roubaix reported that 'a certain woman was shot through the head' for trying to give prisoners bread.[160] By early 1918, unverifiable reports were also reaching the British government of British prisoners being 'shot on sight ... for dropping out to get bread from Belgian civilians'.[161] The International Red Cross received similar

[155] Ibid.

[156] Citation from the unpublished memoirs of George Gadsby in Emden, Prisoners of the Kaiser, p. 115.

[157] 'These women saw us there and they ran out with plates, with potato on. They ran in amongst us and do you know, the Germans halted us and they shouted out an order and the guards went and pushed the women away and then they went in and out of us smashing the plates with their rifle butts.' William Easton interviewed in Emden, Prisoners of the Kaiser, p. 74.

[158] Peter Scholliers and Frank Daelmans, 'Standards of Living and Standards of Health in Wartime Belgium', in Richard Wall and Jay Winter, eds., The Upheaval of War. Family, Work and Welfare in Europe 1914–1918 (Cambridge, 1988), p. 145.

[159] Post-war British and Belgian enquiries failed to find the German soldier who had fired the shot. The child's death later became the subject of a Belgian film after the war and monuments were erected to her at Marchienne-au-Pont and at Monceau-sur-Sambre, where she was born. Éloy Druart, Jusqu'à la mort. Un nid des patriotes. René van Coillie, l'abbé Vital Alexandre, le caporal Trésignies, Yvonne Vieslet (Brussels, 1923), pp. 111–18. www.1914–1918.be/photo.php?image=photos/enfant_vieslet/11vieslet_a.jpg, accessed 25.10.2005. I am indebted to Leen Engelen, University of Louvain, and Professor Sophie de Schaepdrijver, Penn. State, for background information on the Vieslet case.

[160] TNA, WO 32/5188, 33A, Report by a civilian repatriated from Somain, 12.10.1918.

[161] Parliamentary Paper, Cd. 8988, Report on the Treatment by the Enemy of British Prisoners of War behind the Firing Lines in France and Belgium (London, 1918), p. 9.

reports from civilians from northern France being repatriated via Switzerland.[162]

It is clear from the civilian statements that the German treatment of prisoners of war was considered extreme and unacceptable by contemporary commentators. As neutral powers and humanitarian organisations, such as the International Red Cross, were not allowed access to prisoners working for the German army in the occupied territories, civilians took on the role of key witnesses, testifying to the Allies about the prisoner mistreatment they had seen.[163] Those repatriated from occupied France described the condition of prisoners of war as poor and stated that the British prisoners evoked 'pity by their emaciated appearance'.[164] One repatriated civilian stated how at Cambrai the British prisoners 'were not adequately fed and very often the civilian population gave them food'.[165] Another civilian, repatriated from Roubaix, stated that she was imprisoned for sixteen days for giving prisoners food and that, 'although it was forbidden' to help British prisoners, the inhabitants were still managing to supply them with foodstuffs.[166] One repatriated civilian described how at Marchiennes the population was 'moved' by the treatment of the prisoners, one of whom, in 1918, collapsed and died from starvation in the street.[167] In Roubaix, locals affiliated with the French Red Cross even organised a fête in support of prisoners and 'in spite of German orders to the contrary, inhabitants succeeded in giving these prisoners food and clothing'.[168]

The British government, alarmed by the reports it was receiving, tried to interest the Dutch, who had taken over the role of protecting power for British prisoners in Germany following America's entry into the war, to put pressure on Germany to improve the lot of the prisoners working in the occupied territories. In the absence of any neutral inspection reports, however, the Dutch representative van Rappard was unconvinced,

---

[162] ACICR, 431/III/j/c.31, Commission Allemande d'enquête, 431/III, Traitement des PG en France envahie, Rapport de Mr William Cuendet, Président du comité des rapatriés à Zurich au CICR sur la situation des prisonniers dans le nord de la France, 5.9.1917.

[163] The British and French also did not allow the International Red Cross or neutral states to inspect their work camps for German prisoners in their own army zones, with one exception – the French permitted a visit by Gustav Ador from the International Committee of the Red Cross to German prisoners working in the Somme region in November 1916: ACICR, 444/IV/c.59, Letter from Gustav Ador to German Red Cross, Berlin, 20.11.1916.

[164] TNA, WO 32/5188, 33A, Report by a French civilian repatriated from Somain, 12.10.1918.

[165] *Ibid.*, Report by a French civilian repatriated from Cambrai, Hocquet, 12.10.1918.

[166] *Ibid.*, Report by a French civilian repatriated from Roubaix, 12.10.1918.

[167] *Ibid.*, Report by a French civilian repatriated from Marchiennes, 14.10.1918.

[168] *Ibid.*, Report by a French civilian repatriated from Roubaix, 7.10.1918.

believing that the British were exaggerating the problem. Exasperated, the Foreign Office wrote in September 1918 to the British Consul at The Hague, Sir W. Townley, that it

should be glad if you would explain to Monsieur van Rappard that the allegations of gross illtreatment of the prisoners in question have not been founded on the evidence of a small number of prisoners, but on that of a very large number who have escaped at different times from behind the German lines and have given similar accounts of their treatment; that in addition there is a great deal of evidence from prisoners who have been released from permanent internment camps in Germany in which they describe the arrival of large numbers of British prisoners from behind the German lines in a state of exhaustion and disease; that it is certain that among such prisoners a considerable number of deaths have occurred directly resulting from neglect and ill-treatment; that even if the evidence received by His Majesty's Government has been somewhat exaggerated, which there is no reason to suppose, it would still reveal an appalling condition of affairs; and that His Majesty's Government are in fact completely satisfied that the evidence received by them is substantially correct.[169]

By autumn 1918, the evolving battlefield had led to prisoner of war work camps being moved back in tandem with the German retreat.[170] In September, the German army began to evacuate some prisoners to *Stammlager* camps in Germany. However, thousands remained in the occupied zone until the end of the war. In the 4th Army zone alone, on 8 October 1918 there were still 1,048 French prisoners and 6,591 British prisoners in work *Kommandos*. Providing food for these prisoners had become next to impossible for the German army. In September, the *Feldintendantur Gruppe Ieperen* received a message that 'the food for prisoners of war cannot be delivered this month'.[171] On 3 November, the Intendant General of the Field Army (*Generalintendant des Feldheeres*) issued an order that 'due to the present transport situation, the delivery of particular food for prisoners of war is to cease ... Food for prisoners is

---

[169] TNA, WO 32/5188, 24 A, no. 3774, Foreign Office to The Hague, R. Graham for the Secretary of State to Sir W. Townley, 3.9.1918.

[170] At the same time as the British were trying to convince the Dutch to intervene, the principal prisoner illnesses in the occupied zone, dysentery and dropsy, were joined by Spanish influenza. It was reported at the French prisoner of war camp in the Augustinian monastery in Ghent on 9 August, when thirty-eight prisoners out of an overall total of 1,915 were in the military hospital with influenza. At Tourcoing, on the same date, fifty-eight British prisoners out of 700 were sick with the flu. BHStA IV, Kriegsgefangenen-Arbeiter Bataillon, Nr. 29, Abschrift, Bericht über Besichtigung der Gefangenenlager im Bereich des AOK 4, Rekodeis 1 und der BdKM 3 und 5, 9.8.1918.

[171] BA-MA, PH5 / II / 452, Von Seiten des Generalkommandos, Der Chef des Generalstabes, über AOK4, Urgent. Message from Et-Intendantur 4, Nr. 1782/9.

to be allocated from troop food stores.'[172] The number of escapes increased during the final months of the war, due to the inadequate number of German guards available to man prisoner of war work camps and the lack of food.[173] The situation was becoming increasingly unstable as the Allies advanced and the German army tried to evacuate some of its prisoners. On 5 November it was ordered that all transport of prisoners of war through large towns in the occupied territories be avoided due to 'the present mood of the population . . . If prisoner transports through Brussels are unavoidable, the *Kommandantur* is to be informed in advance and numerous guards provided.'[174] It is significant that the German army attempted to evacuate prisoners from the occupied territories as under the pressure of the rapid Allied advance they were no longer evacuating many of their own wounded, who were left behind to be captured by the Allies.[175] Ultimately the German army wished to retain its malnourished labourers right up to the very last days of the war.

Conclusion

The above evidence allows for a number of key conclusions regarding violence against prisoners working for the German army in 1918. First, the overall context of extremely poor living conditions, malnutrition and heavy labour demands was key in facilitating and propagating widespread violence against prisoners. Conditions regarded by the German army in spring 1917 as the most extreme form of prisoner reprisals had become the norm in 1918. Second, German army policy on violence against prisoners was confused and contradictory – certain kinds of violence such as disciplinary punishments or labour under shellfire were at times endorsed by army policy; other kinds of violence were the result of a widespread culture of beatings instigated by guards on their own initiative in order to force prisoners to work. Finally, the violence practised against prisoner of war workers was considered exceptional in the eyes of contemporaries: nowhere is this clearer than in onlookers' accounts of the Armistice period and the liberation of the work camps in the occupied territories.

---

[172] BA-MA, PH5 / II / 452, f. 1, Generalintendant des Feldheeres, IIId. Nr. 223/11.18. Betr. Sonderverpflegung für Kriegsgefangene. Gez. Ritter. Sent to all Gruppenintendanten, 3.11.1918.

[173] BHStA IV, Gen.Kdos IbAK, Bund 38, AOK 18 rm IC, Tgm., 24.9.1918.

[174] BA-MA, PH5 / II / 452, f. 10, Heeresgruppe Kronprinz Rupprecht qu 73990 to AOK 4, 5.11.1918.

[175] ACICR, CR 17–1, Délégation du CI auprés PG allemands 1918–1919, Abschrift Bern, Letter to Herrn Minister von Hindenburg, Abteilung für Gefangenenfragen from Dr. Hahn, Professor d. Hygiene, University of Freiburg i/B., 11.12.1918.

Unchecked, the drive towards extreme forced labour had severe human consequences: many prisoners were in a very poor condition by the Armistice. Reports from German army units during the German retreat stated that some prisoners were too ill to walk. By 7 November 1918, the prisoners of the *Engländer Kommando XI* at Dendermonde were in a very poor condition. A request was made for four horse pairs to help with transport as 'there is a considerable number of sick men among the prisoners who are not capable of making the long marches'.[176]

Eyewitnesses who encountered prisoners in the occupied territories just after their liberation were shocked by the badly malnourished state of the men.[177] The war diary of the Director of Medical Services in the British 2nd Army noted on 6 December 1918 that there were 'various small groups of sick and wounded British prisoners' in neighbouring towns around Spa.[178] It was even rumoured among the prisoners that the British army had ordered that no further liberated captives should be transported through advancing troops in the west, as the sight of malnourished prisoners had so angered British troops on their way to occupy the left bank of the Rhine that the army feared retaliation against German civilians.[179]

A British army memo issued on 16 November, regarding the repatriation of British prisoners of war found in France and Belgium, stated that 'the general principle is that these men have suffered great privations during the time they have spent in the hands of the enemy and they should, therefore, receive the best treatment possible and nothing should be neglected in order to provide this'.[180] Ambulance trains were to be organised rapidly to repatriate these prisoners and army commanders were authorised to provide all medical care necessary.[181] The emphasis on medical care for the prisoners, at a time when British army medical

---

[176] BA-MA, PH5 / II / 452, f. 6, Arb.7.11.1918, Hauptmann an Armee Pferde Inspizienten.

[177] Italian prisoners in the occupied zone were also in poor condition at the Armistice. On 6 November the German commander of the *Italiener Kommando 1* telegrammed AOK 4 to ask for four pairs of horses with harnesses and waggons to carry 'food, furniture, cooking equipment and sick prisoners' during the retreat. BHStA IV, Kriegsgefangenen-Arbeiter Bataillon, Nr. 29, Kriegsgefangenen Inspektion Verkehr mit AOK 4, Italiener Kommando 1 to AOK 4, 6.11.1918.

[178] TNA, WO 95/287, Original War Diary, Director of Medical Services, 2nd Army, October 1918, 6.12.1918.

[179] Interview with Norman Cowan, Emden, *Prisoners of the Kaiser*, p. 168.

[180] SHAT, 16 N 2380, novembre 1918, 48. Copie des instructions données par les anglais pour le rapatriement des prisonniers. 1. Les instructions suivantes sont données comme additif au paragraphe 2 de la lettre no. 648 [QA 1] du 16 novembre relative à l'habillement, la nourriture, le logement et le transport des prisonniers de guerre relachés qui se présentent à nos lignes.

[181] *Ibid.*

resources were already stretched by a flu epidemic, highlights the prisoners' importance for the British authorities.

The French army received similar reports to the British. A telephone message from the French 10th Army to General Headquarters on 16 November stated:

The attention of the High Command is drawn to the lamentable state of physical misery of the French and British prisoners whom the Germans have driven into our lines. These unfortunates are in a terrifying state of thinness and of exhaustion. The Germans have left them without food. A great number of them have not even had the strength to reach our lines and lie in ditches along the roads in front of our front line.[182]

Prisoners flooded across the French lines in the wake of the Armistice. Between 11 November and 16 November 1918, 22,354 French military prisoners and 2,246 British prisoners of war, who had been working in the occupied territories, arrived in the French front line.[183] From Montmédy, a French Député, Mr Renaud, telephoned French Headquarters to say that the town had been flooded by civilians and prisoners of war who had been working for the Germans in Belgium.[184] The French postal censor cited a letter from a civilian written in November which described British prisoners liberated in the occupied territories:

They awake your pity. These are real skeletons and already many have died this night. You see the prisoners arriving, shivering in the street but like paupers with terrible expressions. I feel sick, I can assure you to see them returning in such a state and nothing has been prepared here to receive them which makes us indignant right now.[185]

The same censorship report cited other letters angry at the lack of preparation by the French army for receiving and feeding these men: 'It seems our great administration is not prepared for the peace,' one writer concluded.[186] Another noted that

here prisoners arrive every day who do not know what to do or where to go. The boche officers bring them as far as Pont-à-Mousson but from there on there is nothing organised. Yesterday we had over 1,500 in our town. We set up a

---

[182] *Ibid.*, novembre 1918, GQG, 2e Bureau, Message téléphonique réçu de la Xe Armée. 16.11.1918.

[183] *Ibid*, novembre 1918, État récapitulatif du personnel passé dans nos lignes depuis le 11 nov. 12 heures jusqu'au 16 nov. 12 heures.

[184] *Ibid.*, novembre 1918, Telephone Message from Mr Renaud, Député, EMA, 1er bureau to GQG 1er bureau, 18.11.1918.

[185] SHAT, 16 N 2380, Secret, GQG des Armées du nord et du nord-est, service spécial, contrôl postal aux armées, 24.11.1918.

[186] *Ibid.*

provisional kitchen in our *quartier* and I can tell you that all the inhabitants brought offerings either of money or in kind. Yesterday we gave soup, meat, coffee, tea, chocolate to over 400. You should see how these unfortunates throw themselves on the food.[187]

One civilian in Belgium recalled her first meeting with a British prisoner after the Armistice, who stated,

'We have just been released. We were working in the country and this morning the Huns told us we were free, so off we started. One or two died on the way but further along are a lot more of us with a sergeant.' Sure enough I found them all being taken into different Belgian houses and cared for. These miserable, dirty, vermin-covered ex-prisoners were seated in these beautiful spotless rooms as honoured guests. Many in the houses of people I knew.[188]

Her diary described many of the released prisoners of war as 'pitiable skeletons', several of them 'almost like idiots' due to lack of food. They had been reduced to eating leaves and 'had it not been for food surreptitiously given by Belgian women out of their own scanty store' a greater number would have died.[189] The head of the British Red Cross, Sir Arthur Stanley, echoed these sentiments, writing to *The Times* on 19 December 1918 to tell the British public of the kindness shown to British prisoners of war by Belgian civilians.[190] Annah Peck, an American Mobile Canteen volunteer, met British prisoners travelling on foot who were 'worn and thin and some looked very ill'.[191] They told her they had been released from camps in Belgium at the Armistice and had been aided by Belgian civilians. When William Tucker, a released prisoner, made his way to a Belgian family he knew, the daughter exclaimed at his loss of weight.[192] Tucker described how at the British Headquarters at Tournai:

After several days other prisoners began to crawl in, almost all of them in a condition far more wretched than mine ... Most of the prisoners told the same harrowing story. Soon after the news of the Armistice, the Germans simply scurried off in haste away from possible Allied reach. They abandoned their prisoners, exposed and foodless, to make the best of it. Although scores of prisoners never made it, and finished by the roadsides, I really do not quite know how the Germans could have managed otherwise.[193]

---

[187] *Ibid*. See also *The Times*, 20.11.18, p. 6.
[188] Anonymous diary kept during the occupation of Belgium given to the Anglican chaplain of Brussels, the Reverend Stirling Gahan, Diary of 'Gick', Private papers of the Reverend Stirling Gahan, c/o Gallagher/McCartney family, on loan to Mr Charles Benson, Early Printed Books, Trinity College Library, p. 96, p. 99.
[189] *Ibid*.   [190] Letter from Sir Arthur Stanley, *The Times*, 19.12.1918.
[191] Brown, *The Imperial War Museum Book of 1918*, p. 324.
[192] W. A. Tucker, *The Lousier War* (London, 1974), p. 119.   [193] *Ibid*., p. 121.

Some prisoners from the occupied zone were sent to Germany just prior to the Armistice. Several eyewitness accounts testify that many of these men were in a very poor physical condition. 500 weak and sick men were sent to Döberitz camp, where the International Red Cross found them in December.[194] At Crossen a. Oder camp, Captain John Findlay RAMC reported the arrival of two batches of labour company prisoners on 18 and 24 October 1918. In the first group, 'there were 110 Englishmen – six Englishmen and several other Allied prisoners had died on the way. Many of these 110 died in the next few days of sheer debility due to starvation and neglect. They were all gaunt and haggard and ravenous for food; most of them had oedematis legs.'[195] Of the second group of eighty-six Englishmen, six died on the journey into Germany; many of the rest died in the next few days at Crossen.[196] At Aachen, between September and October 1918, a British prisoner, Private Henry Webb, saw 'a party of about 90 British prisoners' who

had been working behind the lines. They were in a terrible state – simply bones, stinking and verminous and they had no boots and their clothes were in ribbons. We gave them some of our food as they were practically starving. They said they had started 260 strong but the rest had fallen out or died on the way. They had been marched till they could go no farther. I gathered that they had been working on ironworks and on the railways.[197]

Sapper George Waymark, who had continued working at the punishment centre Fort Flines in the occupied territories until late October, was transported to Worms with a large contingent of prisoners from the occupied zone.[198] At Worms camp on 10 November, he wrote in his diary:

I saw two men, or rather skeletons, because they were nothing more. They wore khaki clothes and looked ghastly. I asked them who they were and what regiment they belonged to, but they had lost all power of speech. I don't know whether they were British or not, but they must have been treated hellishly to be in that condition.[199]

The term 'skeleton' was used frequently by onlookers to convey how malnourished these former prisoners from the occupied territories were. One French reporter at Nancy described British prisoners as 'in the

---

[194] ACICR, 432/II/26, 2, Inspection by Siegfried Horneffer and Theodore Aubert, Döberitz camp, 20.12.1918.
[195] TNA, WO 161/97, MO 85, Captain John Findlay, RAMC.
[196] *Ibid.*   [197] TNA, WO 161/100, Interview no. 2724, Private Henry Webb, RAMC.
[198] Worms camp was where other-rank prisoners from Strafkompagnien in the *Etappen-* and *Operationsgebiet* were sent, just days before the Armistice. See HStA STUTT, M.77 / 1, Bd. 1029, Kriegsministerium Unterkunfts-Departement Nr. 2041.9.18 U3, Gerichtlich bestrafte Kriegsgefangene im Armeegebiet, 5.11.1918.
[199] Moynihan, ed., *Black Bread and Barbed Wire*, p. 155.

majority no longer men but shadows clothed in torn rags and so thin!'[200]
A similar account was provided in the post-war memoirs of French
prisoner Robert d'Harcourt, which outlined the horrific state of prisoners
returning to Hammelburg camp after labouring for the Germans at the
front: 'They were moving skeletons, walking phantoms. I will never forget
this Edgar Poe vision. These men – these soldiers – marched, but they
were dead; above each blue coat there was a death head: eyes sunken,
cheekbones standing out, the emaciated grin of skulls in the cemetery...
On their bodies there was no flesh... This was what Germany had done to
French soldiers.'[201]

Even doctors from the International Red Cross, arriving in Germany
after the Armistice to inspect prisoners of war being held in and around
Berlin, were shocked at the condition of some French prisoners who had
been transferred to Germany directly from working in occupied France
and Belgium. These men were suffering from an illness the Red Cross
doctors had never seen before, which they christened 'famine swellings'.[202] The Red Cross team encountered these men at the temporary
hospital on Alexandrinerstrasse in Berlin. Their report gives some indication of the death rates among prisoners who had been working in the
occupied French and Belgian territories:

We have seen several cases of an illness which was fortunately unknown to us, at
Alexanderinerstrasse [sic] Hospital in Berlin: famine oedema (*Hungersoedem*).
This illness we were told had appeared with vigour among certain classes of the
German civilian population and particularly in the prisons. It consists of a complaint characterised by general oedemas (swellings)... There is intense anemia,
extreme emaciation, with loss of 40% of the original weight. The syndrome is
found in men who were forced, for a prolonged period of time, to carry out heavy
labour, while receiving food well-known to have been insufficient. The mortality
rate is up to 50% of cases. Given time, rest and a restorative nutrition [carbohy-
drates, fats] can ensure the disappearance of the oedema swellings and a recovery.
The prisoners suffering from famine oedema that we have seen were employed for
5 to 7 months in the army zone near to the front on heavy labour constructing
railway lines. During this time they were deprived of any communication with
their families and were unable to receive parcels.[203]

The doctors described the state of the French prisoners as deplorable –
their clothes were 'ragged, worn, almost in tatters'.[204] Their underwear

---

[200] Gregor Dallas, *1918. War and Peace* (London, 2000), p 198.
[201] Robert d'Harcourt, *Souvenirs de captivité et d'évasions* (Paris, 1922), p. 194.
[202] ACICR, 432/II/26.B.C [A] Rapport sur la visite de quelques hopitaux et infirmeries des
prisonniers de guerre de l'Entente en allemagne pendant la période de l'armistice
[décembre–janvier 1918–1919] par les docteurs Frédéric Guyot, René Guillermin,
Albert Meyer, délegués du comité international.
[203] *Ibid.*   [204] *Ibid.*

was ripped and some had none. They were suffering from a 'nervous depression which was striking and plain to see'.[205]

Photographs in the Imperial War Museum of malnourished British prisoners of war, taken after the Armistice, illustrate the poor physical condition of some of the liberated men who had been working in the occupied territories.

Thus all the evidence indicates that prisoners working for the German army in the occupied territories endured severe mistreatment in 1918. However, one final crucial piece of information is missing: as with the reprisals of 1917, no figures have been found for British and French prisoner deaths in occupied France and Belgium in 1918. There are a number of reasons for this. First, the occupied zone was beyond the administrative reach of the Prussian *Kriegsministerium*, which recorded death statistics for prisoners in camps in Germany, where camps were under the internal German District Military Commanders. In contrast, the German army in the occupied territories had sole responsibility for recording the deaths of labour company prisoners. Second, the chaos of

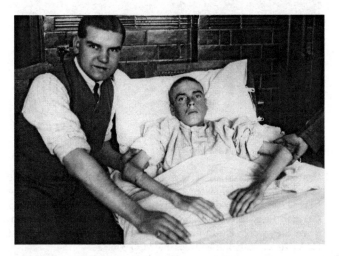

Figure 12. 'Freed from starvation and inhuman treatment, Private Thompson of the Durham Light Infantry, who was reduced to this helpless state through bad and insufficient food and overwork. He was employed in tree felling, which was used for railway sleepers behind the German lines. Photo shows: Private Thompson in bed with two medical orderlies holding up his emaciated arms, 25 October 1918.' IWM HU 65894.

[205] *Ibid.*

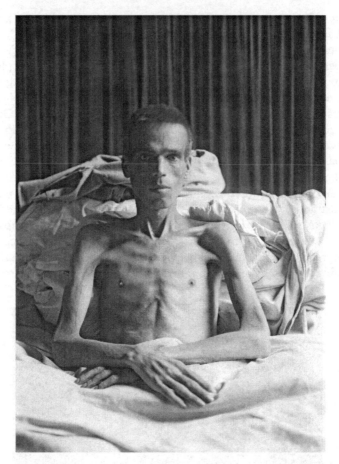

Figure 13. 'Circulation: private. Prisoners of war returned from Germany in an emaciated condition. All had been taken prisoners on May 27th 1918 and then out to work on railway buildings behind German lines until rendered too sick by privations to continue work, when they were sent to Langensalza until returned to England. Private N. A. Veitch, 5th Yorkshires.' IWM Q 31278.

the retreat, the Armistice and revolution severely impinged upon compiling statistical records of prisoner deaths in the occupied territories in the period August–November 1918. Finally, immediately after the war, there was no political will in Germany to try to ascertain statistics. In the initial post-war period, the statistics on prisoner deaths provided by the German government only counted deaths of prisoners in camps in Germany proper – those who died in labour companies in occupied territories were excluded. In fact, the post-war German government informed the Italian Parliamentary Commission for the Investigation of Human Rights Violations Committed by the Enemy of 'the absolute impossibility of indicating the number of dead in the labour companies'.[206] Whether the German army deliberately withheld this information after the war to avoid war crimes trials or paying reparations for the prisoners' treatment, or whether complete records simply had not been kept, is not clear. The destruction of the Prussian army archives at Potsdam in the Second World War means that any records which did exist were destroyed.

Moreover, as this chapter has shown, prisoners who died in the occupied territory were buried there – their graves mixed with those of men who had died from war wounds, making any post-war investigation highly difficult. It is, therefore, impossible to know how many prisoners died as a result of their experiences in labour companies. However, as this chapter has highlighted, despite the absence of any overall figures for the number of prisoners who died in labour companies in occupied France and Belgium, there was ample evidence available to the British and French governments that they had been mistreated.

An additional problem with statistics was that, once the Armistice was signed, prisoners in camps in Germany near to the French or Belgian border, and in particular those in camps located on the left bank of the Rhine, were released by their guards and set out on foot for the Allied lines. The left bank of the Rhine was to be demilitarised under the terms of the Armistice and occupied by the Allies and it appears that prison camp guards took immediate demilitarisation very literally. This complicated the situation, as some of these prisoners arrived at Allied lines in a dishevelled state due to their long journey and not due to forced labour in the occupied territories. One witness reported in a letter that

The French and English who were in Germany near here have started to arrive on foot and in what a state! It is pitiful; they are literally dying of hunger. What a sight! I think that the *boches* have really had it too good to be let shoot off like that – it would be a good thing for us to do in their country (*chez eux*) what they have done in ours.[207]

This led to German claims that the Allies' accusations about prisoner mistreatment in the occupied territories were due to confusion – that prisoners arriving in France in poor condition were themselves to blame, as they had travelled there from camps in Germany on foot instead

---

[206] Giovanna Procacci, *Soldati e prigionieri italiani*, p. 171.
[207] SHAT, 16 N 2380, Secret, GQG des armées du nord et du nord-est, service spécial, contrôl postal aux armées, 24.11.1918.

of waiting in Germany for organised repatriation. General von Winterfeld made precisely this argument to General Nudant, Marshal Foch's representative on the Armistice Commission.[208] Matthias Erzberger, the German representative on the Armistice Commission, reiterated this version of events, claiming at the signing of the prolongation of the Armistice on 13 December 1918 that the prisoners of war by liberating themselves 'had brought on a result that could possibly have been avoided'.[209]

In fact, although large numbers of prisoners arrived from camps in Germany on foot, most reached the Allied lines three to four weeks later than the prisoners from occupied France and Belgium. British prisoners made it clear in their interviews where they had arrived from – their account of their captivity was recorded in some detail. There is no doubt, given the huge amount of evidence, that the Allies liberated large numbers of prisoners of war who had been working for the Germans in the occupied territories and who were in very poor condition. One French report on liberated labour company prisoners noted on 18 November 1918 that

The prisoners in the army zone are no longer in camps as they have been on the march for some time now. We have given orders that they should be handed over to us in groups at certain concentration points but these orders are difficult to carry out. They have fled their *cantonnements* and are welcomed willingly by the local population and one cannot really take severe measures now to stop them.[210]

German guards could not remain with prisoners due to the hostile attitude of the population.[211] The report noted that 'the impossibility of a more organised handover of these prisoners, results from the fact that too little time was allowed the German armies to evacuate'.[212]

Thus prisoners from Germany and from the occupied zones were not mistaken for each other by the Allies. The Permanent Inter-Allied Armistice Commission distinguished between prisoners from camps in Germany and those from the occupied territories in its repatriation plan on 19 November 1918.[213] Regarding prisoners in the occupied territories it noted that a number were still in detachments marching with the

---

[208] 'A Day at the Armistice Commission', *The Times*, 13.12.1918.

[209] Dallas, *1918*, p. 210.

[210] SHAT, 10 N 218, CIPA, sous-commission des PG, Procès-verbal de la conférence du 18.11.1918, 3 heures après-midi au sujet des prisonniers de guerre, 18.11.1918.

[211] *Ibid.*   [212] *Ibid.*

[213] SHAT, 15 N 15, Rapatriement des Prisonniers de guerre, nov–déc 1919, Rapatriement, Inspection des PG Inévacuables, Commission Interalliée de l'Armistice, Général Nudant, 19.11.1918.

German armies in retreat.[214] The Prussian *Kriegsministerium* admitted in a private memo to Matthias Erzberger on 23 November 1918 that the Quartermaster-General in the occupied territories had handed over 'around 59,000 French, 56,000 British and 38,000 Italian prisoners of war' to the Allies.[215] French estimates cited 65,000 French prisoners in the occupied territories on 18 November.[216] These were the German prisoner of war labour company prisoners who had been working in the occupied territories and who had not been evacuated to Germany before the Armistice; these figures give some indication of the extent of the prisoner labour force in the occupied territories in October–November 1918. The Allies were also faced with 184,400 Russian prisoners liberated in the occupied territories, and in the Allied-occupied left bank of the Rhine, to whom they refused entry to France.[217]

Even the sceptic on the British Committee of Enquiry into Breaches of the Laws of War, set up in 1918, Sir Reginald Acland, was won over by the evidence. Unlike the rest of the committee members, by 1922 Acland believed that only two cases of real prisoner abuse had occurred during the war. The first was the eastern front reprisals of 1916. The second was the

ill-treatment of the prisoners, especially during 1918, on the western front. There, again, it is quite obvious, from documents which came into the possession of the committee that the generals – not all of them, thank goodness, but some generals – were directly responsible for the appalling ill-treatment which our men received there.[218]

Indeed, it was the sheer scale of the mistreatment that led to the British pursuing the matter at the Leipzig trials for war crimes in 1921. These trials were a compromise deal made with Germany, whereby it would try suspected war criminals in a German court – the Allies agreed to this after it became clear that Articles 228–30 of the Treaty of Versailles, which allowed for the extradition and trial of suspected German war criminals, were not realistically enforceable. At Leipzig, the German Reich State Prosecutor (*Oberreichsanwalt*) tried a selected number of cases which the

---

214 *Ibid.*
215 BA, R 904/77, f. 3, Kriegsministerium, Unterkunfts-Kriegsabteilung, Nr. 2068.11.18 U.K. to Staatsekretar Erzberger.
216 SHAT, 10 N 218, CIPA, sous-commission des PG, Procès-verbal de la conférence du 18.11.1918, 3 heures après-midi au sujet des prisonniers de guerre, 18.11.1918.
217 ACICR, 432/II/26, 2, Bd., c.44, Exposé de la situation des prisonniers de guerre russe telle qu'elle est comme par l'enquête préliminaire faite en décembre 1918 à Berlin par la délégation du Comité International de la Croix-Rouge.
218 Comments by Sir Reginald Acland on a speech by Lord Cave, *Transactions of the Grotius Society. Problems of Peace and War*, 8 (1922), p. 36.

Allies put forward; following disputes with Germany, the number of cases to be investigated was whittled down to forty-five.

The British put forward cases against seven individuals, to be examined at Leipzig, one of which related to the mistreatment of prisoners held in occupied France in 1918 and two others which related to prisoner beatings in camps in Germany. This chapter opened with a quotation from an account of the evidence presented at this trial taken from a British Parliamentary Paper. The British accused a German camp commandant, Emil Müller, of neglect and violent treatment of prisoners at a work camp at Flavy-le-Martel in 1918. According to one former British prisoner held there, between 5 April and 10 June 1918, seventy British prisoners died of dysentery at this camp where conditions were extremely unsanitary.[219] The British case against Müller at Leipzig was based upon the evidence of such former prisoners. Twenty-seven former British prisoners testified in London and, of these, nineteen made the journey to Leipzig to present eyewitness evidence.[220] Despite their testimony, Müller was acquitted of almost all the charges against him as 'the court ... came to the conclusion that Müller had done his best to improve the conditions of the camp and that his failure to render them satisfactory was due not to his fault but to the lack of assistance given to him by his superiors'.[221] Müller's defence also blamed the British blockade for the lack of available supplies. The only charge on which he was found guilty was that of hitting the prisoners, for which he received six months' nominal imprisonment – the time he had been in detention awaiting trial was deducted from the sentence.[222] J. H. Morgan, British military representative on the Inter-Allied Council, who attended the trial, considered it a farce, noting that Müller, 'a huge man ... habitually thrashed sick men with his stick, kicked them as they lay on the ground ... and amused himself by taking snapshots of them with his camera as they were using an exposed latrine'.[223] The Leipzig court accepted Müller's insistence that he took the photographs 'merely to commemorate his service as commandant'.[224]

It is unlikely that Emil Müller's defence in the Flavy-le-Martel case at Leipzig particularly reflected on what had brought about the catastrophic working conditions for British and French prisoners of war in the occupied territories in 1918. The defence team's task was to show that one man could not be blamed for what were, they argued, the faults of the entire

[219] TNA, WO 161/100, Interview no. 2816, Private John Dixon.
[220] For the statements taken in London see TNA, MEPO 3/1166, German War Criminals, 1921.
[221] Parliamentary Paper, Cd. 1450, *German War Trials. Report*, p. 11.
[222] Hankel, *Die Leipziger Prozesse*, p. 340.   [223] Morgan, *Assize of Arms*, p. 140.   [224] *Ibid.*

German army labour system. The defence claimed that Müller had written to his Divisional Headquarters asking for assistance and supplies but that none had been received owing 'to the great strain put upon German Headquarters Staff by the rapid advance in March 1918, to the fluid state of the front, the number of prisoners taken, the lack of supplies in Germany and the general inability of staff to meet the demands made upon it at this time'.[225] It was claimed that the camp had formerly been a British clearing station and was in poor condition when the Germans occupied it. Müller could not be held responsible 'due to the lack of assistance given to him by his superiors'.[226]

What is perhaps most revealing about this trial is that the appallingly harsh conditions which the prisoners endured at Flavy-le-Martel camp were not disputed by the German court in 1921. Significantly, it was accepted without contention by both the British and the Germans involved in the trial that the camp was overcrowded and unhealthy, leading to many prisoner deaths. Even among the German nationalist circles attempting to defend the German army record at Leipzig, the disastrous health conditions of prisoner work camps in the occupied territories in 1918 were accepted as fact. The evidence was too overwhelming to be challenged. Indeed, the German military evidence on the camp conditions supported the British accusation that they were unsanitary and the camp inadequate. That the work camp was in a dreadful state and prisoners were subjected to violence was not at issue during the trial – what was at issue was *who* was responsible.

This chapter has sought to answer this question, arguing that, as discipline broke down in the German army in 1918, violence against prisoners increased as part of an army culture that at both command levels and lower levels had come to view prisoners *solely* in terms of their labour value to the German war effort. Work outputs took precedence over the prisoners' health, safety and general well-being which were even considered expendable on occasion, on the grounds of military necessity. This was tacitly acknowledged by the OHL's failure to implement protective measures to ensure its malnourished labourers were not overworked, the lack of adequate medical inspections, failure to enforce time off for sick prisoners, exposure to shellfire and failure to prevent beatings by guards. Thus the creation of a forced labour system within the German army dramatically fuelled violence against captives – the dynamic of forced labour in itself was the ultimate key factor that impelled escalation in the German case. Labour demands

---

[225] Parliamentary Paper Cd. 1450, *German War Trials. Report*, p. 11.   [226] *Ibid.*

also took precedence over international law: in 1918, the German army was not only knowingly in breach of the pre-war international law on prisoners, it was also breaching the new treaties on prisoner treatment signed by Germany at Berne and The Hague during 1917 and 1918.[227]

This escalation dynamic, driven by the prioritising of labour output, thus also led to a highly significant dilution of the pre-war distinction in international law and military culture between the prisoner of war and the combatant soldier. Pre-war international law had defined the prisoner of war as a non-combatant figure; in 1918, this distinction began to give way in the German army, as the gap between the forms of violence practised against the enemy on the battlefield and those permissible against prisoner workers was reduced, although it never disappeared – it remained the case that German front soldiers sought to *kill* the enemy on the battlefield, whereas it is important to emphasise that there was never a deliberate policy of shooting labour company prisoners of war. Taboos breached in 1916 and 1917 laid the basis for this process in 1918.

Concomitantly, the distinction between the demands made of the enemy prisoner and those made of the German soldier was disappearing. The ideal of sacrifice had become so all-encompassing and totalised by 1918 that even prisoners of war, who were not part of the nation-in-arms, were to sacrifice their health in the battle zone for Germany. In the cultural context of a total war, extreme battlefield violence became permitted and legitimised as sacrifice – this, in turn, legitimised new forms of violence, including violence against prisoners of war in the German army. Within the logic of this coding, by mid-1918, the calls for total sacrifice by the German army clearly risked endorsing 'total' violence against captives. But were these processes unique to the German army? The next chapter will explore how forced labour evolved in the British and French cases.

---

[227] Article 25 of the 15 March 1918 Berne Accords, signed by France and Germany, stipulated that prisoners should not be forced to work within thirty kilometres of the firing line. BA-MA, PH5 / II / 453, Verfügungen über Kriegsgefangenenangelegenheiten, Bd. 2, f. 92, Abschrift from Generalquartiermeister to all AOKs. In June 1917 and July 1918, Germany signed similar agreements on prisoner treatment with Britain at The Hague. The Berne and Hague agreements related mainly to prisoner exchanges but they also outlined standards for disciplining prisoners and set out rules regarding prisoners' working and living conditions. Signed by representatives of the *Kriegsministerium*, these agreements were publicised within the German army but their stipulations remained largely unenforced in the occupied territories, where German prisoner treatment increasingly deteriorated.

Introduction

As the previous chapter has shown, violence against prisoners in labour
companies was a very significant phenomenon in the German army in
1918. However, if prisoner treatment deteriorated badly in the German
army, what of the French and the British cases? Did forced labour systems
inevitably escalate violent practices against prisoner workers – were
the processes revealed in the previous chapter universal? To investigate
this further, this chapter will explore, as far as sources permit, the ways in
which forced labour developed in Britain and France in 1918. In the British
case, the available sources are limited, which necessitates a focus upon
how prisoner labour was monitored both in the UK and in prisoner of
war labour companies in France. In the French case, the treatment of
German prisoner workers in French prisoner of war labour companies
will be explored. The French case thus facilitates an assessment of whether
it was inevitable, given the totalised battlefield environment where prisoner
labour companies worked, that, by 1918, military violence would spread
into the prisoner labour company system and that prisoner treatment would
deteriorate. Taken together, the two case studies also allow for an examination of how different contextual factors, such as better military resources
and particular cultural attitudes towards prisoners within military and civil
institutions, influenced divergent outcomes to the German case. This
chapter also illustrates the long-term legacy of the intervention of the
British and French governments in 1917 to enforce the thirty-kilometre
rule – this established a strict pattern of government control over prisoner
treatment, which lasted into 1918, contrasting with the German situation,
where the army had far more autonomy in its treatment of prisoner labour.

There are two key overriding differences between the British and
French cases and the German situation that must be emphasised at the
outset. First, Germany, in spring 1918, was overwhelmed by mass captures on a scale that surpassed anything seen in the British and French
armies that year. The German army in the first weeks of the Ludendorff

Offensive captured more prisoners in a shorter space of time than the British or French armies at any point during the war on the western front.[1] Some 75,000 British troops were taken prisoner in the sixteen days between 21 March and 5 April 1918, along with 15,000 prisoners of other Allied nationalities.[2] At no stage in 1918 did either the British or the French army capture as many prisoners in as short a period. British captures in spring 1918 were incredibly low – fewer than a hundred other-rank Germans were captured per week in January and February 1918.[3] Between March and July, British captures never exceeded 2,000 in any one week; between 6 August and 12 August 1918, the number of Germans taken prisoner by the British suddenly jumped from the low hundreds to 19,533.[4] During the two peak periods of mass German surrenders to the British, 20 August to 2 September 1918 and between 17 September and 30 September 1918, the British took 42,753 and 41,062 German prisoners respectively.[5] On both occasions, in fourteen days the British captured fewer than half the 90,000 figure the German army captured in the 21 March–5 April phase. In sum, the British never had to process as many prisoners in as short a period as the German army in spring 1918.

Nor did the French army in 1918 ever take as many prisoners in as short a time as the German army in those first sixteen days of the spring offensive. As in the British case, the French captured very low numbers of Germans in early 1918 – until June, the whole French army never captured more than 2,600 German prisoners a month.[6] In all of January they only captured 296.[7] The number of German prisoners taken by the French suddenly soared in the last fifteen days of July 1918, when 18,021 prisoners were taken.[8] This jump in captures occurred two weeks earlier than the surge experienced by the British army in August 1918, matching the earlier start of the French counterattack. The French army took its highest *monthly* tally of prisoners in 1918 in October, when 36,396 Germans were captured.[9] A further 33,505 German prisoners were taken in the first fifteen days of November 1918.[10] However, this still represents only 69,901 prisoners taken over a six-week period. Therefore, there is some truth in the German army argument that it

---

[1] The Eastern and Italian fronts of course offer a different perspective – the Austro-Hungarian and German victory at Caporetto being one example where the tally of prisoners was much higher.

[2] Kitchen, 'Michael-Offensive', p. 714.

[3] War Office, *Statistics of the Military Effort*, German Prisoners taken by the British Army in France, p. 632.

[4] *Ibid.*   [5] *Ibid.*

[6] These figures are based on an analysis of the États numériques in SHAT, 16 N 525, GQG Bureau de Personnel – Pertes, Dossier 2, Prisonniers de guerre, états numériques, 1917 novembre–1919, février.

[7] *Ibid.*   [8] *Ibid.*   [9] *Ibid.*   [10] *Ibid.*

was initially overwhelmed by prisoners in spring 1918 – although this does not account for the failure to develop administrative systems to deliver parcels to prisoner labour companies in 1918 or the failure to prepare for such high capture rates, repeating the basic error made in 1914 in not adequately planning for prisoners. Moreover, despite all the food supply difficulties, for most of 1918 the German army was able to feed its own fighting soldiers relatively well.[11] It also captured considerable stores of Allied foodstuffs during the spring offensive.[12] The supply of rations and letters to front-line troops, while difficult, never totally broke down. Yet the delivery of parcels to prisoners did.

The second key point that must be emphasised regarding prisoner treatment is that in the British and French armies there was a far more diverse spectrum of colonial, alien civilian internee and immigrant labour sources available. The Allied armies were never as reliant as Germany upon prisoner labour to win the war. In the British army, German prisoner labourers even enjoyed privileged status over colonial workers; Chinese labourers working for the British were sometimes employed up to ten kilometres from the front line.[13] This highlights one further important aspect of the controversy regarding German treatment of prisoners in the occupied territories. It was not only how Germany treated its prisoners that mattered, but rather how this treatment differed from Allied cultural expectations and the Allies' own prisoner treatment. The British and French claimed in 1918 that they treated their prisoners better than the Germans – this was a major factor in their moral condemnation of Germany. But was this claim true? This chapter will now assess the British and French treatment of forced prisoner labour in 1918 in turn.

The 1918 experience of German prisoners of war held by Britain

I am strongly of the opinion that it is economically unsound to ask a man to do strenuous work unless you feed him.[14]

---

[11] Wilhelm Deist, 'Verdeckter Militärstreik im Kriegsjahr 1918?', in Wette, ed., *Der Krieg des kleinen Mannes*, p. 163, footnote 28. The official calorie ration per day was 2,500 for German front soldiers.

[12] Brown, *The Imperial War Museum Book of 1918*, p. 72.

[13] TNA, WO 95/282, Second Army, Deputy Adjutant and Quartermaster General, Jan. 1917–19 Dec. 1917, War Diary November 1917, Proceedings of conference at AHQ at 3 p.m. on 30.11.1917. On Chinese labourers see Xu Guoqi, 'Chinese Laborers in France during the Great War', unpublished paper presented at the Fourth Conference of the International Society for First World War Studies, Washington, 18–20 October 2007, p. 8.

[14] TNA, NATS 1/1331, Interview with Rt. Hon. Ian Macpherson, The Prisoner of War Employment Committee, 22.10.1918.

In 1918, the treatment of British prisoners in Germany was not the only subject of a British government committee investigation. While the Government Committee on the Treatment by the Enemy of British Prisoners of War was carrying out interviews and compiling reports on British prisoners in German captivity, a second committee, appointed by the government, was entrusted with a full-scale examination of how German prisoners were being employed by Britain. This Prisoner of War Employment Committee had a largely economic brief; it was to examine how the labour output of German prisoners held by Britain might be increased. Its existence illustrates the level of civilian government control over the military use of forced prisoner labour in the British case. At first, the committee was only involved in assessing prisoner of war labour in the United Kingdom but, on 19 July 1918, its remit was extended to look at British-run prisoner of war labour companies in France as 'no proper comparison' had been made of how prisoners were employed inside and outside the UK.[15] Using the material gathered by this committee, it is possible to investigate how labour demands influenced prisoner treatment in the British case in 1918, prior to the Armistice, looking first at prisoner labour within the UK and second at the prisoner of war labour company system working for the British army in France, for which, unfortunately, few other sources exist.

The evidence collected by the Prisoner of War Employment Committee reveals several important points. First, the majority of German prisoners taken by Britain were kept in France working in BEF labour companies. There were very few German prisoners actually employed on manual labour tasks in Britain in 1918: on 12 May 1918 there were only 43,140 German prisoners allocated to different economic sectors and of these only 30,480 had actually commenced work.[16] The largest number of prisoners – 9,300 – were working in agriculture. 8,850 were working in building, 3,360 in quarries, 3,250 on timber work and 2,350 on Royal Engineering work.[17] The remainder were manufacturing cement or working on road building. Unlike the German and the French cases, none of these prisoners was engaged in directly manufacturing munitions. Moreover, in contrast to France and Germany, prisoners held in the UK in 1918 were not housed in improvised billets by their employer but were always sent to work from a central established camp, even where prisoners were working on farms,

[15] TNA, NATS 1/568, 40A, Prisoner of War Employment Committee, Prisoner Labour Enquiry, Interim Report, 19.7.1918.
[16] TNA, NATS 1/282, Table showing the distribution of prisoners of war in Great Britain by industry as at 12.5.1918.
[17] Ibid.

a system which ensured adequate prisoner accommodation, although by 1919 this system had changed.[18] Another key factor was that, unlike Germany, the British did not employ German prisoners in mining because of the British trade unions who opposed prisoner labour, fearing it would undercut British miners' wages.[19] Austen Chamberlain pointed out to Lloyd George: 'there is of course no ground in international law for not so employing prisoners and it is only the Trade Union feeling which prevents us from doing it'.[20] In September 1918, Chamberlain even suggested that a 'judicious supply to the press of information about the brutal treatment of British miner prisoners of war in the German mines' might 'start among our Scottish, Welsh or North-country miners a demand for reprisals which might enable us to set apart certain mines to be worked by German prisoners under British foremen'.[21] However, nothing came of the suggestion and German prisoners never worked in UK mines, and were thus spared a dangerous and difficult working environment.[22]

Second, in the UK guards had no role in influencing how fast or effectively prisoners were working. Their sole duty was to prevent any escapes. This contrasted with the pressure upon German guards in the occupied territories to beat prisoners to make them work more. In fact, accounts of German prisoners being beaten in Britain are rare. Only civilian supervisors were responsible for controlling prisoners' output. Indeed, in large camps, guards assigned to prisoner workers were not under the control of the prison camp commandant but were commanded by an entirely different military structure – GHQ home forces.[23] The camp commandant could give the guard direct orders but he could not punish them himself.[24] This led to a particularly relaxed approach towards prisoners from military guards, which the Prisoner of War Employment Committee criticised, stating that guards 'appear in general to take the view that they have nothing to do with the work at all and that so long as they take the prisoners out and bring them back at the proper times they have done all that is required of them'.[25] One farmer, John Steel, who employed prisoners on his farm, stated the guards were never

---

[18] TNA FO 383/506. [19] HLRO, LG F/7/2/16. [20] *Ibid.*
[21] *Ibid.* Underlining in original.
[22] On the dangers of British mines, see Gregory, *The Last Great War*, pp. 278–9.
[23] TNA, NATS 1/1331, Interview with Brigadier General T.E. O'Leary, Second in command to Lieutenant-General Sir Herbert Belfield, Prisoner of War Department at WO, 26.6.1918.
[24] *Ibid.*
[25] TNA, NATS 1/568, 40A, Prisoner of War Employment Committee, Prisoner Labour Enquiry, Interim Report, 19.7.1918.

with the Germans. They are either at the back of the hedge or under a tree in the summer, or somewhere tucked up in the winter. They simply leave the prisoners. They say they have really nothing to do with them, that they bring them to the farm and it is for the farmer to see that they work.[26]

In some cases prisoners were privileged over civilian labourers. At Partington Steel and Iron Company, for example, German prisoners worked a 6 ¾-hour day and their output was 'about one-fifth of the amount done by British labour today'.[27] The company reported persistent slacking and that the 'idleness in which the prisoners are allowed to indulge has a very bad effect on all other classes of labour'.[28] This system where guards were not responsible for prisoners' work rates was considered a waste of manpower by the committee. The British also assigned a much higher number of guards to working prisoners than the French or Germans, which restricted how prisoners could be employed and used up British troops.

Significantly, the cultural attitude to violence towards prisoners was very different among the British military in comparison with its German counterpart. When Colonel Mair, a member of the Prisoner of War Employment Committee, suggested to Colonel Bulkeley, Commandant of Dorchester camp, that repatriated British prisoners of war be used to guard German prisoners, as they might be more enthusiastic about making them work, the conversational exchange was revealing:

> COLONEL MAIR [PRISONER OF WAR EMPLOYMENT COMMITTEE]: It has been suggested that returned prisoners of war from Germany should form the guard. It would be a very good thing if we could give these men something who came back from Germany. They would be much more inclined if they had a bad time in Germany to make the prisoners work?
>
> COLONEL BULKELEY [COMMANDANT, DORCHESTER CAMP]: You would have to be very careful that they did not strike them or something of that sort.[29]

The idea was dropped by the committee.

Third, the Prisoner of War Employment Committee emphasised reward over coercion in order to encourage German prisoners to work. The provision of extra food or pay was seen as the best way to improve output. This was based on information the committee received in consultation. One memo pointed out that

---

[26] TNA, NATS 1/1331, Interview with Mr John Steel, Farmer of Rochford, 7.6.1918.
[27] *Ibid.*, Memo on Prisoner of War Labour Employed by the Ministry of Munitions, Frank Baines, 12.6.1918.
[28] *Ibid.*   [29] *Ibid.*, Interview with Colonel Bulkeley, 21.6.1918.

Punishment is often found to react detrimentally on the work, making the labour sullen and unwilling. Further if certain men are punished very severely on account of withholding their labour, it has been found that throughout the whole camp a consistent witholding of labour is in operation, and as it is impossible to punish the whole camp by detention etc. or loss of rations, the result of such discipline is found to be ineffective.[30]

Pay bonuses, letting prisoners off work early for increased output, or increased food as rewards were used in place of coercion.

The way the British handled a food shortage in relation to German prisoners also differed from the German case. In 1918, many British officials responsible for the employment of German prisoners in the UK called for increased prisoner rations as the only way to increase the amount of manual work a prisoner labourer could do; here the committee listened to both military and civilian employer recommendations, illustrating the broad consultative approach adopted in managing prisoner labour. The consensus was that, unless fed more, prisoners could not be expected to work more. The committee reported that

It has been strongly impressed upon us by the testimony of numerous witnesses representing many branches of labour that a heavy day's work cannot be obtained from the prisoners without some supplement to their present rations. The evidence on this point is overwhelming and all but unanimous ... Money is of little value to the prisoners if they cannot spend it on anything they covet, and of all their desires it seems certain that extra food is uppermost in their minds.[31]

In June 1918, the Prisoner of War Employment Committee recommended providing prisoners with access to extra food.[32] The committee's interim report also recommended making extra food available for sale in prison camp canteens to encourage prisoners to work more. However, in its October 1918 findings, the committee stopped short of recommending extra rations for prisoners, stating, 'the opinion has been expressed in some camps that more work would be done by the prisoners if their ration were increased. There seems to be no direct evidence that the output of the prisoners is curtailed by want of food, and the records of sickness do not provide any justification for the view that the prisoners are underfed.'[33]

[30] *Ibid.*, Memo on Prisoner of War Labour Employed by the Ministry of Munitions, Frank Baines, 12.6.1918.
[31] TNA, NATS 1/568, 40 A, Prisoner of War Employment Committee, Prisoner Labour Enquiry, Interim Report, 40A, 19.7.1918.
[32] TNA, NATS, 1/1331, Prisoner of War Employment Committee, Prisoner Labour Enquiry, draft letter to WO, June 1918.
[33] TNA, NATS 1/569, 34 A, Organisation of Prisoners of War Labour, Memorandum Covering General Conclusions derived from Investigations of Prisoners of War Camps. Twenty-four camps with an aggregate of 14,998 prisoners were assessed by the committee, 8.10.1918.

However, Lieutenant-General Sir Herbert Belfield, head of the Department of Prisoners of War at the War Office, admitted, after the war, that the failure to increase rations to German prisoners had reduced output:

With increasing scarcity of supplies the rations were gradually changed in quality and reduced in amount, until in 1918 the non-worker got little more than a subsistence ration, and the worker no more than was absolutely necessary. It would, indeed, have paid us to feed our working prisoners better, for the general consensus of opinion among employers was that a hard day's work could not be expected from them, but we, at any rate in the United Kingdom, could not increase the ration.[34]

Two important points emerge here. First, Britain, in 1918, was trying to husband its food resources and had cut its allocation to prisoners of war. However, in contrast to the German case, the British accepted that, without an increase in food rations, an increase in prisoner labour output was impossible and would not be demanded of the prisoners. Note Belfield's reference to the attitude among employers. Nowhere was it considered that increased labour output could be forced from prisoners regardless of food intake. Indeed, Colonel Bulkeley, Commandant of Dorchester Camp, even argued for the prisoners' working day to be reduced to six hours only, stating: 'I am a very healthy man but I couldn't do that work on that food.'[35] Thus there was a deterioration in prisoner nutrition in the British case in 1918 but the dynamic of forced labour did not escalate into prisoner starvation.

Second, by late 1918, British public opposition to extra rations for German prisoners was a significant factor in the deterioration in prisoner treatment. Whereas rations for German prisoners working for the BEF in France were increased in 1918 on the recommendations of the committee, it was felt that the same increase could not be granted to German prisoners in the UK because the civilian population, strictly rationed in its own food consumption, would resent it. This public attitude was influenced by information about the treatment of British prisoners by Germany. Sir Ian Macpherson, Undersecretary of State for War, interviewed by the committee in October 1918, argued for prisoner rations in the UK to be increased, stating: 'it is economically unsound to ask a man to do strenuous work unless you feed him'.[36] However, Macpherson warned,

We have all these reports from Germany – most of them unfortunately confirmed – of the wicked treatment which our own men receive, and if it were known in

---

[34] Belfield, 'The Treatment of Prisoners of War', p. 139.
[35] TNA, NATS 1/1331, Interview with Col. Bulkeley, 21.6.1918.
[36] *Ibid.*, Interview with Ian Macpherson, The Prisoner of War Employment Committee, 22.10.1918.

public – however good and sound our economic arguments may be – that we did to a great extent reinforce the constitution of the prisoner by food, I am sure there would be a tremendous outcry. I am sure I am expressing the opinion of the vast majority of the people of this country when I say that if it were known that we gave to German prisoners in this country a proportion of food practically the same – in any case comparable with the ration of our own civil population, while our own prisoners are being overworked and starved I think it would be difficult to defend.[37]

The same problem with public opinion was referred to by Colonel Bulkeley, Commandant of Dorchester Prisoner of War camp, who stated that 'everybody I meet now go [sic] for me about the way the Germans are fed'.[38] French intelligence reported in June 1918 that public opinion in Britain was 'preoccupied' with the fate of British prisoners.[39] The civilian role in Britain was thus not always a positive one in determining prisoner treatment.

In sum, in 1918 the regime of German prisoners working in the United Kingdom involved regulated working hours and a considerable amount of civilian supervision with relatively little military input into how hard prisoners worked. Prisoners also had the opportunity to spend their earnings in camp canteens. However, there had been a reduction in prisoner rations from previous years, which had an adverse effect on prisoner morale. Unlike the German case, this reduction in rations did not significantly impact on prisoner health for three reasons. First, prisoners retained access to canteens, stocked with food, and food parcels. Second, the civilian government was heavily involved in investigating, regulating and advising on changes to prisoner working conditions as illustrated by the role of the Prisoner of War Employment Committee, which kept a close watch on how the reduced rations were influencing prisoner health and called for increased amounts of food to be sold to prisoners through the canteen system. Third, cultural attitudes differed. The reduced rations appear to have been taken into account by employers and civilian supervisors, who set the amount of work to be demanded from the prisoners accordingly. Significantly, employers consulted by the Prisoner of War Employment Committee were largely sympathetic to their prisoner workers.[40] Farmers, in particular, frequently gave their prisoner labourers extra food.

German prisoners working for the British army in prisoner of war labour companies in France experienced a different regime to those

---

[37] *Ibid.*   [38] *Ibid.*, Prisoner of War Employment Committee Meeting, 21.6.1918.

[39] SHAT, 7 N 679, EMA, 2ème bureau, avril 1917–août 1919, Dossier 3, 1.5.1918–15.6.1918, section des renseignements généraux, no. 29, 15.6.1918.

[40] See TNA, NATS 1/1331, Interviews with Major-General Lord Lovat, Sir Frank Baines, Ian Macpherson, Mr John Steel, farmer of Rochford, Mr W. P. Theakston of Huntingdon.

held in the UK. Assessing their experience in 1918 is very difficult due to a shortage of sources, particularly German prisoner testimony – only British sources have emerged for 1918, which is obviously problematic. In October 1918, there were 303 British prisoner of war labour companies in France, comprising some 160,065 German prisoners.[41] By November, German prisoners accounted for 44 per cent of the BEF labour force.[42] In France, German prisoners working in British army prisoner of war labour companies saw their ration increased in 1918, above that received by prisoners in the UK. Sir Frank Baines, Chief Architect at the Office of Works who employed prisoners on projects in Britain and France, told the Prisoner of War Employment Committee:

He did not meet in France signs of real malnutrition or underfeeding. Generally prisoners of war were if anything in a better condition than prisoners in this country; that purely applied to their physical condition. Civilians going over to France are astounded at the quantity of food under military control and that, he thought, probably reacted [sic] in giving prisoners more in France than in England.[43]

However, prisoners in France carried out harder manual work. The Controller of Labour in France, Colonel Wace, informed the Prisoner of War Employment Committee in August 1918 that he considered more work could be got out of German prisoners. He 'was not satisfied unless the task' made the prisoner 'dog tired at the end of the day'.[44] He added 'officers tried to get out [of] the bosche [sic] as nearly as possible the amount of work which the British navvy would do but that was a high standard'.[45] However, he also acknowledged that 'the bosche [sic] works extraordinarily well. There was very little patriotic slacking.'[46] Major Scott-Tucker, in charge of labour discipline, concurred with Wace but added that one German NCO who did slack had recently been court-martialled and received fifty-six days' imprisonment as punishment.[47] Wace pointed out that prisoners were let off work early as a reward if they had finished the task assigned. Wages were also an incentive to work. Prisoners were allowed to buy games, music, musical instruments and even gramophones using any profits made in the camp canteen.[48] Some even bought toys to relieve the monotony of camp life. They could also buy specially censored British newspapers.[49]

[41] Scott, 'Captive Labour', p. 328.   [42] Ibid., p. 319.
[43] TNA, NATS 1/1331, Interview with Sir Frank Baines.
[44] Ibid., Prisoner of War Employment Committee Meeting with Colonel Wace, Controller of Labour in France and Major Scott-Tucker, responsible for labour discipline 12.8.1918.
[45] Ibid.   [46] Ibid.   [47] Ibid.   [48] Scott, 'Captive Labour', p. 328.
[49] Ibid; NATS 1/1331, Interview with Lieut. MacDougall.

The British officers working with prisoners in France were trained for the task. Among the courses British subalterns attended was one on the handling of labour.[50] However, the British privates had little interest in the prisoners' work rate. As in Britain, guards rarely considered that it was their task to make the prisoners work faster or more efficiently. In an interview on 30 July, Sir Frank Baines complained that 'he had never met a guard who was of the opinion that it was his duty to see that the men were keeping to their work'.[51] Baines stated that it was 'lamentable' that the War Office, despite issuing instructions that guards were to make prisoners work efficiently, had not convinced the commandants and the guards in France of this:

> BAINES: what would the W.O. say, that the privates of the guard should be able to insist that these men should go on with their work?
>
> COLONEL MAIR [PRISONER OF WAR EMPLOYMENT COMMITTEE]: I do not think we should have any objection to that provided there was no ill-treatment.
>
> BAINES: the French private himself does it, and does it with the point of the bayonet.[52]

Baines noted with regard to French prisoner labour companies that 'the French were a little bit more drastic and bitter in the treatment of the prisoners'.[53] Clearly British guards enforced a milder discipline at work than that which existed for prisoners working for the French or the German army. Further attempts were made to encourage British guards to make prisoners work efficiently. British instructions on prisoner treatment from 4 September 1918, captured by the Germans, outlined that prisoner guards were 'responsible for maintaining discipline and promoting hard work'.[54] Prisoners who did not work were to have their numbers noted and their names were to be reported back at camp. Freed of the constraints of an occupation situation and dealing with an Allied local population, British guards could afford to be less severe with French or Belgian civilians who tried to communicate with prisoners on matters unrelated to work than their German counterparts – civilians were to be informed that such communication was prohibited and to have their

---

[50] TNA, NATS 1/1331, The Prisoner of War Employment Committee interview with Major-General Lord Lovat, 22.8.1918.

[51] *Ibid.*, Prisoner of War Employment Committee, Interview with Sir Frank Baines, Office of Works, Chief Architect and civilian employer of prisoner of war labour in France and Great Britain, 30.7.1918.   [52] *Ibid.*

[53] *Ibid.*

[54] BA-MA, PH5 / II / 452, f. 140, Übersetzung eines erbeuteten engl. Befehls der 'Linken' 13. Kriegsgefangenen-Halbkompagnie, Besondere Anordnungen für Unteroffiziere und Mannschaften, die zur Bewachung von Kriegsgefangenen kommandiert sind, 4.9.1918.

names taken if they persisted in attempting it. The instructions stated that 'a manly discipline and good work are not obtained by shouting. The best results come if the orders are passed on by the German underofficers and not given to the prisoners directly.'[55] In fact, much of the control of prisoners during labour was carried out by German NCOs who were paid a bonus for this work. This system was found to be highly effective. NCOs largely accepted this role, although there were cases where they were punished with prison terms for telling prisoners to 'go slow'.[56]

In some cases, British guards also fraternised with the prisoners. When the Prisoner of War Employment Committee asked Lord Lovat, Director of Forestry who was responsible for the provision of timber for the troops in France, whether the guards 'sometimes pal up too much with the prisoners'. he admitted that this had been a problem:

I think you always make a pet of something you are looking after every day – just as you would make a pet of a kangaroo. But I want to insist that there is a considerable improvement since March 30.[57]

Convincing guards that they were responsible for making prisoners work effectively was a continual problem in the British prisoner labour company system.

There were three further reasons why German prisoners in British labour companies were largely better treated than their British counterparts in the occupied territories. First, the British kept the thirty-kilometre rule. Prisoner of war labour companies were not to work within thirty kilometres of the front line. This rule could be enforced because the British army had access to other labour sources who could be used nearer to the front. For example, the 2nd Army used British and 'coloured' labour companies wherever it wished, and could use Chinese and alien internee civilian labour companies at up to sixteen kilometres' distance from the front line.[58]

Second, the British had more resources to supply their prisoner of war companies. The logistics of feeding and clothing prisoner of war labour companies were much better in the British army, which, in 1918, did not suffer from the same resource problems hampering the Germans. In a post-war memoir, W. A. Tucker, comparing his treatment by the Germans as a prisoner in occupied France with that of German prisoners taken by Britain, stated:

---

[55] *Ibid.*   [56] TNA, NATS 1/1331, Interview with Major-General Lord Lovat, 22.8.1918.
[57] *Ibid.*
[58] TNA, WO 95/282, Second army HQ, Deputy Adjutant and Quartermaster General, Jan. 1917 to 19 Dec. 1917, Second Army H.Q., 'A' and 'Q' branch, War diary with appendices, Nov. 1917, App. F, Proceedings of conference at AHQ at 3 p.m. on 30.11.1917, Subject: labour.

The Germans did not play the game. I am trying to be fair and not to exaggerate my accounts of their behaviour ... The British at any rate did behave in a proper way to all their prisoners. I had some experience which convinced me that there was little doubt about that. On many occasions my Cyclist Company was called upon to act as sentries over sudden concentrations of German prisoners. The food we gave them was equal in quantity and quality with what was given to British soldiers and the Germans were the first to admit the excellence of these rations compared with what they had been living on before capture. Moreover, the British saw to it that their prisoners were accommodated and clothed in a proper way at the earliest opportunity. A sense of decency demanded that this should be, and it required no authority to dictate it. It was a matter of playing the game.[59]

Third, the system for managing labour in the British army was highly centralised and regulated. Labour companies made up of British soldiers were administered by the same command as those made up of Chinese workers, 'native' colonial workers, alien civilian internees and German prisoners of war. Prisoner of war labour units were thus not part of a separate system but subject to the same labour instructions and control checks as ordinary British infantry labour units. Prisoners carried out the same work as other labour units, except that they were not used inside the thirty-kilometre zone.[60] In the 2nd Army:

In all labour units and prisoner of war companies the working hours per day will be at least 8 exclusive of the time occupied for meals and for going to and from the place of work. If the distance from the place of parade to the work is more than 1½ miles the time taken to march the excess distance may be deducted from the hours of work.

15% of the men will normally be excused from work daily. This will enable each man to have one day's rest in seven. It must be understood that this day off may not be possible when urgent work has to be done.[61]

Prisoner labourers were seen as part of a large labour pool and due to the thirty-kilometre rule were actually privileged over the other types of labour, including British infantry labour units, which had to work closer to the front. Disciplinary charges also reveal that prisoners were not excessively harshly punished in comparison with British soldiers. In the whole conflict, twenty-two military and civilian prisoners of war held by Britain were sentenced to death by military courts.[62] The most common

---

[59] Tucker, *The Lousier War*, pp. 56–7.

[60] IWM, Misc. 214, Item 3104, Report on the administration of labour in XVII Corps, Feb. 1917–Feb. 1918.

[61] TNA, WO 95/282, 2nd Army HQ, Deputy Adjutant and Quartermaster General, Jan. 1917 to 19 Dec. 1917, 2nd Army HQ, 'A' and 'Q' branch, War diary with appendices, Nov. 1917, App. F, Proceedings of conference at AHQ at 3 p.m. on 30.11.1917, Subject: labour.

[62] TNA, WO 161/82, p. 670.

punishment prisoners received was military confinement for six months, one of the lighter punishments available. 2,472 prisoners received this sentence as opposed to 47 who received penal servitude sentences of over a year and 1,191 who were sentenced to imprisonment with hard labour.[63]

It is extremely difficult in the absence of German source material to take this comparison further or to explore how the British labour companies coped with the influx of German prisoners in the last months of the war.[64] By the end of the conflict, German prisoners represented a massive labour force working for the British army: on 11 November 1918 there were 303 British prisoner of war labour companies in France and Belgium containing 178,692 German other ranks.[65] In contrast there were only 64,250 German prisoners of war working in the UK on 7 November 1918.[66] The absence of German testimony or memoirs on British prisoner of war labour companies is remarkable and is matched by an absence of British archive documentation.

However, by late 1918 the British public was certainly convinced that it was treating German prisoners far better than Germany was treating its captive British troops. In September and October 1918, a lively debate on the subject occurred in *The Times*; the newspaper published numerous letters to the editor on the theme of prisoners of war during this period.[67] The British government was heavily criticised for its failure to adopt reprisals against German prisoners which, it was felt, would force Germany to improve its treatment of its British captives. The government was also criticised for the failure of the second Hague Agreement, signed in July 1918, to produce any improvement in Germany's prisoner treatment.[68] Feelings ran high. One letter published in *The Times* on 31 October 1918 came from an anonymous British officer on the western front who stated:

What we all feel so bitterly out here is the treatment of our prisoners. I could hardly believe the monstrous and awful stories one reads about but now I know at first hand from civilians – as does everyone else – of the indescribable brutality and bestial treatment our poor fellows have had to go through . . . many of them perished from murder, starvation and torture. Nothing can ever be written to make those at home realise what our prisoners have suffered. And then our government takes no action whatsoever or none at any rate that is obvious to the public or to the chaps out here . . . At home and out here the German prisoners are not only well treated, but

---

[63] *Ibid.*
[64] TNA, WO 95/4174 contains records of guard unit transfers; no further material on British prisoner labour companies has been found despite an exhaustive search at The National Archives.
[65] Scott, 'Captive Labour', p. 328.   [66] TNA, WO 161/82, p. 634.
[67] See *The Times*, Letters to the editor, 11.9.18; 1.10.18; 3.10.18; 4.10.18; 7.10.18; 10.10.18; 11.10.18; 23.10.18; 31.10.18.
[68] 'A Derelict Agreement', *The Times*, 19.10.1918.

they are absolutely pampered and petted and if anything better fed than the fighting Tommy. One sees batches of them working on roads out here. They loll about smoking and talking and do as much or as little as they please. I don't know what time they start work but they knock off for lunch and cease altogether at 4 pm. They usually have lorries to take them to and from their work and if it is raining I don't believe they work at all. Sunday is a day of rest for them – not for us. Only yesterday I passed a prisoners' camp and saw a mob of them sitting about outside their huts while our Labour Corps men were breaking stones on the road in full view of the camp... We have procured written evidence from civilians of cases where our prisoners have been shot in the street for taking food offered them by civilians. One does not want the brutes ill-treated or starved but why this favouritism?[69]

This source has to be viewed with caution: letters to *The Times* were on occasion orchestrated by the establishment to deliberately provoke a debate on a particular issue. Yet, significantly, even in a letter demanding harsher prisoner treatment, such as this, there is still a strong cultural disapproval of beating German prisoners or starving them; the language is very much the high Edwardian rhetoric of 'fair play', closer to the cultural ideals of British honour espoused by the famous poem 'Vitai Lampada' by Henry Newbolt than the rhetoric of wartime extremes.[70]

Overall, the indications are that conditions for German prisoners working behind British lines remained much better than those for Allied prisoners in occupied territories. The complaints which were made by the German government illustrate this. On 9 October 1918, the German Foreign Office complained about the treatment of German prisoners in three British prisoner of war labour companies – 121, 147 and 71.[71] In prisoner of war labour company 121 the prisoners had only one blanket and had to sleep on the ground. They complained of frequent roll calls and poor food. Many had caught Spanish influenza.[72] In company 147, the accommodation and food were 'extremely inferior (*äusserst minderwertig*)'.[73] Prisoners had been hospitalised suffering from frozen feet or from lice. The water provided to this labour company was dirty. In prisoner company 71, prisoners had to work on Sundays and holidays and received no day off. These were real grievances which show that the British labour company system also saw prisoners' welfare undermined by military necessity. However, they do not compare to the wide range of abuses occurring in the German labour company system. The only very serious complaint here was that men in labour company 71 were not

---

[69] Letter to Editor, *The Times*, 31.10.1918.
[70] On British pre-war definitions of honour and masculinity, see Tosh, 'What Should Historians Do with Masculinity?', pp. 179–202.
[71] BA-MA, PH 2 / 588, f. 156, Nr. 94.11.18.Z.V.I., n. 36, 9.10.1918.
[72] *Ibid.*   [73] *Ibid.*

receiving a day off. Beatings, prisoners collapsing and dying from starvation or enduring work under shellfire are entirely absent. In 1919, the German government admitted that it was 'unlikely' that there were cases of war crimes against German prisoners held by the British.[74] The shortage of sources limits any full comparison of the British and German labour company systems; however, the available evidence suggests that German treatment was worse.

The 1918 experience of German prisoners of war held by France

I have become used to life in my company – that is if the German planes would leave us in peace – which was not the case at the end of July. Only a hair's breadth difference and their first bomb would have fallen directly on our barrack and it would have naturally produced the same result as happened in another company: 92 dead and 70 wounded. You see for us too the war is not over yet and if this distribution of bombs does not stop the best thing for us would be to write to the Red Cross asking for a donation in the form of anti-aircraft guns so that we could defend ourselves against similar attacks.[75]

In contrast to the British case, French prisoner of war labour companies are amply documented, clearly revealing the development of the French army use of forced prisoner labour. By 1 June 1918, France had captured 243,590 German prisoners.[76] Of these 46,664 were working in prisoner of war labour companies for the French army.[77] The remainder had been assigned to work in the French interior or consisted of prisoners who were exempt from working because they were officers or wounded. The French system was highly centralised. The distribution of prisoners of war was decided by the War Committee (*Comité de Guerre*). On 19 May 1918, increased powers were allocated to the *Service Général des Prisonniers de Guerre*, by the French War Ministry.

---

[74] The German government, when establishing a post-war commission to investigate prisoner abuse against Allied prisoners in Germany, stated that it expected the Allies to reciprocate by investigating crimes against German prisoners: 'which it is conceded are not expected as far as prisoners in England are concerned but which are not wholly unfounded as regards prisoners in Russia'. ACICR, 431/III/j/c.31, extract from *The Times*, 'Treatment of Prisoners. German Commission Appointed', 29.11.1918.

[75] German prisoner, working in French prisoner of war labour company 33, to his family, 16 August 1918. SHAT, 16 N 1224, Rapport mensuel sur les renseignements recueillis dans la correspondance des PG de la DE du GAC au courant du mois d'août 1918, QG, 14.9.1918.

[76] SHAT, 16 N 525, État des prisonniers stationnés dans la zone des armées à la date du 1 juin 1918 [captures et évacuations de prisonniers de guerre effectuées dans la quinzaine du 15 mai au 1 juin 1918].

[77] *Ibid.*

This was to set the standards for prisoner treatment and working conditions. The military inspectorate, the *Inspection Général des Prisonniers de Guerre*, which had hitherto controlled these prisoner matters, was henceforth confined to managing the guard system, inspecting camps and enforcing discipline.[78] Within the French system certain special categories of prisoner, such as those from Alsace-Lorraine or Poland, enjoyed a special preferential regime. Wounded prisoners, prisoners who were members of the German army medical services and officer prisoners were also treated differently from the bulk of captives made up of other-rank German soldiers. This chapter will now assess the treatment of other-rank prisoners in French prisoner of war labour companies by looking at French administrative sources, the French postal control reports on German prisoners' letters and German memoirs and interviews, looking in particular at prisoners' rations, disciplinary treatment and working conditions.

Prisoners' rations in France also deteriorated in 1918; however, this was not due to shortages but rather due to the impact of Franco-German negotiations. In 1918, the two Berne Accords, signed between France and Germany in March and April, recognised agreed standards for prisoner rations, punishments, working hours and working conditions. Ironically, this actually meant a cut in bread rations for the average German prisoner in France. Article 26 of the April Berne Accord set rations of 2,000 calories for non-working prisoners, 2,500 for ordinary workers and 2,850 for workers engaged on heavy manual labour.[79] Non-working prisoners and officer prisoners received a daily ration of 350 grams of bread following the Berne Accords; working prisoners received 400 grams.[80] German prisoners had received a ration of 460 grams of meat per week for non-workers and 610 grams for workers prior to the Berne Accords. Following the agreements they only received meat four days a week and their ration was reduced by 3/7ths.[81] A French censor's report noted that German prisoners in prisoner labour companies complained that the 'food was rather insufficient in quantity. The reduction in the bread ration to 400 grams set by the Berne Convention has caused uproar.'[82] The censor summarised several prisoners' comments: 'each prisoner would lose 10 to 15 years off his life on this

---

[78] SHAT, 7 N 1993, Ministère de la Guerre, Sous-Secrétaire d'état de la Justice Militaire, Note pour les Directions et Services, 29.5.1918.

[79] SHAT, 7 N 1993, Ministère de la Guerre, Sous-Sécrétaire d'état de la Justice Militaire. Service général des prisonniers de guerre, à MM. les Généraux Gouverneurs Militaires de Paris et de Lyon, les Généraux commandant les régions, les Commandants régionaux des dépôts de prisonniers de guerre, 15.6.1918.

[80] *Ibid.*   [81] *Ibid.*

[82] SHAT, 16 N 1224, GQG, État-Major, 2e Bureau SRA, Zone des Armées, 1917–1918, DE du GAC, Groupe d'armées de l'est, Direction des étapes, Nord, État-Major, 1er Bureau, Rapport Mensuel de l'Interprète Stagiaire de la DE Nord du GAE, 12.6.1918.

diet; the governments could agree so that prisoners never receive too much but for everything else they cannot agree; the German government was mocking its prisoners and it should watch itself when they are repatriated! The people will not always let themselves be led by the nose.'[83] For Georges Clemenceau, however, the Berne Accords were an important gesture to public opinion, although he confessed to the British that he had no intention of fulfilling all the clauses, particularly those on prisoner exchanges.[84]

Even after the implementation of the Berne Accords, however, the quantity and quality of food received by German captives in France was generally much better than that received by Allied prisoners in Germany in 1918. First, the quality of the French rations had not deteriorated. Second, France adhered strictly to the quantity of rations outlined in the Berne Accords, whereas Germany did not. Many prisoners in France continued to receive a meat ration in 1918, in contrast to Allied prisoners in German labour companies, who never received any meat; although those in French prisoner labour companies obtained meat far less often than those in home front camps.[85] Third, prisoners in France had access to well-stocked canteens which sold food. Finally, prisoners in France – both in the French interior and in prisoner of war labour companies in the army zone – continued to receive parcels. The French censor noted in June 1918 that the parcels always contained 'a high proportion of food items; cakes, biscuits, salami, lard, smoked ham, sugar, jams, tinned food, marmalade, sweets, dried fruit, butter, potatoes and beans'.[86] He also remarked that most of the parcels came from rural Germany or from the Swiss or Dutch Red Cross.[87] German prisoners in France also were regularly able to write and receive letters: one German prisoner remarked 'the post works marvellously now; in sum it is the best thing about captivity'.[88] Another wrote home that all his parcels had arrived and that

---

[83] *Ibid.*, Rapport Mensuel de l'Interprète Stagiaire de la DE Nord du GAE, 12.6.1918.

[84] Clemenceau admitted to the British in a private conversation that he had agreed to the Berne Accords only to quiet public opinion in France, which was clamouring for the government to do something to assist French prisoners. HLRO, LG/F/52/1/33, British Embassy, Paris, confidential, Lord Derby to Arthur J. Balfour, 18.5.1918.

[85] BHStA IV, GenKdos IbAK, Bund 107, Aussagen der am 12.6.18 aus französ. Kriegsgefangenschaft entkommenen deutschen Kriegsgefangenen Untoff. d. L. Hermann Gartner, Musketier Otto Kampe, Musketier Walter Viehrig, 14.6.1918.

[86] SHAT, 16 N 1224, GQG, État-Major, 2e Bureau SRA, Zone des Armées, 1917–1918, DE du GAC, Groupe d'armées de l'est, Direction des étapes, Nord, État-Major, 1er Bureau, Rapport Mensuel de l'Interprète Stagiaire de la DE Nord du GAE, 12.6.1918.

[87] *Ibid.*

[88] *Ibid.*, GAN, DE, État-Major, Service PG, Rapport Mensuel sur les Renseignements recueillis dans la correspondance du mois de Novembre 1917 des Prisonniers de Guerre de la DE du GAN, 22.12.1917.

it was rare for a parcel to go missing in France. It was, he claimed, on the German side that they disappeared.[89]

As in the German case, prisoners working for the French army in the militarised war zone in 1918 experienced worse living conditions than those in prisoner of war camps in the interior of the country. Although standards had improved since early 1917, particularly due to the implementation of the rule that prisoner labour companies could only work at thirty kilometres from the front, these workers still lived in rough accommodation. The thirty-kilometre rule was rigorously kept. Each labour company informed the Rear Zone Administration (*Direction de l'Arrière*) of its distance from the front. On one occasion a company was found to be at twenty-five kilometres from the front. Orders were immediately issued that it be moved back to thirty kilometres.[90] At thirty kilometres prisoners were relatively safe from shells – however, aerial bombardment of work camps was still a danger.[91]

As in the German army, initial conditions after capture were very poor for prisoners taken by the French. While newly taken prisoners were sorted into different categories for divergent treatment – Alsace-Lorrainers, Poles, officers, skilled workers, unskilled workers – they were kept in large collection centres in the army zone where conditions were generally overcrowded with very rudimentary sanitation. The French quarantined their German prisoners for fifteen days in these holding camps. One French report on Allibaudières holding camp was scathing, describing it as poorly built and badly organised.[92] German prisoners who escaped described the holding camps near the front in a very unfavourable light. Two of the main holding camps were at Souilly, already mentioned in chapter 3, and at Connantre. A German prisoner named Streichert who escaped from prisoner of war labour company 19 stated that, at Souilly, prisoners were hit to extract information from them, were fed on watery rice, that almost all the prisoners suffered from frozen hands or feet and that those who reported sick were punished.[93] Another prisoner wrote that he spent three days at Souilly

---

[89] *Ibid.*, Rapport Mensuel sur les renseignements recueillis dans la correspondance du mois de février des prisonniers de guerre de la DE du GAN, 14.3.1918, p. 26.

[90] SHAT, 16 N 2466–2, Inspections des PG, DA GQG État-major, Direction des transports militaires aux armées No. 8633/DTMA compte rendu de l'emplacement des compagnies de PG, 6.12.1917.

[91] SHAT, 16 N 1224, Rapport Mensuel sur les renseignements recueillis dans la correspondance des PG de la DE du GAC au courant du mois d'août 1918, QG, 14.9.1918.

[92] SHAT, 16 N 2466–2, GQG État-major DA. 13.2.18, Compte rendu de mission, Visite du camp de PG d'Allibaudières effectuée le 12.2.1918.

[93] SHAT, 16 N 1224, GQG, État-Major, 2e Bureau SRA, Zone des Armées, 1917–1918, DE du GAC État-Major, Secteur Postal 5, Rapport Mensuel de l'Officier Interprète de la DE du GAC, 19.11.1917.

camp in September 1917 without receiving any food.[94] A prisoner from Connantre camp described it in July as a 'pigsty'.[95] By November 1918 the sanitary situation at Connantre was still problematic. A note for the Medical Service (*Service de Santé*) at General Headquarters, stated that

The holding camp at Connantre … which has 1,800 prisoners does not have a disinfection room nor does it have showers. Please could the necessary equipment be sent to this camp. The prisoners arrive there in large numbers … and are generally in a hideous state of filth. If this situation does not cease one has to fear the outbreak of epidemic sicknesses in this camp.[96]

The poor conditions in French holding camps were just one problem with the French prisoner of war system. While many prisoners working in the interior of France in agriculture or forestry were allowed considerable freedom and were often fed and lodged in small groups by their employers, others set to work in mines or munitions factories fared worse. In general, punishments for misdemeanours were harsh throughout the French system – usually involving long periods in solitary confinement on bread and water.[97] Failed escapers received thirty days' such confinement.[98]

A survey of twelve Bavarian escapers' accounts of conditions in different French prisoner of war camps in 1918 is revealing.[99] In total, in their different interview accounts, the prisoners described eleven camps in the army zone and five camps in the French interior. As regards the army zone camps the following picture emerges: in three of the eleven army zone camps, prisoners were housed in tents; the remainder accommodated captives in wooden barracks, apart from one where the prisoners were held in a riding arena.[100] The bedding situation was mentioned for ten of

---

[94] *Ibid.*   [95] *Ibid.*

[96] SHAT, 16 N 2466–2, 3599/DA Note pour le Service de Santé du GQG, Demande d'une étuve à désinfecter et d'appareils à douches pour le camp d'organisation de Connantre, 8.11.1918.

[97] See Stefan Utsch, *Todesurteil in Tours 1917. Aufzeichnungen des deutschen Kriegsgefangenen 389* (Berlin, 1940), p. 122.

[98] BHStA IV, Gen.Kdos IbAK, Bund 107, Nr. 9739, g O1, Aussagen der am 30.1.1918 aus französ. Kriegsgefangenschaft entkommenen deutschen Kriegsgefangenen, 2.2.1918.

[99] This survey is based upon BHStA IV, Gen.Kdos IbAK, Bund 107, statements from the following German soldiers who escaped French captivity in 1918: Untoff. d. L. Hermann Gartner, Musketier Otto Kampe, Musketier Walter Viehrig, Gefr. Willi Wettig, Inf. Wilhelm Schenk, Inf. Oskar Markert, Gefr. Franz Feldl, Gefr. Walter Siegel, Musk. Johann Holzmann, Unt. Offizier Franz Hiltrop, Reservist Erich Melzner, Ers. Reservist Louis Bode. The eleven army zone camps discussed are: St Hilaire, Allibaudières, Souilly, Vadelaincourt, Vervillers, St Dizier, St Eulien, Châlons-sur-Marne, Mailly, Roye, Liffol-le-Grand. The camps outside the army zone were Rouen, Le Tréport, Etampes, Fort Asnières in Rouen and Montfort sur Maine.

[100] *Ibid.*

these camps: in five, it was relatively good, consisting of bunks or beds and sacks filled with straw and a blanket; in three camps, prisoners received more improvised bedding such as only straw sacks and a blanket or just beds made from hurdles; and in a further two camps, prisoners received no blanket or bedding whatsoever and slept on the ground.[101] In four army zone camps, prisoners stated the guards hit their charges.[102] For six camps, there was no mention of whether heating was available; of the five others where the heating situation was discussed, only one actually had heating. In seven of the eleven camps, prisoners received parcels and post. For ten of the camps, food rations were described in detail. In nine, prisoners received ¼ to ¾ litres of coffee, between ½ to 2 litres of noodles, rice or soup, and 400 to 500 grams of white bread daily; 500 grams was above the Berne accords allocation. This appears to have been standard fare: only one camp did not provide these rations and gave prisoners just 500 grams of bread and water daily. In five of the camps, prisoners reported that the standard fare listed above was added to with vegetables – beans, potatoes or lentils. One lucky camp also received cabbage and turnips and one camp received horse-meat twice a week.[103] In contrast, prisoners in the home front camps received the same food – coffee, soup, noodles and rice but reported a higher bread ration of 600 grams.[104] Their accommodation was also described more favourably and none reported being hit.

Several further important points emerge from the escapers' interviews. First, the average German prisoner in the French army zone usually worked a ten-hour day on heavy manual tasks such as forestry, road building, railway building, quarrying work or loading stores.[105] French military culture was much less concerned about guards cuffing prisoners than was the case in the British army: prisoners were hit on occasion by their guards, although nowhere near as frequently as Allied prisoners in the occupied territories.[106] The above survey shows, in certain camps such as St Hilaire, Souilly, Vadelaincourt and Vervillers, prisoners were openly hit.[107] In contrast to Allied prisoners in the occupied territories, however, almost all German prisoners taken by France were able to notify their relations of their capture relatively rapidly: the longest waiting time was fourteen days before being enabled to write home. Importantly too, none of the escapers mentioned any sickness in the labour companies and there were few complaints about access to medical attention. Clearly, German prisoners in French labour companies were subject to a very rudimentary regime in 1918. However, the extreme conditions inflicted on German prisoners in French labour companies during and immediately after the battle of Verdun were not repeated.

---

[101] *Ibid.* [102] *Ibid.* [103] *Ibid.* [104] *Ibid.*
[105] *Ibid.* [106] *Ibid.* [107] *Ibid.*

German prisoners in French labour companies in the army zone had mixed feelings about their situation, as revealed in extracts from their letters which were cited and summarised in French censorship reports. 'Life is nearly supportable; one single thing is lacking us: liberty!' wrote a prisoner from PG company 52 in February 1918.[108] Another from company 115 told his family not to 'worry about me; I like the work; I have plenty to eat and one is treated according to one's behaviour. Even in enemy country there are good people.'[109] The censor's comments were compiled from the original prisoners' letters, prior to censorship, hence they are a particularly useful source on prisoner perceptions and complaints. The censor did note in March 1918 that most prisoners restricted their letters to discussion of family subjects and of Germany; however, even though prisoners knew their letters were censored, they were surprisingly fortright on their captivity. Some expressed satisfaction at their fate which removed them from the dangers of shells and gas.[110] Many prisoners were happy to be able to sing in choral groups after work.[111] However, other prisoners complained bitterly and compared their situation to that of medieval hermits.[112] The chief complaint was that the rations prisoners received were not adequate for the hard work that was demanded of them.[113] In July 1918, a French censor's report stated:

We cannot pretend no matter how much we might wish to, that there is unanimous satisfaction among our forced guests [nos hôtes forcés] regarding the treatment they have received. Some of them adopt a tragic attitude, claiming they would rather return to the front under a hail of shells and bullets than live in the painful, humiliating situation imposed on them by the 'pays de civilisation' ... However, the majority direct their reproaches and curses at their own government.[114]

Among the resentments prisoners listed against their home government was the call-up to the German army of the remaining male members of their families who had previously been considered too young or too old to fight; captives were also annoyed with the German censor for blacking out large parts of the letters they received from home.[115] However, the censor commented that 'most of the Germans in our charge state that they are satisfied with the way that the French behave towards them. Many of them

---

[108] SHAT, 16 N 1224, Rapport Mensuel sur les renseignements recueillis dans la correspondance du mois de février des prisonniers de guerre de la DE du GAN, 14.3.1918.
[109] Ibid.
[110] Ibid., Rapport Mensuel de l'Interprète Stagiaire de la DE Nord du GAE, 12.6.1918, p. 18.
[111] Ibid.   [112] Ibid.
[113] Ibid., GAE, DE [nord] 1er bureau, Rapport Mensuel de l'Interprète Stagiaire de la DE Nord du GAE. Dated August 1918. Report on July correspondence.
[114] Ibid.   [115] Ibid.

acknowledge that as long as a prisoner stays quiet and does his work properly, not a hair on his head will be touched.'[116]

Prisoners' morale was evidently closely connected to the progress of the German war effort – in part, clearly due to the fact that a German victory would ensure their rapid release. In the postal censor report for July 1918, the censor noted that a proportion of prisoners expressed their dissatisfaction with captivity and their despair at being out of the German offensive. Yet, prisoners, the censor noted, were not depressed. Many were still 'filled with an unquenchable faith in the "right arm of Hindenburg" (in other words in Ludendorff) and are still religiously respectful of the Kaiser', awaiting some action by them which would bring about final victory.[117] However, German war set-backs led to prisoners losing hope in August and September 1918: in August, the censor noted that letters being sent by German prisoners openly discussed disenchantment with the conflict. 'Michael continues to retreat according to what we hear. How is this possible?' wrote a prisoner from prisoner labour company 115 on 28 August.[118] 'I met several new prisoners from the 1919 draft. Well, you know, what I saw and heard there was not very encouraging,' another prisoner from the same company stated.[119] One prisoner told his family: 'You must know that I am a prisoner in France ... I am better here than in the German Michael offensive.'[120] In the August and September reports, there were far fewer complaints about captivity and a general despair at the outcome of the war appeared. Whereas in postal reports from earlier in the year, prisoners were loath to express discouraging sentiments to their families, by August this taboo disappeared.

It is significant that the captive men retained their interest in war news and in wider political issues, including domestic developments within Germany, as this indicates a certain basic level of health that still allowed for continued political debate and commentary. In fact, the references to starvation in the letters between prisoners and the German home front come not from the captives but from the German civilian side. In particular, there was a sharp change of tone in civilians' letters to prisoners working in the army zone between July 1918 and August 1918. German civilians' letters in July complained of food shortages, but the overall outlook was stoic. By August, a tone of despair and hopelessness crept in – sentiments which utterly dominated letters by September. The letters received by prisoners working in the French army zone, who were all other

---

[116] *Ibid.* [117] *Ibid.*

[118] *Ibid.*, Rapport mensuel sur les renseignements recueillis dans la correspondance des PG de la DE du GAC au courant du mois d'août 1918, QG, 14.9.18.

[119] *Ibid.* [120] *Ibid.*

ranks or NCOs, thus reveal the extent of the loss in morale among the lower middle classes and working class in Germany during this period, particularly as large numbers of labour company prisoners' letters and cards, both to and from France, were read to compile the censors' reports: 61,523 in August and 59,263 for September.[121]

News from civilians at home about the deterioration in conditions badly affected labour company prisoners' own morale, as, from August, civilian letters became increasingly negative in outlook. The postal censor reported that many prisoners were receiving news of a breakdown in sexual morality in Germany. One civilian in Koblenz wrote that there was a 'new epidemic of matrimony. If you were here you would be surprised to see them all walking in an interesting manner! You understand: marriage imposes itself.'[122] All the postal reports from prisoner companies also mentioned that prisoners were receiving news of large numbers of deaths from influenza and tuberculosis in Germany in their letters.[123] 'Ah! If you knew how many young women are now dying,' stated a letter writer in Saxony to a prisoner in labour company 26.[124] 'We are all sick – it is due to the food. I would never have believed that we would be brought to this. The food does not suffice to kill us but it is not enough to live on,' a letter from Pomerania to a prisoner stated.[125] 'If you were here you would be amazed at what we are enduring. It is high time that the war finished,' another civilian wrote.[126] German captives in prisoner labour company 114 in September 1918 received news in their post of 120 deaths of civilian acquaintances or relations; prisoner labour company 9 received news of 102 civilian deaths the same month.[127] The impact of so many civilian deaths on morale should not be underestimated – there were only 425 prisoners in each labour company. The French censor noted that in September 1918 'almost all' the letters to prisoners from their families stated that they were unable to send them anything and sought to make the prisoners understand the situation: 'If you knew what we have become I think you would not even dare to ask us for a pin,' a letter from Koenen stated.[128] The censor reports also show a shift in public opinion in Germany towards French treatment of prisoners: German public opinion remained firmly convinced until August 1918

---

[121] Ibid., DE du GAE, État-Major, no. 20, Rapport Mensuel de l'Officier Interprète de la DE du GAE, 14.10.1918.
[122] Ibid., Rapport Mensuel sur les renseignements recueillis dans la correspondance des PG de la DE du GAC au courant du mois d'août 1918, 14.9.1918.
[123] Ibid.   [124] Ibid.
[125] Ibid., DE du GAE, État-Major, no. 20, Rapport Mensuel de l'Officier Interprète de la DE du GAE, 14.10.1918.
[126] Ibid.   [127] Ibid.   [128] Ibid.

that the French were mistreating German prisoners and often mentioned this in their letters. In August and September, however, these comments disappeared.

By late August 1918, some German prisoners in French labour companies in the army zone even acknowledged that despite the work and spartan living conditions their situation was preferable to that of German soldiers or German civilians. 'The food is good ... I have wished many times that you could have as regular and abundant food in Germany, especially the really good white bread which does not exist any more there,' a German prisoner in labour company 31 wrote home.[129] This was an important shift and indicates that, although the French worked their prisoners hard, living conditions in labour companies were, for the majority of German prisoners, largely endurable, a situation which contrasts with the perception of Allied prisoners in the occupied territories in 1918. 'The Frenchman is not mean to us. He who does his work is not unhappy,' a prisoner in labour company 8 wrote.[130] 'I am better here than in the trenches. During the week I go to work and on Sundays I rest. When I return from work at midday I have a hot meal and the most important thing is that in the evening I get a full night's sleep,' another prisoner wrote in September.[131] These letters to Germany informed families that the French were not suffering food shortages. They also served to encourage other German soldiers to surrender.

To conclude, in 1918 German prisoners in the French army zone were worked very hard and received slightly smaller rations than German prisoners in the French interior. However, the evidence suggests that they were subject to less physical violence and received better housing, in purpose-built wooden barracks, than their counterparts in the German-occupied territories, who were often billeted in semi-ruined buildings or factories. Most importantly, they received regular food rations supplemented by parcels from home or neutral charities. They also had regular contact by letter with their loved ones. Overall, in France in 1918, there was less of a difference in prisoner treatment between the army zone camps and those in the French interior than in the German case.

However, it seems that there was a limited deterioration in British and French treatment of prisoners of war during 1918 in comparison to previous years. For prisoners in camps in Britain this was due to the cut in their rations. Similarly, for a proportion of German prisoners in France the Berne Accords resulted in a cut in their bread ration. In other respects, treatment of German prisoners remained largely static for the first half of

---

[129] *Ibid.*   [130] *Ibid.*   [131] *Ibid.*

1918 in the two countries, particularly for those German prisoners in working camps in the army zone who were subject to a very hard regime. Thus overall, the use of forced prisoner labour in the British and French armies did not unleash a violent escalation dynamic against prisoners in 1918 – the deterioration in conditions was limited.

From late July onwards, the huge surrenders of German prisoners placed great strain on British and French holding camps. However, due to the greater food resources of the Allies, the French and British prisoner labour company systems did not collapse under this pressure. The most ironic point about the limited deterioration in prisoner conditions on the Allied side in 1918 was that it occurred at precisely the point when German prisoners' perceptions of captivity became more favourable as captivity became a preferred outcome to fighting on.

Conclusion

If 1940 was, in the words of Marc Bloch's book, France's 'strange defeat', then 1918 represented the strange victory.[132] Sudden triumph came before the military, the politicians or the general public of Britain or France expected it. The rapidity with which events moved between August and November 1918, together with the chaos of the German retreat and the Allied advance, meant that the military bureaucracies struggled to keep pace with what was happening. Even keeping records of what was occurring became problematic. In the midst of the general drama of September, October and November 1918, no administrative systems were in place for dealing with the prisoners of war liberated from working for the German army in the occupied territories. It was simply beyond the British and French armies' capabilities at this point to properly assess or record the scale of prisoner mistreatment in northern France and Belgium. Gathering legal evidence from prisoners about their treatment was last on the agenda; feeding and repatriating them were onerous enough tasks in themselves. Moreover, many prisoners in the occupied territories had been evacuated to camps in Germany in September–October 1918. For the French and British armies at this point, detailed investigation of what had happened to prisoners was impossible.

This confusion which accompanied the end of the war also obscured the key trends in relation to prisoners which were emerging in 1918. The last months of the First World War saw a deterioration in prisoner treatment in the occupied territories, which was the product of cultural

---

[132] Marc Bloch, *Strange Defeat. A Statement of Evidence Written in 1940* (New York and London, 1968)

attitudes within the German military that were dominated by ruthlessness and indifference. In the German case there was no powerful civilian government to control or inspect what was happening. The cultural attitudes which underlay the German army use of prisoners in 1918 effectively marked a break with late nineteenth-century humanitarian ideals of how prisoners should be dealt with.

The Allies, on the other hand, culturally defined themselves against the German pattern of behaviour towards prisoners in 1918, believing that they had upheld the standards of late nineteenth-century humanitarianism. This discourse of difference obscured the reality of the Allies' treatment of prisoners in 1918. For the importance of 1918 was that it showed the prisoner of war labour company – with its implicit acceptance of the idea of forced labour – like the aeroplane, the submarine or poison gas, to be a universal military innovation of the war. It was an innovation common to the Allies and the Germans. Had the German treatment of prisoners in 1918 not deteriorated so badly, more questions would have been raised about the Allies' behaviour. As it was, the German treatment was so bad as to allow the Allies to retain their cultural sense of moral superiority and the German defeat meant Germany was ill-placed to investigate the Allies' use of prisoner labour companies.

Thus the deterioration in German treatment hid the fact that a limited deterioration in prisoner treatment by the Allies also occurred in 1918. In the British case, prisoners in Britain proper were on shortened rations; in the French army, German prisoners were working in prisoner of war labour companies on low rations for long hours in temporary accommodation. In both the British and French cases, a large increase in the numbers of German prisoners in labour companies occurred. Fewer prisoners were being evacuated from the military controlled area to the established camps with their much better leisure and sanitation facilities. Finally, the influx of German prisoners at the end of the war meant that conditions for prisoners in the Allied holding camps deteriorated.

However, perhaps the most important point is that, although a deterioration in prisoner treatment occurred on the Allied side, it was *limited* prior to the Armistice. This limitation was partly due to the greater resources of the Allies. But more importantly it was also due to the different cultural perceptions which underlay Allied behaviour. Cultural attitudes were crucial determinants of the use of the military innovation of prisoner of war labour companies and the treatment of their prisoner members. Both the British and French armies' attitudes towards prisoners were evolving in 1918. In the British case, a very highly developed culture of labour management underscored their treatment of German prisoners. The British applied concepts already developed to deal with their civilian labour force to managing their prisoners of war; it is highly symbolic of this that the British allowed civilians on the Prisoner of War Employment Committee to assess the army's use of prisoner labour in the military zone in France. These cultural attitudes served to limit the military demands made upon prisoners, although in the absence of further German sources the extent to which they protected German prisoners on the ground cannot be fully determined.

The French, despite their often quixotic attempts to reform their prisoner system, failed to establish such a coherent civilian labour management approach. Culturally, the attitudes which informed the treatment of prisoners in the French labour companies were influenced more by prewar French military experiences with forced French labourers, such as French soldiers, prison inmates or colonial subjects, sentenced to hard labour or 'la bagne', rather than civilian worker management. However, the cultural paradigms inherent in the French understanding of the war, such as civilisation against barbarism, and democracy against tyranny, also played a role. It mattered to French self-perception that the 'civilisation' ideals of the French revolution were upheld, ideals which ultimately were universal, not national, in scope. This did not stop the French military employing reprisals or exploiting prisoner labour harshly, but it did limit the level of ruthlessness which was culturally acceptable as direct policy in 1918, prior to the Armistice.

The French military was always aware that it was directly answerable to a civilian government and citizens for whom the civilisation image mattered. It had learnt that lesson during the 1917 spring reprisals. The French military was also continually concerned with public opinion – a concern which even extended to recording German prisoners' attitudes to France in their letters. As long as the war continued, these cultural factors acted to limit the other cultural trend in France towards essentialising the German as a subhuman: the boche enemy who deserved annihilation.[133]

Ultimately the German treatment of Allied prisoners of war in the occupied territories was an important factor in the bitterness which appeared in France and Britain during the initial post-Armistice period. In Britain the issue directly fuelled public anger towards Germany, an anger which was enhanced by the popular belief that Britain had treated its German prisoners well. Britain had not suffered invasion and its soldiers captured by Germany represented the most visible British victims of what was perceived as German 'horror' or *Schrecklichkeit*. In France, the situation was somewhat different. The treatment of French prisoners in the

---

[133] On the essentialist racial discourse against Germans which developed in France see Becker, *Oubliés de la Grande Guerre*, pp. 328–9.

occupied territories in 1918 was less of a focus for public anger, which was also roused by damage to property and industry, general mistreatment of occupied civilians and the invasion atrocities of 1914. However, it did contribute to the climate of extreme anger which emerged in France following the Armistice. This anger helps explain the shift in French cultural attitudes towards German prisoners of war which took place *following* the Armistice in November–December 1918. This was the point when a culture of retribution appeared in France, which was instrumental in defining new boundaries for what was acceptable prisoner treatment in 1919–20. This process occurred at the very moment when the first attempts were made to define the memory of prisoner treatment during the war. It is to this complex and difficult period that this book now turns.

Part III

The end of violence? Repatriation and remembrance

Introduction to part III

By November 1918, there had been radical changes in how the prisoner of war was represented and how prisoners of war were treated. Violence against prisoners had evolved during the conflict to reach a point, in 1918, where it had become a significant military *problem*: it had reached irrational levels in the German army and was spiralling out of control. The primary function of an army is to implement violence in a disciplined way – but violent practices against prisoners had now come full circle, actually undermining obedience to orders in the German case, as harassed guards, faced with impossible labour demands, beat prisoners to force more work out of them. Labour was vital to armies by 1918 – the radicalisation of violent practices against prisoner workers in the German army was counterproductive and inefficient.

Given this scenario there was no longer any meaningful attempt to refer to pre-war international law, which had accorded the prisoner of war legal protections and cultural non-combatant status. The only laws which still retained any validity were the agreements made between belligerents on the basis of reciprocity at The Hague and Berne in 1917 and 1918. However, these were far from satisfactory. Large parts of these agreements had still not been implemented by the end of the war, and those aspects which had come into force – such as the thirty-kilometre rule – had not been uniformly kept.

This is not to say that prisoners everywhere experienced the same *level* of mistreatment by 1918. It is very important to emphasise that the situation that evolved in the western front labour companies was always more extreme than the processes of radicalisation towards prisoners occurring in home front camps in Germany, France and Britain. But, between 1917 and the Armistice, the limits and boundaries that demarcated areas where prisoners were well treated came under increasing strain.

This was the situation when the ceasefire came into force on 11 November 1918. Yet the radicalisation process operating in relation to violence against prisoners of war did not cease with the silencing of the guns. Rather it entered a new phase – one in which radical *representations* of violence against prisoners again dominated public discourse. The ensuing period, between November 1918 and the return of the last German prisoners of war from France in spring 1920, was enormously complex. During this phase, as prisoners were repatriated, societies were confronted with reconciling their wartime expectations and beliefs about prisoner treatment with the emerging reality of what had actually happened, as the large numbers of returning prisoners began to recount their experiences, often emphasising the most harrowing. The impressions which populations and governments gained from returning prisoners of war between 11 November 1918 and spring 1920 fixed the way the wartime treatment of prisoners was initially remembered and historicised; these immediate first post-war impressions were often radical and extreme. The post-war representations of violence against prisoners were also central to the difficult debates regarding how prisoners of war were to be commemorated in each country. Chapter 6 will examine this phase in detail to show how an initial radical memory of prisoner of war treatment developed which culminated in the Leipzig war crimes trials in 1921.

However, after 1921, wartime violence against prisoners of war became a less prominent issue – indeed commemorating prisoners' experiences often became highly problematic. Only once the war ended could countries begin to interpret how their prisoners had been treated in a collective historical sense. Questions arose which had not been relevant while the war continued, such as how the treatment of prisoners of war should be historicised, and whether captives should be compensated. Different strategies were adopted in Britain, France and Germany which channelled the overall memory of the war away from remembering violence itself and towards remembering the consequences of that violence – the war dead, the destroyed landscape and, in the German case, the lost territories; the issue of prisoner mistreatment was marginalised by this shift in focus. The initial radicalisation of post-war memory, which emphasised violent prisoner treatment during the war, was supplanted in Britain, France and Germany during the later interwar period by an emphasis on the battlefield war dead. In particular, the memory of the prisoner labour company system was suppressed. Remembrance practices played a central role in mediating this shift in cultural attitudes.

How this transition from radicalisation of memory to suppression occurred will be explored in chapter 7. It explores why interwar societies were unable to construct a historical narrative of the war that included the prisoner experience, suggesting that the memory of the prisoner of war was ultimately marginalised because it invariably invoked the question of violence against prisoners. This in turn raised the question of who were the *perpetrators* of that violence. In an interwar Europe that lionised ex-servicemen, few were comfortable facing that question.

6 Contested homecomings: prisoner repatriation and the formation of memory, 1918–21

> It is completely natural that the tombs of your compatriots, as those of all the Allied soldiers, should receive the same consideration as our own. Although fate wished it that these comrades should rest in foreign soil, they will find fraternal hands to decorate their sanctuary and piously remember them. Our only wish is that, as a mark of thanks and recognition, those of our own whom we had to leave behind us should also receive from their Allied comrades this mark of friendship.
>
> Extract from a letter sent to the French Consul in Nuremberg by the Association of Ex-Prisoners of War, Nuremberg Branch (*Vereinigung ehemaliger Kriegsgefangener, Ortsgruppe Nürnberg*), explaining why they had laid wreaths on the tombs of French prisoners of war, 29.11.1921.[1]

Introduction

Just days before the signing of the Versailles Treaty, the French artist René Georges Hermann-Paul, a well-established illustrator whose work appeared in leading journals such as *Le Figaro*, *Le Rire* and *Les Droits de l'Homme*, drew the striking depiction of a German prisoner of war which appears in Figure 14. Hermann-Paul portrayed the prisoner as evil and malevolent, a preying figure lurking in the background to destroy French happiness as symbolised by the French mother and her daughter. The title of the picture, '*Bocherie*', draws upon the derogatory name for the Germans, '*Boche*', and is an obvious pun on the French word '*boucherie*' or butchery. The prisoner, who is captioned stating 'They have been really kind. What dirty trick can I do to them before I go?' also represents a clear sexual threat – the French male is absent from this scene, where French womanhood is at the mercy of the dangerous German usurper. The word '*cochonnerie*', with its plural meanings of dirty trick, obscenity or smut, is deeply ambiguous. Clearly, for Hermann-Paul, the German prisoner remained an inherently dangerous figure – a potential perpetrator of violence – even eight months after the fighting had ceased. Hermann-Paul's depiction of the imagined dangers of German prisoner liberation in

[1] MAE, Série Z, Europe Allemagne 1918–1929, no. 187, f. 135, 29.11.1921.

Figure 14. René Georges Hermann-Paul (1864–1940), '*Bocherie*. Le prisonnier: "Ils ont ete bien gentils: quelle cochonnerie vais-je leur faire avant de m'en aller?"' 22 June 1919. Bibliothèque de Documentation Internationale Contemporaine et musée d'Histoire Contemporaine, (BDIC-MHC, Les Invalides) Or F2425 (F).

1919 contrasts strongly with the actual reality which ensued, of former German prisoners, once back in Germany, chivalrously laying wreaths on the graves of their French counterparts in Nuremberg two years later, as described in the quotation which opens this chapter. This contrast neatly exemplifies the enormous gap which developed between French and German views of prisoner repatriation. For France, in the immediate post-war period, German prisoners were dangerous perpetrators to be punished, not victims; they deserved no compassion. For Germany, all prisoners, regardless of nationality were now seen as innocent victims of war.

Thus the representation of the prisoner of war played a fundamental role in stoking European divisions following the Armistice. This chapter focuses upon the key period, from the end of the war in November 1918 to the opening of the Leipzig trials of suspected German war criminals in May 1921, which included several British cases against Germans accused of prisoner mistreatment. This was the phase when the initial 'memory' of prisoner of war treatment was formed across Europe and it will be examined in detail here to illustrate how the question of wartime violence against prisoners made the transition into the immediate post-war period, re-emerging in the form of bitter clashes between 1918 and 1921 over how to remember and commemorate prisoners of war. In France and

Britain, as in Germany, public opinion mobilised around particularly radical understandings of how their prisoners of war had been mistreated – understandings which provided a legitimate platform for societies to express extreme and pent-up feelings of grievance towards the enemy. This process also attributed new values to the violence of the war in all three countries, justifying it in retrospect on the basis of the revelations of late 1918 and 1919 of how the enemy had 'abused' captives. A corollary of this post-war phase was that the figure of the prisoner was again entirely dissociated, for his compatriots, from his previous role as combatant and perpetrator of wartime violence; between November 1918 and the Leipzig trials in 1921, the prisoner of war became a symbol of innocence and of suffering.

The radicalisation of attitudes during the period 1918–21 will be explored here through an analysis of the repatriation of prisoners of war, looking first at the homecoming of Allied prisoners of war to Britain and France and second at the return of German prisoners to the new Weimar state. Repatriation was a fraught and contested process which increased post-war hostility towards the former enemy and also significantly impacted upon the immediate post-war public perception of how prisoners had been treated. Ultimately, this phase was crucial in determining how violence against prisoners was remembered.

Post-war memory narratives: the British and French experience of prisoner repatriation

Hermann-Paul's picture, with its animosity towards German prisoners, accurately illustrates the radical 1919 climate in France. In spring 1919, France held 392,425 German prisoners. A further 320,000 German prisoners were in British captivity.[2] For France, German prisoners represented security, ensuring German compliance with French demands. They also represented a sizeable army of military men to whom Germany had no access. As early as April 1918, the French believed that Germany wanted its prisoners back 'because she wishes to get back military instructors of which she has need'.[3] This mentality continued to govern French perceptions after the Armistice; an emasculated France, which had lost so many men in the war, would be more vulnerable once German prisoners returned home. The repatriation of these prisoners was, as Hermann-Paul illustrated, a lurking issue that threatened French happiness.

---

[2] SHAT, 16 N 525, Number of German prisoners in France on 1.2.1919; TNA, WO 394 and War Office, *Statistics of the Military Effort.*

[3] SHAT, 6 N 114, no. 12, HO, AS échange des prisonniers français et allemand, 30.4.1918.

In addition, Britain and France regarded German prisoners as a bargaining tool and saw their labour as a form of living war reparation. Thus, according to Article 10 of the Armistice Treaty, Germany was obliged to release all Allied prisoners immediately whereas the release date of German prisoners in Allied hands remained indefinite. Initially, the German negotiators viewed this as a temporary stay on German prisoner repatriation which would be remedied as soon as all Allied prisoners reached home. The French viewed the situation rather differently. Immediately following the Armistice, the French army *enlarged* its prisoner of war labour company system, sending German prisoners of war from home front camps all across the country to reconstruct the war-damaged regions in the north. This had the added advantage of removing prisoners from jobs to which demobilised French soldiers were returning. Thus, even after the end of the fighting, the need for forced labour drove an escalatory dynamic leading to a deterioration in prisoner welfare. For France, this use of German prisoners on reconstruction work – and Germany's reaction to it – represented a test of how much the new German regime really wished to atone for the deeds of its wartime predecessor. This cultural understanding framed the initial French retributive refusal to repatriate German prisoners of war.

The Allies' continued refusal to release their German prisoners was also profoundly influenced by their first post-war impressions of how Germany had treated its own captives.[4] The debates about prisoner repatriation concerned far more than merely bringing prisoners of war home. They were also fundamentally about how prisoners had been treated during the war, as the former belligerents built their initial demobilisation identities, each invoking an ideal of justice. The Allies based their right to delay the repatriation of German prisoners upon what they claimed was their morally superior prisoner treatment during the conflict. In a note on 10 May 1919, they refused a German request that German prisoners of war be released on the grounds that 'no comparison is possible between the treatment of prisoners of war by the German government and that of the Allied and Associated powers'.[5] The Allies' own experience of prisoner repatriation in November 1918–January 1919 led them to conclude that Germany had mistreated prisoners and deserved to be punished.

Two important developments in late 1918 fuelled the British and French belief in their superior treatment of prisoners. First, as the war concluded in

---

[4] Although strictly speaking the term Allies refers to all the Allied and Associated Powers involved in the war against the Central Powers, it is used in this chapter to refer to the British and French only.
[5] Doegen, *Kriegsgefangene Völker*, p. 1.

November 1918, a range of Allied wartime eschatological fears regarding their prisoners in Germany appeared to be coming true. The superimposition of the Allies' *expectations* of the state in which they would find their men in German hands at the end of the war on the real events of 1918–19 led to several misinterpretations of what was actually happening in Germany. Second, the repatriation of Allied prisoners from Germany occurred in a situation of unprecedented chaos. This strongly influenced prisoners' memories of their captivity and Allied perceptions of Germany.

To turn first to the Allies' eschatological fears in 1918: Annette Becker and Stéphane Audoin-Rouzeau have highlighted the importance of an eschatological framework during the war: early twentieth-century Europeans often interpreted the conflict in terms of God's judgement upon the world. This framework included certain expectations of an improved, purified or even utopian post-war world which peace would bring.[6] As important, however, as such eschatological hopes, built around the idea of peace, were the concomitant eschatological fears associated with the war ending. One such expectation was that the enemy would suffer apocalyptic collapse. Neither governments nor populations were sure how prisoners of war would emerge from any such total defeat.

There were several recurring Allied expectations regarding the end of the war. First, there was anxiety that Allied prisoners in Germany and the occupied territories would starve to death. There was a widespread fear that peace would reveal that large numbers of Allied prisoners had died during their captivity. Second, there was a popular belief that large numbers of men reported as missing in action would turn out to have been held incommunicado in secret German prisons. One letter writer to *The Times* suggested that such secret British prisoners were working in hidden German mines.[7] This belief was also very prevalent in France, where many families clung to the hope that their missing relative would surface as an unreported prisoner in Germany.[8] Baron d'Anthouard of the French Red Cross blamed this irrational belief on the events of 1914, where many French and British soldiers cut off by the German advance had gone into hiding in the occupied territories.[9] In fact, this belief is likely to have a more obvious and rational origin – the large numbers of prisoners captured by Germany in 1918 whose names had not been passed on to France and Britain.

---

[6] Audoin-Rouzeau and Becker, *14–18. Retrouver la Guerre*, p. 182.
[7] *The Times*, 27.12.1918, Letters to the Editor, p. 7. On these rumours of concealed camps see TNA, FO 383/499.
[8] One French widow's hope that her missing husband is a prisoner forms the basis of the Bertrand Tavernier film *La Vie et rien d'autre* (1989).
[9] D'Anthouard, *Les Prisonniers de guerre français en Allemagne*, pp. 4–5.

Third, the French feared that many Allied prisoners would be infected with potentially lethal diseases with which they could infect the French home population.[10] Fourth, the British feared that the German population in revolution would storm the prison camps to pillage parcels, spread Bolshevism and massacre the prisoners. As Robert Wallace, an Emeritus Professor at the University of Edinburgh, wrote to Woodrow Wilson in 1916, a frustrated Germany might 'at whatever cost of blood and treasure ... murder all the British prisoners in their hands'.[11] In sum, the Allies' expectations were that prisoner repatriation could prove a very disappointing and upsetting experience.

These expectations provided the template for how the Allies interpreted events in November and December 1918. Of the four main imagined 'expectations' the Allies had about the repatriation of their prisoners held by Germany, many appeared in November 1918 to be coming true. The appalling condition of the British and French prisoners liberated in northern France and Belgium, outlined in the previous chapter, proved that the fears of prisoners starving were justified. *The Times* concluded in November on the basis of the liberation of the occupied territories that the shortage of food in Germany in recent months has been 'even worse' than could have been imagined, but that British prisoners had suffered more than the rest of the population.[12] The influenza epidemic which spread throughout the German prison camps in two successive waves in July and in November 1918 appeared to confirm the French fear that prisoners might carry infectious diseases – from July 1918 all ceremonies of welcome in Lyons for French prisoners repatriated from Germany and Switzerland were stopped due to the fear that the prisoners might spread the disease.[13] The German revolution with its similar appearance to what had occurred in Russia the previous year led the British to believe that their fears about the bolshevisation and murder of their prisoners were also prescient. Following the Armistice, there was an immediate breakdown of discipline in German prison camps, which led to prisoner shootings by guards trying to restore order in camps at Langensalza, Stralsund and Mannheim. The Allies quickly interpreted

[10] Dr de Christmas, *Le Traitement des prisonniers français en Allemagne*, pp. 1–7.

[11] Robert Wallace, *Letters to Woodrow Wilson (Aug 30 1914–April 3 1917) about the Prisoners and Hostages in Germany* (London, 1931), p. 11.

[12] Annette Becker, 'Le Retour des prisonniers', in *Finir la guerre, Actes du colloque de Verdun, 12–13 novembre 1999. Les Cahiers de la Paix (finir la guerre)*, 7 (Verdun, 2000), p. 69. Also *The Times*, 16.11.18, p. 6.

[13] Bruno Fouillet, 'La Ville de Lyon au centre des échanges de prisonniers de guerre (1915–1919)', *Vingtième Siècle. Revue d'Histoire*, 86 (April–June 2005), p. 37. On the two waves of influenza in German prisoner of war camps see Gärtner, 'Einrichtung', p. 254.

this in the light of their existing expectations: a massacre of prisoners was imminent. These developments were understood in terms of German violence against helpless captives and through the prism of the fears the Allies had built up around prisoner repatriation. They encouraged existing British and French beliefs that Germany had mistreated its prisoners, and created a strong post-war Allied sense of grievance.

The Allies thus clearly believed an escalation in prisoner mistreatment was occurring in Germany at the end of the war. Yet the reality was very different – there was no significant increase in violence against captives in German home front camps in 1918. Despite the fact that the vast majority of captives were involved in working for the German war economy, and despite the outbreak of revolution in November, which led to a massive breakdown of discipline among the German army personnel responsible for guarding prisoners, the violent patterns which emerged in the occupied territories did not replicate themselves on the German home front.

There is one obvious key explanation for this – British and French prisoners of war in Germany had access to food parcels. This was a major factor as to why no dramatic deterioration in prisoner treatment occurred in Germany in 1918: prisoners' health was protected by this additional food; in turn, this meant prisoners were also capable of working without the need for the constant violent beatings required to force starving or ill men to work on the western front. Although the Allies feared in autumn 1918 that their prisoners were starving in Germany, the success of the parcel system meant that in reality most were adequately fed until the outbreak of revolution. Indeed, British and French officer prisoners actually enjoyed a comfortable standard of living: captive officers were continually able to buy food on the black market through bribing guards. Remarkably, despite the scale of civilian hunger in Germany by the end of the war, parcels for British and French officer and other-rank prisoners of war continued to be delivered; this parcel system only broke down following the onset of the German revolution – something which was beyond the control of the German government or military.[14]

The parcel system worked well until 1918, largely because it was in the interest of both sides. The British and French governments feared public opinion would blame them if their blockade led to prisoners starving, hence their encouragement of parcels and their provision of collective bread and biscuit deliveries to home front German camps. The German

---

[14] ACICR, 432/II/26,2, Bd., c.44. Exposé de la situation des prisonniers de guerre russes telle qu'elle est comme par l'enquête préliminaire faite en décembre à Berlin par la délégation du comité internationale de la Croix-Rouge.

authorities had long encouraged parcels as a way to save food supplies –
in part because in 1915, they had ruthlessly cut prisoner rations to
subsistence level to save food in anticipation of the impact of the Allied
blockade.[15] Although the Hague Convention stipulated that prisoners
should be fed the same rations as soldiers in the captor state's army, the
German government effectively abandoned this regulation: indeed, the
main concern from 1915 on was that prisoners should not be better fed
than German civilians.[16] In April 1916, the Reich Department for
Livestock and Meat Supplies (*Reichstelle für die Versorgung mit Vieh und
Fleisch*) advised the Prussian *Kriegsministerium* that the meat rations for
prisoners be reduced as 'it was not evident why the prisoners should
receive such better meat rations than the civilian population'.[17] In June
1915, General Emil von Friedrich, head of the Accommodation
(*Unterkunft*) Department at the Prussian *Kriegsministerium* which was
responsible for prisoner affairs, even organised a conference for all prison
camp food officers in the Reich on how to feed prisoners as thriftily as
possible.[18]

The parcel system ensured the survival of British and French other-rank
captives in Germany, particularly those who were among the 1.5 million
prisoners of war working for the German war economy by 1918, most of
whom were living in rudimentary working *Kommandos* away from the
main camps: while prisoners assigned to labour on farms were generally
very well fed, those working in mines and factories suffered badly from
overwork and too little food.[19] Parcels were key to the survival of these

---

[15] Hinz, *Gefangen im Großen Krieg*, pp. 203–14, 216.   [16] *Ibid.*

[17] GstA PK, Habt.I.87B.16102, f. 55, Abschrift to Herrn Minister für Landwirtschaft,
Domänen und Forsten, Ernährung der Gefangenen, 14.4.1916.

[18] Prof. Dr. A. Backhaus, *Die Ernährung der Kriegsgefangenen im Deutschen Reiche. Bericht über
den Kursus für Verpflegungsoffiziere der Gefangenenlager vom 22. bis 25. Juni 1915 in Berlin*
(Berlin, n.d. [1915]). Backhaus acted as an advisor to the German authorities on prisoner
nutritional needs; an American critic pointed out that as an agriculture professor he was only
qualified to advise on feeding animals. Hinz, *Gefangen im Großen Krieg*, p. 213.

[19] The International Red Cross inspecting prisoners from *Kommandos* after the Armistice
found that prisoners living with German peasant farmers had fared the best of all non-
officer prisoners: ACICR, 432/II/26,2.c.44, Inspections of Cottbus I, and Cottbus II
camps by Siegfried Horneffer and Theodor Aubert, 18.12.1918. Estimating the number
of prisoners working in agriculture in 1918 is difficult; however, on 10 September 1917
there were 856,062 prisoners of war of all nationalities working in agricultural
Kommandos, and 392,562 in industry – 170,000 of whom were working in mines.
Jochen Oltmer, 'Zwangsmigration und Zwangsarbeit. Ausländische Arbeitskräfte und
bäuerliche Ökonomie im Ersten Weltkrieg', *Tel Aviver Jahrbuch für deutsche Geschichte*,
27 (1998), p. 153. For the argument that prisoners in agriculture were treated more as
normal labourers than captives see Mitze, 'Das Kriegsgefangenenlager Ingolstadt
während des Ersten Weltkriegs', p. 366.

men.[20] Kai Rawe estimates that parcels raised the daily ration of prisoners working in mines in the Ruhr by between 950 and 1,200 calories.[21] This was crucial as their German rations were totally inadequate: by August 1918 prisoner miners in the Ruhr received a meat ration of 200 grams and 175 grams of sausage *per week*.[22] Spanish delegations, inspecting the condition of French prisoners in German home front *Kommandos* as part of Spain's role as the neutral 'protecting power' for French captives in Germany, found that some French prisoners in work *Kommandos* were not receiving regular parcels or the collective bread or biscuit deliveries and were suffering from malnourishment as a result.[23] Lance-Corporal Edward Burley recalled that British prisoners who did not receive parcels were hospitalised at Minden camp in 1917 due to hunger; they had resorted to eating 'potato peelings'.[24]

The parcel system was clearly not flawless: all parcels had to pass through a prisoner's *Stammlager* for censorship before being forwarded, delaying or disrupting delivery, which meant that the parcel situation could vary dramatically between prison camps and *Kommandos* located in the same region by 1918 – Cottbus II in Merzdorff, Brandenburg received no parcels from May 1918 on, whereas prisoners at Brandenburg an der Havel received parcels well into November.[25] Some camp commandants also stockpiled parcels rather than distributing them: at Soltau camp in 1918, 200,000 undelivered packets were discovered after the revolution.[26] The collective biscuit and bread deliveries

---

[20] Conditions in some work *Kommandos* were undoubtedly poor. Arthur Hall, a British prisoner sent to work in a mine at Lorenburg near Holzappel, wrote in his diary in April 1918: 'In a mine again. God help us here.' On 6 May he wrote to his camp commandant in Gießen 're [sic] my position in hell', asking to be returned to the *Stammlager*. Hall, *In Enemy Hands*, p. 104. The British prisoner Arthur Leggett reported how at Friedrichsfeld camp a Russian prisoner would inject men in the leg with benzine, causing them to be hospitalised, so that they could avoid being sent to the Wülfrath punishment *Kommando*. Significantly, this punishment *Kommando*, which worked long hours breaking and loading stone in a quarry, was for recalcitrant German sentries as well as prisoners. In this case prisoners were being punished in the same way as German soldiers. TNA, WO 161/100, no. 1804, Private Arthur Leggett, 6.5.1918.

[21] Rawe, '... *wir werden sie schon zur Arbeit bringen!*', pp. 105–6.   [22] *Ibid.*

[23] *Rapports des délégués du gouvernement espagnol sur leurs visites dans les camps de prisonniers français en Allemagne, 1914–1917* (Paris, 1918), Usine à gaz de Spandau, 23 May 1917, p. 335; *Ibid.*, report on prisoners at Bützow, Müllverwertung [Brandenburg], 31.5.1917, p. 338. See also pp. 158, 233, 289.

[24] TNA, WO 161/99, no. 1032, Lance-Corporal Edward Burley, 7.11.17.

[25] ACICR, 432/II/26 Be, Aubert and Horneffer, Inspections of Cottbus II and Brandenburg a.d.Havel.

[26] Emden, *Prisoners of the Kaiser*, p. 129. See also *Rapports des délégués espagnols*, p. 48, report on Neuburg-sur-Kammel camp, Bavaria.

were also not always sent to the *Kommandos*.[27] However, although other-rank French and British prisoners on the German home front who did not receive parcels did suffer malnutrition and a minority became ill, there are no accounts of multiple deaths from starvation of the kind found for prisoner labour companies in the occupied territories, discussed in the previous part of this book, largely because British and French prisoners receiving parcels, frequently shared with comrades who did not receive food from home.[28] While Italian and Russian prisoners, who had no access to parcels, starved to death in Germany in large numbers in 1918, similar mass deaths from starvation do not appear to have occurred among British and French prisoners. As long as parcel food supplies continued, any escalatory dynamic was limited.

Yet it also appears that popular cultural attitudes additionally limited any radicalisation in prisoner mistreatment on the German home front in 1918. The fact that German society, despite suffering food shortages, generally left the food deliveries for prisoners unmolested reveals a remarkable level of social discipline and an acceptance that prisoners should be provided with additional food from abroad. This was partly also because up until the revolution, the belief continued that these food deliveries were in Germany's interest, providing prisoner workers with food and thereby sparing German food resources. This led to the paradoxical situation whereby British and French prisoners were often better fed than the working-class German civilians they laboured alongside in 1917–18: a British prisoner working near Hagen in late 1917 recalled: 'We worked in company with some civilians, three or four old men and the rest women and girls who seemed astonished at the food we brought with us to eat and complained that they were starving themselves and they certainly looked like it.'[29] The French postal censor even noted in August 1918 that, as regarded food, French prisoners in Germany were 'better treated than the locals'.[30] The censor went on to relate a complaint from a priest in Gondringen who said the five prisoners in his parish ate better than

---

[27] *Rapports des délégués espagnols*, p. 158; TNA, WO 161/99, no. 1060, p. 2200, Interview with Private Edward Page, 15.12.1917.

[28] Private Arthur Robinson, a former British prisoner, reported that while he was in Münster camp in June 1918 he witnessed 'several working prisoners coming from the salt mines and coal mines, who were in a very shocking condition being starved and over worked'. TNA, WO 161/100, Interview no. 2356, Private Arthur Robinson, Interview n.d. One elderly veteran recalled how 'by November ... I had gone down from twelve to six or seven stone ... my head was covered in sores from malnutrition'. Interview with Percy Williams, Emden, *Prisoners of the Kaiser*, p. 164.

[29] TNA, WO 161/99, Interview no. 1082, Private Arthur Filder.

[30] SHAT, 16 N 1224, Rapport Mensuel de l'Interprète stagiaire de la DE Nord du GAE, août 1918, GAE, Nord, 1er Bureau.

anyone else.[31] Yet despite this inequality, there was a surprisingly limited escalation in theft from prisoner food deliveries, even in 1918. The International Committee of the Red Cross received remarkably precise information from the French Red Cross, which from mid-1917 recorded increasing thefts from parcels sent to Germany.[32] For example, the French prisoner *comité de secours* at Altengrabow camp reported that between 23 January 1917 and 10 May 1918 the total amount of material plundered en route amounted to 1,699 boxes of tins, 85 soup tablets, 1 saucisson, 88.25 kilograms of lard, 500 grams of chocolate, 750 grams of rice, 1.625 kilograms of soap and a 50-kilogram box of chocolate sent specially for Christmas.[33] The *Oeuvre Toulousaine de recherches et d'assistance aux prisonniers nécessiteux du Midi* complained to the International Red Cross on 3 October 1918 that it was receiving more and more complaints from Germany about parcels not arriving: 'the parcels of food sent from France do not arrive to our prisoners and deliveries are considerably delayed'.[34] It believed that this was a 'systematic' action by Germany against the prisoners.[35] The French collective biscuit deliveries were weighed leaving Berne and Copenhagen and weighed again on their arrival to allow prisoners and the Spanish inspectors to assess the amount stolen en route.[36] One British prisoner noted that 'it is quite a common thing to see a German sentry walking round with his pocket full of French biscuits which must have been stolen from their supplies'.[37] Yet although theft was widespread, it was only partial pilfering of parcels; a remarkable amount of the food sent still reached the *Stammlager*. Moreover, the items which were arriving in the prison camps from France are revealing. Prisoners were receiving chocolate, soap, lentils, breton sausage, sardines, corned beef, jams, figs, salmon and pâté de foie.[38] These were luxurious foodstuffs in Germany in 1918.[39] Wilhelm Doegen referred bitterly to the fact that 'hungry German guards' had to watch as French and British prisoners received goods from home which were no longer available in

---

[31] *Ibid.*, Rapport Mensuel de l'Interprète stagiaire de la DE Nord du GAE, août 1918, GAE, Nord, 1er Bureau

[32] ACICR, 432/II/26, 2.d.c.44.

[33] *Ibid.*, Altengrabow camp. Königsbrück camp reported in March 1918 that fifty-nine crates had been stolen en route. In January and February 1918, French prisoners at Parchim camp reported the theft of 22 kilograms of soap.

[34] ACICR, 432/II/26,1.c.44.   [35] *Ibid.*   [36] *Rapports des délégués espagnols*, p. 160.

[37] TNA, WO 161/99, no. 1032, Interview with Lance-Corporal Edward Burley.

[38] ACICR, 432/II/26,2.d.c.44.

[39] Importantly, in 1918 there was also some parcel pilfering in France. However, because prisoner rations were better in French camps, theft from parcels had less of an effect on German prisoners' health. SHAT, 16 N 1224, Rapport Mensuel sur les renseignements recueillis dans la correspondance des PG de la DE du GAC au courant du mois d'août 1918, QG, 14.9.1918.

Germany.[40] This was certainly true in some camps; a Canadian prisoner at Friedrichsfeld recalled that

The sentries used to watch us wash in the morning looking at the suds ... It's a wonder we weren't killed half a dozen times for we used to jolly these poor chaps outrageously. 'Is there lots of soap in England?' they would ask. And when we would of course answer 'Yes,' they would say, rather disgustedly: 'no soap in Germany. Everything all gone. No meat, no bread. No potatoes. Everybody's crazy in Germany.'[41]

Professor Engelbert Krebs, a theologian from the University of Freiburg, acting on behalf of the Committee for the Defence of German and Roman Catholic Interests in the World War (*Arbeitsausschuss zur Verteidigung deutscher und katholischer Interessen im Weltkrieg*) argued prisoners had chosen to be fed by parcel 'delicacies' rather than their 'sufficient' German rations; Germany, he wrote in 1917, had let 'not one single prisoner die' from hunger.[42]

In fact, the prisoners' access to such luxurious foodstuffs from parcels gave them considerable leverage to barter both with their guards and with civilians, and this actually appears to have made violence against captives *less* likely in 1918. There was little incentive for guards to mistreat prisoners when bartering with them was more lucrative. A British prisoner, Lance-Corporal Edward Burley, recalled that 'a German will offer 80 marks for a pair of boots and 7 or 8 marks for a tablet of soap'.[43] Burley described how, while working at a brickworks, 'sometimes I talked a little with the civilians who passed by ... and occasionally the children would bring us a couple of apples and ask if we had a pot of fat to give them or a piece of soap'.[44] Prisoners gained power from such transactions: an increase in prisoner–guard fraternisation occurred in 1918 as guards began to barter with prisoners for food. This fraternisation was accelerated by a change in the make-up of the camp guards as in many camps old men and young boys replaced guards who were removed to fight at the front. 'The guards in Germany ... are all men who are totally unfit to go back to the front or else they are composed of civilians with a band round the

---

[40] Doegen, *Kriegsgefangene Völker*, p. 62.

[41] Fred McMullen and Jack Evans, *Out of the Jaws of Hunland. The Stories of Corporal Fred McMullen, Sniper, Private Jack Evans, Bomber, Canadian Soldiers, Three Times Captured and Finally Escaped from German Prison Camps* (New York and London, 1918), p. 119.

[42] Engelbert Krebs, *Die Behandlung der Kriegsgefangenen in Deutschland dargestellt auf Grund amtlichen Materials, von Dr. Engelbert Krebs* (Freiburg, 1917), pp. 48, 135–6. Kurt Flasch, *Die geistige Mobilmachung. Die deutschen Intellektuellen und der Erste Weltkrieg; Ein Versuch* (Berlin, 2000), p. 352.

[43] TNA, WO 161/99, no. 1032, Edward Burley, 7.11.1917.   [44] *Ibid.*

arm or young boys about 16,' one former British prisoner stated.[45] Another said that the guards were young boys of sixteen or older men aged from forty-five to seventy.[46] One guard told a British prisoner that he had fought in 1870.[47] These guards were increasingly disenchanted with the war and had no incentive to drive prisoners hard. One prisoner was told by a guard 'that his children were starving, and that he hoped the war would finish very soon'.[48] Private J. McGinlay was told by his guards in late-1917 that

They were underfed: that they had practically the same food as the prisoners, but the soup was slightly superior. They were all discontented and spoke quite freely of it to me. They told me everybody was discontented about food ... The guards spoke to me about Liebknecht's imprisonment. They said they thought it a shame that a man should be arrested for telling the truth about Germany.[49]

Alec Waugh, a British officer prisoner, wrote of how a German soldier told him in 1918

You are not a father, so you will not understand ... but it is a most terrible thing to watch, as I have watched during the last four years, a little boy growing weaker and paler month after month; and I can tell you that when I look at my little boy, all that I want is that this war should end, I do not care how.[50]

Given the extent of this civilian hunger in Germany, the Allies' fears at the end of the war that their compatriots in German captivity would starve to death were not unrealistic; it remains remarkable that local populations did not plunder the prison camp food stores and that the parcel system continued functioning until the revolution. Yet the Allies fundamentally misinterpreted what was occurring in 1918 and the extent to which the parcel system was successfully protecting prisoners. Their misunderstanding was comprehensible: the death rate for French and British prisoners of war in German home front camps jumped in 1918 and the Allies immediately attributed this to hunger and to German forced labour.[51] Yet, in reality, the main cause does not appear to have been starvation among British and French captives, apart from a small minority of cases; nor does hard labour explain the sudden rise in deaths. There was another reason why prisoners started dying en masse in 1918 – the influenza epidemic which swept the prisoner of war camps.

---

[45] *Ibid.*; also no. 1060, Private Edward Page, 15.12.1917, and no. 1085, Private James Harold, 8.1.1918.
[46] TNA, WO 161/99, no. 1060, Private Edward Page, 15.12.1917.
[47] TNA, WO 161/99, no. 1090, Private Ernest Atkinson, 9.1.1918.   [48] *Ibid.*
[49] TNA, WO 161/99, no. 1092, Private J. McGinlay, January 1918.
[50] Alec Waugh, *The Prisoners of Mainz* (London, 1919), pp. 229–30.
[51] On the rise in the death rate, see Spoerer, 'The Mortality of Allied Prisoners of War'.

Table 7. *Number of British prisoner deaths for each year of the war according to survey of 1,159 burials in Berlin South-western Cemetery.*

1914	1915	1916	1917	1918	1919
14	98	19	75	943	10

This becomes clear from a survey of a large sample of prisoner of war graves. In 1922, the British Imperial War Graves Commission amalgamated the graves of British prisoners in Germany into four major graveyards at Kassel, Berlin, Hamburg and Cologne, with over a thousand burials each, and thirteen other minor burial sites with fewer graves. The grave records for 1,159 prisoners of war who died between 1914 and 1919, buried at one of the four major graveyards, Berlin South-western Cemetery, provide a representative sample from which British prisoner death rates across the war and more particularly, in 1918, can be calculated. Importantly, too, the age of the prisoner at time of death and the cause of death can also be analysed in many cases. The vast majority of these graves – well over a thousand – were of other-rank prisoners. This survey confirms that by far the most deadly year of the war for British prisoners in Germany proper was 1918.[52] For example, of those buried in Berlin South-western cemetery, more prisoners died in May 1918 than died in the whole of 1915 or 1917.

This increase in deaths in 1918 was not simply due to an overall increase in the number of British prisoners in German home front camps. While Germany did dramatically increase the number of British captives it held in 1918, from 45,863 other-rank British prisoners in June 1917 to 177,553 on 10 October 1918 according to Wilhelm Doegen's figures, the majority of these captives remained in the French and Belgian occupied territories after 21 March 1918, as the previous part of this book illustrated.[53] Moreover, the jump in the death rate revealed from the Berlin cemetery grave sample is greater than the jump in the number of prisoners held overall: Germany by October 1918 held four times as many British prisoners as in June 1917, but the grave sample shows the number of deaths in 1918 was 12.6 times higher than 1917.

It is possible that during the latter half of 1918, the increased death rate was influenced by the transfer to German home front camps of prisoner labourers who had been evacuated from occupied France and Belgium;

[52] This finding largely concurs with Mark Sporerer's conclusions that British prisoners had a particularly high mortality rate in 1918: Spoerer, 'The Mortality of Allied Prisoners of War', p. 130.
[53] Doegen, *Kriegsgefangene Völker*, p. 28.

Table 8. *British prisoner death patterns across 1918 based on Berlin South-western Cemetery sample.*

Month	Jan	Feb	Mar	Ap	May	Jun	Jul	Aug	Sept	Oct	Nov	Dec
Deaths	8	5	3	44	117	116	122	41	66	178	163	80

the mortality rate for these prisoners was high, according to British prisoner eyewitnesses. As the previous part of this book has shown, however, until October 1918, prisoners working in occupied France and Belgium who fell ill were usually hospitalised there and buried locally in the event that they died.[54] Therefore, although prisoners from the occupied territories may have slightly influenced the higher death rate in German home front camps, they alone cannot explain the massive extent of the increase.

Instead, the evidence indicates that it was the influenza epidemic of 1918 that was principally responsible for the rise in prisoner deaths. There were two periods of 1918 which saw a higher mortality among prisoners than the remainder of the year: May to July saw the first high wave of deaths; October to November produced the second. This correlates exactly with two waves of influenza which swept Germany in 1918, referred to respectively as the summer epidemic and the autumn epidemic by August Gärtner in the official German medical history of the war.[55]

Early post-war German histories appear to have underestimated the number of prisoners who died from the influenza epidemic – particularly during the second flu wave in October–November 1918, which coincided exactly with the outbreak of revolution, in part because due to revolutionary chaos local prison camp administration collapsed.[56] August Gärtner, in his post-war history, grossly underestimates the influenza mortality rate among prisoners in 1918, claiming that of the 2.4 million prisoners of war held by Germany, *in the whole year* only 217 prisoners died from the flu.[57] Gärtner's figure is totally incorrect given that in just

[54] See chapters 4 and 5 on deaths in the occupied territories. See the case of Private Mowbray Meades, a prisoner of war, who died of pneumonia in July 1918, buried at Lille. www.bbc.co.uk/history/war/wwone/humanfaceofwar_gallery_06.shtml, accessed 17.6.2005.

[55] Gärtner, 'Einrichtung', p. 254. Jay Winter pinpoints three influenza waves in Europe and North America in 1918, occurring in March, October and after the Armistice. According to Winter the post-Armistice influenza wave saw the deadliest form of the virus. See Jay Winter, 'La Grippe Espagnole', in Stéphane Audoin-Rouzeau and Jean-Jacques Becker, eds., *Encyclopédie de la Grande Guerre, 1914–1918. Histoire et culture* (Paris, 2004), pp. 943–8.

[56] Wilhelm Doegen, for example, makes little mention of the influenza epidemic.

[57] Gärtner, 'Einrichtung', p. 254.

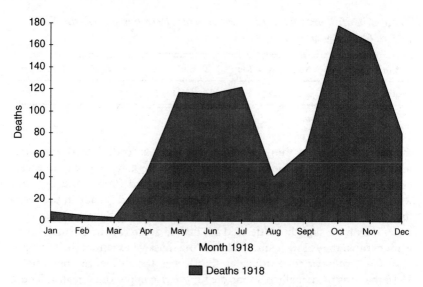

Figure 15. British prisoner death rate in 1918 based upon an analysis of 1,159 prisoner graves in Berlin, South-western Cemetery. Records supplied by the Commonwealth War Graves Commission, Ieper.

one Army Corps area alone, the *I. bayerisches Armee-Korps* region, between 11 October 1918 and 10 November 1918, 291 prisoners died of pneumonia resulting from the influenza epidemic.[58] He appears to have both underestimated influenza deaths and failed to count deaths from influenza complications such as pneumonia or bronchitis.

The two peak mortality periods revealed from the survey of prisoner graves in Berlin South-western Cemetery match other sources. Letters from Germany to German prisoners of war in France described an influenza epidemic among German civilians and in prisoner of war camps in July 1918: 'There is a very large number of sick in the prisoner of war camps, hospitals and forts. A lot have already died. Today again we buried three young Frenchmen aged between 23 and 28 years old,' a correspondent from Gmünd in Württemberg wrote.[59] The French censor noted in his September report on letters from July and August, that 'the flu, known as "Spanish" is raging all across Germany. The announcements of deaths

---

[58] BHStA IV, M Kr 13785, Nachweisung der Sterbefälle von Kriegsgefangenen im Kriege, 1914–1921.
[59] SHAT, 16 N 1224, DE du GAE, État-Major, no. 20, Rapport Mensuel de l'officier interprète de la DE du GAE, 14.10.18.

from pneumonia are very numerous.'[60] 187,000 Germans are estimated to have died of the flu.[61] In comparison, the national death tolls for citizens in France and Britain were estimated at 200,000 and 112,000 respectively.[62]

The influenza killed prisoners of war all across Germany. A French prisoner, Louis Bochet, interviewed in December 1918, recalled how 'around the 20 November 1918 there were a lot of sick in Stuttgart camp. Every day there were 7 or 8 deaths from Spanish influenza.'[63] An Italian prisoner repatriated from Kassel camp reported 'in October there were epidemics of Spanish influenza. There were a lot of deaths, French, English.'[64] On 8 December, the 17th German Army requested a British ambulance train to evacuate 500 sick British prisoners of war being held in a camp at Meschede, where there was an epidemic, reportedly 'due to overcrowding'.[65] In Sprottau prisoner of war hospital in Posen between 5 and 7 December 1918, thirteen prisoners died of flu-related respiratory illnesses.[66] In the first two weeks of December, in the same region, fifty-two French prisoners died from influenza or a subsequent lung infection at Sagan Reserve *Lazarett*.[67] There was also an epidemic at Schneidemühl camp.[68] The International Red Cross, assessing the post-Armistice situation, stated that influenza morbidity rates reached 90 per cent among prisoners in some areas.[69] In contrast, the rate of infection generally among belligerent populations has been estimated at 20 per cent by Jay Winter.[70] Prisoners in German prison camps, therefore, had a much higher rate of infection than civilian populations. The continual movement of prisoners, which was a feature of the German prison camp and *Kommando* work system, helps to explain the spread of the influenza, as

---

[60] *Ibid.*   [61] Dallas, *1918*, p. 199.   [62] *Ibid.*

[63] SHAT, 16 N 1224, Centre de rapatriement de Sarrebourg, Compte rendu des inter-rogatoires, Interrogatoire de Bochet, Louis, vient du camp de Stuttgart, travaillait dans un Kommando à Röhlingen, 7.12.1918.

[64] *Ibid.*, Interrogatoire Dominico Radia, Italian, 12.1.1919.

[65] TNA, WO 95/287, Original War Diary, Director of Medical Services, Second Army, October 1918, 8.12.1918.

[66] SHAT, 7 N 327–1, Kriegsgefangenenlazarett, Sprottau, dem Sanitätsamt VAK, Posen, 7.12.1918.

[67] *Ibid.*, Death certificates for prisoners from Sagan Reserve Lazarett. For an account of deaths from flu by a veteran see Emden, *Prisoners of the Kaiser*, p. 165.

[68] SHAT, 15 N 15, Tgm, Copenhague, 8.12.1918.

[69] Drs Frédéric Guyot, René Guillermin and Albert Meyer, 'La Situation sanitaire des prisonniers de guerre de l'Entente en Allemagne pendant la période de l'armistice (décembre 1918–janvier 1919)', in *Revue International de la Croix-Rouge*, 1e année, no. 2, in *Bulletin International des Sociétés de la Croix-Rouge*, 50e année, nos. 197–202 (January–June 1919), p. 141. See also ACICR 432/II/26,2.c.44 which reports influenza among French prisoners at Münchenberg and Puchheim camps.

[70] Winter, 'La Grippe Espagnole', p. 944.

Table 9. *Prisoners' age at time of death analysed for 674 graves in Berlin South-western Cemetery where the age record is available, 1914–1918.*

Age	18–25	26–35	36–40	41–55	Over 55
Number	328	274	59	12	1

does the fact that prisoners lived in such close proximity to each other. How the influenza first reached the camps remains an open question, although August Gärtner claimed that the civilian population passed on the flu to the prisoners.[71] The prisoner mortality rate was estimated at 25 per cent in the cases where the patient went on to develop pneumonia.[72] Influenza killed extremely rapidly. Its symptoms were terrifying: 'The disease might begin with a violent nosebleed, followed by a high fever, wheezing and finally a choking rattle that sounded like strangulation – for the sick person was indeed being strangled.'[73] Often at the last stage of the illness the patient went black in the face with bleeding from the nostrils.

The influenza epidemic was particularly shocking because of the young demographic it killed. The virus attacked young, previously healthy people especially virulently: prisoners of war who were disproportionately young men of military age were thus particularly vulnerable. An analysis of the 674 prisoner graves in Berlin South-western Cemetery for which age at time of death information is available reveals that 602 of the dead were aged thirty-five or under – 328 of these men were in the 18–25 age bracket.

A final point of importance is that the influenza epidemic was not the sole reason why prisoners died in 1918. Unfortunately, only a small sample of grave records – 212 – provided information as to the cause of death, so this analysis must remain only partial. However, it is clear that in 1918, there was also an increase in prisoners dying as a result of old wounds received at the front and in dysentery deaths. The increase in prisoner deaths from wounds can be attributed to the massive shortage of medical supplies in Germany, which meant that operations, nursing and medical intervention that earlier in the war had saved prisoners' lives were no longer possible. One wounded British prisoner treated at Gießen hospital in June and July 1918 reported that 'There were no drinking vessels; we used the parcel tins. There were no basins to wash in but there

---

[71] Gärtner, 'Einrichtung', p. 254.
[72] Guyot *et al.*, 'La Situation sanitaire', p. 141. Nicole Dabernat-Poitevin, ed., *Les Carnets de captivité de Charles Gueugnier* (Midi-Pyrénées, 1998), p. 221.
[73] Dallas, *1918*, p. 199.

Table 10. *Principal mortality factors in 1918 analysed for the 212 British prisoner graves in Berlin South-western Cemetery where cause of death was recorded.*

Cause	Wounds	Influenza	Pneumonia	Dysentery	Heart failure	Other – TB, diptheria, accident
Number	79	20	57	12	5	39

were two baths, and on one occasion there was hot water . . . There was no cotton wool.'[74] He also reported vermin.[75]

The shortage of medicine was also perceived by contemporaries as a major problem in dealing with the influenza epidemic.[76] In reality the virulence of the virus meant that there was no effective medical remedy available, even in countries not suffering from war shortages.[77] However, the hygiene problems in prisoner of war camps did contribute to infection rates. At the most basic level, prison camps and prison camp sick bays lacked soap for washing, which caused hygiene to deteriorate. The shortage of coal to heat camps was also a problem in some areas – especially as the second flu epidemic among the prisoners broke out in October–November.[78] This was compounded by a shortage of medical personnel – in November, due to the revolution and German demobilisation, military doctors stopped visiting prisoner of war camps.[79] There were local variations, however. A French prisoner, Constant Hallereau, recalled how in his camp at Freiburg 'before the Armistice the sick were neglected and visits by the doctor were rare; after the 11th of November, the sick were better treated'.[80] In some cases, German civilian doctors in local areas were too preoccupied with the civilian flu epidemic to assist. The shortage of medical personnel meant that new infections were not diagnosed and quarantine areas not established.

A comparison of the evidence from Berlin South-western Cemetery with the records of French and British prisoner deaths in the First Bavarian Army Corps region shows that in Bavaria too there was a massive

[74] TNA, WO 161/100, Interview no. 2357, Private Harvey Pink.   [75] *Ibid.*
[76] SHAT, 16 N 1224, Centre de rapatriement de Sarrebourg, Compte Rendu des interrogatoires, 27.11.1918. The shortage of medicines was reported in some camps in the summer of 1917: TNA, WO 161/99, no. 1032, Lance-Corporal Edward Burley, and no. 1085, Private James Harrold.
[77] Winter, 'La Grippe Espagnole', pp. 947–8.
[78] This was the case at Parchim camp. See Guyot *et al.*, 'La Situation sanitaire', p. 141.
[79] BA, R/904/77, f. 29, Regelung betreffend Kriegsgefangene, 16.12.1918.
[80] SHAT, 16 N 1224, Interrogatoire du PG français rapatrié, Constant Hallereau, 41e regiment d'infanterie.

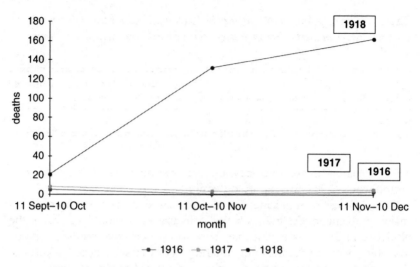

Figure 16. Comparison of French and British prisoner death rates in Stellv. GeneralKommando IbAK (Bavaria) in September–December period, 1916, 1917, 1918. From: BHStA IV, M Kr 13785, Nachweisung der Sterbefälle von Kriegsgefangenen im Kriege, 1914–1921.

jump in prisoner of war deaths in 1918 compared with earlier years. However, there were regional variations regarding which period of 1918 witnessed the greatest mortality rates. The summer influenza epidemic was less deadly in Bavaria. There, it was the winter epidemic of 1918, which saw the death rates among prisoners soar.

As Figure 16 illustrates, the death rate for French and British prisoners of war jumped sharply in the autumn and winter of 1918 compared with the same period in 1916 and 1917. The massive rise in prison camp mortality in 1918 becomes clearer if the deaths of other prisoner nation-alities, such as Russians and Italians, are considered as Table 11 shows.

It is extremely difficult to say whether this increase in prisoner deaths paralleled a large increase in the number of prisoners of war present in the First Bavarian Army Corps region due to a lack of documentation. Bavaria was divided into three Army Corps regions with their headquarters at Munich (First Bavarian Army Corps), Nuremberg (Second Bavarian Army Corps) and Würzburg (Third Bavarian Army Corps), respectively. Two of the largest prisoner camps in the First Bavarian Army Corps region were at Lechfeld and Puchheim.[81] At Puchheim camp,

---

[81] Doegen, *Kriegsgefangene Völker*, pp. 12–23, Verzeichnis der deutschen Kriegsgefangenenlager, deren Kommandanten und die Verteilung der Weltvölker auf die Lager nach dem Stande vom 10 Oktober 1918.

Table 11. *French, British and other prisoner nationality death rates in Stellv.*
GeneralKommando IbAK (First Bavarian Army Corps area).

Week	British deaths	French deaths	Number of British and French deaths	Total prisoner deaths – all nationalities
11 March 1916–10 April 1916	0	3	3	16
11 April 1916–10 May 1916	0	3	3	10
11 May 1916–11 June 1916	0	7	7	23
11 September 1916–10 October 1916	0	5	5	15
11 October 1916–10 November 1916	0	1	1	9
11 November 1916–10 December 1916	0	3	3	7
11 February 1917–10 March 1917	0	2	2	11
11 July 1917–10 August 1917	0	1	1	30
11 August 1917–10 September 1917	0	2	2	19
11 September 1917–10 October 1917	0	3	3	16
11 October 1917–10 November 1917	1	2	3	21
11 November 1917–10 December 1917	1	1	2	98 (82 Italians)
11 February 1918–10 March 1918	3	8	11	58
11 June 1918–10 July 1918	7	11	18	65
11 August 1918–10 September 1918	3	3	6	63 (41 Italians)

Table 11. (*cont.*)

Week	British deaths	French deaths	Number of British and French deaths	Total prisoner deaths – all nationalities
11 September 1918–10 October 1918	2	11	13	60
11 October 1918–10 November 1918	0	128	128 (almost all of pneumonia)	317 (291 are of pneumonia)
11 November 1918–10 December 1918	3	154	157 (pneumonia)	394
11 December 1918–10 January 1919	4	197	201	608 (583 of pneumonia)
11 January 1919–10 February 1919	0 All British have been repatriated	0 All French have been repatriated	0	194 (165 of pneumonia)
11 February 1919–10 March 1919	0	0	0 – all French repatriated	9

Note: Based on the available incomplete data in BHStA IV, M Kr 13785 Nachweisung der Sterbefälle von Kriegsgefangenen im Kriege, 1914–1921.

240 prisoners caught influenza in October 1918, of whom fifty-eight died.[82] From Table 11, it is clear that the British prisoner death rate in Bavaria remained low throughout the war, reflecting the far lower numbers of British prisoners in this region.

In contrast, there were a considerable number of French prisoners in the whole of Bavaria. On 10 October 1918, in all three Bavarian Army Corps regions there were 46,085 French soldiers and 17 French officers in soldiers' camps and 705 French officers and 827 French other-rank prisoners [orderlies] in officers' camps.[83] This represented an overall total of 47,634 French military prisoners in Bavaria in contrast to only

[82] ACICR, 432/II/26,2.c.44, Abschrift, Munich, Dr. Lukas, Oberstabarzt, to Dr Guyot and Dr Guillermin, 4.1.1918.
[83] Doegen, *Kriegsgefangene Völker*, pp. 12–23, Verzeichnis der deutschen Kriegsgefangenenlager, deren Kommandanten und die Verteilung der Weltvölker auf die Lager nach dem Stande vom 10 Oktober 1918.

Table 12. *Number of French and British prisoners of war in Bavaria on 10 October 1918.*

French officers	French soldiers	British officers	British soldiers
722	46,912	221	3,704

Note: taken from 'Verzeichnis der deutschen Kriegsgefangenenlager, deren Kommandanten und die Verteilung der Weltvölker auf die Lager nach dem Stande vom 10 Oktober 1918', Doegen, *Kriegsgefangene Völker*, pp. 12–23.

3,925 British, which helps explain the very low British death rate in 1918 in the First Bavarian Army Corps region.

Between 11 October 1918 and 10 January 1919, 479 French prisoners died in the First Bavarian Army Corps region. Without overall figures for how many French and British prisoners were in the First Bavarian Army Corps region, it is not possible to say whether this increase in deaths was proportional to an increase in prisoners, but given the huge number of deaths from pneumonia it appears plausible to argue that the increase was due to the influenza epidemic and not a simple increase in prisoner numbers. Importantly, the International Red Cross did not attribute the increase in prisoner deaths in Germany to an increase in the number of prisoners in the country.[84] Most observers blamed influenza; however, prisoners believed that malnutrition made captives more susceptible to the epidemic.[85] In reality starvation was not the issue: there was an increase in the death rate in the First Bavarian Army Corps region in late 1918 for prisoners of *all* nationalities – both the British and French prisoners who were receiving parcels and those nationalities which did not have access to parcel food such as the Russians and Italians. However, the belief that starvation was a factor created a sense of grievance in Britain and France towards Germany.

The influenza epidemic fitted perfectly with the eschatological fears harboured by many Allied civilians and prisoners that the war might end in apocalypse. Within Germany, the increase in prisoner deaths also had an impact on prisoners and their guards, causing panic. The prisoners' perception, passed on in letters and in interviews, on their return home, was that captives in German camps were dying in huge numbers. Two

[84] See for the International Red Cross assessment Guyot *et al.*, 'La Situation sanitaire', pp. 137–44.

[85] In fact, malnutrition is unlikely to have been a factor as influenza killed indiscriminately. The highest death tolls worldwide were in the United States, Switzerland and Asia, areas which had not suffered from wartime food shortages. Dallas, *1918*, p. 199.

former French prisoners arriving back in France described the situation in Puchheim camp as 'deplorable. Sanitary conditions extremely bad and around 20 deaths a day from influenza epidemic.'[86] Even without access to statistics it was blatantly obvious to observers that there were a larger number of bodies to bury in 1918 than in previous years. Funerals, grave-digging and an increase in the size of cemeteries had a significant effect on prisoners' mood. The morbid mood among French and British prisoners of war was also augmented by the fact that *other* prisoner nationalities in 1918 were dying of malnutrition. The Danish Red Cross representative Captain Lehrbach reported that 'the Russians are dying like flies'.[87] French prisoners reported to delegates of the International Red Cross that the state of the Russians was 'unimaginable' or that 'they could not understand how these prisoners were still alive'.[88] The news of the Armistice only increased prisoners' alarm – to die a prisoner after the war had actually ended was seen as desperately futile. One British prisoner wrote of the death of a friend on 1 November from

a disease called *Grippe* . . . How he suffered only God knows. The last 3 days or so he turned delirious . . . A prisoner from September 1914, how hard to die with peace so near at hand.[89]

It was this highly negative perception of German prisoner of war camps that thus dominated in Allied military and government circles from mid-summer 1918 to early spring 1919. The Allied experience of prisoner repatriation was greatly influenced by the fear that their prisoners were dying en masse in Germany.

This negative view was compounded by the situation of unprecedented chaos that developed after the Armistice due to the outbreak of the German revolution, which greatly hampered the process of repatriating British and French prisoners from Germany. With the outbreak of revolution, all discipline in prisoner of war camps collapsed as guards left, leaving prisoners to fend for themselves. The British and French repatriation efforts were unable to respond adequately to this chaos. The system of transporting food from outside Germany to the prisoners disintegrated: the deliveries of collective bread from Berne, paid for by the French

---

[86] SHAT, 15 N 15, Rapatriement, Inspection des PG. Inévacuables, nov. 1918–déc. 1919, Tgm to French GQG, 18.12.1918.

[87] ACICR 432/II/26,2, B d, c.44, Exposé de la situation des prisonniers de guerre russe telle qu'elle est comme par l'enquête préliminaire faite en décembre 1918 à Berlin par la délégation du comité international de la Croix-Rouge.

[88] *Ibid.*

[89] Extract from the diary of H. J. Clarke describing the death of Private Charles Kelly, in Hall, *In Enemy Hands*, p. 108.

government, were suspended on 8 November 'due to fears of pillaging'.[90] Parcel delivery to camps ceased completely in many areas; in others the parcels arrived plundered.[91] Even delivery of the insufficient local rations provided by Germany was disrupted.[92] Both the new German government and the Prussian *Kriegsministerium* lost control of the situation. Although still staffed by members of the old regime, the *Kriegsministerium* had lost its administrative power: 'the action of the ministry was practically useless'.[93] The death of the head of prisoner of war issues at the *Kriegsministerium*, General Emil von Friedrich, in late August 1918, added to the difficulties; his successor, General von Fransecky, had had little time to adapt to his new role when the revolution broke out.[94] According to the Danish Red Cross representative in Berlin, Captain Lehrbach: 'Colonel Franzseky [sic] is supposed to be in command of the prisoners' department of the war office but the former sergeant Schlesinger ... is the real Commander in Chief the War Office [sic], as the representative of the workmen's and soldiers' council.'[95] In Bavaria, Kurt Eisner, the leader of the revolution in Munich, sent a telegram to France asking for help, declaring that the Bavarian prisoner of war camps were in crisis.[96]

The dual command structure at the *Kriegsministerium* between Fransecky and Schlesinger was mirrored by the situation on the ground. In some areas camp guards elected their own soldiers' council, while in others the workers' and soldiers' council of the nearest town took charge. One French prisoner described how 'power is shared between the soldiers' councils and the former commandants and as a result there is anarchy almost everywhere'.[97] Some soldiers' councils allowed German officers to continue to administer prison camps provided they followed council orders.[98] Others drove the officers and commandant from the camps and left the running of the camp to the NCOs among the guard. At Mainz prisoner of war camp the commandant was deposed by the local soldiers' council.[99] In Rastatt prisoner of war camp, the use of the bayonet against

---

[90] MAE, Série Z, Europe 1918–1929, Allemagne 181, Prisonniers de Guerre I, Avril 1918–Mai 1921, Tgm from French consul, Berne, to Affaires Etrangères, Paris, 8.11.1918.

[91] General Dupont, 'Une mission en Allemagne. Le rapatriement des prisonniers', in *Revue des Deux Mondes*, 3 (1920), pp. 144–66.

[92] Guyot *et al.*, 'La Situation sanitaire', p. 140.

[93] Dupont, 'Une mission en Allemagne', pp. 144–6.

[94] Thomas Newton, *Retrospection* (London, 1941), p. 263.

[95] The National Archives, Washington, M 367/312 Oct 1918–Jan 1919, f. 0330, American Chargé d'Affaires, Copenhagen to Secretary of State, US, 28.11.1918.

[96] SHAT, 15 N 15, Radiogramme allemand, 10.12.1918, provenance – Nauen.

[97] SHAT, 16 N 1224, Centre de rapatriement de Sarrebourg, Interrogatoire, Sous-Lieutenant Gindre.

[98] Guyot *et al.*, 'La Situation sanitaire', p. 140.   [99] Waugh, *The Prisoners of Mainz*, p. 241.

prisoners was suppressed and guards had their insignia removed.[100] On 21 November the gates of the camp were opened and prisoners were given permission to leave.[101] Across Germany guards stopped enforcing discipline or hygiene regulations.[102] Some camp guards simply self-demobilised, leaving their posts to return home.[103] Other local soldiers' and workers' councils liberated prisoners in their area to create jobs for German workers.[104] Throughout Germany, this process was remarkably non-violent; the priority of guards was to dismantle the prison camp system as rapidly as possible and return home to their families. The socialist language of the revolution also emphasised international working-class solidarity. These factors meant that guards generally tried to act in a conciliatory fashion towards prisoners.

In some camps guards and prisoners celebrated together after the soldiers' council took over.[105] More generally, there was little violence against prisoners from civilians. The International Red Cross observers were amazed at the indifference of German civilians to the former prisoners visiting their towns.[106] In one German town, civilians voluntarily stepped off the pavement and symbolically walked in the gutter to make way for newly liberated British prisoners.[107] Many German socialists believed that the prisoners were fellow victims of an imperialist capitalists' war and made friendly overtures towards prisoners, including printing a pamphlet 'A Parting Word' distributed to British prisoners across Germany after the Armistice.[108] It illustrates the construction of a German collective memory of prisoner mistreatment where prisoner hardship was explained away within the framework of German civilian suffering from the blockade and reciprocal Allied behaviour. The leaflet addressed the prisoners as 'Gentlemen' and informed them that

Your situation has been a difficult one. Our own has been desperate ... Under the circumstances we did our best to lessen the hardships of your lot, to ensure your comfort, to provide you with pastime, employment, mental and bodily recreation. It is not likely that you will ever know how difficult our circumstances

---

[100] SHAT, 7 N 338 Suppl. f. 28, État-Major de l'Armée, Bulletin de renseignements, no. 25, Bade, 25.11.1918.
[101] Ibid.
[102] ACICR, 432/II/262.c.44, Siegfried Horneffer and Theodore Aubert inspection of Döberitz camp, 20.12.1918.
[103] Dupont, 'Une mission en Allemagne', pp. 144–66.
[104] Ibid., p. 147.   [105] Brown, The Imperial War Museum Book of 1918, p. 327.
[106] Guyot et al., 'La Situation', p. 143.
[107] Interview with Ernie Stevens, Emden, Prisoners of the Kaiser, p. 160.
[108] The text of 'A Parting Word' is quoted here from Emden, Prisoners of the Kaiser, p. 163.

have been. We know that errors have been committed and that there have been hardships for which the former system was to blame. There have been wrongs and evils on both sides. We hope that you will always think of that – and be just ... We are sorry that you saw so little of what we were proud of in the former Germany – our arts, our sciences, our model cities, our theatres, schools, industries, our social institutions as well as the beauties of our scenery and the real soul of our people akin in so many things to your own ... We hope that every one of you will go home carrying a message of good will, of conciliation, of enlightenment.[109]

The British prisoners who received the leaflet did not understand its meaning or the revolutionary context that had produced it. Most saw it as a final German insult.[110]

Despite the generally benevolent reaction of the guards to British and French prisoners after the Armistice, however, the situation deteriorated: the prisoners' own reaction to the revolution was a major factor in this. Many captives, upon hearing of the Armistice, refused to continue working for their guards, including work that was for their own benefit such as cleaning their camp or cutting firewood. The functioning of prisoner of war camps and *Kommandos*, some of which contained over 10,000 men, deteriorated badly. A Red Cross inspection of Cottbus I and II camps on 18 December 1918 found overcrowding, insufficient food, insufficient fuel for heating, complete shortage of medical supplies, hygiene regulations abandoned and total disorder.[111] At Döberitz camp prisoners were using the floorboards of their barracks for firewood.[112] Prisoners refused to take any orders from camp guards – encouraged by the knowledge that the guards were highly unlikely to enforce them.[113] A *Kommando* attached to Landau camp working at the Suker factory refused to continue working on 12 November despite the manager's best efforts.[114]

Prisoners of all nationalities on working *Kommandos* flooded back to the nearest main camp (*Stammlager*) in the belief that those in a *Stammlager* would be repatriated more quickly and, in the case of those prisoners on *Kommandos* where food had been scarce, because they thought that in the *Stammlager* they would be better fed.[115] This had disastrous

---

[109] *Ibid.*
[110] Similar leaflets were handed out to prisoners in Wurttemberg by the Executive Ausschuss des Arbeiter- und Soldatenrats, Stuttgart. HStA STUTT, E 135 b, no. 356.
[111] ACICR, 432/II/26,2.c.44, Inspection of Cottbus I and Cottbus II camps by Siegfried Hornelfer and Theodore Aubert. 18.12.1918.
[112] *Ibid.*, Inspection of Döberitz camp, 20.12.1918.
[113] Guyot *et al.*, 'La Situation sanitaire', p. 140.
[114] SHAT, 16 N 1224, Centre de rapatriement de Sarrebourg, Interrogatoire d'André Delanne, 27.11.1918.
[115] Mitze, 'Das Kriegsgefangenenlager Ingolstadt während des Ersten Weltkriegs', pp. 375–7.

consequences as it caused severe overcrowding, administrative chaos and a complete breakdown in discipline. Worse still, it increased the spread of the deadly influenza. There was overcrowding in the hospitals and those with mild influenza were mixed in with serious cases, causing the disease to spread.[116] The International Red Cross sent a medical mission into Germany consisting of three doctors and emergency medical supplies. It found that in some camps German medical orderlies 'refused' to assist the sick prisoners, whereas German doctors continued to care for them 'almost without exception'.[117] In other areas, medical orderlies were given long periods of leave by the local workers' and soldiers' council, leaving sick prisoners without adequate care.[118] However, 'almost everywhere the buildings were dirty; the toilets in particular were completely overflowing and the medical care was insufficient'.[119] International Red Cross observers stated that the 'negligence of the soldiers' councils in failing to observe the recommendations of the doctors aggravated the situation'.[120] This in turn increased the panic of the prisoners and their desperation to leave Germany at once. One of the most serious consequences was that prisoners who developed symptoms kept them secret in the fear that if they were admitted to hospital it would delay their repatriation.[121] The International Red Cross found that 'fearing they will miss the departure of the repatriation trains, prisoners only declare they are sick at the very last moment, thus infecting their comrades in the barracks and not receiving until very late the necessary medical care'.[122]

Given these circumstances, some prisoners reacted violently to the end of the war. French prisoners, hungry, in overcrowded parent camps and faced with an influenza epidemic became extremely frustrated at not being repatriated at once. They began to taunt guards and even to riot. In some camps, such as Friedrichsfeld, Dänholm and Eutin, order collapsed.[123] Prisoners in Strasbourg mutinied and liberated themselves.[124] Some soldiers' councils decided to allow prisoners freedom to come and go from their camps as they pleased.[125] Danzig was flooded with

[116] Guyot et al., 'La Situation sanitaire', p. 140.   [117] Ibid.   [118] Ibid.
[119] Ibid.   [120] Ibid.
[121] Ibid., p. 142. See also SHAT, 16 N 1224, Centre de rapatriement de Sarrebourg, Interrogatoire de André Luncau.
[122] Guyot et al., 'La Situation sanitaire', p. 142.
[123] BA, R 901/77, f. 14, Waffenstillstandskommission, Gef. no. 2194 to Erzberger, Ergebnis der Besprechung vom 10.12.18 über Kriegsgefangenenangelegenheiten, 11.12.1918; Doegen, Kriegsgefangene Völker, p. 10.
[124] SHAT, 10 N 218, CIPA, sous-commission des PG, 18.11.1918, Procès-verbal de la conférence du 18.11.1918.
[125] Guyot et al., 'La Situation sanitaire', pp. 137–44. Also SHAT, 16 N 1224, Centre de rapatriement de Sarrebourg, Compte rendu des interrogatoires, 27.11.1918.

thousands of destitute released prisoners from camps and *Kommandos* in East Prussia.[126] The German government began to fear that prisoners in Germany would revolt en masse.[127]

In particular, French prisoners caused problems in local German towns as, free in public after months or years of captivity, many behaved in an antisocial manner, becoming drunk and disorderly and harassing local women in the street. French prisoners' behaviour was far more violent in this regard than that of other nationalities – they were swift to riot.[128] International Red Cross observers reported how at Stuttgart camp the French prisoners 'at the moment of their departure destroyed and burnt everything they could not bring with them, including things that could have helped the Russians who have nothing. We tried to tell them this but they would not listen.'[129] A French general described French prisoners as difficult to discipline because they were *'exaltés par notre victoire'*.[130] There was marked triumphalist behaviour from French prisoners, which was directed at local German civilians and camp guards. It appears to have been caused by a mixture of vengeance, frustration at their slow repatriation and a desire to compensate for the fact that they had not been in arms defeating Germany at the point of the Armistice. The International Red Cross found 'a state of depression and discouragement' among the French prisoners in many camps due to their disappointed expectation of immediate repatriation following the Armistice.[131] The revolution also meant that prisoners were no longer receiving letters from home, which impacted severely on their morale.[132] In several camps, the situation descended into violence as guards, who had become increasingly nervous of their hungry and disorderly charges, resorted to using their weapons to impose discipline: shooting incidents occurred at camps at Langensalza, Mannheim, Sagan, Stralsund and Stuttgart in the six-week period after the Armistice. In each case, prisoners were wounded or killed by anxious

---

[126] 200,000 Russian prisoners were reported looting in the city. National Archives, Washington, M367/312, Oct 1918–Jan 1919, f. 355, Tgm from Copenhagen to US Secretary of State, 3.12.1918.

[127] Dupont, 'Une mission en Allemagne', p. 147. Also SHAT, 15 N 15, Tgm, M. de la Guerre to Em. Basch at Spa.

[128] SHAT, 15 N 15, Commission allemande d'armistice, Spa, Le Président de la Commission allemande d'Armistice au Président de la Commission Interalliée de l'Armistice, Général Nudant, 7.12.1918.

[129] ACICR, 432/II/26,2.c.44, B f B, Rapport présenté par MM. Correvon et Ch. Müller au CICR sur la mission qui leur fut confiée en Allemagne. Italian prisoners also burnt furniture etc. at Ingolstadt camp Fort VIII prior to leaving. Mitze, 'Das Kriegsgefangenenlager Ingolstadt während des Ersten Weltkriegs', p. 377.

[130] Dupont, 'Une mission en Allemagne', pp. 144–6.

[131] Guyot *et al.*, 'La Situation sanitaire', p. 143.

[132] Dupont, 'Une mission en Allemagne', pp. 145–7.

guards opening fire in response to an incident of ill-discipline – often captives attempting either to leave a camp without permission, to taunt or to riot.[133] In the incident at Langensalza, fifteen prisoners were shot dead and fourteen wounded when guards panicked at the sight of prisoners carrying wood.[134] Ironically, in shooting, guards were to a certain extent using the last resort open to them to restore prison camp discipline – which the Allies were demanding. Yet the remarkable point must be that more such violence did not occur. In the midst of the revolution, German guards remained overwhelmingly restrained in their interactions with British and French prisoners of war, in part, because following the Armistice these captives had gained new status as citizens of the victor nations. The massacre of captives in Germany which the Allies had initially feared in 1918 never materialised – during the Armistice period there was no inevitable dynamic escalation of violence against prisoners within Germany, despite the considerable tensions in the prison camps.

However, not only the German authorities and the prisoners of war were responsible for the strained conditions in the prison camps in 1918; the Allies too contributed to the situation, due to their failure to organise immediate repatriation. The French military were simply overwhelmed by the task. Neither they nor the new German government had exact figures on how many French prisoners were in Germany – the International Red Cross estimated there were 475,000.[135] Other French sources put the figure much higher, at 844,000.[136] In contrast, the British had approximately 190,000 military prisoners to bring home.[137] In addition, there was an unknown number of prisoners in the liberated areas of northern France and Belgium. Within five days of the Armistice, 22,354 French prisoners of war and 2,246 British prisoners liberated from the former German-occupied territories had arrived at the French army front.[138] The French army also faced the daunting reality of the liberation of all

---

[133] Hankel, *Die Leipziger Prozesse*, p. 328.   [134] *Ibid.*

[135] Guyot *et al.*, 'La Situation sanitaire', p. 139.

[136] SHAT, 15 N 15, Rapatriement. Inspection des PG. Inévacuables. nov 1918–décembre 1918. Commission interalliée permanente d'armistice, 19.11.1918; *Bulletin de l'Office d'Information*, Office d'Information des Oeuvres de secours aux prisonniers de Guerre rattaché à l'Agence des Prisonniers de Guerre de la Croix-Rouge française, 1918, p. 3002, cited in Cabanes, 'Finir la guerre', vol. II, p. 416.

[137] Statistics on the number of British prisoners vary. See Table 1 for further details. Wilhelm Doegen states that on 10.10.1918 there were 182,009 British prisoners in Germany. Doegen, *Kriegsgefangene Völker*, p. 28. Given that Doegen's figure cannot include prisoners evacuated from the front between 10.10.1918 and 11.11.1918 or prisoners evacuated from prisoner of war labour companies, it appears likely that the real number of British prisoners in Germany at the Armistice was higher.

[138] SHAT, 16 N 2380, Tgm, État récapitulatif du personnel passé dans nos lignes depuis le 11 novembre, 12 heures jusqu'au 16 novembre, 12 heures.

prisoners in German home front camps on the left bank of the Rhine, which they were due to occupy, as the Germans withdrew in haste under the terms of the Armistice.[139] On 18 November, the French still had no precise information on how many prisoners or camps were located on the left bank of the Rhine.[140] Recognising that getting food through to these prisoners by train was impossible, the first Inter-Allied Armistice Commission repatriation plan, drafted on 19 November, stated that these men would simply have to stay put and rely on the local population for food until the Allied troops took over the running of their camps.[141] The French threatened reprisals if the Germans did not ensure medical care and food for their prisoners on the left bank of the Rhine until their handover.[142] Naturally, the prisoners caught in this situation opted to try to reach France on foot, flooding an already overwhelmed French army, which rushed to establish repatriation centres for them.[143] Across Germany, the distances prisoners attempted to travel were enormous. Some officer prisoners who had left camps in East Prussia arrived at the Swiss border, where they were refused entry and finally ended up in Berlin.[144]

France turned to Britain for assistance but the British initially refused to lend them extra ships to transport prisoners.[145] The British also would not agree to the use of German ships manned by German crews in the Baltic, to repatriate prisoners.[146] The French then turned to the Swiss, who began to repatriate French prisoners using Swiss trains and agreed to send two trainloads of food a day to feed French prisoners in Germany.[147] It was a totally inadequate response to the food needs of the French prisoners in Germany, particularly as upon the Armistice the French had prohibited the sending of all individual parcels. In contrast, the British Red Cross sent trainloads of parcels from Rotterdam immediately after the

---

[139] SHAT, 16 N 2380, Maréchal Foch to US, Belgian and French Commanders in Chief, 16.11.1918, stated that 'the prisoners in the zone being evacuated [by the Germans] have been liberated en masse'.

[140] SHAT, 10 N 218, CIPA, sous-commission des PG, 18.11.18, Procès-verbal de la conférence du 18.11.1918.

[141] SHAT, 15 N 15, Commission Interalliée permanente d'Armistice, Note au sujet des dispositions relatives aux prisonniers de guerre, 19.11.1918.

[142] Ibid., Réponse aux demandes du mémoire du général Nudant au sujet des prisonniers de guerre, C. en Chef des armées alliées, 21.11.1918.

[143] SHAT, 16 N 2380, GQG des armées du nord et du nord-est, État communiqué des centres de triage des PG français venant d'Allemagne, 18.11.1918.

[144] Dupont, 'Une mission en Allemagne', pp. 144–6.

[145] SHAT, 15 N 15, Commandant Poupinel, Compte-rendu des questions traités à la conférence du 18 décembre sur le rapatriement des prisonniers de guerre.

[146] Ibid.

[147] SHAT, 10 N 218, CIPA, sous-commission des PG, Commission Interalliée d'Armistice, Ravitaillement des PG, 20.11.1918.

Armistice direct to the camps.[148] 60–70 per cent of these convoys reached their destination.[149] Georges Cahen-Salvador, head of the French *Service Général des Prisonniers de Guerre*, in his post-war account lauded Allied cooperation in collectively organising the repatriation of their prisoners of war from Germany; in reality the relationship between the British and the French was not unproblematic.[150]

The French had totally unrealistic expectations of the German government and army, insisting that Germany was still obliged to feed prisoners and to provide them with medical care: 'the German government is charged with the <u>entire responsibility</u> for the feeding and medical care of the Entente prisoners until they are handed over to the Allies … At the same time, the Allies will continue to assure <u>additional</u> sources of food and clothing for prisoners as in the past.'[151] The French desire to avoid all dealings with the German administration also delayed matters; Cahen-Salvador told a delegate from the International Red Cross that 'on no account did he desire any involvement of the Germans in the repatriation of French prisoners, except for their provision of military escorts for trains delivering foodstuffs.'[152] Also out of a feeling of 'delicacy' the French initially asked the International Red Cross to organise medical supplies to camps rather than sending in French army medical personnel.[153] There was also an over-reliance upon the new Inter-Allied Armistice Commission, which set up a prisoners of war sub-commission to organise repatriation with the Germans. In conjunction with this sub-commission the French produced three different plans for repatriation on 19 and 28 November and on 4 December.[154] It was only on 6 December that General Dupont arrived in Berlin to begin French repatriation efforts. In contrast, the British Red Cross was already in Berlin and British delegations were already at all the major German and Dutch ports organising loading prisoners onto ships.

General Dupont, in charge of French prisoner repatriation, informed Paris on 19 December that the existing French plan of supplying food to camps by rail from Switzerland was a disaster.[155] Finally, the French government realised that their approach was not working and the

---

[148] 'Prisoners' Parcels', *The Times*, 31.12.1918, p. 4.   [149] *Ibid.*
[150] Cahen-Salvador, *Les Prisonniers de guerre*, p. 277.
[151] SHAT, 15 N 15, Rapatriement des prisonniers de guerre, nov 1918–déc 1919, Ministre de la guerre to MM. le Général Commandant en Chef des Armées du nord et du nord est, 4.12.1918. See also Général Mangin commandant le 10e Armée to Mr le Général Fayolle, Commandant le Groupe d'Armées, 12.12.1918. Underlining in original.
[152] ACICR, 419/XX, Mission Clouzot à Paris, Fontenay sous bois, 8.12.1918.
[153] Guyot *et al.*, 'La Situation sanitaire', pp. 137–44.   [154] SHAT, 15 N 15 and 16 N 2380.
[155] Cahen-Salvador, *Les Prisonniers de guerre*, p. 279.

sub-commission for prisoners of war at Spa was abolished as the French decided on a more direct approach, imitating the British, whose prisoner repatriation was by now already under way.[156] General Nudant, President of the Inter-Allied Armistice Commission, wrote on 15 December 1918 that 'the slowness of the evacuation of our prisoners, due largely to the fact that transport by sea has not yet started together with the critical physical and mental state of our exasperated prisoners makes it absolutely necessary that new methods of evacuation ... be found'.[157] Nothing serves as a better indictment of the French repatriation failure than the fact that over 174,710 French prisoners had effectively walked home before the first organised repatriation began in mid-December 1918.[158] The chaos was almost total: the head of the French Red Cross admitted that neither the number nor the identity of repatriated prisoners was checked.[159]

Organised repatriation of many French prisoners in Germany did not begin until mid-December – no French officers even appeared in the other-ranks' prison camps until this point. In fourteen German regions, French repatriation had not yet begun on 19 December.[160] The first French ship only arrived on 24 December.[161] However, once the French repatriation effort finally began, it operated at an impressive pace, particularly given the hundreds of thousands of French prisoners requiring transport: by 14 January 1919, all French prisoners fit enough to travel had been removed from Germany.[162]

In contrast, the British reacted decisively to prisoner repatriation, even threatening to renew hostilities if the Germans did not re-establish order in their prisoner of war camps. The Württemberg *Kriegsministerium* was informed by Berlin that

A large number of French and British prisoners have been set free either due to orders given by local units or as a result of the carelessness of their guards. A number of them have reached the enemy armies by foot, arriving exhausted and inadequately fed. The British government has protested in the strongest manner

---

[156] *Ibid.*, p. 281; Dupont, 'Une mission en Allemagne', pp. 144–66.
[157] SHAT, 16 N 2380, GQG, État-Major, 1e bureau, General Nudant, Tgm 15.12.1918.
[158] *Ibid.*, 12.12.1918, Transmis au 1er bureau du GQG pour attribution, 2361/DA states that 152,356 French prisoners entered French lines between 18.11.1918 and 9.12.1918. SHAT, 16 N 2380, Tgm, État récapitulatif du personnel passé dans nos lignes depuis le 11 novembre, 12 heures jusqu'au 16 novembre 12 heures states that 22,354 French prisoners arrived between 11.11.1918 and 16.11.1918.
[159] D'Anthouard, *Les Prisonniers de guerre français en Allemagne*, pp. 3–5.
[160] SHAT, 16 N 2380, GQG, 2e bureau, Maréchal Commandant en Chef armées françaises de l'est à Maréchal Foch, 19.12.1918.
[161] Dupont, 'Une mission en Allemagne', p. 153.
[162] SHAT, 6 N 114, Fonds Clemenceau, Message from Général Dupont received 14.1.1919.

and threatened to use force against such a deplorable state of affairs. If, in the future, prisoners of war are not handed over in an orderly manner, a breakdown of the Armistice is to be expected.[163]

While the French tried to plan repatriation through the Inter-Allied Armistice Commission, the British government had circumvented this entire negotiation process, deciding not to appoint representatives to the sub-commission for prisoners of war at Spa.[164] Instead the British handed over the organisation of repatriation to the War Office, which set up an inter-departmental committee with Admiralty, transport, military and civilian input to get repatriation going. This committee did not wait for the results of negotiations with the German Armistice Commission at Spa or for the British military representative, General Ewart, to reach Berlin. Immediately after the Armistice the British Red Cross sent a team to Berlin to coordinate repatriation and food supply to camps with another British Red Cross section in Holland.[165] This led to a quicker improvement in camp conditions for British prisoners than occurred for the French. By 24 December there was 'ample food' reported in all camps in Germany where British prisoners were located and British medical officers had arrived in prisoner camps.[166] The British had repatriated 119,915 prisoners by 31 December – over half their prisoners.[167]

Repatriation was not simply a matter of mass transport logistics, however: the rituals of return, which families, localities and states developed in response to their returning prisoners, were crucial to the former captives' reintegration into their home societies.[168] In this regard, Britain was far more successful than France. The British saw their prisoners of war as heroic victims and even abandoned certain formalities in order that the men could reach home as soon as possible – clearing the interview and quarantine process to just a day or two at the main repatriation centres set up at Dover, Leith, Canterbury and Ripon.[169] Returned prisoners of war received a specially extended two-month leave; initially their French counterparts only received thirty days.[170] Weekly bulletins on the number

---

[163] HStA STUTT, M1/8, Bü. 230, Abschrift, SS. Berlin to Württemb. Ministerium für militärische Angelegenheiten, 27.11.1918.

[164] SHAT, 15 N 15, Note pour M. le directeur général des communications et des ravitaillements aux armées, 13.12.1918.

[165] Dupont, 'Une mission en Allemagne', p. 160.   [166] The Times, 24.12.1918, p. 8.

[167] Ibid., 31.12.1918.

[168] On the rituals of wartime arrival and departure in railway stations, see Gregory, 'Railway Stations. Gateways and Termini'.

[169] Tucker, The Lousier War, p. 123.

[170] SHAT, 16 N 2380, M. de la Guerre, État-major de l'armée, 14.11.1918, Clemenceau to MM. les généraux gouverneurs de Paris, Lyon, les régions 1–13, 18–20 et 21. This was later extended to sixty days.

of British prisoners repatriated were published by *The Times*. Prisoners were honoured by the nation upon their return: train platforms were decorated; bands played on their arrival.[171] The King issued a statement to British prisoners in December, personally apologising to those still in Germany for Christmas and assuring them that they would be brought home soon: 'The King greatly regrets that they should not have returned home before Christmas … He sends them his best wishes for as merry a Christmas as is possible under the circumstances and a happy New Year at home.'[172] Queen Alexandra and Princess Victoria gave out presents and food to repatriated prisoners in London Bridge Station the same month.[173]

The first ships of repatriated British prisoners received a warm welcome at Dover. All the harbour boats sounded their sirens and the town was bedecked with flags.[174] One prisoner described how 'when I got home to Peckham they made a hell of a fuss of me, Union Jacks were flying up the street where I used to live. From one bedroom to another strung across the road was one Union Jack with "welcome home Tom".'[175] Former prisoner W. A. Tucker reported that

all prisoners … suffer a sense of humiliation for having been captured and if only for that reason we did not look for or expect any tumultuous reception on our return home. When on the contrary this did happen it was so totally unexpected … it invoked in us an overwhelming sense of relief and gratitude …[176]

Tucker recalled how waitresses refused to charge him and how 'prisoner-of-war' was even cited on his Army Discharge Certificate in the section listing his military qualifications: 'I know of no other Army which regards capture by the enemy as a military *Qualification* … the intention was compassionate.'[177] Following their return home, every single British prisoner received a letter thanking them for their contribution to the war from the King that described them as 'our gallant officers and men'.[178]

In contrast, French prisoners of war liberated from the occupied territories were initially quarantined for four days, whereas liberated civilian prisoner workers were not quarantined at all.[179] Reports even appeared in the French press criticising conditions for those prisoners of war being repatriated from the army zone who were being held in dirty, overcrowded

---

[171] Dallas, *1918*, p. 240.   [172] 'To British Prisoners in Germany', *The Times*, 27.12.1918.
[173] *Ibid.*   [174] Brown, *The Imperial War Museum Book of 1918*, p. 326.
[175] Interview with Tommy Gay, Emden, *Prisoners of the Kaiser*, p. 184.
[176] Tucker, *The Lousier War*, pp. 122–3.   [177] *Ibid.*   [178] *Ibid.*, p. 182.
[179] SHAT, 15 N 15, C. en Chef des Armées Alliées, no. 747/CR. 23.11.1918.

camps, often waiting over a week for a train home.[180] One prisoner complained that while waiting they were being treated like pariahs.[181] The press reports matched internal army criticism of the condition of the repatriation centres. One report noted: 'the hygiene installations are poor. The men sleep in barracks on a very thin layer of straw. They only receive cold food because there are no beakers or mess kits available to distribute anything else.'[182] In February 1919, the issue was raised in the Chambre des Députés, where Député Léon Pasqual complained at how the repatriated prisoners were treated, demanding that they be spoken to as 'sons of France' and not as 'half-Boches'.[183] The International Red Cross also criticised the lack of heating and poor conditions on the trains repatriating French prisoners.[184] Prisoners received a muted welcome. One former French prisoner stated: 'at Dunkirk, I have to admit it was a disappointment; with all the crowds no one paid any attention to us'.[185] Some commanders even arrested former captives for taking sixty days' leave, because they were unaware of the regulations, which stipulated thirty days' leave for all ex-captives, only extended to sixty days if the captivity had lasted over two years.[186]

There was one additional outcome from the confusion of repatriation. The chaos of the French repatriation meant that men arrived home before their families had been notified that they were on the way; some even avoided officialdom and the *centres du rapatriement* altogether.[187] This gave the families of the missing further hope, which was fed by accounts of missing prisoners of war trapped by unrest in Polish regions of Germany and by the fact that tens of thousands of Allied prisoners, almost all of whom had not been registered and were presumed dead, had emerged from the occupied territories upon their liberation from German prisoner

---

[180] SHAT, 16 N 2380, Extract from *Le Populaire*, 'Comment on traite nos prisonniers', 19.12.1918.

[181] *Ibid.*

[182] *Ibid.*, Compte rendu de mission du médécin principal Raymond, Visite du centre de triage des prisonniers rapatriés de Woippy.

[183] Odon Abbal, 'Les Prisonniers de la Grande Guerre. La captivité. 1914–1954', in Jean-Marie d'Hoop, ed., *Guerres mondiales et conflits contemporains*, 145 (1987), p. 20; see also Odon Abbal, 'Die französische Gesellschaft der Zwischenkriegszeit und die ehemaligen Kriegsgefangenen', in Oltmer, ed., *Kriegsgefangene im Europa des Ersten Weltkriegs*, pp. 298–9.

[184] Cabanes, 'Finir la guerre', vol. II, p. 435.

[185] Relange, *Huit mois dans les lignes allemandes*, p. 13.

[186] Abbal, 'Die französische Gesellschaft der Zwischenkriegszeit und die ehemaligen Kriegsgefangenen', p. 298.

[187] SHAT, 16 N 2380, No.27.510 1/11. M. de la G. Bureau de l'organisation et de la mobilisation de l'armée, 22.12.1918.

of war labour companies.[188] It was little wonder that families of the missing began to believe that their loved one might also prove to be an unregistered prisoner. To satisfy the demands of the families of the missing, the French government increased the staff of its military mission in Berlin and set them to work throughout 1919 locating and registering the graves of dead prisoners and searching for any lost prisoners still in Germany. They only found one, who, ill in hospital, and overlooked during repatriation, was still in Germany against his will.[189] The small number of other former French prisoners discovered had remained clandestinely in Germany by choice, often due to a relationship with a German woman. Eventually, in summer 1919, the French government gave an amnesty to all former French prisoners of war still in Germany so that there was no longer any obstacle to former deserters returning to France.[190]

The British reacted similarly to the French, sending Adelaide Livingstone to assist the British military mission in Berlin to search for prisoner graves and locate the missing.[191] It was an almost impossible task. More efficient than the French, the British had carefully recorded the name and details of each repatriated British prisoner. Indeed, according to one recent assessment by Richard van Emden, on 9 January 1919, the British, cross-referencing their lists of registered prisoners, which had been kept throughout the war, insisted that the Germans should have another 36,000 British prisoners still to repatriate; the Germans had only 13,579.[192] The fate of the 22,421 missing prisoners remained unknown – it is possible that unregistered labour company deaths may account for most of them.

The Allies' perception that their men had simply disappeared within the German camp system caused anger. It fuelled the demand for war crimes trials, to punish those who had mistreated prisoners of war: once it became clear that extraditing suspected war criminals from Germany, as planned under Articles 228–30 of the Treaty of Versailles, was not realistic, the Allies compromised, accepting that the German Reich State Prosecutor would try forty-five cases, selected by the Allies, at Leipzig.

The results merely severely exacerbated French hostility to Germany: at the Leipzig trials, which opened in May 1921, the German defence tried to discredit the evidence of former French prisoners.[193] Following

---

[188] Dupont, 'Une mission en Allemagne', pp. 148–53.
[189] See the case of Felix Grea, SHAT, 7 N 327–1, Mission Militaire Française, Le médécin-major Rodolphe Strauss to Mr le Général Dupont, Berlin, 13.9.1919.
[190] Dupont, 'Une mission en Allemagne', p. 159.
[191] TNA, TS 26/21, German War Trials, Records of Prisoner of War Committee. See also TNA, WO 141/41 and TNA, FO 383/499.
[192] Emden, *Prisoners of the Kaiser*, p. 10.
[193] Horne and Kramer, *German Atrocities*, pp. 348–51.

harassment of French witnesses, the French abandoned the Leipzig trials in disgust to carry out their own trials of all known German war crimes *in absentia* in France.[194] In autumn 1921, Aristide Briand, the French Prime Minister, was lobbied by outraged French ex-prisoners of war associations who wanted renewed action against German war criminals; former French prisoners were deeply angered at the way ex-prisoners' testimony had been challenged by the German defence in court.[195] The French had wanted comprehensive punishment of all perpetrators – not just one or two token cases.[196] In contrast, many British commentators were reasonably satisfied with the limited results of the Leipzig trials. In 1920, the British presented Germany with cases against seven individuals accused of breaching the laws of war: three related to abuses against prisoners and four to war crimes at sea. While not all the original naval cases came to court, all three individuals accused of prisoner mistreatment, Karl Heynen, Emil Müller and Robert Neumann, were successfully tried and found guilty at Leipzig.[197] The three prisoner of war cases dealt with German violence against captives in two camps in Germany, at Pommerensdorf Chemical Works and at the Friedrich der Große mine, as well as at Flavy-le-Martel camp in occupied territory.[198] In the Friedrich der Große case, Karl Heynen, who was in charge of the prisoner working unit at the mine, was sentenced to ten months' imprisonment for beating prisoners; in the Flavy-le-Martel case, Emil Müller, the camp commandant, was sentenced to six months for personal acts of violence against captives and Robert Neumann who was charged with ill-treating prisoners of war at Pommerensdorf Chemical Works received a six-month sentence.[199] While the French understood the Leipzig trials quantitively, in terms of the number of Germans found guilty and sentenced, the British interpreted them symbolically.[200] As the British lawyer Claud Mullins wrote in his 1921 account of the trials: 'the punishment of individual wrong-doers is only part, in my opinion only a secondary part, of the vindication of Law and Humanity. Germany's war criminals were part of the system which produced and encouraged them and the condemnation

---

[194] MAE, Série Y, Internationale, 589, Archives de la mission de l'avocat géneral, Paul Matter, au procès de Leipzig 1921, f. 143, 8.7.1921; Horne and Kramer, *German Atrocities*, pp. 351–3; Hankel, *Die Leipziger Prozesse*, pp. 481–5.

[195] Horne and Kramer, *German Atrocities*, p. 351.

[196] Eduard Clunet, 'Les Criminels de guerre devant le Reichsgericht à Leipzig', *Journal du Droit International*, 48 (Paris, 1921), pp. 440–7.

[197] 'German War Trials', *The American Journal of International Law*, 16, 4 (1922), pp. 629–30.

[198] 'The British Cases', *The American Journal of International Law*, 16, 4 (1922), pp. 633–40.

[199] *Ibid.*

[200] Jean-Jacques Becker, 'Les Procès de Leipzig', in Annette Wieviorka, ed., *Les Procès de Nuremberg et de Tokyo* (Caen, 1996), pp. 51–9; Hankel, *Die Leipziger Prozesse*, pp. 481–5.

of that system is of greater importance than the fate of any individual wrong-doers.'[201] By 1921, the British view was that it was not necessary to try *all* perpetrators – the cases brought by the British at Leipzig were symbolic enough and the trials had successfully served a didactic purpose. By punishing some guilty German perpetrators, as an example, this would teach Germany as a whole the lessons of what Britain considered constituted civilised war practice. In sum, the outcome at Leipzig went some way to salving the British public anger against Germany over prisoner of war mistreatment that had built up in the 1918–21 period.

Whether this was true for British ex-prisoners is another question. Several of the sixty ex-prisoner witnesses who travelled to Leipzig to testify in the three prisoner mistreatment cases had to fortify themselves with drink before embarking on their journey to Germany.[202] Feelings ran high in the run-up to the trials – when the metropolitan police took additional statements at Bow Street police court from ex-prisoner witnesses who were unable to travel to Leipzig, the police feared the public would react violently towards the German representatives sent to attend.[203] In total, over 100 police statements relating to the three British Leipzig prisoner mistreatment cases were taken, at Bow Street and elsewhere from ex-prisoner witnesses, whom the police traced all across the UK.[204] Indeed, as news of the trials spread, many ex-prisoners wrote to the police investigators offering to provide statements on their violent treatment while in German captivity.[205] As one ex-prisoner, T. E. Mann, wrote: 'I myself am still suffering from injuries to my nose caused by the blow of a German rifle butt given for insufficient work accomplished whereas I could scarcely walk owing to weakness due to dysentery. Should you desire testimony from me I should regard it as a duty to dead comrades to give such.'[206] Mann was not called to give evidence as his testimony did not relate to mistreatment at one of the three camps involved in the Leipzig trials.

To conclude, Allied perceptions of prisoner of war treatment during the immediate post-war period were overwhelmingly negative. The chaotic experience of revolution and repatriation left the British and French

---

[201] Claud Mullins, *The Leipzig Trials. An Account of the War Criminals' Trials and a Study of German Mentality* (London, 1921), p. 15; p. 209.

[202] TNA, MEPO 3/1166, DOC Subject: war criminals, Metropolitan police, Criminal Investigation Department, Ref: 222/FC/1, 10/6/1921.

[203] *Ibid.*, Ref: 117403/3, 222/FC/1, 12/5/1921, To superintendant, p. 5.

[204] *Ibid.*, DOC Subject: war criminals, Metropolitan police, Criminal Investigation Department, Ref: 222/FC/1, 10/6/1921.

[205] *Ibid.*, Subject war criminals, Ref: 117403/3, 222/FC/1, 12/5/1921, To superintendant, p. 5.

[206] *Ibid.*, Tunbridge Wells Borough Police – ref. 37/21 to the commissioner of police of the metropolis, enclosed letter from T. E. Mann, 1/5/1921.

with a strong impression that there had been massive prisoner mistreatment in Germany. They blamed Germany for the post-Armistice chaos of the camps and failed to recognise that, in fact, the German revolution was remarkably non-violent towards British and French prisoners of war. The initial Allied 'memory' of German captivity formed during the repatriation phase in 1918–19 was, therefore, a radically negative and anti-German one. The disintegration of the prison camps after the Armistice also impacted on how ex-prisoners recalled their captivity. Although little actual violence occurred in prison camps in Germany after the Armistice, ex-prisoners interpreted the delay in their repatriation and the breakdown in the parcel system as an act of wartime violence against them. Coupled with the outrage at the condition of the prisoners liberated in the occupied territories, this made for considerable anger in Britain and France at German prisoner treatment. This helps to explain why the British and French felt morally justified in withholding their German prisoners after the Armistice.

Post-war memory narratives: the German experience of prisoner repatriation

The German experience of prisoner repatriation was also radically negative and increased hostility towards the Allies in the initial post-war period. In particular, the French decision to use German prisoner labour companies to clear the former battlefields caused immense anger in Germany; this will be explored here through an analysis of the experience of these men and the German response to their treatment. Given the chaos of the French effort to repatriate their own prisoners from Germany and the strains of demobilisation and the influenza epidemic, it seems remarkable that the French government would have attempted an additional mass transport project. But it did. The decision was made the day after the Armistice to move 100,000 German prisoners from camps in the French interior to the devastated northern regions to work on reconstruction and de-mining projects. This was to free up jobs in the interior for returning French servicemen.[207] The decision was taken to move these prisoners despite the protests by several prefects in the devastated areas that they did not want any prisoner labourers in their area, as there was no way of feeding

---

[207] SHAT, 16 N 2466, Compte-rendu de mission, Officier Capitaine de Terrier-Santans, Comité de répartition des prisonniers de guerre en sous-secrétariat de la présidence du conseil, 12.11.1918.

them.[208] These German prisoners joined those already in the army zone in French prisoner of war labour companies. In addition, those prisoners taken in the massive captures of July, August, September and October 1918 were also put directly into army zone prisoner of war labour companies. The men who by their mass surrenders had helped bring the war to a close were now the very Germans upon whom France would exact her revenge. Once again, rank was a decisive factor in determining prisoners' fates – officer prisoners remained in their more comfortable camps in the French interior.

The existing French prisoner of war labour company system in the army zone was massively expanded and its units were symbolically renamed as PGRL companies, which stood for *Prisonniers de Guerre des Régions Libérées*. The administration of prisoner labour companies also changed: the PGRL were placed under the direct authority of the French Prime Minister, Georges Clemenceau, and the French military.[209] The bitterness the French felt at the treatment of their own men in Germany is illustrated by the decision to employ repatriated French prisoners as guards over these German captives.[210] Similarly, in some areas German prisoners clearing the battlefields were forbidden to touch the French dead lest their touch dishonour them.[211] For Clemenceau, the return of France's German prisoners was not to take place until Germany handed over those whom the French accused of war crimes.[212] In the winter of 1918/19 there was considerable support in France for this stance.[213] The view was that, if French soldiers and civilians had to clear the battlefields, then German prisoners should too. The French emphasised Germany's mistreatment of French captives; an Inter-ministerial Commission, led by the *Député* Gratien Candace, investigating German treatment of French prisoners, presented its report to the National Assembly on 11 February 1919, severely condemning German prisoner mistreatment.[214]

Conditions in the French prisoner labour companies in the winter of 1918 and spring of 1919 were very poor. The massive influx of prisoners overwhelmed the French prisoner labour company system, which by spring 1919 contained over 270,000 prisoners.[215] At Connantre camp on

---

[208] *Ibid.*   [209] Delpal, 'Entre culpabilité et réparation', p. 129.
[210] SHAT, 16 N 2380, Compte-rendu de Mission, Officer Capitaine de Terrier-Santans, 18 et 19.12.1918.
[211] Delpal, 'Entre culpabilité et réparation', p. 131.
[212] *Documents on British Foreign Policy, 1919–1939*, E. L. Woodward and Rohan Butler, eds., 1st series, vol. I, 1919 (London, 1947), no. 25, Notes of a Meeting of the Heads of Delegations of the Five Great Powers, 1.8.1919.
[213] Delpal, 'Entre culpabilité et réparation', p. 130.
[214] Candace, *Rapport fait au nom de la Commission des affaires extérieures*.
[215] Delpal, 'Entre culpabilité et réparation', p. 129.

8 November 1918 there were no washing facilities or disinfecting facilities for 1,800 Germans who were 'in a disgustingly dirty condition'.[216] An investigation by General Anthoine on 24 December 1918 found that 'the present organisation of the prisoner labour companies is completely deficient'.[217] Anthoine reported that there was no system of command in place – company commanders were acting completely independently.[218] There was inadequate inspection of work camps.[219] The prisoners had no soap, bandages, access to showers or clean clothes.[220] A military report from the Department of the Somme on 18 March 1919, stated that 'In the whole of the second region there are 78,000 prisoners, of whom 16,000 are sick or mentally ill. Their output is far lower than it should be. In addition the lack of shoes is so bad that among the prisoners at the Amiens citadel, 60 out of 600 could not go to work.'[221] Lieutenant-Colonel Maquard, inspecting the prisoner labour company 113 on 12 February 1919, found that, although bedding and water were satisfactory 'of 338 prisoners there is an average of 60–70 sick per day. In my opinion this high number is due to the lack of cleanliness.'[222] The International Red Cross described the situation in the winter of 1918/19 as 'distressing ... caused by the too hasty sending of prisoners to the zone devastated by war'.[223]

The prisoners were sent to areas of the former battlefields where there was no habitation, road network or access to clean water. The work demanded of them was dangerous and their morale was extremely low, as they faced an ongoing captivity with no fixed date of departure. Self-inflicted violence became a problem: suicide rates jumped in the PGRL.[224] Other forms of violence also emerged; there were strikes and riots by the prisoners, and shootings by guards to restore discipline. An average of 1,500–2,000 'incidents' occurred per month in 1919.[225] The International Red Cross was denied access to the PGRL until May 1919. During its first inspection, its delegates reported that ten prisoners had

---

[216] SHAT, 16 N 2466, 3599/DA, 8.11.1918.

[217] *Ibid.*, GQG Des armées de l'est, État-major, Inspection générale du travail aux armées, No. 58 s/IGT, P. Anthoine, 24.12.1918.

[218] *Ibid.*   [219] *Ibid.*   [220] *Ibid.*

[221] SHAT, 16 N 1663, Visite du 18 mars 1919, reconstitution des régions liberées dans le département de la Somme et la partie ouest de la 2e région, Le général de division Dauvin, Aide-major general du personnel, P. O. Fontenay.

[222] SHAT, 16 N 2732, Rapport du Lt. Col. Maquard, a/s de la cie PG 113 à St Dizier, no.794, 12.2.1919.

[223] Comité International de la Croix-Rouge, *Documents publiés à l'occasion de la Guerre (1914–1919). Rapport de MM. Théodore Aubert et lieutenant-colonel Bordier sur leurs visites aux compagnies de prisonniers de guerre des régions libérées en France, mai–juin 1919* (Geneva, 1919), p. 13.

[224] Delpal, 'Entre culpabilité et réparation', p. 132.   [225] *Ibid.*

been killed by the explosion of shells while clearing the battlefields.[226] As the postal service was non-existent, many prisoners had received no news of their families for months.[227] General Anthoine was placed in charge of the PGRL in May 1919, and he set about improving the prisoners' living conditions. He reported the prisoners' mood as 'sceptical. They say they have been betrayed by the governments and by the German government in particular.'[228] An International Red Cross inspection in the winter of 1919, a full year on from the Armistice, found that the prisoners were well fed and in good physical health, but were still lodged in poor conditions:

Well-built camps are really the exception ... When it rains mud gets in every-where. Although the barracks and tents are heated there were many camps where the prisoners suffered from cold at night. Almost everywhere there is no floor, which is very regrettable during the wet winter months. But when one sees how the local civilians live, often in an even more precarious state, then one realises that it was not possible to do any better.[229]

Hardly surprisingly, the prisoners' letters were somewhat less under-standing: 'I can barely move, and in the camp one sinks up to the knees in filth, food bad, very thin ... the doctor comes here rarely if at all ... thus the prisoners are slowly dying and when will we be released?' one wrote.[230] While the PGRL laboured in poor conditions, those German prisoners still in camps in the French interior enjoyed better treatment: one wrote in 1967 of how prisoners awaiting repatriation enjoyed helping locals with the grape harvest in the French interior in 1919.[231]

Following the Armistice, the British and French declared all previous wartime prisoner exchange agreements null and void, leaving those prisoners due to be exchanged under the Berne Accords bitterly disap-pointed.[232] Worse, wounded or sick prisoners who would previously have qualified for exchange as physically unfit, seriously wounded, *Grands Blessés*, now remained in French or British captivity. After international pressure, the British did finally accept the repatriation of a small number

---

[226] Comité International de la Croix-Rouge, *Rapport de MM. Théodore Aubert et Lieutenant-Colonel Bordier*, p. 17.

[227] *Ibid.*, p. 19.

[228] ACICR, FAW 1, Rentrée des prisonniers allemands chez eux, 1919, août–déc. 1919, Rapport de M. Théodore Aubert sur son voyage à Paris, 26 octobre au 1er novembre 1919.

[229] ACICR, FAW 1, Rentrée des prisonniers allemands chez eux, 1920, Rapport sur la mission en France du Major G. Marcaurd [nov. 1919–fév. 1920]

[230] *Ibid.*, 7.12.1919, Fitz Heine Cie PGRL 233 fowarded to CICR by Volksbund zum Schutze der deutschen Kriegs- und Zivilgefangenen, Ortsgruppe Seelze bei Hannover, 6.1.1920.

[231] BA-MA, Msg 200 / 1187. Account by Carl Schmidt, p. 23.

[232] Becker, 'Le Retour des prisonniers', p. 71.

of wounded and sick prisoners in spring 1919.[233] However, the British and French continued to delay repatriating their German prisoners. Initially, it was stated in Article 214 of the Treaty of Versailles that repatriation would occur after a Peace Treaty came into force. Yet after the Treaty of Versailles was finalised, the Allies agreed that German prisoners would not be repatriated until after the ratification of the treaty by Germany and by three of the other powers involved.[234] Clemenceau also continued to delay any planning for the repatriation of German prisoners by refusing to appoint a French representative to the repatriation commission planned for in Article 215 of the treaty.[235]

It took some time before the German government realised that France saw the prisoners as long-term reconstruction labourers. The new German government initially reacted optimistically to the situation, with Matthias Erzberger, the German representative to the Armistice Commission, proclaiming in December 1918 that the repatriation delay was only a temporary short-term disruption.[236] Having already repatriated British and French prisoners from Germany, it was no longer possible for Germany to inflict reprisals on Allied prisoners to improve French treatment of German captives. All the German government could do was issue verbal protests. This, in turn, led German prisoners and their families to suspect that the Weimar government actually did not wish for the prisoners back and saw them as potential counter-revolutionaries.[237] It was an unfair slur given Erzberger's frustration with the repatriation delay, but it had considerable impact. The prisoners and their families became increasingly alienated from the new German Republic.[238]

Britain initially endorsed the French stance, moving 10,000 prisoners from the UK to France following the Armistice.[239] These men joined 192,298 German prisoners working in France and Belgium in British prisoner of war labour companies.[240] As a result of the massive captures in the last three months of the war, conditions in British prisoner of war

---

[233] Jakob Reinhardt, 'Die Zurückführung der deutschen Kriegsgefargenen aus Frankreich', *Süddeutsche Monatshefte*, 11, 22 (August 1925), p. 11.

[234] ACICR, FAW 1, Rentrée des prisonniers allemands chez eux, Protest note by CICR to Supreme Interallied Council, 22.8.1919.

[235] *Ibid.*

[236] ACICR, FAW 1, Reconstruction des régions devastées, Bulletin de l'office d'information, 15.12.1918, communiqué officiel allemand, signed Erzberger, published in *Frankfurter Zeitung*, 23.11.1918.

[237] Gerhard Rose, *Krieg nach dem Kriege. Der Kampf des deutschen Volkes um die Heimkehr seiner Kriegsgefangenen* (Dortmund, 1920), pp. 9–11.

[238] *Ibid.*, p. 10.   [239] TNA, WO 95/26, Adjutant General's War Diary, March 1919.

[240] TNA, WO 161/82, No. of prisoners in prisoner of war labour companies on 6.12.1918, p. 161.

labour companies deteriorated in winter 1918. The RAMC officer commanding the Fourth Prisoner of War Convalescent Depot at Trouville described the arrival on 7 March 1919 of German prisoners who had been working in British labour companies: 'They were obviously unfit ... Mostly emaciated and melancholie [sic] in appearance.'[241] At his convalescent depot these prisoners enjoyed a milder regime, with circus performances and a Whit Monday sports day.[242] In contrast, those German prisoners being held in prison camps in the UK were very well treated in 1919, as revealed by the Swiss legation reports on its frequent inspections of camps and working units.[243]

Once the Treaty of Versailles was signed, the British and American attitudes changed. They were now keen to return their German charges; the German prisoners themselves were desperate to return home.[244] On 24 July 1919, the liberal press in Britain began to call for the repatriation of the German prisoners.[245] The International Red Cross also issued a formal protest letter to the Supreme Inter-Allied Council on 22 August 1919.[246] At a meeting of the delegates of the five Allied and Associated Powers on 27 August 1919, the British and Americans pressed the French to allow prisoner repatriation to begin before the Versailles Treaty ratification stipulations had been met.[247] The British representative Sir Arthur Balfour stated that the retention of the prisoners was costing the British and Americans 'over £150,000 a day'.[248] Clemenceau refused to compromise, asking the British and Americans to give France their German prisoners instead of repatriating them to Germany. The outcome of the meeting was an agreement that 'an Inter-Allied Commission of one military and one civil [sic] member from each of the five Powers be set up at once to begin repatriation of German prisoners, starting with prisoners held by the British and American armies'.[249] Despite French reluctance, the British and Americans were going ahead with repatriation.

The British began repatriation in September 1919 and it was completed on 1 November 1919.[250] Clemenceau, however, remained obstinate, despite pressure from both Generalissimo Foch and General Anthoine

[241] TNA, WO 95/4/23, War Diary No. 4 Prisoner of War Convalescent Depot, Trouville, 7.3.1919.
[242] Ibid., 8.6.1919; 10.6.1919.   [243] See the numerous reports in TNA, FO 383/506.
[244] See, for example, TNA, FO 383/506, f. 310, petition for release from German prisoners of war in Brocton camp in the UK, 23/3/1919
[245] ACICR, FAW 1, Rentrée des PG allemands chez eux, Memo, n.d.
[246] Ibid., CICR to Conseil suprême Interalliée, Paris, 22.8.1919.
[247] Documents on British Foreign Policy, ed. E. L. Woodward and Rohan Butler, 1st series, vol. I (London, 1947), no. 44, Notes of a Meeting of the Heads of Delegations of the Five Great Powers held in M. Pichon's room at the Quai d'Orsay, 27.8.1919.
[248] Ibid.   [249] Ibid.   [250] TNA, WO 161/82, p. 634.

to repatriate.[251] By October 1919, many in the French army were now in favour of repatriation. General Anthoine told the International Red Cross in October 1919:

Only the action of the Prime Minister is required [to start repatriation]. His restraint is due to motives of internal order, elections, labour needs ... or due to questions of international diplomacy, retention as a means of pressure ... These are the rumours that one hears. It is the affair of Clemenceau alone. In any case the prisoners are profoundly unhappy and the excess of unhappiness makes them eloquent.[252]

French officers in charge of prisoners felt 'separated from their loved ones and were the prisoners of the prisoners of war'.[253] The French position on repatriation had become internationally isolated following the signing of the Peace Treaty and the repatriation of German prisoners by France's Allies. Yet Clemenceau remained adamant; for him, the German prisoners remained perpetrators of the war rather than its victims:

If the repatriation of prisoners by our Allies began in September it is because the French government was unable to oppose it. None of our Allies was as badly injured in its emotions and its interests as the population of the north of France was. How can this population, wandering in the ruins of their homes ... accept to see the German prisoners, employed upon work of the utmost urgency ... leave France before the time appointed by the Treaty of Versailles, which fixed the end of their captivity on the definitive ratification – the entry into force of the treaty?[254]

It was not until 21 January 1920 that France finally began to repatriate her German prisoners of war.[255] For some on the French right, the prisoners' anger towards France remained incomprehensible. Maurice Barrès reported that the repatriated prisoners left with a powerful and 'deaf' hatred for France: 'These German prisoners have no reason to hate us. They hate us all the same.'[256]

In Germany, the Allies' retention of German prisoners of war was seen as irrational, cruel and motivated purely by a vindictive victor's desire for revenge. A massive public campaign was launched to bring the prisoners home. In many cases this campaign was spearheaded by women

[251] SHAT, 6 N 114, Foch to Erzberger, 16.1.1919.
[252] ACICR, FAW 1, Rentrée des prisonniers allemands chez eux, 1919, Rapport de M. Théodore Aubert sur son voyage à Paris le 26 octobre 1919, Meeting with General Anthoine, 30.10.1919, p. 11.
[253] Ibid., Rentrée des prisonniers allemands chez eux 1920.1/1, Rapport au CICR sur la mission en France du Major G. Marcaurd [nov. 1919–fév. 1920].
[254] Becker, 'Le retour des prisonniers', p. 73.
[255] Cabanes, 'Finir la guerre', vol. II, p. 460.
[256] Maurice Barrès, 'Dans quel ésprit les prisonniers allemands quittent la France', Echo de Paris, 8.3.1920.

who wrote to neutral states, to the International Red Cross and even to Clemenceau himself to ask for their menfolk to be returned. The following extract is typical of the letters written to the International Red Cross on behalf of the ill relatives of prisoners, requesting that an individual captive be released: 'His two brothers fell in the war and his mother suffers greatly ... Her health appears very bad.'[257] Often the letters to the Red Cross took the form of all female petitions from German women.[258] Such petitions were a significant form of female political mobilisation. Even children wrote, asking for prisoners to be released. The five Loffler siblings living in Rübgarten, near Tübingen, in Germany, wrote on 9 December 1919 to the International Committee of the Red Cross in Geneva to ask for the return of their eldest brother Wilhelm from France as a Christmas present as: 'Our mother is always crying over our Wilhelm because he still has not come home ... We five siblings beg so dearly for help so that our good Wilhelm can come home to us by Christmas. We wish for no other presents if our brother comes home so that our mother will be well again.'[259] The International Red Cross was no Father Christmas. To all such letters, it replied that it could not intervene in individual cases unless a prisoner was sick.

The anger which Germans felt at the withholding of their prisoners cannot be underestimated. The French chargé d'affaires in Berlin stated 'there is not a day when women do not come to complain in the name of the prisoners' families'.[260] Erzberger received pleading letters from all across Germany.[261] One correspondent wrote in February 1919:

My son was captured after being wounded by shrapnel in October 1918 ... According to his last letter, of 25 December 1918, he was in a British hospital in France. The Prisoner of War Information Association in Wiesbaden told us on the 18th of this month that he is sick with a fever of unknown cause. We are deeply worried about the fate of our 19 year old boy who is barely out of children's shoes.[262]

The son of one prisoner wrote to the International Red Cross to ask if he could take his father's place.[263] Other writers pleaded for the return of prisoners whose mothers or wives were dying, some enclosing medical certificates.[264] A nurse wrote to the International Red Cross:

---

[257] ACICR, FAW 1, Rentrée des prisonniers allemands chez eux, 1919, Elisabeth Müller to CICR, 14.12.1919.
[258] *Ibid.*   [259] *Ibid.*, no. 1/1 août–décembre 1919, Loffler.
[260] Cabanes, 'Finir la guerre', vol. II, p. 454.
[261] BA, WAKO R 904.89, and BA, WAKO R 904.83.
[262] *Ibid.*, Altenkirchen, L. Hilger to M. Erzberger, 22.2.1919.
[263] ACICR, FAW 1, Rentrée des prisonniers allemands chez eux, 1920, 1/1. Red Cross Hannover to CICR, case of August Theile. 22.1.1920.
[264] *Ibid.*

The wife of the prisoner Ersatz Reservist Friedrich Güth ... in Lille depot France is gravely sick and according to the doctor has only a short while left to live. She cries and frets the whole day to see her husband one last time and there are two dependent children, who are robbed of their father and provider through the withholding of the prisoners ... the children will be without protection or help after the death of their mother.[265]

The financial hardship suffered by the families of prisoners led to the Weimar government making a one-off payment of 200 Marks to prisoners' dependants in December 1919.[266]

Demonstrations for the prisoners' return were held in many German urban centres in 1919, often attended by thousands of people.[267] A demonstration held in the fifty-five largest towns in Württemberg on 16 November 1919 attracted over 50,000 people according to the *Volkshilfe für Württ. Kriegs- und Zivilgefangene*.[268] On 9 November 1919, a demonstration at Cologne-Nippes town hall attracted several thousand families.[269] Public mobilisation was swift and occurred at grassroots level. Gerhard Rose, a former leader of the *Volksbund zum Schutze der deutschen Kriegs- und Zivilgefangenen*, described the French refusal to repatriate German prisoners as an action carried out 'to satisfy their hate'.[270] In criticising the French action, Rose spoke for many Germans. Founded after the Armistice, the *Volksbund zum Schutze der deutschen Kriegs- und Zivilgefangenen* had 3,173 local branches across Germany and Rose claimed it had five million members by October 1919, a remarkable popular mobilisation in a country in revolution, although Rose's figure may have been exaggerated: other sources put membership at 350,000 in spring 1920.[271] Those Germans signing up to the *Volksbund* supported its campaign to get the prisoners home, and shared a perception that the French action was unjust. This perception was endorsed by leading German politicians. Walther Rathenau wrote: 'It is outrageous ... that our prisoner fellow citizens do not return home.'[272] He described the situation as 'slavery'.[273] Philipp Scheidemann, German Chancellor in

---

[265] *Ibid.*, Heidelberg, Frau Güth to CICR, 20.11.1919.

[266] *Kölnische Zeitung*, 15.12.1919.

[267] See the letters outlining protests in BA, WAKO R 904.83; ACICR, FAW 1, Rentrée des prisonniers allemands chez eux, dossiers 1919 and 1920; SHAT, 6 N 114.

[268] ACICR, FAW 1, Rentrée des prisonniers allemands chez eux, 1919, Tgm Stuttgart to CICR, 18.11.1919.

[269] SHAT, 6 N 114, Le Maréchal Foch to Mr le Président du Conseil, Ministre de la Guerre, 15.11.1919.

[270] Rose, *Krieg nach dem Kriege*, p. 54.

[271] *Ibid.*, p. 51; see Pöppinghege's contrasting figures: Rainer Pöppinghege, '"Kriegsteilnehmer zweiter Klasse"? Die Reichsvereinigung ehemaliger Kriegsgefangener, 1919–1933', *Militärgeschichtliche Zeitschrift*, 64 (2005), p. 401.

[272] *Frankfurter Zeitung*, 1.2.1919.   [273] *Ibid.*

spring 1919, stated: 'I believe the whole world must join with us in crying out against this last insult to all humanity.'[274] There was considerable hostile German press coverage of the French decision throughout 1919, with headlines such as 'the heartless war against German mothers and women'.[275]

The year following the war thus saw a radicalisation of German war memory around the image of the suffering innocent German prisoner. The Allies' retention of German prisoners became a popular metaphor for what Germans perceived as the wider unjust punishment of their country by their enemies. The prisoner repatriation issue was thus interpreted as a tale of German victimisation. A key part of this process was the emergence of a powerful German narrative in 1919 in popular publications, press and political circles that portrayed Germany's own wartime prisoner treatment as chivalrous, honourable and fair; wartime German violence against Allied prisoners was utterly occluded. This discourse created the impression that the Allies had no just moral grounds for their action in withholding German captives. While it initially developed in support of the campaign for the release of German prisoners from Allied captivity, ultimately it determined the popular German understanding of Germany's own prisoner of war treatment long after the prisoner repatriation phase had ended. It also reflected an economic imperative to exonerate Germany from prisoner mistreatment accusations: annex one to part VIII of the Treaty of Versailles held Germany responsible (under Article 232) for the 'damage caused by any kind of maltreatment of prisoners of war', and for 'the cost of assistance by the Government of the Allied and Associated Powers to prisoners of war and to their families'.[276]

This radicalisation of a German sense of victimisation across 1919 can clearly be seen to have affected the main German domestic investigation into whether the German army had mistreated Allied prisoners. In November 1918, only weeks after the Armistice, Matthias Erzberger, head of the German Armistice Commission, appointed the well-known pacifist and international law expert Professor Walther Schücking of Marburg University to head an independent German commission of enquiry into Allied accusations of prisoner mistreatment.[277] Erzberger initially

---

[274] *Ibid.*, 7.2.19.   [275] *Deutsche Allgemeine Zeitung*, 16.8.1919.
[276] Doegen, *Kriegsgefangene Völker*, pp. 1–2; Versailles Treaty, Annex 1 to Article 232, Articles 214–24, no. 1 and no. 6. See also Institute of International Affairs, *A History of the Peace Conference of Paris*, vol. III (London, 1920), Appendix 1, pp. 209–11.
[277] For a brief history of the commission see Hankel, *Die Leipziger Prozesse*, pp. 321–32. On Schücking's pacifism during the war see David Welch, *Germany, Propaganda and Total War, 1914–1918. The Sins of Omission* (London, 2000), p. 137.

emphasised that the commission was to objectively investigate possible German war crimes; its establishment was to show 'that the new Republican German government has decided to act harshly and without regard for rank or position against each individual who is guilty of breaching either the orders of the authorities or the laws of humanity in his treatment of prisoners'.[278] However, Erzberger's comments revealed the problem that was to dog the commission – it could not conceive that prisoner mistreatment might actually have been ordered by the German High Command. The Schücking Commission was initially relatively objective, setting out to establish through a case-by-case examination whether international law had been broken. Indeed, Schücking admitted that it was modelled on the British Government Committee on the Treatment by the Enemy of British Prisoners of War, which had impressed German observers during the conflict.[279] The Commission drew on the Reichstag peace movement's work during the war to investigate and criticise crimes against Allied prisoners of war.[280] By December 1918, Professor Schücking had accumulated 1,100 volumes of individual cases of complaints.[281] Faced with an overwhelming task of investigation, the commission narrowed its field of enquiry to serious cases where prisoners had died or cases where the Allies had issued diplomatic protest notes.[282]

The move by Erzberger to establish the Schücking Commission reflected the view of many left-wing and centre liberal German lawyers, administrators and politicians in November and December 1918 who believed that the only way to heal the wounds of the war was to strengthen and rebuild international law.[283] Walther Schücking even wrote a book on the need to restore international law, which he considered to be 'in crisis' following the conflict.[284] At the first sitting of the Schücking Commission in December 1918, he spoke of the 'general impression of the present day that only a return to the idea of law can save us all from the terrible misery caused to the civilised world by the war for power'.[285] However, by 1920,

---

[278] Hankel, *Die Leipziger Prozesse*, p. 325.

[279] ACICR, 431/III/j/c.31, Walther Schücking, 'Die deutsche Untersuchungskommission. Völkerrechtswidrige Behandlung der Kriegsgefangenen', *Deutsche Allgemeine Zeitung*, 23.12.1918.

[280] ACICR, 432/II/26,2.c.44, Commission neutre à Berlin – 1918, 432/II/26.B.b, Mission Bossier, 17.12.1918.

[281] *Ibid.*   [282] Hankel, *Die Leipziger Prozesse*, p. 326.

[283] See, for example, Clemens Plassmann, *Die deutschen Kriegsgefangenen in Frankreich 1914–1920. Beiträge zur Handhabung und zum Ausbau des internationalen Kriegsgefangenenrechtes, von Clemens Plassmann* (Berlin, 1921).

[284] Walther Schücking, *Die Völkerrechtliche Lehre des Weltkrieges* (Leipzig, 1918), pp. 1–2.

[285] *Berliner Tageblatt*, 5.12.18, 'Die Behandlung der Kriegsgefangenen. Die erste Sitzung der Untersuchungskommission.'

when the Commission published its first report into prisoner abuses, it had become partisan, consulting few Allied witnesses and accepting the word of senior German military figures without question. It found individual prison camp guards guilty of breaching international law in only four cases, three of which occurred after the Armistice.[286] In twenty-one cases the commission was unable to reach a conclusion, due to insufficient evidence, and in eleven cases the commission found no breach of international law had taken place.[287] Deference to the German military was a major problem for the civilians sitting on the commission. Ultimately, its report almost entirely exonerated Germany.[288]

At the same time as the Schücking Commission was established, the Prussian Ministry for War, the *Kriegsministerium*, also issued its own defence of German prisoner treatment. General von Fransecky, the post-war head of the prisoner of war department at the *Kriegsministerium*, appointed Wilhelm Doegen to produce a book on Germany's prisoner treatment.[289] Doegen was a former *Gymnasium* school teacher who had spent the war visiting German home front prisoner of war camps to research and record the different languages spoken by prisoners of war with the Prussian Phonogram Commission, in order to advance the academic study of linguistics. Selected for his credentials as a civilian and a scholar who had worked with prisoners of war, Doegen was provided with access to *Kriegsministerium* archives and, in 1919, published *Kriegsgefangene Völker. Der Kriegsgefangenen Haltung und Schicksal in Deutschland*, a whitewash defence of Germany's prison camp system which promoted the idea that French prisoners had sabotaged the German war effort; a second edition was published in 1921. The French Ambassador to The Netherlands described the book in damning terms as 'a pamphlet which illustrates the extent of the violence which the Berlin Government is using to excite the German people against France'.[290] Doegen's book emphasised that Germany had treated its prisoners in exemplary fashion and utterly played down prisoner deaths or violent treatment; needless to say, prisoner labour companies in France and Belgium or German reprisal measures were scarcely mentioned in this work.

---

[286] Hankel, *Die Leipziger Prozesse*, pp. 329–32.   [287] *Ibid.*
[288] *Die Behandlung der feindlichen Kriegsgefangenen. Amtlicher Bericht der Kommission zur Untersuchung der Anklagen wegen völkerrechtswidriger Behandlung der Kriegsgefangenen in Deutschland* (Berlin, 1920).
[289] Doegen, *Kriegsgefangene Völker*, p. 1.
[290] MAE, Série Z Europe 1918–1929, Allemagne 181, Prisonniers de Guerre I, Avril 1918–May 1921, no.186, légation de la Republique Française aux Pays-Bas, M. Charles Benoît, Ministre de la Rep. Française aux Pays-Bas à son Excellence Mr le Ministre des Affaires Etrangères, 24.12.1919.

Doegen's claims that Germany had treated its prisoners well reflected one aspect of the German defensive argument that developed in 1919; another key element was the contention that the Allies were being hypocritical in punishing Germany while ignoring their own prisoner mistreatment. The Allies' insistence on prosecuting Germans who had mistreated Allied prisoners while letting any Allied prisoner abuse go unpunished was seen as hugely unfair; it further fuelled a sense of German victimisation. Germany had released all Allied prisoners, including those serving jail terms for disciplinary crimes, under the terms of Article 218 of the Armistice Treaty. The German response was to call for reciprocity, claiming that the Allies too had committed prisoner abuses. In 1919, the German Foreign Office published an English translation of a 1918 book, *Die Gefangenen-Misshandlungen in Entente-Ländern*, under the English title *Maltreatment of Prisoners in Allied Countries*, which recounted incidents of mistreatment of German prisoners in Allied countries in an effort to make Germany's case abroad.[291] In 1921, with the active support of the Reich Association of Ex-Prisoners of War (*Reichsvereinigung ehemaliger Kriegsgefangener*), Clemens Plassmann published a book indicting French treatment of German prisoners.[292]

This German defensive campaign continued until well into the 1920s. An inherently contradictory German discourse on prisoner treatment developed which claimed that Germany had treated Allied prisoners humanely, while also arguing simultaneously that any German mistreatment only mirrored prisoner abuses carried out by all belligerents. Official investigations continued to largely exonerate Germany: the parliamentary Commission of Enquiry established by the Weimar National Assembly to investigate the origins of the war, wartime peace initiatives and the causes of the defeat directed its third subcommittee to focus on the violation of the laws of war, including prisoner of war abuses.[293] When the Commission published the results of its 1919–28 investigation in a multi-volume series, *Völkerrecht im Weltkrieg*, one and a half volumes were dedicated to the subject of prisoner treatment. The Commission's findings rebutted the Allies' accusations, often with detailed German counter-accusations.[294] The result thus largely

---

[291] Auswärtiges Amt, *Die Gefangenen-Misshandlungen in Entente-Ländern. Noten der deutschen Regierung an die Neutralen Staaten* (Berlin, 1918). Translated as: *German Government. Maltreatment of Prisoners in Allied Countries. Notes by the German Government to Neutral States* (Berlin, 1919).

[292] Plassmann, *Die deutschen Kriegsgefangenen in Frankreich 1914–1920*.

[293] Horne and Kramer, *German Atrocities*, pp. 338–9.

[294] Reichstag, *Völkerrecht in Weltkrieg*, vol. III, part I, *Verletzungen des Kriegsgefangenenrechts* (Berlin, 1927).

reproduced the main Allied and German propaganda narratives of the war. However, the Independent Socialist (USPD) members of the subcommittee produced a sharply dissenting minority report which found that prisoners in Germany had suffered excessively harsh disciplinary measures and that German reprisals against prisoners had been unjustifiable in international law.[295] The USPD went on to construct its own narrative around prisoner mistreatment, in which it was the capitalist war that was to blame for all prisoner abuses. Overall, the Commission's divided conclusions on violence against prisoners reflected Germany's internal left–right political polarisation and the competition among opposing factions as to which political identity represented the legitimate heir to the *Kaiserreich*.

Thus although Germany was violently politically fragmented between 1919 and 1921, the defensive narrative on the prisoner of war issue was supported by most of the political spectrum – even if right-wing groups were the most active in promoting it. The moderate Republican press did admit that prisoner abuses had occurred, but argued that these were isolated incidents. It outlined during the Leipzig trials that it was the duty of civilised people to rejoice at the 'harsh Leipzig judgements', while insisting that they would reveal the cruelties which had occurred to be 'isolated facts, not the result of a system. We are not a barbaric people.'[296] Only a small number of isolated left-wing voices courageously called for greater interrogation of Germany's own mistreatment of its prisoners, such as the pacifist Walter Oehme, who wrote in 1920 of terrible conditions endured by Russian prisoners in German prison camps after the Armistice, or Lili Jannasch, who tried to inform the German public of Allied evidence of German prisoner abuses.[297] Some former guards also spoke out, such as an ex-prison camp guard going by the anonymising name of Frank Furter, who in a strong critique of the punishment of low-ranking German individuals for prisoner mistreatment at the Leipzig Trials admitted in the journal *Das Tagebuch* that prisoner beating was widespread and that the senior commanders were responsible for it, stating that: 'In a Field Hospital (*Lazarett*) I saw prisoners who, after weeks of work behind the front, were literally skeletons, lousy and beaten, in a state of collapse … *Hungertyphus* the doctor called it. However, he

---

[295] *Ibid.*, vol. III, part I, pp. 24–7.

[296] MAE, Série Z, Europe 1918–1929, Allemagne 181, Prisonniers de Guerre I, avril 1918–mai 1921, f. 296, Consulat général de France en Wurttemburg, Direction des affaires politiques Europe, to M. le Président du Conseil, Ministre des Affaires Étrangères, Paris, n.d. [1921].

[297] Walter Oehme, ed., *Ein Bekenntnis deutscher Schuld. Beiträge zur deutschen Kriegsführung* (Berlin, 1920), pp. 70–3; Lilli Jannasch, *Untaten des preussisch-deutschen Militarismus im besetzten Frankreich und Belgien* (Wiesbaden, 1924), pp. 16–27.

did not report it as this "would bring nothing but useless trouble".'[298] The left-wing author Kurt Tucholsky, writing in *Die Welt am Montag* in 1921 in the context of the Leipzig Trials, decried the general trend of propagating information about atrocities against German prisoners without considering Germany's own prisoner mistreatment:

War and the military are to blame both for the culprits and the victims of such atrocities. It is not possible to tell people that killing and gassing each other on the battlefield is fine, while the enemy has to be treated with respect in the camps. All countries are guilty of committing atrocities and one has to start with oneself. Thousands upon thousands of atrocities have been committed against helpless men and the French refuse to follow up those crimes. However, what about ourselves? Nobody who admits that German soldiers committed crimes as well can expect others to sentence their war criminals if we ignore ours.[299]

Such rhetoric attempted to suggest to the German public that German prisoner mistreatment had occurred. It met with little success. By 1921, with German hostility to the Leipzig Trials at its height, the dominant attitude was one of denial that Germany had mistreated Allied prisoners. This was reinforced by such right-wing authors as August von Gallinger, who the same year published *Die Gegenrechnung*, a book containing accusations by former German prisoners of the Allies, damning Britain and France for their prisoner mistreatment.[300] A special edition of the *Süddeutsche Monatshefte*, devoted entirely to Gallinger's accusations, accused the Allies of spreading lies about German prisoner treatment. 'We know how the enemy prisoners in Germany were treated,' the editor stated in its introduction. 'I was myself during the war asked to donate to help provide foreign-language books for prisoners in Germany.'[301] The implication was clear – the German reader should trust his or her own memory above the Allied accusations and prisoner testimony. The subjective individual experience of seeing several prisoners well treated locally was enough from which to generalise the overall situation of millions of Allied prisoners in Germany and the occupied territories. This was a perfect means of ensuring that a collective amnesia developed as regarded wartime German prisoner treatment in mines, factories and the occupied zones. The German public did not understand that verified accounts of

---

[298] Frank Furter, 'Sergeant Heynen und das Völkerrecht', *Das Tagebuch*, 2, 22, 4.6.1921.

[299] Kurt Tucholsky, writing under the pseudonym Ignaz Wrobel, 'Gegenrechnung', *Die Welt am Montag*, 27 JG, Nr. 31, 1.8.1921. I am grateful to Vanessa Ther for drawing my attention to this source.

[300] August von Gallinger, *The Countercharge. The Matter of War Criminals from the German Side*. (Munich, 1922 [German edition, 1921]).

[301] Foreword by Paul Nikolaus Cossmann, Prof. Dr. August Gallinger, 'Gegenrechnung', *Süddeutsche Monatshefte* (June, 1921).

mistreatment by newly liberated prisoners from the occupied territories had radicalised the British call for war crimes trials; many genuinely believed that the Allied accusations were entirely fabricated.[302] Gerhard Rose, of the *Volksbund zum Schutze der deutschen Kriegs- und Zivilgefangenen*, attributed all the reports of starving British prisoners which appeared in the British press at the Armistice to 'atrocity propaganda', planned and invented by the British government in order to convince the British public to support its desire to detain German prisoners of war.[303]

The German mood in December 1918 was recorded by a British journalist in Cologne, who told locals that, 'whereas German prisoners sent back from England are in the best of physical condition, our own prisoners come back to us in a terrible state due to starvation and ill-treatment', only to receive the reply that 'they may have suffered somewhat general food shortage and in isolated instances may have been harshly used, but the French treated our prisoners abominably and what went on at Stratford camp … would make one's hair stand on end'.[304] There was no recognition of the mistreatment of Allied prisoners in the occupied territories: in the German version of events, the Allied food blockade had brought suffering to all, prisoners and German civilians alike, and additional anger was stoked by the continuing blockade of Germany after the war had ended.[305] The British journalist concluded that he had 'carried on conversations like this literally for hours with Germans of high education, men in position to know the facts and have not extracted a single admission that the German nation is anything but the innocent victim of aggression and slanders of jealous rivals'.[306] The head of the French military mission in Berlin after the Armistice found the same attitude:

Germans living in the interior of the country, who only saw the prisoners from the main camps, relatively well housed, sufficiently fed thanks to food deliveries from France, were sometimes surprised at our reproaches and did not want to believe they were well founded. It was still the 'it is not true' of the Manifesto of 93. There is no one more deaf than he who does not wish to hear.[307]

An American lieutenant sent to Germany to supervise the repatriation of Allied prisoners of war summed up the mood in Berlin in December 1918 in the words of a popular street song: 'The war is over now. We are at peace. Let us forget, Comrade.'[308]

Ultimately, this failure to acknowledge prisoner abuse on the German side proved significant for several reasons. First, the German army

---

[302] Dallas, *1918*, p. 240.   [303] Rose, *Krieg nach dem Kriege*, p. 29.
[304] 'Impenitent Germany', *The Times*, 30.12.1918, p. 7.   [305] *Ibid.*
[306] *Ibid.*   [307] Dupont, 'Une mission en Allemagne', p. 159.   [308] Dallas, *1918*, p. 273.

treatment of prisoners of war, as labourers and on reprisals, was remarkably harsh – particularly in 1917 and 1918 – exceeding in scale any
mistreatment patterns on the Allied side; the failure to rigorously investigate and condemn the new violent practices against prisoners which had
emerged in the German army meant they were effectively tacitly pardoned,
although the Allies can also be criticised for their failure to investigate their
own prisoner abuses, particularly in North Africa and in French labour
companies in 1916. Second, the failure to inform the German public about
the mistreatment of Allied prisoners led to it attributing the Allies' accusations to propaganda. It meant that the German public and many of
Germany's civilian politicians had no chance of understanding the real
motivations behind the Allies' refusal to repatriate German captives.
Third, the failure of the new German government to indict its predecessor
for its prisoner of war treatment epitomised its general reluctance to firmly
discredit the Kaiser's regime or, more particularly, to discredit the German
army – a failure which had serious long-term consequences as loyalties to
the old regime went unchallenged. A comprehensive Weimar government
investigation of army practice could potentially have challenged such pro-
army attitudes. In particular, the Weimar failure to expose the German
army's behaviour towards Allied prisoners in labour companies in 1918
left the stab-in-the-back legend of a noble German army unquestioned.
By failing to take the initiative, the Weimar government also allowed the
German right to remobilise around prisoner of war issues and to use the
broader German campaign to get the Allies to repatriate their German
prisoners to regain popular support and undermine the government for
failing to bring the prisoners home.

Finally, the failure to accept that any German mistreatment of prisoners
had occurred was also a failure to accept defeat. By contesting the Allies'
right to hold onto German captives, Germany was also contesting the
Allies' right to treat it as a vanquished power. The Allies' refusal to repatriate their German prisoners brought home the reality of Germany's
military defeat, a reality which many Germans did not wish to face.
A British officer prisoner, Alec Waugh, was told by a German teacher in
November 1918 that 'what hurts our pride more than anything is the
thought that we release prisoners instead of exchanging them. It shows us
so clearly that we are beaten.'[309] Nothing could more clearly symbolise the
powerless military situation and diplomatic isolation of Germany following
the Armistice.

---

[309] Waugh, *The Prisoners of Mainz*, pp. 232–8.

Conclusion

The repatriation of prisoners which followed the end of the war was marked by violent polemic, bitterness and misunderstanding; during this repatriation phase, wartime violence against captives was a dominant public theme and diametrically opposed Allied and German post-war narratives on prisoner of war treatment were established. Between 1918 and 1921, former belligerents' impressions of the enemy's prisoner treatment radicalised significantly; this contributed to new negative interpretations of the former enemy which remobilised popular hostilities. Revelations about real violence against captives underpinned the violent rhetoric of these public debates: the British and French were enraged by appalling German prisoner treatment in occupied France and Belgium. However, they were also angered by the effects of the influenza epidemic and German revolutionary chaos – which they mistakenly interpreted in late 1918 as a deliberate German policy of mass death, violence and starvation in German home front prisoner camps. Their reaction, the withholding of German prisoners in Britain and France, was a punitive response enacted against German captives – it exposed large numbers of German prisoners to a dangerous working environment, clearing the former battlefields, and caused enormous psychological suffering to prisoners and their families.

Little common understanding existed in the immediate aftermath of the war between the Allies and Germany. This was exacerbated by ignorance on the Allied side of the real political and economic conditions prevailing in Germany and the huge emotional impact of the retention of German prisoners upon a population already bitterly disappointed by defeat and the failure of Wilson's fourteen points to materialise as a basis for negotiations. On the German side, the gap in understanding was exacerbated by the failure to recognise the very real grievances the British and French felt at how their men had been treated while prisoners of war. With the issue of prisoner repatriation such a source of contention and rival discourses between November 1918 and 1921, it is little wonder that the reality of what had happened to prisoners during the war itself also became shrouded in confusion and polemic, ironically at the very point where national investigations were taking place. The contested narratives about repatriation help to explain why interwar societies ultimately found it impossible to accurately assess what had actually happened to prisoners during the war.

To return, in concluding, to the Nuremberg Association of Ex-Prisoners of War referred to at the opening of this chapter, who, in November 1921, like many other local German prisoner of war veterans' associations laid wreaths on Allied prisoners' tombs.[310] The intention was to show Germany was an honourable, chivalrous country, making real efforts at reconciliation; it was also to symbolise emphasise that all prisoners were equal victims of the war. The Nuremberg ex-prisoners called upon the French to respond in kind at the graves of German prisoners in France, thereby equating the French and German prisoner dead and implying a universality of prisoner suffering. In many ways, this was a heartfelt act: these former prisoners were using the graves of the French prisoners in Germany as proxy sites of mourning for their own lost comrades who now lay in French soil. However, this action by German prisoner of war veterans also epitomises the disparity in understanding between the two sides by 1921. The Allied contention was that prisoners had not 'universally' suffered equally; they believed Germany had treated its prisoners far worse than the Allies had behaved towards their captives. For the Allies, between 1918 and 1921, the key issue was how British and French prisoners had ended up in graves in Germany, rather than how those graves were honoured. Given such gaps in understanding, little conciliation was possible on prisoner issues in the immediate post-war period; prisoner repatriation proved a divisive, antagonistic process.

[310] MAE, Série Z, Europe 1918–1929, Allemagne 187, f. 135, 29.11.1921.

La Grande Illusion: the interwar historicisation
of violence against prisoners of war, 1922–39

> We three can do nothing until we meet again.
>> Inscription on a British prisoner of war grave at Kassel-Niederzwehren
>> Commonwealth War Graves Cemetery, Kassel, Hessen, Germany.

> *Rauffenstein*: I do not know who is going to win this war, but I do know
> one thing: the end of it, whatever it may be, will be the end of the
> Rauffensteins and the Boeldieus.
> *De Boeldieu*: But perhaps there is no more need of us.
>> Extract from the film *La Grande Illusion*, directed by Jean Renoir, 1937.[1]

Introduction

Up until 1921, discourses on violent prisoner treatment, often based on
real wartime events, continued to dominate in Britain, France and
Germany; the experience of prisoners whose captivity was uneventful
was largely excluded from public discussion. However, the following
years saw a cultural shift away from this emphasis upon violence against
prisoners. Almost all of the wartime references to prisoners of war explicitly or implicitly related acts of violence by the enemy towards them; yet by
the early 1930s, the mistreatment of prisoners of war had become a
marginal issue. This was in a large part due to a change in the public
mood in the mid-1920s in favour of European reconciliation: emphasising
wartime violence by the enemy against helpless captives became incompatible with the new pacifist consensus, which promoted dismantling
wartime hatreds. To re-engage with the former enemy in peacetime, it
proved necessary to forget their wartime prisoner mistreatment.

This selective amnesia regarding violence against prisoners of war,
which developed in Britain, France and Germany during the interwar
period, ultimately was also a major factor in the gradual disappearance of
prisoners from the history of the war more generally: captivity as a wartime
experience was increasingly excluded from both popular and official

---

[1] Jean Renoir, *La Grande Illusion*, trans. M. Alexander and A. Sinclair (London, 1968),
p. 71.

commemoration and historicisation of the conflict between 1922 and 1939 in all three countries, although this process occurred much earlier in Britain and France than in Germany. Historians agree that until recently 1914–18 prisoners were absent from the historiography of the First World War.[2] However, as this chapter will show through a detailed analysis of interwar Britain, France and Germany, this process of exclusion actually began during the interwar period, when, as it became expedient to forget violence against prisoners in the interests of conciliation, it ultimately became problematic to include prisoners in the commemoration and historicisation processes at all; they were gradually omitted altogether from public remembrance. Even the most disturbing, large-scale and highly visible innovation in captivity – prisoner of war labour companies – was already ostensibly forgotten by the mid-1930s, despite having been an obvious feature of the conflict. Public debates about First World War prisoner mistreatment petered out by the early 1930s.

This process of interwar amnesia was gradual and complex. Defining how societies 'forget' is as difficult for the historian as defining the different ways societies collectively 'remember', a subject which continues to produce historiographical debate as to whether interwar remembrance showed continuity with the traditions of the pre-war period or whether modernist forms of expression predominated; whether there is even such a thing as 'collective' memory is also contested.[3] For the purposes of this chapter, historical amnesia will be defined as both the absence of the social articulation of past experiences or discourses and their conscious suppression through the construction of an invented past. It will be argued here that 'forgetting' violence against prisoners of war was a multi-faceted process: the memory of prisoner mistreatment did not disappear instantly after the peak of official interest in the subject in 1919–21; rather, it first mutated. What presaged 'forgetting' was a form of memory disruption, a

---

[2] On the absence of historiography on First World War prisoners of war until the 1990s see Speed, *Prisoners, Diplomats and the Great War*, p. 8; Becker, *Oubliés de la Grande Guerre*, p. 15; Abbal, *Soldats oubliés*, p. 7; Rachamimov, *POWs and the Great War*, p. 3 and Hinz "'Die deutschen 'Barbaren' sind doch die besseren Menschen'", p. 340.

[3] See Adrian Gregory, *The Silence of Memory. Armistice Day 1919–1946* (Oxford and Providence, 1994), pp. 2–4; Jay Winter, *Sites of Memory, Sites of Mourning. The Great War in European Cultural History* (Cambridge, 1995), Introduction, pp. 1–11; Samuel Hynes, *A War Imagined. The First World War and English Culture* (London, 1990); Mosse, *Fallen Soldiers*; Paul Fussell, *The Great War and Modern Memory* (London, 1977); Modris Eksteins, *Rites of Spring. The Modern in Cultural History* (New York, 1989); Jay Winter and Emmanuel Sivan, eds., *War and Remembrance in the Twentieth Century* (Cambridge, 1999), p. 1. On the concept of 'collective memory' see Pierre Nora, ed., *Realms of Memory. The Construction of the French Past*, vol. I: *Conflicts and Divisions* (New York, 1996), p. 1; Maurice Halbwachs, *On Collective Memory* (Chicago and London, 1992 [1941]); Étienne François and Hagen Schulze, eds., *Deutsche Erinnerungsorte*, 3 vols. (Munich, 2001).

reinvention or reselection of what aspects of prisoner of war life would be remembered. This reselection was based upon what interwar societies valued and what they perceived as historically important. Ex-prisoners were themselves directly involved in this process: in the 1920s, prisoners of war influenced the public perception of captivity through memoirs and, in France and Germany, veterans' associations, which were active in trying to promote awareness of the wartime prisoner experience. The most important aspect of this memory disruption was the discarding of the discourse of violence, which had been so interwoven with the prisoner of war narrative during the war and the immediate post-war years in Britain, France and Germany, in favour of a discourse of reconciliation.

Made during the French Popular Front, Jean Renoir's film *La Grande Illusion* clearly illustrates this process. Perhaps the most famous interwar portrayal of First World War prisoners of war, the film depicts life in an officer prisoner of war camp, where the majority of prisoners are airmen.[4] The film, therefore, represents the capture experience and imprisonment of a privileged minority. Prison life in an officers' camp is portrayed as tolerable, with parcel supplies from home and Germans whose behaviour is largely defined by old code of honour niceties – the film highlights Franco-German dialogue and understanding, as the conversation quoted at the opening of this chapter, between a prisoner, the French aristocratic officer de Boeldieu, and his class counterpart, the aristocratic German camp commandant von Rauffenstein, played by Erich von Stroheim, lamenting the loss of aristocratic solidarity, illustrates. The prisoner is depicted as a conciliatory, not a divisive figure, who symbolises a shared humanity. It is all a long way from the entrenched bitternesses of 1919–21.

Renoir's narrative choices are highly revealing of the ways in which the prisoner experience was being interpreted by the 1930s; it is not discussed in terms of German aggression, violence or military atrocities. Rather, it is the foil for a wider discussion of the war: the prison camp experience is used as a setting for a broader narrative about social interactions between men, the collapse of the class system and European reconciliation. And, most significant of all, the camp world is open to being fictionalised in ways that allow the narrative to deal with these themes; although Renoir did consult with former prisoners when preparing the film, a tacit recognition that the subject matter of the prison camp was still to some extent a sensitive issue, he was able to include scenes that were historically

---

[4] Airmen often had a less violent capture experience: in the British case, we know that the German capture of British airmen was often markedly chivalrous. See the many accounts of capture by British airmen who were taken prisoner in TNA, AIR 1/501/15/333/1 Interrogative reports by escaped or repatriated prisoners of war, RFC or RAF, 1915–1918.

unrealistic, without provoking any public outcry. In his letters, Renoir acknowledged that his aim was to make a work of art, not a documentary:

The goal of this film is not to describe the life of French prisoners in German camps during the war. It is a confrontation between different types of men ... The President of the League of Wartime Escapees, Mr Richard, and a commission of escapees with whom we had important discussions before starting the film, know this very well as we agreed with them that the scenes which later would allow Commandant von Rauffenstein and Capt de Boeldieu to confront each other had no place in a purely documentary account of the lives of the prisoners.[5]

Here Renoir recognised his need for artistic licence, although he also desired that the 'framework' of captivity 'be reconstructed with the greatest possible exactitude' out of 'respect for the men who suffered in these prisons' – an acknowledgement that prisoner hardship had occurred.[6] But Renoir's prison camp was not about the real experiences of prisoners; the depiction of dialogue with the enemy was what interested him, not violence. This was also reflected in his decision to depict the Germans humanely: 'in our film, there is no "boche" guard; there is a *German* guard'.[7] All of this was perfectly legitimate as Renoir was working at the level of myth and allegory to create a cinematic narrative. However, through this shift in emphasis, one of the most important issues during the war, violence against prisoners of war, is occluded in the film. In this regard, *La Grande Illusion* is precisely that – an illusion, albeit a magnificent artistic one. The deterioration in other-rank prison camp life in Germany in 1917 and 1918 is not depicted, apart from a brief scene with angry, hungry Russians. The darker side of life for other-rank prisoners – harsh working conditions in the labour companies in the occupied territories, the factory, the mine, reprisal camps – is absent. The consequences of this outlasted the 1930s; the film's artistic excellence – cinematography, narrative, use of symbolism and its commercial and enduring success – meant that for many viewers its conciliatory portrayal became the abiding image of the First World War prison camp.

Renoir's film is but one example, albeit an extremely influential one, of the changing ways in which the interwar period perceived First World War prisoner treatment. It illustrates the complexity of the relationship between memory, cultural representations and the shifting historicisation of captivity. Such interwar reinterpretations of the prisoner experience

---

[5] Letter from Jean Renoir to Albin Michel and Jean des Vallières, June 1937, 'Origins of scenes from "La Grande Illusion" called into question by Albin Michel and Des Vallières', in David Thompson and Lorraine LoBianco, eds., *Jean Renoir. Letters* (Boston and London, 1994), p. 32.

[6] *Ibid.*, p. 38.   [7] *Ibid.*, p. 36.

deserve detailed attention as they raise difficult questions about linkages, continuities and breaks in European history between the two world wars. For interwar representations of prisoners which played down violence against captives only gradually came to dominate and always co-existed uneasily with sublimated private memories; for the same reason, the subsequent public marginalisation of the subject of wartime captivity by the 1930s was never a truly 'total' amnesia in Britain, France and Germany. As Jay Winter has argued, there were many different 'memory sites', both public and private, through which the war was understood in the interwar years.[8] However much interwar histories marginalised or omitted prisoners, there were many people living in Europe at the outbreak of the Second World War who still had private personal memories of prisoner treatment during the First. Given these hidden connections, it is clear that the interwar amnesia on captivity masked the survival of private memories, even if prisoner treatment disappeared from public debate. This chapter will now examine in detail how the memory of violence against prisoners of war became increasingly marginalised in interwar Britain, France and Germany, leading to all three countries ultimately repressing the broader history of wartime captivity by the 1930s.

The need to forget? British society and the memory of prisoner mistreatment

One of the key reasons why the memory of violence against prisoners matters to a society is the likelihood of repetition: where societies feel that violent imprisonment is likely to recur in the future, the memory of past prisoner mistreatment remains important. This was the case in the immediate post-war years, when former prisoners and their societies openly engaged with the memory of violence against prisoners during 1914–18. In particular, there was a sense among former prisoners that something had gone wrong with war, and indeed with European culture, that had led to the more violent forms of captivity that emerged during certain phases of the conflict. Prisoner mistreatment was thus initially something to be solved rather than forgotten. In Britain and France, this led to calls for war crimes trials; in Germany, there were demands that international law be revised in order to protect prisoners more effectively.

In Britain, however, following the Leipzig trials in 1921, the public and the establishment rapidly lost interest in accounts of violence against prisoners. The subject disappeared from public debate. For example, the results

---

[8] Winter, *Sites of Memory, Sites of Mourning*, p. 1.

of the official post-war British enquiry into German prisoner abuses, based on interviews with former prisoners, which referred to a 'system' of German mistreatment, were ultimately never published during the interwar years.[9] The Leipzig Trials created a sense that the issue had been dealt with. Public silence, however, was also due to a change in attitudes which served to silence the memory of prisoner mistreatment; this shift in attitudes was not challenged by ex-prisoners in Britain, who did not significantly mobilise to publicise their wartime experiences.

Two issues, in particular, clearly reveal this interwar change in attitudes in Britain: first, an analysis of the key figures involved with the question of prisoner of war treatment during the war reveals that in the interwar period they modified how they wrote and spoke about prisoners to play down mistreatment issues. For example, Lieutenant-General Herbert E. Belfield, who had been head of the Department of Prisoners of War at the War Office, changed his tone markedly by the early 1920s. The wartime suspicions and animosities articulated in the diary he kept at the Hague Conference in June 1917, where he met with a German delegation to discuss prisoner treatment, were markedly different from his speech to the Grotius Society on 6 November 1923.[10] In his 1917 diary, Belfield made continual anti-German comments, referring to 'the brutal treatment' to which British prisoners had been subjected.[11] In his 1923 speech, however, he was far less critical of Germany, considering, for example, that the 'infliction of heavy punishments' on British prisoners was legal as prisoners were subject to the German military code.[12] Similarly revealing was a debate at the Grotius Society in London, in 1922, where Sir Reginald Acland, a former member of the Committee of Enquiry into Breaches of the Laws of War, challenged the former Home Secretary, Viscount George Cave, on his claim that there had been widespread prisoner mistreatment by Germany.[13]

These changes in attitude were not due to any post-war crisis of faith in the evidence of mistreatment gathered during the war; on the contrary, those who had compiled this evidence were rewarded in the interwar years. The head of the Government Committee on the Treatment by the Enemy of British Prisoners of War, Sir Robert Younger, was made Baron Blanesburgh for his part in collecting evidence of German prisoner mistreatment. Adelaide Livingstone, the remarkable American woman who had coordinated the

---

[9] Morgan, *Assize of Arms*, vol. I, p. 140.

[10] IWM, 91/44/1 HEB 1/1 Papers of Lieutenant-General Sir Herbert Belfield, Director of Prisoners of War 1914–1920, Diary of the conference at The Hague, 23 June–7 July 1917; Belfield, 'The Treatment of Prisoners of War', pp. 131–47.

[11] *Ibid.*   [12] *Ibid.*

[13] Comments made by Sir Reginald Acland on a speech by Lord Cave, *Transactions of the Grotius Society. Problems of Peace and War*, 8 (London, 1922), p. 36.

running of the Government Committee on the Treatment by the Enemy of British Prisoners of War from 1915 to 1918, was made a Dame in 1918 for her war work. She was appointed head of the War Office mission to search for the missing in France and Flanders 1919–20 and subsequently became Assistant Director of Graves Registration and Enquiries in Central Europe 1920–2.[14] This was a truly remarkable career for a young woman and confirms that Livingstone's wartime investigations and reports were well regarded. Yet although the wartime evidence of German prisoner mistreatment was not discredited, it was no longer seen as relevant: after the Leipzig trials, the issue was considered resolved in Britain. The emphasis shifted to promoting European reconciliation, not pursuing war crimes issues; this change in attitude even affected those who had collected ex-prisoner testimony in the first place: Adelaide Livingstone's subsequent career is illustrative of this post-war shift to pacifism. Her experiences between 1914 and 1918 mobilised her to campaign vigorously for peace in the interwar years. She became involved with the League of Nations and later campaigned against European rearmament through the Peace Ballot of European populations in the 1930s, which petitioned people to vote symbolically against war. She was Director of Special Activities to the League of Nations Union between 1928 and 1934 and Secretary to the National Declaration Committee between 1934 and 1935, during which time she organised the peace ballot, publishing a book on its results.[15] Later she served as secretary and subsequently vice-chairman of the International Peace Campaign, 1936–40. The promotion of peace was more important to Livingstone than the re-opening of old wounds about prisoners of war.

The second issue which clearly reveals this interwar change in British attitudes is the prisoner memoir: between 1921 and 1939, the vast majority of prisoner memoirs published in the UK were by officer prisoners, who experienced little wartime mistreatment. The wartime discourse on violence against other-rank captives was virtually absent in memoirs; officer prisoners' jocular accounts of escape flourished in its place. These accounts were particularly noteworthy for their playful tone – many deliberately depicted prisoner of war camps as a kind of public school with barbed wire.[16] One described escape as 'very like one of

---

[14] Adelaide Livingstone died in 1970. From *Who Was Who, 1961–1970*, vol. VI (London, 1972).

[15] *Ibid.*; Adelaide Livingstone, *The Peace Ballot. The Official History with a Statistical Survey of the Results* (London, 1935).

[16] For typical examples see Godfrey Walter Phillimore, *Recollections of a Prisoner of War* (London, 1930); H. G. Durnford, *The Tunnellers of Holzminden. With a Side-Issue* (Cambridge, 1930); Wallace Ellison, *Escapes and Adventures* (Edinburgh and London, 1928).

those board games we used to play as boys – the game was tireless. The camp was the board.'[17] In 1931, the BBC even organised a series of sixteen talks by officers who had escaped from Germany during the Great War, most of whom in the 1920s had already written a memoir on their escape.[18] It is a mark of the cultural shift towards reconciliation that had occurred since the early 1920s that three German officer escapers who had broken out of British camps were included; in contrast, the voice of British other-rank prisoners, who had experienced a completely different and far harsher captivity than officers, was largely absent.[19] Such was the interest in the radio talks that it was decided to edit them into a book, *Escapers All*, which duly appeared in 1932. The introduction by J. R. Ackerley is revealing. Ackerley openly acknowledged the narrative shift that had occurred since the conflict:

A good many of the books which have been published in all countries about escaping, especially those published during or soon after the war, are coloured with the animosities and prejudices of that time, and I believe that a number of their authors could now wish this otherwise. This book, however, will not concern itself with the treatment of prisoners of war or the conditions in which they lived, excepting in so far as these are a relevant background to their adventures of escape. Prisoners of war were treated the same in every country that took part in the war, and when they received – as they occasionally did receive in all countries – real kindness and consideration, then we may be surprised and grateful that such good qualities managed to survive the poison and the pettiness of those times.[20]

The *mistreatment* of prisoners had become taboo, even though implicit in Ackerley's comments was the idea that prisoners had been the target of enemy hatreds. As Ackerley's comments illustrate, in Britain the emphasis on violence against captives gave way after the Leipzig Trials to a purely social narrative of officer prison camp life, which allowed British commentators to engage in a conciliatory way with Germany; a similar shift is also evident in the difference between statements made by officer prisoners during the war to the British Committee on the Treatment by the Enemy of British Prisoners of War and their more light-hearted interwar memoirs.[21] By the 1930s, the desire for reconciliation took precedence over all else, stifling any accurate historicisation of violence against

---

[17] H. G. Durnford, ed., *Tunnelling to Freedom and Other Escape Narratives from World War One, Hugh Durnford and Others*, Introduction by J. R. Ackerley (New York, 2004). Unabridged reproduction of *Escapers All. Being the Personal Narratives of Fifteen Escapers from War-Time Prison Camps, 1914–1918* (London, 1932), p. 14.

[18] *Ibid.*, publisher's note, p. 7.   [19] Durnford, ed., *Tunnelling to Freedom.*   [20] *Ibid.*, p. 15.

[21] TNA, WO 161/96, Interview no. 323 with Lieut. D. Grinnell-Milne; TNA, WO 161/96, Interview no. O.416, 2nd Lieut. H. G. Durnford; Durnford, *The Tunnellers of Holzminden*; Duncan Grinnell-Milne, *An Escaper's Log* (London, 1926).

prisoners, as illustrated in 1935 when the British Legion hosted a visit to Brighton by German ex-prisoners of war. The Germans were greeted by the former commandant of the camp for German prisoners of war at Camberley; as a token of their friendship, the German ex-prisoners presented the mayor of Brighton with a miniature swastika banner.[22]

This interwar shift towards privileging a non-violent image of captivity went largely unchallenged, because, unlike Germany and France, ex-prisoners of war did not mobilise collectively in Britain in any significant numbers to raise awareness of other-rank prisoners' wartime experiences.[23] In 1926, a British Association of Ex-Prisoners of War was established which was still in existence in 1933. It had very close ties with the British Legion, however, and its membership was small. On 28 January 1928, it organised the first separate public commemoration of prisoners of war in Britain, a march through London which ended at the Cenotaph; about 600 members of the Association attended and a wreath was laid at the Cenotaph by the mother of a prisoner who died in captivity.[24] This ceremony briefly became an annual event in the early 1930s.[25] The Association of Ex-Prisoners of War also published a newsletter on matters of interest to prisoners during the same period and held an annual dinner, as well as organising dances. However, according to its own newsletter, its activities were very limited; it lamented that only a small number of ex-prisoner veterans had become involved.[26] The only other prisoner of war groups that emerged were a handful of small clubs set up around individual camps, and these, like the interwar memoirs, were often focused upon officers. They organised reunions, rather than campaigning for ex-prisoners' rights or publicising mistreatment issues and were modelled upon the gentlemen's clubs, which were such an important part of British upper-class male socialisation.[27] The vast majority of British ex-prisoners did not develop any separate veteran group identity. Indeed, many remained on the fringes of British society more generally: the police

---

[22] 'German Ex-Servicemen at Brighton', *The Times*, 21.6.1935; 'German Ex-Soldiers' Visit to England', *The Times*, 25.6.1935.

[23] BA, R 8095/3, ReK, Bericht aus der Besprechung mit Herrn von Hünefeld und Major Fitzmaurice (British Legion) am Montag den 25 Juni 1928 im Hotel Kaiserhof. Es sprachen vor die Kameraden von Lersner und Dr Givens; Graham Wootton, *The Official History of the British Legion* (London, 1956), Appendix 2, p. 313.

[24] *The Times*, 'War Prisoners at the Cenotaph', 30.1.1928.

[25] *The Times*, 'Ex-Prisoners of War at the Cenotaph', 4.5.1931.

[26] See The Association of Ex-Prisoners of War's newsletter, *The Kriegsgefangener. The Association of Ex-Prisoners of War*, March and June 1933 editions.

[27] See the report on the Holzminden reunion dinner, *The Times*, 25.7.1938. On the British tradition of male clubs, see John Davidson Ketchum, *Ruhleben. A Prison Camp Society* (Toronto and Oxford, 1965), p. 178.

reports from 1921 on ex-prisoners interviewed in preparation for the Leipzig Trials emphasised the poverty of many of the men. Several were unemployed and six of the ex-prisoner witnesses who travelled to Leipzig had to have suits bought for them in order to render them presentable in court.[28]

However, the main reason for the weakness of the British Ex-Prisoner Association was that the British Legion was so powerful; in the interwar period, it successfully recruited and united British veterans and lobbied on their behalf, making no distinction between former prisoners and other categories of ex-servicemen; thus many former prisoners joined it. The success of the Legion, which included veterans of all ranks and from all services, as well as the war-disabled, meant that fragmented special-interest veterans' groups remained remarkably weak in Britain. Its work facilitated what Adrian Gregory has described as the remarkably smooth reintegration of British veterans into civil society – even if, as he argues, ex-servicemen had little control over public commemoration of the war, which always prioritised the civilian bereaved over veterans.[29] Formed in 1921, the British Legion was an amalgamation of four earlier veterans' associations: the National Federation of Discharged and Demobilised Sailors and Soldiers; Comrades of the Great War; the National Association of Discharged Sailors and Soldiers; and the Officers' Association. The fifth veterans' association, the radical left-wing National Union of Ex-Servicemen, disappeared during the 1920s. Significantly, none of these initial veterans' groups focused upon prisoners of war.

One further reason for the absence of any significant ex-prisoner mobilisation in interwar Britain was that the state did not stigmatise captivity: there was no cultural distinction made between prisoners of war and combatants who had never been captured. The treatment of prisoner of war graves highlights this. The Imperial War Graves Commission established and maintained cemeteries for prisoner of war graves in Germany which were identical to those built for the battlefield dead in France, even including the same headstone design; thus, in contrast to the graves of French prisoners of war in Germany, dead British prisoners were interred in what were clearly *combatant* burial grounds. This move undermined initial public opposition to leaving prisoners' graves in Germany.[30] Following the

---

[28] TNA, MEPO 3/1166, Subject: war criminals, Metropolitan Police Criminal Investigation Department, Ref: 222/FC/1, To: Superintendant 10/6/1921.

[29] Gregory, *The Silence of Memory*, p. 4, and pp. 51–2.

[30] Philip Langworth, *The Unending Vigil. The History of the Commonwealth War Graves Commission* (Barnsley, 2003 [1967]), p. 122.

investigation by the British military mission in Berlin into what had happened to missing prisoners, the Imperial War Graves Commission registered and amalgamated all British prisoner of war graves into four large graveyards at Kassel, Berlin, Hamburg and Cologne, with over a thousand burials, and thirteen other minor burial sites with fewer graves. A Federal German Law in 1922 assured security for the cemeteries, which had a full-time British staff appointed to tend them.[31] Families were able to request a personal inscription to be placed on the grave headstone. At Kassel graveyard, the cemetery entrance was flanked by two beehive-style fort towers, symbolically protecting the sleeping dead within. In contrast, the graves of German prisoners of war who died in the UK received no special treatment and were only amalgamated into a centralised prisoner of war graveyard at Cannock Chase in 1964.[32]

There was one final factor which silenced the public debate on wartime violence against prisoners in interwar Britain: this was the growing belief that all wartime accounts of atrocity had been fabricated by the state. Promoted particularly vigorously by the British Member of Parliament and anti-war campaigner Sir Arthur Ponsonby, in his 1928 book *Falsehood in Wartime*, this belief profoundly undermined any attempt to discuss the reality of wartime prisoner mistreatment.[33] Ponsonby's work directly discredited the testimony of prisoners of war: 'Stories of the maltreatment of prisoners have to be circulated deliberately in order to prevent surrenders. This is done, of course, by both sides.'[34] He used examples of cases where undoubtedly the British government had invented or exaggerated atrocity tales, such as the story of the crucified Canadian, to argue that all propaganda on prisoner mistreatment was invented. Ponsonby's work reflected a growing interwar attitude in Britain, particularly prevalent by the 1930s, that propaganda lies, including those about violence against prisoners of war by the enemy, had contributed to keeping the population fighting, thereby sustaining the war unnecessarily. Such attitudes made it impossible for ex-prisoners to publicly discuss their experiences of mistreatment without risking being accused of war-mongering: there was no public appetite for such testimony by the 1930s.

Ponsonby's work was illustrative of the wider shift in how the war was understood in Britain by the early 1930s as a catastrophic disaster and a needless waste of lives. Given the extent of anti-war feeling, the only discussion of violence against prisoners of war still possible was that which served an anti-war message, as illustrated by the 'literature of

---

[31] *Ibid.*
[32] www.cannockchasedc.gov.uk/cannockchase/wargraves.htm, accessed 10.8.2005.
[33] Ponsonby, *Falsehood in Wartime.*   [34] *Ibid.*, p. 22.

disenchantment' writers, many of whom, including Vera Brittain and R. C. Sherriff, used violence against the German prisoner as the ultimate symbol of the futility of war and man's common humanity.[35] When the young German, significantly described as the 'BOY', appears on stage at the end of Sherriff's influential play *Journey's End*, the purpose is to reveal the ludicrous nature of war, where one boy dies in a raid to capture another:

> [Suddenly the BOY falls on his knees and sobs out some words in broken English.]
>
> GERMAN: Mercy – mister – mercy!
> S-M: Come on lad, get up.
> [With a huge fist he takes the BOY by the collar and draws him to his feet. The BOY sobs hysterically ...][36]

A similar use of the German prisoner was also made powerfully by Siegfried Sassoon. For example, his poem 'Atrocities' uses prisoners to depict the wartime enemy as victim:

> You told me, in your drunken-boasting mood,
> How once you butchered prisoners. That was good!
> I'm sure you felt no pity while they stood
> Patient and cowed and scared, as prisoners should.
> How did you do them in? Come don't be shy:
> You know I love to hear how Germans die,
> Downstairs in dug-outs. 'Camerad!' they cry;
> Then squeal like stoats when bombs begin to fly.[37]

Yet ironically, while the 'literature of disenchantment' emphasised the German captive, portraying him in a human light, it largely ignored the British prisoner. Left out of the iconic literature, which would go on to dominate British popular memory of the war, the British prisoner never entered the collective national consciousness. German wartime violence against British prisoners was deliberately 'forgotten' in the interwar period and former British prisoners acquiesced in this amnesia. As a result, it ultimately proved impossible to incorporate British prisoners' experience of captivity into the interwar historicisation of the war in Britain.

---

[35] Brittain, *Testament of Youth*, p. 376.

[36] R. C. Sherriff, *Journey's End* (London, 1929), p. 74.

[37] This poem was originally published in 1919. Rupert Hart-Davis, ed., *The War Poems of Siegfried Sassoon* (London, 1983), p. 145. Copyright Siegfried Sassoon by kind permission of the Estate of George Sassoon and Barbara Levy Literary Agency. The poet Herbert Read makes similar use of the German prisoner in his poem 'The Scene'. Herbert Read, *Collected Poems 1913–1925* (London, 1927), p. 83.

Poilus or *prisonniers*? The memory of violence against prisoners of war in interwar France

In contrast to the British case, in France in the 1920s ex-prisoners of war were extremely active in publicising their accounts of prisoner mistreatment in Germany. This was because French ex-prisoners, unlike their British counterparts, faced significant discrimination from their own government. The elites of French interwar society were far more suspicious of prisoners of war in the 1920s than their British or German counterparts. The mood is illustrated by the title of a 1922 article in the *Almanach of Combatants and Victims of the War*: 'The Prisoners Were Combatants'.[38] In neither Britain nor Germany was it necessary to issue any such reminder. Former French prisoners of war found that government and military circles did not categorise them as former combatants, seeing captivity as a boon: 'After all, preserving one's life is quite something. To keep your life is worth suffering a little hunger,' was how one French senator countered prisoners' demands for equal recognition with other ex-servicemen, in 1931.[39]

French ex-prisoners were thus forced to campaign, against considerable stigma throughout the 1920s, to obtain the same rights that were accorded automatically to other former combatants who had not been captured: for example, repatriated prisoners received the non-combatant demobilisation allowance rate and French prisoners who died in captivity were initially refused the citation '*mort pour la France*'.[40] As a consequence their children were not entitled to the special status of 'orphans of the nation' (*pupilles de la nation*) with its concomitant welfare benefits, which was accorded to the children of those who died at the front.[41] It took three years before the law was modified on 26 January 1922 to allow those who had died in captivity the right to the same citation as battlefield dead. Prisoners also faced real difficulties obtaining a pension for injuries or illnesses caused by the war, particularly as in many cases they no longer had the necessary papers to prove the origin of their complaint.[42] As late as 1929, the historian Odon Abbal claims that only 60 per cent of French ex-prisoners who were entitled to a pension because of sickness or wounds had been able to obtain one.[43]

---

[38] J. Segonzac-Volvey, 'Les Prisonniers furent des combattants', in *Almanach du combattant et des victimes de la guerre* (Paris, 1922), p. 187, cited in Odon Abbal, 'Un combat d'après-guerre. Le statut des prisonniers', *Revue du Nord*, 80, 325 (1998), pp. 405–16.

[39] *Ibid.*, p. 415. Becker, *Oubliés de la Grande Guerre*, p. 369.

[40] Abbal, 'Un combat d'après-guerre', pp. 407–8. [41] *Ibid.*

[42] *Ibid.*, pp. 409–10. [43] *Ibid.*, p. 410.

This interwar suspicion that prisoners were cowards or deserters had its roots in the massive captures of August and September 1914, when France's military fate hung in the balance and the large number of prisoners taken by Germany led to suspicions that French soldiers were letting themselves be captured too easily.[44] On 28 November 1914, Joffre had decided that any combatant captured unwounded by the Germans would be the subject of a military investigation.[45] This suspicion of prisoners resurfaced after the repatriation of liberated captives to France. Prisoners were also affected during the 1920s, by the growing focus upon the front combatant, which came to obscure all other war sacrifices, as the cult of those who had died on the battlefield was glorified above all else.[46] Relegated to a poor third place in terms of suffering behind the battlefield dead and the civilians of the devastated northern regions, French prisoners of war were suspected of having had an easy war.

This suspicion against ex-prisoners lasted into the 1930s. Most famously, 1936 saw the right-wing press, in particular *L'Action Française*, engage in a witch-hunt against the Minister of the Interior in Léon Blum's Popular Front government, Roger Salengro, because he was a former prisoner of war, accusing him of deserting; in fact, Salengro's only crime was to have been captured. Tormented by the accusations, Salengro committed suicide in November 1936.[47]

Given this context, large numbers of former prisoners in France joined the main French ex-prisoners' association, the *Fédération nationale des anciens prisonniers de guerre* (later renamed the *Fédération nationale des anciens prisonniers de guerre, évadés et otages*), which actively campaigned for greater rights for ex-prisoners and sought to raise public awareness about the harsh wartime experiences of prisoners in German captivity; it had 60,000 members in 1935.[48] Politically on the centre-right, the *Fédération* produced a monthly newsletter from 1921, which was still in existence in 1929.[49] Many French former prisoners also joined other non-prisoner veterans' associations such as the *Union Fédérale* or the *Union*

---

[44] SHAT, 7 N 143, EMA, 1er Bureau, Prisonniers de guerre français, Ministère de la Guerre, cabinet du ministre, Circular from Ministre de la Guerre, 16.12.1914.
[45] *Ibid.*   [46] Becker, *Oubliés de la Grande Guerre*, p. 367.
[47] Thomas Ferenczi, *Ils l'ont tué! L'Affaire Salengro* (Paris, 1995), pp. 8–9. http://membres. lycos.fr/histoiredefrance/articles/personnalites/Salengro.htm, accessed 31.5.2005.
[48] Antoine Prost, *In the Wake of War. 'Les Anciens Combattants' and French Society, 1914– 1939* (Oxford and Providence, 1992), p. 40. Becker, *Oubliés de la Grande Guerre*, p. 368.
[49] Bibliothèque de Documentation Internationale Contemporaine, Université de Paris-X, Nanterre (BDIC-MHC Nanterre), *APJX pour prisonniers français en Allemagne. Lettre mensuelle de la Fédération Nationale des Anciens Prisonniers de Guerre*, 1921–août/sept. 1929 (nos. 1–86) G F P 708. This later became the *Journal des anciens prisonniers de guerre, évadés, otages*, Oct. 1929. G F P 708.

Nationale de Combattants. However, even the post-war mobilisation of ex-prisoners was affected by the stigma against captivity: ex-prisoners who had escaped founded their own veterans' association, the *Union des Évadés de Guerre*, in 1918, to differentiate themselves from those who had remained in captivity.[50] With a maximum of 16,000 members, the *Union des Évadés* was made up of former officer prisoners.[51] The main French prisoner veterans' association, the *Fédération nationale des anciens prisonniers de guerre*, regarded the *Union des Évadés de Guerre* as an illegitimate attempt to divide those who had suffered together in captivity, pointing out that one prisoner's escape often depended on the aid of many others who had remained behind.[52] The conflict between the two associations was at times bitter. In 1927, the *Union des Évadés* even sent a declaration to the Senate, urging it to refuse to pass an indemnity that would compensate former prisoners for the money their families had spent on food parcels.[53] It felt that those who had remained in prison camps deserved no such special compensation. Ultimately, ex-prisoners did not receive any recompense during the interwar period for the huge sums that their families had spent on food parcels – a draft proposal for compensation in 1933 estimated that collectively the families of French prisoners had sent 1,254,308.125 francs' worth of parcels themselves and had paid Swiss agencies to send a further 6,144,000 francs' worth.[54]

Despite the stigma attached to captivity, however, French ex-prisoners waged a very active campaign to be treated in the same way as other former combatants, winning considerable support in parliament. There were 293 *Députés* in the parliamentary 'Group for the Defence of Former Prisoners of War' in May 1923, who campaigned for greater compensation for ex-prisoners.[55] The main prisoner veterans' association, the *Fédération nationale des anciens prisonniers de guerre*, also had the support of the main French veterans' association, the *Union Nationale des Combattants*, in its campaigns for better compensation for prisoners; the former head of the French *Service Général des Prisonniers de Guerre*, Georges Cahen-Salvador, also assisted by raising the profile of prisoner sufferings.[56] In 1929, Cahen-Salvador wrote the sole interwar French history of prisoners of war, as the

---

[50] Abbal, 'Un combat d'après-guerre', p. 412.   [51] *Ibid.*, p. 413.
[52] BDIC-MHC Nanterre, O pièce 14505, Fédération nationale des anciens prisonniers de guerre, évadés et otages, pamphlet, *Les Prisonniers de guerre*, n.d.
[53] Abbal, 'Un combat d'après-guerre', pp. 412–13.
[54] SHAT, 6 N 442, no. 1706, Chambre des Députés, Annexe au procès-verbal de la 2e séance du 31 mars 1933, Proposition de loi tendant à attribuer une indemnité de nourriture et d'entretien aux anciens prisonniers de guerre, pendant la durée de leur captivité au cours de la guerre, 1914–1918.
[55] Abbal, 'Un combat d'après-guerre', p. 411.   [56] *Ibid.*, p. 410.

only book in the Carnegie Series to deal with prisoners of war of any nationality.[57] By this point a member of the French delegation to the League of Nations, Cahen-Salvador believed that

in the ten years since the peace has been signed we have not yet made known the long martyrdom of prisoners of war ... This account is an act of witness and gratitude owed to those not spared the anguish of exile, to those who departed this life on foreign soil, those who suffered and those who through their dignity and courage taught the enemy to respect them.[58]

French ex-prisoners campaigned for both public recognition and financial redress. One of their key financial demands was that Germany be forced to pay the outstanding wages due to former captives for their wartime work: it was policy during the war in Britain, France and Germany that for security reasons other-rank prisoners only received a fraction of their wages each week in coupons which could only be used at the prison camp canteen. Their surplus earnings were recorded as savings in their camp or working unit account book, to be paid out to them when they were released at the end of the war. However, due to the chaos of repatriation from Germany, many Allied prisoners were never paid this money; in retaliation, German prisoners were not paid their outstanding wages on leaving France and Britain. Those leaving France were given certificates instead, by the French government, stating what money was owed them.[59]

In 1926, the French and German governments came to a final deal on prisoner compensation, which included these unpaid prisoner earnings. The settlement greatly favoured France: the French received 13 million francs in compensation for French ex-prisoners; the Germans received only 4.5 million francs in compensation for German ex-prisoners who had worked for France.[60] The imbalance was stark: this settlement included not only the pay due to German prisoners for 1914–18 but also the wages due for the extra work carried out by German prisoners to restore the devastated regions of France between November 1918 and spring 1920, which even at the time had been paid at a fraction of the wages of a French civilian labourer. The French negotiators offered only partial reimbursement and secretly admitted that the deal was unfair to Germany, which

---

[57] Cahen-Salvador, *Les Prisonniers de guerre*; *Dictionnaire Biographique, 1961–1962*, 5th edn (Paris, 1963), entry for Georges Cahen-Salvador (1875–1963), p. 636.

[58] Cahen-Salvador, *Les Prisonniers de guerre*, p. 8.

[59] BA, R 8095.5, Reichsverein. ehem. Kriegsgefangener e.v., Bundestag, 4.6.26.

[60] Centre des Archives Économiques et Financières, Savigny-le-Temple, B/0061026/1, Direction du mouvement général des fonds, 1919–1926, Compte spécial des échanges de monnaies allemandes, 1919–1926, Rapport au Ministre au sujet de l'accord signé à Berlin le 30 octobre 1926 concernant les avoirs des prisonniers de guerre.

could have challenged it under international law.[61] However, Germany gave in. Yet ultimately this deal did not prove the financial recompense that French ex-prisoners had campaigned for: wrangling over how best to distribute this 13 million francs meant that the money did not reach the individual French ex-prisoners directly concerned.

However, perhaps the most important aspect of the French ex-prisoners' campaign was their demand for public recognition of their sacrifices. This manifested itself most clearly in their demand to force the French government to treat the graves of French prisoners the same as those of combatants who fell on the battlefield and to repatriate French prisoners' bodies from Germany in the 1920s, something it had initially declined to do.[62] The ex-prisoners' campaign was highly emotive, forcing a reluctant French government to give way. As one former prisoner, Eugène-Louis Blanchet wrote:

Frenchmen, do you not think that German earth is too cold and heavy to guard such bodies? ... We do not wish that French mothers and French wives should go each year on All Souls' Day to weep in German cemeteries in the midst of those who killed their fathers, their sons, their husbands.[63]

The government estimated the cost of the repatriation of prisoners' bodies at 7,420,846 francs – 818 francs per body moved from Germany to a special prisoner of war graveyard which was built for this purpose at Sarrebourg and 1,224 francs per body returned to its family for burial.[64] Using the information regarding the location of French prisoner graves in Germany, which had been collected in 1919 by the initial post-war French military mission under General Dupont, made up of twelve officers, seventeen *sous-officiers* and three civilians, sent to Berlin to find missing prisoners, the repatriation of bodies was finally completed by 1926; the French government also requested the International Red Cross in Geneva to go through all its files to help locate the graves of French captives.[65] Nothing could better symbolise the success of the French ex-prisoners' mobilisation than the fact that the opening of the prisoner of war graveyard at Sarrebourg in Alsace, close to the battlefield where Major-General

[61] *Ibid.*

[62] ACICR, 448/VII/c.65; See also Francis Grandhomme, 'Une manifestation du devoir de mémoire. L'inauguration du cimitière des prisonniers de la grande guerre, Sarrebourg, 12 septembre 1926', Association Nationale du Souvenir de la Bataille de Verdun, *Les Cahiers de la Grande Guerre*, 28 (2001), pp. 35–7.

[63] Becker, *Oubliés de la Grande Guerre*, p. 362.   [64] SHAT, 10 N 194, D.1. Annexe.

[65] SHAT, 7 N 362, supplément, Paris, Le Président du Conseil, M. de la G. à Mr le Maréchal Commandant en Chef les Armées Alliées, État nominatif du personnel désigné pour faire partie de la mission de recherche des disparus, 31.7.1919; Djurović, *L'Agence Centrale de Recherches du Comité International de la Croix-Rouge*, p. 72.

Stenger, one of the German individuals the French put forward for trial for war crimes at Leipzig, had shot French prisoners of war out of hand in 1914, was carried out with all the pomp and ceremony due to dead combatants.[66] Symbolically, the sculpture chosen for the cemetery was one of prisoner agony, a man on his knees, his head thrown back in torment, which had been made during the war in Grafenwöhr camp in Bavaria.[67] The repatriation of prisoner bodies and the establishment of the Sarrebourg prisoner of war graveyard marked a major victory for ex-prisoners in their campaign against the marginalisation of their experience in official war remembrance.

However, prisoners not only pursued moral recognition for their experiences through their collective actions: they also sought it through individual writings. French ex-prisoners of all ranks produced memoirs prolifically during the interwar period, as a way of publicising their experiences; in contrast to the British case, memoir writing was not largely restricted to former officers.[68] This explains why the memory of the harsher experiences of wartime captivity, which were almost all confined to other-rank soldier prisoners, continued to exist in the 1920s in France, long after it had been excluded from the public sphere in Britain. Violence against captives was central to the image of captivity which ex-prisoners depicted in their writings, in part reflecting the proactive campaign to convince the public that prisoners were not shirkers; Fernand Relange's memoir, Huit mois dans les lignes allemandes, published in 1919, is a typical example. Relange sought to prove that prisoners were not cowards, opening his memoir with extracts from his two citations for bravery prior to his capture.[69] He went on to describe in detail the starvation and harsh labour conditions endured by French prisoners kept working for the German army in the occupied territories in 1918.

For some, memoirs were a duty. As Robert d'Harcourt wrote in 1922 of his captivity in Germany: 'In spite of our legitimate hatred of the German, I would say even because of this hatred, so that it can be rigorously and

---

[66] Grandhomme, 'Une manifestation du devoir de mémoire', pp. 22–4; Horne and Kramer, German Atrocities, p. 348.

[67] Grandhomme, 'Une manifestation du devoir de mémoire', p. 27.

[68] A survey of the original card catalogues of the BDIC-MHC Nanterre, the Weltkriegssammlung in the Staatsbibliothek zu Berlin and the British Museum, London provides the titles of 170 memoirs published between 1919 and 1941 written by British and French prisoners captured by Germany and German prisoners held by Britain or France. Of these 73 were written by French ex-prisoners, 62 by German ex-prisoners and 35 by British ex-prisoners.

[69] Relange, Huit mois dans les lignes allemandes. See also the descriptions of captivity in BDIC-MHC Nanterre, O pièce 14505. Fédération nationale des anciens prisonniers de guerre, évadés et otages, pamphlet, Les Prisonniers de guerre, n.d.

exactly justified, it is an absolute duty for those of us who have seen them from up close, to only write and tell of them what is true.'[70] For Harcourt, his memoir was a way of exorcising the harsh experiences of his captivity and showing that prisoners too had fought their own wartime battles. His attempts to escape, recounted in detail, highlight this.[71] Indeed, ex-prisoners generally sought to portray captivity as a legitimate form of wartime combat for France, as an interwar pamphlet produced by the *Fédération nationale des anciens prisonniers de guerre* illustrates:

> In olden times the courage of each man was the essential factor in victory ... But what was possible in olden times when hand-to-hand combat determined victory has become difficult with modern methods whose destructive power is unimaginable for those who have never lived the life of the trenches, who have not been involved in titanic battles or been on a lunar landscape in the middle of swathes of asphyxiating gas, under machine-gun tornados, attacking determined men .... At a moment inscribed only on the wheel of fortune, one of these adversaries may surrender, not because of weakness but because he has no other means left of resisting.[72]

The pamphlet emphasised how French prisoners of war, despite enduring hardships, fought on against Germany during their captivity by sabotaging crops and industry; they continued to act as combatants even while incarcerated:

> There are numerous facts which we could cite, because there were hundreds of thousands of isolated prisoners, left to their own resources, exposed to the reprisals of their captors who, away from the limelight, magnificently carried out their duty ...[73]

One former prisoner, Charles Chassé, an English teacher at the Lycée de Brest, in a speech at the school prize-giving in 1919, even described the continued fight by prisoners during their captivity as a key contributing factor to French victory: for Chassé, French prisoners had acted as 'missionaries of the Republic', political indoctrinators of the German peasant population.[74] They were not cowards, but agents of French victory: it was their parcels that shattered local confidence that the German submarines were starving out the Allies; it was their table manners, teaching German peasants in some areas to eat from plates rather than from a collective shared pot, and their superior knowledge of farming, teaching German farmers how to sow seeds properly, that taught Germans to respect

---

[70] D'Harcourt, *Souvenirs de captivité et d'évasions*, p. 12.   [71] *Ibid.*

[72] BDIC-MHC Nanterre, O pièce 14505. Fédération nationale des anciens prisonniers de guerre, évadés et otages, pamphlet, *Les Prisonniers de guerre*, n.d.

[73] *Ibid.*

[74] BDIC-MHC Nanterre, O pièce 15505, Lycée de Brest, 12.7.19, M. Chassé, pp. 16–18.

France.[75] Above all, they taught German civilians that France was a land of ease, without *Ersatz*, where moderate work secured a comfortable life for all, because France 'was a Republic; because France did not have a Kaiser or a Kronprinz'.[76] Yet, despite this vindication of captives as combatants, Chassé also made sure to emphasise his front experience, outlining the lack of fear he felt during battle: 'full of enthusiasm ... without a single reservation'.[77] This was the glorification of battle of the former prisoner, determined in his speech to allay any suspicions of cowardice.

This depiction, which dominated in the majority of French ex-prisoners' accounts, of captives as combatants who continued to fight for France despite violent German mistreatment was not uncontested, however; precisely because not all prisoners had suffered in Germany, it proved impossible for ex-captives to sustain a uniform image of German brutality. The gap between captivity experiences of ease and hardship was evident even to ex-prisoners: in his speech, Charles Chassé pointed out that prisoners' accounts often sounded contradictory because 'certain forest *Kommandos* and almost all the mine *Kommandos* without exception (in particular the salt mines) were hell (*bagnes*) right up to the day of the Armistice; they did not ration the spade and bayonet blows'.[78] However, 'in certain peasant families in contrast ... the prisoners were treated as children (and some as masters) of the house'.[79]

It was this very contradictory nature of the different types of captivity experience that fed the idea in France that prisoners had had an easy time during the war: it even led some ex-prisoners to challenge accounts of violent captivities, attributing them to false wartime propaganda. In 1925, Georges Connes, a former officer prisoner in Germany, wrote in his memoir of his experience:

I am going to say something that might be considered shocking: if by our own choice and use of means to kill, we have been more monstrous in this war than ever before, the horror of the treatment of prisoners is far from having increased proportionately, and I am not at all certain that such treatment has not been better than ever, given the enormous number of prisoners.[80]

Intended as a response to a negative memoir of captivity by Thierry Sandre, entitled *Le Purgatoire*, Connes' memoir contested the accounts

[75] BDIC-MHC Nanterre, O pièce 15505, Lycée de Brest, Année scolaire 1918–1919, Discours prononcé à la distribution des prix le 12 juillet 1919, par M. Chassé, pp. 1–20.
[76] *Ibid.*, p. 18.   [77] *Ibid.*   [78] *Ibid.*, p. 12.   [79] *Ibid.*, p. 13.
[80] Georges Connes, *A POW's Memoir of the First World War. The Other Ordeal*, ed. Lois Davis Vines (Oxford and New York, 2004), p. 4; see also the reconciliatory narrative by Jacques Rivière, *L'Allemand. Souvenirs et réflections d'un prisonnier de guerre* (Paris, 1918).

of his fellow ex-prisoners who emphasised mistreatment; writing against the dominant popular view of captivity, he was ultimately unable to find a publisher for his work, which did not appear in print until 2001.[81]

In some ways, Connes' memoir resembles the more famous critique by the French interwar writer Jean Norton Cru, who, in 1929, claimed that many of the writings of his fellow ex-combatants were inaccurate or exaggerated.[82] Yet Connes, who had spent his captivity within the relatively protected confines of a prisoner of war camp for officers, raised inherent contradictions in his text. He sought to justify his position and, in so doing, alluded to a different wartime reality to the version of captivity he wished to present.

Basically, all prisoners witnessed the same things, minor incidents compared with the realities of war. Only a few have dared to create literary works out of these petty annoyances and the insignificant exchange of jabs that took place far from the real battlefield. When all is said and done, we must realise that prisoners of war slept inside most nights, away from the risk of mutilation and death, and we had something to put in our bellies almost every day. Being in the habit of only talking about what I know first-hand I will limit my account to the experiences of the officers, *referring only occasionally to the Russian officers, who practically starved to death by the thousands.* While not intending to underestimate the moral suffering of prisoners of war (*I know many did not make it back*), I remind myself that the proportion of fatalities among prisoners during and after captivity was much smaller than among the men who fought and were not captured.[83]

The interwar privileging of the battlefield dead had been internalised by Connes, altering how he saw the experience of captivity. Yet although Connes wished to argue that captivity was the better fate, he could not entirely reconcile this with his underlying knowledge of the darker aspects of imprisonment, which he had been spared. The desire to write a reconciliatory text, showing the enemy in a human light, lay behind Connes' textual inconsistencies: 'It was in the other ordeal, in the prisoner of war camps, that we could learn, if we did not already know it, that a man is a man and nothing more. Nothing very admirable, whatever the colour or shape of his clothes or the language he speaks.'[84]

By the early 1930s, however, such pacifist attitudes became more common among former French prisoners. There were two reasons for

---

[81] Georges Connes, *L'Autre Épreuve. Souvenirs hétérodoxes de captivité, 1916–1919* (Paris, Montreal, Budapest, 2001).

[82] Connes, *A POW's Memoir of the First World War*, p. 1; Cru, *Témoins*. On Norton Cru's work see Leonard V. Smith, 'Jean Norton Cru and Combatants' Literature of the First World War', *Modern and Contemporary France*, 9, 2 (2001), pp. 161–9.

[83] Connes, *A POW's Memoir of the First World War*, p. 1. Italic emphasis mine.

[84] *Ibid.*, p. 6.

this. First, the general growth of the pacifist movement among French veterans also had an influence upon ex-prisoners.[85] The détente which followed the 1925 Locarno Treaty facilitated German veterans' associations sending representatives to the 1928 Luxembourg Congress, organised by the Inter-Allied Federation of Ex-Combatants, the *Fédération Interalliée des Anciens Combattants* (FIDAC), an umbrella association which linked war veterans from Allied countries. Such encounters between French and German ex-servicemen gradually changed the cultural climate. Perhaps the most dramatic meeting was the enormous 12 July 1936 demonstration at Verdun, where veterans from all over France, joined by their German and Italian counterparts, took an oath declaring their desire for peace.[86] As in the British case, this growth of pacifism led to a reassessment of the meaning of 1914–18 captivity: the enemy of the prisoner was no longer perceived as Germany, but rather modern war itself. At a pacifist exhibition organised in the early 1930s by the Catholic activist Marc Sangnier, a photograph of French prisoners bore the caption: 'They have known fatigue, neglect, reprisals and hunger. Question them, however; they have not learnt to hate men but to hate war.'[87]

Second, the signing of a new, third, Geneva Convention, in 1929, dedicated totally to prisoner of war treatment, which went far beyond the existing first two Conventions of 1864 and 1906, which dealt with the treatment of the enemy wounded in battle, restored former prisoners' faith in international law.[88] In 1923, the tenth conference of the International Red Cross laid the groundwork for this additional 1929 convention, which addressed in detail the precise abuses that had occurred during the First World War.[89] Indeed, the legacy of the First World War was omnipresent during its drafting: Gustav Rasmussen, a Danish plenipotentiary and the Danish chargé d'affaires at Berne, even dedicated his account of the drafting of the 1929 convention to 'the unknown prisoner of war'.[90] The new convention was created specifically because international and national observers, such as the International Red Cross, knew that prisoner mistreatment had occurred during the conflict.[91] Their acknowledgement of the need for a new convention was in itself a form of official recognition for ex-prisoners and a vindication of the claims

---

[85] Antoine Prost, *Les Anciens Combattants, 1914–1940* (Paris, 1977), pp. 121–3.
[86] *Ibid.*, p. 123.   [87] Becker, *Oubliés de la Grande Guerre*, p. 370.
[88] See Wylie, 'The 1929 Prisoner of War Convention', pp. 91–111.
[89] Comité International de la Croix-Rouge, 'Le Code du Prisonnier. Rapport présenté par le Comité International à la Xme Conférence', *Revue Internationale de la Croix-Rouge*, 3e Année, 26, in *Bulletin International des Sociétés de la Croix-Rouge*, 52e Année, nos. 221–6 (January–June 1921), pp. 100–29.
[90] Rasmussen, *Code des prisonniers de guerre*, pp. 1–11.   [91] *Ibid.*

of those who stated they had been mistreated. By 1929, many veterans were strongly in favour of this revision of international law: the 1928 FIDAC Luxembourg Congress even drafted its own list of proposals for a new international law to protect prisoners, blaming the failure of international law during the war for their sufferings; much of this text overlapped with the 1929 Geneva Convention.[92] Among the German veterans who participated in this process at the Congress was Dr Joachim Givens, from the main German ex-prisoners of war association, the *Reichsvereinigung ehemaliger Kriegsgefangener*.[93] The 1929 Geneva Convention ultimately meant that many contemporaries felt reassured that prisoner mistreatment was less likely in future wars. The fear of repetition had been significantly reduced, allowing ex-prisoners to culturally demobilise. By the mid-1930s, in France, there was a shift away from ex-prisoners' demands for justice and their emphasis upon violent prisoner mistreatment, which had dominated the 1920s image of the prisoner, towards more social and reconciliatory portrayals of captivity. It is this change that is reflected in *La Grande Illusion*.

The general shift towards pacifism meant that discussion of wartime violence against French prisoners became much rarer by the late 1930s. Ex-prisoners and the French public alike now prioritised European reconciliation, fearing the outbreak of another conflict. As Reid Mitchell has written of prisoner memory after the American Civil War, 'The price of reconciliation was – as so often occurs – a blurring of the historical reality. It was easier to forget prisoners of war than to seek justice.'[94] Captivity remained a problematic subject in France throughout the interwar period: greatly stigmatised in the 1920s, by the following decade it was marginalised because it was only possible to mention in ways that promoted reconciliation. This impeded any accurate interwar French historicisation of prisoner treatment.

The way prisoners were 'forgotten' in interwar France was thus very different to the British case. Whereas in Britain, no distinct historicisation of captivity took place because ex-prisoners' experiences were amalgamated into a generic, shared combatant memory, particularly through the British Legion, in France, the experience of prisoners of war was initially deliberately excluded from the official history of the war. Amnesia in France was imposed upon prisoners from within their own society, which, suspicious of their surrender, wished to exalt the heroic front

---

[92] BA, R 8095.4.   [93] *Ibid.*
[94] Reid Mitchell, '"Our prison system supposing we had any". Die Kriegsgefangenenpolitik der Konföderierten und der Unionisten im Amerikanischen Bürgerkrieg', in Overmans, ed., *In der Hand des Feindes*, p. 213.

combatant dead. This process of marginalising the memory of captivity was continually challenged by French ex-prisoners throughout the 1920s. Ultimately, it is ironic that during the interwar period the French government was reluctant to commemorate the very prisoner mistreatment it had so carefully chronicled in its own wartime propaganda. Against this cultural consensus, French prisoners fought a courageous but ultimately unsuccessful battle for a place in the national memory throughout the interwar period using memoir testimony and their veterans' associations. However, by the 1930s, with war in Europe again looming, the historicisation of their First World War captivity experiences was subordinated to the imperatives of French appeasement.

Writing the history of prisoners of war in interwar Germany

Ironically, it was German prisoners of war who enjoyed the most positive recognition from their compatriots in the 1920s. At first glance this appears inexplicable. After all, the massive surrenders of 1918 were a major factor in Germany's defeat. However, no significant interwar stigma, comparable to that which occurred in France, developed in Germany in the 1920s towards those who had returned from captivity. In fact, ex-prisoners, far from being marginalised, enjoyed considerable historical and political attention and consideration at the national level. However, the historical narrative on captivity which German ex-prisoners ultimately promoted revolved around the prison camp experience as one of social and national regeneration, emphasising the political lessons about 'community' which German society could learn from the prisoners' comradeship as well as the need for European reconciliation through a revision of the Versailles Treaty in Germany's favour. Discussion of prisoner mistreatment was marginalised within this overall discourse, which portrayed the prisoner as an agent for positive social change rather than a victim: when violence against captives was mentioned by ex-prisoners, it was usually in order to promote an anti-war message as part of this ex-prisoners' mission to improve German society.

There were several reasons for the largely positive status of German ex-prisoners. First, the circumstances surrounding repatriation help to explain why this situation developed. German prisoners were a major political issue in 1919 and 1920 because of the Allies' decision to delay their release. Consequently, as the previous chapter has shown, they became a symbolic rallying point, not only for the German right, but for the entire German political spectrum. Perhaps the only thing which all of Germany agreed on in 1919–20 was that the Allies' refusal to let German prisoners home to their families, over a year after the war had ended, was morally wrong. This created a groundswell of popular goodwill towards prisoners among the general public. It also created an element of fear: the left felt it was necessary to reach out to former German prisoners who had missed the events of the revolution and were resentful that the new government had not obtained their release earlier; the right felt it was necessary to welcome German prisoners because they might make valuable reactionary fighters, especially given the various right-wing plans to carry out a putsch in Germany in 1919 and 1920.[95] In the early Weimar Republic, in which every political faction was eager to increase its support, there was no bloc that wished to alienate former prisoners.

The prisoners' own attitudes, however, were highly complex: the French action in retaining German prisoners meant that anti-French feeling was prevalent among many repatriated German captives, as well as a dislike of the Weimar State; as one pamphlet put it: 'Embittered men are travelling home. Embittered against the foreign state which treated them harder than necessary and held them prisoner longer than was just; embittered also against the homeland, whose indifference and lack of energy they believe to be partly responsible for their fate.'[96] However, many of these repatriated prisoners also returned home strongly anti-war. Others, in particular those arriving from Russia, arrived in Germany with pro-Bolshevik attitudes. The same pamphlet reported that 'a large number of those prisoners who have returned from Russia have joined with those elements of the population who have set about the most threatening resistance to the rebuilding of our economic and political life'.[97] The belief among German right-wing groups was thus that providing support for prisoners would prevent them turning to Bolshevism. In the immediate aftermath of the war, the German political centre and right therefore endorsed an inclusive memory of the German combatant that did not discriminate against ex-prisoners.

In particular, this context meant that there was widespread political support for the main German ex-prisoners of war veterans' association, the centre-right *Reichsvereinigung ehemaliger Kriegsgefangener* (ReK), because it was seen as a stabilising, bourgeois, conservative influence that would help stop former prisoners becoming Bolsheviks. Founded in order to prevent looting in Constance during the German revolution by Freiherr

---

[95] On putsch plans see Horne and Kramer, *German Atrocities*, pp. 337–41.

[96] Gustav Boehmer, *Denkschrift über die Forderung der Kriegsgefangenen auf volle Gleichberechtigung mit den sonstigen Heeresangehörigen* (Berlin, 1919), pp. 1–5.

[97] *Ibid*. On repatriated prisoners becoming Bolsheviks see Ian Kershaw, *Hitler*, vol. I: *Hubris, 1889–1936* (London, 2001), p. 123.

Wilhelm von Lersner, a former officer prisoner, from a group of fellow prisoners on one of the last trainloads of German captives exchanged by France in November 1918, the ReK rapidly became a significant lobby group, agitating for the release of German prisoners still held by the Allies.[98] Claiming 30,000 members by the late 1920s, the success of the ReK was the second key reason for the high profile of captivity in the German historicisation of the war in the 1920s. Indeed, the historian Rainer Pöppinghege points out that at its height in spring 1921 the ReK claimed to have 400,000 members, representing roughly a third of all ex-prisoners.[99] It was extremely well connected: while its membership came from all backgrounds, its leadership was largely from the upper classes and the aristocracy. The ReK described itself as a *Frontkämpferverband*, and, in contrast to France, this claim by German ex-prisoners to 'front combatant' status was never really substantially challenged by German politicians or the public, although within the ReK the ex-prisoners themselves continually felt insecure, believing that society viewed them suspiciously, as 'second-class veterans' compared to other ex-servicemen.[100] Throughout the 1920s and early 1930s, the ReK campaigned successfully for both the financial and moral recognition of ex-prisoners' sacrifices.

The ReK initially campaigned alongside its sister lobby group, the *Volksbund zum Schutz der Deutschen Kriegs- und Zivilgefangenen*, an organisation founded in December 1918 for the families and friends of German prisoners, for the Allies to release their German captives; in Berlin in 1921 the ReK held a mass protest to highlight the plight of German prisoners held back in France due to the fact that they were serving prison sentences for misdemeanours committed during captivity.[101] In 1919, it also produced pamphlets that were distributed to newly repatriated prisoners which explained the changes that, during their absence, the revolution had brought about in Germany; these pamphlets were largely supportive of Weimar democracy.[102] With the repatriation of the majority of German prisoners of war from France in spring 1920 and from Russia in 1922,

---

[98] Rose, *Krieg nach dem Kriege*, pp. 45–6.

[99] BA, R 8095.5; Pöppinghege, '"Kriegsteilnehmer zweiter Klasse"?', p. 401. There were a handful of other very small local ex-prisoner associations in existence in Germany in the 1920s such as the Kameradschaft ehemaliger Kriegsgefangener Dresden or the Vereinigung ehemaliger Kriegsgefangener in Sibirien (Breslau), none of which developed beyond a single local grouping. Pöppinghege, '"Kriegsteilnehmer zweiter Klasse"?', p. 396.

[100] BA, R 8095.1, Aktenvermerk. Betr. Rücksprache mit Ministerialrat Schreiber, Finanzministerium am 11.6.1929. Pöppinghege, '"Kriegsteilnehmer zweiter Klasse"?', p. 403.

[101] *Ibid.*, pp. 399–400.

[102] Freiherr Wilhelm von Lersner, *Gefangenschaft und Heimkehr* (Berlin, 1919); Freiherr Wilhelm von Lersner, *Wir Gefangenen und die Not der Heimat* (Berlin, 1919).

however, the ReK and the *Volksbund* switched from lobbying for prisoners' repatriation to campaigning for prisoners' rights. Despite the much more favourable cultural attitudes to ex-prisoners in Germany, there remained inequalities in the financial compensation offered to prisoner veterans for their time in captivity in comparison with non-prisoner ex-servicemen.[103] The *Volksbund* campaigned to change what it viewed as discriminatory regulations against ex-prisoners, which meant that captivity only counted as a service period if the prisoner concerned had suffered particular danger to his life and health.[104] It also campaigned for prisoners to be paid for their time in captivity, and for outstanding acts of bravery during captivity to be eligible for military awards.[105] Together with the ReK, it was extremely successful: after negotiations, obtaining agreement in 1921 that prisoners would be compensated for outstanding wartime pay.[106] In 1919, Finance Minister Bernhard Dernburg also made a fund of 20 million marks available to assist needy prisoners of war during their repatriation.[107]

Between 1919 and 1922, the ReK focused on assisting former prisoners to reintegrate into German society, advertising jobs and housing in its newsletter, *Der Heimkehrer*, which it produced from 1918 to 1929.[108] It lobbied political parties to adopt the issue of prisoner welfare, holding regular flag days to raise money and public awareness of former prisoners, many of whom found themselves disadvantaged in finding employment due to the fact that they had been released long after the majority of German soldiers had been demobilised and returned to work.[109] The ReK also liaised with the German equivalent of the Imperial War Graves Commission, the *Volksbund Deutsche Kriegsgräberfürsorge*, to ensure the upkeep of German prisoner of war graves in France and Russia.[110] Although the ReK went bankrupt in the 1923 German inflation crisis, von Lersner rapidly refounded it the following year; although membership never returned to the high figures of the early 1920s, the association

---

[103] BA, R 8095.5, Anträge zum Bundestag 1926, 4.-6. Juni in Remagen am Rhein.
[104] Boehmer, *Denkschrift über die Forderung der Kriegsgefangenen.*   [105] *Ibid.*
[106] Pöppinghege, '"Kriegsteilnehmer zweiter Klasse"?', p. 403.   [107] *Ibid.*
[108] BA, R 8095.5, 11. Bundestag der Reichsvereinigung ehemaliger Kriegsgefangener, n.d. For copies of *Der Heimkehrer*, see Archives of the League of Nations, United Nations Library, Geneva, 1708 Registry International Labour Office, Refugees mixed archival group – Fonds Nansen, Registry files (1920–1924) Box R 1708, 73 files, *Der Heimkehrer*, 1920–1922. *Der Heimkehrer* was still in existence in 1929. See BA, R 8095.1, Aktenvermerk, 21.6.1929, Betr. Entschädigungsfragen. Rücksprache mit Kamerad Pfandner vom Reichsbund der Kriegsbeschädigten am 21. Juni 1929.
[109] BA, R 8095.1, Aktenvermerk. Besprechung mit Fräulein Klante 29.12.1928; BA, R 8095.5, 11. Bundestag der Reichsvereinigung ehemaliger Kriegsgefangener, n.d.
[110] BA, R 8095.1, Aktenvermerk. Besprechung mit Volksbund Deutsche Kriegsgräberfürsorge, 19.12.28.

remained a significant, well-connected force.[111] Through the efforts of the ReK's patron, Elsa Brändström, a Swedish woman known to ex-prisoners as the 'angel of Siberia' because of her work bringing supplies personally to prison camps in Russia during the war, for which she was considered for the Nobel Peace Prize in the early 1920s, two sanatoria for disabled ex-prisoners, Marienborn and Gut Schreibermühle, as well as an orphanage called Neusorge for the children of German prisoners who had died in captivity, were established.[112] The ReK was also keen to commemorate those prisoners who had died in captivity. Initially it considered adopting the memorial built by Allied prisoners at Soltau camp, to those of their number who had died, for this purpose, before deciding that a memorial to Allied prisoners would not work as a memorial to the 'sacrificial death' ('*Opfertod*') of German prisoners of war.[113] Disagreements about how to finance a memorial further delayed the project.[114] However, in 1931 the ReK finally erected its own memorial to dead prisoners of war, symbolically located at the Tannenberg National War Memorial, highlighting the extent to which the German nationalist right accepted ex-prisoners; indeed, the head of the Tannenberg Memorial Committee, Generalmajor Hans Kahns, gratified the ReK by describing the dead prisoners as 'front warriors in the purest sense of the word', echoing the claim of von Lersner the previous year that 'whoever fell into captivity fought for his country in the most advanced front position'.[115]

Through the ReK's lobbying for prisoners' rights on pension and other welfare issues, its leadership soon came to be seen as a stabilising political intermediary between the Weimar government and ex-prisoners. Yet, although it claimed publicly to be politically neutral throughout its existence, in reality the ReK was deeply ambiguous about the Weimar Republic: its leaders were typical early Weimar conservatives, who had initially supported the new state out of fear of Bolshevism. They moved further to the right as the 1920s continued, campaigning openly against the Versailles Treaty, as illustrated by their 1923 pamphlet *Friedensdiktat, Rechtsungültigkeit. Das Friedensdiktat, seine Rechtsungültigkeit und die Mittel,*

---

[111] BA, R 8095.5, 11. Bundestag der Reichsvereinigung ehemaliger Kriegsgefangener, n.d.
[112] Rachamimov, *POWs and the Great War*, pp. 164–9, 222; BA-MA, Msg 200 / 454, 'Die Idee von Neusorge'. Norgard Kohlhagen, *Elsa Brändström. Die Frau, die man Engel nannte* (Stuttgart, 1991), p. 173.
[113] Klaus Otte, *Lager Soltau. Das Kriegsgefangenen- und Interniertenlager des Ersten Weltkriegs (1914–1921). Geschichte und Geschichten* (Soltau, 1999), pp. 301–2.
[114] BA, R 8095.5, Entwurf einer Aktennotiz, ReK und VeK.
[115] Pöppinghege, '"Kriegsteilnehmer zweiter Klasse"?', p. 410.

sich von ihm zu befreien and, in particular, the 'war guilt' clause.[116] This right-leaning campaign against Versailles raised tensions within the organisation. Unusually for Weimar veterans' associations, the ReK had managed to remain unified during the revolutionary period; an ReK memo noted: 'We were all proud of the fact that despite revolution and internal conflicts, the ReK was the only organisation in which everyone was united. No other veterans' organisation could boast similar unity.'[117] Indeed von Lersner believed that no revision of Versailles could be achieved unless Germans from right and left united and for this reason insisted on proclaiming that the ReK was above party politics and neutral on domestic political divisions.[118] By 1925, however, a split became unavoidable due to the ReK's campaign against Versailles and, in particular, the anti-Versailles Mühlhaus programme put forward by the ReK leadership in 1925: some members of the ReK branches in Bremen and in Berlin, where the ReK was SPD-dominated, broke away to found a smaller rival, pacifist association, the *Arbeitsgemeinschaft der Vereinigung ehemaliger Kriegsgefangener Deutschlands* (VeK), which campaigned against the idea of military service and promoted the Republic.[119] The VeK viewed the ReK's programme as too nationalist, its leadership as dominated by right-wing ex-officers and its campaign against the 'war guilt' clause in the Treaty of Versailles as reactionary.[120] However, the two organisations did occasionally still coordinate their efforts in the late 1920s when campaigning on prisoner financial compensation issues.[121]

By the late 1920s, the ReK leadership was espousing increasingly *völkisch* ideas, promoting the idea of the German need for greater 'living space' (*Lebensraum*), which echoed the rhetoric of the National Socialist party.[122] Yet for the ReK, its conservative German nationalism was not incompatible with pacifism – throughout its existence, it claimed to be

---

[116] Berlin, Staatsbibliothek, Weltkriegsammlung, Krieg – 1914, 26883, Reichsvereinigung ehemaliger Kriegsgefangener e.v., Bundesleitung, *Friedensdiktat, Rechtsungültigkeit. Das Friedensdiktat, seine Rechtsungültigkeit und die Mittel, sich von ihm zu befreien* (Berlin and Magdeburg, 1923). Pöppinghege, '"Kriegsteilnehmer zweiter Klasse"?', p. 405.

[117] BA, R 8095.5, Entwurf einer Aktennotiz, 20., ReK und VeK.

[118] BA, R. 8095.1, Aktennotiz, Freiherr von Lersner, 26.8.1929.

[119] BA, R 8095.5, Entwurf einer Aktennotiz, ReK und VeK. The ReK had over 400 local groups, the VeK 20. The VeK produced its own newsletter *Daheim*. BA, R 8095.5, Rundschreiben der VeK, n.d. [1926]. Pöppinghege, '"Kriegsteilnehmer zweiter Klasse"?', p. 404.

[120] BA, R 8095.5, Aktennotiz über die Tagung in Aschersleben am 29.1.1927.

[121] Pöppinghege, '"Kriegsteilnehmer zweiter Klasse"?', p. 407.

[122] Freiherr von Lersner spoke of the 'German living space emergency' ('*Deutsche Raumnot*') as the greatest hindrance to peace at the 11th Bundestag der Reichsvereinigung ehemaliger Kriegsgefangener: BA, R 8095.5, 11. Bundestag der Reichsvereinigung ehemaliger Kriegsgefangener, n.d.

staunchly anti-war and avoided extreme nationalistic statements.[123] Its conservative leaders contended that the injustice of the Treaty of Versailles was the barrier to reconciliation between the peoples of Europe and that a strong Germany on the international stage would lead to greater European harmony. The organisation thus saw itself as promoting European reconciliation and peace, through revision of Versailles, sending a delegation to the 1928 Luxembourg Congress of the *Fédération Interalliée des Anciens Combattants*; it also had intensive contact with French and British veterans.[124] It also supported the plans to revise international law to provide better protection for prisoners; indeed Dr Joachim Givens, a member of the ReK leadership, was part of the official German delegation to the negotiations for the new 1929 Geneva Convention on prisoners of war.[125] The ReK also became part of the umbrella group the *Deutsche Kriegsgefangenenliga*, which represented the main Austrian, German and Czechoslovak ex-prisoner of war associations at the international level.[126]

Within this context, prisoner mistreatment was narrated by the ReK only in terms of its potential anti-war message: the ReK maintained that it had a responsibility to publicise the worst experiences of captivity as a warning to society about the horrors of war. The founder of the ReK, Wilhelm von Lersner, outlined in a speech in 1922 that

We former prisoners of war know all too well that we as the defeated will not win the trust of the victor with the call 'Never again war', and we do not make this statement to convince the victor; but because we have recognised the greatness of this precept . . . There is one thing we plan to do in this time of internal battle, and that is to ensure that the call 'Never again war' will apply to our own people![127]

The ReK's commemoration of prisoner mistreatment in the First World War thus occurred within the framework of its anti-war campaign, believing that through such commemoration society might learn valuable lessons. At a meeting in January 1929, von Lersner stated that 'in order to preserve the memory of the terrible experiences of captivity as a warning to future generations, it is absolutely necessary to collect everything which

---

[123] Pöppinghege, '"Kriegsteilnehmer zweiter Klasse"?', p. 411.   [124] *Ibid.*, p. 419.
[125] *Ibid.* See also Wilfried Rogasch, 'Zur Geschichte der Sammlung', in Rosmarie Beier and Bettina Biedermann, eds., *Kriegsgefangen. Objekte aus der Sammlung des Archivs und Museums der Kriegsgefangenschaft, Berlin und des Verbandes der Heimkehrer, Kriegsgefangenen und Vermisstenangehörigen Deutschlands e.V., Bonn–Bad Godesberg im Deutschen Historischen Museum, 30. Oktober 1990 bis 30. November 1990* (Berlin, 1990), p. 12; BA, R 8095.3; BA, R 8095.1, Aktenvermerk. Betr. Archiv und Museum der Kriegsgefangenschaft, Unterredung mit Herrn Rudolf Lissmann, 23.2.1929.
[126] Pöppinghege, '"Kriegsteilnehmer zweiter Klasse"?', p. 396.
[127] Rogasch, 'Zur Geschichte der Sammlung', p. 12.

is needed as a basis for the historical examination of prisoner of war captivity'.[128] In a radio speech in 1930, to mark the French evacuation of the Rhineland, von Lersner also emphasised that it was the task of ex-prisoners to teach society the positive lessons from captivity: ex-prisoners could, he believed, help dismantle harmful class structures by recounting the positive 'classless' national nature of the prison camp society as a model '*Volksgemeinschaft*'.[129]

Ex-prisoners in this discourse were no longer victims but proactive prophets: they could, the ReK felt, promote the reordering of society along what they saw as the positive values of the shared prison camp community. They could also warn of the evils of war, thereby preventing its repetition. The ReK thus passionately promoted the memory of prisoners of war during the interwar period, financially supporting the publication of studies on prisoner of war history and setting up an archive for documents and artefacts from captivity.[130] The ReK even planned to establish a scholarship for a university student to research the history of prisoners during the conflict.[131] By 1929, the ReK was planning a prisoner of war museum.[132] For former German prisoners, unable to visit the graves of their comrades who died in France, Britain or Russia, this historicisation of the prisoner experience was both a form of mourning and commemoration.

As part of this historicisation process, the ReK supported a wide range of historical publications on prisoners' wartime experiences. Reflecting its claim to be politically neutral, it did not limit its support to publications on the treatment of German prisoners abroad but was also interested in work on the social life of Allied prisoners in Germany. It had its own publishing company, Verlag ReK, and also worked with the Ost-Europa Verlag.[133] Thus it was possible for the ReK to write a short foreword endorsing a nationalist collection of prisoner reminiscences in 1929, while at the same time sponsoring the publication of a key study of prisoner theatre which presented a much milder version of First World War captivity.[134] This

---

[128] BA, R 8095.1, Aktenvermerk. Aussprache über Archiv und Museum der Kriegsgefangenschaft am 9. Januar 1929.

[129] Pöppinghege, '"Kriegsteilnehmer zweiter Klasse"?', pp. 404, 415.

[130] BA, R 8095.1, Aktenvermerk. Aussprache über Archiv und Museum der Kriegsgefangenschaft am 9. Januar 1929.

[131] BA, R 8095.1, Aktenvermerk, Betr. Archiv und Museum der Kriegsgefangenschaft, Unterredung mit Herrn Rudolf Lissmann, 23.2.1929.

[132] BA, R 8095.1, Aktenvermerk Betr. Archiv und Museum der Kriegsgefangenschaft, Unterredung mit Herrn Rudolf Lissmann, Frankfurt a/M. 23.2.1929.

[133] BA, R 8095.1, Aktenvermerk. Aussprache über Archiv und Museum der Kriegsgefangenschaft am 9. Januar 1929.

[134] Fritz Ibrügger, ed., *PG Feldgraue in Frankreichs Zuchthäusern* (Hamburg, 1929), p. 8; Hermann Pörzgen, *Theater ohne Frau. Das Bühnenleben der kriegsgefangenen Deutschen, 1914–1920* (Berlin and Königsberg, 1933).

ReK work overlapped with a broader cultural interest among Weimar academic circles in the prisoners of war of 1914–18.[135] Drawing on German academia's wartime interest in camps as sociological and anthropological sites of study, scientists, psychiatrists and social researchers in Weimar rushed to analyse the lessons on human sexuality, language and communication forms which the history of prisoner of war camps might reveal.[136] The famous sexologist Magnus Hirschfeld was one example, studying prisoner sexuality.[137] Such sociological academic studies were often international in scope and aspired to impartial objectivity.

As a result of the work of the ReK, by 1933 the German prisoner of war was fully integrated into the historicisation of the war in Germany. This is clearly illustrated by Hitler's recognition of the association upon coming to power in January 1933. While the republican, pacifist VeK was forced to disband in spring 1933, the ReK was initially encouraged by the new regime: both Hindenburg and Hitler sent greetings by telegram to its annual meeting in July. There was jubilation among the ReK membership at Hitler's wording: 'I greet the honourable comrades who fell into captivity and who are members of the front soldiery (*Frontsoldatentum*) called to work to create the new Germany.'[138] The ReK leadership, already ideologically distant from the Weimar state and parliamentary democracy by 1933, saw Hitler's telegram as an official recognition of the ex-prisoner by the new Nazi regime; they had no difficulty after this point in believing that Hitler's plans overlapped with their own ideas regarding *Volksgemeinschaft* and putting national unity above party in-fighting.[139] Indeed, when the ReK organised a major exhibition in Hamburg in July 1933 on the prisoner of war, von Lersner's opening speech declared that: 'our *Reichsvereinigung*, in which from the beginning men of all classes and educational backgrounds, shoulder to shoulder as comrades, shared the

---

[135] An example of the ReK's international approach was the Austrian study of prisoners in all countries involved in the war, by Hans Weiland and Leopold Kern, the cover of which showed prisoners of all nationalities as the links in a circular chain – British, French, Japanese, American, German, Serb, Turkish, etc. symbolically displayed united. Weiland and Kern, eds., *In Feindeshand*, vol. II. The ReK had a close relationship with the Austrian BeöK and they coordinated on this project.

[136] Stefan Wangart and Richard Hellmann, *Die Zeitung im deutschen Gefangenen- u. Interniertenlager. Eine Bibliographie* (Bühl and Baden, 1920).

[137] For German socio-cultural research on prisoners see Magnus Hirschfeld, ed., *Sittengeschichte des Weltkrieges*, 2 vols., vol. II (Leipzig and Vienna, 1930); Hans Bayer, *Das Presse- und Nachrichtenwesen der im Weltkrieg kriegsgefangenen Deutschen* (Berlin, 1938); Pörzgen, *Theater ohne Frau*; Karl Scharping, *In russischer Gefangenschaft. Die kulturellen und wirtschaftlichen Leistungen der Kriegsgefangenen in Russland* (Berlin, 1939); Prof. Dr. Christoph Beck, *Die Frau und die Kriegsgefangenen*, 2 vols. (Nuremberg, 1919).

[138] Pöppinghege, '"Kriegsteilnehmer zweiter Klasse"?', p. 420.   [139] *Ibid.*, p. 421.

same fate, has always been the best example of National Socialism'.[140] Yet despite the ReK leadership's newfound enthusiasm for Nazi ideology, the organisation was still resolutely anti-war: the purpose of the Hamburg exhibition was to show 'the terrible conditions of captivity in which hundreds of thousands of our people suffered through depression, homesickness, privation and strain' and to counter the 'false image' of captivity which Dr Joachim Givens, the ReK exhibition organiser, claimed had developed in films.[141] On 22 July 1933, the ReK became part of the Kyffhäuserbund veterans' association and the year concluded with further official recognition, as President Hindenburg officially received three representatives of the ReK at the Presidential Palace to commemorate the anniversary of the founding of the organisation.[142] Hindenburg outlined how he believed that 'the bravest and most courageous who held out longest at the front' were those captured.[143] The ReK later laid a wreath on his behalf, in memory of the 165,000 German prisoners they claimed had died in captivity.[144]

However, the reality was that these 1933 events would turn out to be the pinnacle of official recognition of the ReK. The anti-war aims of the association were not in keeping with Nazi ideology: in the new National Socialist Germany, the ReK found it impossible to found their planned museum.[145] Von Lersner was also privately uneasy when the ReK was 'aryanised' under the Nazi regime; he felt that the anti-Semitic exclusion of Jewish veterans broke with the ideal of national unity.[146] In 1934, the patron of the ReK, Elsa Brändström, chose to emigrate to America with her husband, a Christian Socialist politician who opposed the Nazis.[147] Ultimately, in 1936 the ReK was liquidated as part of the *Gleichschaltung* policy of the Nazi state and the *Nationalsozialistische Kriegsopferversorgung* took over its role.[148] The reasons behind this are not clear, but it seems likely that the ReK's anti-war stance was one factor. In addition, the ReK represented an independent political grouping and a potential moderate right-wing alternative to Nazi ideology which could not be allowed within a dictatorship. Perhaps most importantly, the memory of German surrenders in the First World War was no longer palatable as Germany

---

[140] Rogasch, 'Zur Geschichte der Sammlung', p. 13.   [141] *Ibid.*

[142] BA-MA, Msg 200 / 106, ff.1–3, text of the meeting between Hindenburg and the ReK representatives, Freiherr Wilhelm von Lersner, Paul Peddinghaus and Prof. Gustav Boehmer, 20.12.1933.

[143] *Ibid.*   [144] *Ibid.*   [145] Rogasch, 'Zur Geschichte der Sammlung', p. 13.

[146] Pöppinghege, '"Kriegsteilnehmer zweiter Klasse"?', p. 421.

[147] Kohlhagen, *Die Frau, die man Engel nannte*, pp. 141–4. On Elsa Brändström's life see Eduard Juhl, Margarete Klante and Herta Epstein, *Elsa Brändström. Weg und Werk einer grossen Frau in Schweden, Siberien, Deutschland, Amerika* (Stuttgart, 1962).

[148] Rogasch, 'Zur Geschichte der Sammlung', p. 13.

remobilised in the mid-1930s: they undermined the regime's false *Dolchstoß* legend of the 'stab-in-the-back' that the defeat in 1918 was all the fault of German civilians who failed to hold out on the home front. German soldiers who had been captured alive did not fit with the extreme warrior rhetoric of Nazism.

The power of the ReK and its willingness to promote the memory of captivity was one important reason why the history of prisoners of war was so present in 1920s Germany. However, there was a final factor as to why prisoners of war were so central to interwar German memory of the conflict, in contrast to the French and British cases. Political activists on the German nationalist right sought to discredit the Allies by promoting a vitriolic propaganda narrative based on archive material that emphasised Allied mistreatment of German captives. Thus, in the German case, it was not only prisoner veterans but also political propagandists who were largely responsible for deliberately sustaining a wartime discourse on prisoner mistreatment into the late 1920s. The politicised function of this right-wing mistreatment narrative, intended to mobilise reactionary opinion within Germany against the Allies, meant that it was distinct from that of the ReK, which, when it referred to prisoner mistreatment, framed it in terms of an educational, reconciliatory anti-war pacifism.

For certain groups on the German right, such as former army officers and the civil servants at the Foreign Office, who retained their positions following the 1918 revolution, returning German prisoners suddenly became immensely useful. They could provide accounts of Allied war crimes such as battlefield shootings of captives or cruelties during captivity, which could be used to counter the Allies' war crimes accusations against Germany. From 1914, the Prussian *Kriegsministerium* had contained a section called the *Militär-Untersuchungstelle für Verletzungen des Kriegsrechts* (Military Office for the Investigation of Breaches of the Laws of War), dedicated to collecting evidence on Allied war crimes, including the abuse of prisoners. From mid-1919, this section was instructed to sift the evidence it had gathered to find anything which could be used to defend Germans accused of war crimes and threatened with Allied extradition.[149] The Weimar government was keen to protect these men:

The Cabinet cannot publicly act to protect the accused. Minister Erzberger believes it would be best if those who consider that they might be in danger disappear within the Reich ... Minister Reinhard suggests that they should flee to neutral countries. Each individual must organise his own passport but no difficulty

[149] BHStA IV, M Kr, 14128, Nr. 5289, Ministerialrat Sperr, Stellv. Mitglied des Reichsrats to das Staatsministerium des Äußern, Vertraulich! 1.11.19.

or hindrance will be put in his way ... Both ministers have given assurances that funding will be provided ... The Ministry for Foreign Affairs will put no obstacles in the way of these individuals leaving the country.[150]

Wartime archives on the Allies' treatment of German prisoners were seen as a valuable source for German counter-propaganda. In January 1919, an official at the Bavarian *Ministerium für militärische Angelegenheiten* (formerly the Bavarian *Kriegsministerium*) fumed at an article in the French press that reported prisoner mistreatment at Parchim camp: 'If we allow this campaign of lies to continue without defending ourselves, the same thing will happen as during the war – it will be believed.'[151] He wrote that

The best approach is to strike back by opening the archives in which the sworn statements of our prisoners of war have been deposited and offer the French these huge amounts of monstrous material ... No one from the Entente ever felt it incumbent upon himself to stop the Russians while they were still their ally, from using our prisoners to build the Murman railway, on which task thousands died. If the Entente knowingly falsely accuses us of the persecution of the Armenians, then it is itself guilty by association of the murder of our prisoners in Romania and Russia. The French in any case have no right to protest, their treatment of our prisoners involved the devilish invention of physical and moral tortures worthy of their savage colonial troops.[152]

Using the wartime prisoner archives in this way became official post-war German policy, despite the fact that many of the archive sources on Allied prisoner mistreatment were unverified or accounts based on hearsay. In 1919, the German Foreign Ministry even co-opted a group of ex-prisoners from the ReK to produce a white book on French treatment of German prisoners, giving them access to the former Prussian *Kriegsministerium* archives.[153] The German Foreign Ministry also produced an official book of prisoner testimony based on extracts from the diplomatic notes it had sent to neutral governments to publicise Allied crimes against German prisoners.[154] It also published a propaganda tract accusing French colonial troops of killing Germans they had captured.[155]

Archives were not only used for official propaganda. Large amounts of dubiously gathered and unverified wartime archival material was also leaked to right-wing writers for popular books which would influence

---

[150] *Ibid.*
[151] BHStA IV, M Kr 14128, Eilmittelung an AII, Nr. 4069, from Rosshaupter, 11.1.1919.
[152] *Ibid.*
[153] Rose, *Krieg nach dem Kriege*, p. 46. The white book which resulted from this collaboration was entitled *Deutsche Kriegsgefangene in Feindesland. Amtliches Material, Frankreich* (Berlin and Leipzig, 1919).
[154] Auswärtiges Amt, *Die Gefangenen-Misshandlungen in Entente-Ländern.*
[155] Auswärtiges Amt, *Liste über Fälle, die sich auf plannmäßige Ermordung und Misshandlung.*

public opinion; German prisoners of war were now the favoured sons of
the German right. Such archive prisoner testimony appears in a 1921
book by August Gallinger, *Gegenrechnung. Verbrechen an kriegsgefangenen
Deutschen*, which provided a German list of Allied 'war criminals' to
counter the Allies' extradition demands.[156] Gallinger also published an
English version of this work entitled *The Countercharge*, which reproduced
statements by German prisoners on Allied atrocities.[157] A similar work by
Hans Weberstedt, *Frankreichs wahres Gesicht. Das Buch der blau-weiß-roten
Schande; die deutsche Gegenliste*, published in 1926, reproduced statements
on French atrocities against prisoners. The book was intended to 'inform
the German people and all people of the earth' of the truth about France's
war crimes against German prisoners who 'felt the culture of the "*Grande
Nation*" on their own bodies'.[158] Its political aim was clear: 'Whoever
reads this book will be finally healed of the germ of reconciliation between
the peoples and will surely no longer believe in understanding and the
madness of pacifist views (*pazifistische Wahngebilde*).'[159] Many of the
extracts it reproduced had been leaked from the archives of sworn official
statements taken during the war, often based on hearsay or second-hand
information.[160] The international political climate in the 1920s was such
that former German prisoners of war suddenly became a very welcome
propaganda commodity for right-wing reactionary propagandists in
Germany. Even Ludendorff in his memoirs described German prisoners
as 'the very flesh of our flesh', and outlined how their mistreatment had
created bitterness.[161] For Germany the prisoner issue was a remarkably
versatile theme for retaliating against former enemies: in contrast to
Britain and France, where the issue of prisoner mistreatment focused
upon one perpetrator, Germany, the German right accused multiple
nations of mistreating German prisoners, focusing in particular on
France, Romania and Russia with fewer references to Italy and Britain.

This was not only a top-down right-wing campaign in German society.
Unlike in France and Britain, because of the controversy over extraditing
Germans accused of war crimes and the Leipzig Trials, there was a real
mobilisation in Germany to refute the prisoner abuses of which its own

---

[156] August Gallinger, *Gegenrechnung. Verbrechen an kriegsgefangenen Deutschen* (Leipzig and
Munich, 1921).
[157] Gallinger, *The Countercharge*.
[158] Hans Weberstedt, *Frankreichs wahres Gesicht. Das Buch der blau-weiß-roten Schande. Die
Deutsche Gegenliste* (Erfurt, 1926), Foreword. The appendix to the book included a
counter-list of Allied war criminals.
[159] *Ibid.*
[160] For another example of such propaganda see 'Die Bestie in Menschen', *Süddeutsche
Monatshefte* (July 1923).
[161] Erich von Ludendorff, *My War Memories*, 2 vols., vol. II (London, 1919), p. 453.

army stood accused. Multiple right-wing memoirs by ex-prisoners supported the German right's campaign to show that the Allies had mistreated German captives.[162] One typical example was Fritz Ibrügger's book *PG Feldgraue in Frankreichs Zuchthäusern*, a collection of accounts by German prisoners held by France, published in 1929. Ibrügger dedicated the book to 'German youth, the bearer of the future Germany ... called to bring the seed of 1914 to 1924 to fruit'.[163] He cited a proto-fascist poem that declared: 'German brothers make room for the "we"! Bury the little "I" in you. That little "I", it must go – Germany, Germany must remain!'[164] The book went on to reproduce accusations of French cruelty to prisoners and to reassert the injustice of withholding prisoners after the war had ended. Emphasising accounts of violence against Germans held captive by the Allies provided a defeated power with a noble narrative of victimhood at the hands of its victors. Moreover, the right frequently advocated the persecution argument that German prisoners were victims because they were *Germans*, which racialised German suffering. The question of prisoner of war commemoration in Weimar Germany was thus not only about remembrance but also about forming right-wing political identities.

In the face of this right-wing discourse, the German political centre and left were largely impotent. In the early Weimar years, the government focused upon countering the Allies' accusations that Germany had mistreated Allied prisoners by verifying the accuracy of their allegations – hence the attempt, through the Schücking Commission, to examine Germany's prisoner treatment.[165] However, successive Weimar governments did little to combat the interwar right-wing polemic that the Allies had mistreated German captives – indeed the published findings of the Weimar National Assembly parliamentary enquiry *Völkerrecht im Weltkrieg* actually reinforced some of the right-wing claims by reproducing wartime accusations of prisoner abuse by the Allies.[166]

Thus, in the German case, three key factors – the late release of German prisoners with the widespread popular campaign for their repatriation that ensued, the higly active and well-connected ReK veterans' association for ex-prisoners, and the right-wing political propaganda campaign that

---

[162] See Ernst Hermann, *Kriegsgefangen im Westen. Nach dem Tagebuch eines Gefangenen der 249 POW Coy in France* (Jena, 1933); Ernst Oswald Mueller, *Gefesseltes Heldentum. Erlebtes und Erschautes als Gefangener in Frankreich u. Afrika* (Leipzig, 1933); Heinz Thuemmler, *P.G. 905. Frankreichs Verrat an der weißen Rasse* (Leipzig and Naunhof, 1933). In addition, according to Georg Wurzer, some 150 memoirs were published by Germans who had been prisoners in Russia: Georg Wurzer, 'Deutsche Kriegsgefangene in Russland im Ersten Weltkrieg', in Overmans, ed., *In der Hand des Feindes*, p. 365.

[163] Ibrügger, ed., *PG Feldgraue in Frankreichs Zuchthäusern*, p. 8.   [164] *Ibid.*

[165] Hankel, *Die Leipziger Prozesse*, pp. 326–32.

[166] Reichstag, *Völkerrecht im Weltkrieg*, vol. III.

accused the Allies of mistreating German captives during the war –
ensured that German prisoners of war were central to the 1920s historicisation of the conflict in a way that differed from Britain and France.
German ex-prisoners of war were not marginalised or silenced in the
1920s. It was only when the Nazis came to power that a separate prisoner
of war memory was dismantled when the ReK was abolished in the mid-
1930s in the Nazi restructuring of veterans' organisations. As the Nazi
state set about dismantling the Treaty of Versailles, which had been a key
mobilising reason for the German right to maintain its politicised discourse about Allied prisoner mistreatment, the right-wing polemic on
Allied wartime prisoner abuse also died away. Thus a form of amnesia
regarding the history of prisoner of war treatment also emerged in Germany
by the mid-1930s, albeit largely artificially imposed from above by the
totalitarian Nazi state, which did not wish to emphasise 1914–18 captivity
or prisoner mistreatment but rather to glorify war. It is perhaps the ultimate
irony that such amnesia about First World War prisoner of war
camps developed under a regime which, from 1933 on, operated its own
new repressive concentration camp system for civilian prisoners within
Germany. The ReK's rhetorical lauding of the prisoner of war camp as a
site where German prisoners of war were reformed into the perfect wartime
Volksgemeinschaft, 'becoming free through renewal' (*Durch Neuwerden zum
Freiwerden*) was quickly supplanted by the Nazi ideological vision of the
concentration camp as the locus for reforming 'dissidents' perceived as
threatening the *Volksgemeinschaft* in the 1930s.[167]

Conclusion

In the immediate aftermath of the First World War, the dominant wartime
belief that the enemy had violently mistreated prisoners of war still prevailed in Britain, France and Germany. However, as this chapter has
shown, during the 1920s in Britain and France, and in the early 1930s
in Germany, the question of the violent mistreatment of prisoners gradually disappeared from public debate. Although the processes behind this
evolution of interwar memory were very different in each country, the
outcome was ultimately surprisingly similar by the mid-1930s: the history
of captivity became marginalised and eventually excised altogether from
the national historicisation of the war. In all three cases, this marginalisation of the history of prisoners began with a process of redefinition.
Contemporary cultural structures served to repress or distort the history

---

[167] Pöppinghege, '"Kriegsteilnehmer zweiter Klasse"?', p. 416.

of captivity during the 1920s by privileging certain narratives of prisoner treatment over others: in Britain, class hierarchies repressed the harsh captivity experience of other-rank ex-prisoners; in France, the clash over who had the right to be commemorated as a combatant eclipsed any debate over prisoner mistreatment; and in Germany, the whole question of prisoner abuse was subsumed into the propaganda needs of the German right. The growing focus upon commemorating the dead combatant in all three countries also undoubtedly played a role in deflecting post-war attention from prisoner mistreatment, as did the need to demobilise wartime hatreds and historicise the conflict without jeopardising Europe's uneasy peace – certain war memories of brutal captivities became impossible to publicly articulate in peacetime because they were too divisive, either internationally or internally; the German right wing's deliberate use of divisive prisoner atrocity propaganda was the one noteworthy exception to this process. There was also a sense among contemporaries that the cruelties of the war were all too visible and too well known; as a result, they did not recognise that there was any need to revisit or particularly single out any one aspect of the conflict such as captivity.

Thus, in many quarters, there was a move away from depicting violence as a component of captivity and towards a gentler, more social memory of camp life; this was partly a radical process, a means of breaking with the past which entailed a reimagining of the wartime captivity experience with the purpose of occluding certain aspects. Yet it occurred within the confines of traditional forms of popular expression, carried out by very mainstream traditional agents of social memory – memoirs and veterans' associations. The reintegration of former captives into peacetime communities was part of this process, limiting what ex-prisoners, too, could tell in the post-war years: in interviews during the war, the culture of conflict with its emphasis upon shaming the enemy appears to have allowed prisoners to describe being beaten.[168] During the interwar period, with the return to peacetime norms of masculinity, it became more difficult for men to articulate or revisit such experiences, which showed them in a powerless or humiliated light. This helps explain why in the interwar period ex-prisoners frequently sought to depict themselves as mastering their captivity; it may also explain why allusions to the sexual abuse of prisoners are so rare.[169]

---

[168] See the interview collections in: TNA, WO 161/98; WO 161/99; WO 161/100; SHAT, 7 N 1187, Attachés militaires Pays-Bas. Déclarations de prisonniers de guerre français évadés à la légation de France à la Haye, 1915–1916.

[169] During the course of this study only one reference to sexual abuse was found – an article in the *Münchener Augsburger Abend Zeitung*, 'sadisme français', 25.12.1920, which relates an account of a French guard raping a German prisoner. The account is allegorical in tone and appears to have been fabricated.

Overall, interwar attempts to portray captivity in ways that avoided discussing wartime violence proved difficult to sustain – the very presentation of a partial, sanitised version of prisoner history suggested the excluded subject of captivity violence which was being ignored. This was an additional important factor in why interwar attempts to incorporate captivity into the commemoration of the war were unsuccessful.

It was thus not the case that, once the war ended, wartime accounts of prisoner of war mistreatment were found to have been invented or untrue – in fact, many had been based on real incidents of violence. Rather it was the case that, by the 1930s, societies had ultimately opted to avoid any thorough objective examination of the realities of wartime violence against captives; writing this history proved too fraught. As a result, Britain, France and Germany failed to historicise war violence against prisoners and consequently to develop any broader analytical conclusions about how the war had led to new dyanamics developing between captivity, forced labour and violence. The overall outcome was a tacit form of amnesia by the late 1930s in all three countries, regarding First World War captivity, an amnesia based upon choosing silence.

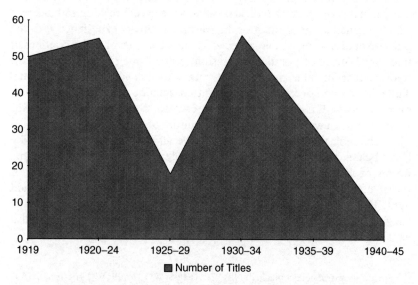

Figure 17. Survey of the publication dates of 217 interwar titles on prisoners of war in Germany, Britain and France found in the original card catalogues of Trinity College Library, Dublin; the BDIC-MHC, Nanterre; the Weltkriegsammlung in the Staatsbibliothek zu Berlin; and the British Museum.

A survey of the number of publications relating to First World War prisoners of war during the interwar period in all three countries illustrates the changing status of the subject in the public sphere and the fluctuating onset of this amnesia in the 1930s, as shown in Figure 17. It reveals two peaks in prisoner publications occurring in 1920 and 1930 and a trough which corresponded with the Locarno spirit of *rapprochement*. From 1930 on, however, there was a steady decline in new publications on wartime captivity. This decline has to be contextualised; the vast majority of interwar books written on the war were obsessed with war origins and high politics.[170] Not only prisoners of war but also the ordinary soldier combatant was often left out of such narratives, while public commemorations focused upon the dead. However, this survey does suggest a significant decline in public interest in the 1930s in publications specifically on captivity.

Yet for all the amnesiac qualities of the late 1930s, the question of 1914–18 prisoner treatment re-emerged once the Second World War began. Partly this was because the outbreak of a second conflict reawakened fears that there might be a repetition of wartime mass captivity and prisoner mistreatment – fears which had been so instrumental in driving the narrative about violence against prisoners of war as well as ex-prisoners' peace campaigns in the 1920s. Partly too, it was because of the propaganda value of old atrocity stories for remobilising populations to fight. But ultimately, this re-emergence also testifies to the fact that interwar attempts to resolve the memory of prisoner of war treatment in the First World War had failed. There was no historical consensus about what had happened by the outbreak of the Second World War, precisely because societies had ultimately adopted an amnesiac approach in the 1930s. This meant that in 1939–45 much about First World War prisoner treatment remained unknown, unclear and open to manipulation, as the following epilogue will briefly discuss.

---

[170] See Prost and Winter, *The Great War in History*, pp. 34–58.

Epilogue: the legacy of First World War captivity in 1939–45

It is beyond the scope of this study to compare the nature of captivity and violence against prisoners of war in the two world wars; any such comparison requires a book in its own right. The purpose of this epilogue, however, is simply to suggest that hidden influences from the First World War played a role in shaping prisoner of war captivity in Britain, France and Germany during the 1939–45 conflagration, although the widespread interwar amnesia that developed by the 1930s in these three countries regarding First World War prisoner treatment makes it extremely difficult to trace this process. To what extent the previous conflict was a factor in determining Second World War captivity still remains largely unexplored in the existing historiography. Recently there has been a major upsurge in historical studies on prisoners of war in 1939–45, with new work by Bob Moore, Rüdiger Overmans, Simon Paul Mackenzie and Frank Biess, among others.[1] Yet we still know too little about the legacy of First World War

---

[1] For an overview of recent trends in the historiography of Second World War prisoner of war captivity see Ilse Dorothee Pautsch, 'Prisoners of War and Internees in the Second World War – a Survey of Some Recent Publications', *Contemporary European History*, 12, 2 (2003), pp. 225–38. See also Sibylle Scheipers, ed., *Prisoners in War. Norms, Military Culture and Reciprocity in Armed Conflict* (Oxford, 2009); Bob Moore and Barbara Hately-Broad, eds., *Prisoners of War, Prisoners of Peace. Captivity, Homecoming and Memory in World War Two* (Oxford and New York, 2005). Moore in particular has published widely on Second World War prisoners: see Bob Moore, 'Turning Liabilities into Assets: British Government Policy towards German and Italian Prisoners of War during the Second World War', *Journal of Contemporary History*, 32, 1(1997), pp. 117–36, and Bob Moore and Kent Fedorowich, *The British Empire and Italian Prisoners of War* (London, 2002). See also Overmans, ed., *In der Hand des Feindes*; Gerhard Hirschfeld, ed., *The Policies of Genocide. Jews and Soviet Prisoners of War in Nazi Germany* (London, 1986); Arieh J. Kochavi, *Confronting Captivity. Britain and the United States and their POWs in Nazi Germany* (Chapel Hill, 2005); and Frank Biess, *Homecomings. Returning POWs and the Legacies of Defeat in Postwar Germany* (Princeton and Oxford, 2006). On British prisoners in Germany in the Second World War, see Neville Wylie, *Barbed Wire Diplomacy. Britain, Germany and the Politics of Prisoners of War, 1939–45* (Oxford, 2010); Adrian Gilbert, *POW. Allied Prisoners in Europe 1939–1945* (London, 2006); S. P. MacKenzie, *The Colditz Myth. British and Commonwealth Prisoners of War in Nazi Germany* (Oxford, 2004), and Mackenzie, 'The Treatment of Prisoners of War in World War II'. On Canadian prisoners see Vance, *Objects of Concern*. On French prisoners in the Second World War see the work

captivity upon prisoner treatment during the Second World War, the extent of continuities and discontinuities between the two conflicts or indeed the links between civilian and prisoner of war captivities.[2] In addition, whether First World War captivity may have influenced interwar incarceratory systems, in Soviet Russia or Francoist Spain for example, also remains unexplored.[3] As regards prisoner of war treatment in Britain, France and Germany, only a few historians have discussed the question of links between the two world wars and they have come to widely different conclusions, with Annette Becker contending that the severe 1914–1918 treatment of French military and civilian prisoners of war served as a precedent for Second World War atrocities against prisoners in Germany, while Odon Abbal argues against viewing the two wars as linked.[4] Indeed for Becker, 'one root of the political and human failure we associate with the Holocaust and responses to it was an epistemological block, an unwillingness or inability to acknowledge and integrate the atrocity of the previous world war'.[5] Richard Speed interprets prisoner abuse in the Second World War as a clear break with prisoner treatment in the First

---

of Yves Durand: *La Captivité. Histoire des prisonniers de guerre français: 1939–1945* (Paris, 1981), and *La Vie quotidienne des prisonniers de guerre dans les stalags, les oflags et les kommandos, 1939–1945* (Paris, 1987), as well as Sarah Fishman, *We Will Wait. Wives of French Prisoners of War, 1940–1945* (New Haven, 1991). Fabien Théofilakis is also completing a new study on German prisoners of war in France during the final phase of the Second World War. See his recent article 'La Sexualité du prisonnier de guerre. Allemands et Français en captivité (1914–1918, 1940–1948)', *Vingtième Siècle*, 99, 3 (2008), pp. 203–19. See also the useful article by Neville Wylie on interwar regulation: Wylie, 'The 1929 Prisoner of War Convention'.

[2] Although we lack a specific monograph comparing prisoner of war captivity in both wars, some comparative work has been done on the question of war violence and wartime mobilisation. See Audoin-Rouzeau *et al.*, *La Violence de guerre, 1914–1945*; see also the study by Nicolas Beaupré, Anne Duménil and Christian Ingrao, eds., *1914–1945. L'Ère de la Guerre*, 2 vols, vol. I: *Violence, mobilisations, deuil. 1914–1918* (Paris, 2004), and that by Bruno Thoss and Hans-Erich Volkmann, eds., *Erster Weltkrieg – Zweiter Weltkrieg. Ein Vergleich. Krieg, Kriegserlebnis, Kriegserfahrung in Deutschland* (Paderborn, 2002). See, in particular, Benjamin Ziemann's chapter on violence in this Thoss and Volkmann volume: Benjamin Ziemann, '"Vergesellschaftung der Gewalt" als Thema der Kriegsgeschichte seit 1914. Perspektiven und Desiderate eines Konzeptes', pp. 753–9. Omer Bartov's work also looks at how combatant violence in the First World War may have influenced the Holocaust: see Bartov, *Murder in Our Midst*. Gerd Krumeich's recent book also considers the influence of the Great War upon National Socialism: Gerd Krumeich, ed., *Nationalsozialismus und Erster Weltkrieg* (Essen, 2010).

[3] On the Gulag system, see Stephen Wheatcroft, 'The Scale and Nature of German and Soviet Repression and Mass Killings, 1930–1945', *Europe-Asia Studies*, 48, 8 (1996), 1319–53; and also Anne Applebaum, *Gulag. A History* (London, 2003); on Francoist camps see Julius Ruiz, 'A Spanish Genocide? Reflections on the Francoist Repression after the Spanish Civil War', *Contemporary European History*, 14, 2 (2005), pp. 171–91; Peter Anderson, 'The Chetwode Commission and British Diplomatic Responses to Violence behind the Lines in the Spanish Civil War', *European History Quarterly* (forthcoming).

[4] Abbal, *Soldats oubliés*; Becker, *Oubliés de la Grande Guerre*.

[5] Becker, 'Suppressed Memory of Atrocity', p. 66.

World War, which he concludes was largely humane, governed by entirely benevolent attitudes towards prisoners in Germany, France and Britain.[6] More generally, there is also a shortage of work that compares prisoner treatment in eastern Europe in both world wars: Rüdiger Overmans, in a short chapter comparing prisoner treatment trends in Russia and Germany across the two conflicts, concludes that, during the Great War, Russia showed greater signs of radicalisation towards captives than Germany; the inverse, he argues, was true for the Second World War.[7]

The lack of more comparative studies is not surprising: the significant structural differences between captivity in the two world wars makes comparing them deeply problematic, even if one restricts the comparison to Britain, France and Germany. First, most obviously, the totalitarian nature of the Nazi German state set it apart from the French and British liberal democracies in 1939, in a way that differed considerably from the smaller contrast between authoritarian Wilhelmine Germany and its liberal democratic French and British opponent states in 1914–18; this makes comparison of historical processes within the three countries in the Second World War much less straightforward than for the Great War. Second, very clearly, any comparison has to recognise that, in the case of Germany in 1939–45, the ideological conceptualisation of the purpose of captivity was radically different to 1914–18: the Nazi state saw the prison camp not merely as a location for confining prisoners of war for the duration of the conflict but also as an instrument for purging civilian dissidents as well as exterminating those groups classified as racially undesirable according to the Nazi world view. The German Second World War camp system was thus a tool of genocide as well as a location for prisoner of war confinement; any comparative study of prisoners of war must grapple with this unique, 'dual' function of the German camp network driven by Nazi exterminatory racial ideology. The use of camps to deliberately implement mass genocide marked a major break with the earlier war: in particular, the racialised anti-Semitism of the Nazi regime and its use of death camps to gas Europe's Jewish population had no precedent in the 1914–18 German prison camp network. Indeed, in the First World War Jewish prisoners of war were often favoured as translators

---

[6] Speed, *Prisoners, Diplomats and the Great War*.

[7] Rüdiger Overmans, '"Hunnen" und "Untermenschen" – deutsche und russisch/sowjetische Kriegsgefangenschaftserfahrungen im Zeitalter der Weltkriege', in Thoss and Volkmann, eds., *Erster Weltkrieg – Zweiter Weltkrieg*, p. 364.

and even allowed to keep Jewish religious holidays.[8] The way that forced labour was often deliberately used in camps and work units to advance the genocidal aims of the Nazi regime by intentionally working captives to death also differed from 1914–18. The 'dual' genocidal and confinement functions of the Nazi camp system thus contrasts dramatically with the more logistically driven 'dual' captivity system that emerged during the First World War, which divided prisoners between army labour companies and homeland prisoner of war camps according to labour needs and which developed not only in Germany but also in other countries, including Britain and France. This is not to say that continuities between the two conflicts do not exist; however, it is to suggest that the most important links between 1914–18 and 1939–45 captivity are more likely to be found in terms of shifting and radicalising ideas regarding the prisoner of war forced labour unit, its nutrition and its living conditions, rather than in the establishment of extermination camps to implement Nazi racial ideology in the Second World War, which marked a radical break in European history.

The third structural problem with comparing captivity in both world wars is the difficulty of integrating the extreme nature of Nazi German treatment of one group of combatant prisoners of war – Soviet prisoners of war – into any overall comparative analysis. In the Second World War, western front and eastern front prisoners of war, captured by Germany, were treated very differently: while French and British prisoners were largely contained in prisoner of war camps or sent to working units that were similar to their First World War counterparts, Soviet prisoners of war were often held in spartan camps with extremely high mortality rates or simply killed outright. During the Second World War, 5,754,000 Soviet prisoners were captured by the Germans, of whom between 3,290,000 and 3,700,000 died.[9] More Russians died in German prisoner of war camps in the years 1941–5 'than in all of World War One'.[10] In other words, while western front captives experienced the confinement function of the Nazi camp system, their eastern front Soviet counterparts, stigmatised within Nazi ideology on both racial and political grounds as Slavs and Communists, were subjected to both the confinement *and* the genocidal functions of the Third Reich's camp network. Any comparative

---

[8] BA-MA, PH 5 II / 453, Armee-Oberkommando 4, Abt.Ic.A., Verfügungen über Kriegs-gefangenenangelegenheiten Band 2, Jan 1918–Nov 1918, f.00243, Generalintendant des Feldheeres, 14.1.18, III.d.no.1066/1.18, Betr: Mazzoth für Kriegsgefangene.

[9] Speed, *Prisoners, Diplomats and the Great War*, p. 2. Overmans estimates approximately 5.2 million Soviet prisoners captured by Germany of whom approximately 3 million died. See Overmans, '"Hunnen" und "Untermenschen"', pp. 352 and 356.

[10] Tony Judt, *Postwar. A History of Europe since 1945* (London, 2005), p. 19.

examination of both world wars thus faces the difficult question of how to incorporate this internal radical contrast in eastern front and western front prisoner treatment within the Nazi German system during the Second World War. Attempting comparative work on German captivity in both world wars also necessitates engaging with the fraught question of Soviet mass mistreatment of their 3 million German prisoners – an estimated third of whom died – and how this influenced the post-war German memory of Second World War captivity.[11]

In fact, the extremes of violence against prisoners of war that emerged on the eastern front in 1941–5 marked such a radical break in twentieth-century European history that comparison becomes highly problematic: any discussion must thus recognise that any continuities with the First World War occurred against the backdrop of this major eastern front rupture with the norms of 1914–18. The mass deaths of Soviet prisoners of war in Germany simply have no parallel in First World War captivity: even if the earlier war did establish the crucial precedent of differentiated treatment and increased exposure to violence for particular nationalities, thereby undermining the idea of a standard universal treatment for all prisoners as enshrined in international law, differentiation between captives was largely on political-strategic grounds in 1914–18, rather than the racialised criteria which developed in 1939–45.[12] More generally, on the battlefield, there was simply no parallel during the First World War with Nazi Germany's racialised war of extermination in the East: the German-Soviet front in 1941–5 saw a policy of no quarter and harsh prisoner treatment widely practised by both sides.[13] The patterns of fighting and of capture in the west also differed in 1939–45. This was not a rerun of trench warfare: Britain had very few German prisoners until 1942 and the French, occupied in 1940, were not in a position to imprison prisoners of war in France until 1944.[14] Rather the French concern for much of the Second World War was for their 1,800,000 servicemen who were

---

[11] Overmans, '"In der Hand des Feindes"', p. 14.
[12] I have discussed this in more detail elsewhere. See Heather Jones, 'A Missing Paradigm? Military Captivity and the Prisoner of War, 1914–1918', *Immigrants and Minorities*, 26, 1/2 (2008), pp. 19–48.
[13] Stefan Karner, 'Konzentrations- und Kriegsgefangenenlager in Deutschland und in der Sowjetunion. Ansätze zu einem Vergleich von Lagern in totalitären Regimen', in Overmans, ed., *In der Hand des Feindes*, pp. 387–412.
[14] J. Anthony Hellen, 'Temporary Settlements and Transient Populations. The Legacy of Britain's Prisoner of War Camps 1940–1948', *Erdkunde*, 53 (1999), p. 197; Fabien Théofilakis, 'Les Prisonniers de guerre allemands en mains françaises au sortir de la Seconde Guerre Mondiale. Gestion et enjeux', unpublished paper, p. 2, paper kindly provided by the author.

prisoners of war in Germany.[15] All these major structural differences mean that a three-way study of British, French and German captivity in the Second World War poses greater challenges than for the 1914–18 conflict, where the differentials between the three countries are far smaller.

Yet, despite these major structural differences between prisoner treatment in the two world wars, it is worth looking more closely at how the earlier conflict influenced its successor and how radical ruptures and longer-term hidden continuities interacted. Several important precedent trends must be noted: first, the First World War established the norm that prisoners would be fed from parcels, rather than, as outlined in international law, by the captor nation. This occurred once again in the Second World War, when British and American prisoners lived largely off parcels sent to Germany and Italy.[16] Second, 1914–18 set the precedent of ignoring international law regarding prisoners of war when this was in the national interest, in favour of reprisals to influence the enemy or when necessary to increase prisoners' labour output. Third, the First World War established the important precedent of neutral inspections of camps as a means of protecting prisoners of war; however, it also led to an over-confidence, regarding the power of inspections to curtail abuses. A naive trust in positive inspection reports may to some extent have blinded the ICRC to the changed, genocidal nature of the German camp system in 1939–45. Finally, the First World War established the precedent of the camp as a site of educational experimentation, where prisoners could take classes in languages, politics and history; the Allies' introduction of re-education classes for Nazi prisoners in the Second World War can be seen as a progression from this earlier development. Certainly, some prisoners themselves linked the programmes: a German prisoner held by the British army in the Rhineland wrote in 1946 of how, almost thirty years before, in 1916, he had been captured by the British and that he viewed the denazification camp at Wilton Park in terms of his earlier First World War captivity at Donnington Hall officers' camp:

The aims which the work in Wilton Park serves are not strange to me. At Donnington Hall, Nottingham, my officer's [sic] camp at that time, which obviously in many respects resembled the Wilton Park course camp, interest for me and many other comrades especially the younger ones was awakened in the problems which now stand on the Wilton Park syllabus.[17]

[15] Rüdiger Overmans, 'The Repatriation of Prisoners of War once Hostilities are Over. A Matter of Course?', in Bob Moore and Barbara Hately-Broad, eds., *Prisoners of War, Prisoners of Peace* (Oxford and New York, 2005), p. 17.

[16] Gilbert, *POW. Allied Prisoners in Europe*, pp. 97–100.

[17] TNA, FO 371/55689, C3783, A. Münzebrock to Major-General Strong, FO, 4.4.1946. I am grateful to Riccarda Torriani for alerting me to this source.

One can also ask whether the anthropological and linguistic studies of prisoners of war which took place in prisoner of war camps in Germany and Austria-Hungary during the First World War served in any way as a precedent for scientific experimentation on prisoner of war and civilian victims in the German camp system in 1939–45.[18] Anthropological research was also carried out in prisoner of war camps in Britain in 1914–18; one study measured men from different regions of Germany in order to highlight their racial differences.[19]

Overall, however, these continuities largely illustrate that the earlier war provided a logistical model, not an ideological one, for the later conflict. In a practical sense, the memory of 1914–18 prisoner treatment bequeathed certain legacies to 1939–45. The *Stammlager, Kommando* and prisoner of war labour company systems in Germany provided both a logistical model and a vocabulary for later Second World War prisoner of war *Stalags* and working units. Indeed, in some countries the same sites were used again in 1939–45: Britain resurrected its First World War Isle of Man camp for the internment of aliens.[20] Theresienstadt and Mauthausen in Austria, Auschwitz in Poland and Ohrdruf in Germany, all part of the First World War prisoner system, became notorious concentration camps in the Second World War.[21] Other trends also repeated themselves: the French in 1945–8 used German prisoners as a source of reparations labour in a similar way to 1918–20.[22] Once again, the organisation of food for these prisoners proved problematic; it was only in 1947 that the International Red Cross found their food situation had normalised.[23] Again, too, after the Second World War there was a period of memory disruption, a series of silences and amnesias regarding prisoner mistreatment – whether this followed the same patterns as 1919–39 merits

---

[18] A Prussian Phonogram Commission was established to record and study the diverse languages of prisoners in German camps; other anthropological studies of prisoners were carried out in Austria-Hungary. See Doegen, *Kriegsgefangene Völker*, p. 1; Andrew D. Evans, 'Capturing Race. Anthropology and Photography in German and Austrian Prisoner-of-War Camps during World War I', in Eleanor M. Hight and Gary D. Simpson, eds., *Colonialist Photography. Imagining Race and Place* (London, 2002), pp. 226–56; Jürgen-K. Mahrenholz, 'Zum Lautarchiv und seiner wissenschaftlichen Erschließung durch die Datenbank IMAGO', in Marianne Bröcker, ed., *Berichte aus dem ICTM-Nationalkomitee Deutschland, Band XII, Bericht über die Jahrestagung des Nationalkomitees der Bundesrepublik Deutschland im International Council for Traditional Music (UNESCO) am 08. und 09. März 2002 in Köln* (Bamberg, 2003), p. 139.

[19] F. G. Parsons, 'Anthropological Observations on German Prisoners of War', *The Journal of the Royal Anthropological Institute of Great Britain and Ireland*, 49 (1919), pp. 20–35.

[20] Hellen, 'Temporary Settlements and Transient Populations', p. 197.

[21] Marie-Anne Matard-Bonucci and Édouard Lynch, *La Libération des camps et le retour des déportés* (Paris, 1995), p. 63.

[22] Théofilakis, 'Les Prisonniers de guerre allemands en mains françaises', p. 2.

[23] *Ibid.*, p. 6.

further research. All these points indicate that the legacy of First World War captivity largely emerged in 1939–45 through what Isabel V. Hull has defined as 'habitual practices, default programs, hidden assumptions and unreflected cognitive frames' which influenced organisational and military action. This epilogue will now briefly highlight some examples of how this process operated, considering as evidence several 'hidden assumptions' and 'default programs' from 1914 to 1918 which can be identified in Second World War belligerents Britain and Germany.[24] The more complicated situation of France, with its experience of defeat and Armistice in 1940, followed by occupation, necessitates a more developed asymmetric comparison, which lies beyond the scope of this short case study.

Perhaps one of the most important examples of such 'hidden assumptions' about captivity was the belief in Germany in 1939 that the country had wasted precious food resources on prisoners at the expense of the civilian population during the First World War. As Georges Connes wrote in 1925, 'there are Germans who think that these prisoners were the cause of their country's downfall'.[25] This was the theme of a 1939 official German Wehrmacht publication, *Kriegsgefangene*, which also reproduced documentary and photographic evidence of sabotage by Allied prisoners gathered during the First World War by the Prussian *Kriegsministerium* in order to show that, by damaging crops, prisoners had exacerbated food shortages.[26] Its introduction stated that the book should act as 'an admonition and a warning for every member of the *Volk*. The enemy remains the enemy.'[27] In *Kriegsgefangene*, the prisoners were blamed for food shortages and – by derivation in the Nazi view of why the war ended, which was based upon the stab-in-the-back legend – for the collapse of the German home front. A skewed memory of 1914–18 was constructed to harden attitudes to prisoners in 1939–45.

Further 'hidden assumptions' about First World War captivity emerge in other Second World War German texts: a 1940 book whose title translates as *British 'Humanity' against the Unarmed* by Arthur Finck illustrates a prevalent Second World War German belief that in the Great War, Britain had successfully concealed its war crimes because

Germany at that time was not able to match the British propaganda. Its leaders did not recognise the danger and allowed this massive deception of humanity to occur. They had to hand material in abundance, which they could have used to reveal the

[24] Hull, *Absolute Destruction*, p. 2.   [25] Connes, *A POW's Memoir of the First World War*, p. 5.
[26] Wehrmacht, *Kriegsgefangene! Auf Grund der Kriegsakten bearbeitet beim Oberkommando der Wehrmacht* (Berlin, 1939).
[27] *Ibid.*, Preface.

truth ... For this reason we are publishing the documents of the Foreign Ministry and the former Prussian Ministry of War on the fate of prisoners of war in England during the World War, and leaving it up to each reader to come to their own conclusion.[28]

To produce atrocity propaganda for his 1940 readership, Finck thus resorted to reproducing accounts of First World War Allied prisoner mistreatment from the archives of the Prussian *Kriegsministerium* in what was an example of a 'default' return to the earlier interwar practices of the German right wing. In a similar propaganda vein, a number of memoirs by German ex-prisoners held in France during the First World War, which emphasised the harshness of French captivity, were published in 1940.[29] The interwar controversy over First World War prisoner mistreatment clearly partially revived: a 1941 published German Ph.D. dissertation sought to prove by studying newspapers produced in 1914–18 prisoner of war camps in Germany that the Allied accusations, 'led principally by the French', that the Germans had mistreated prisoners were simply a fabricated polemic.[30] The fact that such newspapers were only produced in *Stammlager* or officers' camps, to which the majority of prisoners working in *Kommandos* by 1916 had no access, was not mentioned.[31]

Another example of the 'hidden assumptions' and 'default programs' linking the two wars through the interwar period is illustrated by two German cartoons, one from 1915 and one from 1933, which replicate the same 'joke', merely switching the subject from a Russian prisoner of war being 'improved' by his stay in a German camp in the 1915 version to a 'noble Communist' being 'improved' by the camp experience in the 1933 version.[32] The sequence of images of a prisoner having his hair cut and being washed, resulting in his relatives being shocked at his new appearance, which they blame on 'mistreatment', was absolutely identical in the two cartoons, reproduced here. In both cases, the humour masks mistreatment: the 'cartoon' joke at the Russian prisoners' expense was published in 1915 – just after typhus swept through the German camps,

[28] Arthur Finck, *Britische 'Humanität' gegen Wehrlose. Die Misshandlung deutscher Gefangener in England während des Weltkrieges* (Stuttgart and Berlin, 1940).

[29] See Karl Kirchhoff, *Von Hölle zu Hölle. Erlebnis einer französischen Kriegsgefangenschaft* (Gütersloh, 1940); Carl Berger, *Sieben Jahre in Frankreichs Kerkern* (Berlin, 1940); Utsch, *Todesurteil in Tours 1917*; Karl Wilke, *Tage des Grauens. Frankreichs 'Humanität'* (Berlin, 1940). Ibrügger's book was also reissued in 1941: Ibrügger, ed., *PG Feldgraue in Frankreichs Zuchthäusern*.

[30] Rudolf Häussler, *Das Nachrichten- und Pressewesen der feindlichen Kriegsgefangenen in Deutschland, 1914–1918*, published doctoral thesis, University of Leipzig (Berlin, 1941).

[31] On access to newspapers, see Pöppinghege, *Im Lager unbesiegt*.

[32] Figure 18 is also reproduced in Hinz, '"Die deutschen 'Barbaren' sind doch die besseren Menschen"', p. 358.

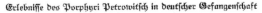

Figure 18. 'The Experience of Porphyri Petrowitsch in German Captivity'. Caption reads: 'When after 11 months he sent his photograph back to his loved ones at home, they cried in horror "For pity, what must our poor little dove have had to suffer from those cursed sausage-makers."' 'Die Erlebnisse des Porphyri Petrowitsch in deutscher Gefangenschaft', in *Simplicissimus*, Jg. 20 (1915), Nr. 19 (10.8.1915), p. 227.

killing many Russian prisoners; the anti-Semitic 1933 cartoon depicts the brutal concentration camp experience of Communists, Jews and others in the Third Reich as funny.

In British Second World War publications, 'hidden assumptions' about the lessons of captivity in the 1914–18 conflict can also be found. J. H. Morgan, the former British military representative on the Inter-Allied Council who had been in charge of a sub-commission of the control commission for the disarmament of Germany from 1919 to 1923, published a

Figure 19. 'The Noble Communist in the Concentration Camp'. The sequence of captions reads: 'arrest', 'clean-up', 'cut (hair and beard)', 'fresh air', 'photograph'. The last caption, an anti-Semitic depiction of Jewish customers in Berlin's Romanesque Café, reads: 'When his photograph arrives six weeks later in Café Megalomania: "Horrible! What the poor man must have gone through."' Der Edelkommunist im Konzentrationslager', *Kladderadatsch*, 14.5.1933, illustration no. 26 in Richard J. Evans, *The Coming of the Third Reich* (New York, 2004).

history of the 'disarmament of Germany and her rearmament 1919–1939' in 1945.[33] His book emphasised British foolishness in not pursuing the German perpetrators of crimes against British prisoners of war in 1914–18. Morgan identified the Leipzig Trials as a major error by Britain.[34] He also believed that the Reichstag Enquiry set up by Weimar to investigate the conduct of the war had failed:

It was sitting at the time of our arrival in Berlin. A pertinacious Reichstag deputy pressed Bethmann-Hollweg as to why, when Chancellor, he had tolerated these iniquities in Belgium ... The Imperial Chancellor ... let the cat out of the bag. The German High Command, he pleaded, had silenced all his protests with the curt reply, '*In war we must stop at nothing.*' It was the voice of tradition.[35]

Morgan clearly saw the origins of the 1939–45 conflict in German military culture during the previous war: 'As it was in 1914, so it was in 1919. So it is now ... The inflammatory passages of *Mein Kampf* in which he [Hitler], declares that Germany would never rest until she had achieved the annihilation (*die Vernichtung*) of France are neither as new nor as transient as some amongst us fondly believed in the years of "appeasement".'[36] Morgan was not the only British observer to look to the earlier war for lessons: in February 1940, the British Minister for War was asked in the House of Commons whether arrangements were being made, '*as in the last war*, for German prisoners to be hired out for manual labour on estates and farms, or by contractors for works of afforestation, agricultural operations, land drainage, road making etc.'[37] The response was negative, but the terms of the question are revealing. Even where decisions were being made to break with the patterns established in the First World War, they were being framed in reference to it – it remained a latent model. Even in America in 1941, James Morgan Read highlighted what he claimed was 'false' First World War 'atrocity propaganda', including accounts of prisoner mistreatment, as an admonition to the American public to stay neutral.[38]

'Hidden assumptions' formed in the First World War may also have influenced ex-prisoners who held important positions during the 1939–45 conflagration. That Charles de Gaulle was a prisoner in Germany in 1914–18 is well known.[39] Less well known is that Adolf Hitler served at one point as a guard at Traunstein prisoner of war camp between November 1918 and late January 1919, precisely the period when conditions in

---

[33] Morgan, *Assize of Arms*, vol. I, pp. 139–41.   [34] *Ibid.*   [35] *Ibid.*, p. 216.   [36] *Ibid.*
[37] Hellen, 'Temporary Settlements and Transient Populations', p. 197. Italics mine.
[38] Read, *Atrocity Propaganda*.
[39] Annette Becker, 'Charles de Gaulle, prisonnier', in Institut Charles de Gaulle/Historial de Péronne, *De Gaulle soldat 1914–1918* (Paris, 1999), pp. 98–115.

Bavarian camps deteriorated rapidly.[40] A large number of the prisoners of war in Traunstein camp at this time were Russians. In August 1919, Hitler worked on a German army propaganda course designed to reindoctrinate German prisoners of war who had recently been repatriated and who had arrived back in Germany with what were termed 'Bolshevik' political tendencies.[41] Hitler's subsequent attitudes to both Russian prisoners of war and German prisoners of war taken prisoner by the enemy must have been influenced by these encounters. The terrible condition of Russian prisoners in Germany after the Armistice was likely to reinforce prejudices against Slavs as uncivilised. The fact that German prisoners of war were repatriated to Germany having picked up left-leaning political views in captivity may also have been a factor in his later contempt for German troops who surrendered. Moreover, there was a significant number of former prisoners of war among the fifteen top officials of the German ministerial bureaucracy and the SS who met with Reinhard Heydrich at the infamous Wannsee conference in January 1942, where the escalation of the Holocaust was planned. Of the seven who had served in the 1914–18 conflict, four had been prisoners of war.[42] Two were held by the French and two by Russia. One of those present, Dr Alfred Meyer, State Secretary at the Ministry for the Occupied Eastern Territories, had been a prisoner of the French from 1917 until 1920. In 1942, he was a key figure in the mass deportations of Soviet forced labourers.[43] His concept of prisoner labour may well have been influenced by his earlier captivity experience: whether he drew upon the organisational structure of the prisoner of war labour company of 1914–18 when setting up the much harsher slave labour system he organised in 1942 simply remains unknown.

Hitler's adversary, Winston Churchill, also had direct experience of 1914–18 prisoner treatment. As outlined in chapter 2, in 1915 Churchill was involved in the policy of reprisals launched against German submarine prisoners, which badly backfired.[44] While First Lord of the Admiralty, he was also exposed to the ideas of the First Sea Lord, Sir John Fisher, who wanted to shoot German prisoners of war as a reprisal for German Zeppelin attacks on Britain.[45] Similar continuities in personnel can be found elsewhere: Robert Vansittart, the viscerally

---

[40] Kershaw, *Hitler*, vol. I: *Hubris*, p. 117.   [41] *Ibid.*, p. 123.

[42] They were: Otto Hofmann (1896–1982), SS Race and Settlement; Wilhelm Kritzinger (1890–1947), Reich Chancellery; Dr Roland Freisler (1893–1945), Reich Ministry of Justice; and Dr Alfred Meyer (1891–1945), Reich Ministry for the Occupied Eastern Territories. Mira Bihaly and Gerhard Schoenberner, eds., *House of the Wannsee Conference. Permanent Exhibit, Guide and Reader*, English version (Berlin, 1999), pp. 54–67. I am grateful to Mark Jones for bringing this source to my attention.

[43] *Ibid.*   [44] Gilbert, *Churchill*, p. 296.   [45] *Ibid.*

anti-German Permanent Undersecretary at the Foreign Office during the Second World War, had formed his dislike of Germany while working in the Foreign Office Department of Prisoners of War under Lord Newton between 1916 and 1918.[46] Some British interrogators working with German prisoners in 1939–45 had also worked in the same job in 1914–18: the head of a British interrogation centre at Kensington Palace Gardens, where German prisoners of war were mistreated in the Second World War, Lieutenant-Colonel Alexander Scotland, had been awarded an OBE for his services interrogating German prisoners of war during the 1914–18 conflict.[47] For another British interrogator, the silence of Second World War German prisoners was directly attributable to lessons learned from the previous conflict: 'After the Great War, the German General Staff declared our Intelligence to be the best in the World, and it appears that this praise is well justified judging from the prudent way in which present German P.W. conduct themselves when under interrogation.'[48] In some cases, this was about more than abstract continuities. Some men experienced captivity in both world wars: a German woman writing in 1946 to the International Red Cross at Geneva of her brother Emil, aged forty-nine, a prisoner of war of the Soviets, outlined how: 'he took part in the 1914 World War and was only released in 1920 from French captivity. He has sacrificed many years for a Fatherland that today lies in ruins, precisely through the fault of people without a conscience.'[49]

Ultimately, it is not the intention here to overstate the direct links between the two wars. However, it is clear that First World War captivity influenced Second World War attitudes and decisions in both representational and practical ways which deserve further attention. Although the memory of prisoners of the 1914–18 conflict was not often overtly referred to, it was present in the cognitive frame of reference of many involved in the 1939–45 war, particularly at the outset. This explains why the invading German army in 1940 destroyed the monuments at Monceau-sur-Sambre and Marchienne-au-Pont erected to Yvonne Vieslet, the Belgian child shot trying to give food to a prisoner in 1918, and why it removed large amounts of war archive material relating to prisoners of

---

[46] Robert Vansittart, *Black Record. Germans Past and Present* (Melbourne, 1941); Vansittart, *The Mist Procession.*

[47] Ian Cobain, 'The Secrets of the London Cage', *The Guardian*, 3.4.2006.

[48] George Eckert Institut, Brunswick, Nachlass T. J. Leonard, Box 8, folder 'Anweisungen über Behandlung von Kriegsgefangenen', n.d. lecture notes for instructing British troops on interrogating German prisoners, 1939–45.

[49] ACICR, G 25/36, Plaintes générales, France 1946–1947, v.669, G17/134/13, Letter from Trude Fuhr-Keller, 30.10.1946.

war, from Belgium and France, to Germany.[50] The politics of memory were hugely important to this 1940 invasion. The historical image of the 1914–18 conflict, and German prisoner treatment in particular, was clearly still being defined a year into the Second World War. Ultimately, as this example illustrates, the failure to investigate prisoner treatment during the interwar period and the amnesia which came to surround the subject meant that the First World War was a murky, subjective frame of reference for those involved with prisoner issues in the Second. As a result, we still do not know enough about the extent of the continuities and discontinuities which link captivity in the two conflicts.

[50] www.charleroi-decouverte.be/index.php?id=113, accessed 2/3/2010. On the removal of archive files see Horne and Kramer, *German Atrocities*, p. 404. Among the archives stolen were files from the Service Historique de l'Armée de Terre and the Archives of the French Foreign Ministry.

Conclusion

A number of assumptions regarding the First World War can be revised in light of this study. First, mass captivity was absolutely central to the conflict. It can no longer be seen as a marginalised sideshow or treated only as part of the social history of the home front, set apart from the violence of the Great War. Nor can violence against prisoners of war be solely discussed in terms of the moment of capture on the battlefield; this book has shown that violence during captivity was also significant and that it offers valuable insights into the radicalising tendencies which the war unleashed within societies.

One of these radicalising tendencies was a drive towards extremes in the textual and visual representation of prisoners of war in all three countries which, in turn, exacerbated an escalation in violent practices against prisoners, to varying degrees in each national case. Representations emerge here as having a powerful role in shaping the public expectations of captivity and the kinds of violence against prisoners that occurred. This is the reason for the sustained focus upon the interaction between representations of violence and violent practices in this book.

Second, many of the representations of violence against prisoners of war in the public domain were based upon real incidents. This book rejects the idea that First World War propaganda was largely exaggerated or fabricated. Instead it shows that there was a close, interactive relationship between propaganda and reality, which provides valuable insights into the information channels which operated within wartime societies. Violence against captives cannot be simply attributed to wartime myths or exaggerations; it was a real and widespread phenomenon. Nor can representations be seen as simply media tales or images with no real impact: this study has shown that the representation of violence had a significant effect on changing the image of enemy captivity, which, by the end of the conflict, was powerfully associated with violent treatment. In this regard, one can identify a brutalisation process occurring within societies during the war, as civilian perceptions of enemy captivity became far more extreme and, in certain social quarters, popular attitudes towards enemy captives hardened.

Third, if there was one central consequence of this radicalisation, it was the blurring of the distinction between the prisoner of war, a non-combatant category, and the enemy combatant soldier. The usual definition of total war focuses on the extent to which a conflict differentiates between civilians and soldiers; yet the collapse of the distinction between the prisoner of war and the combatant enemy can also serve as a way of measuring totalisation.[1] This distinction, as enshrined in international law, clearly began to break down as the Great War went on. Indeed, the overall trend was away from adhering to the regulation of prisoner treatment in international law in favour of bilateral interim agreements or reprisals; the idea of treating all prisoners universally also collapsed as certain national groups or ethnicities were singled out for privileges or punishment. Increasingly the Hague Convention was completely ignored. The Geneva Convention clauses, regarding the treatment of enemy wounded taken prisoner, fared a little better and continued to be generally observed to the end of the conflict. However, the war set a dangerous precedent of jettisoning international law when it suited the captor state; later wars would dramatically build on this trend.

This major weakening of international law has to be seen within a broader context, however; other cultural limitations on violence against prisoners clearly remained in place. These were sufficiently powerful to restrain escalation within certain thresholds: the fact that the majority of British, French and German prisoners of war in the three countries studied survived their captivity is proof of this, as is the fact that wounded prisoners were often provided with medical care and that the rules of class continued to be respected; indeed, the protection accorded to officer prisoners throughout the war suggests that class was a much more deeply ingrained ideology in European societies than pre-war international law. The Great War can thus best be described as a phase during which a 'culturally bounded' radicalisation of violence against prisoners occurred.

Perhaps the best way of accounting for why radicalisation always operated within certain thresholds is to recognise the pivotal role played by civilians; while military decision-making was crucial to the kinds of violence against prisoners that emerged in the First World War, it was never completely disconnected from civilian opinion. This brings us to the fourth key conclusion of this study: First World War escalation was not inevitable nor irreversible. And it was often determined by civilian reaction. Radicalisation of violence against enemy prisoners remained a negotiated process which was conveyed, approved or restricted through public

---

[1] Stig Förster, 'Introduction', in Chickering and Förster, eds., *Great War, Total War*, p. 8.

reactions. Polities and armies were constantly influenced by this, as they took decisions on prisoner of war policies. Indeed, as this study has shown, radicalisation processes could be effectively reversed when the public rejected them: the British Admiralty's failed reprisal attempt in 1915 and the French government's intervention to improve prisoner treatment in French prisoner of war labour companies in 1917 are cases in point, where public opinion forced governments to halt escalation. The role of civilians can thus be likened to that of a pendulum; at some points in the war, and, in particular, within the democratic states, civilian responses served to check violence against captives. At other points, they exacerbated it, as when civilians behaved hostilely to prisoners arriving in Germany and France in 1914.

First World War captivity can thus no longer continue to be seen as an unmitigated prisoner of war humanitarian success story. Although the parcel system and neutral intervention undoubtedly saved lives, the need for parcels actually points to a more negative trend, the increasing reluctance of captor states to take full responsibility for feeding prisoners; much of the civic response to sending aid to prisoners overseas was also motivated by nationalism and a desire to help the war effort. It was closely linked to the belief that prisoners were being mistreated by the enemy, as much an illustration of the mobilisation of wartime fears and hatreds as of straightforward humanitarianism.[2]

The fifth major contention of this study is that both fatal *and* non-fatal forms of violence against prisoners must be studied if the range of different forms of radicalisation occurring in the three countries during the war is to be fully understood. Killing was obviously the most extreme form of violence; it cannot be reduced to the same level as more minor violent practices that humiliated, coerced or disciplined. Yet, while acknowledging this differentiation, this study shows that it is important not to ignore non-fatal forms of violence in captivity. Although, as discussed in the introduction to this book, levels of fatal violence only ever affected a minority of prisoners directly, what emerges here is how important the radicalisation of non-fatal forms of violence was during the war, particularly in German captivity and, during certain phases of the conflict, in parts of the French system too. Even given the fact that prisoners working in agriculture in all three countries were largely excluded from violent mistreatment, this radicalisation still affected large numbers of captives.

What is particularly interesting in this regard is how during the war traditional prisoner of war scourges such as epidemics or hunger were now

[2] Jones, 'International or Transnational?'

seen as unacceptable extremes; these older forms of prisoner mistreatment co-existed with the new, much more radical, forms of violence seen during reprisals and in labour companies. Yet although only the latter can truly be identified as demonstrating new 'totalisation' processes at the heart of the war, the changing public attitude to traditional forms of prisoner mistreatment is a revealing indication of the increasingly total mobilisation of public opinion in response to the conflict. As a result, both fatal and non-fatal violence were pivotal to how contemporaries understood captivity. Historians need to consider the legacy of both in any overall assessment of how the First World War contributed to radicalised twentieth-century attitudes towards captives.

This brings us to the final, and most important, conclusion of this book: the First World War has to be seen as absolutely pivotal in the development of forced labour in the twentieth century. The dual system of prisoner labour companies on the western front and home front camps that emerged during the conflict was a dramatic structural innovation, a clear example of how the pressures of fighting 'total war' led all three states studied here to develop more 'total' forms of captivity, using the new prisoner labour company system. Here, what Roger Chickering has identified as the improvised, contingent nature of the totalising processes at the heart of the war emerges very clearly.[3] In response to the sudden new mass prisoner phenomenon, a consequence of the unprecedented scale of the conflict, armies opted to radicalise the use of forced labour in ways that exposed captives to increased violence; indeed, in the German case, a prisoner labour company system was created which by 1918 operated explicitly through coercing prisoner workers using constant violence. This set a dangerous precedent that the life of the prisoner labourer was expendable when this was in the interest of the captor army.

The prisoner labour company illustrates radicalisation at a number of levels: it shows that Britain, France and Germany were prepared to openly flout international law that prisoners should not be put to work directly on their captor state's war effort; it reveals what was clearly a universal trend at the heart of the conflict towards the increased acceptance of forced labour. Indeed prisoners, who were paid only a tiny wage in camp coupons and who had no certainty of when they would be released, come close to meeting Stanislaw Swianiewicz's definition of slavery, a permanent condition of total ownership of a socially segregated individual by another person or institution.[4] The labour company appears to have

---

[3] Chickering and Förster, eds., *Great War, Total War*, pp. 35–53.
[4] Stanislaw Swianiewicz, *Forced Labour and Economic Development. An Enquiry into the Experience of Soviet Industrialization* (Oxford, 1965), p. 21.

been an inherent product of military thinking rather than restricted to any one culture. Faced with a need for manpower, similarly structured innovations in forced prisoner labour emerged in all three armies. How badly they treated that labour differed; the necessity for it in all three cases was not questioned.

The Great War thus ended with two captivity models *in situ*. It is not implausible to suggest that, after 1939, in the absence of the pressures of trench warfare, the British reverted to structuring their prisoner of war camps along the lines of the First World War home front prisoner of war camp system model. Nor is it implausible to posit that, in contrast, in the Second World War, Germany radically developed its *univers concentrationnaire* in ways that drew upon both the First World War prisoner labour company idea and the home front camp system, now combined with Nazi ideological aims and the regime's experiences of using concentration camps and prisons in the 1930s. France, defeated in 1940, was largely spared from the need to revisit its First World War lessons in captivity administration. The German prisoner of war labour company system in the occupied territories of Belgium and northern France thus shows us the radicalisation dynamic possible where the German army was presented with absolute control of captives, without the civilian supervision or intervention which was present in the British and French cases and also to a limited extent, in the German home front camps. While recognising that the German army did make some efforts in 1918 to protect prisoner health in order to preserve its captive labour pool, the drive to extremes which ensued in the occupied territories in 1916–18 was an ominous portent for later developments.

This has throughout been a comparative study with the aim of showing how comparison can redefine our understanding of the war. And it has highlighted the very real similarities between the three countries studied here – particularly their common resort to prisoner of war forced labour as well as the broadly equivalent structural innovations they made to deal with the organisation of wartime captivity. It has contended that forms of radicalisation regarding captivity violence were occurring at different speeds in all three states at the level of representations and practices. Yet its ultimate conclusion is that major, highly significant differences also emerge between these countries regarding the use of violence against prisoners of war. A spectrum of radicalisation is clearly identifiable, with Germany at the most extreme end. German prisoner treatment was simply more ruthless than the other two cases, where the civilian state had greater input into the control of military prisoners. In its dealings with captives, it comes closest to the model of the First World War as a 'total war', in terms of its response to the totalising pressures the conflict unleashed. This is particularly clear in the prisoner reprisal sequences in 1916 and 1917, detailed in this book, where it is not possible to attribute violent radicalisation simply to the German army's economic need for prisoner labour. Here this study differs from Uta Hinz's conclusions that the deterioration of prisoner treatment in the German case was primarily driven by economic factors.[5] Military cultural attitudes were as important determinants.

Yet if there is a *Sonderweg* to emerge from this study, it is actually Britain, where, throughout the war, violence against prisoners remained far less acceptable than in France or Germany and where cultural constraints acting against radicalisation proved particularly powerful.[6] It is as important to question why, with regard to its German captives, Britain proved so surprisingly resilient to escalation as to focus upon why Germany proved so susceptible. France, in contrast, emerges in an interim position on the radicalisation spectrum; in 1916–17, it was following a similar trajectory to Germany, with increasing use of violence in French prisoner of war labour companies, a trajectory it abandoned following government intervention in 1917 to stop prisoner abuses. Thus the comparison of violence against prisoners of war highlights broader, deeper differences in how national cultures responded to the pressures of wartime.

For all of the above reasons, it is important that captivity in the First World War receive far greater attention. It was, as this book has shown, an integral part of the war. It was also fundamentally a transnational phenomenon, which merits comparative study. The focus in this conclusion has been largely upon the broader structural implications of this history. However, it is appropriate to end with a reminder of the individual human suffering which it also encompassed. On 29 November 1918, a German schoolgirl, Piete Kuhr, went to lay a wreath on the grave of a French prisoner in an act of pacifist protest at the hatreds the war had engendered. The inscription on the grave where Kuhr laid her wreath illustrated the personal cost which captivity could entail. It read:

> 'À toi mes pensées
> et mes larmes,
> tous les jours.'[7]

---

[5] Hinz, *Gefangen im Großen Krieg*, p. 362.

[6] On the longer-term historical context of this British exceptionalism, see Adrian Gregory, 'Peculiarities of the English? War, Violence and Politics. 1900–1939', *Journal of Modern European History*, 1, 1 (2003), pp. 44–59; Jon Lawrence, 'Forging a Peaceable Kingdom. War, Violence and the Fear of Brutalisation in Post-First World War Britain', *Journal of Modern History*, 75, 3 (2003), pp. 557–89.

[7] Mihaly, *'Da gibt's ein Wiedersehn!'*, p. 379. The inscription translated reads: 'To you my thoughts and my tears, all my days.'

Glossary of foreign terms

Auswärtiges Amt	German Ministry for Foreign Affairs
Etappengebiet	Area to the rear of the German front
Generalquartiermeister	German Army Quartermaster-General
Grand Quartier Général	French General Headquarters
Großes Hauptquartier	German General Headquarters
Kommando	Detachment of prisoners in Germany working outside their prison camp
Kriegsgefangener	German term for Prisoner of War
Lazarett	A German military hospital
Ministère de la Guerre	French Ministry of War
Oberste Heeresleitung	German Army Supreme High Command
Operationsgebiet	Area of German front-line military operations
Poteau	A punishment practised against prisoners held by Germany involving the prisoner being tied to a post or tree
Preußisches Kriegsministerium	Prussian Ministry of War
Prisonnier de guerre	French term for prisoner of war
Stammlager	A principal prison camp within the German system which administered multiple prisoner *Kommandos*
Zone des Armées	Militarised zone to the rear of the French front lines

Bibliography

ARCHIVE SOURCES

IRELAND

The National Archives of Ireland
M 6808, shelf 3/478/9 P. Aylward

Trinity College Library, Dublin (TCD)
War 1914–1918. Misc. Pamphlets on War:

TCD 135.d.21, 22
TCD 74.a.94
TCD German Atrocity Drawings,
Unpublished Selection, 940.3.E.6.

UNITED KINGDOM

**The National Archives (formerly the Public Record Office),
London (TNA)**

*Foreign Office: Consular Department: General Correspondence
from 1906*
FO 369/1450 K 15026 Maj. Gen. Sir Herbert Belfield, 'Report on Directorate of
   Prisoners of War', September 1920

*Foreign Office 383: Prisoners of War and Aliens Department: General
Correspondence from 1906, 1915–1919*
FO 383/267 Germany, Prisoners, 1917
FO 383/268 Germany, Prisoners, 1917
FO 383/269 Germany, Prisoners, 1917
FO 383/304 Germany, Prisoners, 1917
FO 383/407 Germany, Prisoners, 1918
FO 383/499 Germany, Prisoners, 1919
FO 383/506 Germany, Prisoners, 1919

Foreign Office 371: General Correspondence 1946
FO 371/55689, C3783

Foreign Office Embassy and Consulates, United States of America,
General Correspondence, Prisoners (War), Nos. 1–36, 1918
FO 115/2434 Prisoners (War) nos. 16–34 Propaganda (British) Nos 1–36, 1918

Records of the Metropolitan Police Office
MEPO 3/1166 Office of the Commissioner, Correspondence and Papers:
International Crime, 1921

War Office
WO 32: War Office and Successors: 1845–1945 Registered Files,
Conventions and International Agreements: Prisoners of War (Code 55B)
WO 32/5365 Proposal whereby German prisoners captured by British may be
handed over to French authorities, 1914
WO 32/5098 Communications with The Hague and agreements concerning
employment of prisoners near firing zone, 1916–1917
WO 32/5381 Employment and treatment of British prisoners of war by Germans
behind firing lines, 1917–1918
WO 32/5188 Alleged ill-treatment of British prisoners and of their employment
within 30 kilometres of front line, 1917–1918
WO 32/5373 Responsibility of War Office regarding repatriation, exchange and
internment of prisoners of war, 1916–1917
WO 32/5371 Plea for action to improve conditions of 39 British 'reprisal' prisoners
at Halle, Germany, 1915
WO 32/5369 Reports on condition of British prisoners in Germany; relief measures, 1914–1915
WO 32/5367 Royal Warrant and rules for maintenance of discipline among
prisoners, 1914–1915
WO 32/5608 German Commission on alleged ill-treatment of British prisoners of
war, the Wittenberg Case and trial and execution of Captain C. Fryatt of the
S. S. Brussels
WO 32/5396 Decorations and medals: General (Code 50 (A)): Question of
awards and mentions for prisoners of war, 1917–1919
WO 32/5456 Legal and Judicial: Courts Martial (Code 67 (C)): Authorisation
for General Trenchard commanding Independent Force, Royal Air Force, to
convene General Courts Martial and Military Courts for prisoners of war, 1918
WO 32/15541 Prisoner of war, Capt. Lt Franz Rintelen: transfer to authorities in
USA, 1915–1918
WO 32/4868 Pay and allowances (officers): General (Code 39 (A)): Issue of pay to
officers who are prisoners of war, Army Order, 1915
WO 32/15506 Prisoner of war: Parole (Code 91 (E)): Withdrawal of parole given
by officers to the Dutch authorities

WO 95: War Office: First World War and Army of Occupation, War
Diaries 1914–1923
WO 95/26 Branches and Services: Adjutant General, Jan. 1916–Dec.1919
WO 95/33 Branches and Services: Quarter-Master General, Jan.–Mar. 1917

WO 95/267 1st Army, 21 Labour Group Headquarters May–Oct. 1917

WO 95/282 Headquarters Branches and Services: Adjutant and Quarter-Master General, Jan. –Dec. 1917

WO 95/287 Headquarters Branches and Services: Director of Medical Services, May 1918–Mar. 1919

WO 95/358 2nd Army, 12 Labour Group Headquarters, July–Oct. 1917; 29 Labour Group Headquarters, July–Oct. 1917

WO 95/429 July–Oct. 1917, 3rd Army, 9 Headquarters Labour Group; May–Sept 1917, 13 Headquarters Labour Group; May–Oct. 1917, 34 Headquarters Labour Group; May–Oct. 1917, 49 Headquarters Labour Group

WO 95/517 4th Army, June 1916–Apr. 1917, 12 Labour Battalion, Devonshire Regiment; 53 Labour Group Headquarters May–Oct 1917; 70 Labour Group Headquarters Aug. –Oct. 1917; 49 Labour Company May–Aug. 1917

WO 95/4123 Lines of Communication; Prisoner of War Convalescent Depot (Havre) Apr. 1917–Mar. 1919; 4 Prisoner of War Convalescent Depot (Havre) Mar.–July 1919

WO 95/5040 Advanced Base and Defences, Nov 1918.–Apr. 1920 9 Prisoner of War Labour Corps; Jan. 1919–Apr. 1920, 10 Prisoner of War Labour Corps; Nov. 1918–Jan. 1920, 11 Prisoner of War Labour Corps; Sept 1919–Apr. 1920, 13 Prisoner of War Labour Corps; Jan. 1919–Apr. 1920, 17 Prisoner of War Labour Corps; May 1919–Feb. 1920, 18 Prisoner of War Labour Corps; Jan. 1919–Oct. 1919, 19 Prisoner of War Labour Corps

WO 141: War Office: Documents removed from the general series of War Office registered files WO 32 because they were considered sensitive, 1912–1946

WO 141/9 Formation of 'Irish Brigade' among prisoners of war in Germany, 1915–1921

WO 141/15 Sir Roger Casement's visits to Irish prisoners in Limburg Camp, 1916

WO 141/38 Enquiry into the surrender of the 1st Gordon Highlanders in Aug. 1914, 1923

WO 141/41 Execution of four men of the Royal Navy Division for alleged murder of a German soldier, 1919–1920

WO 142: War Office: Reports, minutes of committees and papers on Chemical Warfare 1905–1967

WO 142/177 Interrogation of prisoners, Reports Nos. F/M/H1-H18, 1915–1918

WO 158: War Office: Military Headquarters: Correspondence and Papers, First World War

WO 158/907 General von Lettow's force: treatment of troops as prisoners of war, Dec. 1918

WO 161: War Office: Miscellaneous Unregistered Papers, First World War

WO 161/82 Armies at home and abroad, 1914–1920: statistical abstract

WO 161/88 Reports and assessments, German casualties, Aug. 1914–Dec. 1915

WO 161/89 Monthly summaries, German casualties, Aug. 1914–Apr. 1916

WO 161/90 Notes and press cuttings, German casualties, July 1915–Mar. 1916

WO 161/91 Statistical analysis, German casualties, Sept. 1915

WO 161/95 Committee on the Treatment of British Prisoners of War: Interviews and Reports, officers' reports, Aug. 1915–Mar. 1917

WO 161/96 Committee on the Treatment of British Prisoners of War: Interviews and Reports, officers' reports, Apr. 1917–Jan. 1919

WO 161/97 Committee on the Treatment of British Prisoners of War: Interviews and Reports, medical officers' reports, Aug. 1915–Jan. 1919

WO 161/98 Committee on the Treatment of British Prisoners of War: Interviews and Reports, other ranks' reports, Oct. 1915–Aug. 1916

WO 161/99 Committee on the Treatment of British Prisoners of War: Interviews and Reports, other ranks' reports, May 1917–Jan. 1918

WO 161/100 Committee on the Treatment of British Prisoners of War: Interviews and Reports, other ranks' reports, Dec. 1917–Feb. 1919

WO 161/101 Committee on the Treatment of British Prisoners of War: Indexes to Interviews and Reports, Aug. 1915–Feb. 1919

WO 162: Unregistered papers of the Adjutant General relating to organisation, mobilisation and recruitment, medical arrangements for and casualty statistics and papers of various military actions; prisoners of war ... 1715–1971

WO 162/341 Report on the work of the Prisoners of War Information Bureau: includes examples of administrative papers, hospital and internment reports, 1 Aug. 1914–Dec. 31 1920

WO 394: War Office: Department of the Secretary, C5 Statistics Branch: Statistical Abstracts 1916–1920

WO 394/1 Statistical Abstracts of information regarding the armies at home and abroad 1916, Nov.–1917, Mar., Nos. 1–5

WO 394/2 Statistical Abstracts of information regarding the armies at home and abroad 1917, Apr.–June, Nos. 6–8

WO 394/3 Statistical Abstracts of information regarding the armies at home and abroad 1917, July–Sept., Nos. 9–11

WO 394/4 Statistical Abstracts of information regarding the armies at home and abroad 1917, Oct.–Nov., Nos. 12–13

WO 394/5 Statistical Abstracts of information regarding the armies at home and abroad 1917, Dec.–1918, Jan., Nos. 14–15

WO 394/7 Statistical Abstracts of information regarding the armies at home and abroad 1918 Apr.–May, Nos. 18–19

WO 394/8 Statistical Abstracts of information regarding the armies at home and abroad 1918, June–July, Nos. 20–21

WO 394/9 Statistical Abstracts of information regarding the armies at home and abroad 1918, Aug.–Sept., Nos. 22–23

Ministry of Transport
*MT 9 Board of Trade and Ministry of Transport and successors: Marine,
Harbours and Wrecks (M, H and W Series) Files, 1854–1969*
MT 9/1176 Prisoners of war (Code 106): Peace Conference – Points for discussion, 1918
MT 9/1211 Prisoners of war (Code 106): Segregation – German Merchant Navy officers 1918
MT 9/1227 Prisoners of war (Code 106): Repatriation, 1914–1918
MT 9/1249 Prisoners of war (Code 106): Reports on visits to camps
MT 9/1597 Prisoners of war (Code 106): Treatment and maintenance, 1917–1923

*MT 23 Admiralty, Transport Department: Correspondence
and Papers*
MT 23/393 Prisoners of war. Office memorandum concerning expenses incurred in connection with combatant prisoners in Naval custody, 1915
MT 23/559 Employment of German prisoners of war. Report of Principal Naval Transport Officer, France, after the French Military Authorities' Conference, 1916
MT 23/561 German prisoners of war. Suggestion for employing these for discharging coal hulks at Portland, 1916
MT 23/622 Exchange of incapacitated prisoners of war by British hospital ship, 1916
MT 23/682 Employment by the French of German prisoners of war at Havre. Report of Principal Naval Transport Office, France, 1916
MT 25/18 Repatriation of German prisoners of war, 1918; repatriation of British prisoners of war from Germany to Holland, 1918

Ministry of National Service
*NATS 1 Files relating to matters of permanent interest dealt with by the
Trade Exemptions, Medical, Labour Supply, Finance and Organisation,
Recruiting and Recording Departments of the Ministry of National
Service, 1914–1920*
NATS 1/282 Agreement between Board of Agriculture, War Office and Ministry of National Service concerning release of 30,000 Grade 1 men; substitution of German prisoners of war and war work volunteers, 1918
NATS 1/567 Prisoners of War Committee: Constitution and function; policy file, 1917–1918
NATS 1/568 Prisoners of War Committee Labour Policy: extension of Prisoners of War Committee to enquire into conditions of labour, remuneration and supervision of prisoners of war, 1918
NATS 1/569 Prisoners of war: inspection of camps by Ministry of National Insurance; utilisation of prisoners, enquiry, 1918
NATS 1/1330 Reports on prisoner of war camps, 1918
NATS 1/1331 Prisoner of War Employment Committee, 1916–1918
NATS 1/1332 Prisoner of War Employment Committee, 1917–1918

Ministry of Health MH 106, War Office: First World War Representative
Medical Records of Servicemen 1912–1921
MH 106/1979 German prisoners of war, 26 Oct. 1916–15 June 1917

Air Service AIR 1, Air Ministry: Air Historical Branch (Series 1)
1794–1974
AIR 1/501/15/333/1 Interrogative reports by escaped or repatriated prisoners of war, RFC or RAF, 1915–1918
AIR 1/605/16/15/246 Miscellaneous reports on prisoners of war, civilian internees and deserters, 1917–1918
AIR 1/910/204/5/826 German Air Force Intelligence on Western Front, prisoner of war reports, Jan.–June 1916
AIR 1/910/204/5/827 Intelligence: German Air Force reports from crew of Zeppelin L 15, Apr. 1916
AIR 1/1206/204/5/2619 Reports by repatriated or escaped RAF officer prisoners of war, 1918–1919
AIR 1/1289/204/11/62 Interrogation Reports on German Air Service prisoners of war, Jan.–Aug. 1916
AIR 1/1649/204/95/1 Reports on missing aircrew, Nov. 1917–Oct. 1918
AIR 1/1649/204/95/8 Casualties and prisoner of war correspondence, Feb. 1918–Feb. 1919
AIR 1/1993/204/273/182 Military Courts on enemy prisoners of war, July–Nov.1918
AIR 1/2154/209/3/312 Bomb targets: prisoner of war camps in Germany, RU.967, May–Oct. 1918
AIR 1/2251/209/54/29 Reports on interrogation of escaped British prisoners of war, Nov. 1916–Apr. 1917

Home Office HO 45, Registered Papers, 1839–1979
HO 45/10764/270829 Commissions and Committees: Committee on the Treatment by the Enemy of British Prisoners of War, 1914–1919
HO 45/10881/340700 War: Employment of prisoners of war in agriculture, 1916–1918

Cabinet
CAB1/22/3 Jan. 2, 1917, Reprisals for outrages against prisoners of war
CAB 24/63 Sept. 12, 1918, Prisoners of war. Summary of reprisals taken by the British and German governments since the beginning of the war
CAB 24/111 February 26, 1920, First, Second and Third Reports from the Committee of Enquiry into Breaches of the Laws of War
CAB 42/21/6 Oct. 12, 1916, Minutes etc. (Submarines, The Balkans, Prisoners of War, Man-Power)

Ministry of Munitions
MUN 4/6527 Labour: Control, Training etc.: Employment of labour on army contracts; employment of prisoners of war in France, and of imported labour, Feb. 1916–June 1918

Admiralty
ADM 1, Admiralty and Ministry of Defence, Navy
Department: Correspondence and Papers, 1660–1976
ADM 1/8388/237 Prisoners of War. War Office Bureau of Information opened – questions as to Naval Prisoners, 1914
ADM 1/8393/304 Prisoners of War in Germany, 1914
ADM 1/8419/103 Legality of prisoners of war in Germany being forced to work on farms, 1915
ADM 1/8434/283 Blockade of Germany. Question of sending food parcels to prisoners of war at Doeberitz, 1915
ADM 1/8446/15 Procedure to be adopted regarding Prisoners of War captured from Enemy Submarines, 1916
ADM 1/8489/109 Employing of German prisoners of war in the docks, 1917
ADM 1/8506/265 Prisoners of War, Notification of escapes and recaptures. Home Office circulars issued to Police etc. 1917

ADM 131, Admiralty, Plymouth Station: Correspondence, 1842–1969
ADM 131/86 Mobilisation: recruiting and manning ... treatment and accommodation of enemy prisoners of war, July 1914–

ADM 137, Admiralty: Historical Section: Records used for Official History, First World War
ADM 137/3885 Specifications and reports of patrols of German submarines and prisoner of war statements, 1916
ADM 137/3868 Miscellaneous papers: prisoners of war; the press; pan-German policy ... 1914–1918
ADM 137/3855 Copies of letters of German prisoners of war, interned at Donnington Hall, passing to and from USA

TS/26 Records created or inherited by the Treasury Solicitor and HM Procurator General's Department: War Crimes Papers, The Great War 1914–1918, Alleged War Criminals 1918–1922
The Leipzig Trials: TS 26/907; TS 26/908; TS 26/909; TS 26/21

Churchill Archives Centre, Churchill College, University of Cambridge

Papers of Sir Maurice Hankey (1877–1963)
Diaries: HNKY 8/1 (Sept. 1917); HNKY 8/2 (Oct. 1917); HNKY 8/4 (Jan. 1918); HNKY 1/3 (30.4.1917–19.7.1918)

Papers of Major General Sir Edward Spears
SPRS 1/54 British Military Mission to Paris, 1919

Imperial War Museum, Department of Documents, London (IWM)
Misc. 214, Item 3104, Report on the administration of labour in XVII Corps Feb. 1917–Feb. 1918
92/46/1 Diary of Surgeon Lieutenant Commander A. J. Gilbertson, RNVR
93/21/1 Diary of Nestor Hersent, St Leger, 1916

91/44/1, *Papers of Lieutenant-General Sir Herbert Belfield*
HEB 1/1 Conference at The Hague, 23 June–7 July 1917
HEB 2 Notebook of points for discussion at Berne Conference
HEB 4 Diary of the 1917 Hague Conference by Lieutenant-General Sir Herbert Belfield
HEB 5 Official Report of Commons debates for 8 Feb 1915, 3 March 1915 and 29 October 1918. Official Report of Lords Debates, 24 April 1918

House of Lords, Record Office (HLRO)

Papers of Andrew Bonar Law
BL/50/3/45 Report on the condition of German submarine prisoners in the UK, 1915
BL/81/3/5 Correspondence on prisoner reprisals, 1917

Papers of David Lloyd George
LG/D/17/6/31 Correspondence with Albert Thomas and U. F. Wintour on use of German prisoners as labour in France, 1916
LG/F/170/4/1 Memo on cabinet discussion of establishment of interdepartmental committee on prisoners of war, n.d. (late 1918)
LG/14/4/32 Correspondence on prisoner reprisals, spring 1917
LG/F/9/1/24 Note on prisoner repatriation, n.d. (1919)
LG/E/3/18/5 Letter from British Consulate, Rotterdam, 20.10.1916
LG/F/52/1/33 British Embassy, Paris, 18.5.1918, Letter from Lord Derby to Arthur J. Balfour reporting on a meeting with Clemenceau
LG/F/7/2/16 Letter from Austen Chamberlain to Prime Minister Lloyd George. 7.9.1918 on possible use of German prisoners of war in British mines

University of Birmingham Library, Special Collections
Acc.18F/1/52 Diaries of Llewellyn H. Gwynne, Bishop of Khartoum, Army Chaplain (4th Class) 1914–1915, Deputy Chaplain-General 1915–1919

The Commonwealth War Graves Commission (formerly the Imperial War Graves Commission) (IWGC)

Records of British prisoner of war graves in the following cemeteries
Aachen Military Cemetery – Nordrhein-Westfalen
Bad Bergzabern Cemetery – Rheinland Pfalz
Berlin South-western Cemetery – Brandenburg
Bocklemund New Jewish Cemetery – Cologne, Nordrhein-Westfalen
Bonn North Cemetery – Bonn, Nordrhein-Westfalen.
Cologne Memorial – Cologne, Nordrhein-Westfalen
Cologne Southern Cemetery – Cologne, Nordrhein-Westfalen
Deutz Jewish Cemetery – Cologne, Nordrhein-Westfalen
Euskirchen New Town Cemetery – Nordrhein-Westfalen
Gießen Jewish Cemetery– Gießen, Hessen
Göttingen Jewish Cemetery – Göttingen Niedersachsen

Hamburg Cemetery – Hamburg
Hasenheide Garrison Cemetery – Berlin, Berlin
Koblenz Jewish Cemetery – Koblenz, Rheinland-Pfalz
Münster Haus Spital [sic] Prisoners of War Cemetery – Munster, Nordrhein-Westfalen.
Niederzwehren Cemetery – Kassel, Hessen
Worms (Hochheim Hill) Cemetery – Worms, Rheinland-Pfalz

Cambridge University Library (CUL)

Jenkinson Collection
Wrc.16.102 *Die Behandlung der feindlichen Kriegsgefangenen. Amtlicher Bericht der Kommission zur Untersuchung der Anklagen wegen Völkerrechtswidriger Behandlung der Kriegsgefangenen in Deutschland* (Berlin, 1920)

FRANCE

Archives Nationales, Paris (AN)

F23 Versements des Ministères et Services extraordinaires du temps de guerre – 1914 et années suivantes
F.23.5 Prisonniers de guerre civils et militaires 1917–1918, Internées civils français et étrangers (1916–1918) conférences de Berne et exécutions des accords relatifs aux internés civils, 1918

AJ 30. 277–295 prisonniers de guerre; fiches individuelles et dossiers généraux 1915–1920
AJ 30.277 Alsace-Lorraine

Ministère du Commerce
F 12 7802 Rapatriement de prisonniers de guerre, 1918–1919

Ministère des Travaux Publics
F 14 11329 Emploi des prisonniers de guerre dans les ports, mai 1915–décembre 1915; prisonniers dans les carrières et mauvaise volonté des prisonniers de guerre allemands, janvier 1918–juin 1918
F 14 11330 *Ibid.* janvier 1918–janvier 1919 et juillet 1918–janvier 1920

Prefects' Reports, 1914
F7.12936; F7.12937; F7.12939

Archives du Ministère des Affaires Étrangères, Quai d'Orsay, Paris (MAE)

Correspondance politique et commerciale 1897–1918, Première partie, Nouvelle série. Guerre 1914–1918, Dossier général
82 jan. 1917
83 fév. 1917

Correspondance politique et commerciale 1897–1918, Première partie, Nouvelle série, Guerre 1914–1918, Droit de la guerre sur terre
1114 Rapports du Ministère de la Guerre, 1914–1915 Allemagne, Autriche. Dossier général I, 1914, juillet–décembre
1115 Accusations allemandes, oct. 1914–déc. 1915
1116 Accusations allemandes, janv. 1916–mai 1916
1124 Grande Bretagne, 1915–1918

Correspondance politique et commerciale 1897–1918, Première partie, Nouvelle série, Guerre 1914–1918, Maroc
288 Mission Militaire française, 1915–1916
392 Travaux publics dossier général, 1915–1916
384 Travaux publics chemins de fer 1915, fév.–1916, janv.

État numérique des fonds de la correspondance politique et commerciale (nouvelle série) 1897 à 1918, supplément, Maroc
468 Mission militaire française, Services de sûreté 1914–1916, corps d'occupation, justices de paix, 1912–1916

Correspondance politique et commerciale 1914–1940. Serie A. Paix
64 Violations du droit; responsabilités, sanctions, représailles, 1916, juillet–1920, décembre
80 Conditions militaires de la Paix, Prisonniers de guerre, juillet–octobre 1919

Correspondance politique et commerciale 1914–1940, Série Z, Europe, Allemagne 1918–1929
181 Prisonniers de guerre, avril 1918–mai 1921
182 Allemagne. Prisonniers de guerre
187 Sépultures militaires 1919, avril–1923, juin
589 Archives de la mission de l'Avocat général Matter au procès de Leipzig, 1921

Service Historique de l'Armée de Terre, Vincennes (SHAT)

Répertoire des archives du Maroc, serie 3 H (1877–1960)
3 H 260 Cabinet militaire de la résidence générale, affaires en rapport avec le 2ème bureau: ... Rapatriement vers la Suisse de grands blessés allemands prisonniers au Maroc (1915–1916)

Série N 1872–1919
3 N 10 Comité de Guerre, Échange de prisonniers de guerre
5 N 131 Cabinet du Ministre, Dossiers Clementel et Albert Thomas: comptes rendus de mission concernant les ressources industrielles et les fabrications de guerre, octobre 1914–mai 1915
5 N 159 Cabinet du Ministre, Messages téléphones, télégrammes et traductions de télégrammes chiffrés reçus, classés par pays, France ... les prisonniers de guerre, juin–août 1917
5 N 166 Cabinet du Ministre, Angleterre, Documents provenant principalement du GQG britannique, de l'attaché militaire, du ministre des munitions à

Londres, de la marine, des affaires étrangères, de la mission militaire à Folkestone et du 'secretary post office' concernant . . . les prisonniers de guerre, décembre 1916–juillet 1917. Renseignements sur messages téléphones et télégrammes, Angleterre, déc. 1916–juillet 1916, Prisonniers de guerre français et étrangers, déc. 1916–mars 1917

5 N 167 Cabinet du Ministre, Angleterre, Prisonniers britanniques

5 N 187 Cabinet du Ministre. Messages téléphones, télégrammes et traductions de télégrammes chiffrés reçus, classés par pays . . . l'espionnage et le rapatriement des prisonniers de guerre

5 N 270 Cabinet du Ministre. Questions diverses 1915–1920. Camps d'officiers prisonniers en Allemagne (fin. 1915).

5 N 556 Cabinet du Ministre, Bureau des Informations Militaires, 1915–1919. Prisonniers de guerre allemands

6 N 21 Fonds Buat . . . Alsace-Lorraine: organisation administrative de l'Alsace-Lorraine par les autorités militaires, traitement des prisonniers de guerre (novembre 1914–août 1915) Alsaciens-Lorrains prisonniers de guerre, nov. 1914–août 1915, Dossier 16

6 N 22 Fonds Buat . . . rapports des médecins rapatriés d'Allemagne notamment au sujet du traitement des prisonniers de guerre (septembre 1914–juin 1915)

6 N 23 Fonds Buat, État-Major de l'Armée de Terre, Fonds Buat, Correspondance août 1914–octobre 1915 . . . travail des prisonniers de guerre (1er avril 1915)

6 N 47 Fonds Gallieni, Renseignements divers, juin 1915–février 1916, Documents concernant l'Allemagne et l'Autriche du 25 juin 1915 au 31 décembre 1915

6 N 53 Fonds Clemenceau, Dossiers personnels du Président du conseil, Ministre de la guerre. 1917–1919 . . . Incident Foch-Clemenceau à propos du rapatriement des prisonniers allemands et correspondance échangé avec le secrétaire d'état allemand Erzberger (janvier–février 1919)

6 N 110 Fonds Clemenceau, Prisonniers de guerre 1915–1918, Inspection générale des prisonniers de guerre: circulaires concernant notamment le régime des prisonniers, l'administration de ceux-ci, la discipline, la surveillance, la correspondance, le travail, l'alimentation et la santé, journal hebdomadaire (mars–décembre) 1916

6 N 114 Fonds Clemenceau, Allemagne, 1914–1921 . . . correspondance entre Foch et Clemenceau pendant les tractations de la conférence de la paix, rapatriement des prisonniers de guerre allemands

7 N 143 E. M. A. 1er Bureau 1914–1918, Effectifs, Prisonniers de guerre français. Classement méthodique, Rapatriés, rapatriés sanitaires, rapatriés et évadés . . . militaires tombés valides entre les mains de l'ennemi

7 N 327–1 suppl. Deuxième Bureau de l'EMA, Documents sur l'Armée allemande et les manoeuvres de l'armée française: correspondance et télégrammes de la mission militaire française à Berlin

7 N 334 suppl. d.1 interrogatoires de militaires rapatriés d'allemagne comme grands blessés et malades, renseignements receuillis dans les correspondances adressés aux prisonniers de guerre allemands 1915–1919.

7 N 338 Suppl. EMA, 2e Bureau de l'EMA Dossier 1. Renseignements sur la Bataille de la Somme: traduction de documents allemands, comptes rendus d'interrogatoires de prisonniers (1916–1917)

7 N 362 suppl. État-Major de l'Armée, deuxième bureau de l'EMA, section des missions, d.2, organisation et fonctionnement de la mission militaire française à la recherche des disparus en Allemagne (1919–1926); d.3, mission de recherche des disparus en Allemagne: gestion du personnel officier 1919–1927

7 N 576 EMA, 1er Bureau, 4e section et 5e section nouvelle, Pertes, États récapitulatifs des pertes des armées; états numériques des officiers et hommes de troupe morts ou disparus, dénombrements mensuel des renseignements relatifs aux pertes; morts, disparus et prisonniers comptés dans les dépôts, pertes en Orient; pertes d'après les archives administratives, 1914–1918

7 N 679 EMA, 2e Bureau, Bulletin d'information de quinzaine no. 5, 20 juin 1917

7 N 999; 7 N 1000; 7 N 1001: EMA, 2e Bureau, Pontarlier: rapports mensuels concernant principalement la France, l'Autriche-Hongrie et la Suisse, rapports sur le camp d'Auch, sur la correspondance des familles allemandes avec les prisonniers en France et sur la correspondance des prisonniers de guerre français internés en Suisse, sur le courrier saisi à bord des bateaux et sur la presse suisse germanophile, octobre 1915–mai 1918

7 N 1187 Attachés militaires Pays-Bas, Déclarations de prisonniers de guerre français évadés à la légation de France à la Haye, 1915–1916

7 N 1585 Attachés militaires en Suisse, 1913–1915, Prisonniers de guerre en Allemagne

7 N 1993 EMA, 3e Bureau, Prisonniers de guerre: organisation, personnel, locaux, utilisation de la main-d'œuvre, carte des camps 1914–1919

7 N 2015 EMA, 3e Bureau. ... reseignements donnés à l'ennemi par des prisonniers

7 N 2105 EMA, Section d'Afrique, agissements anti-français en Afrique du Nord ... prisonniers de guerre envoyés au Maroc et en Algérie, août 1914–juin 1923

7 N 2107 EMA, Section d'Afrique ... Prisonniers de guerre indigènes évadés, août 1914–décembre 1920

7 N 2189 EMA, Section d'Afrique, Contentieux et justice militaire, prisonniers de guerre: prisonniers français musulmans en Allemagne, prisonniers et suspects divers, 1915–1919

10 N 194 Commission d'enquête des marchés de l'état, Marchés des cerceuils et de croix, exhumations, regroupement de sépultures, restitution de corps aux familles, rapatriement de corps de prisonniers de guerre et de militaires décédés à l'étranger, 1919–1926

10 N 218 Commission Inter-Alliée Permanente de l'Armistice (CIPA), Service des prisonniers de guerre, 1918–1920

12 N 3 Sous-secrétariat d'état de l'administration ... les prisonniers de chaque nationalité faits par les belligérants, 1914–1921

15 N 15 suppl. Grand Quartier Général des armées alliées, Direction générale des communications et des ravitaillements aux armées, Attribution de matériel de guerre abandonné par les allemands, rapatriement des prisonniers de guerre français, allemands et serbes, nov. 1918–déc. 1919

15 N 15 Rapatriement des prisonniers de guerre, nov. 1918–déc 1919, Dossiers 44, 45, 46 Rapatriement, Inspection des PG. Inévacuables, nov. 1918–déc. 1919

16 N 525 GQG, 1er Bureau, Pertes, statistiques sur les pertes, statistiques par affaires, par armes; pertes des armées Alliées; contingents indigènes; disparitions; prisonniers de guerre, 1914–1918

16 N 1224 GQG, 2e Bureau, Rapports Mensuels des officiers interprètes sur la situation politique, économique, morale et sanitaire en Allemagne, d'après le contrôle de la correspondance des prisonniers (zone des armées); interrogatoires des prisonniers français rapatriés, concernant notamment la révolution allemande, octobre 1917–janvier 1919

16 N 1663 Comptes rendus des séances et correspondance diverse concernant la commission ministerielle des villes bombardées, le comité spécial pour la reconstitution des moyens d'habitation, le comité spécial de reconstitution des régions envahies, le comité consultatif d'action économique, les comités du 'secours national' et du 'village reconstitué', documents de principe et documents divers concernant les regions liberées et la reorganisation des territoires reconquis, aide apportée aux populations, liste d'habitants recupèrés, ravitaillement, 1916–1919

16 N 2380 GQG, Direction de l'Arrière, Organisation: étapes. Évacuations de prisonniers rapatriés, nov. 1918–septembre 1919, Organisation et principes diverses

16 N 2382 GQG, Direction de l'Arrière, Organisation: étapes. Évacuations de prisonniers rapatriés, novembre 1918–septembre 1919. États. Décembre 1918–janvier 1919

16 N 2466 GQG, Direction de l'Arrière, Main d'oeuvre et PG, Prisonniers de guerre: organisation, 1915–1919, Inspection des camps

16 N 2467; 16 N 2468; 16 N 2469; 16 N 2476: GQG, Direction de l'Arrière, Compagnies de PG travailleurs: constitution, mouvements, affectations d'unités, emploi, discipline, travail, 1916–1919

16 N 2732 GQG, Direction de l'Arrière, Inspection des unités indigènes d'étapes et des PG de la Zone des Armées, Minutes de rapports sur les inspections des compagnies de PG 1916–1919

16 N 2947 GQG, TOE Turquie: Comptes rendus sur la propagande musulmane faite parmi les prisonniers arabes et notamment algériens en Allemagne

16 N 3017 GQG, 3e Bureau TOE, puis 3e Bureau A. ... Pratiques odieuses de l'autorité allemande à l'égard de nos prisonniers de guerre, no.179

19 N 512 IIe Armée. DES (1). Formations de prisonniers de guerre: archives du camp de PG de Souilly et du groupement de compagnies de PG; notes et circulaires, correspondance diverse, avril 1916–octobre 1918

Série N 1920–1940
6 N 442 Statuts des anciens prisonniers de guerre (1933)

Centre des Archives Économiques et Financières, Savigny-le-Temple
B/0061026/1 Direction du mouvement général des fonds, 1919–1926

B/0060829 Rapatriement des prisonniers de guerre allemands, rédition des avoirs monétaires des PGA liberés (1929–1951)

Archives Départementales de l'Aude, Carcassonne
9 R 1 Dépot d'officiers allemands prisonniers de guerre à la caserne du château à la cité de Carcassonne
2 R 15 Circulaires concernant les prisonniers, aide apportée aux militaires blessés, aux prisonniers; pain de guerre des prisonniers
2 R 16*–18* Listes des prisonniers du département par arrondissement et par commune, 1914–1918
4 M 1859 Archives de l'Hérault. Mesures particuliers en temps de guerre. Suspects d'un point de vue national, déserteurs, étrangers, propagande pacifiste, réunions politiques, syndicales et corporatives, prisonniers de guerre, surveillance, correspondance postale suspecte, interception: permis de séjour aux étrangers; état moral de la population, enquête: rapports de police, PV de gendarmerie, correspondance 1914–1916

Archives Départementales de la Loire
AD 3R 64 Prisonniers de Guerre. Assistance

Bibliothèque de Documentation Internationale Contemporaine-Musée d'Histoire Contemporaine (BDIC-MHC)

I. BDIC-MHC UNIVERSITÉ DE PARIS X-NANTERRE
O pièce 15505 Chassé, Charles, Lycée de Brest, Année scolaire 1918–1919, Discours prononcé à la distribution des prix le 12 juillet 1919
4 Delta 26 Dossier, BDIC Allemagne, Prisonniers Allemands après l'Armistice 1918, German leaflet about a collection to be held in support of prisoners of war, 1919, entitled 'Wie sie leiden'
F pièce 158 (16) (F) La politique allemande dans les camps de prisonniers de guerre belges, Curiosités de guerre belges, juillet, 1917, no.16
O pièce 21353 Merkblätter für die Besichtigung der Gefangenenlager in Afrika
O 745 (21) col. Werner, Georges, 'Les prisonniers de guerre', extract in Académie de Droit International, *Recueil des Cours*, 1928
O pièce 14505, Fédération Nationale des anciens prisonniers de guerre, évadés et otages, *Les Prisonniers de guerre* (Paris, n.d.)
S 9794 (1) *Le Sort des prisonniers de guerre. Qui considère-t-on comme prisonnier de guerre* (Bruxelles, n.d.)
F pièce 114 (F), Belot, *Derrière les barbelés. Scènes de la vie des prisonniers de guerre* (Roanne, n.d.)

II. BDIC-MHC, LES INVALIDES.
ART WORK VIEWED:
Or 2059 D. Widhopff, 'Remords: Qu'elle est jolie cette petite française, et comme elle ressemble à celle que nous avons fusillé dans les tranchées ... après', Dans un hôpital: femme secourant prisonniers allemands blessés. Crayon

Est F2.349 Jean-Louis Forain, L'École des héros: 'Comment vous avez attrapé ça? – Je soignais leurs blessés' (1915). Deux enfants s'adressant à un soldat mutilé. Lithographie

Est 1125.D.61.108 Jean-Louis Forain, Souvenirs d'enfant (Les prisonniers passent) 'Dis maman! ... c'est-il ceux-là qui ont tué papa?' (1916). Mère et petite fille, colonne de prisonniers qui passe. Publié dans Le Figaro, 23.11.1916

Est F 2384 Jean-Louis Forain, Prisonniers Boches: 'Est-ce que ce sont aussi des soldats? On le croyait ...' (1916). Dialogue entre un garçonnet et un poilu, Au fond près de ruines, prisonniers allemands et leur sentinelle (Le Figaro, 1.3.1916; 1.11.1916; 23.2.1916)

Or 1233 Pierre Gérbaud, 'Assassin inconscient, 14–18, Soldat français qui vient d'abattre un prisonnier allemand'. Crayon, fusain

Or SA 79 A.-M.Gilbert, 'Prisonniers! Chouette! ... Nous v'là assurés sur la vie!' 1916, Prisonniers allemands derrière les barbelés. Aquarelle

Or F3 1307–1320 [F] Marcel-Eugène Louveau Rouveyre, 'Prisonniers allemands, gare de Mantes' (Seine et Oise) 1914. 10 fusains

Or F3 1278[F] Marcel-Eugène Louveau Rouveyre, 'Étude des boches'. Crayon

Or F2. 555 [F] Henry Geoffroy, 'Les Enfants héroïques', Enfant défendant un soldat, 1914, Officier allemand ordonnant à un jeune homme de donner le coup de grâce à un blessé

Or F1 222 [F] Daniel de Theureude de Losques, 'Prisonniers allemands – Meaux le 24 août 1914'. Crayon, aquarelle

Or 243 Pierre-Paul Montagnac, 'Prisonniers allemands à la corvée de pommes de terre 1914–1918'

Or 572 Charles Picart-le-Doux, 'Prisonnier allemand vu de dos', 1914–1918, Crayon

Or F3 633 [F] F. Rousselin, 'Prisonniers allemands employés dans les bois de Blércourt, Verdun à la construction de routes pour accéder à la côte 304'. Blércourt, 1917. Prisonniers travaillant dans un chemin creux. Incre de chine

Or PE 107 Jules Adler, 'Prisonnier du fort de Douaumont, Politisch, Camp de Souilly, février 1917'

Or PE 111 Jules Adler, 'Prisonnier de Douaumont, Linderer, Bavière, camp de Souilly, 6.2.1917', Prisonnier assis. Fusain et pastel jaune

Or F2430 [F] René Georges Hermann-Paul, 'De Soissons à l'Argonne – Mein Gott, vous n'êtes donc pas défaitistes, 24.7.1918'. Fantassin français et prisonnier de guerre allemand

Or F2.425[F] René Georges Hermann-Paul, 'Bocherie. Le prisonnier: ils ont été bien gentils. Quelle cochonnerie vais-je leur faire avant de m'en aller, 22.6.1919'. Femme jouant avec son enfant; derrière un arbre prisonnier allemand, Pince et lavis à l'encre de chine

Or F 2432 [F] René Georges Hermann-Paul, 'Encore des américains! Mais qu'est-ce qu'il attend Hindenburg pour faire son offensive?' Deux prisonniers allemands regardant des soldats américains qui débarquent

Or F2 399 [F] René Georges Hermann-Paul, 'La réponse de Verdun, Le voilà le chemin de la paix! 20.12.1916'. Soldats français, prisonniers allemands. Crayon, fusain

Or F2.412 [F] René Georges Hermann-Paul, 'La carte de pain, "Ne grogne pas, le boche écoute!"' 24.1.1918. Deux femmes et un prisonnier allemand devant une boulangerie
Or 4949 René Georges Hermann-Paul, 'Le prisonnier' 1914–1918, Un prisonnier allemand surveillé par un soldat français. Aquarelle
Est FL 1837 André Warnod, 'Les Prisonniers de Guerre!' (Prisonniers français arrivent en Allemagne; Au fond une foule qui hurle)
Est F 287 André Warnod, 'Au poteau' (Mersebourg camp)
Est FL 1834 André Warnod, 'L'hôpital' (Mersebourg camp, Allemagne). Un prêtre avec un prisonnier de guerre mourant

Bibliothèque Nationale de France (BNF)
Zeitung für die deutschen Kriegsgefangenen (Paris, 1915)
Wöchentliche Nachrichten im Kriegsgefangenen-Lager Tours, juin 1918–juin 1919, Tours

GERMANY

Bundesarchiv, Berlin-Lichterfelde (BA)

Waffenstillstandskommission
R 904/77 Kriegsgefangene, Dez. 1918–März 1919, Nr. 41, Bd. 1, Generalia, Schriftw. etc. betr. Rückbeförderung der feindl. und Zurückhaltung der deutschen Kriegsgefangenen. Einsetzung einer Kommission zur Untersuchung der Anklagen wegen völkerrechtswidriger Behandlung der Kriegsgefangenen in Deutschland (27/30.11.1918)
R 904/81 Gen. Kriegsgefangene, Dez. 1918–Juni 1919, Nr. 41, Bd. 5, Professor Schücking, Kommission zur Untersuchung über Behandlung der feindlichen Kriegsgefangenen [sic]
R 904/82 Gen. 9.3–21.3.1919, Nr. 41, Bd. 6, Zuschriften von Angehörigen deutscher Kriegsgefangener (auch von Vereinen), Enthält nur: Vorschlag v. Conr. Meissner, dir. Der Graf v. Reventlow-Criminil'schen Besitzungen, anstelle der Kriegsgefangenen deutsche Strafgefangene zum Wiederaufbau der zerstörten Gebiete zu verwenden, 9.3.1919
R 904/83 spez. Kriegsgefangene, Nov.1918–März 1919, Nr. 42, Schriftwechsel (zahlr. Privatbriefe!) Alphabet. geordnet, zahlreiche Einzelfälle, auch über Verhaftete aus dem bes. Gebiet – K. M. übersendet Abschr. der eidl. Aussage des Stabsarztes Dr. Essen betr. die Behandlung deutscher Heeresangehöriger u. des deutschen Sanitätspersonals in den belg. Gefangenenlagern, 5.3.1919
R 904/88 spez. Kriegsgefangene, 18.12.1918–13.1.1920, Nr. 46, Professor Schücking: Kommission zur Untersuchung über Behandlung der feindlichen Kriegsgefangenen [sic], spez. Protokolle der Kommissionssitzungen, Untersuchungen u. Urteile (Abschriften) Tätigkeitsbericht, Schriftwechsel mit Erzberger
R 904/89 Kriegsgefangene I. Jan–Febr. 1919, Nr. 47, Bd. Zuschriften von Angehörigen deutscher Kriegsgefangener (auch von Vereinen) spez. Inhalt der Zuschriften; Bitten um Befreiung der deutschen Kriegsgefangenen,

Behandlung derselben in Feindesland, Bitte um Nachforschungen etc. damit oft verbunden Lob für oder Angriffe gegen Erzberger

Auswärtiges Amt

R 901/54389 Gefangenschaft, Kriegsgefangene, Juni 1915–Dez. 1918
R 901/84189 Konferenz über Gefangenenfragen, Hague 1918, AA III b
R 901/84255 Gefangenenlager in Deutschland, Kassel
R 901/84451 Gefangenenlager in Deutschland, AA IIb Akten betreffend das Gefangenenlager in Stettin
R 901/84490 Auswärtiges Amt, IIIb Akten betreffend die Gefangenenlager im besezten Gebiete
R 901/84525 Auswärtiges Amt IIIb Akten betreffend Besichtigungen der Gefangenenlager in Frankreich und Deutschland durch das Rote Kreuz vom Juni 1915 bis Februar 1916, Militärwesen, Nr.184, Frankreich Lager

Auswärtiges Amt: Nachrichten- und Presseabteilung

R 901/54400 Vergeltungsmaßregeln, Repressalien, Bd. 1, Jan. 1917–Nov. 1918
R 901/54403 Misshandlung verwundeter Gefangener, Bd. 1, Jan. 1917–Nov. 1920
R 901/54405 Greuel an Militärpersonen an der Front, Bd. 1, Februar 1917–Nov. 1918
R 901/54408 Kriegsgefangene auf Schiffen und in beschossenen Städten, Bd. 1 Februar 1917–Juni 1918
R 901/54409 Verwendung von Gefangenen in der Feuerzone, Bd. 1, Jan. 1917 – Nov. 1918
R 901/ 54410 Wirtschaftliche Ausnutzung von Gefangenen, Bd. 1, Jan. 1917–Juni 1920
R 901/54411 Militärische Ausnutzung von Kriegsgefangenen, Bd. 1 Jan. 1917–Juli 1920
R 901/54412 Besichtigung von Kriegsgefangenen, Bd. 1, Jan. 1917–Feb. 1920
R 901/54423 Behandlung von Kriegsgefangenen in Deutschland, Bd. 1, Aug. 1918–Okt. 1920

Reichsvereinigung ehemaliger Kriegsgefangener
Miscellaneous unsorted papers:
R 8095/1; R 8095/2; R 8095/3; R 8095/4; R 8095/5

Bundesarchiv-Militärarchiv, Freiburg (BA-MA)

Bestand Msg 200 Elsa-Brändström-Gedächtnisarchiv-Sammlung Kriegsgefangenenwesen

Msg 200 / 106 Besuch einer Absendung der Reichsvereinigung ehemaliger Kriegsgefangener bei Reichspräsident von Hindenburg am 20 Dez. 1933. Aufzeichnung des Gesprächs mit dem Reichspräsidenten (Kopie)
Msg 200 / 203 Gedächtnisfeier der Reichsvereinigung ehemaliger Kriegsgefangener in Köln und Hamburg. Freiherr von Lersner und Propst Juhl als Teilnehmer (2 Fotos) 1959–1969

Msg 200 / 224 Inder. Behandlung und Verpflegung indischer Kriegsgefangener im Gefangenenlager Wittenberg. Bericht von Oberleutnant Jantzen. 1914–1915

Msg 200 / 327 Die Kriegsgefangenenlager in Frankreich, Korsika und Nord Afrika. Allgemeiner Lagebericht und Gesamtberichte

Msg 200 / 330 Das Liederbuch von Carcassonne, 1917

Msg 200 / 427 Rose, Gerhard. Aus den Erfahrungen einer vierjährigen Gefangenschaft in Algerien und Frankreich (*Deutsch-Medizinische Wochenschrift*, 10.7.1919, S. 771–773)

Msg 200 / 454 Programms eines Kinderspiels auf Schloss Neusorge mit Fotografien 1924. Foto des Neusorge-Zöglings Kurt Siebke

Msg 200 / 559 Ansicht des Kriegsgefangenenlagers 'Stobs' in Schottland 1918

Msg 200 / 590 Otto von Waterstorft: Gefangennahme, Verhältnisse im Kriegsgefangenenlazarett und im Kriegsgefangenenlager Brest/Bretagne, 1914

Msg 200 / 926 Aufzeichnungen eines deutschen Kriegsgefangenen über seine Erlebnisse in französischer Gefangenschaft. 1914–1919. Deutsche Kriegsgefangene in Frankreich – DRK (Deutsches Rotes Kreuz) Wochenbericht Nr. 68 vom 11.3.1916

Msg 200 / 1187 'Es war vor 50 Jahren'. Erinnerungen eines deutschen Kriegsgefangenen in Frankreich während des ersten Weltkrieges (1917–1920) von Karl Schmidt (um 1967)

Msg 200 / 1247 Feldpostkarten aus britischer Gefangenschaft: Parent Camp Bramley, Southend-on-sea Handforth, 1916–1918

Bestand PH 2 Kriegsministerium

PH2 / 25 Schwarzen Liste derjenigen Engländer, die sich während des Krieges gegenüber deutschen Heeresangehörigen völkerrechtswidrigen Verhaltens schuldig gemacht haben (mit Vernehmungsprotokollen der Zeugenaussagen) 1915–1919

PH2 / 26 Kriegsministerium. Militär-Untersuchungsstelle für Verletzungen des Kriegsrechts. Kriegsrechtsverstöße englischer Truppen gegen Deutsche Heeresangehörige in der Kampfzone (1914, 1917–1918). Denkschrift über die seit Ende des Jahres 1917 neu festgestellten Völkerrechtsverletzungen englischer Truppen mit Vernehmungsprotokollen der Zeugenaussagen. Hierin: englische Kriegsrechtsverstöße in Belgien und Frankreich 1914–1918. Völkerrechtsverletzungen, Greuel etc. 1918–1921

PH2 / 33 Kriegsministerium. Militär-Untersuchungsstelle für Verletzungen des Kriegsrechts. Anlagenband II zu der Liste derjenigen Franzosen, die sich besonders roh und grausam gegen deutsche Gefangene gezeigt haben

PH2 / 36 Interner Wochen Bericht Nr. 68 des deutschen Roten Kreuzes-Ausschuss für deutsche Kriegsgefangene, 2.4.1916

PH2 / 588 Schwarze Liste derjenigen Engländer, die sich während des Krieges gegenüber deutschen Heeresangehörigen völkerrechtswidrigen Verhaltens schuldig gemacht haben

Bestand PH 2 Kriegsministerium, Teil 2 (from former DDR archives)

PH 2 / 592 Aufstellung über strafbare Handlungen durch Heeresangehörige im besetzten Gebiet, 1914–1918

PH 2 / 595 Aktenverzeichnis der Leipziger Verteidigungsstelle über Verfahren gegen Kriegsbeschuldigte, die aufgrund des Gesetzes zur Verfolgung von Kriegsverbrechen und Kriegsvergehen vom 18. Dez. 1919 vom Reichsgericht in Leipzig untersucht bzw. verurteilt wurden, 1919

Bestand PH 5 Oberkommandos

PH 5 / 185 Bd. 10: Aug.–Sept. 1914. hierin Anl.z.KTB, Transportbewegungen: 11.8.–28.9.1914. Anl. z.KTB, Gefangene: 20.8.–1.9.1914

Bestand PH 5 II Armeen (AOKs)
Armeeoberkommando 4

PH 5 II / 442 Verfügungen und Schriftwechsel des Inneren Dienstes der Militärgefangenen-Kompagnien. Feb. 1917–Nov. 1918. 4.1.16.1./14. Enthält u.a.: Heranziehen von Heeresunfähigen zum militärischen Arbeitsdienst, Stärkenachweisung für eine Kriegsarbeiter-Kompagnie, Bekleidung und Ausrüstung

PH 5 II / 446 Aufstellungen über alliierte Kriegsgefangene im Bereich der 4. Armee. March–Aug 1918. 4.1.16.1/18

PH 5 II / 447 Monatsberichte über Gefangenenlager. Enthält u.a. Meldungen über Stärke, Zustand, Verpflegung und Unterkunft. Karte mit Einzeichnungen der Gefangenenlager. Jan. 1918–Nov. 1918. 4.1.16.1/19

PH 5 II / 448 Meldungen über eingebrachte Kriegsgefangene. Apr. 1918–Juli 1918

PH 5 II / 449 Schriftwechsel über die Rückführung von französischen und englischen Kriegsgefangenen hinter die 30 km Feuerlinie. Enthält auch: Armee Befehl über Verschiebung der südlichen Armeegrenze, vom 3.6.1918. März 1918–Sept. 1918

PH 5 II / 452 Verfügungen über Kriegsgefangenenangelegenheiten. (Bd. 1 und 2) Jan. 1918–Nov. 1918. 4.1.16.1/24 a+b

PH 5 II / 453 Verfügungen über Kriegsgefangenenangelegenheiten. (Bd. 1 und 2) Jan. 1918–Nov 1918. 4.1.16.1/24 a+b

PH 5 II / 454 Verfügungen über Kriegsgefangenenangelegenheiten. Febr. 1915–Okt. 1918. 4.1.16.1/25

PH 5 II / 455 Verfügungen über Kriegsgefangenenangelegenheiten. (Bd. 1 und 2) Sept. 1914–Dez. 1917. 4.1.16.1/26a+b. Enthält u.a.: Erlass der Obersten Heeresleitung über Behandlung von Kriegsgefangenen zur Erhaltung der Arbeitskraft (Juli 1917); Aufstellung der zur 4. Armee gehörigen Kriegsgefangenenlager (17.8.1917)

PH 5 II / 456 Verfügungen über Kriegsgefangenenangelegenheiten. (Bd. 1 und 2) Sept. 1914–Dez. 1917. 4.1.16.1/26a+b. Austausch Arbeitsgeschädigter Kriegsgefangener; Armeebefehl mit Richtlinien zu Gefangenenvernehmungen und –abschub (Juli 1917)

PH 5 II / 457 Verfügungen über Kriegsgefangenenangelegenheiten, enthält u.a.: Einsatz für Bahnbau; Austausch französischer Kriegsgefangener; Leitpunkte für die Rückführung von Kriegsgefangenen; Berner Vereinbarungen zwischen Deutschland und Frankreich vom 26.4.1918 über Behandlung von Kriegsgefangenen und Zivilpersonen (Broschüre)

PH 5 II / 458 Arbeitseinsatz von Kriegsgefangenen Facharbeitern im Bergbau und Schiffsbau. Mai 1918–Okt. 1918. 4.1.16.1/28

PH 5 II / 459 Einsatz von Kriegsgefangenen und Zivilarbeitern zum
Stellungsbau im Bereich des AOK 4 (Hermann-Stellung) Juni 1917–Sept.
1918. 4.1.16.1/29
PH 5 II / 463 Aufstellen von belgischen Strafgefangenen-Arbeiter-Bataillonen.
Apr. 1918–Nov. 1918. 4.1.16.1/32. Enthält ... Zustandsberichte der Lager.
Rückführung von französischen und belgischen Strafgefangenen aus Deutsch-
land in das Etappengebiet zur Arbeit in Strafgefangenen-Arbeiter-Bataillonen
PH 5 II / 470 eingegangene Funksprüche über die Behandlung der belgischen
Bevölkerung und der Kriegsgefangenen. März 1917–Okt. 1918, 4.1.16.1/38

Nachlass Otto Josef Richard Franz von Trotta General Treyden
Behandlung der Kriegsgefangenen im ersten Weltkrieg auf beiden Seiten
(persönliches Kriegstagebuch von Hptm. Otto von Trotta gen. Treyden)
N 233 / 32; N 233 / 33; N 233 / 35; N 233 / 46; N 233 / 51

Militärgeschichtliche Sammlung
2/2361: Artillerie-Regiment 3. Kriegstagebuch des Majors a.D. Koebke. Bd. 1,
Einleitung und Mobilmachung, Westl. Kriegsschauplatz, 1914

Politisches Archiv des Auswärtigen Amtes, Berlin (AA)

*Akten betreffend den Krieg 1914. Grausamkeiten in der Kriegsführung
und Verletzungen des Völkerrechts*
Aug.–Sept. 1914: R 20880; R 20881; R 20882; R 20883

Abteilung A. Geheime Akten betreffend den Krieg 1914
Geheim Unternehmungen und Aufwiegelungen gegen unsere Feinde – unter den Iren
R 21154 2/16.11.14–15.12.14
R 21157 5/1.2.15–20.2.15

*Akten Krieg 1914. Unternehmungen und Aufwiegelungen gegen unsere
Feinde – Tätigkeiten in Gefangenenlagern*
R 21244 1/10.14–5.2.15/
R 21245 2/6.2.15–12.4.15/

Akten betreffend Freigabe der Kriegsgefangenen von 1919
R 22601 Pol. 9. Freigabe der Kriegsgefangenen/1/ 1.5.19–16.7.19

*General Hauptquartier Akten betreffend Kriegsgefangene: Austausch
und Entlassung. Juli 1915–April 1917*
R 22213

Bayerisches Hauptstaatsarchiv, Abteilung IV Kriegsarchiv, Munich (BK)

*Etappen-Inspektion 6; Et. Magazine; Et. Kdo. 16; Mobile Et.
Kommandaturen*
Et.Insp.6. Bund 141 (IVb) Etappenarzt, Obergeneralarzt Dr. Schiller,
Überwachung der Gesundheitsverhältnisse in den Kriegsgefangenenlagern
und Militärgefängnissen

Etappen-Inspecktion 6. Armee, Bund 203 des Engländer Kommandos III, Lohnlisten und Verpflegsrapporte der gefangenen Engländer und Russen, Sept. 1917–Feb. 1918

Etappen-Inspektion 6. Armee, Bund 202 Kriegsgefangenen-Erholungsheim 526 Kloster Wez-Welwein [sic], Kriegsbesoldungsrapporte Sept. 1917–Januar 1918, Mannschafts-Lohnung und Verpflegung, Sept.–Nov. 1918

Etappen-Inspektion 6. Armee, Et.Insp. Gef.kdo. Bund 199 Der Gefangenen-Inspektion, Kriegstagebuch 11.5.1917–30.6.1917; Kriegstagebuch 1.7.17–30.9.17; Kriegstagebuch 1.10.1917–31.12.1917; Kriegstagebuch 1.1.1918–31.3.1918; Personalverzeichnisse 16.11.17–28.4.1918

Kriegsgefangenen-Lager, Arbeitskommandos, Bewachungskompagnien

Kr. Gef. Arb. Batl. 29. Bund 3

Eisenbahn-Tr. Rekodeis

Eisenbahn-Tr. Rekodeis 1, Heeresarchiv München Gruppe II, Kriegstagebuch 2.8.14–20.10.17, Bund 4 Akt 1, entries for 19.1.1916 and 21.1.1916

Stellv. Generalkommando III. A.K. und Abw. Amt.

Stellv. Gen. Kdo. III. A.K. Bund 291.Teil 1. Ehemalige Kriegsgefangene, E. K. Eisernes Kreuz für ehemalige Kriegsgefangene

Generalkommandos I A.K., II A.K.

Gen. Kdo. I.b.A.K, Bund 38. K. G. Kriegsgefangene, Juli–Oktober 1918. Allg. u. besonders

Gen. Kdo. I.b.A.K, Bund 183. K. G. Akten des Generalkommandos I. Armee-Korps, XXIV, Kriegsgefangene. Generalia und Spezialia. Generalkommando I. bayer. Armee-Korps Abt. I m. Registratur, XXIV Kriegsgefangene Allg. 1914–1918, Bes. 1914–1918; 1. Offiziere 1914–1915; 2. Mannschaften 1914–1916

Gen. Kdo. I.b.A.K, Bund 107 (IV), Nachrichten, A Gefangenenvernehmungen und Aussagen zurückgekehrter Deutscher aus franz. Gefangenschaft, Aug 1916–Juni 1918

Generalkommando des II. bay. Armee Korps, Bund 177, Akten des Generalkommandos II B. Armee-Korps, 1 Justiz-Pflege,Verletzungen des Kriegsrechts

I. bay. Reserve Division, Bund 30, 1915

Stellv. Generalkommando I. Armee Korps

Stellv. Gen. Kdo. I. Armee Korps, Bund 916 Beilage zu den Mitteilungen des K.M. für Truppenaufklärung Nr. 9, 1918

Stellv. Gen. Kdo. I. A.K. Bund 985 Verkehr mit Kriegsgefangenen 1915–1918, Beifügungen, Auszeigen, Beschäftigung der Kriegsgefangenen

Stellv. Gen. Kdo. I. A.K. Bund 1539 Überwachung des Postverkehrs der feindlichen Kriegsgefangenen und der deutschen Kriegsgefangenen

Stellv. Gen. Kdo. I. A.K. Bund 1709 Presse, Propaganda

Bestand Kriegsministerium, M Kr, Band II, pp. 45–7, Kriegsgefangene
M Kr 1630 Kriegsgefangene, August–September 1914
M Kr 1631 Kriegsgefangene, Oktober 1914
M Kr 1674 Austausch, Okt. 1915–1916
M Kr 1682 Kriegsgefangene, Rückkehr aus Kriegsgefangenschaft, 1919
M Kr 1687 Kriegsgefangene, Unter-Akt. I, Mai 1917–Juli 1917

M Kr Mobilmachung XVI-Mob. 11606–14464 Repertorium,
Kriegsministerium, Band 6
M Kr 12912 Postverkehr mit Kriegsgefangenen
M Kr 13785 Nachweisung der Sterbefälle von Kriegsgef. im Kriege, 1914–1921
M Kr 13799 Feindliche Greueltaten im Kriege, 1914
M Kr 14126 Verletzungen des Kriegsrechts, Bd. I, 1914–1915
M Kr 14127 Verletzungen des Kriegsrechts, Bd. II, 1915–1918
M Kr 14128 Verletzungen des Kriegsrechts, Bd. III, 1918–1922

Library Collection
BK, no. 2950, Dr. G. Seiffert, Lager Lechfeld, 'Hygienische Erfahrungen bei Kriegsgefangenen'. Sonderdruck aus der *Münchener Medizinische Wochenschrift* (1915), Nr. 1, pp. 35–6 and Nr. 2, pp. 68–70

Geheimes Staatsarchiv Preußischer Kulturbesitz, Berlin-Dahlem (GStA PK)

Preußisches Ministerium für Wissenschaft, Kunst und Volksbildung
I.HA Rep. 76.VIIIB.1685 Angelegenheiten des Roten Kreuzes, Bd. 5, Jan. 1913–Dez. 1925
I.HA Rep. 76.VIIIB.1694 Erlaubnis zum Gebrauch des Roten Kreuzes, Okt. 1911–Sept. 1914
I.HA Rep. 76.VIIIB.1695 Ministerium des Innern. Medizinal Abteilung. Akten betreffend der Erlaubnis zum Roten Kreuzes [sic]
I.HA Rep. 76.VIIIB.1700 Akten betreffend ... Roten Kreuz (Vaterländische Frauenvereine Bestand), Bd. 3, Apr. 1912–Okt. 1914
I.HA Rep. 76.VIIIB.1701 Dem Roten Kreuz angeschlossene Vereine (Vaterländische Frauenvereine), Bd. 4, Nov. 1914–Marz 1916
I.HA Rep.76.VIIIB.1703 Vaterländische Frauenvereine, Bd. 2 Jan. 1908–Apr. 1915
I.HA Rep. 76.VIII.B.4263 Typhuserkrankungen in der Provinz Hessen-Nassau, Bd. 3, Okt. 1914–Sept. 1926

Preußisches Ministerium des Innern
I.HA Rep. 77. Tit. 1713. Spez. I. Nr. 73. b.1, Korps der Land-Gendarmerie, Special-Akten betreffend Mobilmachung 1914, 1.8.1914–31.1.1919

Preußisches Ministerium für Landwirtschaft, Domänen und Försten
I.HA Rep.87B.16098 1914–1915 Maßanhmen aus Anlass des Krieges 1914, Beschäftigung von Kriegsgefangenen und Arbeitslosen

I.HA 87B.16099 1915–1918 Abteilung IaV, Akten betreffend Beschäftigung von Kriegsgefangenen und Arbeitslosen

I.HA 87B.16102 1916–1917 Die Beschäftigung von Kriegsgefangenen und Arbeitslosen (Vorschläge hierzu, bzw. hinsichtlich der Unterbringung) Anträge auf Überlassung

I.HA 87B.16103 1917–1921 Die Beschäftigung von Kriegsgefangenen und Arbeitslosen (Vorschläge hierzu, bzw. hinsichtlich der Unterbringung) Anträge auf Überlassung

Musikabteilung, Lautarchiv, Humboldt Universität
Miscellaneous Recordings from the Prussian Phonogram Commission of prisoners of war in German camps

Württembergisches Hauptstaatsarchiv, Stuttgart (HstA STUTT)

E 135 a Landesausschuss der Soldatenräte Württembergs 1918–1919 (Microfilm)
Nos. 226; 227

E 135 b Landesausschuss der Soldatenräte Württembergs 1918–1919 (Microfilm)
Nos. 356; 524; 693; 781; 820; 932; 992; 1039;1098;1109;1119;1181;1283; 1222

Bestand M 1 / 3 Kriegsministerium Zentral Abteilung
M 1 / 3 Bund 526 Neuorganisation des Staatlichen Lebens nach dem Kriege
M 1 / 3 Bund 527 Sammlung von Unterlagung über Verletzungen des Völkerrechts im Krieg und über das Schicksal und die Behandlung deutscher Kriegsgefangener (mit einschlägigen Berichten); allgemeine Kriegsgefangenenangelegenheiten 1914–1919

Bestand M 1 / 8 Kriegsministerium: Medizinalabteilung (1855) 1874–1920
M 1 / 8 Bund 224 Juli–Sept. 1917, Kriegsgef. des 1. Weltkrieges, Allgemeines und Einzelfälle; Maßnahmen zur Gegensteuerung in Folge von Unterernährung von ausfallenden Kriegsgefangenen Arbeitskräften; Besprechungsergebnis von britischen und deutschen Regierungsvertretern in Den Haag über die Behandlung von Kriegsgefangenen und Durchführung eines größeren Gefangenenaustausches

Bestand M 77/1 Stellvertretendes Generalkommando XIII. Armeekorps 1914–1918 mit Vorakten ab 1878 und Nachakten bis 1925 (1942)

Offiziersabteilung (IIa)
M 77 / 1 Bund 296 Austausch, Berne
M 77 / 1 Bund 297 Stellv. Generalkommando XIII (x.w.) Armeekorps IIa Akten betr Kriegsgefangenenlager und Kriegsgefangene, vom 30.10.16 - 4.3.20

Abwehr- und Sicherheitsabteilung (IIe)
M 77 / 1 Bund 924 deutsche Kriegsgefangene, Deserteure

M 77 / 1 Bund 930 Rückkehr deutscher Kriegs- und Zivilgefangener aus dem Ausland, April–Sept. 1918
M 77 / 1 Bund 969, Strafverfahren no. 48; no. 60; no. 46

Justizabteilung- Unterabteilung b (IIIb) Kriegsgefangene
M.77 / 1 Bund 1024 Bestrafen Kriegsgefangenen [sic] wegen Fluchtversuchen, Durchführung militärgerichtlicher Verfahren gegen Kriegsgefangene, strafgerichtliche Verfolgung der Kriegsgefangenen in Vorzugslagern
M.77 / 1 Bund 1027 Bestrafung des Geschlechtsverkehrs Kriegsgefangener mit deutschen Frauen, Jan., März 1918.
M.77 / 1 Bund 1029 Abschub der Kriegsgefangenen der Entente, Nov.–Dez. 1918

M 83 Strafverfahren
M 83 Bund 56a Strafverfahren wegen Meuterei
M 83 Bund 59 Émile Baben

M 280 Archiv-Verzeichnis der Mob. Etappen-Kommandanturen XIII.
A. K. Etappen und Arbeitsformationen
M 280 Bund 20 Mob. Etappen-Kommandantur Nr. 63 (früher 2/XIII Montmedy), Schriftstücke über franz. Kriegsgefangene 1914–April 1916; Gefangene 1915–1917
M 280 Bund 32 Arbeiten für Kriegsgefangene [sic] 28.12.15–9.6.16, 12.5.16–27.10.16
M 280 Bund 56 Mob. Etappen Kommandantur 103 (früher 4/XIII Tourcoing), Gefangenenwesen, Aug. 1917–Juli 1918

Nachlass Franz Ludwig von Soden, 1873–1945
M 660 / 038 Bund 16 Grundlegende Befehle des Armee-Oberkommandos 1, Abtg 1a
M 660 / 038 Bund 17 Befehle vom Chef des Generalstabes des Feldheeres an verschiedene Oberkommandos
M 660 / 038 Bund 20 März–Aug. 1917, verschiedene Befehle des Armee-Oberkommandos 1
M 660 / 038 Bund 21 Apr.–Juni 1917, grundlegende Befehle des Armee Oberkommandos 1, Abtg 1a

Nachlass Gleich
M 660 Oberstleutnant Gerold von Gleich, Meine Erlebnisse im Feldzug 1914

Nachlass Flammer
M 660 Nachlass Generaloberarzt Dr. Max Erwin Wilhelm Flammer

George Eckert Institut, Brunswick
Nachlass T. J. Leonard, Box 8, folder 'Anweisungen über Behandlung von Kriegsgefangenen', n.d. lecture notes for instructing British troops on interrogating German prisoners, 1939–45

ITALY

Vatican Archive, Rome (ASV)

Affari Ecclesiastici Straordinari, Stati Ecclesiastici, 1916–1918, pos. 1403–1404
Fasc. 539; Fasc. 540 Prig. francesi in Germania; Da alcuni parenti di francesi civili e di militari prig. di g. in Germania, arrivano alla S. Sede informazioni e domande di aiuto perché venga migliorata la situazione, il trattamento e l'assistenza spirituale degli stessi prigionieri.

Affari Ecclesiastici Straordinari, Stati Ecclesiastici, 1916–1918, pos. 1412
Fasc 550 Iniziativa della S. Sede contro le rappresaglie sui prig. di Guerra; Informazioni di Mons; Marchetti sulla questione delle rappresaglie; Proposta della S.S. ai governi di Germania, Francia, Inghilaterra, Austria-Ungheria, Russia e Belgio

Affari Ecclesiastici Straordinari, Stati Ecclesiastici, 1919–1922, pos. 1445
Fasc. 591 Nouvo intervenuto della S. Sede per la liberazione dei prig. tedeschi

Sacra Congregazione degli Affari Ecclesiastici Straordinari, Germania, anno 1917–1918, pos. 1634–1635
Fasc. 863 1917–1918. Interessamento della S. Sede in favore di prigionieri francesi
– suppliche di aiuto per attivare lo scambio di notizie con i prigionieri
– lettera del Cardinale Segretario di Stato al Ministro di Prussia presso la S. Sede.

Segretaria di Stato, Guerra 1914–1918, rubrica 244,
Fasc. 18 Diario (1914) S. E. Mgr. Tacci, Nuncio Apostolico, Belgio
Fasc. 51 Initiativa del S. Padre per l'abolizione delle misure di rappresaglie escercite sui prigionieri di guerra
Fasc. 52 Iniziatione del S. Padre per rimpatrio dei medici e sanitare prigionieri di guerra
Fasc. 53 Initiazione del S. Padre per l'abolizione delle rappresaglie in genere 1916
Fasc. 132 Prigionieri tedeschi
Fasc. 137 Évêche de Versailles, Charles Fibier, 20.9.1915, enclosure: mémoire, redigé sous la foi du serment par Monsieur l'abbé Truffant diocese de Lille et mémoire redigé sous la foi du serment par Mr l'abbé Aubry, du diocèse de Beauvais

SWITZERLAND

Archives of the International Committee of the Red Cross, Geneva (ACICR)

Archives du Comité international de la Croix Rouge, Agences de Bâle et de Trieste; Agence Centrale des Prisonniers de Guerre (ACPG), Groupe 400, Prisonniers de Guerre: Archives Générales de l'ACPG 1914–1918
411/IX/c.10 Conférence Angleterre-Allemagne-Danemark, La Haye, juillet, 1917

411/XXIV/c.12 Conférence France-Allemagne, Berne, avril 1918
419/VIII/c.26 Missions d'étude. Mission Chenevière, Crosnier en Angleterre, Londres, oct. 1918
419/XIX/c.26 Missions d'étude. Mlle Cramer, MM. Werner et Boissier à Berlin, oct. 1918
419/XX/c.26 Missions d'étude. Clouzot à Paris, déc. 1918
431/III/j/c.31 Traitement Général des prisonniers, Commission Allemande d'Enquête
431/V/c.32 Traitement des prisonniers en Angleterre
432/II/8/c.41 Mission Blanchod et Speiser au Maroc (déc. 1915, janv. 1916)
432/II/10/c.37 Mission Vernet et de Muralt en Tunisie (janv. 1916)
432/II/11/c.41 Mission Schatzmann et O. L. Cramer en Algérie (oct. 1915, janv. 1916)
432/II/12/c.41 Mission Blanchod et Speiser en Allemagne (mars–avril 1916)
432/II/26,1.c.44 Délégation neutre à Berlin, nov. 1918
432/II/26,2.c.44 Délégation neutre à Berlin, nov. 1918
434/VII/c.50 Correspondance des prisonniers de guerre dans la zone des armées
444/I/c.59 Zone des armées et prisonniers de guerre nouvellement capturés. Détermination de la zone des armées
445/II/c.60 Représailles. Représailles contre intellectuels
445/III/c.60 Représailles dites du Dahomey et des camps d'Afrique
444/IV/c.59 Zone des armées et prisonniers de guerre nouvellement capturés. Visites de p.g. dans la zone des armées
445/IV/c.61 Représailles. Envoi des prisonniers anglais sur la frontière russe en représailles de l'emploi dans les ports français des prisonniers allemands faits par les anglais (1916–1917)
445/V/c.61 Représailles allemandes envers un certain nombre d'officiers français à la suite de l'embarquement des prisonniers allemands sur les navires-hôpitaux
445/VI/c.61 Représailles dans la zone des armées (1917). Zone des armées allemandes
445/VII/c.61 Représailles divers envers les officiers
445/VIII/c.61 Représailles allemandes envers les aviateurs nouvellement capturés
445/IX/c.61 Représailles diverses
446/III/c.62 Camps de propagande et enrôlement des étrangers
448/VII/c.65 Inhumations et exhumations. Exhumations et transferts de corps

Fonds de Watteville, 1919–1921
FAW 1 c.1 Rentrée des prisonniers allemands chez eux
FAW 140–3 c.14 Allemands en France – Traitement, corresp. de p.g. en France, p.g. allemands dans la zone des armées . . . envoi des wagons en France (linge et vêtements)
FAW 432 c.20 Relations avec les puissances protectrices et les délégués neutres – visites de camps
FAW 400 c.20 Transfert de corps de France en Allemagne
FAW 431 c.20 Traitement général des p.g.
Uncatalogued: c.29 1914–1920 rapports et témoignages
CG1CS c.5 and c.6 Violation des Conventions
CR 17 c.7 Délégation du C.I. auprès des p.g. allemands
G 25/36 Plaintes générales, France, 1946–1947, v.669

Archives of the League of Nations, Geneva
1708 Registry International Labour Office, 1919 Refugees mixed archival group –
Fonds Nansen, Registry files (1920–1924) Box R 1708, 73 files 1920–1922
IPBA 480 International Peace Bureau, 1914
P.153 Lyautey, Louis Hubert Gonzalve, 1854–1934, Archives du Maréchal
Lyautey, 1875–1915

UNITED STATES OF AMERICA

The National Archives, Washington
*Records of the Department of State relating to World War One and its
termination 1914–1929*
Illegal and Inhumane Warfare, August–October 1914
Roll 367.356; Roll 367.357; Roll 367.358

Prisoners of war
Roll 367.284 Dec. 1914–Mar.1915
Roll 367.310 Feb. 1917
Roll 367.312 Oct. 1918–Jan. 1919

IRELAND

Private collections
Papers of the Bennett family in possession of Dr Douglas Bennett, Dublin
Papers of The Royal Dublin Fusiliers Association in possession of Tom Burke,
University College, Dublin
Papers of the Reverend Stirling Gahan, Chaplain to Edith Cavell in possession of
the Gallagher/McCartney family, Donegal (on loan to Mr Charles Benson,
Trinity College Library)

PUBLISHED PRIMARY SOURCES

NEWSPAPERS AND PERIODICALS

Ireland
The Tipperary Star (Aug.–Sept.1914)
The Tipperary People (Aug.–Sept. 1914)
The Irish Times (1914)
The Wesley College Quarterly (1914–1919; special edition on prisoners of war, 1919)

Britain
The Times (1914–1919)
The Manchester Guardian (1915)
The Transactions of the Grotius Society (1921–1924)
The Army Quarterly (1934)

France
Le Temps (1917)
L'Illustration (1914; 1917; 1919)
L'Humanité (1914)

Germany
Vorwärts (1917)
Kölnische Zeitung (1919)
Süddeutsche Monatshefte:
Kriegsgefangen (March 1916)
In Englischer Gewalt (April 1916)
Was wir litten (special edition on prisoners of war, January 1920)
Gegenrechnung (special edition on prisoners of war by Prof. Dr. August Gallinger, June 1921)
Die Bestie in Menschen (July 1923)

Prison camp magazines
Le Canard de Nuremberg (1916–1918)
Le Sans Fil, the weekly magazine of prisoners at Stendhal camp, editor Marceau Lizarot, year 1, issues 1–4 (December 1916–January 1917)

OFFICIAL PUBLICATIONS

Britain
Collected Diplomatic Documents Relating to the Outbreak of the European War (London, 1915)
Documents on British Foreign Policy, 1919–1939, ed. E. L. Woodward and Rohan Butler, 1st series, vol. I, 1919 (London, 1947)
Documents on British Foreign Policy, 1919–1939, ed. W. N. Medlicott, Douglas Dakin and M. E. Lambert, 1st series, vol. XVI (London, 1968)
Foreign Office, *The Treatment of Prisoners of War in England and Germany during the First Eight Months of the War* (London, 1915)
Hansard, *The Parliamentary Debates*, Official Report, 5th series, vol. LXVIII, 11 November–27 November 1914 (London, 1914)
The Parliamentary Debates, Official Report, 5th series, vol. CX, 15 October 1918–21 November 1918 (London, 1918)
The Horrors of Wittenberg. Official Report to the British Government (London, 1916)
Joint War Committee of the British Red Cross Society and the Order of St John of Jersusalem in England, *Reports by the Joint War Committee and the Joint War Finance Committee of the British Red Cross Society and the Order of St John of Jerusalem in England on Voluntary Aid Rendered to the Sick and Wounded at Home and Abroad and to British Prisoners of War 1914–1919* (London, 1921)
National War Aims Committee, *Prisoners of Prussia. Official Report on the Treatment of British Prisoners by the Enemy during 1918* (London and Edinburgh, 1918)
Parliamentary Paper, Cd. 964, *Report on the Treatment by the Enemy of British Officers, Prisoners of War in Camps under the 10th (Hanover) Army Corps up to March 1918*. London, 1918, misc. no. 28, 1918 (London, 1918)
Parliamentary Paper Cd. 1450, *German War Trials. Report*, vol. XII, 1921 (London, 1921)
Parliamentary Paper, Cd. 7815, *Correspondence between His Majesty's Government and the United States Ambassador Respecting the Treatment of German Prisoners of War and Interned Civilians in the United Kingdom*, misc. no. 5, 1915 (London, 1915)

Parliamentary Paper, Cd. 7816, *Correspondence between His Majesty's Government and the United States Government Respecting the Rights of Belligerents*, misc. no. 6, 1915 (London, 1915)

Parliamentary Paper, Cd. 7894, *Report of the Committee on Alleged German Outrages Appointed by His Britannic Majesty's Government and Presided Over by the Right Hon. Viscount Bryce, O.M.* (London, 1915)

Parliamentary Paper, Cd. 8084, *Report on the Transport of British Prisoners of War to Germany, August–December 1914*, misc. no. 3, 1918 (London, 1918)

Parliamentary Paper, Cd. 8087, *Correspondence with the German Government Respecting the Death by Burning of J. P. Genower, Able Seaman, When Prisoner of War at Brandenburg Camp*, misc. no. 6, 1918 (London, 1918)

Parliamentary Paper, Cd. 8224, *Report by the Government Committee on the Treatment by the Enemy of British Prisoners of War Regarding the Conditions Obtaining at Wittenberg Camp during the Typhus Epidemic of 1915*, misc. no. 10, 1916 (London, 1916)

Parliamentary Paper, Cd. 8236, *Correspondence with the United States Ambassador Respecting the Transfer to Switzerland of British and German Wounded and Sick Combatant Prisoners of War*, misc. no. 17, 1916 (London, 1916)

Parliamentary Paper, Cd. 8323, *Correspondence with His Majesty's Minister at Berne Respecting the Question of Reprisals against Prisoners of War, September 1916* (London, 1916)

Parliamentary Paper, Cd. 8351, *Report on the Typhus Epidemic at Gardelegen by the Government Committee on the Treatment by the Enemy of British Prisoners of War during the Spring and Summer of 1915*, misc. no. 34, 1916 (London, 1916)

Parliamentary Paper, Cd. 8480, *Correspondence Respecting the Use of Police Dogs in Prisoners' Camps in Germany*, misc. no. 9, 1917 (London, 1917)

Parliamentary Paper, Cd. 8590, *An Agreement between the British and German Governments Concerning Combatant and Civilian Prisoners of War*, misc. no. 12, 1917 (London, 1917)

Parliamentary Paper, Cd. 8615, *Report of the Joint Committee Appointed by the Chairmen of Committees of the House of Lords and the House of Commons to Enquire into the Organisation and Methods of the Central Prisoners of War Committee* (London, 1917)

Parliamentary Paper, Cd. 8988, *Report on the Treatment by the Enemy of British Prisoners of War Behind the Firing Lines in France and Belgium*, misc. no. 7, 1918 (London, 1918)

Parliamentary Paper, Cd. 9106, *Report on the Treatment by the Germans of Prisoners of War taken during the Spring Offensives of 1918*, misc. no. 19, 1918 (London, 1918)

Parliamentary Paper, Cd. 9150, *Report on the Employment in Coal and Salt Mines of the British Prisoners of War in Germany*, misc. no. 23, 1918 (London, 1918)

Parliamentary Recruiting Committee, *The Truth about German Atrocities. Founded on the Report of the Committee on Alleged German Outrages* (London, 1915)

The Reception of Wounded Prisoner Soldiers of Great Britain in Switzerland (London, 1916)

War Office, *Reprisals against Prisoners of War. Correspondence between the International Red Cross Committee and the British Government* (London, 1916)

Statistics of the Military Effort of the British Empire during the Great War, 1914–1920 (London, 1922)

Younger, Robert, *The Horrors of Wittenberg. Official Report to the British Government* (London, 1916)

France

Candace, Gratien, *Rapport fait au nom de la Commission des affaires extérieures*, no. 5676, Chambre des Députés, onzième législature, session de 1919, annexe au procès-verbal de la 2e séance du 11 février 1919 (Paris, 1919)

Ministère des Affaires Étrangères, *Germany's Violations of the Laws of War 1914–15*, trans. J. O. P. Bland (London, 1915)

Rapports des Délégués du Gouvernement espagnol sur leurs visites dans les camps de Prisonniers français en Allemagne 1914–1917 (Paris, 1918)

Le Régime des prisonniers de guerre en France et en Allemagne au regard des conventions internationales, 1914–16 (Paris, Imprimerie Nationale, 1916)

République Française, *Documents relatifs à la Guerre–1914–1915–1916–1917. Rapports et procès-verbaux d'enquête de la Commission institué en vue de constater les actes commis par l'ennemi en violation du droit des gens (décret du 23 septembre 1914). Rapports VI–VII–VIII–IX* (Paris, Imprimerie Nationale, 1917)

Germany

Auswärtiges Amt, *Deutsche Kriegsgefangene im Feindesland. Amtliches Material. Frankreich* (Berlin and Leipzig, 1919)

Die Gefangenen-Misshandlungen in Entente-Ländern. Noten der deutschen Regierung an die Neutralen Staaten (Berlin, 1918), translated as: *German Government. Maltreatment of Prisoners in Allied Countries. Notes by the German Government to Neutral States* (Berlin, 1919)

Liste über Fälle, die sich auf planmäßige Ermordung und Misshandlung einer größeren Zahl von deutschen Kriegsgefangenen durch farbige Truppen beziehen (Berlin, 1919)

Völkerrechtswidrige Verwendung farbiger Truppen auf dem europäischen Kriegsschauplatz durch England und Frankreich (Berlin, 1915)

Backhaus, Prof. Dr. A., *Die Ernährung der Kriegsgefangenen im Deutschen Reiche. Bericht über den Kursus für Verpflegungsoffiziere der Gefangenenlager vom 22. bis 25. Juni 1915 in Berlin* (Berlin, n.d. [1915])

Die Behandlung der feindlichen Kriegsgefangenen. Amtlicher Bericht der Kommission zur Untersuchung der Anklagen wegen völkerrechtswidriger Behandlung der Kriegsgefangenen in Deutschland (Berlin, 1920)

Doegen, Wilhelm, *Kriegsgefangene Völker*, vol. I: *Der Kriegsgefangenen Haltung und Schicksal in Deutschland* (Berlin, 1919 [1921])

Handbuch über den Königlich Preußischen Hof und Staat für das Jahr 1914 (Berlin, 1913)

Handbuch über den Königlich Preußischen Hof und Staat für das Jahr 1918 (Berlin, 1918)

Reichsarchiv, *Der Weltkrieg 1914 bis 1918. Die militärischen Operationen zu Lande*, 14 vols. (Berlin, 1925–44), *Das deutsche Feldeisenbahnwesen*, vol. I: *Die Eisenbahnen zu Kriegsbeginn* (Berlin, 1928)

Reichstag, *Das Werk des Untersuchungsausschusses der Verfassunggebenden Deutschen Nationalversammlung und des Deutschen Reichstages, 1919–1928, Verhandlungen, Gutachten, Urkunden,* ed. Eugen Fischer, Berthold Widmann, Walther Boch, Walter Schücking, Johannes Bell, Georg Gradnauer, Rudolf Breitscheid and Albrecht Philipp, 3rd series, *Völkerrecht im Weltkrieg,* vol. III, parts 1 and 2 (Berlin, 1927)

Reichswehrministerium, *Sanitätsbericht über das Deutsche Heer (Deutsches Feld- und Besatzungsheer) im Weltkriege 1914/18,* 3 vols, (Berlin, 1934–8)

Schjerning, Prof. Dr. Otto von, ed., *Handbuch der ärztlichen Erfahrungen im Weltkriege, 1914–1918,* vol. VII: Wilhelm Hoffmann, ed., *Hygiene* (Leipzig, 1922)

Wehrmacht, *Kriegsgefangene. Auf Grund der Kriegsakten bearbeitet beim Oberkommando der Wehrmacht* (Berlin, 1939)

BOOKS, PAMPHLETS AND ARTICLES 1880–1922

A History of the Conference of Paris, vol. III: *The Armistice Agreement* (London, 1920)

Accord entre le gouvernement français et le gouvernement allemand concernant les prisonniers de guerre (Vevey, 1918)

Andler, Charles, *'Frightfulness' in Theory and Practice, as Compared with Franco-British War Usages* (London, 1916)

Anlagen zur Kriegs-Sanitätsordnung [KSD Anl.] vom 27 Januar 1907 (Berlin, 1907)

Anonymous, *A German Deserter's War Experience* (London, 1917)

   Black List and Blockade. Interview with Rt. Hon. Lord Robert Cecil M.P. (London, 1916)

   Does the British Navy Take Prisoners? (London, n.d. [1916])

   Französische Grausamkeiten. Auszüge aus der Vernehmungen heimgekehrter Kriegsgefangener (Tübingen, 1920)

   Frightfulness in Retreat (London, New York and Toronto, 1917)

   Kriegsgefangene in Deutschland / Prisonniers de guerre en Allemagne / Prisoners of War in Germany (Fribourg, c.1916)

   The Men who Tidy Up. By One Who Has Served in a British Labour Battalion (London, 1917)

   To Make Men Traitors. Germany's Attempts to Seduce Her Prisoners of War (London, 1918)

Armin, A., ed., *Die Welt in Flammen. Illustrierte Kriegschronik, 1914* (Leipzig, 1915)

Aus dem Kriegsgefangenen-Lager Mannheim (Mannheim, 1916)

Ausschuß für Rat und Hilfe Abteilung Vermissten-Suche in Frankfurt am Main, ed., *Aus deutschen Kriegsgefangenenlagern* (Frankfurt am Main, 1915)

Backhaus, Prof. Dr. A., *Die Kriegsgefangenen in Deutschland. Gegen 250 Wirklichkeitsaufnahmen aus deutschen Gefangenenlagern* (Siegen, 1915)

Barclay, Thomas, *Law and Usage of War – A Practical Handbook* (London, 1914)

Beck, Prof. Dr. Christoph, *Die Frau und die Kriegsgefangenen,* 2 vols., vol. I: *Die deutsche Frau und die fremden Kriegsgefangenen,* vol. II: *Die fremdländischen Frauen und die deutschen Kriegsgefangenen* (Nuremberg, 1919)

Bédier, Joseph, *German Atrocities from German Evidence* (Paris, 1915)

Benjamin, Walter, 'Critique of Violence' (1921), in Marcus Bullock and Michael W. Jennings, eds., *Walter Benjamin. Selected Writings,* vol. I: *1913–1926* (Cambridge, Mass., and London, 1996), pp. 236–52

Bericht über die Tätigkeit der Abteilung für kriegsgefangene Deutsche, 1914–1919 (Kiel, 1919)

Blücher, Evelyn, *An English Wife in Berlin. A Private Memoir of Events, Politics and Daily Life in Germany throughout the War and the Social Revolution* (London, 1920)

Boehmer, Gustav, *Denkschrift über die Forderung der Kriegsgefangenen auf volle Gleichberechtigung mit den sonstigen Heeresangehörigen* (Berlin, 1919)

Bower, Graham, 'The Laws of War. Prisoners of War and Reprisals', in *Problems of the War*, vol. I: *British Institute of International and Comparative Law. Papers Read before the Society in the Year 1915* (Oxford, 1915), pp. 15–31

'The British Cases', *The American Journal of International Law*, 16, 4 (October 1922), 633–40.

British Red Cross Society, *The Work of the Committee, 1916–1919, British Red Cross Society and Order of St. John of Jerusalem in England, Central Prisoners of War Committee* (London, 1919)

Brown, James Scott, ed., *The Hague Conventions and Declarations of 1899 and 1907. The Carnegie Endowment for International Peace* (Washington, D.C., and Oxford, 1915)

Bury, Herbert, *Here and There in the War Area* (London, 1916)

Capitain, Edmund C., 'La Rentrée des prisonniers en Allemagne', *Revue Internationale de la Croix-Rouge*, 2e année, 15, in *Bulletin International des Sociétés de la Croix-Rouge*, 31e année, nos. 209–14 (January–June 1920), 245–9

Cave, George, 'Address to the Seventh Annual General Meeting of the Grotius Society', *Transactions of the Grotius Society. Problems of Peace and War*, 8 (1922), xv–xliii

Cazal-Gamelsy, Georges, *Une épidémie dans un camp de prisonniers, contribution à l'étude clinique du typhus exanthématique* (Toulouse, 1920)

Central Committee for National Patriotic Organisations, *The Story of British Prisoners* (Cambridge, 1999 [1915])

Christmas, Dr de, *Le Traitement des prisonniers français en Allemagne d'après l'interrogatoire des prisonniers ramenés d'Allemagne en Suisse* (Paris, 1917)

Clunet, Édouard, 'Les Criminels de guerre devant le Reichsgericht à Leipzig', *Journal du Droit International*, 48 (Paris, 1921), 440–7

Comité International de la Croix-Rouge, 'Le Code du Prisonnier. Rapport présenté par le Comité International à la Xme Conférence', *Revue Internationale de la Croix-Rouge*, 3e année, no. 26, in *Bulletin International des Sociétés de la Croix-Rouge*, 52e année, nos. 221–6 (January–June 1921), 100–129

Documents publiés à l'occasion de la Guerre de 1914–1915. Rapports de MM. Dr C. de Marval (3ème et 4ème voyages) et A. Eugster (2ème voyage) sur leurs visites aux camps de prisonniers en France et en Allemagne (Geneva, 1915)

Documents publiés à l'occasion de la Guerre de 1914–1915. Rapports de MM. Ed. Naville, V. van Berchem, Dr C. de Marval et A. Eugster sur leurs visites aux camps de prisonniers en Angleterre, France et Allemagne (Paris and Geneva, 1915)

Documents publiés à l'occasion de la Guerre Européenne 1914–1916, Rapports de M. le Dr A. Vernet et M. Richard de Muralt sur leurs visites aux dépôts de prisonniers en

Tunisie et de MM. P. Schazmann et Dr O.-L. Cramer sur leurs visites aux depôts de prisonniers en Algérie en décembre 1915 et janvier 1916 (Geneva, 1916)
Documents publiés à l'occasion de la Guerre (1914–1919). Rapport de MM. Théodore Aubert et Lieutenant-Colonel Bordier sur leurs visites aux compagnies de prisonniers de guerre des régions liberées en France, mai–juin 1919 (Geneva, 1919)
'Le Rapatriement des prisonniers', *Revue Internationale de la Croix-Rouge*, 1er année, 2, in *Bulletin International des Sociétés de la Croix-Rouge*, 50e année, nos. 203–8 (July–December 1919), 1322–34

Corbett-Smith, A., *The Marne and After. A Companion Volume to 'The Retreat from Mons'* (London, New York, Toronto, Melbourne, 1917)
The Retreat from Mons by One Who Shared in It (London, New York, Toronto, Melbourne, 1917)

d'Anthouard, A. de, *Les Prisonniers allemands au Maroc. La campagne de diffamation allemande. Le jugement porté par les neutres. Le témoignage des prisonniers allemands* (Paris, 1917)
Les Prisonniers de guerre français en Allemagne, leur ravitaillement depuis l'armistice, leur rapatriement, les réparations qui leur sont dues. Rapport (Paris, 1919)

Dautrey, Marie-Joseph, *Deux epidémies de typhus exanthématique dans les camps de prisonniers d'Allemagne, Langensalza et Cassel, 1915*, published doctoral thesis (Nancy, 1919)

Deutsche Kriegsgefangenen-Fürsorge Bern, *Atlas der Gefangenenlager in Frankreich in neun Karten* (Bern, 1918)

Dupont, General, 'Une mission en Allemagne. Le rapatriement des prisonniers', *Revue des Deux Mondes*, 57 (May–June 1920), 144–66.

Evans, A. J., *The Escaping Club* (London, 1921)

Filliol, V., *La Guerre et les chemins de fer. Étude de la nouvelle réglementation des transports par chemins de fer avec l'examen de la jurisprudence parue depuis la mobilisation* (Paris, 1917)

French, Field Marshal Sir John, *1914* (London, 1919)

Furter, Frank, 'Sergeant Heynen und das Völkerrecht', *Das Tagebuch*, 2, 22 (4.6.1921), 675–9

Gallinger, August, *Gegenrechnung. Verbrechen an kriegsgefangenen Deutschen* (Leipzig and Munich, 1921). Translated as: *The Countercharge. The Matter of War Criminals from the German Side* (Munich, 1922)

Garner, James Wilford, *International Law and the World War* (London, 1920)

Gärtner, August, 'Einrichtung und Hygiene der Kriegsgefangenenlager', in Otto von Schjerning, ed., *Handbuch der ärztlichen Erfahrungen im Weltkriege 1914/18*, vol. VII: *Hygiène*, ed. Wilhelm Hofmann (Leipzig, 1922)

Gautier, Alfred, 'Traitement des prisonniers de guerre en Allemagne', *Revue Internationale de la Croix-Rouge*, 2e année, no. 1, in *Bulletin International des Sociétés de la Croix-Rouge*, 31e année, nos. 209–14 (January–June 1920), 689–95

Gerard, James W., *Face to Face with Kaiserism* (New York, 1918)
My Four Years in Germany (New York, 1918)
'The German Treatment of Prisoners', *The New Statesman*, 5 (1 May 1915), 76–7
'German War Trials', *The American Journal of International Law*, 16, 4 (October 1922), 628–31

Goschen, Edward, *The One Condition of Peace* (London, 1916)

Guyot, Frédéric, René Guillermin and Albert Meyer, 'La Situation sanitaire des prisonniers de guerre de l'Entente en Allemagne pendant la période de l'armistice (décembre 1918–janvier 1919)', *Revue Internationale de la Croix-Rouge*, 1e année, no. 2, in *Bulletin International des Sociétés de la Croix-Rouge*, 50e année, nos. 197–202 (January–June 1919), 137–44

Hall, William Edward, *International Law* (Oxford, 1880)

Harrison, Austin, 'Our Duty to the Prisoners', *The English Review*, 20 (April–July, 1915), 237–40

Harvey, F. W., *Comrades in Captivity. A Record of Life in Seven German Prison Camps* (London, 1920)

Hedin, Sven, *With the German Armies in the West* (New York and London, 1915)

Hopkins, Tighe, *Prisoners of War* (London and Kent, 1914)

Institute of International Affairs, *A History of the Peace Conference of Paris*, vol. III (London, 1920)

International Law Association, *Report of the Twenty-Ninth Conference held at the Town Hall, Portsmouth, England, May 27th–31st 1920* (London, 1920)

Keble, Howard, *'The Quality of Mercy'. How British Prisoners of War Were Taken to Germany in 1914* (London, 1918)

Kempf, Rosa, 'Die deutschen Kriegsgefangenen und die deutschen Frauen', *Die Frau*, 28 (1920/21), 330–4

Kluck, General Alexander von, *The March on Paris and the Battle of the Marne, 1914* (London, 1920)

Krebs, Engelbert, *Die Behandlung der Kriegsgefangenen in Deutschland, dargestellt auf Grund amtlichen Materials* (Freiburg, 1917)

Kriegsgefangenschaft in Frankreich. 131 Ansichten aus deutschen Gefangenenlagern in Frankreich mit erläuterndem Text (Basel, 1916)

Larmandie, Hubert de, *Les 100 numéros du Petit Français, organe authentique des officiers français prisonniers à Brandenbourg et Halle* (Paris, 1917)

Laurens, Jean-Pierre, *Prisonniers de guerre. Cahier à la mémoire des compagnons de captivité du camp de Wittenberg* (Paris, 1918)

Lectures on Land Warfare for Infantry Officers (London, 1922)

Leete, Alfred, *The Bosch Book* (London, 1917)

Lersner, Freiherr Wilhelm von, *Gefangenschaft und Heimkehr* (Berlin, 1919)
   Wir Gefangenen und die Not der Heimat (Berlin, 1919)

Link, Arthur S., ed., *The Papers of Woodrow Wilson*, vol. LVI: *1919* (Princeton, 1987)

Les Lois de la guerre. Prisonniers allemands et prisonniers français. Comment l'Allemagne et la France observent les conventions de la Haye (Paris, 1915)

Lunn, Sir Arnold Henry Moore, *Was Switzerland Pro-German?* (London, 1920)

McCarthy, Daniel J., *The Prisoner of War in Germany. The Care and Treatment of the Prisoner of War with a History of the Development of the Principle of Neutral Inspection and Control* (New York, 1918)

The Manchester Guardian Illustrated History of the War (London, 1920)

Monvoisin, Georges, *Le Typhus exanthématique, son traitement par les injections intraveineuse de sérum de convalescents; à propos de l'épidémie de typhus du camp de prisonniers de Wittemberg (1914–1915)* (Paris, 1919)

Mullins, Claud, *The Leipzig Trials. An Account of the War Criminals' Trials and a Study of German Mentality* (London, 1921)

Munthe, Axel, *Red Cross and Iron Cross. By a Doctor in France* (London, 1930 [1916])

Newcombe, Luxmoore and John H. E. Winston, *A Prisoners-of-War Library* (Aberdeen, 1919), reprinted from *The Library Association Record*, vol. XXI (September 1919).

Oehme, Walter, ed., *Ein Bekenntnis deutscher Schuld. Beiträge zur deutschen Kriegsführung* (Berlin, 1920)

Oppé, Ernest F., *Prisoners of War in Germany. A Personal Note by E.F.O.* (Aldershot, February, 1919)

Page, Arthur, *War and Alien Enemies. The Law Affecting their Personal and Trading Rights and Herein of Contraband etc.* (London, 1914)

Parsons, F. G., 'Anthropological Observations on German Prisoners of War', *The Journal of the Royal Anthropological Institute of Great Britain and Ireland*, 49 (1919), 20–35

Peschaud, Marcel, *La Guerre et les transports. Politique et fonctionnement des transports par chemin de fer pendant la guerre* (Paris and New Haven, 1926)

Phillimore, Geo. G. and Hugh H. L. Bellot, 'Treatment of Prisoners of War', *Transactions of the Grotius Society. Problems of Peace and War* 5 (1919), 47–64.

Phillipson, Coleman, *International Law and the Great War* (London, 1915)

Plassmann, Clemens, *Die deutschen Kriegsgefangenen in Frankreich 1914–1920. Beiträge zur Handhabung und zum Ausbau des internationalen Kriegsgefangenenrechtes, von Clemens Plassmann* (Berlin, 1921)

Pope-Hennessy, Una, *Map of the Main Prison Camps in Germany and Austria* (London, 1918)

Powys, A. R., *Homeward Journey 1918. A Letter by A. R. Powys* (Somerset, 1986)

Psychologische Beobachtungen in d. Vermissten- u. Kriegsgefangenenfürsorge. Auszug aus d. Jahresbericht d. Bezirksausschusses Gießen für Vermisste u. Kriegsgefangene (Hamburg, 1918)

Règlement sur le droit de la guerre et instruction sur le service des prisonniers de guerre (Paris, 1915)

Rivière, Jacques, *L'Allemand. Souvenirs et réflections d'un prisonnier de guerre* (Paris, 1918)

Rose, Gerhard, *Krieg nach dem Kriege. Der Kampf des deutschen Volkes um die Heimkehr seiner Kriegsgefangenen* (Dortmund, 1920)

Roxburgh, Ronald Francis, *The Prisoners of War Information Bureau in London. A Study* (London, 1915)

Sachsse Kapitän z. S. and Cossmann, früher Oberleutnant d. R., eds., *Kriegsgefangen in Skipton. Leben und Geschichte deutscher Kriegsgefangener in einem englischen Lager* (Munich, 1920)

Schücking, Walther, *Die Völkerrechtliche Lehre des Weltkrieges von Walther Schücking* (Leipzig, 1918)

Sorel, Georges, *Reflections on Violence* (New York, 1941 [1908])

Steen, T. E., *Négociations pour les prisonniers de guerre* (Paris, *c.*1918)

Stiehl, O., *Unsere Feinde. 96 Charakterköpfe aus deutschen Kriegsgefangenenlagern* (Stuttgart, 1916)

Struck, Hermann, *Kriegsgefangene. Ein Beitrag zur Völkerkunde im Weltkriege. 100 Steinzeichnungen* (Berlin, 1916)

Thomsen, Andreas, *Ein Vorschlag zum Schutz unserer Kriegs- und Zivilgefangenen in Feindeshand gegen Tötung und Misshandlung* (Hanover, 1915)

The Times History of the War vol. VI (London, 1916)

Timsit, Gaston, *Contribution à l'étude de typhus exanthématique par la relation de cas observés au camp de prisonniers de guerre de Cassel* (Algiers, 1915)

Vassaux, Eugène, 'Des prisonniers de guerre et des otages en droit romain et en droit français', doctoral thesis (Paris, 1890)

Vischer, A. L., *Die Stacheldraht-Krankheit. Beiträge zur Pyschologie des Kriegsgefangenen* (Zurich, 1918). Translated as: *The Barbed Wire Disease. A Psychological Study of the Prisoner of War* (London, 1919)

Wangart, Stefan and Richard Hellmann, *Die Zeitung im deutschen Gefangenen- u. Interniertenlager. Eine Bibliographie* (Buehl and Baden, 1920)

Wehberg, Hans, *Das Beuterecht im Land und Seekriege* (Tübingen, 1909). Tanslated as: *Capture in War on Land and Sea* (London, 1911)

Wharton, Edith, *Fighting France, from Dunkerque to Belfort* (London, 1915)

French Ways and Their Meaning (London, 1919)

In Morocco (New York and London, 1920)

The Marne. A Tale of the War (London, 1918)

BOOKS, PAMPHLETS AND ARTICLES 1923–1945

Ackerley, Joe Randolph, ed., *Escapers All. Being the Personal Narratives of Fifteen Escapers from War-Time Prison Camps 1914–1918* (London, 1932)

The Prisoners of War. A Play in Three Acts (London, 1925)

Anonymous, *Französische Grausamkeiten. Auszüge aus den Vernehmungen heimgekehrter Kriegsgefangener* (Tübingen, 1926)

Armstrong, Harold Courtenay, *On the Run. Escaping Tales* (London, 1934)

Baden, Prince Max von, *The Memoirs of Prince Max of Baden*, 2 vols., vol. I (London, 1928)

Bayer, Hans, *Das Presse- und Nachrichtenwesen der im Weltkrieg kriegsgefangenen Deutschen* (Berlin, 1938)

Beckh, Emil, *Die wissenschaftlichen und rechtlichen Verhältnisse der Bayerischen 6. Reserve – Division im Großen Krieg 1914–1918* (Nuremberg, 1925)

Belfield, Lieutenant-General Sir Herbert Eversley, *The Belfield Family* (London, 1930)

'The Treatment of Prisoners of War', *Transactions of the Grotius Society. Problems of Peace and War*, 9 (1923), 131–47

Bloch, Marc, 'A Contribution towards a Comparative History of European Societies', in Marc Bloch, *Land and Work in Medieval Europe* (London, 1967), pp. 45–69

'Réflexions d'un historien sur les fausses nouvelles de la Guerre, 1921', in Marc Bloch, *L'Histoire, La Guerre, La Résistance*, ed. Annette Becker and Étienne Bloch (Paris, 2006), pp. 293–316

Strange Defeat. A Statement of Evidence Written in 1940 (New York and London, 1968)

Brittain, Vera, *Testament of Youth* (London, 1978 [1933])

Cahen-Salvador, Georges, *Les Prisonniers de guerre (1914–1919)* (Paris, 1929)

Chapman, Guy, *A Passionate Prodigality. Fragments of an Autobiography* (London, 1965 [1933])

Clemenceau, Georges, *Grandeurs et misères d'une victoire* (Paris, 1930)

Cohen-Portheim, Paul, *Time Stood Still. My Internment in England 1914–1918* (London, 1931)

Cron Hermann, *Geschichte des deutschen Heeres im Weltkriege, 1914–1918* (Berlin, 1990 [1937]). Translated as: *Imperial German Army, 1914–1918. Organisation, Structure, Orders of Battle* (West Midlands, 2001)

Crozier, Frank Percy, *The Men I Killed* (London, 1937)

Cru, Jean Norton, *Témoins. Essai d'analyse et de critique des souvenirs de combattants édités en français de 1915 à 1928* (Paris, 1929)

Doegen, Wilhelm, 'Die feindlichen Kriegsgefangenen in Deutschland', in Max Schwarte, ed., *Der Große Krieg, 1914–1918*, 10 vols., vol. III: *Die Organisationen der Kriegsführung* (Berlin, 1923), pp. 205–20

    ed., *Unter fremden Völkern. Eine neue Völkerkunde* (Berlin, 1925)

Dorgelès, Roland, *Le Cabaret de la belle femme* (Paris, 1928)

Druart, Éloy, *Jusqu'à la mort. Un nid des patriotes. René van Coillie, l'abbé Vital Alexandre, le caporal Trésignies, Yvonne Vieslet* (Brussels, 1923)

Durnford, Hugh G., *The Tunnellers of Holzminden. With a Side-Issue* (Cambridge, 1930)

    ed., *Tunnelling to Freedom and Other Escape Narratives from World War One* (New York, 2004 [1932])

Ewart, Wilfred, *When Armageddon Came. Studies in Peace and War* (London, 1933)

Fay, Sir Sam, *The War Office at War* (London, 1937)

Finck, Arthur, *Britische 'Humanität' gegen Wehrlose. Die Misshandlung deutscher Gefangener in England während des Weltkrieges* (Stuttgart, 1940)

Freud, Sigmund, *Civilization and Its Discontents* (New York, 1930)

Graves, Robert, *Goodbye to All That* (London, 1929)

Halbwachs, Maurice, *On Collective Memory* (Chicago, 1992 [1941])

Häussler, Rudolf, *Das Nachrichten- und Pressewesen der feindlichen Kriegsgefangenen in Deutschland 1914–1918* (Berlin, 1940)

Hirschfeld, Magnus, ed., *Sittengeschichte des Weltkrieges*, 2 vols. (Leipzig and Vienna, 1930)

His, Wilhelm, *Die Front der Ärzte* (Bielefeld and Leipzig, 1931)

Huber, Michel, *La Population de la France pendant la Guerre* (Paris, 1931)

James, Lionel, *Times of Stress* (London, 1929)

Jannasch, Lilli, *Untaten des preussisch-deutschen Militarismus im besetzten Frankreich und Belgien* (Wiesbaden, 1924). Translated as: *German Militarism at Work. A Collection of Documents* (London, 1926)

Jünger, Ernst, *Storm of Steel* (New York, 1996 [1929])

    ed., *Das Anlitz des Weltkrieges. Fronterlebnisse deutscher Soldaten* (Berlin, 1930)

'Kriegsgefangen im Westen', *The Army Quarterly*, 29, 1 (1 October 1934), 171–2

Kuncz, Aladór, *Black Monastery* (London, 1934)

Livingstone, Adelaide, *The Peace Ballot. The Official History with a Statistical Survey of the Results* (London, 1935)

Ludendorff, Erich von, *My War Memories 1914–1918*, 2 vols. (London, 1919)

Maurice, John Frederick, *Governments and War. A Study of the Conduct of War* (London, 1926)

Mayence, Fernand, *Die Legende der Franktireurs von Löwen. Antwort auf das Gutachten des H. Professors Meurer von der Universität Würzburg* (Louvain, 1928)

McDonagh, Michael, *In London during the Great War. The Story of a Journalist* (London, 1935)

Morgan, J. H., *Assize of Arms. Being the Story of the Disarmament of Germany and her Rearmament*, 2 vols., vol. I (London, 1945)

Newsum, Henry Neill, *Behind a Mask* (Lincoln and London, 1932)

Newton, Lord Thomas, *Retrospection* (London, 1941)

Plassmann, Clemens, 'Die völkerrechtlichen Grundlagen des Kriegsgefangenenwesens ins Jahre 1914', in Max Schwarte, ed., *Der Große Krieg, 1914–1918*, 10 vols., vol. III: *Die Organisationen der Kriegsführung* (Berlin, 1923), pp. 147–58

Ponsonby, Arthur, *Falsehood in Wartime. Containing an Assortment of Lies Circulated throughout the Nations during the Great War* (London, 1928)

Pörzgen, Hermann, *Theater ohne Frau. Das Bühnenleben der Kriegsgefangenen Deutschen 1914–1920* (Königsberg, 1933)

Rasmussen, Gustav, *Code des prisonniers de guerre. Commentaire de la Convention du 27 juillet 1929, relative au traitement des prisonniers de guerre* (Copenhagen, 1931)

Read, Herbert, *Collected Poems 1913–1925* (London, 1927)

Reichsvereinigung ehemaliger Kriegsgefangener e.v., Bundesleitung, *Friedensdiktat, Rechtsungültigkeit. Das Friedensdiktat, seine Rechtsungültigkeit und die Mittel, sich von ihm zu befreien* (Berlin and Magdeburg, 1923)

Reinhardt, Jakob, 'Die Zurückführung der deutschen Kriegsgefungenen aus Frankreich', *Süddeutsche Monatshefte*, 11, 22 (August 1925), 1–29

Remarque, Erich Maria, *All Quiet on the Western Front* (London, 1996 [1929])

Renn, Ludwig, *Nachkrieg. Roman* (Berlin, 2004 [1930])

Renoir, Jean, *La Grande Illusion*, Film, Paris UGC Video (1990 [1937])

Rosenberg, Curt H., 'International Law Concerning Accidents to War Prisoners Employed in Private Enterprises', *The American Journal of International Law*, 36, 2 (1942), 294–8

Sassoon, Siegfried, *Memoirs of an Infantry Officer* (London, 1930)

Scharping, Karl, *In russischer Gefangenschaft. Die kulturellen und wirtschaftlichen Leistungen der Kriegsgefangenen in Russland* (Berlin, 1939)

Sherriff, R. C., *Journey's End* (London, 2000 [1929])

Thieme, Georg, *Vor 20 Jahren. Deutsches Arzttum im Weltkrieg* (Leipzig, 1935)

Thuliez, Louise, *Condemned to Death* (London, 1934)

Tierce, Antoinette, *Between Two Fires* (London, 1931)

Vansittart, Robert, *Black Record. Germans Past and Present* (Melbourne, 1941)

Wallace, Robert, *Letters to President Woodrow Wilson (Aug 30 1914–April 3 1917) about the Prisoners and Hostages in Germany* (London, 1931)

Weaver, Lawrence, *The Scottish National War Memorial at the Castle, Edinburgh. A Record and Appreciation* (London, 1928)

Weberstedt, Hans, *Frankreichs wahres Gesicht. Das Buch der blau-weiß-roten Schande. Die deutsche Gegenliste* (Erfurt, 1926)
Weiland, Hans and Leopold Kern, eds., *In Feindeshand. Die Gefangenschaft im Weltkrieg in Einzeldarstellungen*, 2 vols. (Vienna, 1931)
Wharton, Edith, *A Son at the Front* (London, 1923)
Who Was Who, vol. II: *A Companion to Who's Who Containing the Biographies of Those Who Died During the Period 1916–1928* (London, 1929)
Who Was Who, vol. III: *A Companion to Who's Who Containing the Biographies of Those Who Died During the Period 1929–1940* (London, 1941)
Wilke, Karl, *Prisoner Halm. Die Geschichte einer Gefangenschaft* (London, 1931)

PRISONER OF WAR MEMOIRS

British memoirs

Austin, L. G., *My Experiences as a German Prisoner* (London, 1915)
Bond, Reginald Coppleston, *Prisoners Grave and Gay* (Edinburgh and London, 1935)
Ellison, Wallace, *Escapes and Adventures* (Edinburgh and London, 1928)
Green, Arthur, *The Story of a Prisoner of War by No. 6646, 1st Somerset Light Infantry* (London, 1916)
Grinnell-Milne, Duncan, *An Escaper's Log* (London, 1926)
Hay, Major M. V., *Wounded and a Prisoner of War* (Edinburgh and London, 1930 [1916])
Lorimer, Austin, *My Experiences as a German Prisoner* (London, 1915)
McMullen, Fred, and Jack Evans, *Out of the Jaws of Hunland. The Stories of Corporal Fred McMullen, Sniper, Private Jack Evans, Bomber, Canadian Soldiers Three Times Captured and Finally Escaped from German Prison Camps* (London and New York, 1918)
Moloney, William O' Sullivan, *Prisoners and Captives* (London, 1933)
Phillimore, Baron Godfrey Walter, *Recollections of a Prisoner of War* (London, 1930)
Thomas, Cecil, *They Also Served. The Experiences of a Private Soldier as Prisoner of War in German Camp and Coal Mine 1916–1918* (London, 1939)
Tucker, W. A., *The Lousier War* (London, 1974)
Waugh, Alec, *The Prisoners of Mainz* (London, 1919)

French memoirs

Arvengas, Gilbert, *Entre les fils de fer. Carnet d'un prisonnier de guerre 1914–1917* (Paris, 1918)
Blanchet, Eugène-Louis, *En représailles* (Paris, 1918)
    La Haine qui meurt (Paris, 1932)
Blanchin, Léon, *Chez eux. Souvenirs de guerre et de captivité* (Paris, 1916)
Caubet, Georges, *Instituteur et Sergent. Mémoires de guerre et de captivité* (Carcassonne, 1991)
Charrier, Marcel, *Notre évasion d'Allemagne. Épisode de la Grande Guerre 1914–1918 par un vendéen sapeur au 6ème génie* (Luçon, 1931)
Connes, Georges, *L'Autre Épreuve. Souvenirs hétérodoxes de captivité, 1916–1919* (Paris and Montreal, 2001). Translated as: *A POW's Memoir of the First World War. The Other Ordeal*, ed. Lois Davis Vines (Oxford and New York, 2004)

Dufour, Jean-Jules, *Dans les camps de représailles* (Paris, 1918)
Gueugnier, Charles, *Les Carnets de captivité de Charles Gueugnier, 1914–1918* (Toulouse, 1998)
Harcourt, Robert de, *Souvenirs de captivité et d'évasion* (Paris, 1922)
Hennebois, Charles, *Journal d'un grand blessé. Aux mains d'Allemagne* (Paris, 1916)
Moussat, Émile, *L'Âme des camps de prisonniers. Récits d'éxil en Allemagne de 1914 à 1918* (Paris, 1935)
Relange, Fernand, *Huit mois dans les lignes allemandes. Souvenirs d'un prisonnier de Belleherbe* (Besançon, 1919)
Riou, Gaston, *The Diary of a French Private. War Imprisonment 1914–15* (Paris, 1916)
Warnod, André, *Prisoner of War (in Germany) with Sketches by Author* (London, 1916)

German memoirs
Berger, Carl, *Sieben Jahre in Frankreichs Kerkern* (Berlin, 1940)
Cohen-Portheim, Paul, *Time Stood Still. My Internment in England 1914–1918* (London, 1931)
Ernst, Hermann, *Kriegsgefangen im Westen nach dem Tagebuch eines Gefangenen der 249 POW Coy in France* (Jena, 1933)
Frerk, Fr Willy, *Kriegsgefangen in Nordafrika. Aus dem Tagebuche des deutschen Gardegrenadiers Eduard von Rohden* (Siegen, 1917)
Ibrügger, Fritz, ed., *PG Feldgraue in Frankreichs Zuchthäusern* (Hamburg, 1929)
Kirchhoff, Karl, *Von Hölle zu Hölle. Erlebnis einer französischen Kriegsgefangenschaft* (Gütersloh, 1940)
Müller, Ernst Oswald, *Gefesseltes Heldentum. Erlebtes und Erschautes als Gefangener in Frankreich u. Afrika* (Leipzig, 1933)
Richert, Dominik, *Beste Gelegenheit zum Sterben. Meine Erlebnisse im Kriege 1914–1918*, ed. Angelika Tramitz and Bernd Ulrich (Munich, 1989)
Rocker, Rudolf, *Hinter Stacheldraht und Gitter. Erinnerungen aus der englischen Kriegsgefangenschaft* (Berlin, 1925)
Schubert, Gustav, *In Frankreich kriegsgefangen. Meine Erlebnisse auf dem Vormarsch der 1. Armee durch Belgien und Frankreich sowie in der französischen Kriegsgefangenschaft* (Magdeburg, 1915)
Thuemmler, Heinz, *P.G. 905. Frankreichs Verrat an der weißen Rasse* (Leipzig and Naunhof, 1933)
Utsch, Stefan, *Todesurteil in Tours 1917. Aufzeichnungen des deutschen Kriegsgefangenen 389* (Berlin, 1940)
Wilke, Karl, *Tage des Grauens. Frankreichs 'Humanität'* (Berlin, 1940)
Winter-Heidingsfeld, Heinz von, *Menschen in Käfigen. Ein P. G. Tagebuch* (Berlin, 1918)

SECONDARY LITERATURE, 1945–2011

BOOKS AND ARTICLES

Abbal, Odon, 'Un combat d'après-guerre. Le statut des prisonniers', *Revue du Nord*, 80, 325 (1998), 405–16

'Die französische Gesellschaft der Zwischenkriegszeit und die ehemaligen Kriegsgefangenen', in Jochen Oltmer, ed., *Kriegsgefangene im Europa des Ersten Weltkriegs* (Paderborn, 2006), pp. 295–308

'Le Maghreb et la Grande Guerre. Les camps d'internement en Afrique du Nord', in Jean-Charles Jouffret, ed., *Les Armes et la Toge. Mélanges offerts à André Martel* (Montpellier, 1997), pp. 623–35

'Les Prisonniers de la Grande Guerre. La captivité: 1914–1954', *Guerres mondiales et conflits contemporains*, 147 (July 1987), 5–30

'Santé et captivité. Le traitement des prisonniers français dans les hôpitaux allemands', in *Actes du Colloque 'Forces Armées et société'* (Montpellier, 1987), pp. 273–83

Soldats oubliés. Les prisonniers de guerre français (Esparon, 2001)

Absalom, Roger, 'Hiding History. The Allies, the Resistance and the Others in Occupied Italy 1943–1945', *The Historical Journal*, 38, 1 (March 1995), 111–31.

Afflerbach, Holger, *Falkenhayn. Politisches Denken und Handeln im Kaiserreich* (Munich, 1994)

Agamben, Giorgio, 'The Camp as the *Nomos* of the Modern', in Hent de Vries, ed., *Violence, Identity and Self-Determination* (Stanford, 1997), pp. 106–17

Homo Sacer. Sovereign Power and Bare Life (Stanford, 1998)

Remnants of Auschwitz. The Witness and the Archive (New York, 2002)

State of Exception (Chicago and London, 2005)

Allen, Tony, *British Prisoners of War, 1914–1918* (York, 1999)

German Prisoners of War, 1914–1918 (York, 1999)

Anderson, Benedict, *Imagined Communities. Reflections on the Origins and Spread of Nationalism* (New York and London, 1991)

André, François Victor, *Les Raisins sont bien beaux. Correspondance de guerre d'un rural: 1914–16* (Paris, 1977)

Applebaum, Anne, *Gulag. A History* (London, 2003)

Archer, John, and Jo Jones, 'Headlines from History. Violence in the Press, 1850–1914', in Elizabeth A. Stanko, ed., *The Meanings of Violence* (London and New York, 2003), pp. 17–31

Arendt, Hannah, *Eichmann in Jerusalem. A Report on the Banality of Evil* (London, 1994)

On Violence (London, 1970)

Ashworth, Tony, *Trench Warfare 1914–1918. The Live and Let Live System* (London, 2000)

Auclert, Jean-Pierre, *La Grande Guerre des crayons. Les noirs dessins de la propagande en 1914–1918* (Paris, 1981)

Audoin-Rouzeau, Stéphane, *Les Armes et la chair. Trois objets de mort en 14–18* (Paris, 2009)

Cinq deuils de guerre 1914–1918 (Paris, 2001)

L'Enfant de l'ennemi 1914–1918. Viol, avortement, infanticide pendant la Grande Guerre (Paris, 1995)

Men at War, 1914–1918. National Sentiment and Trench Journalism in France during the First World War (Leamington Spa, 1992)

Audoin-Rouzeau, Stéphane, and Annette Becker, *14–18. Retrouver la Guerre* (Paris, 2000)

'Violence et consentement. La "culture de guerre" du premier conflit mondial', in Jean-Pierre Rioux and Jean-François Sirinelli, eds., *Pour une histoire culturelle* (Paris, 1997), pp. 251–71

Audoin-Rouzeau, Stéphane, Annette Becker, Christian Ingrao and Henri Rousso, eds., *La Violence de guerre 1914–1945. Approches comparés des deux conflits mondiaux* (Paris, 2002)

Audoin-Rouzeau, Stéphane, and Jean-Jacques Becker, *La France, la nation, la guerre: 1850–1920* (Paris, 1995)

eds., *Encyclopédie de la Grande Guerre, 1914–1918. Histoire et culture* (Paris, 2004)

Auriol, Jean-Claude, *Les Barbelés des bannis. La tragédie des prisonniers de guerre français en Allemagne durant la Grande Guerre* (Paris, 2002)

Barthas, Louis, *Les Carnets de guerre de Louis Barthas, tonnelier 1914–1918* (Paris, 1997)

Bartov, Omer, *Murder in Our Midst. The Holocaust, Industrial Killing and Representation* (Oxford, 1996)

Bass, Gary Jonathan, *Stay the Hand of Vengeance. The Politics of War Crimes Tribunals* (Princeton, 2000)

Beaupré, Nicolas, Anne Duménil and Christian Ingrao, eds., *1914–1945. L'Ère de la Guerre*, 2 vols., vol. I: *Violence, mobilisations, deuil. 1914–1918* (Paris, 2004)

eds., *14–18. Aujourd'hui, Today, Heute*, vol. IV: *Marginaux, marginalité, marginalisation* (Paris, 2001)

Beauvoir, Simone de, *Memoirs of a Dutiful Daughter* (London, 1959)

Becker, Annette, 'Charles de Gaulle, prisonnier', in Institut Charles de Gaulle/ Historial de Péronne, *De Gaulle soldat 1914–1918* (Paris, 1999), pp. 98–115

Les Cicatrices rouges 14–18. France et Belgique occupées (Paris, 2010)

Les Monuments aux morts. Patrimoine et mémoire de la Grande Guerre (Paris, 1988)

Oubliés de la Grande Guerre. Humanitaire et culture de guerre, 1914–1918. Populations occupées, déportés civils, prisonniers de guerre (Paris, 1998)

'Le Retour des prisonniers', in *Finir la guerre, Actes du colloque de Verdun, 12–13 novembre 1999. Les Cahiers de la Paix*, 7 (Verdun, 2000), pp. 67–78

'Suppressed Memory of Atrocity in World War I and Its Impact on World War II', in Doris L. Bergen, ed., *Lessons and Legacies VIII. From Generation to Generation* (Illinois, 2008), pp. 65–82

'Des vies déconstruites. Prisonniers civils et militaires', in Nicolas Beaupré and Christian Ingrao, eds., *14–18. Aujourd'hui, Today, Heute*, vol. IV: *Marginaux, marginalité, marginalisation* (Paris, 2001), pp. 79–110

War and Faith. The Religious Imagination in France, 1914–1930 (Oxford, 1998)

Becker, Jean-Jacques, *1914. Comment les français sont entrés dans la guerre. Contribution à l'étude de l'opinion publique printemps–été 1914* (Paris, 1977)

The Great War and the French People (Providence and Oxford, 1985)

'Les Procès de Leipzig', in Annette Wieviorka, ed., *Les Procès de Nuremberg et de Tokyo* (Caen, 1996), pp. 51–9

Beckett, Ian F. W., and Keith Simpson, *A Nation in Arms. A Social Study of the British Army in the First World War* (Manchester, 1985)

Beier, Rosmarie, and Bettina Biedermann, eds., *Kriegsgefangen. Objekte aus der Sammlung des Archivs und Museums der Kriegsgefangenschaft, Berlin, und des Verbandes der Heimkehrer, Kriegsgefangenen und Vermisstenangehörigen Deutschlands e.V.* (Bonn-Bad Godesberg and Berlin, 1990)

Bendick, Rainer, 'Les Prisonniers de guerre français en Allemagne durant la guerre de 1870–71', in Sylvie Caucanas, Rémy Cazals and Pascal Payen eds., *Les Prisonniers de guerre dans l'histoire. Contacts entre peuples et cultures* (Toulouse, 2003), pp. 183–95

Bergeot, Laurent, Fabienne Bliaux, Jean-Michel Declerq, Anne Dopffer, Karine Jagielski, Frédéric Panni, Frédérique Pilleboue, Cécile Rat, Dominique Roussel, eds., *Réconstructions en Picardie après 1918* (Paris, 2000)

Berlin, Jörg, ed., *Die deutsche Revolution 1918/19. Quellen und Dokumente* (Cologne, 1979)

Bessel, Richard, *Germany after the First World War* (Oxford, 1993)

Best, Geoffrey, *Humanity in Warfare. The Modern History of the International Law of Armed Conflicts* (London, 1980)

Bianchi, Bruna, *La Violenza Contro la Popolazione Civile nella Grande Guerra. Deportati, Profughi, Internati* (Milan, 2006)

Bieber, Benjamin, *Wie Kriege enden. Die Reintegration von Soldaten in Nachkriegsgesellschaften* (Hamburg, 2002)

Biege, Bernd, *Helfer unter Hitler. Das Rote Kreuz im Dritten Reich* (Hamburg, 2000)

Biess, Frank, *Homecomings. Returning POWs and the Legacies of Defeat in Postwar Germany* (Princeton, 2006)

Bihaly, Mira, and Gerhard Schoenberner, eds., *House of the Wannsee Conference. Permanent Exhibit. Guide and Reader* (Berlin, 1999)

Bird, J. C., *Control of Enemy Alien Civilians in Great Britain, 1914–1918* (New York, 1986)

Birnstiel, Eckart, and Rémy Cazals, eds., *Ennemis fraternels 1914–1915. Hans Rodewald, Antoine Bieisse, Fernand Tailhades. Carnets de guerre et de captivité* (Toulouse, 2002)

Bishop, Alan, and Mark Bostridge, eds., *Letters from a Generation. First World War Letters of Vera Brittain and Four Friends* (Boston, 1999)

Blyth, Ronald, *Akenfield. Portrait of an English Village* (London, 1969)

Bouloc, François, '"Profiteurs" et "profitants" de la Grande Guerre en Aveyron. Traits et faits divers d'un phénomène d'opinion', *Revue du Rouergue*, 70 (Summer 2002), 183–207

Bourke, Joanna, *Dismembering the Male. Men's Bodies, Britain and the Great War* (London, 1996)
  An Intimate History of Killing. Face-to-Face Killing in Twentieth-Century Warfare (London, 1999)

Bourne, J. M., *Britain and the Great War* (New York and London, 1989)
  Who's Who in World War One (London and New York, 2001)

Bowgen, Alan, 'British Army PoWs of the First World War', *Ancestor. The Family History Magazine of the Public Record Office*, 6 (February/March, 2002), 34–9

Breuilly, John, 'Introduction. Making Comparisons in History', in John Breuilly, ed., *Labour and Liberalism in Nineteenth-Century Europe. Essays in Comparative History* (Manchester and New York, 1992), pp. 1–25

Brittain, Vera, *Chronicle of Youth. Great War Diary 1913–1917*, ed. Alan Bishop (London, 2000)

Brown, Malcolm, *The Imperial War Museum Book of 1918. Year of Victory* (London, 1998)

Brown, Malcolm, and Shirley Seaton, *Christmas Truce* (London, 2001)

Burdick, Charles, *The German Prisoners of War in Japan, 1914–20* (London, 1984)

Bussière, Eric, Patrice Marcilloux and Denis Varaschin, eds., *La Grande Reconstruction. Reconstruire le Pas-de-Calais après la Grande Guerre. Actes du colloque d'Arras 8 au 10 novembre 2000* (Dainville, 2002)

Canini, Gérard, 'L'Utilisation des prisonniers de guerre comme main d'oeuvre 1914–1916', in Gérard Canini, ed., *Les Fronts invisibles. Nourrir, fournir, soigner. Actes du colloque international sur la logistique des armées au combat pendant la première guerre mondiale organisé à Verdun les 6, 7, 8 juin 1980* (Nancy, 1984), pp. 247–61.

Caucanas, Sylvie, Rémy Cazals and Pascal Payen, eds., *Les Prisonniers de guerre dans l'histoire. Contacts entre peuples et cultures* (Toulouse, 2003)

Charles, Christophe, *La Crise des sociétés impériales. Allemagne, France, Grande Bretagne, 1900–1940. Essai d'histoire sociale comparée* (Paris, 2001)

Chickering, Roger, *Imperial Germany and the Great War 1914–1918* (Cambridge, 1998)

Chickering, Roger, and Stig Förster, eds., *Great War, Total War. Combat and Mobilization on the Western Front, 1914–1918* (Cambridge, 2000)

Clarke, Ken, *Clarke's Camberley at War (1914–1918)* (Camberley, 1986)

Clausewitz, Carl von, *On War* (Ware, 1997 [1832])

Clout, Hugh, *After the Ruins. Restoring the Countryside of Northern France after the Great War* (Exeter, 1996)

Cobain, Ian, 'The Postwar Photographs That British Authorities Tried to Keep Hidden', *The Guardian*, 3 April 2006.

Cochet, François, *Soldats sans armes. La captivité de guerre. Une approche culturelle* (Brussels, 1998)

Cohen, Deborah, 'Comparative History. Buyer Beware', in Annette M. Marciel, Daniel S. Mattern and Christof Mauch, eds., *Bulletin of the German Historical Institute, Washington*, 29 (Fall 2001), pp. 23–34

Colley, Linda, *Captives. Britain, Empire and the World, 1600–1850* (London, 2003)

Conteh-Morgan, Earl, *Collective Political Violence. An Introduction to the Theories and Cases of Violent Conflicts* (New York and London, 2004)

Cook, Graeme, *Break Out. Great Wartime Escape Stories* (London, 1974)

Cook, Tim, 'The Politics of Surrender. Canadian Soldiers and the Killing of Prisoners in the Great War', *The Journal of Military History*, 70, 3 (2006), 637–65

Cool, Karolien, *Het Leven van de Vlaamse krijgsgevangenen in Duitsland in de Eerste Wereldoorlog* (Brussels, 2002)

Cummings, E. E., *The Enormous Room* (London, 1978)

Dabernat-Poitevin, Nicole, ed., *Les Carnets de captivité de Charles Gueugnier* (Midi-Pyrénées, 1998)

Dagan, Yael, 'La Demobilisation de Jacques Rivière, 1917–1925', *Cahiers du Centre de recherches historiques*, 31 (2003), 131–53

Dallas, Gregor, *1918. War and Peace* (London, 2000)

Daniel, Ute, *The War from Within. German Working-Class Women in the First World War* (Oxford and New York, 1997)

Daniel-Wieser, Florence, *Otages dans la Grande Guerre. Destins de prisonniers et civils lorrains* (Nancy, 2005)

Davis, Belinda, *Home Fires Burning. Food, Politics, and Everyday Life in World War I Berlin* (Chapel Hill, 2000)

Davis, Gerald H., 'National Red Cross Societies and Prisoners of War in Russia, 1914–1918', *Journal of Contemporary History*, 28, 1 (1993), 31–52

'Prisoners of War in Twentieth Century War Economies', *Journal of Contemporary History*, 12 (1977), 623–34

Deist, Wilhelm, *Militär- und Innenpolitik im Weltkrieg 1914–1918* (Düsseldorf, 1970)

'Verdeckter Militärstreik im Kriegsjahr 1918?' in Wolfram Wette, ed., *Der Krieg des kleinen Mannes. Eine Militärgeschichte von unten* (Munich and Zurich, 1995)

Delpal, Bernard, 'Entre culpabilité et réparation. La douleureuse situation des prisonniers de guerre allemands maintenus en France au temps du Traité de Versailles', in Nicolas Beaupré and Christian Ingrao, eds., *14–18 Aujourd'hui, Today, Heute*, vol. IV: *Marginaux, marginalité, marginalisation* (Paris, 2001), 124–37

'Prisonniers de guerre en France 1914–1920', in André Gueslin and Dominique Kalifa, eds., *Les Exclus en Europe 1830–1930* (Paris, 1999), pp. 144–59

Dictionnaire Biographique, 1961–1962, 5th edn (Paris, 1963)

Djurović, Gradimir, *L'Agence Centrale de Recherches du Comité International de la Croix-Rouge. Activité du CICR en vue du soulagement des souffrances morales des victimes de guerre* (Geneva, 1981)

Dollery, Brian, and Craig R. Parsons, 'Prisoner Taking and Prisoner Killing. A Comment on Ferguson's Political Economy Approach', *War in History*, 14, 4 (2007), 499–512

Dollinger, Hans, *Der Erste Weltkrieg in Bildern und Dokumenten* (Munich, 1965)

Duffy, Christopher, *Through German Eyes. The British and the Somme 1916* (London, 2006)

Durand, Yves, *La Captivité. Histoire des prisonniers de guerre français: 1939–1945* (Paris, 1981)

La Vie quotidienne des prisonniers de guerre dans les stalags, les oflags et les kommandos, 1939–1945 (Paris, 1987)

Duroselle, Jean-Baptiste, *La Grande Guerre des Français 1914–1918. L'Incompréhensible* (Paris, 2002)

Eckart, Wolfgang U., 'Epidemien', in Gerhard Hirschfeld, Gerd Krumeich and Irina Renz, eds., *Enzyklopädie Erster Weltkrieg* (Paderborn, Munich, Vienna and Zurich, 2003), pp. 458–60

Eksteins, Modris, *Rites of Spring. The Modern in Cultural History* (New York, 1989)

Emden, Richard van, *Prisoners of the Kaiser. The Last POWs of the Great War* (Barnsley, 2000)

Espagne, Michel, 'Sur les limites du comparatisme en histoire culturelle', *Genèses*, 17, 1 (1994), 112–21

Evans, Andrew D., 'Capturing Race. Anthropology and Photography in German and Austrian Prisoner-of-War Camps during World War I', in Eleanor M. Hight and Gary D. Simpson, eds., *Colonialist Photography. Imagining Race and Place* (London, 2002), pp. 226–56

Farcy, Jean-Claude, *Les Camps de concentration français de la Première Guerre Mondiale* (Paris, 1995)

Feldman, Gerald D., *Army, Industry and Labor in Germany, 1914–1918* (Princeton, 1966)

Feltman, Brian K., 'Tolerance as a Crime? The British Treatment of German Prisoners of War on the Western Front, 1914–1918', *War in History*, 17, 4 (2010), 435–58

Ferenczi, Thomas, *Ils l'ont tué! L'Affaire Salengro* (Paris, 1995)

Ferguson, Niall, *The Pity of War. Explaining World War I* (London, 1998)

'Prisoner Taking and Prisoner Killing in the Age of Total War. Towards a Political Economy of Military Defeat', *War in History*, 11, 2 (2004), 148–92

Ferro, Marc, *La Grande Guerre. 1914–1918* (Paris, 1990 [1969])

Fine, Martin, 'Albert Thomas. A Reformer's Vision of Modernization, 1914–32', *Journal of Contemporary History*, 12 (1977), 545–64

Fischer, Fritz, *Germany's Aims in the First World War* (London, 1967)

Fishman, Sarah, *We Will Wait. Wives of French Prisoners of War, 1940–1945* (New Haven, 1991)

Fitzpatrick, Matthew P., 'The Pre-History of the Holocaust? The Sonderweg and Historikerstreit Debates and the Abject Colonial Past', *Central European History*, 41 (2008), 477–503

Flasch, Kurt, *Die Geistige Mobilmachung. Die deutschen Intellektuellen und der Erste Weltkrieg; Ein Versuch* (Berlin, 2000)

Fletcher, Jonathan, *Violence and Civilization. An Introduction to the Work of Norbert Elias* (Cambridge, 1997)

Flood, P. J., *France 1914–1918. Public Opinion and the War Effort* (Basingstoke, 1990)

Foucault, Michel, *Discipline and Punish. The Birth of the Prison* (London, 1979)

Fouillet, Bruno, 'La Ville de Lyon au centre des échanges de prisonniers de guerre (1915–1919)', *Vingtième Siècle: Revue d'Histoire*, 86 (April–June 2005), 25–42

François, Étienne, and Hagen Schulze, eds., *Deutsche Erinnerungsorte*, 3 vols. (Munich, 2001)

Fridenson, Patrick, ed., *The French Home Front, 1914–1918* (Oxford, 1992)

Fulbrook, Mary, ed., *German History since 1800* (London, 1997)

Fussell, Paul, *The Great War and Modern Memory* (London, 1977)

Garrett, Richard, *Prisoner of War. The Uncivil Face of War* (Newton Abbot, 1981)

Gatrell, Peter, 'Prisoners of War on the Eastern Front during World War I', review article in *Kritika. Explorations in Russian and Eurasian History*, 6, 3 (Summer 2005), 557–66

'Refugees and Forced Migrants during the First World War', *Immigrants and Minorities*, 26, 1/2 (2008), 82–110

Geinitz, Christian, *Kriegsfurcht und Kampfbereitschaft. Das Augusterlebnis in Freiburg. Eine Studie zum Kriegsbeginn 1914* (Essen, 1998)

Gellner, Ernest, *Nationalism* (London, 1997)

Gerwarth, Robert, and Stephan Malinowski, 'Der Holocaust als "kolonialer Genozid"? Europäische Kolonialgewalt und nationalsozialistischer Vernichtungskrieg', *Geschichte und Gesellschaft*, 33 (2007), 439–66

Geyer, Michael, 'Insurrectionary Warfare. The German Debate about a *Levée en masse* in October 1918', *Journal of Modern History*, 73 (2001), 459–527

'Rückzug und Zerstörung 1917', in Gerhard Hirschfeld, Gerd Krumeich and Irina Renz, eds., *Die Deutschen an der Somme, 1914–1918. Krieg, Besatzung, Verbrannte Erde* (Essen, 2006), pp. 163–78.

The Stigma of Violence, Nationalism and War in Twentieth-Century Germany', *German Studies Review*, 15 (1992), 75–110

'War and Terror. Some Timely Observations on the German Way of Waging War', *AICGS Humanities*, 14 (2003), 47–69

Gibson, Craig, 'The British Army, French Farmers and the War on the Western Front', *Past and Present*, 180, 1 (2003), 175–240

Gilbert, Adrian, *POW. Allied Prisoners in Europe 1939–1945* (London, 2006)

Gilbert, Martin, *Churchill. A Life* (London, 2000)

The First World War (London, 1995)

The Routledge Atlas of the First World War (London, 1994)

Grandhomme, Francis, 'Internment Camps for German Civilians in Finistère, France (1914–1919)', *The Historian*, 68, 4 (Winter 2006)

'Une manifestation du devoir de mémoire. L'inauguration du cimitière des prisonniers de la Grande Guerre, Sarrebourg, 12 septembre 1926', Association Nationale du Souvenir de la Bataille de Verdun, *Les Cahiers de la Grande Guerre*, 28 (2001), 21–56

Gregory, Adrian, *The Last Great War. British Society and the First World War* (Cambridge, 2008)

'Peculiarities of the English? War, Violence and Politics. 1900–1939', *Journal of Modern European History*, 1, 1 (2003), 44–59

'Railway Stations. Gateways and Termini', in Jay M. Winter and Jean-Louis Robert, eds., *Capital Cities at War, Paris, London, Berlin, 1914–19, A Cultural History*, vol. II (Cambridge, 2007), pp. 23–56

The Silence of Memory. Armistice Day 1919–1946 (Oxford and Providence, 1994)

Grupp, Peter and Maria Keipert, eds., *Biographisches Handbuch des deutschen auswärtigen Dienstes 1871–1945* (Paderborn, Munich, Vienna and Zurich, 2000)

Guéno, Jean-Pierre, and Yves Laplume, *Paroles de poilus. Lettres et carnets du front (1914–1918)* (Paris, 1998)

Gullace, Nicoletta, 'Sexual Violence and Family Honor. British Propaganda and International Law during the First World War', *The American Historical Review*, 102, 3 (1997), 714–47

Hall, Malcolm, *In Enemy Hands. A British Territorial Soldier in Germany, 1915–1919* (Stroud, 2002)

Hankel, Gerd, *Die Leipziger Prozesse. Deutsche Kriegsverbrechen und ihre strafrechtliche Verfolgung nach dem Ersten Weltkrieg* (Hamburg, 2003)

Hankey, Lord Maurice, *The Supreme Command 1914–1918*, 2 vols. (London, 1961)

Hanna, Martha, *The Mobilization of Intellect. French Scholars and Writers during the Great War* (Cambridge, Mass., and London, 1996)

Hart-Davis, Rupert, ed., *The War Poems of Siegfried Sassoon* (London, 1983)

Haste, Cate, *Keep the Home Fires Burning. Propaganda in the First World War* (London, 1977)

Haupt, Hans-Gerhard, and Jürgen Kocka, 'Comparative History. Methods, Aims, Problems', in Deborah Cohen and Maura O'Connor, eds., *Comparison and*

History. Europe in Cross-National Perspective (New York and London, 2004), pp. 23–40

Hayward, James, *Myths and Legends of the First World War* (Sutton, 2002)

Hellen, J. Anthony, 'Temporary Settlements and Transient Populations. The Legacy of Britain's Prisoner of War Camps 1940–1948', *Erdkunde*, 53 (1999), 191–219

Henig, Ruth, *The Origins of the First World War* (London and New York, 1993)

Herbert, Ulrich, *A History of Foreign Labor in Germany, 1880–1980. Seasonal Workers / Forced Laborers / Guest Workers* (Michigan, 1990)

Herwig, Holger, *The First World War. Germany and Austria-Hungary, 1914–1918* (London, 1996)

Hight, Eleanor M., and Gary D. Simpson, eds., *Colonialist Photography. Imagining Race and Place* (London, 2002)

Hingorani, R. C., *Prisoners of War* (Dobbs Ferry, N.Y., 1982)

Hinz, Uta, '"Die deutschen 'Barbaren' sind doch die besseren Menschen". Kriegsgefangenschaft und gefangene "Feinde" in der Darstellung der deutschen Publizistik 1914–1918', in Rüdiger Overmans, ed., *In der Hand des Feindes. Kriegsgefangenschaft von der Antike bis zum Zweiten Weltkrieg* (Cologne, Weimar and Vienna, 1999), pp. 339–62

'Fuir pour la patrie. Officiers prisonniers de guerre en Allemagne, 1914–1918', in Institut Charles de Gaulle/Historial de Péronne, *De Gaulle soldat 1914–1918* (Paris, 1999), pp. 48–57

Gefangen im Großen Krieg. Kriegsgefangenschaft in Deutschland, 1914–1921 (Essen, 2006)

'Kriegsgefangene', in Gerhard Hirschfeld, Gerd Krumeich and Irina Renz, eds., *Enzyklopädie Erster Weltkrieg* (Paderborn, Munich, Vienna and Zurich, 2003), pp. 641–6

'Prisonniers', in Stéphane Audoin-Rouzeau and Jean-Jacques Becker, eds., *Encyclopédie de la Grande Guerre, 1914–1918. Histoire et culture* (Paris, 2004), pp. 777–84

Hirschfeld, Gerhard, ed., *Keiner fühlt sich hier mehr als Mensch. Erlebnis und Wirkung des Ersten Weltkriegs* (Frankfurt am Main, 1996)

ed., *The Policies of Genocide. Jews and Soviet Prisoners of War in Nazi Germany* (London, 1986)

Hirschfeld, Gerhard, Gerd Krumeich, Dieter Langewiesche and Hans-Peter Ullmann, eds., *Kriegserfahrungen. Studien zur Sozial- und Mentalitätsgeschichte des Ersten Weltkrieges* (Essen, 1997)

Hirschfeld, Gerhard, Gerd Krumeich and Irena Renz, eds., *Enzyklopädie Erster Weltkrieg* (Paderborn, Munich, Vienna and Zurich, 2003)

Holmes, Richard, *The First World War in Photographs* (London, 2001)

Hoover, Herbert, *The Memoirs of Herbert Hoover. Years of Adventure, 1874–1920* (London, 1952)

Höpp, Gerhard, *Muslime in der Mark. Als Kriegsgefangene und Internierte in Wünsdorf und Zossen, 1914–1924* (Berlin, 1997)

Horne, John, ed., *Labour at War, France and Britain, 1914–1918* (Oxford, 1991)

State, Society and Mobilization in Europe during the First World War (Cambridge, 1997)

'War and Conflict in Contemporary European Society, 1914–2004', *Zeithistorische Forschungen / Studies in Contemporary History*, Online-Ausgabe, 1 (2004), H3, URL: www.zeithistorische-forschungen.de/16126041-Horne-3-2004

Horne, John, and Alan Kramer, *German Atrocities, 1914. A History of Denial* (New Haven and London, 2001)

'German "Atrocities" and Franco-German Opinion, 1914. The Evidence of Soldiers Diaries', *The Journal of Modern History*, 66, 1 (1994), 1–33

Hull, Isabel V., *Absolute Destruction. Military Culture and the Practices of War in Imperial Germany* (Ithaca and London, 2005)

Hunt, Lynn, 'French History in the Last Twenty Years. The Rise and Fall of the Annales Paradigm', *Journal of Contemporary History*, 21, 2 (1986), 209–24

Hüppauf, Bernd, 'Kriegsliteratur', in Gerhard Hirschfeld, Gerd Krumeich and Irina Renz, eds., *Enzyklopädie Erster Weltkrieg* (Paderborn, Munich, Vienna and Zurich, 2003), pp. 177–91

ed., *War, Violence and the Modern Condition* (Berlin, 1997)

Hynes, Samuel, *A War Imagined. The First World War and English Culture* (London, 1990)

Inglis, Brian, *Roger Casement* (London, Sydney and Auckland, 1973)

Isnenghi, Mario, and Giorgio Rochat, *La Grande Guerra 1914–1918* (Milan, 2000)

Jackson, Robert, *The Prisoners 1914–1918* (London, 1989)

Jahr, Christoph, *Gewöhnliche Soldaten. Desertion und Deserteure im deutschen und britischen Heer 1914–1918* (Göttingen, 1998)

'"Der Krieg zwingt die Justiz ihr Innerstes zu revidieren." Desertion und Militärgerichtsbarkeit im Ersten Weltkrieg', in Ulrich Bröckling and Michael Sikora, eds., *Armeen and ihre Deserteure. Vernachlässigte Kapitel einer Militärgeschichte der Neuzeit* (Göttingen, 1998), pp. 187–221

Jeanneney, Jean-Noël, 'Les Archives des commissions de Contrôle postal aux armées (1916–1918), une source précieuse pour l'histoire contemporaine de l'opinion et des mentalités', *Revue d'Histoire moderne et contemporaine* (Jan–March 1968), 209–33

Jeffrey, Keith, *Ireland and the Great War* (Cambridge, 2000)

Jeismann, Michael, *Das Vaterland der Feinde. Studien zum nationalen Feindbegriff und Selbstverständnis in Deutschland und Frankreich 1792–1918* (Stuttgart, 1992)

Jones, Edgar, 'The Pyschology of Killing. The Combat Experience of British Soldiers during the First World War', *Journal of Contemporary History*, 41 (2006), 229–46

Jones, Heather, 'Encountering the "Enemy". Prisoner of War Transport and the Development of War Cultures in 1914', in Pierre Purseigle, ed., *Warfare and Belligerence. Perspectives in First World War Studies* (Boston and Leiden, 2005), pp. 133–62

'The Final Logic of Sacrifice? Violence in German Prisoner of War Labor Companies in 1918', *The Historian*, 68, 4 (2006), 770–91

'The German Spring Reprisals of 1917. Prisoners of War and the Violence of the Western Front', *German History*, 26 (2008), 335–56

'International or Transnational? Humanitarian Action during the First World War', *European Review of History*, 16, 5 (2009), 697–713

'A Missing Paradigm? Military Captivity and the Prisoner of War, 1914–1918', *Immigrants and Minorities*, 26, 1/2 (2008), 19–48

Jones, Heather, Christoph Schmidt-Supprian and Jennifer O'Brien, eds., *Untold War. New Perspectives in First World War Studies* (Boston and Leiden, 2008)

Judt, Tony, *Postwar. A History of Europe since 1945* (London, 2005)

Juhl, Eduard, Margarete Klante and Herta Epstein, *Elsa Brändström. Weg und Werk einer grossen Frau in Schweden, Siberien, Deutschland, Amerika* (Stuttgart, 1962)

Karner, Stefan, 'Konzentrations- und Kriegsgefangenenlager in Deutschland und in der Sowjetunion. Ansätze zu einem Vergleich von Lagern in totalitären Regimen', in Rüdiger Overmans, ed., *In der Hand des Feindes. Kriegsgefangenschaft von der Antike bis zum Zweiten Weltkrieg* (Cologne, Vienna and Weimar, 1999), pp. 387–412

Keegan, John, *The Face of Battle. A Study of Agincourt, Waterloo and the Somme* (London, 1976)

The First World War (London, 1998)

Kelly, Phyllis, *Love Letters from the Front* (Dublin, 2000)

Kershaw, Ian, *Hitler*, vol. I: *Hubris, 1889–1936* (London, 2001)

Ketchum Davidson, John, *Ruhleben. A Prison Camp Society* (Toronto and London, 1965)

Kirchner, Klaus, ed., *Flugblatt-Propaganda im 1. Weltkrieg, Europa*, vol. II (Erlangen, 1992)

Kitchen, Martin, *The German Offensives of 1918* (Stroud, 2001)

'Michael-Offensive', in Gerhard Hirschfeld, Irena Renz and Gerd Krumeich, eds., *Enzyklopädie Erster Weltkrieg* (Paderborn, Munich, Vienna and Zurich, 2004), pp. 712–15

The Silent Dictatorship. The Politics of the German High Command under Hindenburg and Ludendorff, 1916–1918 (London, 1976)

Knox, MacGregor, 'Weltkrieg und "Military Culture". Kontinuität und Wandel im deutsch-italienischen Vergleich', in Sven Oliver Müller and Cornelius Torp, eds., *Das Deutsche Kaiserreich in der Kontroverse. Eine Bilanz* (Göttingen, 2008)

Kochavi, Arieh J., *Confronting Captivity. Britain and the United States and their POWs in Nazi Germany* (Chapel Hill, 2005)

Kocka, Jürgen, 'Asymmetrical Historical Comparison. The Case of the German *Sonderweg*', *History and Theory*, 38, 1 (2002), 40–50

Facing Total War. German Society, 1914–1918 (Leamington Spa, 1984)

Köhler, Gottfried, *Die Kriegsgefangenen-, Internierten- und Militärlager in Österreich-Ungarn 1914–1919 und ihre Feldposteinrichtungen* (Graz and Linz, 1991)

Kohlhagen, Norgard, *Elsa Brändström. Die Frau, die man Engel nannte* (Stuttgart, 1991)

Koller, Christian, 'The Recruitment of Colonial Troops in Africa and Asia and their Deployment in Europe during the First World War', *Immigrants and Minorities*, 26, 1/2 (2008), 111–33

Kramer, Alan, *Dynamic of Destruction. Culture and Mass Killing in the First World War* (Oxford, 2007)
'The First Wave of International War Crimes Trials. Istanbul and Leipzig', *European Review*, Academia Europaea, 14, 4 (2006), 441–55
'Prisoners in the First World War', in Sibylle Scheipers, ed., *Prisoners in War. Norms, Military Culture and Reciprocity in Armed Conflict* (Oxford, 2009), pp. 75–91
Krumeich, Gerd, '"Saigner la France"? Mythes et réalité de la stratégie allemande de la bataille de Verdun', *Guerres Mondiales et Conflits Contemporains*, 182 (1996), 17–30
ed., *Nationalsozialismus und Erster Weltkrieg* (Essen, 2010)
Kudrina, Iulia, 'Das Dänische Rote Kreuz in den Jahren des Ersten Weltkrieges', *Zeitgeschichte (Austria)*, 25, 11–12 (1998), 375–9
Kuprian, Hermann J. W., and Oswald Überegger, eds., *Der Erste Weltkrieg im Alpenraum. Erfahrung, Deutung, Erinnerung / La Grande Guerra nell'arco alpino. Esperienze e memoria* (Innsbruck, 2006)
Lafitte, François, *The Internment of Aliens* (London, 1988)
Langworth, Philip, *The Unending Vigil. The History of the Commonwealth War Graves Commission* (Barnsley, 2003 [1967])
Lawrence, Jon, 'Forging a Peaceable Kingdom. War, Violence and the Fear of Brutalisation in Post-First World War Britain', *Journal of Modern History*, 75, 3 (2003), 557–89
Leidinger, Hannes, 'Gefangenschaft und Heimkehr. Gedanken zu Voraussetzungen und Perspektiven eines neuen Forschungsbereiches', *Zeitgeschichte (Austria)*, 25, 11–12 (1998), 333–42
Leidinger, Hannes, and Moritz, Verena, 'Verwaltete Massen. Kriegsgefangene in der Donaumonarchie 1914–1918', in Jochen Oltmer, ed., *Kriegsgefangene im Europa des Ersten Weltkriegs* (Paderborn, 2006), pp. 35–66
Le Naour, Jean-Yves, *Misères et tourments de la chair durant la Grande Guerre. Les mœurs sexuelles des Français 1914–1918* (Paris, 2002)
Lerchenmueller, Joachim, '"The Wretched Lot" – A Brief History of the Irish Brigade in Germany 1914–1919', in Gisela Holfter and Joachim Lerchemueller, eds., *Jahrbuch des Zentrums für deutsch-irische Studien / Yearbook of the Centre for Irish-German Studies* (Limerick, 1998/9), pp. 95–115
Leven, Karl-Heinz, *Die Geschichte der Infektionskrankheiten. Von der Antike bis ins 20. Jahrhundert* (Landsberg/Lech, 1997)
Levi, Primo, *If This Is a Man – The Truce* (London, 1987 [1958])
Levie, Howard S., 'Prisoners of War and the Protecting Power', *The American Journal of International Law*, 55, 2 (1961), 374–97
Liulevicius, Vejas Gabriel, *War Land on the Eastern Front. Culture, National Identity and German Occupation in World War I* (Cambridge, 2000)
Lüdtke, Alf, and Bernd Weisbrod, eds., *No Man's Land of Violence. Extreme Wars in the 20th Century* (Göttingen, 2006)
Macintyre, Ben, *A Foreign Field. A True Story of Love and Betrayal during the Great War* (London, 2001)
Mackenzie, S. P., *The Colditz Myth. British and Commonwealth Prisoners of War in Nazi Germany* (Oxford, 2004)

'The Ethics of Escape. British Officer POWs in the First World War', *War in History*, 15, 1 (2008), 1–16

'The Treatment of Prisoners of War in World War II', *The Journal of Modern History*, 66, 3 (1994), 487–520

Macmillan, Margaret, *Peacemakers. Six Months that Changed the World* (London, 2001)

Mahrenholz, Jürgen-K., 'Zum Lautarchiv und seiner wissenschaftlichen Erschließung durch die Datenbank IMAGO' in Marianne Bröcker, ed., *Berichte aus dem ICTM-Nationalkomitee Deutschland. Bericht über die Jahrestagung des Nationalkomitees der Bundesrepublik Deutschland im International Council for Traditional Music (UNESCO)* (Bamberg, 2003), pp. 131–54

Matard-Bonucci, Marie-Anne, and Édouard Lynch, *La Libération des camps et le retour des déportés* (Paris, 1995)

Mauran, Hervé, 'Une minorité dans la tourmente. Évacuation, internement et contrôle des Alsaciens-Lorrains en France (1914–1919)', *Bretagne 14–18*, 3 (2002), 101–29

Mayer, Laurence, *Victory Must Be Ours. Germany in the Great War, 1914–1918* (London, 1995)

Mazower, Mark, *Dark Continent. Europe's Twentieth Century* (London, 1998)

'Violence and the State in the Twentieth Century', *American Historical Review*, 107, 4 (2002), 1158–78

McCoubrey, Hillaire, *International Humanitarian Law and the Regulation of Armed Conflicts* (Aldershot, 1990)

McDonald, Lyn, *And They Called It Passchendaele. The Story of the Third Battle of Ypres and of the Men who Fought in it* (London, 1990)

The Roses of No Man's Land (Harmondsworth, 1993)

The Somme (London, 1983)

McPhail, Helen, *The Long Silence. Civilian Life under the German Occupation of Northern France 1914–1918* (London, 1999)

Messinger, Gary, *British Propaganda and the State in the First World War* (Manchester, 1992)

Michel, Marc, 'Intoxication ou "brutalisation". Les représailles de la Grande Guerre', in Nicolas Beaupré and Christian Ingrao, eds., *14–18. Aujourd'hui, Today, Heute*, vol. IV: *Marginaux, marginalité, marginalisation* (2001), 175–97

Middlebrook, Martin, *The Kaiser's Battle: 21 March 1918. The First Day of the German Spring Offensive* (London, 1978)

Mihaly, Jo, *'Da gibt's ein Wiedersehn!' Kriegstagebuch eines Mädchens 1914–1918* (Freiberg and Heidelberg, 1982)

Mitchell, Reid, '"Our prison system, supposing we had any". Die Kriegsgefangenenpolitik der Konföderierten und der Unionisten im Amerikanischen Bürgerkrieg', in Rüdiger Overmans, ed., *In der Hand des Feindes. Kriegsgefangenschaft von der Antike bis zum Zweiten Weltkrieg* (Cologne, Weimar and Vienna, 1999), pp. 211–34

Mitze, Katja, *Das Kriegsgefangenenlager Ingolstadt während des Ersten Weltkriegs*, published doctoral thesis (Münster, 1999)

'"Seit der Babylonischen Gefangenschaft hat die Welt nichts derart erlebt". Französische Kriegsgefangene und Franctireurs im Deutsch-Französischen Krieg 1870/71', in Rüdiger Overmans, ed., *In der Hand des Feindes.*

Kriegsgefangenschaft von der Antike bis zum Zweiten Weltkrieg (Cologne, Weimar and Vienna, 1999), pp. 235–54

Moore, Bob, 'Turning Liabilities into Assets. British Government Policy towards German and Italian Prisoners of War during the Second World War', *Journal of Contemporary History*, 32, 1 (1997), 117–36

Moore, Bob, and Kent Fedorowich, *The British Empire and Italian Prisoners of War* (London, 2002)

Moore, Bob, and Barbara Hately-Broad, eds., *Prisoners of War, Prisoners of Peace* (Oxford and New York, 2005)

Morton, Desmond, *Silent Battle. Canadian Prisoners of War in Germany, 1914–1919* (Toronto, 1992)

Mosse, George L., *Fallen Soldiers. Reshaping the Memory of the World Wars* (Oxford, 1990)

The Nationalization of the Masses. Political Symbolism and Mass Movements in Germany from the Napoleonic Wars through the Third Reich (Ithaca and London, 1991)

Moynihan, Michael, ed., *Black Bread and Barbed Wire. Prisoners in the First World War* (London, 1978)

Nachtigal, Reinhard, *Kriegsgefangenschaft an der Ostfront, 1914 bis 1918* (Frankfurt am Main, 2005)

'The Repatriation and Reception of Returning Prisoners of War, 1918–22', *Immigrants and Minorities*, 26, 1/2 (2008), 157–184

Russland und seine österreichisch-ungarischen Kriegsgefangenen (1914–1918) (Remshalden, 2003)

'Seuchenbekämpfung als Probleme der russischen Staatsverwaltung. Prinz Alexander von Oldenburg und die Kriegsgefangenen der Mittelmächte', *Medizinhistorisches Journal*, 39 (2004), 135–63

'Seuchen unter militärischer Aufsicht in Rußland. Das Lager Tockoe als Beispiel für die Behandlung der Kriegsgefangenen 1915/16', *Jahrbücher für Geschichte Osteuropas*, 48 (2000), 363–87

Naimark, Norman, *Fires of Hatred. Ethnic Cleansing in Twentieth-Century Europe* (Cambridge, Mass., 2001)

Noakes, Jeremy, 'Review of Jörg Später, *Vansittart. Britische Debatten über Deutsche und Nazis, 1902–1945* (Göttingen, 2003)', *German Historical Institute London, Bulletin*, 27, 2 (November 2005), 93–101

Nora, Pierre, ed., *Realms of Memory. The Construction of the French Past*, 3 vols., vol. I: *Conflicts and Divisions* (New York, 1996), and vol. III: *Symbols* (New York, 1998)

Noriel, Gérard, *Sur la 'crise' de l'histoire* (Paris, 1996)

Offenstadt, Nicolas, *Les Fusillés de la Grande Guerre et la mémoire collective, 1914–1999* (Paris, 1999)

Offer, Avner, *The First World War. An Agrarian Interpretation* (Oxford, 1989)

Oltmer, Jochen, 'Zwangsmigration und Zwangsarbeit. Ausländische Arbeitskräfte und bäuerliche Ökonomie im Ersten Weltkrieg', *Tel Aviver Jahrbuch für deutsche Geschichte*, 27 (1998), 135–68

ed., *Kriegsgefangene im Europa des Ersten Weltkriegs* (Munich, Paderborn, Zurich and Vienna, 2006)

Otte, Klaus, *Lager Soltau. Das Kriegsgefangenen- und Interniertenlager des Ersten Weltkriegs (1914–1921). Geschichte und Geschichten* (Soltau, 1999)

Overmans, Rüdiger, '"Hunnen" und "Untermenschen" – deutsche und russisch/sowjetische Kriegsgefangenschaftserfahrungen im Zeitalter der Weltkriege', in Bruno Thoss and Hans-Erich Volkmann, eds., *Erster Weltkrieg – Zweiter Weltkrieg. Ein Vergleich. Krieg, Kriegserlebnis, Kriegserfahrung in Deutschland* (Paderborn, 2002), pp. 335–65.

'"In der Hand des Feindes". Geschichtsschreibung zur Kriegsgefangenschaft von der Antike bis zum Zweiten Weltkrieg', in Overmans, ed., *In der Hand des Feindes. Kriegsgefangenschaft von der Antike bis zum Zweiten Weltkrieg* (Cologne, Weimar and Vienna, 1999), pp. 1–40

'The Repatriation of Prisoners of War once Hostilities Are Over. A Matter of Course?', in Bob Moore and Barbara Hately-Broad, eds., *Prisoners of War, Prisoners of Peace* (Oxford and New York, 2005), pp. 11–22

ed., *In der Hand des Feindes. Kriegsgefangenschaft von der Antike bis zum Zweiten Weltkrieg* (Cologne, Weimar and Vienna, 1999)

Parker, Peter, *The Old Lie. The Great War and the Public School Ethos* (London, 1987)

Parmiter, Geoffrey de C., *Roger Casement* (London, 1936)

Pautsch, Ilse Dorothee, 'Prisoners of War and Internees in the Second World War – a Survey of Some Recent Publications', *Contemporary European History*, 12, 2 (2003), 225–38

Pedroncini, Guy, *Les Mutineries de 1917* (Paris, 1967)

Pöppinghege, Rainer, 'Belgian Life behind German Barbed Wire', in S. Jaumain, M. Amara, B. Majerus and A. Vrints, eds., *Une guerre totale? La Belgique dans la Première Guerre Mondiale. Nouvelles tendances de la recherche historique* (Brussels, 2005), pp. 207–21

Im Lager unbesiegt. Deutsche, englische und französische Kriegsgefangenen-Zeitungen im Ersten Weltkrieg (Essen, 2006)

'"Kriegsteilnehmer zweiter Klasse"? Die Reichsvereinigung ehemaliger Kriegsgefangener 1919–1933', *Militärgeschichtliche Zeitschrift*, 64 (2005), 391–423.

Powell, Allan Kent, *Splinters of a Nation. German Prisoners of War in Utah* (Salt Lake City, 1989)

Power, Samantha, *'A Problem from Hell'. America and the Age of Genocide* (London, 2003)

Procacci, Giovanna, 'Les prisonniers italiens. Mémoire de la captivité', in Jean-Jacques Becker et al., eds., *guerre et cultures, 1914–1918* (Paris, 1994), pp. 322–8

Soldati e prigionieri italiani nella grande guerra, con una raccolta di lettere inedite (Turin, 2000)

Prost, Antoine, *Les Anciens Combattants et la société française, 1914–1940*, 3 vols. (Paris, 1977). Translated as: *In the Wake of War. 'Les Anciens Combattants' and French Society, 1914–1939* (Oxford and Providence, 1992)

'Les Limites de la brutalisation. Tuer sur le front occidental, 1914–1918', *Vingtième Siècle. Revue d'Histoire*, 81 (2004), 247–68

'Verdun', in Pierre Nora, ed., *Realms of Memory. The Construction of the French Past*, 3 vols., vol. III: *Symbols* (Chichester and New York, 1998), pp. 376–401

Prost, Antoine, and Jay Winter, *The Great War in History. Debates and Controversies, 1914 to the Present* (Cambridge, 2005)

Purseigle, Pierre, 'La Guerre au miroir de l'humour en France et en Grande Bretagne', *Histoire et Sociétés*, vol. I: *La Modernisation de l'Europe occidentale dans les années vingt* (2002),134–7
ed., *Warfare and Belligerence. Perspectives in First World War Studies* (Boston and Leiden, 2005)
Purseigle, Pierre, and Jenny Macleod, eds., *Uncovered Fields. Perspectives in First World War Studies* (Boston and Leiden, 2004)
Rachamimov, Alon, 'Alltagssorgen und politische Erwartungen. Eine Analyse von Kriegsgefangenenkorrespondenzen in den Beständen des Österreichischen Staatsarchivs', *Zeitgeschichte, Austria*, 25, 11–12 (1998), 348–56
'The Disruptive Comforts of Drag. (Trans)Gender Performances among Prisoners of War in Russia, 1914–1920', *The American Historical Review*, 3, 2 (2006), 362–82
'Imperial Loyalties and Private Concerns. Nation, Class and State in the Correspondence of Austro-Hungarian PoWs in Russia, 1916–1918', *Austrian History Yearbook*, 31 (2000), 87–105
POWs and the Great War. Captivity on the Eastern Front (Oxford and New York, 2002)
Rawe, Kai, '. . . *wir werden sie schon zur Arbeit bringen'. Ausländerbeschäftigung und Zwangsarbeit im Ruhrkohlenbergbau während des Ersten Weltkrieges* (Essen, 2005)
Read, James Morgan, *Atrocity Propaganda, 1914–1919* (New Jersey, 1941)
Reeves, Nicolas, 'Cinema, Spectatorship and Propaganda. "Battle of the Somme" (1916) and Its Contemporary Audience', *Historical Journal of Film, Radio and Television*, 17, 1 (March 1997), 5–29
Reid, Patrick, and Maurice Michael, *Prisoner of War* (London, 1984)
Reiter, Andrea, *Narrating the Holocaust* (London and New York, 2000)
Renoir, Jean, *La Grande Illusion*, trans. M. Alexander and A. Sinclair (London, 1968)
Richard, Ronan, 'Réfugiés, prisonniers et sentiment national en milieu rural en 1914–1918. Vers une nouvelle approche de l'Union Sacrée', *Annales de Bretagne et des Pays de l'Ouest*, 105 (1998), 111–28
Ring, Friedrich, *Zur Geschichte der Militärmedizin in Deutschland* (Berlin, 1962)
Ritter, Gerhard, *The Schlieffen Plan. Critique of a Myth* (New York, 1958)
Robertson, David, *Deeds Not Words. Irish Soldiers and Airmen in Two World Wars* (Dublin, 1998)
Rogasch, Wilfried, 'Zur Geschichte der Sammlung', in Rosmarie Beier and Bettina Biedermann, eds., *Kriegsgefangen. Objekte aus der Sammlung des Archivs und Museums der Kriegsgefangenschaft, Berlin, und des Verbandes der Heimkehrer, Kriegsgefangenen und Vermisstenangehörigen Deutschlands e.V., Bonn-Bad Godesberg im Deutschen Historischen Museum, 30. Oktober 1990 bis 30. November 1990* (Berlin, 1990), pp. 12–92
Rohkrämer, Thomas, *Der Militarismus der 'kleinen Leute'. Die Kriegervereine im Deutschen Kaiserreich 1871–1914* (Munich, 1990)
Roth, Andreas, '"The German Soldier Is Not Tactful". Sir Roger Casement and the Irish Brigade in Germany during the First World War', *The Irish Sword. The Journal of the Military History Society of Ireland*, 19, 78 (Winter 1995), 313–32

Rother, Rainer, ed., *Der Weltkrieg 1914–1918. Ereignis und Erinnerung* (Berlin, 2004)

Ruiz, Julius, 'A Spanish Genocide? Reflections on the Francoist Repression after the Spanish Civil War', *Contemporary European History*, 14, 2 (2005), 171–91

Rusel, Jane, *Hermann Struck (1876–1944). Das Leben und das graphische Werk eines jüdischen Künstlers* (Frankfurt am Main, Berlin, Bern, New York, Paris and Vienna, 1997)

Sanders, M. L., and Philip M. Taylor, *British Propaganda during the First World War, 1914–18* (London and Basingstoke, 1982)

Scally, Derek, 'German Town Restores Cross that Remembers Deaths of Irish Prisoners', *The Irish Times*, 19 November 2007.

Scheipers, Sibylle, ed., *Prisoners in War. Norms, Military Culture and Reciprocity in Armed Conflict* (Oxford, 2009)

Scholliers, Peter and Frank Daelemans, 'Standards of Living and Standards of Health in Wartime Belgium', in Richard Wall and Jay Winter, eds., *The Upheaval of War. Family, Work and Welfare in Europe 1914–1918* (Cambridge, 1988), pp. 139–58

Schumann, Dirk, 'Europa, der Erste Weltkrieg und die Nachkriegszeit. Eine Kontinuität der Gewalt?' *Journal of Modern European History*, 1, 1 (2003), 24–43.

'Gewalt als Grenzüberschreitung. Überlegungen zur Sozialgeschichte der Gewalt im 19. und 20. Jahrhundert', *Archiv für Sozialgeschichte*, 37 (1997), 366–86

Scott, Peter T., 'Captive Labour. The German Companies of the B.E.F., 1916–1920', *The Army Quarterly and Defence Journal*, 110, 3 (July, 1980), 319–31

Segesser, Daniel Marc, 'The Punishment of War Crimes Committed against Prisoners of War, Deportees and Refugees during and after the First World War', *Immigrants and Minorities*, 26, 1/2 (2008), 134–56

Seipp, Adam, *The Ordeal of Peace. Demobilization and the Urban Experience in Britain and Germany, 1917–1921* (Farnham and Burlington, 2010)

Sémelin, Jacques, 'Introduction. Violences extrêmes. Peut-on comprendre?' *Revue Internationale des Sciences Sociales*, 174 (2002), 479–81.

Sewell, William H., 'Marc Bloch and the Logic of Comparative History', *History and Theory*, 6 (1967), 208–18

Sheffield, Gary, *Forgotten Victory. The First World War, Myths and Realities* (London, 2001)

Sheehan, James, 'What It Means to Be a State. States and Violence in Twentieth-Century Europe', *Journal of Modern European History*, 1, 1 (2003), 11–23

Siann, Gerda, *Accounting for Aggression. Perspectives on Aggression and Violence* (London, Sydney and Boston, 1985)

Smith, Anthony D., *The Ethnic Origins of Nations* (Oxford, 1986)

Smith, Leonard V., *Between Mutiny and Obedience. The Case of the Fifth French Infantry Division during World War One* (Princeton, 1994)

'Jean Norton Cru and Combatants' Literature of the First World War', *Modern and Contemporary France*, 9, 2 (2001), 161–9

Smither, Roger, '"A Wonderful Idea of the Fighting". The Question of Fakes in "The Battle of the Somme"', *Historical Journal of Film, Radio and Television*, 13, 2 (1993), 149–69

Sofsky, Wolfgang, *Traktat über die Gewalt* (Frankfurt, 1996)
Violence. Terrorism, Genocide, War (London, 2003)

Speed, Richard B. III., *Prisoners, Diplomats and the Great War. A Study in the Diplomacy of Captivity* (New York and London, 1990)

Spoerer, Mark, 'The Mortality of Allied Prisoners of War and Belgian Civilian Deportees in German Custody during the First World War. A Reappraisal of the Effects of Forced Labour', *Population Studies*, 60, 2 (2006), 121–36

Stanko, Elizabeth A., ed., *The Meanings of Violence* (London and New York, 2003)

Stevenson, David, *1914–1918. The History of the First World War* (London, 2004)

Stibbe, Matthew, *British Civilian Internees in Germany. The Ruhleben Camp, 1914–1918* (Manchester, 2008)
'Civilian Internment and Civilian Internees in Europe, 1914–20', *Immigrants and Minorities*, 26, 1/2 (2008), 49–81
German Anglophobia and the Great War 1914–1918 (Cambridge, 2001)
'The Internment of Civilians by Belligerent States during the First World War and the Response of the International Committee of the Red Cross', *Journal of Contemporary History*, 41, 1 (2006), 5–19
'Introduction. Captivity, Forced Labour and Forced Migration during the First World War', *Immigrants and Minorities*, 26, 1/2 (2008), 1–18
'A Question of Retaliation? The Internment of British Civilians in Germany in November 1914', *Immigrants and Minorities*, 23, 1 (March 2005), 1–29

Storz, Dieter, *Kriegsbild und Rüstung vor 1914. Europäische Landstreitkräfte vor dem Ersten Weltkrieg* (Herford, Berlin and Bonn, 1992)

Strachan, Hew, *The First World War*, vol. I: *To Arms* (Oxford, 2001)

Streit, Christian, 'Partisans-Resistance-Prisoners of War', *Soviet Union/Union Soviétique*, 18, 1–3 (1991), 259–76

Swianiewicz, Stanislaw, *Forced Labour and Economic Development. An Enquiry into the Experience of Soviet Industrialization* (Oxford, 1965)

Terraine, John, *Douglas Haig. The Educated Soldier* (London, 1963)

Théofilakis, Fabien, 'La Sexualité du prisonnier de guerre. Allemands et Français en captivité (1914–1918; 1940–1948)', *Vingtième Siècle*, 99 (2008), 203–20

Ther, Philipp, 'Beyond the Nation. The Relational Basis of a Comparative History of Germany and Europe', *Central European History*, 36, 1 (2003), 45–73

Thiel, Jens, *'Menschenbassin Belgien'. Anwerbung, Deportation und Zwangsarbeit im Ersten Weltkrieg* (Essen, 2007)

Thompson, David, and Lorraine LoBianco, eds., *Jean Renoir. Letters* (London and Boston, 1994)

Thoss, Bruno, and Hans-Erich Volkmann, eds., *Erster Weltkrieg – Zweiter Weltkrieg. Ein Vergleich. Krieg, Kriegserlebnis, Kriegserfahrung in Deutschland* (Paderborn, 2002)

Tiepolato, Serena, 'L'Internamento di civili prussiani in Russia (1914–1920)', in Bruna Bianchi, ed., *La Violenza Contro La Popolazione Civile Nella Grande Guerra* (Milan, 2006), pp. 107–27

Tilly, Charles, *The Politics of Collective Violence* (Cambridge, 2003)

Todman, Dan, *The Great War. Myth and Memory* (New York and London, 2005)

Tosh, John, 'What Should Historians Do with Masculinity? Reflections on Nineteenth Century Britain', *History Workshop Journal*, 38, 1 (1994), 179–202

Treffer, Gerd A., 'Die dritte Stufe knarrt. Wie Charles de Gaulle, der Mitbegründer der deutsch-französischen Freundschaft, im Ersten Weltkrieg Deutschland kennen lernte – und gleich wieder daraus flüchten wollte', *Die Zeit*, 33 (5.8.2004), 82

Die ehrenwerten Ausbrecher. Das Kriegsgefangenenlager Ingolstadt im Ersten Weltkrieg (Regensburg, 1990)

Tuchman, Barbara, *The Proud Tower. A Portrait of the World before the War. 1890–1914* (London, 1966)

Ullmann, Hans-Peter, *Das Deutsche Kaiserreich 1871–1918* (Frankfurt am Main, 1995)

Ulrich, Bernd, *Die Augenzeugen. Deutsche Feldpostbriefe in Kriegs- und Nachkriegszeit, 1914–1933* (Essen, 1997)

'Feldpostbriefe des Ersten Weltkrieges. Möglichkeiten und Grenzen einer alltagsgeschichtlichen Quelle', *Militärgeschichtliche Mitteilungen*, 53, 1 (1994), 73–83

Ulrich, Bröckling, ed., *Armeen und ihre Deserteure. Vernachlässigte Kapitel einer Militärgeschichte der Neuzeit* (Göttingen, 1998)

Urban, Frank, *Ned's Navy. The Private Letters of Edward Charlton from Cadet to Admiral. A Window on the British Empire from 1878 to 1924* (Shrewsbury, 1998)

Vance, Jonathan, *Death so Noble. Memory, Meaning and the First World War* (Vancouver, 1997)

Objects of Concern. Canadian Prisoners of War through the Twentieth Century (Vancouver, 1994)

ed., *Encyclopedia of Prisoners of War and Internment* (Santa Barbara, 2000)

Vansittart, Robert, *The Mist Procession. The Autobiography of Lord Vansittart* (London, 1958)

Véray, Laurent, *Les Films d'actualité français de la Grande Guerre* (Paris, 1995)

Verhey, Jeffrey, *The Spirit of 1914. Militarism, Myth and Mobilisation in Germany* (Cambridge, 2000)

Vincent, C. Paul, *The Politics of Hunger. The Allied Blockade of Germany 1915–1919* (Athens, Ohio, and London, 1985)

Wachsmann, Nikolaus, '"Annihilation through Labor". The Killing of State Prisoners in the Third Reich', *The Journal of Modern History*, 71, 3 (1999), 624–59

Wall, Richard, and Jay Winter, eds., *The Upheaval of War. Family, Work and Welfare in Europe 1914–1918* (Cambridge, 1988)

Wasserstein, Bernard, *Barbarism and Civilization. A History of Europe in Our Time* (Oxford, 2007)

Watson, Alexander, *Enduring the Great War. Combat, Morale and Collapse in the German and British Armies, 1914–1918* (Cambridge, 2008)

Weber, Thomas, *'Our Friend "the Enemy"'. Elite Education in Britain and Germany before World War I* (Stanford, 2008)

Wegner, Bernd, ed., *Wie Kriege entstehen. Zum historischen Hintergrund von Staatkonflikten* (Paderborn, Munich, Vienna and Zurich, 2003)

Weindling, Paul, *Epidemics and Genocide in Eastern Europe, 1890–1945* (Oxford, 2000)

Weisbrod, Bernd, 'Violence et culture politique en Allemagne entre les deux guerres', *Vingtième Siècle. Revue d'Histoire*, 34 (1992), 113–25

Welch, David, *German Propaganda and Total War, 1914–1918. The Sins of Omission* (London, 2000)

Werner, Michael, and Bénédicte Zimmermann, 'Beyond Comparison. Histoire Croisée and the Challenge of Reflexivity', *History and Theory*, 45, 1 (2006), 30–50

Wette, Wolfram, ed., *Der Krieg des kleinen Mannes. Eine Militärgeschichte von Unten* (Munich and Zurich, 1995)

Whalen, Robert Weldon, *Bitter Wounds. German Victims of the Great War, 1914–1939* (London and Ithaca, 1984)

Wheatcroft, Stephen, 'The Scale and Nature of German and Soviet Repression and Mass Killings, 1930–45', *Europe-Asia Studies*, 48, 8 (December 1996), 1319–53

Wheeler-Bennett, John W., *Brest-Litovsk. The Forgotten Peace, March 1918* (London, 1963)

Who Was Who, vol. VI: *A Companion to Who's Who Containing the Biographies of Those Who Died during the Decade 1961–1970* (London, 1972)

Wieviorka, Annette, ed., *Les Procès de Nuremberg et de Tokyo* (Caen, 1996)

Williamson, Samuel R. Jnr, and Peter Pastor, eds., *Essays on World War One. Origins and Prisoners of War* (New York, 1983)

Willis, Edward Frederick, *Herbert Hoover and the Russian Prisoners of World War I. A Study in Diplomacy and Relief, 1918–19* (Stanford, 1951)

Willis, J. F., *Prologue to Nuremberg. The Politics and Diplomacy of Punishing War Criminals of the First World War* (Westport, Conn., and London, 1982)

Wilson, Trevor, 'Lord Bryce's Investigation into Alleged German Atrocities in Belgium, 1914–15', *Journal of Contemporary History*, 14, 3 (1979), 369–83

The Myriad Faces of War. Britain and the Great War 1914–1918 (Cambridge, 1986)

Winchester, Barry, *Beyond the Tumult* (London, 1971)

Winter, Denis, *Haig's Command. A Reassessment* (London, 1992)

Winter, Jay M., *The Experience of World War I* (London, 2003)

The Great War and the British People (London and Basingstoke, 1985)

'La Grippe Espagnole', in Stéphane Audoin-Rouzeau and Jean-Jacques Becker, eds., *Encyclopédie de la Grande Guerre, 1914–1918. Histoire et culture* (Paris, 2004), pp. 943–8

'Military Fitness and Civilian Health in Britain during the First World War', *Journal of Contemporary History*, 15 (1980), 211–44

Sites of Memory, Sites of Mourning. The Great War in European Cultural History (Cambridge, 1995)

Winter, Jay M., and Jean-Louis Robert, eds., *Capital Cities at War. Paris, London, Berlin, 1914–1919*, vol. I (Cambridge, 1997)

Capital Cities at War. Paris, London, Berlin 1914–19. A Cultural History, vol. II (Cambridge, 2007)

Winter, Jay M., and Emmanuel Sivan, eds., *War and Remembrance in the Twentieth Century* (Cambridge, 1999)

Wotton, Graham, *The Official History of the British Legion* (London, 1956)

Wurzer, Georg, 'Deutsche Kriegsgefangene in Russland im Ersten Weltkrieg', in Rüdiger Overmans, ed., *In der Hand des Feindes. Kriegsgefangenschaft von der Antike bis zum Zweiten Weltkrieg* (Cologne, Weimar and Vienna, 1999), pp. 363–87

Wylie, Neville, 'The 1929 Prisoner of War Convention and the Building of the Interwar Prisoner of War Regime', in Sibylle Scheipers, ed., *Prisoners in War. Norms, Military Culture and Reciprocity in Armed Conflict* (Oxford, 2009), pp. 91–111.

Barbed Wire Diplomacy. Britain, Germany and the Politics of Prisoners of War, 1939–45 (Oxford, 2010)

'Prisoners of War in the Era of Total War', *War in History*, 13, 2 (2006), 217–33

Yerly, Frédéric, 'Grande guerre et diplomatie humanitaire. La mission Catholique Suisse en faveur des prisonniers de guerre (1914–1918)', *Vingtième Siècle*, 58 (1998), 13–28

Ziegler, Susanne, 'Die akustischen Sammlungen. Historische Tondokumente im Phonogramm-Archiv und im Lautarchiv', in Horst Bredekamp, Jochen Brüning and Cornelia Weber, eds., *Theater der Natur und Kunst. Essays. Wunderkammern des Wissens* (Berlin, 2000), pp. 197–207

'"Stimmen der Völker". Das Berliner Lautarchiv', in Horst Bredekamp, Jochen Brüning and Cornelia Weber, eds., *Theater der Natur und Kunst. Katalog. Eine Ausstellung der Humboldt-Universität zu Berlin 10. Dezember 2000 bis 4. März 2001* (Berlin, 2000), pp. 117–28

Ziemann, Benjamin, *Front und Heimat. Ländliche Erfahrungen im südlichen Bayern 1914–1923* (Essen, 1997). Translated as: *War Experiences in Rural Germany, 1914–1923* (Oxford and New York, 2007)

'Germany after the First World War – a Violent Society? Results and Implications of Recent Research on Weimar Germany', *Journal of Modern European History*, 1, 1 (2003), 80–95

'"Vergesellschaftung der Gewalt" als Thema der Kriegsgeschichte seit 1914. Perspektiven und Desiderate eines Konzeptes', in Bruno Thoss and Hans-Erich Volkmann, eds., *Erster Weltkrieg – Zweiter Weltkrieg. Ein Vergleich. Krieg, Kriegserlebnis, Kriegserfahrung in Deutschland* (Paderborn, 2002), pp. 753–9

THESES AND DISSERTATIONS

Beaupré, Nicolas, 'Les Écrivains français et allemands de la Grande Guerre (1914–1920)' (Doctoral thesis, University of Paris X – Nanterre, 2002)

Cabanes, Bruno, 'Finir la Guerre. L'expérience des soldats français (été 1918-printemps 1920)' (Doctoral thesis, University of Paris I – Panthéon Sorbonne UFR d'histoire, 2002)

Feltman, Brian K., 'The Culture of Captivity: German Prisoners, British Captors, and Manhood in the Great War, 1914–1920' (Doctoral thesis, The Ohio State University, 2010)

Lerner, Paul, 'Hysterical Men. War, Neurosis, and German Mental Medicine, 1914–1921' (Doctoral thesis, Columbia University, 1996)

Rachamimov, Alon, 'Marginalized Subjects. Austro-Hungarian POWs in Russia 1914–1918' (Doctoral Thesis, Columbia University, 2000)

Solassol, Stéphane, 'La Réciprocité dans le Droit de la Guerre' (Doctoral thesis, Université de Caen-Basse Normandie, 2003)

Thiel, Jens, 'Belgische Arbeitskräfte für die deutsche Kriegswirtschaft. Deportation, Zwangsarbeit und Anwerbung im Ersten Weltkrieg' (Doctoral thesis, Humboldt-Universität zu Berlin, 2003)

Wilkinson, Oliver, 'Captured! What was the Experience of a British Prisoner of War during the First World War?' (Undergraduate Thesis, University of Lancaster, 2007)

UNPUBLISHED PAPERS

Anderson, Peter, 'The Chetwode Commission and British Diplomatic Responses to Violence behind the Lines in the Spanish Civil War', *European History Quarterly* (forthcoming).

Becker, Annette, 'Prisonniers civils et militaires, représailles et boucliers humains, 1914–1918', paper presented at the international conference 'La Captivité et les prisonniers de guerre. Aspects politiques, sociaux et psychologiques de l'histoire de la Première Guerre Mondiale', Moscow, 4–5 December 1997

Egger, Matthias, 'Austro-Hungarian Prisoners of War in Russia and Italy, 1914–1922. Their Administration by the Austro-Hungarian and Subsequent Austrian Government', paper presented at the conference 'Other Combatants, Other Fronts. Competing Histories of the First World War', Fifth Conference of the International Society for First World War Studies, London, 10–12 September 2009

Guoqi, Xu, 'Chinese Laborers in France during the Great War', paper presented at the Fourth Conference of the International Society for First World War Studies, Washington, 18–20 October 2007

Kramer, Alan, 'Deutsche Kriegsverbrechen 1914/1941. Kontinuität oder Bruch?', forthcoming in the Hans-Ulrich Wehler Festschrift

'The Origins of the Concentration Camp System in Central Europe? Italian Prisoners of War in Austria-Hungary, 1915–1918', paper given to the Modern European History Research Seminar, Trinity College Dublin, 11 October 2007

'Italienische Kriegsgefangene im Ersten Weltkrieg', paper presented to the SFB Kriegserfahrungen, Tübingen, 7 May 2004

Rein, Leonid, 'Voices from Captivity. Letters of German POWs in England during World War 1', paper presented at the conference 'Captivity from Babylon to Guantánamo', University College, London, 10 November 2005

Schroer, Timothy, 'The Birth of Codified Racial Segregation of Prisoners of War', paper presented at the conference 'Other Combatants, Other Fronts. Competing Histories of the First World War', Fifth Conference of the International Society for First World War Studies, London, 10–12 September 2009

Steinbach, Daniel, 'Challenging European Colonial Supremacy. The Internment of "Enemy Aliens" in British and German East Africa during the First World War', paper presented at the conference 'Other Combatants, Other Fronts. Competing Histories of the First World War', Fifth Conference of the International Society for First World War Studies, London, 10–12 September 2009

Stibbe, Matthew, 'Elsa Brändström and the Reintegration of Returning Prisoners of War and their Families in Post-War Germany and Austria', paper provided by the author

Théofilakis, Fabien, 'Les Prisonniers de guerre allemands en mains françaises au sortir de la Seconde Guerre Mondiale. Gestion et enjeux', paper provided by the author

WEBSITES

www.cannockchasedc.gov.uk/cannockchase/wargraves.htm Accessed: 10.8.2005

http://home.arcor.de/kriegsgefangene/cemetery/cannockchase.html Accessed: 10.8.2005

www.dhm.de/presseinfos/2001020701.html Accessed: 14.9.2005

www15.bni-hamburg.de/bni/bni2/neu2/getfile.acgi?area=geschichte&pid= 131 Accessed: 27.10.2005

www.1914–1918.be/photo.php?image=photos/enfant_vieslet/11vieslet_a.jpg Accessed: 25.10.2005

www.bbc.co.uk/history/war/wwone/humanfaceofwar_gallery_07.shtml Accessed: 17.6.2005

www.bbc.co.uk/history/war/wwone/humanfaceofwar_gallery_06.shtml Accessed: 17.6.2005.

http://membres.lycos.fr/histoiredefrance/articles/personnalites/Salengro.htm Accessed: 31.5.2005

www.bautz.de/bbkl/b/brandstroem e.shtml Accessed: 30.12.2005

Index

Lightning Source UK Ltd.
Milton Keynes UK
UKOW04f0627230914

239024UK00015B/520/P